Midwest Studies in Philosophy
Volume IX

D1306120

MIDWEST STUDIES IN PHILOSOPHY

EDITED BY PETER A. FRENCH, THEODORE E. UEHLING, JR., HOWARD K. WETTSTEIN

Many papers in MIDWEST STUDIES IN PHILOSOPHY are invited and all are previously unpublished. The editors will consider unsolicited manuscripts that are received by January of the year preceding the appearance of a volume. All manuscripts must be pertinent to the topic area of the volume for which they are submitted. Address manuscripts to MIDWEST STUDIES IN PHILOSOPHY, University of Minnesota, Morris, MN 56267, or Department of Philosophy, University of Notre Dame, Notre Dame, IN 46566, or Trinity University, San Antonio, TX 78284.

The articles in MIDWEST STUDIES IN PHILOSOPHY are indexed in THE PHILOSOPHER'S INDEX.

Midwest Studies in Philosophy Volume IX Causation and Causal Theories

Editors

PETER A. FRENCH
Trinity University
THEODORE E. UEHLING, JR.
University of Minnesota, Morris
HOWARD K. WETTSTEIN
University of Notre Dame

University of Minnesota Press • Minneapolis

Published by the University of Minnesota Press,
2037 University Avenue Southeast, Minneapolis, MN 55414
Printed in the United States of America.

Library of Congress Cataloging in Publication Data
Main entry under title:
Causation and causal theories.

(Midwest studies in philosophy; v. 9)
1. Causation – Addresses, essays, lectures. I. French,
Peter A. II. Uehling, Theodore Edward. III. Wettstein,
Howard K. IV. Series.
BD541.C19 1984   122   84-2349
ISBN 0-8166-1349-4
ISBN 0-8166-1352-4 (pbk.)

This volume is dedicated to
the memory of
J. L. Mackie

Midwest Studies in Philosophy
Volume IX
Causation and
Causal Theories

Midwest Studies in Philosophy
Volume IX

Is the Causal Structure of the Physical Itself Something Physical?

HILARY PUTNAM

I

According to David Hume, thinking is just a matter of "association of ideas." According to many contemporary philosophers, understanding our words is a matter of grasping their "conceptual roles in the language.[1] Sometimes the conceptual role of the words in a language is thought of as something associated with the whole language, something not separable from the skills of confirming and disconfirming sentences in a language, deducing consequences from hypotheses stated in the language, etc.—so that talk of the "conceptual role" of an isolated word or sentence would be, strictly speaking, incorrect—and sometimes it is thought of as something that a single word or single sentence can have.

In either case, insofar as mastering "conceptual roles" is learning what to believe (with what degree of confidence) under various conditions of prior belief and sensory stimulation, these accounts are still associationist. We are represented as probabilistic automata by such accounts—systems having "states" that are connected by various "transition probabilities" to one another and to sensory inputs and motor outputs. (Some authors suggest that we might be systems of probabilistic automata rather than single automata, but this does not affect the point I am making). If you think of the states of these automata as "mental states" (possibly unconscious ones) and the transition probabilities as the "rules of association," then you will see that this is just a sophisticated and more mathematical version of Hume's "association of ideas." A big change is that it is not only conscious "mental states" that are associated; the connection between two conscious mental states may be mediated by a long string of unconscious associations of more than one kind. Another big change is that an "idea," in the sense of a concept, is identified with a program or program-feature rather than a single mental entity. Still, our theory of understanding, to the extent one has been suggested, is a direct successor to Hume's.

3

Hume's account of causation, on the other hand, is anathema to most present-day philosophers. Nothing could be more contrary to the spirit of recent philosophical writing than the idea that there is nothing more to causality than regularity or the idea that, if there is something more, then that something more is largely subjective. One recent writer even speaks of his doctrine as belief in "non-Humean causation."[2]

I want to suggest that there is a certain absurdity in trying to hold on to an associationist account of understanding while believing in "non-Humean causation." Hume's problems with causation *ought to be* problems for contemporary philosophers, if they thought through their own doctrines.

To explain what I mean, I must first set aside the anachronistic suggestion that Hume thought one can define 'A causes B' as 'if A, then immediately afterwards B', or something of that kind. Hume was not a twentieth-century linguistic philosopher trying to translate sentences in ordinary language into an "ideal language," or a "conceptual analyst" in the style of Moore and Broad.

What Hume held was that the circumstances under which we think or say that A causes B are characterized by certain objective properties (regular succession and the possibility of filling in intermediate causal links so that the causal action is via contiguity in space and time). He did not claim that we think or say 'A causes B' *whenever* these properties are present. But he seems to have thought that what makes us regard some regularities (in which the contiguity conditions are satisifed) as noncausal or coincidental and others as causal is largely subjective: a matter of human psychology, not of something that is present in Nature in the latter class of cases and absent in the former. His important thesis was negative, not positive. He did not say we can define 'causes' in noncausal terms, much less attempt to actually do it, but he maintained that the idea that in some cases the cause does not merely precede the effect but actually (in some "thick" sense) necessitates the effect is totally unintelligible. (He explained the almost irresistible temptation to think something like this in terms of a theory of projection—we project our feeling of necessitation, which is itself an epiphenomenon of the habit of expectation we have built up, in Hume's view, onto the external phenomena.)

What I want to say is that once one has "bought" an associationist account of understanding, then the *other* famous Humean doctrines—the "idealist" doctrines as well as the "sceptical" doctrine about causality—are almost forced upon one.

To see why this is so, let us recall the antirealist arguments that I employed in *Reason, Truth and History*—the model theoretic arguments against realism, in particular.[3] I showed that an ideal set of operational and theoretical constraints on sentence acceptance at most fixes the truth value of whole sentences. If one is inclined to think that "survival value" somehow determines what sentences are true under which conditions, which sentences should be believed under which conditions of "sensory stimulation," which "motor responses" one should make when one believes which sentences; then, I argued, even if this is right, such "evolutionary" considerations cannot do better than (suitable) operational and theoretical constraints can do; again, only the truth value of whole sentences gets fixed (in various actual and possible situations). This leaves the reference of most signs within the sentence underdetermined, in a very radical way. Even a function that specifies the truth value of "a cat is on a mat" in all possible worlds does not suffice to rule out that "cat" refers to cherries in the actual world (chapter II).

Robert Shope has summed up my argument so well in a recent review (to appear in *Philosophy and Phenomenological Research*) that I take the liberty of quoting him:

> Constraints, e.g., that "cat" be applicable to an object upon inspection, or, e.g., that our employing "cat" be linked to a causal chain of the appropriate type, will fail to provide a general account of reference. For invoking such constraints still fails to explain how the word "inspection" or the words describing that particular type of causal chain get their reference. This is because the set-theoretical technique [the one I employ in chapter II] shows that the string of signs saying that the constraint is met . . . would remain true if the word 'inspection' had a different interpretation. So assumption of a metaphysical realist perspective leaves us in an epistemological impasse. It allows us no way of telling, on the basis of what is going on within our minds, whether the occurrence of the thought that the constraint is being conformed to indicates the *right* actual relation, R, holds between the word "inspection" in our thought and the world.

The standard "realist" response to this sort of argument is to say that all my argument shows is that what is "going on within our minds" does not fix the "right" reference relation, R. ("*You* know which one that is," says the metaphysical realist, in effect.) There are constraints built into physical reality (i.e., into the external world) that single out the "right" reference relation. (David Lewis even uses the phrase 'natural constraint' in this sense—to mean, *not* a constraint that, when described by a string of signs, seems natural subjectively, but a constraint that is *imposed*—and, apparently *interpreted*—by Nature herself.) What is wrong with this response?

What is wrong is that Nature, or "physical reality," in the post-Newtonian understanding of the physical, has no semantic preferences. The idea that some physical parameter, or some relation definable in terms of the fundamental parameters of physics, simply cries out for the role of mapping our signs onto things has no content at all.

Consider, for example, the way in which Lewis himself suggests that Nature might interpret our signs for us. The "natural constraint" that (together with other constraints imposed by *us*) fixes the reference of our words is that certain words— the natural kind terms—should *refer to 'elite' classes*.[4] What is 'eliteness'? Lewis does not say. He just postulates that there must be a special family of sets, the 'elite' sets, such that physical reality itself insists that (*ceteris paribus*) our natural kind terms have sets in that family as their extensions.

Donald Davidson, on the other hand, has suggested that whereas a set of "true sentences" is somehow fixed, it is not fixed by a relation of reference. Seeking a theory of the mysterious relation R that 'hooks language onto the world' is just a mistake, Davidson thinks. Rather, *any* of the "reference-relations" whose existence I proved, any of the relations that maps signs onto things in such a way that the truth conditions come out right (up to logical equivalence)—call these *admissable* relations—is equally kosher.[5] On Lewis's view, there *must be* a singled out R, otherwise physics itself is impossible. On Davidson's view there is no such relation nor do we need one. Who is right?

It is easy to show that not only would we have the same experiences *in all possible worlds* on either theory, but that all physical events (events described in terms of the fundamental magnitudes of physics) would be the same. The same physical theory would be true on Davidson's view as on Lewis's. So the question— if it is an intelligible question—which of these two theories is right is certainly not an empirical question.

I myself find both views incoherent. Lewis's view requires us to believe that some sets of things *identify themselves* as "natural kinds"; Davidson's requires us to believe in a world of things in themselves that have no determinate relations to our language.

The way out that most materialists (metaphysical realists of the physicalist persuasion) prefer is to think of *causation* (understood in a "non-Humean" way) as the relation that (somehow) does the "singling out." *Causation*—real necessitation —has so much dignity, as it were, that it seems absurd that the existence of admissible relations that map the two-place predicate 'causes' onto relations other than the *real* relation of causation (the one with all that dignity) should have any philosophical significance at all. The world has, as physicalists are fond of saying, a "causal structure," and the reference relation R is singled out from the huge set of admissible relations by that causal structure (somehow).

It is just at this point that three of Hume's concerns—the concern with understanding, the concern with causation, and the "idealism"—become relevant to our present-day discussion.

Let *causation** be the image of the term 'causes' under any nonstandard reference relation—any admissible relation R^* that is *not* the 'right' relation (you know, R). (I am speaking within the metaphysical realist picture, of course—my own view is that the whole picture is a mistake.) Then, if God had picked R^* instead of R to be the "right" relation (or if "physical reality" had), all these physicalists would now be worshiping Causation* instead of Causation.

On the "conceptual role" theory of understanding—the theory that I described as a neoassociationism—there is *no* respect in which Causation* is any less appropriate a referent for the term 'causes' than is Causation itself. The *-concepts fit the conceptual role semantics every bit as well as the R-concepts (the ones picked out by the "right" relation).

This is the problem the physicalist faces: his metaphysical realism makes him want to hang onto the image of language as "hooking onto" the world via a "right" relation R. His neoassociationist account of understanding, however, commits him to an account of how we understand *all* of our notions—including the notion of causation itself—which has nothing to do with R. The conceptual role semantics—the schedule of associations—fits cats*, mats*, causation* perfectly, in the sense that our inductive and deductive inferences are valid and invalid exactly as often whether "physical reality" picks R or R^* to put our terms in correspondence with things in the world. An associationist or neoassociationist account of understanding simply turns reference, conceived of as an explanatory relation between what is "going on in our minds," on the one hand, and mind-independent entities, on the other, into a bit of superstition. The materialist ends up looking like a believer in occult phenomena, such as magic, divine intervention, or inexplicable noetic rays running from referents to signs.

What I have just sketched (in modern dress) is how an associationist theory of understanding naturally leads to scepticism about our ability to refer to a discourse-independent (or mind-independent) external world.

Criticizing this argument, Michael Devitt[6] and (independently) Clark Glymour[7] have suggested that the "right" reference relation is something they refer to as 'causal connection'. And they reject my charge that they are postulating an obscure or occult kind of "metaphysical glue" binding the term 'causal connection' (or the term 'reference') to R. 'Causal connection' is attached to R by causal connection, not by metaphysical glue, they write. But this is, in fact, just to say that R (causal connection) is *self-identifying*. This is to repeat the claim that a relation can at one and the same time be a physical relation and have the dignity (the built-in intentionality, in other words) of choosing its own name. Those who find such a story unintelligible (as I do) will not be helped by these declarations of faith.

There are, basically, two ways a metaphysician can go at this point. He may try to keep the idea that causation is just a physical relation in the sense of being definable in terms of the fundamental magnitudes (field tensors, etc.) of physics. In this case he (1) abandons the attempt to explain how one physical relation should have the dignity—or intentionality—that enables it to fix reference, when another—causation*—does not. (Of course, causation* can be defined in terms of the fundamental* magnitudes just as causation can be defined in terms of the fundamental magnitudes, *if* causation *can be* so defined. And the fundamental* magnitudes, by virtue of the logical equivalences between statements about them and statements about the fundamental magnitudes, are represented by the same operators on Hilbert space as the fundamental magnitudes; it makes no difference to *physics* whether we describe the world in terms of the fundamental magnitudes or the fundamental* magnitudes.) (2) He takes on the task of carrying out a formidable reduction program.

The other way he can go is to say that causation is not definable in terms of the fundamental parameters of physics and to say that it has a special intentionality. (Perhaps this is what its "non-Humean" character consists in. If A causes B then A *explains* B; and explanation is connected with reason itself.) This, as I understand him, is Richard Boyd's approach. Boyd would defend including such a mysterious relation as "non-Humean causation" in a materialist ontology by arguing that science itself needs to postulate such a relation.

As far as fundamental physics is concerned, I have already indicated why I think that such views are wrong. Quantum mechanics has no realist interpretation at all, which is why it is an embarrassment to materialists (generally they write as if quantum mechanics did not exist). But if we make quantum mechanics look classical by leaving out the observer and the observer's side of the cut between system and observer, or if we confine attention to prequantum mechanical physics, then the world looks like this: there is a closed system (in classical physics this could be the whole physical universe) that has a maximal state at each time (along each time-like hyperplane). There is a well-defined mathematical function that determines the state at all earlier and later times (depending on the characteristics of the system). The equations of motion (e.g., the Dirac equation) enable one to determine this function. If one says, "The states do not merely succeed one another in the way the theory says; each state *necessitates* the succeeding states," then one is not reporting the content of classical physics, but reading in a metaphysical interpretation that physicists have long rejected as unnecessary. Even the time-directedness of causal processes disappears in fundamental physics.

When we come to sciences less fundamental than fundamental particle phsyics, say sociology or history, or even to evolutionary biology, or even to chemistry or solid-state physics, then, of course, we find that causation-as-bringing-about is invoked constantly, in the guise of disposition talk ("the gazelle's speed *enables* it to outrun the lion most of the time"), in the guise of counterfactuals ("the salt would have dissolved if the solution had not been saturated"), and in the guise of "causes"-statements ("the extreme cold caused the material to become brittle"). Even in fundamental particle physics such talk becomes indispensable when we *apply* the physics to actual systems that are (of course) *not* the whole universe-regarded-as-a-closed-system. But the *ontology* – the *Weltbild* – of materialist metaphysics is, remember, the ontology of the universe-as-a-closed-system-from-a-God's-eye-view; and it is precisely *this* ontology and this *Weltbild* that has no room for "non-Humean causation."

One way of reconciling the indispensability of causation-as-bringing-about in daily life and in applied science with the fact that *no* mysterious relation of "non-Humean causation" figures in the world picture of fundamental physics at all was suggested by Mill (and revived by John Mackie).[8] Fundamental physics implicitly defines a notion Mill called "the total cause" (at a given time). In post-Einsteinian physics, we might define the total cause at time t_0 of an event A (at a time subsequent to t_0) to be the entire three-dimensional space-time region that constitutes the bottom of A's light cone at the time t_0. Any aspect of this region that is sufficient to produce A (at the appropriate time t_1) by virtue of the Dirac equation (or the appropriate equation of motion) may also be called a 'total cause' of A.

When we say that the extreme cold (at t_0) caused the material to be brittle (at t_1), then we do not mean that this was the total cause of the material's becoming brittle (even given the cold at t_0, the material would not have become brittle if a heater had been present and preset to turn on immediately after t_0, for example). What we do, according to Mill and Macie, is *pick out* a part of the total cause that we regard as important because of its predictive and explanatory utility. If we discover that the cold was correlated with something that by itself provides an explanation of the material's becoming brittle, and the material will become brittle even in the absence of the cold if this correlated factor is still present, then we will change our inference-licensing practice and we will also select a different part of the total cause to call "the cause'. Which is "the cause" and which a "background condition" depends on a *picking out*, an act of *selection*, which depends on what we know and can use in prediction; and this is not written into the physical system itself.

If we postulate a "non-Humean causation" in the physical world, then we are treating causation-as-bringing-about as something built into the physical universe itself: we are saying that the physical universe distinguishes between "bringers-about" and "background conditions." This seems incredible; after all, if heaters were normally set to turn on when a place got cold, then we might very well choose to say that the cause of the material's becoming brittle was that the heater malfunctioned and allowed the place to get cold (which is quite different from saying that the extreme cold at t_0—prior to when the heater would have turned on—is the cause). Like counterfactuals, causal statements depend on what we regard as a "normal" state of affairs, what we regard as a state of affairs "similar" to the actual, and so on. For example, when a heater is present, then we regard it as "normal" that it should turn on at the preset time, and this is a reason for singling out the "exceptional" part of the total situation—the heater's failing to turn on—as a "cause" and not as a "background condition." On the other hand, every concrete situation has infinitely many exceptional or improbable features, and we do *not* single out most of these, nor do we accept counterfactuals to the effect that had *they* been different, then the material would not have become brittle. Rejecting these counterfactuals, in turn, involves considering certain nonactual "possible worlds" as sufficiently "similar" (or better, sufficiently cotenable, in Goodman's sense)[9] with the actual world (in the light of which contrary-to-fact-supposition is being thought about) to serve as counterexamples to counterfactuals. Is all *this* supposed to be "built into physical reality"?

The view of those who answer "yes" seems to be a desperate attempt to combine a medieval notion of causation (a notion according to which what is normal, what is an explanation, what is a bringer-about, is all in the essence of things themselves and not at all contributed by our knowledge and interests) with modern materialism.

On the other hand, the view of those who answer "no" (and give the sort of reasons Mill and Mackie give) creates a new kind of dualistic cut between what is "really there" (the physical system with its "states" and the law determining how they succeed one another in time) and the referring, knowing, interested mind that picks out some aspect of what is really there as "the cause" when it finds it can use that aspect in predictions that are important for it, issues "inference licenses," considers nonactual situations as "similar to the actual" (or as similar as can be expected, given that the antededent of a counterfactual is supposed to be true in them), and thus determines an *epistemic* distinction between a "cause" and a "background condition." How does this mind get to be able to *refer* to the mind-independent world? Answer "via the relation of causal connection," and you have slipped back to treating causation as something "out there" and not simply "epistemic."

Notice that Hume's project was to distinguish between what "really exists," in the metaphysician's sense (or what "really exists" *as far as we can know*) and what we "project." Notice further that both Mackie and Boyd *accept* Hume's project. Boyd says, in effect, "Causation really exists—none of it, not one bit, is a projection," and Mackie says, "Much of it is projection."

The reason I don't regard either the "yes" answer or the "no"answer to the question "Is causation-as-explanation built into physical reality?" as acceptable is that I find the whole notion of being "built into physical reality" or of "really existing" in the metaphysician's sense without content.

A first stab at another way of looking at the whole question might come from recalling that whether causation "really exists" or not, it certainly exists in our "life world." What makes it "real" in a *phenomenological* sense is the possibility of asking "Is that really the cause?"—i.e., of *checking* causal statements, of bringing new data and new theories to bear on them.

If we say this, while leaving aside the problematical idea of "really existing," then we have a picture not too different from Wittgenstein's or Austin's, or, for that matter, Husserl's. The world of "ordinary language" (the world in which we actually live) is full of causes and effects. It is only when we insist that the world of ordinary language (or the *Lebenswelt*) is defective (an ontological "jungle," vague, gappy, etc.) and look for a "true world" (free of vagueness, of gaps, of any element that can be regarded as a "human projection") that we end up feeling forced to choose between the picture of "a physical universe with a built-in structure" and "a physical universe with a structure imposed by the mind," not to mention such pictures as a physical-universe-plus-a-mysterious-relation-of-"correspondence," or a-physical-universe-plus-mysterious-"essences"; to choose, that is, between pictures that are at once terribly alluring and perfectly contentless.

To recapitulate: I have argued that materialism, which conceives of persons as automata, inherits Hume's problems. A neoassociationist theory of understanding (the probabilistic automaton model) renders it unintelligible that anything in the mind/brain can bear a *unique* correspondence to anything outside the mind/brain. (Of course, everything corresponds in *some way or other* to everything else; the problem is how any *one* correspondence can be singled out as "the" relation between signs and their referents.) In this sense, Hume's difficulties with objective reference to an external world are difficulties for the materialist too.

Moreover, if the physical universe itself is an automaton (something with "states" that succeed one another according to a fixed equation), then it is unintelligible how any particular *structure* can be singled out as "the" causal structure of the universe. Of course, the universe fulfills structural descriptions—in *some way or other* it fulfills every structural description that does not call for too high a cardinality on the part of the system being modeled; once again, the problem is how any *one* structure can be singled out as "the" structure of the system.

If we say that the structure of the physical universe is singled out by the *mind*, then we either put the mind outside the universe (which is to abandon materialism) or else we are thrown back to the first problem: the problem of how the signs employed by the mind can have a determinate "correspondence" to parts and aspects of the universe. If we say that the causal structure of the physical universe is "built into" the physical universe, then we abandon materialism without admitting that we are abandoning it; for all we do in this case is to project into physical system properties (for example, being a "background condition," being a cause, being cotenable with the antecedent of a counterfactual) that cannot be properties of matter "in itself." In this sense, Hume's difficulties with objective necessitation are difficulties for the materialist too.

There are those who would say, "So much the worse for materialism," while keeping Hume's project (of dividing reality into what is "really there" and what is a human projection). But attempts to build a metaphysical system that is not materialist always appear as mere culture curiosities. We cannot really go back to the Middle Ages or to Plato's time. If science does not tell us what is "really there" in the metaphysical sense, then neither does anything else. What has collapsed is the attempt to divide mundane reality, the reality of the *Lebenswelt*, into Real Reality and Projection.

II

Up to now I have looked mainly at efforts by philosophers who are both physicalists and metaphysical realists (call them "materialists"). Now, I wish to begin by looking at some very influential writings by a philosopher who is a physicalist but *not* a realist – W. V. Quine.

Quine regards the counterfactual idiom as hopelessly subjective and (for this reason) to be shunned in scientific work. On the other hand, he has no objection to individual dispositional predicates, e.g. *soluble*, and employs them freely in his own philosophy of language. How does he reconcile these views?

Quine employs two ideas: one well understood but of limited applicability, and the other very ill understood, even by Quine's many admirers.

The first is the idea of a *natural kind*.[10] A natural kind is, for example, the class of things with a given microstructure, e.g., the soluble things. (Quine assumes that there is what he calls a 'chemical formula' for solubility.) Quine's basic claim is that we can identify the dispositional property (solubility) with the corresponding microstructure.

One reason that this idea is of limited applicability is that many dispositions cut across natural kinds. Being *poisonous*, for example, cannot be identified with the possession of any one microstructure (membership in any one natural kind) because there is no such one microstructure (no such one natural kind). (The stimulus meanings of sentences are dispositions, in Quine's view[11] – the most important dispositions there are, for Quine's philosophy of language – and Quine himself points out that there is no *one* microstructure that is common to all human brains with a given speech-disposition.)

This is not the feature of Quine's account that I wish to concentrate on, however. The second idea that Quine uses needs a little explaining. This is the idea that truth and reference are "disquotational."

A dispositional predicate—say 'soluble'—can stand for a nondispositional microstructural property, in Quine's view, *even if we cannot say which one*. Our question is, how does this come about?

The problem that Quine might seem to face is the following. If what associates a particular microstructure M with the predicate 'is soluble' is the fact that M *explains* the event of this substance dissolving when it is put in water, the event of this other substance dissolving when it is put in water, and so on, then we need a notion like "explanation" to describe the association in question. But Quine does not regard explanation as a precise notion (he has balked in print at talk of "laws," for example, and he detests counterfactuals), and he certainly would not admit "explains' as a primitive notion in his ideal language (the "first-class conceptual system").

Of course, there are other possibilities one might try. One might say that what associates the microstructure M with the predicate is the fact that *scientists* have identified the microstructure in question with solubility, or will in the future. But what if we are dealing with a disposition whose microstructural basis scientists will never discover? The human race may become extinct in the next hundred years; but Quine would still let us talk of "the stimulus meaning of 'Lo, a rabbit,'" and would say that this stimulus meaning was a dispositional predicate that applied to a class of organisms—the class of all organisms in a certain *disjunction* of microstates —even though it is virtually certain that we could not discover the description of that disjunction in a hundred years (or ever). One might talk about what scientists would discover if investigation continued indefinitely, but this would be to employ a counterfactual (with a very vague and problematic antecedent, to boot).

What is often missed by readers of Quine is that this is no problem at all for him, given his view of language (but for reasons that are unacceptable to realists).

We have been speaking as if reference were a relation between things in a mind-independent world and bits of language. But this is a picture that Quine rejects. For Quine, truth is "immanent truth"—that is, to say *"Snow is white" is true* is to reaffirm "Snow is white" and not to ascribe a mysterious property called 'truth' to "Snow is white." Similarly, we might say that for Quine reference is "immanent reference"—to say *"Cat" refers to cats* is to say only that cats are cats,[12] and not to say that a mysterious relation called 'reference' obtains between the word "cat" and cats. Any definition of reference that yields the truisms "'Cat' refers to cats," "'Electron' refers to electrons," etc., will do. We do not have to *first* "put the words in correspondence with objects" and *then* utter these statements to declare which objects our words correspond to; our Skinnerian schedule of conditioning enables us to use the words (which is all understanding them involves, in Quine's view), and the truisms just mentioned give a way of *adding* the word 'refers' to our language, which ensures that it will have the property we want—that we can use the word 'refers' to give a disquotational definition of truth (for the sublanguage that does not contain 'semantical' words).

Now, since the question "How does language hook on to the world?" is a *pseudoquestion* on this view (because languages "hook onto the world" only *relative* to a translation manual into *my* language, and *my* language hooks onto the world "transparently," via the disquotational account of reference and truth), the question that *is* a question for a correspondence theorist – "How do dispositional (or any other) predicates 'hook onto' the right objects and properties?" is also a pseudoquestion. If my evolving doctrine contains the sentence "Having the same stimulus meaning as 'Lo, a rabbit!' is being in any microstructure in a cerain (unspecified) set S," then, according to my evolving doctrine, it is *true* that the predicate "has the same stimulus meaning as 'Lo, a rabbit!'" is true of all and only those things that have a microstructure in some set S of microstructures, whether we shall ever be able to define S or not. The realist objection, "Yes, it is true *according to your doctrine*, but is it really true?" is only intelligible as a request to reexamine my doctrine *scientifically*. As a philosophical request to explain how this *can* be true if no such set S has been (or ever will be) "singled out," it is unintelligible; the doctrine Quine calls 'Ontological Relativity' is supposed to show that *that* sort of philosophical request is impossible to meet.

In sum, if the theory that microstructures *are* what dispositions turn out to be is a "good" theory (scientifically speaking), then it becomes true – or as true as anything is, in a Quinian way of thinking – as soon as we adopt it. The work of actually *reducing* dispositions one by one to (disjunctions of) microstructures is unnecessary. We have all the advantages of "theft over honest toil."

The price one pays for Quine's solution to the metaphysical problem is abandoning the idea that truth is a substantial notion, the idea that truth-or-falsity is a genuine parameter with respect to which we appraise one another's utterances and writings. When I say that I am trying to decide whether what you have said or written is true, then, in Quine's view, all I mean is that I am making up my mind whether to "assent." But this is to give up what is right in realism. The deep problem is how to keep the idea that statements are true or false, that language is not mere noise and scribbling and "subvocalization," without being driven to postulate mysterious relations of correspondence. Quine's view is not the cure for metaphysical realism but the opposite pole of the same disease.

III

John Mackie's *The Cement of the Universe* does not pretend to offer definitive solutions to the problem we have discussed, but it does present the different strands of the problem of causation in a remarkably sensitive way. Dealing in chapter 8 with the crucial question, in what sense there is an objective "causal link" to be found in Nature, Mackie suggested that this link consists in certain kinds of qualitative and structural persistence and continuity. An example may help to explain what he had in mind.

Consider simple cases of collision, say a baseball bat striking a baseball. In these cases, something quite specifiable "persists," namely the momentum of the bat. One can treat this momentum as an enduring quantity (a vector quantity: one possessing a direction as well as a magnitude), and its "persistence" is described by the law of the conservation of momentum.

Unfortunately, there does not appear to be any *one* quantity that is conserved in every case of what we describe as causation. To explain how Mackie would probably meet this objection, let us look at a different sort of case.

Suppose the valve on a boiler sticks and the boiler explodes. This is not a case of a quantity 'persisting' from the sticking to the explosion nor of something changing continuously from the sticking to the explosion. Indeed, from an "objective" point of view it might well seem that the valve plays no more of a part in the production of the explosion than any piece of the boiler of comparable surface area. Yet we describe the sticking of the valve as the "cause" of the explosion, and not the presence of X, where X is an arbitrary small piece of the boiler.

What Mackie would do in such a case is distinguish between the "neolithic" (*sic*) statement that the sticking of the valve caused the boiler to explode, which he regards as having an epistemic element and hence as not "simply true," and the "law of working" that is exemplified in the case described. The law of working would simply be that the increase in the temperature of the steam produces a continuous increase in the pressure of the steam against the boiler until the appropriate coefficient of strength of the material of the boiler is exceeded. (A second law of working would describe the flying apart of the material when this limit is reached.) An ordinary language counterfactual (which is *not* "simply true") tells us that steam would have escaped (bringing down the pressure—and hence exemplifying yet another "law of working") if the valve had not stuck. The "neolithic" statement is epistemic in the way the counterfactual is epistemic, but the success of all this talk that is "neolithic" and "not simply truth" is explained by something that is objective and in nature—that is, the continuous changes of temperature and pressure described by the several "laws of working." It is *these* that constitute the "causal link" (which Mackie equates with the "necessitation").

Even if Mackie could specify the different sorts of statements he is prepared to count as "laws of working," and thereby indicate what sorts of "structural and qualitative" persistence and continuity should count as "causal links," very little of what philosophers call 'causal connection' turns out to be objective on such a story. "Causal theories" of this and that typically assume that statements to the effect that X brought about Y are "simply true," in Mackie's phrase, and this is just what Mackie is prepared to give up.

Indeed, it is not clear to what philosophical problem Mackie's theory actually speaks. He suggests that he is speaking to Hume's problem, but how? True, temperature and pressure increase continuously when a boiler explodes. But temperature[*] and pressure[*] (the images of the terms 'temperature' and 'pressure' under any admissable nonstandard reference relation) also increase continuously; indeed "the temperature increased" and "the temperature[*] increased" have the same-truth-value not just in the actual world but in all possible worlds. Yet it seems sticky to say that the objectivity of the causal nexus consists in the continuity of the increase of temperature* and in the continuity of the increase of pressure.* In some places Mackie uses frankly epistemic considerations to decide what is and what is not the right sort of persistence: it would be *suprising*, he argues, if a particle that has moved in a straight line ceased to do so in the absence of a force. But this appeal to what we find "surprising" undercuts the whole enterprise of answering Hume.

IV

The idea that we have found the Furniture of the Universe when we get down to such things as the conservation of energy and momentum (and, in classical physics, of matter) represents the idea I have already criticized, the idea that the world picture of fundamental physics is metaphysically "complete." This picture and the dualist picture of the mind "imposing" a structure on the material world, "singling out" conditions as background conditions and events as "bringers about," employing counterfactual conditionals and "neolithic" causal statements as inference licenses, etc., are made for each other.

We might be saved from this particular sterile clash of views if we paused to reflect that science itself, and not just "ordinary language," is deeply pluralistic in its ontology. Physics may — sometimes — present the world in the language of functional dependence, but evolutionary biology, for example, explains evolutionary survival in terms of "neolithic" causal and dispositional concepts. Gazelles survived because they could outrun lions and other predators; that is a perfectly good "scientific explanation," and it claims, among other things, that gazelles would not have escaped if they had not run so fast. The causal structure of the world is not physical in the sense of being built into what we conceive of as physical reality. But that doesn't mean that it is pasted onto physical reality by the mind. It means, rather, that "physical reality" *and* "mind" are both abstractions from a world in which things having dispositions, causing one another, having modal properties, is simply a matter of course. Like all matters of course, causality can be seen as either the most banal or the most mysterious thing in the world. As is so often the case, each of these ways of seeing it contains a profound insight.

Notes

1. For example, H. Putnam (one of my former selves), "Reference and Understanding," in my *Meaning and the Moral Sciences* (London, 1976), 97-122. My present view, e.g., "Computational Psychology and Interpretation Theory," in *Philosophical Papers*, vol. 3 *Realism and Reason* (Cambridge, 1983) is that a holistic "conceptual role" account is the correct account (of what goes on in us when we understand a language) at one level of description but not at another. It *is* the correct account at the computation level (describing the brain as if it were a computer), but not at the intentional level. In my present view, intentional predicates, e.g., "is speaking a language," "means that there are a lot of cats in the neighborhood," "understands those words," are not reducible to computational or computational-cum-physical predicates any more than physical predicates are reducible to phenomenal ones. (See also, "Reflections on Goodman's *Ways of Worldmaking*" in *Realism and Reason*.)

2. R. Boyd, "Materialism without Reductionism: What Physicalism Does Not Entail," in *Readings in the Philosophy of Psychology*, edited by N. Block (Cambridge, Mass., 1980), 67-106.

3. *Reason, Truth and History* (Cambridge, 1981), chap. 2 and appendix.

4. I am quoting from an unpublished lecture by Lewis titled "Putnam's Paradox." Lewis credits the idea of "elite" classes to G. H. Merrill.

5. "A Coherence Theory of Truth and Knowledge," delivered at the Kant/Hegel Congress in Stuttgart, August 1981. It may be that I have misinterpreted Davidson and that he would say that the truth conditions must "come out right" up to a notion of equivalence stronger than logical equivalence (say, one determined by translation practice). However, it is mysterious how a constraint on the *verbal-form* of truth conditions could operate to narrow down the set of reference relations beyond the requirement that the truth conditions come out right up to logical equivalence (a requirement that depends only on the notion of *truth*, which is primitive in Davidson's theory). I suspect that Davidson equivocates between rejecting the "correspondence" picture and wanting to say that there are a number of "correspondences," not a single distinguished one.

6. "Putnam on Realism," unpublished.

7. "Conceptual Scheming or Confessions of a Metaphysical Realist," *Synthèse* 51 (1982): 169-80.

8. *The Cement of the Universe* (Oxford, 1974), 60-64.

9. *Fact, Fiction and Forecast*, 4th ed. (Cambridge, Mass., 1982), chap. I.

10. *Ontological Relativity and Other Essays* (New York, 1969), chap. 5.

11. *Word and Object* (Cambridge, 1960), 33-34.

12. More precisely, it is to say that the word 'cat' belongs to a certain recursively defined set of ordered pairs that includes the pair consisting of the word spelled 'c'-'a'-'t' and the set of cats. The statement *'cat' refers to cats* is a logical consequence of *'cat' is spelled 'c'-'a'-'t' and the set of cats is the set of cats* when the "disquotational" definition of reference is applied. Note that this is not at all a correct logical consequence on the intuitive notion of "reference."

Causes, Causity, and Energy

HECTOR-NERI CASTAÑEDA

Our ordinary concept of causality is—as David Hume wisely underscored—the concept in which an event or change *produces* another event or change. This production is the central core of causation, and the objective component of it Hume analyzed as constant conjunction. As is well known, Hume emphasized that our notion of production or causation has a subjective component, namely, the illusion of a certain necessity in the connection between cause and effect. Typically, the critique of Hume has centered on his attack upon, and on his theses about, necessity. But the core idea of production has been generally kept out of the dialectical stage. Here I will put necessity aside and bring this very idea of *production* to the center of the stage. I propose to explore the most general logical and ontological features of production. The most intriguing feature is the deep connection between production and energy. But as it will become apparent from the ensuing discussion, that deep connection is mediated by a more general concept of world-orderliness that I shall dub *causity*. Thus, the general principles here formulated belong to the philosophical foundations of thermodynamics.

I. ENTRY RAMP: PRODUCTION AND HUME'S CAUSAL GENERALIZATIONS

1. Some Data about Causality

There are two fundamental data about our concepts and views of causation and causal laws, which we cannot neglect, namely:

(C.1*) We are often more certain that an item c has caused an item e than of any causal law under which c and e fall. We may, of course, be sure of many laws of nature (formulated for closed systems), whether causal or not, that impinge upon (or govern) the context in which c and e occur.

(C.2*) We establish causal generalizations on the basis of singular causal instances.

By (C.2*) true causal generalizations are truly *causal* generalizations: that is, instances of sequences of certain types of events are indeed related by causality.

2. Hume's Causal Generalizations

Humean generalizations, i.e., statements about constant conjunctions, are not truly causal. They are, according to Hume, formulations of universal coincidence. This is objectively the whole of causality in the Humean view. Is this correct? Let us consider a typical example carefully scrutinized by Hume, precisely to make his point. Let us examine his scrutiny:

> Here is a billiard-ball [let us call it *ball B*] lying on the table, and another [let us call it *ball A*] moving towards it with rapidity. They strike; and the ball [*B*], which was formerly at rest, now acquires a motion. *This is a perfect instance of the relation of cause and effect* as any which we know, either by sensation or reflection. Let us therefore examine it. 'Tis evident, that the two balls touched one another before *the motion was communicated* and there was no interval betwixt the shock and the motion. *Contiguity* in time and place. . . . *Priority* in time. . . . But this is not all. Let us try *any other balls* of the same kind in like situations, and we shall always find, that the *impulse of the one produces motion in the other*. Here therefore is the *third* circumstance, *viz*, that of a *constant conjunction* betwixt the cause and the effect. Every object like the cause, *produces* always some object like the effect. Beyond these circumstances . . . I can discover nothing in this cause. The first ball [*A*] is in motion; touches the second [B]; immediately the second is in motion; and *when I try the experiment* with the same balls or like balls, in the same circumstances, I find, that upon the motion and touch of the one ball, motion always follows the other. In whatever shape I turn this matter, and however I examine it, I can find nothing farther.

This is Hume's own remarkable and pithy summary of his discussion of causality (*A Treatise of Human Nature*, edited by L. A. Selby-Bigge [Oxford, 1978], 649ff). It makes almost palpable how there is no logical necessity in the motion of ball *B* following the touching of ball *B* by ball *A*. On this we cannot gainsay Hume. And we must not quibble with him about his claim that he finds in the situation nothing farther than the three elements he has enumerated. But we must ask whether there is in that situation anyting *further*, anything that we can find. Let us, therefore, scrutinize the situation Hume has described in full detail.

The following points emerge under attentive scrutiny of Hume's billiard balls *A* and *B*.

Point 1. Hume agrees with most of us in the above data. His example of an ordinary billiard ball hitting another is a perfect—even paradigmatic—example of causation. Of course, we may not be able to tell whether the billard balls on a given table are ordinary billard balls, or whether the table itself is ordinary. But we can be sure that if they are ordinary we are seeing a perfect case of causation.

Point 2. Patently, the three circumstances Hume mentions are present in the situation.

Point 3. The condition of constant conjunction is, of course, not perceived. And Hume's discussion of it is very instructive. We must go over it very slowly. To establish the requisite constant conjunction Hume, very revealingly, does not refer us to his past experiences of previous collisions of balls A and B, where the full resemblance of the object involved should prove helpful. He does not even allude to past experiences of other billiard balls, or other objects in motion colliding with each other. Hume proceeds to "try any other balls of the same kind in like situations." He also tries the same balls A and B. In all, he turns to future cases. Of course, his claim that the collision between balls A and B is a perfect example of causality depends *psychologically* on past cases: he needs the past cases to *be able* to make the claim. But when it comes to *justifying* the claim, Hume marches into the future for the appropriate evidence. After all, the claim of causation is about the whole of time. Yet there is something perplexing here. How does Hume expect to verify conclusively the causal claim by considering just a few, or many, other cases? The future time goes *much* beyond the time during which he performs his experiments. Since the generalization is not logically necessary, on Hume's official causal theory the confidence he shows about his causal claim is merely an expression of his habit of inferring motion in the likes of B from motion in the likes of A. But we shall not comment any further on this aspect of Hume's view.

Point 4. Hume is sure that he has found all the causality he wishes to establish with his experiments on collisions of balls similar to A and B. He says most deliberately: "and we *shall always* find, that the impulse of the one [ball] *produces* motion in the other [ball]" (emphasis is added). And he has repeated many a time that the verb 'produces' is just another synonym of 'causes'.[2] Hume is so sure that the striking of one ball by another causes, produces, motion in the stricken ball every time it is stricken, even though he has considered just a few instances. The point is that *Hume establishes the causal generalization by induction from the singular causations*! This is precisely the most fundamental datum $(C.2^*)$ displayed above. Indeed, Hume's discussion is a brilliant application of both data $(C.1^*)$ and $(C.2^*)$ above. Yet it is not clear what right he has to do so.

Hume's inductive procedure is misleadingly represented in his explicit claim that "Every object like the cause, *produces* always some object like the effect" (emphasis added). Although we can know a priori that a cause produces its effect, we cannot know a priori that a given event is a cause of another, nor can we tell a priori what the relevant likenesses are.

Point 5. Yet Hume's discussion reveals an important datum about causality encapsulated in the principle just quoted, namely, the *piggybackness of causality*:

$(C.3^*)$ If an item c causes an item e, then there are properties ϕ-ness and $\$$-ness, and circumstances Z such that: if c is ϕ, e is \$, c is in Z, and whatever item of the same category as c is ϕ and in Z causes an item that is \$ and is of the same category as e.

Obviously, like (C.1*) and (C.2*), (C.3*) is only a criterion of adequacy for any account of causality.

Point 6. Up to this point Hume's text is clear. Yet he repeats his discussion, except for one thing. He makes a list of what he finds in each experiment, and now he lists: the contiguous succession, the contiguous location, and the constant conjunction of the events composing each experiment. Since to cause and produce are the same thing, the list does not include production. All those three elements comprise all the production of the motion in ball B by the striking of it by ball A. But it is patent to the attentive eye that those three elements do not amount to such production. Yet, as Hume correctly says, using data (C.2*), he has been examining a perfect example of causation. We must, therefore, delve into the situation and try to pinpoint the most crucial element Hume has not been able to find: namely, the *production* of the motion in ball B by its being struck by ball A.

3. The Production of Motion in Hume's Ball B

Evidently, the contiguity of the constant succession of the striking of ball B by ball A and the motion of ball B is not exactly the production of that motion by that striking. Yet that production is there, as Hume stresses. Perhaps we can find this production if we somehow manage to eliminate it from the situation without tampering with the Humean contiguous constant conjunction. We must, therefore, perform a *Gedankenexperiment* that conforms to the following:

Desideratum. The experiment must maintain: (i) the collision of ball A with ball B; (ii) the motion of ball B; (iii) the immediate and contiguous succession of the collision of both balls and the motion of B; and (iv) the truth of the universal contiguous conjunction of similar collisions and similar motions. But (v) the experiment must not preserve the production (or causation) of the motion of ball B by the collision of both balls.

Spelling the desideratum out makes it embarrassingly easy to provide examples illustrating it. A simple example is this:

(G.-C) Here is billiard ball B lying on the table and ball A is moving toward it with rapidity. There is, however, a mechanism M under the table such that when ball A reaches ball B, mechanism M will both stop ball A cold and prevent ball B from moving. There is, besides another mechanism M', such that it is timed by a certain clock to release the hold, if any, of M on B and set B in motion at an appropriate speed precisely at the moment that M stops ball A cold. Thus, when the collision takes place, ball B moves as if it had been caused to move by its collision with ball A.

Clearly all five clauses of our desideratum are fulfilled. The example is better than

what Hume's discussion required. We have added the condition on the appropriateness of the speed of motion, which Hume did not consider. Obviously, the example
can be enriched so as to meet an improved example of Hume's that brings in relevant features of mechanics that Hume ignored, e.g., the direction of the motions
and the velocities and masses of the balls in question. We shall assume that they are
all incorporated in (G.-C).

The superficial moral of experiment (G.-C) is that Humean generalizations of
constant conjunctions may hold, not only because they describe universal coincidences, but also because they may be partly causally true and partly coincidentally
true.

In (G.-C) we have hypothesized two causal mechanisms M and M', which together bring about the coincidence of the two causal paths. We have removed the
obvious causal connection between the motion of ball B and the collision between
the two balls by linking them to two different causal chains. But what exactly is to
remove the causal connection? Let's ponder this question.

Mechanism M literally *absorbs* the motion of ball A, and mechanism M' *produces* the motion of ball B. We have merely introduced, a Humean might remark,
new sequences of contiguous constant successions of changes. He will insist that we
are simply dealing with new Humean generalizations. Perhaps. Yet we have already
accomplished something noteworthy: we have *drained* causation from those Humean
sequences of contiguous constant successions. Clearly, the recipe is ready at hand:
we can introduce at any point in a causal path a pair of counterbalancing mechanisms, like M and M', such that one deviates causality from its normal path, while
the other mechanism reintroduces causality at the very same spatiotemporal point
of deviation. The problem of pinning production or causation down remains. What
exactly is that which can be drained or detoured from a causal path, and can be
taken from another causal path and reinstituted at the points of detour?

II. CAUSITY, MOTION, AND ENERGY

What, then, is present in the causal relation between the collision of ball A with
ball B and the motion of ball B? We can say with Hume that the collision *produced*
the motion in ball B. But wait! Ball A was moving in the direction of ball B with
rapidity. The collision of the two balls *communicated* motion from ball A to ball B.
This is an element present in all of Hume's experiments with his billiard balls and
with his objects similar to them in similar circumstances of collision. He didn't
dwell upon it, it is true. Yet that seems, on reflection, to be a most crucial element
missing in his examination of the billiard ball collision. Indeed, the collision of the
balls produced, not merely motion in ball B, as Hume reports, but produced—
and this is of the utmost importance—a very particular motion in ball B. The motion of ball B is characterized by a set of features (like velocity, direction, mass of
ball B) that connect directly to similar features of the motion of ball A. The collision of the balls produces motion in ball B in the sense that motion *transfers* from
ball A to ball B, but also in the sense that crucial features of the motion of A either

also transfer to the motion of ball B or are connected to features of the latter motion in specified ways. The heart of production, or causation, seems, thus, to be transfer or transmission. In Hume's example there is literally a transfer of motion and direction, etc., from ball A to ball B. Yet the *transfer* of motion is precisely the aspect of his perfect example of causation that Hume did not take into account. Our example (G.-C) gets rid of the causal connection between the two balls, and between their collision and the motion of ball B, just by eliminating the transfer of motion from ball A to ball B.

Causation and transfer of motion are in Hume's example either the same thing, but only contingently the same, or at least partially overlapping. But we *cannot* in general identify the transfer of motion with causation. This is already forcefully suggested by our example (G.-C). In it the transfer of the motion of ball A to mechanism M, we said absorbs that motion, is the causation of *some* state in M. Naturally, mechanism M may absorb the motion of ball A by this motion being transmitted to a moving part of M. But it is an open question, to be determined empirically, whether M can absorb the motion of ball A without replicating it.

There is, however, something perplexing about a transfer of motion. We seem to be hypostatizing motion. On the other hand, the motion of an object is rather a string of successive states of the object in question, each state lasting only an instant or a moment. Thus, the view that the motion of ball A is destroyed (perhaps only in part, if ball A bounces from ball B at a lower speed) and that the motion of ball B is created at the appropriate subsequent instant looks better. But at the surface ontological level, the level at which we deal with causes either in daily experience or in scientific research, it really does not matter whether we suppose that something passes, so to speak, bodily across time from the cause to the effect, or we merely suppose that something in the cause is destroyed at the moment of causation while a counterpart, even replica, of it is created in the effect. Whatever the profound metaphysics of time and causality may be, the crucial thing is that on the surface of it *causation is communication and transmission* of something in the cause to the effect, whether by replication or by actual carrying over across time. This transfer of something, including the transfer of certain orderliness, is the substance of causation.

In our example (G.-C), nothing leaves ball A to go to ball B. Mechanism M absorbs the motion of ball A fully. But it is not required that anything in mechanism M receives that motion—although something may do so. In any case, we know that there are causes that do not, at least in appearance, involve motion. But perhaps every case of causation is at bottom the transfer of motion from the cause to the effect, or from the objects involved in the event that is the cause to the objects involved in the event that is the effect. This is an empirical matter that we cannot decide by means of philosophical reflection on the general nature of causality. The fundamental point is that in causation there is a transfer (or metaphysical replication) of *something* in the setup containing the cause to the setup containing the effect. For convenience, neutrally, so as to beg no empirical issues, let us dub *causity* that, in general, which is characteristically transferred from the causal network to the effectal network. Thus, with the same neutrality we adopted in the preceding paragraph regarding the transfer of motion, we shall speak of the *transfer of causity*. And as before, we allow that there may not be a literal transfer across time of some selfsame item, but only an appropriate matching of a vanishing causity at a given spatiotemporal position and a contiguous creation of causity—perhaps of a different species—at an adjacent, or the same, space-time location.

Here we cannot enter into a discussion about whether causity is motion or momentum, or whether causity is something else, or perhaps something generic that allows of several different specifications. Empirical considerations suggest that motion itself is not causity, but that it just happens that when, as in Hume's billiard ball example, motion is transferred there is also a transmission of causity. As things are conceived nowadays by scientists, it is a safer bet to equate causity with *energy*. We must insist, however, that this equation manifests a *contingent identity*. To be sure, what exactly causity is is a topic for scientific investigation. At our level of philosophical reflection all we can say here is that causation is much more than universal coincidence of properties of events in contiguous succession. Causation is a very special transfer of something from the causal setup to the effectal setup. Philosophy can and should formulate some of the most general and pervasive principles or laws governing that transfer, but it cannot substitute for scientific research. On the other hand, philosophy must provide a foundation for scientific theorizing about causity.

Perhaps what is nowadays called energy is all the causity there is in the world. But perhaps there are still unknown forms of energy = causity. And perhaps there are further forms of causity that should better not be called energy because of their anomalous or bizarre properties. Perhaps psychological logical interaction involves peculiar specifications of causity. Questions such as these are not strictly philosophical, but belong rather to the empirical disciplines.

To some extent the transfer of the motion in ball A to ball B in their collision is a transfer of causity, although perhaps not all the causity spread about in ball A that is involved in the collision. To that extent Hume's own example shows that causity is a quantity that can be divided: some amount of motion and causity stays in bouncing ball A, and some amount of motion and causity transfers to ball B. Example (G.-C) merely shows that the total causity embodied in the motion of ball A can be transferred to mechanism M. Thus, the causity present in the causal setup can be fragmented and spread about among the objects comprising the effectal setup.

To the extent htat the motion of ball A is tantamount to causity, we are dealing with what may be called *active causity*. To the extent that objects have causal powers, we may speak of *potential causity*. But we shall not go into this here.

III. CAUSITY, EXISTENCE, AND ETIOLOGICAL PROPERTIES

1. Causity and Existence

The preceding discussion reveals that causity is not existence. Undoubtedly, temporal slices or states of the universe or of a thing might be said to inherit existence from their immediate predecessors. But the mere transfer of existence amounts to mere succession. Indeed, we can view Hume's account of causation as the mere transfer of existence along universal coincidences of properties alongside time.

Existence is not a quantity, nor does it allow of degrees. Existence is exactly the same everywhere. On the other hand, causity is a quantity and must be measurable.

2. Causity and Objects

Causity is measurable and appears in amounts that are divided in its transference from the causal setup to the effectal setup. But amounts of causity are not objects. For instance, in our current view of the world, the transfer of energy from the cause-involved objects to the effect-involved objects is not the transfer of one object from the former to the latter group. To be sure, most of the objects in a causal setup continue existing in the effectal setup, and they continue existing with most of their causal powers, i.e., with their reserves of causity. Yet their continued existence with their amounts of causity across time is *not* the transfer of causity that constitutes causation. Nevertheless, causity is partly transferred in causation across a time T by continuing to be attached to the objects that undergo the relevant causal changes at time T as the totality of the causal powers of the objects involved in the causal reaction. Causity is not a part of an object, but migrates from object to object riding on the backs of the objects that abide in the causal transaction. Causity, like space, time, and motion, remains an abstract quantifiable structure that unifies sets of objects into tightly organized systems. An obvious feature of that systematic unification is the unity of a *T-causally closed sector* of the universe, viz., a sector such that all the changes in it straddling time T preserve causity. Perhaps the only sector of the universe that is causally closed at all times is the universe itself.

3. The Dependency of Causity on Etiological Properties

We have already noted the principle $(C.3^*)$ of the piggybackness of the causal relation. It is also a principle of the piggybackness of causity. Although causity is a structure that unifies the patterns of changes that objects can undergo, causity is a dependent structure and the causal powers of objects are dependent properties. They depend on properties that objects must possess for causity and causal powers to come into being. We may call all those properties that ground causity and causal powers *etiological properties*, leaving it open whether all nondependent properties that objects can have by themselves are etiological. Causity is not an etiological property. In particular, since causity abides through causal transactions, it cannot be identical with any of the properties that objects change in such transactions.

The dependency of causity and causal powers on etiological properties is an ontological constraint on the realm of possible worlds. There is no possible world in which causity is preserved through the changes across a given time T without there being an orderly succession of the properties of changes or of the preservation of objects across T. To illustrate, it would be to postulate a world full of energy without the regular pattern of changes that make energy measurable. The postulation of energy would be entirely gratuitous to say the least. Naturally, as pointed out right at the inception of our discussion of Hume's example, there can be regularities in the events in the world without there being causation; hence, regularities of events do not necessitate any amount of causity. Conversely, causity grounds regularities. The transfer of causity across a time of change forces an orderly succession of the properties involved in the change. This is so even if the amount of causity is not preserved in the universe.

Causity is so intimately bound up with transfer and preservation across time that one cannot help asking whether the postulation of enduring objects involves the postulation of causity, whether substance and causation go conceptually hand in hand. The correct answer to this question seems to me to be emphatically affirmative. But we will not explore the connections between causity and substance here.

IV. FOUNDATIONS OF THE MEASUREMENT OF CAUSITY

A change is the succession of incompatible properties across a given time. A caused change is a change involving a transfer of causity across the time of the change. A caused change is, thus, productive; but the causity transmitted from the causal setup to the effectal setup does not belong to the change, but to the setups in question. *A caused change is causative preserving*, but not causity increasing. *Uncaused changes can be causity increasing.*

At any rate, the measurement of causity is the measurement of the causity spread about in the causal and effectual setups. We measure the causity of the objects involved in the change and the circumstances of the change. Here we are interested in the most basic and pervasive principles of causity measurement.

The most elementary principles required for the measurement of causity ground with the ontologico-epistemological dependency principle (C.3*) quoted above. They are:

(C.M.1) Causity is measurable.

(C.M.2) *Causity dependency.* Sets of properties, not the individual properties of an object, or field of objects, are assigned (by nature, of course) amounts of causity.

(C.M.3) *The possibility of epiphenomenalism.* The amount assigned (by nature) to a set of properties may be zero.

A set S of properties is epiphenomenal for an object, if and only if the properties of S are causally inefficacious: they have no causity. Which properties — perhaps psychological properties — are epiphenomenal is an empirical issue of the greatest importance to be decided by scientific research.

Principle (C.M.2) is founded on (C.M.1). By nature assigning causity to sets of properties, rather than individual properties, it makes measurement manageable. For causity (e.g., energy) to be measurable it must appear in finite amounts. But then not all properties of an object can be assigned nonzero amounts of causity, unless, of course, these amounts form a convergent series. The reason is clear: every object has an infinity of properties. For instance, given the infinitely divisibility of space, each object has an infinity of relations to portions of space, or the bits of matter that occupy such portions. More safely, for any property Pness that an object o has there is the infinity of properties o also has of the form being P or (P and Q) for any property Qness, whether o is Q or not. Thus, (C.M.2) cuts across these infinities.

The partition of the properties of an object o into sets of logically equivalent properties does not guarantee the finitude of the amount of causity assigned to o. The set of such sets may be infinite. We need another assumption to secure the needed finitude of the causity of each object.

The assumption that the sets of properties in a causal setup be assigned causity in amounts that lie in a convergent series will do. But it is a very drastic assumption. It presupposes too much causal holism: that somehow *all* the properties of the objects be taken together by nature in the assignment of causity amounts; furthermore, since the order of the terms of a convergent series is crucial, that assumption postulates an absolute causal ordering of all the properties or sets thereof, and there is little evidence of such holistic absolute ordering.

In the case of some particular properties we may certainly find that the assignment of causity to families of them is the sum of convergent series. If the space occupied by an object o is infinitely divisible, since presumably every part of o will have some causity, then the total amount C of causity assigned to o is also infinitely divisible. Then the assignments of all the amounts of causity assigned to the infinitely many parts of o will converge to C. In such cases we will have integrable continuous functions measuring the causity of an object along certain families of properties.

Regardless of the ultimate grounds for finitude, we have that:

(C.M.4)   *Causity finitude.* The total amount of causity possessed by an object and the total amount of causity assigned to every set of properties are both finite.

(C.M.5)   *Causal closure.* If a set S of properties of an object o is assigned an amount C of causity, then S is closed under logical equivalence. That is, if a property Pness is in S and Qness is equivalent to Pness, then Qness is also in S.

(C.M.6)   *Additivity of causity.* If an object o is made up of objects a and b, then the causity of o = the causity of a + the causity of b.

For convenience we shall speak of *representative causal subsets* of sets of causally equivalent properties. Two properties are causally equivalent if they belong to one and the same set to which some amount of causity is assigned. Given a set S of sets of causally equivalent properties, we can always consider a subset of s of S

whose members are pairwise not logically equivalent such that each member of s is a member of just one member of S. To the extent that nature is prodigal in its distribution of causity, it assigns causity to representative unit sets. Patently, when causity is assigned to a set that is not a unit set we confront a law of nature, namely, the law that establishes the *causal equivalence* of the members of the set. Such laws are not, strictly speaking, causal laws, because they do not furnish specific conditions for measuring the amount of causity that transfers from the causal setup to the effectal setup. Such laws simply establish that each of the members of the given set, even though not logically equivalent, can be indistinctly used as members of a representative set in the computation of causity measurements. For that reason we shall call such laws *laws of causal equivalence*. Obviously:

(C.M.7) *Causal economy*. The more economical nature is in its distribution of causity, the more laws of causal equivalence order the universe.

As far as mere causation goes, the universe could have a history of steadily increasing total causity. In such a case there are uncaused changes, i.e., changes in which the effectal setup has more causity than the causal setup, and the new, additional causity comes from nowhere. But the universe would be gaining a certain increase in orderliness.

On the other hand, as far as mere causation goes, the universe could have had a history of decreasing causity. This means that it would have become more disorderly. Undoubtedly, the actual history of the universe can combine both decreases and increases of causity. In particular, the universe can conserve its total amount of causity even though in some sectors causity decreases while in others causity increases.

A fully deterministic universe is one in which causity remains constant not only in toto, but at every change. This does not mean, of course, that causity is constant at every space-time position. Thus the conservation of causity (or energy) at every change is only a necessary condition of determinism.

Minimizing Arbitrariness:
Toward a Metaphysics of Infinitely Many
Isolated Concrete Worlds

PETER UNGER

A particular fact or event often appears arbitrary and puzzling, until it is exhibited as the outcome of certain causal processes. Usually, though not always, such a causal explanation helps to relieve the feeling of arbitrariness, at least for a while. But it is easy and natural for our feeling to reassert itself: We are moved to ask why just *those* causal processes governed the situation of that fact or event, rather than some others. To deal with this further, larger question, often we can exhibit those causal processes as being, themselves, the results of, or certain specific instances of, prior or more general causalities. Or, much the same, we can redescribe the initial particular fact, and perhaps the cited cause as well, and display the items thus described as an instance of some very general, fundamental law or phenomenon.[1] But any of this will only push the question back one step more. For we can always press on and ask: Why is it that just *that* very general phenomenon, or law, should be so fundamental, or indeed obtain at all, in the world in which we have our being? Within the usual framework of explanation, law and causation, there seems no place for such curiosity to come to rest. There seems no way for us to deal adequately with the brute and ultimate *specificity* of the ways in which almost everything appears to happen. And what seems worse, the specific character of certain of these laws or ways, even of quite fundamental ones, often seems so quirky, the very height of arbitrariness.

For an example of what I mean, why is it that, as science says, there is a certain particular upper limit on velocities for all (ordinary) forms of physical objects (which is, in familiar conventional units, very nearly 186,000 miles per second)? Why does just *this* limit obtain and not some other one, or better, some *range of variation* of uppermost speeds? Why must causal processes involving motion all conform to *this particular* restriction, rather than to some other, or to no such restriction at all?

For another example, why is it that almost all of the matter that there is comes in just *three* (rather small) sorts of "parcels" (protons, electrons, and neutrons)? Why not so much matter coming in just *two* sorts of parcels, at the level now in question, or better, just *one* sort?

For a third example, we may consider what current science takes to be the basic (types of) physical forces of nature: As of this writing, scientists recognize exactly four of these forces. At the same time, physicists are hard at work seeking to unify matters at least somewhat, so that there will be recognized no more than three such basic forces, possibly fewer.[2] Certain deep intellectual feelings, feelings that are, I believe, shared by many scientists, philosophers, and others, motivate this reduction. Along such reductionist, unifying lines, these *rationalist feelings* will not be much satisfied until we think of our world as having, at base, only one sort of basic physical force (or, alternatively, having none at all, forces then giving way to some more elegant principle of operation).

1. TWO FORMS OF RATIONALISM

How far can these rationalist feelings be followed? Unless his world is so chaotic as to be beyond any apparent cooperation, for a scientist it will almost always be rational to follow them as far as he can: Reduce the specificities of one's world to a very few principles, maybe one, operating with respect to a very few (kinds of) substances, maybe one; further, have the ultimate quantitative values occurring in the principles be as simple and unquirky as possible.

If scientists are *extremely* successful in satisfying these feelings, a philosopher (who may of course also be a scientist) might rest content with just those findings. Such a philosopher will hold a unique and beautifully simple principle to hold sway over *all* of (concrete) reality. Let me call this philosopher a *moderate rationalist.*

Another sort of philosopher will press on with these feelings, even in the face of the enormous scientific success just imaginatively envisioned. He is an *extreme rationalist*, and even in that happy situation, he will say this: Though the working of *our world* is as elegant as might be, why should *everything* there is behave in accord with just *this* specific principle? Why should *any* specific way, even a most metaphysically elegant, be preferred to any *other* specific way for a world to be? Why shouldn't there be *somewhere*, indeed be *many domains*, where things are less beautifully behaved? If so, then, *over all*, everything there is will be metaphysically most elegant, the *universe as a whole* preferring *no specific* way to any other, but, rather, giving each and every way its place and due. With a suitably enormous infinite variety of independent domains, of mutually isolated concrete worlds, we will have, over all, *the least arbitrary universe entire*; otherwise we will not, over all, have so little arbitrariness.

Both of these forms of rationalism are appealing to our deep rationalistic feelings (even while we have other feelings that go against them both). In this paper, I will not substantially favor either form over the other. Nor will I argue that it is most rational for us to adopt either of the rationalisms. My aim will be avowedly rationalist, but it will also be modest: I will be arguing that, at least in the evidential situation in which we do find ourselves, the metaphysics proposed by an extreme rationalist (for any evidential situation) should be taken very seriously. In other words, at least in our actual evidential situation, we should take very seriously a metaphysics of infinitely many mutually isolated concrete worlds.

Now, though it is not quite so dominant as it was some years ago, a heavily empiricist approach to concrete reality is, still, much more fashionable than a more rationalist approach. Accordingly, many philosophers will tell us not to worry about any apparent brute and fundamental arbitrariness in nature, which we seem to see and are, in fact, at least somewhat troubled by. Taken altogether, they will say, things just are the specific way that they are or, if one insists in putting it so, the specific way they happen to be.

Perhaps this basic empiricist attitude is unobjectionable; I do not know. Although I find it somewhat unappealing, perhaps there is no way it can be faulted. At the same time, there seems nothing that requires us to prefer this fashionable approach and to reject a more rationalist approach to all of concrete reality.

2. A RATIONALIST MOTIVATION FOR CONCRETE POSSIBLE WORLDS

In our physical science, I am told, certain magnitudes are taken as fundamental and universal. For instance, an example already cited, there is a fundamental upper limit on the velocity of any (normal) particle or signal. But, why just *that* upper limit, for *all* such speeds, everywhere and always? Why not just a bit more speed allowed or, alternatively, not even that much, if not around here and now, then many, many galaxies away, or many, many eons from now?

Consider a physical theory according to which there was a limit on speeds, but one that varied with the place of the mover in question. This might be due to, as the theory says, the mover's place being under an influence that varies with respect to place — for example, the influence of vast structures of intergallactic structures of matter, which surround any given place in all, or many, directions. On such a theory there would be no universality to, and thus no universal preference for, just the limit in our (only pretty big) neighborhood. Far away enough over there, the limit would be higher; and far enough away over *there*, it would be lower. Because it would not be universal, our neighborhood speed limit would not seem, or be, so arbitrary. By localizing our specificity, we minimize the arbitrariness that is associated with it.

A strategy of localization, it seems to me, does have its merits. But the present attempt at applying the strategy has at least two difficulties. First of all, according to what science seems to tell us, there is little or no evidence for thinking that our world conforms to the sort of theory just considered. Rather, available evidence seems to indicate the opposite: (Even if given infinite space) we'll get the same speed limit for *every* (big) neighborhood, no matter how remote from ours it may be.[3] (Morever, there seems to be a lot of evidence that we don't have infinite space, or infinite time.) So an attempt at spatial localization does not in fact seem feasible.

Second, and perhaps more important, any imagined law of variation of speeds would *itself* have some numbers constant for it. And then we might ask: Why should velocities vary with surrounding spaces in just *that* way, with just *those* constants constraining variation? Why shouldn't the regularities of varying speeds be otherwise, other than they happen to be in our whole physical world?

To remove or to minimize this remaining arbitrariness, we might try to "localize" the mode of spatial variation, too, staying with our general strategy. But how are we to do so? We might stretch things out over time: Different variation factors for different vast epochs. But the same problems arise here, too. First, what evidence there is about physical time is not so congenial. And, more fundamentally, there will be left as universal (and unexplained) some factors for variation over time of the space-variation constant(s). Why should just *those* temporal factors hold, and hold universally? Why not some others? Either we must admit defeat or we must reach out further, in order to achieve a *new form of localizing*.

Having used up all of space and time, even assuming both are infinite in all their directions, where do we go? We must expand our idea of the "entire universe," of all that there is. But in what way? A certain philosophical conception of *possible worlds* might provide the best route for our rationalistic localizing strategy. Indeed, it might provide the only route. It is my rationalist suggestion, then, to try to make more sense of concrete reality by adopting a metaphysics of many concrete worlds.

3. TWO APPROACHES TO A METAPHYSICS OF ISOLATED CONCRETE WORLDS: THE RATIONALIST AND THE ANALYTIC

It will be in a tentative and an exploratory spirit that I will advocate a metaphysics of many concrete words. The view I will favor is at least very similar to, and is perhaps the very same as, the view of such worlds developed by David Lewis.[4] My present motivation for taking such a view seriously, however, is quite different from his (main) motivation. The differences are such, it will emerge, that my approach is aptly called *rationalist*, or rationalistic, whereas his approach might better be called *analytic*, or analytical. It seems true however, that, at least in their main elements, the rationalist approach and the analytic approach are entirely compatible with each other.

Let us suppose the two approaches are indeed compatible. Then whatever motivation each yields can add to that from the other, so as to make more acceptable their shared metaphysical position. It is my hope that this is so.

At the same time, there are those philosophers unfriendly to this metaphysics for whom, I suppose, Lewis's analyses themselves are entirely unhelpful and implausible. Now, insofar as my rationalistic approach can be made appealing, such thinkers will have, perhaps for the first time, at least some motivation for accepting a metaphysics of many concrete worlds.

4. POSSIBLE WORLDS AS CONCRETE ENTITIES

It is fashionable for philosophers to talk of possible worlds. But much of this talk seems metaphorical, or heuristic, at best. This observation has moved several philosophers, J. L. Mackie being notable among them, to question the (significance of) this fashion. In his *Truth, Probability and Paradox*, Mackie writes ". . . talk of possible worlds . . . cries out for further analysis. There are no possible worlds except the actual one; so what are we up to when we talk about them?"[5] In my opinion, these words express a dilemma felt by many philosophers, though Mackie expresses it in a somewhat oblique and indirect way.

More directly put, the dilemma is this: Philosophical accounts of possible worlds fall into either of just two baskets. In the first basket are accounts where 'possible world' is to denote some "abstract entity," such as a set of mutually consistent propositions that, together, purport to describe comprehensively the world in which we live. Presumably, just one of these sets yields a completely successful description, all the others than failing.

Whatever their philosophical value, such accounts use the expression 'possible world', and even the word 'world', in a way that is bound to mislead. For such accounts, the world in which we live is *not* a possible world at all, let alone the most vivid and accessible example of one. For we live in a world consisting, directly and in the main, of stones, animals, people, and suchlike, not of sentences or propositions (however numerous and well behaved). We live in a world that is, at least in the main, *concrete*. So it is most unclear how any other candidate worlds, on the one hand, and the world we live in, on the other, might be suitably related so that *all* of them are *worlds*. Such accounts, then, tend to collapse into mere heuristic devices, even if some may be very helpful heuristically.

In the second basket, we find the story told by David Lewis and variants upon it. On such accounts, possible worlds are concrete entities, generally constituted of smaller concrete things that are at them, or in them. In this central respect, all of the (other) possible worlds are just like the actual world, the world in which *we* live. On this sort of account, the relations between worlds are just those of qualitative similarity and difference, as regards the various respects in which these concrete entities may be compared. These relations are of the same sort as some of those that obtain between "lesser" objects, e.g., between individual inhabitants, whether of the same world or of different ones.

On Lewis's treatment of worlds and their parts, no object can be at, or be a part of, more than one world, while every concrete object is at, or is a part of, at least one world. So each concrete entity that is itself not a world, but is only a world-part, is a part of exactly one of the infinity of concrete worlds.[6] I shall assume this treatment in what follows. I will advocate a many worlds metaphysics where each chair and each person, for examples, are at one and only one concrete possible world: A given chair, or a given person, is just at its own world and, thus, is *not identical* with *any* chair, or *any* person, that is at *any other* world. At most, the others are (mere) *counterparts of* the concrete objects first considered.

How does such a story go as regards relations of space, time and causality? First, there are some tiny worlds; the whole world here is, say, a single space-time point. Beyond those, the concrete inhabitants of a given world are related spatially and/or temporally and/or causally to at least some other inhabitants of that same world, so the world forms a spatial and/or temporal and/or causal system. But inhabitants of *different* worlds do *not* bear any of these relations to each other, nor does any complete world bear any to any other complete world. Causally, spatially, and temporally *isolated* from each other are the infinity of worlds.

In this second sort of account, it seems to me, it is clear enough, and not misleading, how the others, like the actual world, should *all* be *worlds*. But there is another sort of trouble with this account: It seems incredible, crazy, way beyond the reach of any even halfway reasonable belief.

So this is, in brief, our dilemma of possible worlds. On any account where matters are not incredible, things seem badly obscure or misleading. On any where things seem much less misleading, we face a "universe" that seems utterly incredible. What are we to do?

Formally, at least, there are three alternatives: First, we just don't take talk of possible worlds to be literal or serious; we treat it as *at best* a helpful heuristic. Second, we work out some way in which it's clear how both some abstract structures, on the one hand, and our actual concrete selves and surroundings, on the other, can all be worlds. Finally, we try to make a story of isolated concrete realms somewhat more credible, or less incredible.

Largely by way of a rationalist strategy of "localizing" specificity so as to minimize arbitrariness, we will be attempting the third alternative. So, we are at once involved in two tasks: One, making our own world seem more intelligible by incorporation of it into a relevantly vaster universe; two, making sense of other worlds by showing how they can form a system, a vast universe, by reference to which our actual world can be seen as being less disturbingly peculiar.

5. THE ANALYTICAL MOTIVATION FOR CONCRETE POSSIBLE WORLDS

At least for the most part, the analytical motivation for the metaphysics of many concrete worlds is best provided by Lewis. He does this in, among other writings, his early paper "Counterpart Theory and Quantified Modal Logic" and, later on, in his book *Counterfactuals.*[7] For present purposes, I might assume a familiarity with that motivation, especially as there is little of it that I can express as well as Lewis already has done. Still, as some may want reminding of the relevant aspects of the works in question, I will attempt a sketch of the analytical motivation here, a sketch that must be as crude as it is brief.

Now, some of the things believed by us are clear enough as regards their content. For example, it is relatively clear what is believed when I believe that the chairs in my living room are arranged in a rectangular pattern. In contrast, other things we believe seem to be quite obscure and even mysterious: that the chairs in my living room *might have been* arranged in a circular pattern (instead of in a rectangular pattern). Now, either we construct some theory, some analysis, of the content of the latter beliefs that renders the obscurity and mystery superficial, thus removing or at least lessening it, or else we leave things alone, our opinions then continuing to be fraught with mystery. The latter alternative is philosophically unappealing. Hence, there is motivation to construct a clarifying analysis.

On Lewis's analysis, we quantify over, or refer to, concrete objects that are other than our actual world or any part thereof. So the believed proposition that the chairs in my living room *might have been* arranged in a circular pattern is understood, *roughly*, as the proposition that there are worlds with chairs very similar to my living room chairs in rooms very similar to my living room, all in a very similar set of relations (mainly of "possession") to people very similar to me, and in at least some of those worlds the relevant chairs *are* arranged in a circular pattern. The subtlety of Lewis's analysis lies, of course, in the details that make such a rough treatment as the one above into a very much smoother treatment. But the general point is clear enough even now: the more mysterious "might have been" is understood in terms of the quite straightforward "are." By acknowledging many *more* chairs, rooms, and people than we ordinarily envision, we can understand everything here believed in terms of rather unmysterious relations—similarity and also circular arrangement—obtaining among suitably "full-blooded," unmysterious objects—chairs, rooms, and people.

Of particular interest to Lewis and to many other philosophers are our beliefs in counterfactual conditional propositions. An example is (my belief that) if the chairs in my living room were arranged in a circular pattern (instead of their actual rectangular one), then I would have been displeased at their arrangement. When reflected upon, such propositions appear to involve very mysterious nonexistent situations. But we believe many of these propositions to be true. So, again, a clarifying analysis is wanted.

Lewis offers an analysis that is of a piece with that offered for the simpler modal beliefs just considered. For our example, the analysis proceeds at least roughly as follows: There are the many worlds; among them are some where there is someone much like me who has his living room chairs arranged circularly; among these worlds some differ more than others from our world; in the ones that differ least—scarcely at all, except for the arrangement of such chairs—the chair owner, or any chair owner most like me, is displeased at the circular arrangement of his living room chairs.

As before, so again: By admitting lots more chairs, rooms, and people than are usually entertained, and by admitting lots more worlds for all those things to be in, we can understand accepted propositions in a manner that renders them relatively straightforward. We can understand them in a way that dispels much of the air of mystery that initially seems to surround them.

Sometimes we are in a mood when philosophical analyses seem of substantial value. When I am in such a mood, Lewis's analyses of the noted propositions often, though not always, strike me as accurate enough to be of value. Sometimes we are

in a very different mood: How can any proposition apparently so fraught with obscurity, mystery, and problems be equivalent to one that is so very much more
straightforward and, apparently, problem free? The mood this question signals is
hardly pecliar to our thought about modals and counterfactuals, much less to Lewis's
analyses thereof. The same doubts concern, for example, analyses of propositions
about knowing, where the statement doing the analyzing seems so very much more
free of all sorts of skeptical problems and paradoxes than does the knowledge claim
itself. Further examples abound; the philosophical situation is quite a general one.

When we doubt the value of philosophical analysis, two things can be tried.
First, we can try to show ourselves, via subtle psychological explanations, that two
propositions can indeed be equivalent, in as serious a sense of "equivalent" as we
might wish, and yet *strike us* as being so different in those respects just noted. With
enough ingenuity, perhaps this can be done for a substantial range of interesting
proposed analyses; perhaps it can be done, in particular, for Lewis's analyses of
modal and counterfactual propositions. But maybe that won't really work well, either generally or for the particular cases currently in focus.

A second thing we might try is to construe a proposed analysis as an *explication*. Now, we take what we begin with as inherently problematic, not just of a
form that, typically, engenders illusions of real problems in beings with minds like
ours. In a sense, what we begin with is beyond full redemption. Then, explicating,
we do this, or something of the like: We put forth something that preserves a relatively unproblematic core, but then only such a core, of that which we find so
problematic. Generally, an explication will add something to the core that it preserves. When something is added, the addition will dovetail well with what is preserved from the original; it will yield something very much "along the lines" of the
original problematic thought, but, at the same time, it will be relatively clear and
problem free. We can, then, have a variety of explications of any given problematic
thought, none of which is equivalent to that thought or to each other, but none of
which differs very greatly in content from the original thought. Each of these, if
there is more than one, will be a *good* explication of that troublesome original.

I do not think that Lewis ever offers his system as (part of) a program for
such explications, not analysis proper. Yet I feel free to take it either way and, depending on how I feel about analysis itself, sometimes I take it in one way, sometimes in the other. Whether taken as analysis proper or as explication, Lewis's proposals can give us some analytic motivation for the metaphysics of many worlds.

Somewhat conservatively, I'd like to say this: Either Lewis's proposals provide accurate analyses, as he intends, or, if not that, then at least they provide good
explications of those troublesome thoughts to which he turns his attention. That is
something I'd like to say. Is it true? I am uncertain.[8] Fortunately, we need not decide this issue here.

As will be remembered, our own project is to present appealingly the *rationalist*
approach to many worlds, not the analytical one. Even so, we will continue to refer
to Lewis's motivation. This is understandable. By noting its contrasts with the analytical approach, we can help make clearer the rationalist approach we are proposing.

6. THE MUTUAL ISOLATION OF THE MANY CONCRETE WORLDS

To minimize arbitrariness, and make the world more intelligible, we need to employ our strategy of localization. Then any particular way things happen will be less than universal and will be offset by, and thus not preferred to, other ways things happen elsewhere. This gives an argument for the causal isolation of concrete worlds and their respective inhabitants.

Suppose there is a concrete world A and another one B with, say, an individual rock, a, an inhabitant of A and not of B and an individual window, b, a part of B and not of A. Can rock a have any effect upon window b, perhaps if accelerated to some enormous velocity and at once being exceedingly massive?

Suppose that a interacted with b so that it broke b or, perhaps, so that it turned b into a translucently colored, purple window. Then there would be certain laws, or regularities, or whatever, that governed or described the way that at least some objects of A interacted with at least some objects of B. However interesting or uninteresting to us in their formulation, any such law would have *some particular character*. We can then ask: Why do the interacting objects of A and those of B interact in *just that* way, or in *just those* ways, and not in some other manner? Why is the character of their interaction just the way it in fact happens to be? We face the threat of arbitrariness.

Our strategy is to localize any such threatening arbitrariness. We implement it, in this case, by having A and B as two (only *somewhat* isolated) *realms* of just one *world*. (We can talk of these realms, of course, as worlds, but then we use 'world' in a new sense. To avoid needless ambiguity, let's not now talk in that way.) Then the way in which realms, or objects in realms, interact in this world, W_1, will be just one way things happen in the universe entire. There will also be (infinitely) many other worlds, $W_2, W_3, \ldots, W_n, \ldots$, in each of which there are two realms that interact in *other* ways. And there will be infinitely many *other* worlds with *no* interacting realms. And there will be infinitely more *still* other worlds with *three* interacting realms, and so on. Now, all of these worlds together allow us to see as local any specific manner of the interacting of any objects. But they can do that only if they themselves are all mutually isolated and present no higher-order interactions of any particular character or manner whatsoever. Thus, from the point of view of our strategy, there must be largest *isolated* concrete parts of the universe entire. It is these concrete items that we have been calling *worlds* and that, quite understandably, we will continue to speak of with that appellation.

Perhaps the argument just given is, even in its own rationalist terms, somewhat incomplete. Suppose that for any given world, W_1, there is interaction between it and *every other* world of an enormous infinity of worlds. Then there might be no arbitrariness for a given interaction law and each of the, say, two worlds it relates. For a world with just the character of either one of the two will interact in each of an infinity of other lawful ways with (at least) one world with just the character of the other. And perhaps we can generalize from two worlds, and pairwise interaction, to any number whatever. Then there will be, even across worlds, objects interacting in every imaginable way and then some; no way of interacting will be preferred to any other.

Is so *very* much *interaction* for a world a coherent possibility? Can there really be *laws* operating in *such* multiplicity at all, or any such *infinitely various causality?* I think not.

Suppose, as may be, that this negative thought is misplaced. Then there still remains one rationalist line of argument for causal isolation: It is at least somewhat arbitrary that a given world, any world, interacts *at all* with any other world, whether the world interacts with only one other world or whether with an enormous infinity. Interaction is one specific way of relation, and noninteraction is another; so neither happens universally. For any candidate world of any character, at least one such candidate interacts with other candidates and also, elsewhere in the universe entire a duplicate candidate doesn't interact. The candidate that does interact is but a realm of a larger world, the world itself containing such interaction but not interacting. Only the duplicate candidate that fails to interact is a proper world and not a realm, or inhabitant, of a world. Whatever interacts, then, is not a world; so there are infinitely many concrete worlds, none of them interacting.

The rationalist approach argues for causal isolation among real concrete worlds. The analytical approach moves us in the same direction: It often seems puzzling what is claimed where we say one event *caused* another. So we want a clarifying analysis of what it is for one particular thing or event to cause another. Now, following a suggestion of Hume, Lewis and others have attempted to analyze such singular causal judgments in terms of counterfactual conditional statements involving the (alleged) cause and the (alleged) effect.[9] Very *roughly*, "c caused e" is analyzed as: if c had not occurred, then c would not have occurred. (To make matters smoother, the analyzing counterfactual must be made more complex and must also be understood in a suitably context-sensitive manner.) Hard as the work is to smooth things out adequately, the underlying idea is intuitive and appealing.

Now, as a formal possibility, one may adopt some such counterfactual analysis of causality and, at the same time, have no theory of counterfactuals themselves. But, at best, that would be displaying two apparent mysteries as being at base one. So we are moved to adopt a clarifying analysis of counterfactuals as well.

As indicated previously, Lewis's analysis of counterfactuals is a promising view. Wedding this analysis to a counterfactual analysis of causation gives one an analysis of causation in terms of relatively straightforward (noncausal) relations among concrete worlds and inhabitants thereof.

With this background well enough in view, we ask: What does the analytical approach indicate, or perhaps even require, as regards causal relations between concrete worlds? There occur two sorts of argument: a "cautionary" one and a more substantive one.

The cautionary argument: Propositions about causal relations in a given world are, as remarked, analyzed in terms of (less mysterious) noncausal relations between the relevant parts of that world and certain parts of other worlds. Now, providing that these worlds do not themselves enter into causal relations, there will not lurk somewhere in the relations analytically employed a circularizing causal feature. But if there are causal relations between worlds, as well as within worlds, there is at least a threat of circularity.

The substantive argument: Any propositions as to transworld causation will be unanlyzable in terms of the theory. Then they will be without any noncircular analysis and, requiring one as they do, these propositions will have a content at least as mysterious-seeming as our more ordinary causal judgments. So there will be an insoluble problem just in case some such positive propositions are true. Given this approach, we conclude that there are no true propositions stating transworld causal relations.

If the inhabitants of any given world never interact with those of any other, then the items from the different worlds will not be *connected* in any realistic way. So they won't form very much of a unified system. Still, if the inhabitants from different worlds were spatially related, they would be in a system of spatial relations, and that would satisfy our idea of unity to some considerable degree. Likewise, if the events of one world were related temporally to those of others, then that would be an inclusive temporal system that could play some unifying role. But, it can be argued, these relations do not obtain, nor do any other "dimensional" relations.

We have just supposed a separation between causal relations, on the one hand, and relations of space and time on the other. But perhaps there really is no such separation. Rather, space, time, matter, energy, and causality, in a suitably general sense of this last term, must all be understood in terms of each other. So a real space has causal properties that influence the course of matter and energy in it over time. The causal features of a space are inherent to, inseparable from, its real geometry. Now, some (whole) spaces will bend light rays a certain amount in a certain direction, others more so and others less. Still others will leave the light's path unbent. As the former spaces will be understood as influencing the light's path in (what are to us) more striking ways, so the latter may be understood as influencing it, too, but in what are (regarded by us as) less striking ways. Well beyond this example, the considerations can be generalized. So causality cannot be removed from realistic spatial and temporal relations between concrete items, that is, from any spatiotemporal relations that might suitably serve to connect them into a unity. If this is right, then the arguments just preceding, as they undermine *all* alleged transworld causal relations, will, in particular, undermine any arguments relevant to any alleged transworld spatial and temporal relations. In conclusion, any (inhabitant of any) concrete world will be spatially and temporally unconnected with any other (inhabitant of any other) concrete world.

Suppose one has no belief in what I've just said. Suppose one thinks, instead, that space and time really are independent, in every important sense or way, from questions of causal relation. Even so, our rationalist approach will lead one to think that the concrete worlds are isolated spatially and temporally.

Recall our discussion of section 2. We saw there that, in order to implement our strategy of localization satisfactorily, we need a universe entire that comprises much more as to space and as to time than all of the time and space of our world (even if our space and time are infinite in all their directions). We need, that is, a universe comprising infinitely many spaces and times and infinitely many worlds of which those are (some of) the dimensions. These worlds will not themselves be spatially or temporally related, for that would fuse into one the various spaces, and the various times, needed as distinct for a full implementation of our localizing strategy. From our rationalist perspective, therefore, we are motivated to accept the idea of many concrete worlds that are each totally isolated from all of the others.

7. ON THE RESISTANCE TO THE IDEA OF INFINITELY MANY ISOLATED CONCRETE WORLDS

Let us confront the great resistance people feel toward the view of many mutually isolated concrete worlds. For unless we unearth implicit factors of resistance and promise to do something to disarm them, any more positive steps toward greater credibility are likely to fall on deaf ears. Why, then, are so very many philosophers, as indeed they are, so terribly resistant to such a view? Why do people think it so crazy to consider such a view a serious candidate for acceptability?

The metaphysics we propose to take seriously posits a group of concrete worlds with two salient features. First, *infinite diversity*: every way for anything to be, or behave, is a way that (some) things are, or do behave, if not in a particular given world (say, the actual world), then in some other one. Second, *total isolation*: each world is totally isolated from every other world. Each of these two features does, as a matter of psychological fact, promote much resistance to our metaphysical view.

The matter of infinite diversity has been rather extensively discussed in the literature. For example, this diversity has been thought to undermine the rationality of predictions about the actual world, and it has been thought to foster an attitude of indifference toward our own future actions and their consequences.[10] Does the infinite diversity implicit in our metaphysics have such dire implications, otherwise avoidable? If so, then that would be reason, even if not conclusive reason, to reject the metaphysics.

Especially in his most recent writings, Lewis has argued, convincingly to my mind, that there are no such problems stemming from a metaphysics of infinitely many concrete worlds, but only various confusions to such a threatening effect.[11] Although it would be useful for still more to be said to counter this source of resistance, there is not now an acute need to do so.

I turn, then, to spend some energy meeting resistance stemming from the other main feature of our metaphysics, total isolation. The total isolation of each world promotes two main sorts of worry. One of them is more blatant and obvious; the other, I think, is more profound. Both merit some discussion in the present essay.

The more obvious worry is this: in that there is total isolation of worlds, there is, in particular, complete causal isolation among them. So nothing in our world, ourselves included, will ever interact with any other world, or anything in any other world. Accordingly, the metaphysics in question posits all sorts of things that none of us ever will, or ever can, connect with any experience or observation. Worlds there are with cows that fly, and with particles generally like our electrons but a hundred times as massive. As we are causally isolated from these worlds, cows, and heavy electrons, we can never perceive them, nor any of their causes or effects. So it seems that we can never have any experiential reason for thinking there to be such things. But if no experiential reason for such a thought as to such contingent existents, then no reason is possible for us at all. Such a rarified metaphysics is difficult even to tolerate, let alone to find at all acceptable.

This worry can be met in either of two main ways. As I understand him, Lewis would meet it by arguing that we need not have *experiential* reason to believe in such otherworldly things to accept them with reason. Rather, adequately searching ratiocination about contingency and necessity, conducted (largely) a priori, will give us reason enough for our metaphysical view.[12] This is, or is very close to, a position of extreme rationalism. Now, whatever the strengths and the weaknesses of this sort of answer, there is another way to meet the worry in question.

From a position of moderate rationalism, we can argue that there can be some *very indirect experiential* evidence for the idea of such outlandish, isolated entities. Near this paper's end, in sections 10 and 11, I will attempt such an argument. Moreover, I will there argue that we *now do have* some such indirect experiential reason, or evidence. But, as indicated, this argument will have to wait.

For there is another worry stemming from causal isolation that is, though less obvious, philosophically deeper and more important. That deep worry is this: According to so much of our commonsense thinking, all of concrete reality forms a single, unified system of concrete objects. We are among the objects of the system, as are our parts and the particular experiences and thoughts we produce, or enjoy, or suffer. So are the many things around us. Each of these objects is, somehow or other, temporally related to every other one. Each of those that are in space at all (and *maybe* all of them are in space) is spatially related to all the other spatially located objects. Finally, there is at least a presumption regarding any two concrete objects that they are both embedded in (at least) one causal, or quasi-causal, network or system.

However well or badly conceived it may be, this aspect of common sense is very important to us. For it would serve to satisfy our belief, perhaps even our desire, too, that all of reality be sufficiently *unified*, at least all of concrete reality. Or so we are given to think. For, as we usually reckon matters, without causal, spatial, and temporal relations among them, the concrete entities that exist will not be sufficiently *connected* for all of them to be parts of a universe that is an intelligible unity or whole.

The view of isolated concrete worlds, with their mutually isolated different inhabitants, does not allow for these wanted connections. Thus it does *not* present all of the concreta there are as forming, or as belonging to, what is an encompassing *unity*.

Let us now turn to deal with this negative thinking, proceeding by stages through the next two sections.

8. THE UNIVERSE ENTIRE, THE OBJECTS IN IT, AND CONDITIONS OF UNITY

In the face of this negative conclusion, how might we make less incredible a metaphysics of infinitely many concrete worlds? They, and their respective inhabitants or parts, will be utterly isolated from, and unconnected with, each other. Yet we do believe that they all belong, somehow, to one universe entire. How can they be so unconnected and yet participate in an appropriate *unity*, so as to achieve this belonging?

We want a credible answer. But it is important not to expect too much from a candidate answer. For we might well be confused, at least much of the time, in our conception of what the *whole* universe *is*. We might often be prone to take it to be very much like one of its mere parts or constituents, whereas it may in fact be very unlike any constituent, however great, that it ever might have. If we are prone to such a confusion, then we might be prone to think like this: The conditions of unity for the universe entire must be very like those for certain of its objects, in particular like those for some grand and complex possible world. Now, the unity conditions for individual worlds are rather stringent; perhaps each part of any such world must be at least temporally related to (at least some) other parts. Hence, we might conclude, the universe itself must have all its part in such a connected system. From this perspective, perhaps a badly confused one, the metaphysics of possible worlds will seem to yield a universe so many of whose parts are so very, very inappropriately related.

It is my suspicion that, at bottom, this line of thinking, or at least one rather like it, is the main cause of resistance to the metaphysics we are trying to advocate. So I will argue for the inappropriateness of any such line of thinking.

The universe or, as we may say somewhat artfully, the *universe entire* is very different indeed from anything else there is, or ever may be. For the universe entire is, of necessity, more *inclusive* than anything else and, indeed, is absolutely all-encompassing. As it is distinguished from all else by this feature, there is nothing else required to guarantee its existence. In particular, we do not need any distinctness, or boundary conditions, required for at least many lesser objects, perhaps for all.[13]

In the case of such lesser objects as require some such broadly construed boundary conditions, and perhaps all of them do, how are the conditions to be fulfilled positively? Suppose that the object is concrete and not infinitesimal. So it has concrete parts that are so related as to constitute it, but not any other object. So each such object has, for a plausible suggestion, a special *cohesive* unity that holds between all of its parts, in virtue of which they are *all* of *its* parts and in virtue of which *it* is *just that object*, none other. An example: The stars in our galaxy are united, via mutual spatial and (other) causal relations; these unifying relations distinguish the galaxy they thus form from the rest of the actual world. So, deriving from these relations of unity, there is the distinctness required for our galaxy to be a genuine object.[14]

Because the universe entire is guaranteed unique in any case, there need not be any unity imposed on, or found in, its parts to generate the distinctiness for it that, perhaps, every object must have. Even if the universe is wholly concrete, as many nominalists believe, this will be so. Accordingly, when the object of our consideration is the universe entire, we may relax our usual requirements for unity.

9. A SORT OF UNITY FOR A UNIVERSE OF MANY ISOLATED CONCRETE WORLDS

On a metaphysics of many concrete worlds, the universe entire will not be unified through connecting relations among its main concrete parts. But this does not mean that the universe will not be a unity. For it, or the concrete aspect of it, might be unified in some other way, where connections and dimensional relations are not the unifying factors. But, then, *how* might such a universe still qualify as a unity?

Being sympathetic with my rationalist project, though not going so far as to believe in it, David Lewis has offered me in conversation a highly appealing answer. Let me try to recount it, develop it a little, and then notice its implications (as Lewis has done) for a metaphysics of (infinitely) many unconnected concrete worlds.

Consider a circle dance with boys and girls partnered one to one. After going through a certain sequence of steps, a dance unit, the boys and girls change partners; perhaps each girl goes one boy in the clockwise direction, each boy then going one girl in the counterclockwise direction. With new partners, the boys and girls go through the dance unit sequence again. And, then, they change partners again in the aforesaid manner, and so on.

Consider three variations of this dance. In the first, each girl dances with all the boys except for two; no girl gets all the way around the circle nor, then, does any boy. On this variation, the dance is, with respect to major elements, *incomplete*. In the second variation, each girl dances with each boy exactly one time; so everyone goes right around the whole circle and then stops. This variation has the dance being relatively *complete*. A third variation has each girl dance with each boy once and, then, dance a second time with each of her first two partners. So everyone goes right around the circle and then some. On this variation, the dance will be *redundant*, in a salient and relevant way. The second variation is, I suggest, more of a unity than either the first or the third: For, unlike the first, it is complete and, unlike the second, it is not redundant.

The unity of just the middle (second) dance will be clear enough, I think, whether the dance is taken as a particular occurrent event (concrete) or whether as an (abstract) choreographic structure. Of course, all three variations must be treated the same with respect to such a further consideration. But that is easily enough accomplished. In such a case, connecting relations—causal, spatial, and temporal— will be alike for the three variations; either they will be present in all or else absent in all. As far as such relations go, then, the question of unity should receive the same answer in each of the three cases. But, whether such relations are all absent or whether all present, that question receives a different answer for the second variation, a positive answer, than it does for the first and the third. So, for the question of unity, whether related items be concrete or whether abstract, connecting relations are not always crucial. On the contrary, at least for a certain range of cases, the combination of relevant completeness and nonredundancy can make for unity.

Let's consider another example, one that seems more directly concerned with nature itself, indeed with fundamental features of nature. Consider, first, a concrete world with exactly three types of fundamental particles: one type has mass and positive electric charge, one type has mass and negative electric charge, and, finally, one type has no mass and positive electric charge. Consider, next, a world that has each of these three types of basic particles and, also, just one more type: a sort of particle that has no mass and negative electric charge. The second world is, I suggest, more of a unity than is the first, even though there is no relevant difference in connecting relations between the two cases. For the second world, though not the first, is relevantly complete.

Explicitly suppose that each type of particle is instanced an equal number of times, in both of the aforesaid worlds and, thus, in particular in the second, more complete one. Now consider a third world that has, as regards fundamental particles, just the same four *types* as in the second world. But, unlike in the second world, in this third there are many more particles of the fourth type, with negative electric charge and no mass, than there are of the other types, the numbers for the three others being, again, exactly the same. This world is, it seems to me, less of a unity than is the second world, again despite no relevant difference in any connecting relations. And the reason for this is, it appears, that there are *extra*, or *redundant*, particles of the fourth type in this world. Of these three worlds, just the second one has both a relevant completeness along with a relevant lack of redundancy. Because of that, just this second world is (much of) a unity, whereas the first and third worlds are not. Connecting relations for the small concrete items have nothing to say in the matter; but, apparently, a good deal gets said anyway. So, by themselves, the combination of relevant completeness and nonredundancy can make for unity and can do it in what would appear to be quite an extensive range of cases.

Contemplating our main subject, the suggestion is that the universe entire, as a universe (whose concrete aspect is one) of many isolated concrete worlds, is a case in this extensive range. The main relevant elements are the concrete worlds. When will there be a universe that is a unity? When the worlds altogether exhibit completeness, but do not exhibit redundancy. Well, when will *that* be?

The universe will be complete providing that every way that a world could possibly be is a way that some world is.[15] What are the possibilities here? As far as the details go, I have no way of knowing. But we need not say what they are. To help ensure the wanted completeness, though, we should have a *very liberal* conception of possibility at work. We need not, I think, allow "situations that are to make true statements that are contradictory." But our range of possibilities, our range of various worlds, must be enormously abundant; in an old-fashioned word, we need a *plenitude*. So our range of metaphysical possibilities must include, I imagine, many that are quite beyond our own abilities to conceive of in any illuminating way or detail, as well as many that may at times seem mere fabrications of mind-spinning: As a (self-styled) rationalist, I need unity for the universe entire. For this unity, I need an *extremely great infinite variety* of worlds; without so very many qualitatively different worlds, we'll lack completeness and, thus, lack unity.

For unity we need nonredundancy as well, not just completeness. What does this mean for the ultimate case, presently being considered, of the universe entire, with its infinitely many varied worlds? In particular, does it mean that no world has any qualitative duplicate? It would be nice and neat if it did mean that. However, nonredundancy will not yield as much as that, I am afraid, but rather will yield this slightly weaker proposition: Either each world is without qualitative duplicate or else if any world does have at least one duplicate, then each world has as many duplicates as does every other world.

With completeness and nonredundancy thus available, we have a universe entire that is at least something of a unity. Indeed, as suggested in the section just preceding, it might be a unity of the only sort one should ever expect for the universe entire. At any rate, the foregoing considerations do a fair amount, I think, to motivate serious consideration for a metaphysics of infinitely many isolated concrete worlds. But, especially from our rationalistic perspective, some new problems seem to arise.

Suppose that each concrete world had exactly seven duplicates. Then there would be exactly eight worlds of each character. There would be *unity* enough, for there would be completeness along with no relevant redundancy. Still, the universe imagined seems highly *arbitrary*: Why should there be just *eight* worlds of each character, rather than some other number? Our rationalist feelings are repelled by the suggestion of such an eightfold way.

Well, how many worlds are there of each character? The rationalist aspects of my mind find two answers that seem at least somewhat more appealing than any others: one and, at the other extreme, an *infinite* number of each character.[16] The latter answer, infinity, itself raises questions as to what *size* of infinity we have at hand. As this further question appears to find no motivated answer, there seems to be a preference, generated thereby, for the former. In addition, the former answer—no duplicate for any world—might find some adequate indiscernibility argument in its favor, though really good indiscernibility arguments are, I think, very hard to come by. At any rate, all things considered, I hesitantly advocate the answer, *one*. So, I thus advocate a metaphysics of an *extremely* great infinity of mutually isolated concrete worlds, not even one of which is duplicated even once in the universe entire.[17]

10. EMPIRICAL SCIENCE AND METAPHYSICS

The arguments so far presented for our many worlds metaphysics, both rationalist and also analytical, are a priori, either entirely or at least to a very high degree.

Except for purposes of illustration and exposition, (virtually) no appeal is made to our sensory experience. Now, perhaps the matters here treated are, indeed, always best treated by way of some such a priori approach. Given the nature of these matters, that is not implausible. On the other hand, it may be that, instead, certain of these matters should receive a more empirical treatment, a treatment that contains both elements of experience and those of pure reason, and each to a significant degree. Let me try to explain and motivate this mixed, more empirical treatment, and then examine some of its consequences.

Near the beginning of this paper, it will be remembered, I said that any given universal limit on velocities, as it gave absolute universality to some special, particular feature of things, would be arbitrary; it would, indeed, be highly arbitrary, too much so to be tolerated by a rationalist approach to the universe entire. In the spirit of this enquiry, I will stand by this statement, which seems correct from any rationalist approach that is even moderately vigorous or pure. But, then, I went on to say, or at least to imply, that it would be *just* as arbitrary to have *no* velocity limit as universal. This is, or is very close to, the position of extreme rationalism. Although this further contention can be made appealing from a rationalist perspective, it does not seem to be required by such a perspective, as was the previous statement. In other words, from a general rationalist point of view, it does not seem, or does not always seem, so *highly arbitrary* to have *no* such *universal* limit as it does to have any *given* universal limit.

Suppose that this is indeed the case. Then a world where there is no such limit will, other things equal, be a less arbitrary world than a world where there is such a limit, whatever the limit's particular value. The following question then arises: Which is a less arbitrary *universe entire*, a universe that contains only a world (or worlds) of the first, less arbitrary sort or a universe that contains that and, besides, all those worlds that are more arbitrary ones? From a purely a priori stance, there is something to be said for each of the two alternatives.

On the one hand, a universe entire that contains even the more arbitrary worlds does not prefer any world to any other one. So on the vastest scale we can (yet) conceive, the universe will not then show any preference. That makes such a universe, with infinitely many concrete worlds, seem less arbitrary than a more restrictive universe entire.

On the other hand, a universe with such arbitrary worlds seems to have all sorts of quirky, mutually isolated brute facts: There's this world with just this upper limit, and there's that world with just that one, and there's nothing grander in the world that displays these two isolated brute facts as various *instances* of, or *outcomes* of, some *deeper, less quirky* reality.

Suppose that the second sort of universe entire contains, as does the first, (infinitely) many concrete worlds but all with no universal velocity limits. Suppose, further, that it contains worlds that have, even as quite fundamental features of them, arbitrary features. For example, suppose that some form of quantum theory governs many of these worlds, as it seems to govern the actual world, so that only *certain* configurations of "small particles" ever obtain. *Other* configurations are never found anyplace in these worlds. Now, a universe entire that contained certain sorts of more arbitrary worlds, say, quantum worlds, but failed to contain other sorts, say, worlds with universal speed limits, would, it seems from a rationalist perspective, clearly be more arbitrary than a universe that excluded no world at all. If this is right, then the dilemmatic question we are facing reduces to another one.

Suppose that there is at least one world that is as free of natural arbitrariness as can be. Vague as my formulation of it is, we will entertain this supposition. Now we may ask: Which is the less arbitrary, a universe entire that contains only such a least arbitrary world, or a universe that has every sort of world there might be, however quirky and peculiar? From a purely rationalist perspective, this question seems impossible to decide.

Now, the case for a universe entire with just a metaphysically best world is *helped* if it can be shown, a priori, that there is only *one* world that is least arbitrary. The case for having all worlds is *helped* if it can be shown, a priori, that there is *no uniquely* least arbitrary world. But, whether or not either of these alternatives can be argued a priori, such considerations are less than decisive. So it is that, from our rationalist perspective, a priori arguments can take us only so far in the matter of whether there are, in the universe entire, many concrete worlds or only one, the actual world. At least, this is how the question often does appear.

With this appearance before us, the suggestion arises that we import some empirical evidence into our discussion. Conjoined with some appropriate a priori reasoning, perhaps such evidence can point the way toward a rational stance for us in the matter, at least rational from our general rationalist perspective. For this to happen successfully, we must import the evidence quite indirectly. This is, or is very close to, the position of moderate rationalism.

Suppose the world we live in, our actual world, provided us with sensory evidence that did much to support a conception of it as highly unarbitrary. Somewhat specifically, what do I mean by this supposition? I am uncertain. Nonetheless, these may be some illustrative examples: Evidence indicated that the real geometry of our world was Euclidean, so that there was zero curvature to space everywhere; the world seemed to be spatially and temporally infinite in all directions, rather than of some specific finite size and age; matter did not mainly come in three main types of "elementary particles," but only in one type or, perhaps better still, in different numbers of types in different very large regions and eras. I think that you may be getting the idea.

Further suppose that, as more experiments were performed and observations made, they tended to support a conception of our world where it appeared increasingly less arbitrary. According to available evidence, our world seemed, more and more, to be very nearly the metaphysically best, most elegant world. There was, in a phrase, epistemological convergence toward the metaphysically best world.

In such epistemic circumstances, it would be rational, at least from a rationalist perspective, to give credence to the following propositions. First, that our world was the least arbitrary world. And, second, that our world was the only world there was at all.

The rationality of the first of these propositions is, I presume, acceptable enough for such a context. But how do we move from it to get the second as well? Here is an argument that is, I think, suggestive and even appealing, though quite far from being conclusive.

There is an enormous infinity of candidate worlds, or "designs for worlds." There is even a very great infinity of such candidate worlds with a place for intelligent, philosophical beings. In this latter great infinity, the number of least arbitrary candidates, only one, is very small in comparison to the number of those more arbitrary than the minimum. Now, if all of these candidates were successful, it would be *highly* unlikely that we should find ourselves in the least arbitrary one. But, we are assuming, that is just the sort of world in which we are. So it is highly unlikely that they are all successful. We accept the very likely idea that is the negation.

Furthermore, it would be more arbitrary for some and not all of such (more arbitrary) candidates to be successful than it would be for none of them to be. So, on our perspective, and given that evidence, it would be rational to accept the idea that our world, the (minimally arbitrary) actual world, is the only world in the universe entire.

We may perhaps agree that in the face of certain "favorably convergent" evidence, and given our rationalist perspective, it would be rational to accept a metaphysics where the actual world is the only world and to reject our metaphysics of many concrete worlds. On the other side of the coin, we may then also agree that in the face of very different evidence, which supported a conception of our actual world as a very quirky, highly arbitrary world, the reverse would be rational: At least from our rationalist perspective, we may then accept our metaphysics of infinitely many concrete worlds and reject a metaphysics of the actual world as the only concrete world. Or, at the least, in such an evidential situation, it would be rational for our rationalist to take many worlds metaphysics very seriously and to be somewhat doubtful about the more ordinary view. This is (a modest form of) moderate rationalism.

As in the previous sections, the material so far presented in this one is purely (or almost purely) a priori argument. What we have newly done so far is to add some *a priori epistemological arguments*, concerning how a rationalist might best interpret various sorts of evidence, to an a priori metaphysics already in place. Let's now inject some empirical evidence itself into the mix of our available considerations.

Well, then, what *is* the available empirical evidence, and what *does* it indicate about the actual world? As empirical science presents it to us, is the world we live in, the world of which we are a part, is this a world notable for its lack of natural arbitrariness? Far from it, the actual world, our evidence seems to indicate, is full of all sorts of fundamental arbitrary features, quirks that seem both universal for the world and absolutely brute. The particular universal limit on velocities in our world is just one conspicuous example. Another is the apparent ultimate, universal validity of quantum physics. A third is the tripartite division of most matter. And so on, and so forth.

According to available evidence, and to such a theory of our actual world as the evidence encourages, the actual world has nowhere near the lack of arbitrariness that rationalist intuitions find most tolerable. To satisfy the rationalist approach, our evidence tells us, we must look beyond the reaches of our actual space and time, beyond our actual causal network. For there to be a minimum of arbitrariness in the universe entire, indeed anything anywhere near a minimum, we might best understand the universe as including, not only the actual world, but infinitely many other concrete worlds as well.

There are other options, of course. Perhaps most conspicuously, there is this: Our available evidence is, at this time, badly misleading. Almost as conspicuous is this: Our scientists are insufficiently imaginative to articulate an intellectually satisfying cosmology, one much more elegant than any now available, that even our present evidence supports. Such options as these are not highly irrational. And they do hold out the hope for a universe entire whose concrete parts are all part of one vast causal, dimensional network, all satisfyingly interconnected. (The question arises: When, even if perhaps not now, *would* we have enough evidence about the world around us, and about our ability at theory formation, to make these options appear as dogmas, and rightly so?) But, just as these options are now worth at least our serious consideration, so, too, is our hypothesized metaphysics of many concrete worlds.

11. THE TWO FORMS OF RATIONALISM AND THE ANALYTICAL APPROACH

We have just explored a form of rationalism that is rather open to empirical evidence, even while it constrains interpretation of such evidence. This moderate rationalism strikes a nice balance, I think, between respect for intuitions of reason and respect for sensory experience. For that balance, we must pay a price.

Extreme rationalism, unlike moderate rationalism, will *always* work hand in hand with the analytic motivation for many concrete worlds. No matter what the empirical evidence, such an extreme view runs, it can have no bearing on the question of the structure of the universe entire. Rather, it can only inform the inhabitants of any given world, one of infinitely many, as to the features of their world; empirical evidence just helps them learn which of all the worlds is their world.

On this more rigid view, it is supposed that, no matter what the empirical evidence, the least arbitrary *universe* is (the) one where every world that can possibly be is a world that does exist. So, with extreme rationalism, all the worlds are there in any case. So a real model is always available for a Lewis-type treatment of our (superficially) mysterious beliefs. Extreme rationalism, then, is guaranteed to work hand in hand with the analytical approach to many concrete worlds.

With a moderate rationalism, the analytically wanted worlds won't always be available: In certain evidential situations, we do well to suppose that they are not. For moderate rationalism, there is no guarantee of partnership with the analytical motivation. That is the price of this more flexible form of rationalism.

Is this price exorbitant; or is the empirically open form of rationalism at least the equal of, and maybe superior to, the form that is guaranteed to coincide with our analytical motivation? This question is, I believe, a difficult one to answer, even in a mildly satisfactory way. But, fortunately for present purposes, we need not address this difficult question.

The reason for this happy state of affairs is, of course, pretty obvious: For us, such evidence as would threaten a partnership between moderate rationalism and the analytical motivation is utterly hypothetical. Our actual evidence poses no such threat at all. For there is precious little in our available experience to indicate that our world is the metaphysically best world that there is, and there is much to indicate that, on the contrary, it is highly arbitrary in various fundamental respects.

Perhaps in any case whatsoever, but certainly given our actual experience, a metaphysics of infinitely many isolated concrete worlds is a view to be taken very seriously. To be sure, such a view has its unattractive aspects. But so, too, does any serious alternative position of which we are aware.[18]

Notes

1. See Donald Davidson, "Causal Relations," *Journal of Philosophy* 64 (1967).

2. I usually get my science from the popular press. For example, see Timothy Ferris, "Physics' Newest Frontier," *New York Times Magazine*, 26 September 1982.

3. There may be some special exceptions to this that science recognizes. But my point does not depend on whether or not that is so.

4. Lewis has published a very large body of work developing this view. One good place to look for a statement of this metaphysics is in his book *Counterfactuals* (Oxford, 1973), especially on pp. 84-91.

5. J. L. Mackie, *Truth, Probability and Paradox* (Oxford, 1973), 90. This passage is quoted by Robert Stalnaker in his paper "Possible Worlds," *Nous* 10 (1976).

6. This idea of "world-bound individuals" wants convincing argument. In a recent paper, "Individuation by Acquaintance and by Stipulation," *Philosophical Review* 92 (1983), Lewis offers an argument for the idea from his analytical approach. The argument is on pp. 21-24. Now, even discounting the small gap in the reasoning that Lewis points out in his footnote 15, I find the argument less than fully convincing, only somewhat persuasive. In conversation, Dana Delibovi has suggested an argument for this idea from the rationalist approach. But that argument, too, leaves something to be desired. For now, I will adopt this idea as a working assumption. It makes for a more elegant system, and I know of nothing wrong with it.

7. The mentioned paper originally appeared in *Journal of Philosophy* 65 (1968); the book is that cited in note 4.

8. The philosophical literature contains ever so many criticisms of Lewis's analyses. A couple of prominent examples, fairly representative of the lot, are Alvin Plantinga's "Transworld Identity or World-bound Individuals?" in Milton Munitz, ed., *Logic and Ontology* (New York, 1973) and Robert Adams's "Theories of Actuality" in *Nous* 8 (1974). I believe, but am not certain, that Lewis defends his analyses adequately against such objections, especially in various of the postscripts in his *Philosophical Papers*, vol. 1 (Oxford, 1983), and that his treatment is also well defended by others, such as Allen Hazen in his "Counterpart-theoretic Semantics for Modal Logic," *Journal of Philosophy* 76 (1979).

9. See David Lewis, "Causation," *Journal of Philosophy* 70 (1973), for an early statement of such an analysis.

10. For a prominent example, see the paper by Robert Adams cited in note 8.

11. See the postscripts in his *Philosophical Papers*, vol. 1, especially the postscripts to "Anselm and Actuality."

12. For example, see Lewis's *Counterfactuals*, especially pp. 88-91.

13. As I must do for the remark to stand, I use the terms of difference in a very lenient manner. So, I regard as distinct two overlapping objects. Indeed, if a certain bronze statue is one thing and a piece of bronze in exactly the same space at the same time is another, then, in my sense of 'distinct', each of those objects is distinct from the other.

14. I take seriously the view that what counts as an object is relative to the context in which it is claimed that a candidate is an object, and that part of the context is the perhaps temporary interests of the speaker or of some assumed audience. So what is an object might be interest-relative. Even if that is indeed the case, the present points remain unaffected.

15. On Lewis's analytic approach, a way for a thing to be just is a thing that is that way. So a way for a world to be just is a world that is that way. *For the analytical approach*, the sentence "Every way that a world could possibly be is a way that some world is" will express a tautology, a proposition that will hold true even if there is only one (concrete) world or even none at all. *Relative to that approach*, such an apparently useful sentence will not, in fact, allow us to express what we want to express, namely, the relevantly *plenitudinous* character of the group of concrete worlds.

Both the analytic approach and also the rationalist approach require a plenitude of concrete worlds, an enormous infinity of various concrete worlds. It is also important to an advocate of either approach that he be able to express this required plenitude. This *problem of expressing the plenitude* was raised by Peter Van Inwagen and sharpened to this present form by Lewis.

A tautology will not express the required plenitude properly, nor will it express anything of much metaphysical interest. So, what are we to do. As rationalists, our problem is not acute because we can give up our partnership with the analytic approach. Then we can express our plenitude by taking possibilities, including "designs for possible worlds," as appropriate abstract structures. Then we can say: Every possibility for a world, or every design for a possible world, is *realized by* at least one concrete world. But, as advocates of a metaphysics of many concrete worlds, we rationalists hope that we do not have to give up this partnership.

For the analytical approach, the problem is an acute one. The matter may not be one of do or die; after all, at least in philosophy, no problems for views have an absolutely crucial bearing. But this is a very serious problem for the analytical approach.

16. At the very outset, the answer *none* also seems appealing. But given the existence of the actual world, that answer is soon excluded. As we are given that, we ignore this appeal.

17. Inconclusive as this argument is, it is something. In contrast, the analytical approach seems to give no way at all for motivating any answer to this question of qualitatively identical worlds. Perhaps that is why Lewis does not advocate any position on this question. Though it is not wanted without some supporting argument, some position on this question is wanted.

18. For very many of the thoughts that help to shape this paper, I am greatly indebted to David Lewis. Anyone who has read from the paper's beginning to this point would be apt to think my debt to him is a very large one; it is even larger than one would be apt to think.

For useful ideas and suggestions, I am also indebted to Dana Delibovi, Allen Hazen, Thomas Nagel, John Richardson, and, especially, Peter Van Inwagen.

The Direction of Causation
and the Direction of Time

DAVID H. SANFORD

It is, it seems, a fundamental fact that the future is due to the present, or, more mildly, is affected by the present, but the past is not. What does this mean? It is not clear and, if we try to make it clear, it turns into nonsense or a definition . . .

Frank Ramsey

I. Fixity

J. L. Mackie published three different accounts of the direction of causation. The earliest appeared in "The Direction of Causation:"

If A and B are causally connected in a direct line, then B is causally prior to A if there is a time at which B is fixed while A is not fixed otherwise than by its causal connection with B.[1]

Although Mackie used the phrase *causally connected in a direct line* in chapter 7 of *The Cement of the Universe*, it does not occur in the more complicated account of causal priority he offered in this book.[2] I have argued elsewhere that the second acacount has difficulties that the first account avoids.[3] Both accounts distinguish the tasks of determining the causal order of particular events and determining the orientation or direction of this order.[4] Although there are disanalogies between temporal order and causal order, the distinction in the temporal case is helpful in understanding the distinction in the causal case. The fact that B is temporally between A and C, which can be expressed either by (A, B, C) or by (C, B, A), does not imply whether A is earlier or later than B. Given the temporal order of events, the determination of temporal direction is a further task. Similarly, the fact that B is causally between A and C does not imply whether A causes B or B causes A. Given that events are causally connected in a direct line, determination of the causal direction is a further task.

If A and B are each occurrences, and neither is earlier than the other, they are simultaneous; whatever temporal relation one has to a third occurrence C the other has too. There is no causal analogue to simultaneity. If A neither causes nor is caused by B, it does not follow that whatever causal relations one has to a third occurrence C the other has as well. Items in one causal order need not be causally related to items in another causal order. It is, however, possible that a third occurrence C has the same causal relation to both A and B. This is a causal fork.

Causal forks can provide counterexamples to regularity theories of causation. Mackie discusses the following example: Day after day, workers in London stop work immediately after the hooting of the hooters in Manchester.[5] We do not want to explain this regularity by supposing that there is a direct causal connection between the Manchester hooters and the London workers. There is, rather, a common cause, its being five o'clock, responsible for both the hooting in Manchester and the workers' behavior in London. Mackie was mistaken, I believe, to suggest that the distinction between causal forks and events causally connected in the direct line should be drawn by an account of causal priority. The distinction can be drawn without reference to direction. "Causally connected in a direct line with" is non-transitive. A causal fork exists when something C is causally connected in a direct line with both A and B, A and B are distinct, but A and B are not causally connected in a direct line with each other. After an account of causal ordering establishes the existence of such a causal fork, an account of causal direction can establish whether C is a common cause or a common effect of A and B.

In this essay, I will be concerned with both temporal direction and causal direction. One reason Mackie was unwilling simply to define causal direction in terms of temporal direction is that he thought it was at least conceptually possible that a cause should occur later than its effect. I will not explore this putative possibility very deeply, but I do maintain that it is at least conceptually possible that a cause should occur no earlier than its effect; and this provides sufficient motivation for not identifying causal priority between causally connected items with temporal priority.

Although Mackie refuses to make this identification, his notion of fixity is explained by reference to temporal priority. An event A is fixed before time t if either A occurs before time t or something causally sufficient for A occurs before time t. 'Causally sufficient' here should not be identified either with 'causes' or with 'is a sufficient cause'.[6] Mackie does not assume that every cause is causally sufficient for its effect, and he does not assume that anything causally sufficient for an event is one of its causes. If A is causally necessary for B, then B is causally sufficient for A, even if A is a cause of B.

Talk of fixity suggests a picture both familiar and obscure. The past is wholly fixed, but the future is not. More and more events become fixed as time passes. Fixity is a property that events acquire by the passage of time. Every event that has happened or is happening has it. Some events that will happen do not have it yet.

D. H. Mellor vigorously opposes this picture.[7] He holds that although events themselves are often changes, and consist of changes, events do not themselves change in any respect. They do not acquire the property of fixity. Events happen or occur, but there is no need to regard *having happened* as a property events acquire by happening. Instead of saying that more and more events become fixed as time passes, we should say that if time t' is later than time t, more events have happened before t' than before t. I think that although Mackie is attracted by the picture of becoming fixed as acquiring the property of fixity, he neither accepts it explicitly nor requires it for his treatment of causal direction.

Ignore, for a moment, that an event is fixed at time t when an earlier event occurs at t which is causally sufficient for it. Consider only pairs of events in which one is fixed when the other is not only because one happens before the other. Notice that there is a difference between the following two views:

(1) If A and B are causally connected in a direct line, A causes B if and only if A is earlier than B.

(2) If A and B are causally connected in a direct line, A causes B if A is earlier than B.

The second can allow simultaneous causation so long as some principle for determining causal betweenness and thus for ordering events as causally connected in a direct line does not imply that causal ordering mirrors temporal ordering. Once direction is determined between any two members of a causal order, direction is determined between members of every pair in the order. If events are ordered (A, B, C) and C causes B because, in accord with (2), it is earlier than B, then B causes A even though B may be no earlier than A. If the principle of causal ordering determines the order (A, B, C) and yet allows both A and C to be earlier than B, then it, together with (2), implies mutual causation. If this is an incoherent result, either (2) or the principle of ordering must be rejected or revised. View (2) must be revised in any case if we want to allow the possibility of temporally backward causation which is not also a case of mutual causation and thus also a case of temporally forward causation. I have no strong desire to allow for backward causation, but I shall nevertheless suggest one way (2) might be revised to allow it.

(2') If A and B are causally connected in a direct line, A causes B if A is earlier than B and there is no overriding reason to regard B as a cause of A.

In the situation schematically described above, there is a competition between 'A causes B' and 'C causes B' because both A and C are earlier than B, although B is causally between A and C. If temporal precedence in one case overrides it in the other, the second pair exhibits temporally backward causation. Overriding is presumably determined by how the causal order (A, B, C) fits into a larger causal order. If the causation of B by A does not fit into any larger causal order, the causation of B by C does, and the causation of A by B is required to fit A into any larger causal order; then B causes A despite the fact that A is earlier than B. Mackie describes imaginary examples of precognition.[8] I doubt that there are any actual examples.

Now I return to the aspect of fixity that we have been neglecting. If A is causally sufficient for B, then B is fixed as soon as A is fixed. Fixity of this kind produces a certain dilemma of determinism for Mackie's account of causal direction. One alternative of the dilemma was mentioned by Mackie himself.[9] If the world has existed forever and is totally determined, then every occurrence in it has been fixed forever, and no occurrence, on Mackie's account, is causally prior to any other. Although we may believe neither that the world has existed forever nor that it is totally determined, it seems strange that these two beliefs together should be inconsistent with a belief in causal priority.

The other alternative of the dilemma is described by J. A. Foster.[10] Suppose that some occurrences are undetermined, that at some time before such an occurrence nothing obtains that is causally sufficient for it. Suppose, for example, that when a steel ball bearing falls on a knife edge, it is undetermined whether it will bounce to the right or to the left. The knife edge is fastened over a V-shaped trough. If the ball bounces to the right, it will roll down the right-hand side of the trough to the bottom; if it bounces to the left, it will roll down the left-hand side to the bottom. In these circumstances, the ball's hitting the knife edge is causally sufficient for its ending up at the bottom of the trough; the occurrence of its reaching the bottom of the trough is fixed as soon as it hits the knife edge. The ball actually bounces to the right, and its reaching the bottom of the trough is fixed before it bounces to the right. Thus, according to Mackie's account, its reaching the bottom of the trough is causally prior to its bouncing to the right. Even if we want to allow the possibility of backward causation, we do not want to count this as an example of it. Something has gone wrong.

There is a tension in Mackie's discussion of causation, and not only in his account of causal priority, between the assumption and rejection of determinism. Mackie explicitly denies that an event is caused only if some earlier event is causally sufficient for it.[11] On the other hand, his notion of an *inus* condition, an *insufficient* but *non-redundant* part of an *unnecessary* but causally *sufficient* condition, applies only when there is a causally sufficient condition. I am going to follow Mackie's example of defining an *inus* condition to see whether we can define a similar notion that applies to indeterministic as well as deterministic causation. Such a notion should be useful in emending Mackie's notion of fixity, and I think it will also be theoretically interesting in other ways.

II. SUFFICING

The following paragraph is taken from G. E. M. Anscombe's inaugural lecture "Causality and Determination":

> Since Mill it has been fairly common to explain causation one way or another in terms of 'necessary' and 'sufficient' conditions. Now "sufficient condition" is a term of art whose users may therefore lay down its meaning as they please. So they are in their rights to rule out the query: "May not the sufficient conditions of an event be present, and the event yet not take place?" For "sufficient condition" is so used that if the sufficient conditions for X

are there, X occurs. But at the same time, the phrase cozens the understanding into not noticing an assumption. For "sufficient condition" sounds like: "enough". And one certainly *can* ask: "May there not be *enough* to have made something happen—and yet it not have happened?"[12]

What does it mean to say there was *enough*? About the same time as Anscombe's lecture, Fred I. Dretske and Aaron Snyder, working independently of her, were thinking similar thoughts. They describe a device the activation of which results in the shooting of a cat, and they attempt to define a notion of causal sufficiency such that the activation is causally sufficient for the cat's death even though relevantly similar cats would not be shot in relevantly similar cases. They write:

> This conception is captured by the idea that, fundamentally, a sufficient condition is *all that is necessary*. Hence, in this sense, we may define "A is causally sufficient$_0$ for B" as: given A, nothing else is necessary for the occurrence of B. (In order to allow for causal sequences, what we require is, strictly speaking, that there be nothing else which is necessary for B for which anything other than A is necessary; we discuss this complexity later.)[13]

They have in mind a complexity of the following sort: A is necessary for B, and B is necessary for C. This does not entail, but neither should it preclude, that A is sufficient$_0$ for C. Given A, it is not strictly true that nothing else is necessary for the occurrence of C; for B is also necessary for the occurrence of C. If nothing other than A is necessary for B, however, the fuller version of the definition can be satsified in this case.

Unfortunately, the definition is not satisfiable by causal sequences containing more than three members. Lengthen the sequence above by adding an additional link: C is necessary for D. Then it is impossible, on the above definition, that A is sufficient$_0$ for D. There is something other than A, namely C, necessary for D for which something other than A, namely B, is necessary.

We could avoid this difficulty by replacing "for which anything other than A is necessary" in the above definition by "for which anything is necessary for which A is not necessary." But this suggestion also has a difficulty that can be seen by considering a miniature Galton board of the kind used to display probability distributions. Imagine that ten knife edges or pins are arranged in a triangular array as follows:

$$1$$
$$2 \quad 3$$
$$4 \quad 5 \quad 6$$
$$7 \quad 8 \quad 9 \quad 10$$

A ball dropped on pin 1 bounces to the left or to the right, and it is not determined beforehand which way it will bounce. It either hits pin 2 or hits pin 3, bounces again in an undetermined way, and so forth. Let '(n)' abbreviate 'the ball hits pin n'. We would like to say that (2) is sufficient$_0$ for (5). In the common sense of *sufficient*, although (5) is sufficient neither for (8) or for (9), it is sufficient for (8) or (9). In the circumstances, if (5), there is no possibility but that either (8) or (9). But if (5) is sufficient for (8) or (9), then (8) or (9) is necessary for (5). So something other than (2) is necessary for (5). Is (2) necessary for (8) or (9)? It is not. There are three possible paths from (1) to (8) or (9) that do not contain (2).

I want to follow Dretske and Snyder in taking *necessary for* as primitive in defining *enough* or *all that is necessary*. Since 'sufficient' is such a well-entrenched technical term in philosophy, I shall use the term 'suffice' instead of 'sufficient$_0$'. There are many ways one might try to emend the definitions we have considered so far. Instead of sketching further attempts that have difficulties, I turn to the one I shall advocate.

If I am allowed the suspect word 'unredundant', I can use the reverse acronym 'suni' to indicate something like the dual of Mackie's notion of an *inus* condition. A *suni* condition is a condition that is a *sufficient* but *unredundant* part of a *necessary* but (possibly) *insufficient* condition. I understand '*suni*' to function grammatically like 'necessary' and 'sufficient'. On my view of conditionship, '*A* is a sufficient condition of *B*' entails, but is not entailed by, '*A* is sufficient for *B*'. In the Galton board example above, where I claimed that (8) or (9) was necessary for (5), I would deny that (8) or (9) was a necessary condition for (5). With the present notion, I want to leave room to distinguish "*A* is a suni condition of *B*" from the weaker "*A* is *suni* for *B*." (I would argue that a parallel distinction is desirable for Mackie's notion of *inus*.)

A is *suni* for *B*:   There is an *X* such that (*A* or *X*) is necessary for *B*, and *X* is not necessary for *B*.

When this definition is satisfied, there is something necessary for *B*, namely (*A* or *X*). (*A* or *X*) is possibly insufficient for *B* in the sense that the satisfaction of the definition does not require it to be sufficient for *B* in the classical sense: it may be causally possible for either *A* or *X* to obtain even though *B* does not obtain. On the other hand, if (*A* or *X*) is sufficient for *B* in the classical sense, the definition may still be satisfied. The sense in which *A* is sufficient for (*A* or *X*) is logical. The second conjunct of the definition, '*X* is not necessary for *B*', ensures that *A* is not a redundant disjunct with respect to the necessity of (*A* or *X*) for *B*. Since *X* alone is not necessary for *B*, the disjunction of *A* with *X* makes a real contribution to the necessity of (*A* or *X*) for *B*. It is not required that *X* make a real contribution. When *A* is necessary for *B*, *X* can be anything that is not itself necessary for *B*. So if *A* is necessary for *B*, *A* is a *suni* for *B*. The interesting case is when *A* is a *suni* for *B* even though *A* is not necessary for *B*.

Here is a first attempt at a definition of *suffices* in terms of *suni*:

A suffices for *B*: *A* is *suni* for everything necessary for *B*.

Notice how this definition applies to the earlier example. (2) suffices for (5). Although (8) or (9) is necessary for (5), (2) is a *suni* (8) or (9). For there is something, namely (3), such that (2) or (3) is necessary for (8) or (9), and (3) by itself is not necessary for (8) or (9). Notice also how this definition is not satisfied by a case in which we want to deny the presence of *all that is necessary*. Just the scratching of a match does not suffice for its lighting, for the presence of oxygen is necessary for lighting, and the scratching of a match is not *suni* for the presence of oxygen.

This definition, however, fails to accommodate the possibility of interference. I want to say that in our Galton board example, (1) suffices for (10). Once a ball hits pin 1, nothing else is necessary for it to bounce down to pin 10 (although the chances are only 1 in 8 that it will reach pin 10.) The fact that (6) is also necessary for (10) is not a difficulty, because (1) is *suni* for (6). The difficulty is that, strictly speaking, there are indefinitely many noninterferences that are also necessary for (10). It is necessary that you do not reach in and catch the ball before it reaches pin 10. It is necessary that you do not knock the device off the table before the ball reaches pin 10. It is necessary that the world not vanish into nothingness before the ball reaches pin 10.

The possibility of interference raises exactly the same kind of difficulty for Mackie's notion of an *inus* condition. Mackie appears to think it is not a serious difficulty:

> Interference is the presence of a counteracting cause, a factor whose negation
> is a conjunct in a minimal sufficient condition (some of) whose other con-
> juncts are present.[14]

When *A* is an *inus* condition of *B*, an insufficient but nonredundant part of an unnecessary but sufficient condition *C* of *B*, then for every factor *I* that could interfere with the presence or production of *B* in presence of *A*, the absence of *I* is a component of *C*. Similarly, one might maintain, when *A* is *suni* for *B*, then so is each complex that contains *A* together with the absences of any factors that might interfere with the presence or production of *B* in the presence of *A*. The trouble with these suggestions is that they require infinite complexity. Once we start listing things that could interfere, there seems to be no end. However many specific conjuncts we add to *C* or conjoin with *A*, there will always be some kind of possible interference we have not covered.

I suggest that we use the distinction between presences and absences, between occurrences and nonoccurrences, to account for the phenomenon of interference. Although the distinction has its difficulties, I think it is clear enough to serve our purposes. Presences and occurrences can compete with and preclude each other. If the glass is full of beer, it is not also full of milk. If I am running, I am not also sitting. Absences and nonoccurrences do not compete with or preclude each other. If the glass contains no beer, it can also contain no milk, no cognac, no orange juice, and so forth. If I am not running, I can also be not sitting, not writing, not reading, and so forth. Complementary pairs, such as running and not running, being full of beer and not being full of beer, cannot both be negative; but it is not obvious to me that every complementary pair contains one negative member. For our purposes, we can treat all questionable cases as positive. My point is that an absence of interference really is an absence. For the ball to reach pin 10, it is necessary that you *not* knock the device off the table. This does not say that something must be present for the ball to reach pin 10; it says only that an event of a certain kind cannot occur. So I suggest the following revision of our definition of *suffices*:

A suffices for B: A is *suni* for everything positive necessary for B.

This revision also handles another difficulty with the earlier definition. One thing necessary for (10) is that not-(2), and not-(5), and not-(9). If (1) and (2), (2) is not regarded as *interfering* with (10) precisely because there is something, (1), *suni* for both (2) and (10). The fact that the ball's not hitting pin 2 is necessary for the ball's hitting pin 10 does not count against (1)'s sufficing for (10), on the revised definition, because the ball's not hitting pin 2 is not positive; it is only an absence or nonoccurrence.

What is it for something to interfere with the presence or production of *B*? It is for something *C* to suffice for the absence of *B* despite the fact that something *A* suffices for *B* and does not suffice for *C*. Interference should be distinguished from prevention. "Prevent" is a success word. If *B* is prevented, then *B* does not occur. But something can interfere with the production of *B* and *B* be produced despite the interference. Something can interfere with an interference. If I throw a wrench into the works, you may pull it out before the damage is done.[15]

When *A* occurs, *A* suffices for *B*, and nothing interferes with the production of *B*, *B* may still fail to occur. When the ball drops on pin 1, the chances are that it will not hit pin 10 even though nothing interferes with its hitting pin 10. It is therefore appropriate to ask, when *A* suffices for *B* and nothing interferes, what the probability is of *B*'s occurrence given *A*. *A* is sufficient for *B*, in the classical sense, when the probability is 1. *A* necessitates *B* when it occurs if it is sufficient for *B* and nothing interferes.[16] If not all causes necessitate, the world is not wholly deterministic.

The notion of probability can enter our discussion in another way when we notice that the definition of *suffices* differs from the Dretske-Snyder definition of $sufficient_0$ in an important respect. As they understand "*all that is necessary*," it does not presuppose that *something* is necessary. Mackie describes an indeterministic slot machine that sometimes delivers a chocolate bar "for no reason that is discoverable even in principle."[17] Even when something occurs, say the insertion of a shilling, of a kind that always is followed by the delivery of a chocolate bar, Mackie denies in this case that the delivery of the chocolate bar is caused. Causation, he holds, requires the occurrence of a distinct causally necessary condition. I am inclined to agree. On my definition of *suffices*, the insertion of the shilling does not suffice for the delivery of a chocolate bar simply because nothing is necessary for the delivery of a chocolate bar. Sometimes it just happens; and even if it happens immediately after the insertion of a shilling, it might have just happened then anyway. Dretske and Snyder, on the other hand, are inclined to allow that *A* can be $sufficient_0$ for *B* even though nothing is necessary for *B*. As their definition stands, it appears that if nothing is necessary for *B*, then anything at all is $sufficient_0$ for *B*. This undesirable result can be avoided by allowing, in a case where nothing is necessary for B, that A suffices for B if the occurrence of B is more probable when A is present than when A is absent.

III. FIXITY REPLACED

If A occurs before B, A suffices for B, but A does not necessitate B, it seems inappropriate to say that the occurrence of B was fixed as soon as A occurred. For the purpose of entertaining another revision of Mackie's definition of causal direction, let us say that A is *sufficed* before time t if A occurs before t or something occurs before t that suffices for A.

> (2″) If A and B are causally connected in a direct line, A causes B if A is sufficed earlier than B and there is no overriding reason to regard B as a cause of A.

The final clause about the absence of overriding reasons, as before, is optional. It can be omitted if we do want to allow for the possibility of backward causation.

The distinction between ordering and direction, as before, allows for simultaneous causation even though causal priority is defined by temporal priority. One might wonder whether there is any reason to bring fixing or sufficing into an account of causal priority if one does not want to allow for the possibility of backward causation. Certain cases of simultaneous causation are allowed that would not be allowed otherwise. When A and B are causally connected in a direct line and simultaneous, it is possible that one is sufficed earlier than the other. Suppose that something C that suffices for A occurs before anything that suffices for B and that there is something necessary for B for which nothing sufficed until after C occurred.

One horn of the dilemma considered earlier, Foster's example, ceases to be a difficulty. Although the ball's hitting the knife edge does not fix its bouncing to the right, in Mackie's sense, it does suffice for its bouncing to the right.

The other horn of the dilemma, however, might appear at first sight to be made more difficult than before. If the world is not completely deterministic, then not all occurrences are fixed forever, but it seems that all occurrences might still be sufficed forever. But the logical features of sufficing make this unlikely. Consider an occurrence E for which both B and D are necessary. Suppose that A suffices for B and C suffices for D. It does not follow that something suffices for E. A need not be *suni* for D; and if it is not, it will not suffice for E. A and C together need not be *suni* for B and D separately; and if they are not, A and C together also will not suffice for E. Even if every occurrence is sufficed before it occurs, the multiplicity of independent necessary conditions for many occurrences makes it unlikely that every occurrence is sufficed forever.

I hope my revisions of Mackie's treatment of the direction of causation helps to show how his general approach applies to an indeterministic world. I turn now to a fundamental objection to defining causal priority by reference to temporal priority.

IV. SCEPTICISM ABOUT TEMPORAL PRIORITY

There is still something theoretically unsatisfactory about definitions (2), (2'), and (2''). As John Earman puts it:

> The next problem which leaps to mind is why Mackie's definition of fixity is slanted in favor of the past. It is true that we feel the past is settled and fixed in a way the future is not; but in so far as I can make any sense out of this feeling, it derives from the belief that causal influences "go" in the future direction but cannot "go" in the past direction. It is exactly this belief which is in question.[18]

If, by reference to temporal priority, we could produce an account that accords with all our ordinary judgments of causal priority, including cases of simultaneous causation and perhaps even backward causation, this would still not explain why effects depend on their causes in a way that causes do not depend on their effects, or why, generally, what is later depends on what is earlier in a way that what is earlier does not depend on what is later. The attempt to explain temporal priority by reference to causal priority can lead at best to an uninformative circle if causal priority is itself defined by reference to temporal priority.

I shall address this problem by responding to an argument by Graham Nerlich for the sceptical conclusion that there really are no objective facts that ground the admittedly inescapable feelings that there are these one-way temporal and causal dependencies. Nerlich suspects that "cause is an anthropocentric, coarse-grained concept powerless to explain the fundamental nature of time."[19] He develops an example to show that, in ordinary situations, events make things to have happened earlier as easily as they make things happen later. He admits that we cannot usually intend to do something to make something to have happened earlier and that "we seem to feel conceptual outrage at the idea that any event can stand to earlier events in ways at all like the ways in which causes stand to their effects and which leads us to think of causes creating effects."[20] Nerlich thinks, however, that this sense of outrage, rather than being grounded on a correct metaphysical understanding of how events in the world are objectively related, results from facts about our subjective temporal experience, facts that tempt us to entertain the confused metaphysical views that time flows and that "the past is somehow there (though less real than the present) and that the future is nothing at all."[21]

Nerlich spells out a seven-step argument for the conclusion that in an ordinary situation, an event can cause and make to have happened an earlier event. The central contentions of the argument can be summarized as follows:

    I.   If A is a necessary condition of B, then B is a sufficient condition of A.

    II. If A is an occurrent causally sufficient condition of B, A is a cause of B.

Refinements of II necessary to handle cases of overdetermination and causal premption are not to the point because there are plenty of cases in which these complications are absent. Any emendation of II by adding a reference to time order begs the question at issue. If A is both a causally necessary and causally sufficient condition of B, then, by I, B is a sufficient condition of A. By II, then, B is a cause of A even if A is earlier than B.

I reject assumption I, and I have developed an account of conditionship according to which I is false.[22] Conditionship is nonsymmetric, on my view; not just anything should be counted as a condition of anything else, even if the presence of one requires the presence of the other. The following two arguments are fallacious in the same way:

A is a condition. A is sufficient for B.

Therefore, A is a sufficient condition of B.

John is a son. John is considerate of Mrs. Smith.

Therefore, John is a considerate son of Mrs. Smith.

Just as the second conclusion requires not merely that John is a son, but that he is a son of Mrs. Smith, the first requires not merely that A is a condition, but that it is a condition of B.

A is a condition of B only if there are admissible circumstances in which everything necessary for A is necessary for B. The notion of 'admissible circumstances' is intended to let us ignore cases of overdetermination and standby causes and cases in which the laws are different from the relevant laws in the actual situation. All actual circumstances are admissible. Drinking cyanide is a condition of death because there are admissible circumstances in which everything necessary for drinking cyanide is necessary for death. If there happens to be someone ready to shoot the intended victim to death in case he does not drink the cyanide, this standby cause is ignored in determining conditionship. Death is not a condition of drinking cyanide because there are no admissible circumstances in which everything necessary for death is necessary for drinking cyanide. Although all my examples of conditions in "The Direction of Causation and the Direction of Conditionship" are causal, I intended my account of conditionship to apply to noncausal conditions as well. Having a true belief is a necessary condition of knowledge, but knowledge is not a sufficient condition, or any kind of condition, of having a true belief.

I would still propose that in an account of causal priority, Mackie's requirement of temporal priority and fixity be replaced by a requirement of one-way causal conditionship. If A and B are causally connected in a direct line, A is a cause of B if A is a causal condition of B and B is not a causal condition of A. A can still be a cause of B even if A and B are causal conditions of each other so long as A and B are members of a larger causal order whose direction is determined by another pair related by one-way conditionship.

Nerlich is willing to accept my argument for the nonsymmetry of conditionship and to reject assumption I. He thinks no such assumption is needed to argue for the existence of backward causation in common, everyday situations. My account of conditionship, he claims, provides no non-question-begging grounds for holding that earlier events are causally sufficient conditions for later events while denying that later events are causally sufficient conditions, in the same ordinary circumstances, for earlier events.

Nerlich's problem example deals with a clock that keeps perfect time. Although it runs neither slow nor fast, it does not always show the correct time. At 11:30 a.m. it is ten minutes slow, and at 12:30 p.m. it is ten minutes fast. It is interfered with exactly twice, at 11:45 and at 12:15, and it is advanced ten minutes each time. The clock, as one can infer from the story told thus far, tells the correct time after the first adjustment until the second adjustment. Nerlich says that he does not think it matters how these adjustments occur. I think that it could matter, but I would like to deal with the example without appealing to causal directionality involved in the adjustments.

The 11:45 adjustment is naturally regarded as a sufficient condition in the circumstances for the clock's telling the correct time at noon. The circumstances include the clock's running perfectly, its being ten minutes slow at 11:30, and, except for the 11:45 adjustment, its not being interfered with between 11:30 and noon.

The problem concerns the 12:15 adjustment. Why should it not similarly be regarded as a sufficient condition in the circumstances for the clock's telling correct time at noon? The circumstances include the clock's running perfectly, its being ten minutes fast at 12:30, and its not being interfered with, except for the 12:15 adjustment, between noon and 12:30. If there are reasons, based on my account of conditionship, for denying that the 12:15 adjustment is a sufficient condition of the noon reading, will there not be similar reasons for denying that the 11:45 adjustment is a sufficient condition for the noon reading?

Nerlich mistakenly claims that on my account of *sufficient condition*, neither the 11:45 adjustment nor the 12:15 adjustment counts as a sufficient condition of the noon reading. Although correcting the misunderstanding on which this claim is based will not help deal with Nerlich's main point, it will enable us to detect similar mistakes elsewhere. If *necessary for* and *sufficient for* are to be explained by reference to the impossibility of certain states of affairs existing together, it is essential that there be some prohibition of redundancy. Striking a match is not, strictly speaking, sufficient just by itself for the match's lighting. There is no law of nature L such that the following is true:

It is impossible that (Match M is scratched & L & Match M does not light).

Some other factors in the situation have to be added to the conjunction. But we cannot add just any factor that actually obtained. If match M was not actually scratched, for example, we cannot add it. The following is indeed true:

It is impossible that (Match M is scratched & L & Match M does not light & Match M is not scratched).

But this should not be taken to show that the scratching match M is sufficient for its lighting, or that its lighting is necessary for its being scratched. (Remember that with our additional requirement for conditionship, we distinguish *necessary (sufficient) for* from *necessary (sufficient) condition of.*) The conjunct "Match M does not light" in the statement above can be replaced by anything or by nothing, and the resulting statement will still be true. The truth of the above statement does not show any connection between the scratching (or nonscratching) of match M and anything else.

The sufficiency of Match M's being scratched for its lighting is shown if there is *some* true statement of the form:

It is impossible that (Match M is scratched & Match M does not light & . . .)

in which none of the otherwise appropriate conjuncts makes any conjunct redundant. It is not required that *every* true statement of this form be nonredundant, for such a requirement can never be satisfied. Nerlich is correct to point out that if we consider the 11:59 reading as a relevant factor, then the 11:45 change is superfluous in explaining the noon reading. But this does nothing to show that mention of the 11:45 change is superfluous in every explanation of the noon reading.

Louis E. Loeb makes a mistake of just this kind in his discussion of Mackie's *inus* conditions. According to Loeb, "Mackie's analysis would virtually abolish causes from the natural world."[23] Loeb correctly argues that given almost any causal factor C relevant to an occurrence E, there will be some minimal sufficient condition for E that does not contain C. All that Mackie requires, however, is that C be a component of some minimal sufficient condition, not that it be a component of every minimal sufficient condition.

Although Nerlich is wrong to claim that given my prohibition of redundancy in explanations of sufficiency, neither the 11:45 nor the 12:15 adjustment is a sufficient condition of the noon reading, his central challenge is independent of this claim. How can the earlier and later adjustments be distinguished as conditions? How, without assuming the putative facts about temporal priority we seek to explain, can we argue that the earlier adjustment really is a condition of the noon reading while the later adjustment is not?

In Nerlich's example, the supposition that the clock keeps perfect time is the analogue of a lawlike natural regularity. But a simpler example poses the same puzzle. Consider a clock face with no works behind it. The hands are moved twice. Before 11:45, the clock face reads 11:50. The hands are advanced ten minutes at 11:45 so that the clock reads 12:00, as it does until 12:15, when the hands are advanced another ten minutes. Given that the clock has no works, and that it reads 12:10 after 12:15, why should the 12:15 adjustment not be counted as a condition of the noon reading?

Once we understand the form of Nerlich's puzzle, we see that it arises everywhere. For a still simpler example, let us consider a body that moves in accord with Newton's first law of motion: every body continues in its state of rest or of uniform motion in a right line unless it is compelled to change that state by forces impressed upon it. Suppose that a body moves uniformly in a right line from a to c. A force is impressed upon it at point b; it changes direction and moves from b to c. The solid line in the accompanying diagram indicates the actual path of the body.

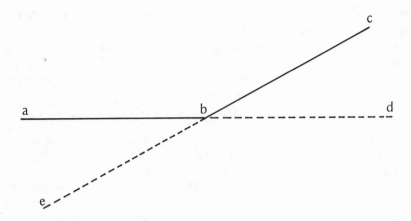

The broken lines indicate the alternative paths mentioned in the consequents of these competing subjunctive conditionals:

If no force had been impressed upon the body at *b*,
(i)   it would have moved uniformly in the right line *abd*.
(ii) it would have moved uniformly in the right line *ebc*.

These subjunctive conditionals should be distinguished from the following indicative conditionals:

If no force has been impressed upon the body at *b*,
(i′) it has moved uniformly in the right line *abd*.
(ii′) it has moved uniformly in the right line *ebc*.

Indicative conditionals like these are not relevant to determining the direction of causation. If no force has been impressed upon the body at *b*, then conditional (i′) is false, for its consequent is false – the body in fact moved along path *bc*, not along path *bd*.

Many writers look to counterfactual subjunctive conditionals not merely to explain the direction of causation but also to explain causal connection in general. When Mackie abandoned his attempt to account for the direction of causation by reference to fixity, he suggested an account in terms of conditionals.

> . . . If on a particular occasion A's doing X is causally related to B's doing Y, and if they had not been so related but things had otherwise been as far as possible as they were, A would still have been doing X but B would (or might) not have been doing Y, then A's doing X is conditionally and causally prior to B's doing Y.[24]

I think this account fits our common opinions about causal priority in examples where the cause and effect are so related that there is a clear sense in talking about the occurrence or nonoccurrence of one with or without the occurrence of the other. Flipping a switch and the light's going on are causally related, and if they were not, but things had otherwise been as far as possible as they were, the switch would have been flipped while the light stayed off. Although Nerlich can challenge our preference for taking earlier respects of similarity to be more important than later respects—why not say that the light would have gone on without the switch being flipped?—Mackie can reply that we have experience of switches being flipped unconnected to lights. But I think that Nerlich's example, and my variations on it, show that the applications of Mackie's account are limited. I do not see how to apply Mackie's test to these examples. What is it to suppose that an adjustment of clock hands is not causally related to a clock reading or that the impression of a force on a moving body is not causally related to its path? In these cases there seems to be no causal chain such that we can suppose that the connecting links are missing.

The competing pair of counterfactual conditionals (i) and (ii) concern the absence of a force impressed on a moving body rather than the absence of a causal connection between a moving body and an impressed force. The problem of finding an objective reason for our natural preference for (i) can be viewed as an instance of Nelson Goodman's Problem of Relevant Conditions. Given the counterfactual supposition that no force was impressed, we would like to take the actual path ab as cotenable with this supposition. If the body was moving along path ab and no force was impressed upon it, then, according to Newton's first law, it continued moving in the right line abd. But what reason do we have, besides an appeal to the very temporal asymmetry we seek to explain, not to take the actual path bc as cotenable with the supposition? If the body was moving along path bc and no force had been impressed upon it, then according to Newton's first law, it would have been continuing in motion along the right line ebc.

All the physical processes in this example are reversible. The actual path of the body, its reversal, the two possible paths mentioned in (i) and (ii), and their reversals are all in accord with Newton's first law. It is difficult to see how our preference for (i) over (ii) depends on our assuming that some irreversible process, not yet mentioned, must be occurring. Nor should we expect to find an objective basis for this preference in the time-symmetric equations of physics. We should not assume that if there is an objective basis, it is expressible by equations. I would compare equations, in this respect, with truth-functional conditionals. Both are useful as premises of inference. The direction of inference need not follow the direction of dependence. A conditional can be true in virtue of an event of one sort depending causally on an event of another sort, but the conditional itself is not suited to express this dependence. An equation, similarly, can be true in virtue of a quantity of one sort depending on a quantity of another sort, but the equation itself is not suited to express this dependence.

We may suppose, in our example, that the body moves through a dark vacuum, that no heat is dissipated by the impression of the force at b, that the body leaves no traces, and that the impression of the force leaves a trace only by altering the body's path. On this supposition, we still want to accept (i) and to reject (ii). If there is an objective reason for saying that the force at b causes the body to move in the direction of c rather than causes it to have moved from the direction of a, we should not expect to find it in signals diverging outward from a point source or in thermodynamic asymmetries. We may suppose that our example concerns the path of a molecule, with the force impressed by collision with another molecule, that these molecules are part of a gas in a state of high entropy, and that the entropy has not changed significantly and will not change significantly for a long time. This supposition is also irrelevant to our preference of (i) over (ii). If the asymmetry here is objective, it is difficult to see how it can be connected with a change in entropy.

A philosopher who doubts the existence of an objective ground for our preference of (i) over (ii) will not argue that (ii), on the contrary, should be preferred to (i), or that (i) and (ii) should both be accepted and causation viewed as running both forward and backward in time. In questioning the ground of our preference, the philosopher means to undermine the supposed objectivity of one-way causal dependence. In maintaining that our preference of (i) over (ii) is due to our subjectively slanted view of time, the philosopher may, of course, attempt to explain this subjective slant by reference to entropy or de facto irreversible processes. I shall not argue against subjectivist views on this matter except by attempting to describe an objectivist alternative that will appear more plausible.

Can comparisons of similarity between possible worlds help ground our preference for (i) over (ii)? The two possible worlds described in the consequents of (i) and (ii) appear to be equally similar to the actual world, in which a force was impressed upon the body. One coincides exactly with the actual world before the body reaches b, and the other coincides exactly with the actual world after the body reaches b. We cannot simply take earlier similarity to be more important than later similarity without begging the question we are attempting to answer. And it is difficult to see how an appeal to some further similarity between worlds can support our attaching more importance to the earlier similarity than to the later one.[25]

I would approach subjunctive, counterfactual conditionals in a manner more like Nelson Goodman's treatment in chapter 1 of *Fact, Fiction and Forecast* than in the manner of the currently more popular possible-world semantics. Rather than seek to locate appropriate standards of similarity between possible worlds, I would like to find appropriate standards for selecting features of the actual situations that should be considered along with the counterfactual supposition of the antecedent. Although I have been representing the problem of defending the objectivity of the earlier/later asymmetry as the problem of finding an objective reason for accepting conditional (i) rather than conditional (ii), I do not see a solution to the first problem as following as a corollary to an adequate general account of conditionals. I think, rather, that an adequate general account of conditionals requires a solution to the problem of temporal asymmetry.

In another essay, I have argued against the notion of counterfactual dependence.[26] The acceptability of a counterfactual conditional does not coincide in any useful way with the dependence of what is mentioned in the consequent on what is mentioned in the antecedent. A counterfactual conditional may be acceptable in virtue of one of several patterns of dependence. Rather than attempting to explain causal, temporal, or any other kind of dependence by reference to acceptable conditionals, I claim, we should refer to patterns of dependence in accounting for the acceptability of counterfactual conditionals. Whereas what is mentioned by the antecedent of some acceptable counterfactuals would have depended on what is mentioned by the consequent, the pattern of dependence relevant to both (i) and (ii) in the present example is of the more ordinary kind. The acceptability of each conditional rests on whether the event mentioned in the consequent would have resulted from something, the event mentioned in the antecedent, or some unmentioned actual event, or the event mentioned in the antecedent together with some unmentioned actual event. What we need is an objective reason for thinking that had no force been impressed upon the body at point b, the body's subsequent path would have depended on its earlier path rather than the other way around.

V. DEPENDENCE AND THE FLOW

In *The Cement of the Universe*, Mackie's most vivid expression of the view that there is some kind of one-way dependence of later states on earlier states does not appear in chapter 7, "The Direction of Causation," which is preoccupied with the possibility of backward causation, but in chapter 8, "The Necessity of Causes." I will work toward an answer to Nerlich's challenge by defending, in part, the following passage:

> The dictum that 'the universe needs to know where to go next' may require some explanation and defence. I am suggesting that there is some truth in the notion that what happens next *flows from* what is there already. The immediate future is, so to speak, *extruded* by the present and the immediate past.[27]

The appeal of this imagery, I believe, is independent of whatever importance or objectivity we attach to the notions of past, present, and future. After Nerlich comments that "we seem to feel conceptual outrage at the idea that any event can stand to earlier events in ways at all like the ways in which causes stand to their effects and which lead us to think of causes creating effects," he suggests that this sense of outrage "springs from those (seeming) facts about time that tempt us to say that it flows, that the past is somehow there (though less real than the present) and that the future is nothing at all."[28] I believe that the feeling of conceptual outrage can be preserved without attaching any ontological importance to the present or the *now*. The last sentence in the passage from Mackie is just a special instance of the more general claim that precedes it. The state of the world is, so to speak, extruded by its immediately earlier state. It is not extruded by its immediately later state. This metaphor does not require reference to the present and so does not require supposing that the present somehow has a greater degree of reality than the future, or that being future and being past are objective properties that events respectively lose and acquire by the passage of time.

There are many three-dimensional objects, such as telephone wires, that have a much longer spatial extension along one dimension than the other two, but when they are considered four-dimensionally, as Mackie says, they "have a considerable temporal persistence as well as spatial extension, and so come out not as worms but as thin but two-dimensionally extended spatio-temporal sheets."[29] A spatially rather than temporally extended space-time worm would be the history of a three-dimensional object that is huge along just one spatial dimension and that exists for a very brief time. Mackie takes the prevalence of temporally extended over spatially extended space-time worms to confirm the appropriateness of his extrusion metaphor.[30] John Earman objects both to the metaphor and to Mackie's defense of the metaphor.

> The only way this 'so to speak' is cashed in is by means of the further claim that the ideas of flow and extrusion help to explain the (alleged) fact that most long space-time "worms" are temporal rather than spatial. I see no need for such a metaphysical explanation over and above what physics tells us. And, in any case, the crucial asymmetry Mackie needs is otiose for purposes of the explanation; for the explanation would work just as well if the immediate past were extruded from the present and the immediate future.[31]

I agree that Mackie does not succeed in defending the view that later states depend on earlier states any more than earlier states depend on later ones. But I think that the prevalence of temporally extended space-time worms still provides partial support for Mackie's metaphor. It is more appropriate to talk of extrusion or dependence along a temporal dimension than along a spatial dimension.

Spatial dimensions are not dimensions of dependence, which is not to deny that there are relations of dependence through space. The table top remains above the floor only because it is supported at each end by the legs. When one end of the table is pushed, the other end moves. Given a rigid object of a certain shape, the position and motion of some of its parts are determined by the position and motion of other of its parts. But given just the nature of the occupants of a limited spatial region, little follows about the occupants of adjacent spatial regions. Laplace's calculator, knowing the total state of a closed system during a short temporal interval, can predict and retrodict more or less accurately, depending on whether the laws of working are more or less deterministic, states of the system at other times. The calculator cannot, from knowing the total state of a system in a short spatial interval — from knowing everything that goes on in a limited spatial region throughout time — figure out the states of the system at other places. A sudden change from air to wood along a spatial dimension, as at the boundary of a wooden table top, violates no law. A sudden change from air to wood along a temporal dimension would be a miracle. Laplace's calculator performs inferences of two kinds, prediction and retrodiction. If all the laws he uses are time-symmetric, he need not be able to tell the difference. But to repeat points made earlier, the direction of inference need not be the direction of dependence; and if there is a direction of dependence, we should not expect to find it indicated by time-symmetric equations.

I believe that the same notion of conditionship that accounts for causal dependence and various kinds of noncausal dependence also accounts for temporal dependence. Consider a persisting object that exists before, during, and after some time t. Some states of the object before t are conditions of some of its states after

t, but none of its states after t are conditions of any of its states before t.[32] That is, on my account of conditionship, there are admissible circumstances—usually the actual circumstances—in which everything necessary for its being in some state it is in before t is necessary for its being in some state it is in after t, but not everything necessary for its being in any state it is in after t is necessary for it being in any state it is in before t.

There are many ways of regarding a thing as being in a state. A choice of two true state descriptions, one of an object's states before t and one of its states after t, may imply that the object changed in a certain respect, or may imply that it did not change in a certain respect, or may imply nothing either way. If the states of a uniformly moving body are described in terms of direction, for example, the two descriptions may imply that the body did not change direction. If the states are described in terms of position, two descriptions of the same body covering the same time intervals as before may imply that it did change position. Both changes and nonchanges exhibit one-way conditionship.

If an object persists unchanged in a certain respect, it is necessary that nothing changed it. In addition to this negative condition, there is generally a positive condition for a thing's remaining in a state throughout a temporal interval, namely that it be in that state during the earlier part of the interval. Its being in the state earlier is thus a condition of its being in the state later, since everything necessary for its being in the state earlier is necessary for its being in the state later. But its being in the state later is not a condition of its being in the state earlier, for something is necessary for its being in the state later, namely the nonexistence of some interference that changed it, which is not necessary for its being in the state earlier. Knowledge of noninterference may, of course, be necessary to infer a thing's earlier state from knowledge of its later state. Interference can go in either direction.

If an object changes in a certain respect, it is generally necessary that something changed it. Which earlier states of the object are necessary for the newly acquired state depends on the nature of the change. When a table, for example, is painted with opaque paint, its earlier color is not a condition of its later color, but there are still properties of its surface necessary for it to take paint. The later state is not a condition of the earlier state because not everything necessary for the later state is necessary for the earlier state.

Let us say that a state of an object is internally independent if no state of the object at any other time is a condition of its being in this state at any given time. The qualification 'generally' in the last two paragraphs is intended to accommodate the putative logical possibility that there are some internally independent states. If the character of an image projected on a movie screen is regarded as a state of the screen, and if we ignore the persistent phyical properties of the screen that enable it to reflect a projected image, the image-state of a movie screen at any given time can be regarded as internally independent. It is, at any rate, independent of the image-states of the screen at other times. Most states of a movie screen, such as its having a certain shape, size, position, reflective characteristics, and so forth, at a given time, are not internally independent.

My view of one-way temporal dependence appears to conflict with metaphysical views others have advocated. The following principle, which Descartes took as an axiom, may be interpreted as saying that every state of any object is internally independent:

> The present time has no causal dependence on the time immediately preceding it. Hence, in order to secure the continued existence of a thing, no less a cause is required than that needed to produce it at first.[33]

To express this view yet again, this time using Mackie's imagery, the universe never knows where to go next. It always needs to be told. The immediate future is independent from the present and the immediate past, not extruded by it. The immediate future is always extruded by something else. According to occasionalism, although all states of objects are internally independent, they are all dependent on God.

Let us say that a state of an object is totally independent if nothing is a condition of its being in this state at any given time. Radical occasionalism, an extreme view that probably has no defenders, although Hume sometimes sounds like one, holds that every state of any object is totally independent. The universe never knows where to go next, and there is nothing to tell it where to go next. Where it goes next is always a matter of pure chance. The appearance of persisting objects results from the astounding inexplicable coincidence that qualities happen to persist through time in a largely coherent way. It is as if a movie film randomly assembled from frames that were themselves randomly produced, so there are no genuine connections between any two frames or between each of two frames and something else, should just happen to be indistinguishable from a movie of an ordinary persisting object that changes in some respects while it does not change in other respects. On my view, radical occasionalism makes this movie film analogy incoherent. Radical occasionalism has no resources to ground the part of the analogy that stipulates that the independent frames are assembled in some order or other. Given three totally independent frames A, B, and C, there is nothing to distinguish the order (A, B, C) from the orders (B, A, C) or (A, C, B); and even if there were one order rather than another, there is nothing to give such an order a direction.

The view of Mackie's I am defending is contrary to Descartes's axiom and incompatible with ordinary Cartesian occasionalism.[34] Although it is unclear whether the dependence is best regarded as causal, the present time does depend on the time immediately preceding it. Nothing is needed to secure the continued existence of a thing except its prior existence and the absence of any interference with its persistence.

In our example of a moving body, the body's moving along a certain path before it reaches point b is a condition of its moving along whatever path it does move along after it reaches point b. The later path is not a condition of the earlier path. The later path depends not only on the earlier path but also on what does or does not happen to the body at point b. The earlier path does not depend on what happens at point b.

In Nerlich's clock example, the 11:45 change is a condition of the noon reading, and the 12:15 change is not a condition of the noon reading. Everything necessary for the 11:45 change is necessary, in the circumstances, for the noon reading. Something necessary for the 12:15 change, namely the existence of the clock at 12:15, and thus also the existence of the clock during the interval between noon and 12:15, is not necessary for the noon reading. For a clock to read 12:00 noon at noon it is not necessary that the clock continue to exist after noon.

Suppose that no clock can exist at the same time Thor throws his most terrible lightning bolt. Two subjunctive conditionals compete in a now-familiar way. If Thor had thrown his terrible lightning bolt at noon:

(i*) The clock would have existed before noon but not after noon; it would have ceased to exist at noon.

(ii*) The clock would have existed after noon but not before noon; it would have started to exist at noon.

Although I do not take the acceptability of conditionals like (i*) rather than (ii*) to constitute the one-way dependence of later states on earlier states, I take the general principle that earlier states are conditions of later states, but not the other way around, to explain the acceptability of (i*) rather than (ii*).

If I am right about the prevalence of one-way conditionship, and thus one-way dependence, through time, one might still ask why it is that the dependence runs from earlier to later rather than the other way around. I suggest this is like asking why six o'clock is one hour later than five o'clock rather than one hour earlier. If the temporal dimension is the dimension of dependence, and temporal order is the order of dependence, then temporal direction is the direction of dependence. There is no separate, independent principle of temporal direction that happens to coincide with the direction of dependence exemplified by ordinary persistent objects.

Time is like a river and love is like a lion's tooth. The similes are not apt in every respect. Love is not coated with a hard, white substance like enamel. Time does not move. Insofar as they embody the myth of passage or temporal motion, I do not want to defend Mackie's metaphor of extrusion or the more familiar metaphor of flow. I have tried to abstract and defend the literal appropriateness of another feature of the motion metaphors and similes often used to talk of time. The constitution of a flowing river depends on what its constitution was upstream, not upon what it will be downstream. The character of something extruded depends on the shape of the nozzle and the character of what is pushed through it, and not the other way around. There is also a one-way dependence through time. Later states depend on earlier states, and not the other way around. As Ramsey puts it, it is a fundamental fact that the future is affected by the present, but the past is not.[35] I have attempted to make this clearer without turning it into nonsense. If I have turned it into a definition, then I hope the definition is an informative one that applies to the actual world.

Mackie suggests extending the notion of causation "to include the relation between the earlier and later phases of the existence of any material object."[36] He says that "basic laws of working are, in part, forms of persistence."[37] I have not addressed the question of how causal conditions are best distinguished from conditions of other kinds, and I think that philosophy still lacks an adequate account of the distinction. Whether or not the one-way dependence exhibited by persistence through time is regarded as causal, it does support Mackie's reference to temporal priority in his explanation of fixity. On my view, however, considerations of the same sort that support a reference to temporal priority, namely the appeal to nonsymmetric conditionship, can replace the notion of fixity in an account of the direction of causation.

Notes

1. *Philosophical Review* 75 (1966):457.

2. Oxford, 1974, 190. Hereafter, I refer to this book as *Cement*.

3. David H. Sanford, "The Direction of Causation and the Direction of Conditionship," *Journal of Philosophy* 73 (1976):193-207.

4. I have also discussed this topic in my review of *Hume and the Problem of Causation* by Tom L. Beauchamp and Alexander Rosenberg, *Nous* 17 (1983).

5. *Cement*, pp. 83-86.

6. D. H. Mellor, in "McTaggart, Fixity and Coming True," *Reduction, Time and Reality*, edited by Richard Healy (Cambridge, 1981), 79-97, represents Mackie as defining *fixity* by reference to *is a sufficient cause of* (94), which leaves Mackie's account of causal direction open to an unjustified charge of circularity.

7. Ibid. Also see Mellor's *Real Time* (Cambridge, 1981).

8. *Cement*, 173-79.

9. *Cement*, 191-92.

10. "Testing the Cement: An Examination of Mackie on Causation," *Inquiry* 18 (1975): 487-98.

11. *Cement*, 40-43.

12. *Metaphysics and the Philosophy of Mind*, vol. 2 of *The Collected Philosophical Papers of G. E. M. Anscombe* (Minneapolis, 1981), 135.

13. "Causality and Sufficiency: Reply to Beauchamp," *Philosophy of Science* 40 (1973):290.

14. *Cement*, 76.

15. Anscombe concludes "Causality and Determination" by saying, "The most neglected of the key topics in this subject are: interference and prevention" (*Metaphysics and the Philosophy of Mind*, 147). I hope my present brief discussion serves at least as a beginning of an adequate treatment of these topics.

16. I regard this as a paraphrase of Anscombe's definition of a *necessitating cause*, ibid., 144.

17. *Cement*, 41.

18. "Review of *The Cement of the Universe*," *Philosophical Review* 85 (1976):392. Mellor raises a similar objection in "McTaggart, Fixity, and Coming True," 94-95.

19. "Time and the Direction of Conditionship," *Australian Journal of Philosophy* 57 (1979):14.

20. Ibid., 4.

21. Ibid.

22. See the article referred to in note 3.

23. "Causal Theories and Causal Overdetermination," *Journal of Philosophy* 71 (1974):535. I am partly responsible for the occurrence of this mistake in Nerlich's article, for I failed to detect it and thus made no attempt to correct it in our correspondence that preceded the publication

of this article. Professor Nerlich provided some useful comments on an earlier version of my paper. He has not seen an advance copy of the present version.

24. J. L. Mackie, "Mind, Brain, and Causation," *Midwest Studies in Philosophy* 4 (1979): 24. Although in this article Mackie adopts my suggestion that the direction of causation be explained by reference to the direction of conditionship, he also says, and I agree, that his account of the direction of conditionship is rather different from mine.

25. Even if I accepted David Lewis's description of the standard resolution in his "Counterfactual Dependence and Time's Arrow," *Nous* 13 (1979):455-76, I would not know how to makes similar remarks in his review of *The Cement of the Universe*.

26. David H. Sanford, "Conditionals and Dependence" (forthcoming).

27. *Cement*, 225.

28. "Time and the Direction of Conditionship," 4.

29. *Cement*, 227.

30. *Cement*, 226-28.

31. "Causation: A Matter of Life and Death," *Journal of Philosophy* 73 (1976):12. Earman makes similar remarks in his review of *The Cement of the Universe*.

32. I assume, of course, that for some true descriptions that apply to a thing at time t, there is no corresponding state of that thing at time t. It may be true of this sea today that there will be a sea fight on it tomorrow, but I do not count among the states of the sea today its *being the location of a sea fight tomorrow*.

33. Axiom II of "Arguments Demonstrating the Existence of God and the Distinction between Soul and Body, Drawn up in Geometrical Fashion," appended to *Reply to the Second Set of Objections*.

34. It is compatible with a proposition of Descartes's most profound follower. See Spinoza's *Ethics*, Part III, Prop. 6.

35. Or, as David Lewis puts it, "The literal truth is just that the future depends . . . on the present. It depends, partly, on what we do now. . . . The past would be the same, however we acted now. It is . . . independent of the present" ("Counterfactual Dependence and Time's Arrow," 462-62). I think that Lewis does not succeed in making this clear with his notion of *counterfactual dependence*. As I argue in "Conditionals and Dependence," although objective relations of dependence ground acceptable counterfactual conditionals, there is no useful sense of dependence that can be defined by reference to acceptable counterfactuals. If the river at this point had been different, it would have been correspondingly different upstream. I see no point in concluding from this that the character of the river upstream depends — counterfactually depends — on its character downstream. The genuine dependence runs in the other direction.

36. *Cement*, 156.

37. *Cement*, 221.

Mackie and Shoemaker
on Dispositions and Properties

ALEXANDER ROSENBERG

In "Dispositions and Powers," J. L. Mackie identifies three different "ontological views about dispositions":

> The first is the one Armstrong calls phenomenalist and ascribes to Ryle: we attribute a minimal disposition, which is in effect to assert a conditional or set of conditionals, themselves to be interpreted as inference tickets; but this does not mean anything is going on in the things to which we attribute the disposition which is not going on in similar things from which we withhold this description.

> The second is the 'realist' view, that dispositions have occurrent (and concurrent) categorical bases consisting of properties which are not in themselves peculiarly dispositional, though they may be introduced in the dispositional style and may be known only as the bases of these dispositions; although the dispositional descriptions are conditional-entailing, the properties to which they point are only contingently related to the displays of the dispositions.

> The third is what we may call the rationalist view; dispositions (while still being intrinsically dispositional and conditional-entailing) are real occurrent states of the object, different from anything a realist would call a categorical basis (which may or may not be there as well), but actually present both when the disposition is being manifested and when it is not.[1]

The first of these views Mackie says may sometimes be right, though in general it is unlikely; the second is prima facie a plausible hypothesis; and "the third view can be firmly rejected." (p. 143) Mackie's endorsement of the realist view about dispositions is actually much stronger. For his final conclusion is that while most properties, including the most basic ones, like mass, "are introduced in a dispositional style and are known only or mainly by way of the effects they have or would have in such-and-such circumstances, . . . it is reasonable to postulate bases

77

for them which are not distinctively dispositional, which are neither mere networks of minimal dispositions nor properties whose presence would entail the conditionals by which the dispositions are displayed." (p. 153) In fact, Mackie endorses the "thesis that no properties are in themselves dispositional." (p. 146)

As with many of the doctrines Mackie defended, the motivation for the view of dispositional properties that he offers in "Dispositions and Powers" is largely epistemological. His wider aims are to defend a moderate empiricism, and his arguments against a variety of ontological views have been uniformly epistemological. His objection to the existence of irreducibly dispositional properties is characteristic of this style of argument.

> There are at least two reasons for doubting whether there are any distinctively dispositional properties in [the rationalist's] sense. First it seems quite unnecessary to postulate them. Why should we insert this extra element between the non-dispositional behavior and the causal behavior? It looks like a fiction generated by treating as the name of a separate entity the dispositional style of describing the basis by way of the causal behavior. Secondly, the suggestion that there are such properties is in open conflict with Hume's principle that there can be no logical connections between distinct existences. For if fragility in this sense were an intrinsic property of the glass, then [the glass's fragility, its] being struck, and [its] breaking would all be distinct existences, and yet on this view, the conjunction of the first two would entail the third. The ontological claim that dispositions or powers exist as real stages of things seems to result from an unhappy mixing up of two points which are separately legitimate: that a dispositional—and therefore condition entailing—*description* may be justified, and that a fragile glass, for example, differs intrinsically and categorically—namely in molecular structure—from a superficially similar glass that is not fragile. (p. 137)

Epistemological arguments for strong metaphysical conclusions are now much less common than they have been in the recent past. This makes Sidney Shoemaker's arguments[2] against views that Mackie defended all the more striking. Although Shoemaker does not cite Mackie, his thesis is the direct denial of Mackie's, for he describes it as "the view that properties just are powers, or that all properties are dispositional, [even though] . . . a thing's powers or dispositions are distinct from, because 'grounded in', its intrinsic properties." (p. 115) Moreover, Shoemaker describes his own arguments for this conclusion as "broadly speaking, epistemological." Since I share Mackie's motivation and believe that the views it sustains are correct, I attempt in this paper to construct an assessment of Shoemaker's theory, in their spirit.

I

According to Shoemaker, "what makes a property the property it is, what determines its identity, is its potential for contributing to the causal powers of the things that have it." (p. 114) "For something to have a power . . . is for it to be such that its presence in circumstances of a particular sort will have certain effects." (p. 113) Properties are thus clusters of causal powers. Shoemaker qualifies and restricts his claim in one important respect. He excludes from the purview of this analysis the so-called "Cambridge properties" that have bedeviled discussions of change and of causation. Thus the predicate 'being one hundred miles from the current heavyweight boxing champion of the world' may be true of an object, but it does not designate a "real" property of it, a property to which Shoemaker's theory is meant to apply. Cambridge predicates are "true of a thing, not because (or only because) of any properties it has, but because something else, perhaps something related to it in certain ways, has certain properties." (p. 112) In his discussion Shoemaker employs the term "Cambridge-property," thus leaving it unclear how his denial of their reality is to be understood. (Of this more below.)

The following identity conditions for properties are offered: "properties are identical, whether in the same possible world or in different ones, just in case their coinstantiation with the same properties give rises to the same causal powers." (p. 122) As Shoemaker candidly admits, this criterion is circular in several respects. Not only does the criterion explicitly cite the very notion it gives the identity conditions of, but the determination of sameness of causal powers, of circumstances and of effects, themselves all involve appeals to sameness of properties. These circularities are held by Shoemaker to be unavoidable because notions of property, causal power, event, similarity, persisting substance "belong to a system of interrelated concepts, no one of which can be explicated without the use of the others." (p. 123)

But matters are more serious than this, for the doctrine that the identity of a property is given by its associated causal powers makes these powers essential to it, and "this has a very strong consequence, namely that causal necessity is just a species of logical necessity."

> If the introduction into certain circumstances of a thing having certain properties causally necessitates the occurrence of certain effects, then it is impossible, logically impossible, that such an introduction could fail to have such an effect and so logically necessary that it has it. To the extent that causal laws can be viewed as propositions describing the causal potentialities of properties, it is impossible that the same properties should be governed by different causal laws in different possible worlds, for such propositions will be necessarily true when true at all. (p. 124)

Shoemaker adds however, that although they are necessary truths, the causal laws fixed by properties are not analytic, or knowable a priori. He avails himself of Saul Kripke's case for the view that there are necessary a posteriori truths, which can only be known empirically.[3] This "theory can allow that our knowledge of these potentialities is empirical, and that it is bound to be only partial." (p. 124) Nevertheless, Shoemaker's conclusion is, not surprisingly, the direct denial of Mackie's starting point. For whereas Mackie excludes the rationalist theory that there are any irreducible causal powers, on the strength of Hume's dictum that there are no necessary connections, Shoemaker concludes from his account of properties that "I thus find myself, in what I once would have regarded as reactionary company, defending the very sort of 'necessary connection' account of causality which Hume is widely applauded for having refuted." (p. 133)

As noted above, the arguments for this theory of properties, and its "reactionary" ramifications, are described by Shoemaker as "broadly speaking, epistemological. Only if some causal theory of properties is true, I believe, can it be explained how properties are capable of engaging our knowledge, and our language, in the way they do." (p. 116) Now, in one sense this claim is undoubtedly true, and the plethora of causal theories of our knowledge of anything and everything is vivid testimony to its truth. Indeed, Mackie admits as much in the passage quoted at the beginning of this paper. But few theories that explain our knowledge on the basis of causal connections to its objects have the strong consequences of Shoemaker's. Indeed, the real source of his conclusions is not epistemological; but as the coda to the sentence just quoted hints, it is the connection widely averred between identity conditions and essentiality, and not epistemology, that grounds Shoemaker's argument.

Shoemaker's epistemological argument proceeds by inviting us to suppose what he hopes to refute: that the identity of properties is "logically independent" of their causal potentialities. If this were so, the following untoward consequence for our knowledge of properties and objects would ensue: (1) there may be what have been called nomological danglers (though Shoemaker does not use this term), properties that make no causal contribution to the character of objects that manifest them; (2) there could be distinct and different properties with indistinguishable causal powers; (3) a property could have different causal powers over time so that an object's powers might remain entirely constant while its properties changed, or might retain all its properties while changing its powers. Among the further repurcussions of these possibilities, there are the following: (4) all judgments of overall-resemblance between objects would be ungrounded, for we would not have good evidence that our enumeration of shared properties was complete or even covered more than an infinitesimal fraction of the properties of objects, properties beyond our acquaintance because of their causal isolation. (5) Moreover, it would be impossible for us to know that two objects shared even a single property, since even if they did, the possible shuffling of causal powers might preclude any evidence that this was so; (6) indeed, we would not even be able to know whether an object had retained or changed its properties, since the same causal powers might be associated with different properties, and the same property with different causal powers; finally, (7) "there would be no way in which a particular property could be picked out to have a name attached to it; and even if, *per impossible*, a name did get attached to a property, it would be impossible for any one to have any justification for applying the name on particular occasions." Presumably, these possibilities constitute a reductio ad absurdum of the denial that properties are clusters of causal powers, because *we* do have knowledge of properties.

Several of these possibilities do not really undermine our knowledge, and, moreover, Shoemaker's own theory seems to raise obstacles to our knowledge of properties at least as serious as those that he hopes to circumvent. The first untoward possibility he mentions seems little more than the contradiction of Shoemaker's thesis. The second, that there might be distinct properties with identical powers, would certainly preclude our ever distinguishing them, but it requires a strong principle of verificationism to deny their possibility on this ground alone. Indeed, both the first and second possibilities seem to be assumed to be intelligible in the controversies over whether empirically indistinguishable, mutually incompatible theories disagree about any fact of the matter or not as well as discussion of epiphenomenalism and anomalous monism in the Philosophy of mind. If the third possibility were actual, then though we might be unable to acquire any knowledge of properties, we would not really require any either, so far as providing ourselves with causally relevant information is concerned. If a property changed its causal powers, or at least those on which our knowledge of it relies, it would indeed be inaccessible, but also irrelevant for understanding the causal transactions in which objects are engaged. As for the properties of objects remaining the same while the causal powers that constitute these properties change, this is no mere possibility but in quantum mechanical preparations seems to be an actuality. What makes quantum behavior in accordance with Bell's inequality so mysterious is that the conditional causal powers of microparticles change in ways we hold to be independent of the very properties these conditional powers reflect.

The possibility that an object's causal powers may change while *all* its properties remain constant is of course ruled out just because a causal power is a property; on the other hand, it is not obvious that causal knowledge requires the judgments of *overall-similarity*, or even the sharing of single properties that possibilities (5) and (6) preclude. Even were the notion of overall-similarity not a will-o-the-wisp, our causal knowledge requires only that objects share small numbers of causal powers, not that they share all or even one property, *over and above causal powers.*

Now, since causal powers of objects are themselves properties, all of Shoemaker's objections to a nondispositional theory of properties must apply to these powers as well. This means of course that we cannot circumvent his objections by simply focusing on causal powers and surrendering knowledge of properties as a prize not worth the effort. On the other hand, it remains a mystery how it is that we acquire knowledge of properties through acquaintance with their causal powers. For the latter are themselves properties, and so presumably have their identities fixed by further essential causal powers. I shall return to the problems associated with this regress below. For the moment, however, consider how Shoemaker's doctrine deprives us of knowledge of properties more directly. There are many properties of objects that we believe to be open to direct inspection: their composition, internal structure, perhaps their color, their mass, etc. Of course, some of these properties may not be intrinsic or monadic properties of objects, but relational ones (color is an obvious and historically vexed example of the latter sort). Our knowledge of the existence of various properties is based on causal relations between objects bearing these properties and our sensory apparatus. In spite of the inductive risks this causal connection generates, we are quite confident that at least some of the predicates that our language provides do express properties.

But if Shoemaker is correct, we have no more right to be confident about any of the properties *we believe there are* than we have confidence in the nomological generalizations that express their relations to one another. For some properties, like the strangeness, color, and charm of quarks, this is a reasonable attitude, but is it so for all properties? It is widely believed that we can acquire knowledge of properties independent of knowledge of, or even the existence of, nomological generalizations in which they figure. Indeed, it is a platitude of epistemology that we acquire such knowledge first, and it is a necessary preliminary to the inductive search for causal laws. This is one reason why Goodman's new riddle of induction is so haunting: we are certain that green and blue are real properties, while grue and bleen are not, even though we cannot make a well-grounded, evidential distinction between the generalizations in which these properties figure.

It is a fact that the discovery of laws has sometimes led to the repudiation of belief in a property (for example, it is said that there is no such property as 'containing dephlogisticated air' because we have discovered that there are no laws in which a predicate allegedly describing such a property figures); but if Shoemaker is correct, there is no property we have any right to confidence in the existence of until we have confidence in our knowledge of the laws in which it figures. We may be confident that there are properties, because we are confident that there are laws, but we cannot be confident that any of our predicates expresses a property, or which property it expresses, until we have knowledge of *all* the laws of nature. For whereas the predicates that figure in any given low-level, empirical, lawlike sentence (for example) may remain fixed throughout the theoretical changes that may eventuate in the true total science, the inevitable changes in other laws, especially the more theoretical ones that explain derived, observationally discoverable, general laws, will regularly change our beliefs about the causal powers of the properties expressed by predicates in the lower level laws.

Thus we will have no assurance that there is such a property as, say, charge, nor will we know what that property is until its causal powers, its essence, have been disclosed to us by whatever ultimate physical theory lies beyond quantum electrodynamics. And of course since true total science does not wear this label on its sleeve, we shall, on Shoemaker's view, never know whether any of our predicates pick out properties or not, even when and if they do. This skeptical conclusion about our current and future knowledge about any and all properties is at least as great as the skepticism Shoemaker seeks to forestall.

It is of course open to accept this skeptical conclusion and to hold that it remains forever a hypothesis whether any of our predicates denote a property. One doubts that this is a conclusion Shoemaker is eager to embrace.

One reason to withhold attribution of this skeptical thesis to Shoemaker is his own persistent contrast between what he identifies as real properties, like being made of steel or being knife shaped, and Cambridge properties, like being grue or being bleen. Apparently we know the former two for real properties and the latter as mere Cambridge properties, and Shoemaker offers us a sort of recipe for coming by this knowledge:

> Roughly, if a question about whether [a] thing has a property at a place and time concerns a genuine non-relational property, the question is most directly settled by observations and tests in the immediate vicinity of that place and time. . . . (p. 121)

But to allow that we distinguish real properties and mere Cambridge properties in the actual world empowers us to describe and consider possible worlds in which what are real properties of our world are but Cambridge properties, and this possibility severs the connection between properties and laws that Shoemaker claims to have uncovered. Consider the property of being made of steel, which we identify in the actual world through its causal powers, like that of combining with the property of being knife shaped in objects that have the causal power of cutting bread. The property of being made of steel has been identified in our world through the fact that it has clustered together with other properties and causal powers hitherto. Now, consider a possible world identical in history to the actual world up until some time t. Suppose that after t, being made of steel no longer clusters with being knife shaped to cut bread. In this possible world, of course, the causal laws must be different from those that operate in the actual world, and in this possible world we would be obliged to search for some underlying property of steel things that is the real locus of their bread cutting powers. We would withdraw the claim that it was the property of being made of steel that accorded the conditional power of cutting bread and reclassify this property as a mere Cambridge property of, among other things, knives, a Cambridge property that we had hitherto mistakenly supposed to be a real property. But, it may be asked, on what grounds does one claim to have identified the *same* item in this possible world as we identify in the actual world: after all, one is a mere Cambridge property and the other is a real property. Well, as Shoemaker says, "There is a close linkage between identity across time and identity across possible worlds." (p. 119) Our reason for saying that we have identified the same item, the same property, in both worlds is that the histories of the two worlds are identical up until time t. Until this time, 'being made of steel' expressed the same properties; to say that it does not thereafter, or that it never did express the same property, is simply to deny that we can identify and reidentify properties in the actual world. For in the actual world we have no more resource for doing this than its actual history and our knowledge of it.

If we can distinguish real properties and Cambridge properties in our world, then there can be possible worlds in which any and all of the real properties of the actual world are themselves Cambridge properties. In other words, the properties we know and identify may be known and identified at other worlds, worlds at which the causal laws relating properties are different. This conclusion, so utterly at variance with Shoemaker's, can only be avoided by denying that we can know of the existence of and identify Cambridge properties in the actual world, i.e., distinguish them from real properties, as Shoemaker does in example and argument. Indeed

Shoemaker is committed to the incoherence of the notion of a Cambridge property.

II

Shoemaker's appeal to epistemological considerations in behalf of metaphysical conclusions is unusual, especially since he holds that the metaphysical necessities he uncovers have no epistemic payoffs: we cannot know a priori any of the necessary truths whose necessity the metaphysical conclusions vouchsafe. In fact, the seventh and last of his untoward epistemological consequences of the denial that properties are causal powers essentially is the really serious argument for his view, and it is not particularly epistemological. For all parties must agree that reidentifying properties is crucial to their epistemic roles, no matter what their nature. Moreover, it is through their role in securing the identity of properties that causal powers acquire their logical connection with properties, and it is on this that Shoemaker's most controversial theses hinge. For it is indeed the case that we identify properties by their causal powers. If, as is widely held, the identity criteria for any kind reflect the essential or necessary properties of instances of the kind, it must follow that the causal powers of a property are connected to it necessarily. This is all the argument that Shoemaker really needs for his claims.

Let us accept the philosophical doctrines about identity, essence, and reference on which Shoemaker's theses hinge. However, it seems that cleaving to these doctrines makes it even more mysterious how we secure reference to properties, on Shoemaker's theory of them. Since, as we have seen, one cannot know that there is a cluster of causal powers associated with any predicate actually in use, because of the inadequacy and incompleteness of contemporary science, it follows that the criterion of identity that Shoemaker provides (properties are identical just in the case that their causal powers are) can have no firm application to decisions about whether predicates we use express properties, or whether two predicates express the same property or not. It will certainly be impossible to infer from the limited similarity of physical appearance at particular places and times, under particular conditions, of two distinct objects, that they share any properties in common, since such local similarities will be dependent on their other properties and ours as perceivers, as well as on the properties of conditions of observation, and may be the results of the clustering of very disparate causal powers.

Thus the implicit generality that Shoemaker accords to properties in virtue of the causal character of their identity criteria blocks the kind of identification and reidentification necessary for attaching a name to a property, or justifiably applying that name on other occasions. Of course, if we sever the causal theory of properties from the notion that causation is an implicitly general relation, whose individual instantiations obtain in virtue of general regularities, then this problem does not arise. If we can have *direct* knowledge of the causal powers of particular objects in particular settings, as the rationalist supposes, without having to appeal to contingently discoverable laws that subsume their behavior, then we could ground our identification and reidentification of properties on our knowledge of the causal powers of these particular objects.

This revision of Shoemaker's doctrine would be more in accord with our intuition that we do have direct knowledge of the existence and identity of at least some properties, or at least inductively less risky knowledge of them than of any laws in which they might figure. But this revision will turn Shoemaker's theory into the denial of the claim that all properties are dispositional, for dispositional ones are just those that do reflect the same inductive risk as laws do; the properties whose causal powers we can identify directly, without a detour through the discovery of causal laws, are the paradigm nondispositional, or manifest properties, whose existence Shoemaker denies.

If properties are clusters of causal powers and if causal powers are properties, then causal powers are themselves clusters of causal powers. In spite of the circularity of the relations among properties and causal powers, it may be hoped that causal powers could be graded along a dimension of more and more generality and fundamentality. After all, properties will be those entities denoted by the predicates of causal laws, and if laws reflect an axiomatic hierarchy, then we may be able to read off not only the causal powers that there are, from laws, but also how they cluster to generate the properties that they constitute. Thus, there will be a descent of causal powers until we reach the properties mentioned in the ultimate, unexplained laws of physics. If Shoemaker is correct, these properties will have to be dispositional because all properties are. On the other hand, they cannot themselves be composed of further causal powers, more fundamental than they are, for they are the properties related by the most fundamental laws of physics. There seems no alternative short of accepting that such properties will not be dispositional after all, except that of endorsing the view of them that Mackie dubbed the "rationalist" one.

If we exclude an infinite regress of more and more fundamental causal powers, we must reflect on the nature of the most fundamental of them. What will they be like? They will presumably be dispositional and not manifest properties of the fundamental constituents of matter or regions of space time. In particular, they will be the dispositions to have physical effects under given physical conditions described in the causal regularities they are called upon to explain. But this will run them afoul of Mackie's objection to the rationalist thesis that there are such purely dispositional properties.

Mackie attacks the version of this rationalist thesis defended by Rom Harré (whom Shoemaker cites in his own footnotes as expounding a view similar to his own).[4] According to Harré, the regress of deeper and deeper causal regularities, each explaining behavior of successively more fundamental entities by appeal to more fundamental properties, can only be brought to a halt by appeal to basic unexplicated powers, attributed to entities that are themselves characterized only by these powers. Mackie criticizes this view as:

> either confused or evasive. One possibility is that it is only the style of reference to these entities that is characteristically disposition, that the entities characterized only by their powers are merely *temporarily* ultimate, they are

merely the last items we have so far introduced in the regress of explanations. If so this closing of the regress is only verbally satisfactory. We are just saying that there is something here which does work in the way observed or inferred. When we later discover more about the natures of these entities, the connections between their natures and what they do will still be contingent and Humean; we shall merely have taken a further step in the regress, not resolved it into something essentially different. . . .

Alternatively if he [Harré, or other "rationalists"] postulates that there are, at some level, entities whose powers are part or the whole of their natures, then he would be introducing what I have called distinctively dispositional, conditional-entailing properties. These would indeed terminate the regress of explanation absolutely, not merely temporarily, and would give us something radically different from the 'irrational', Humean, regular sequence. And this is strongly suggested when Harré speaks about 'ultimate entities' which 'must be point centres of mutual influence, that is centres of power.' . . . . But this distinctive doctrine would be achieved only at the cost of violating . . . the central and overwhelmingly plausible [of Hume's theses] that there are no logical connections between distinct existences. (pp. 138-39)

Now, of course Shoemaker explicitly rejects this "central and overwhelmingly plausible" thesis of Hume's, so that the cost of Harré's distinctive doctrine of "centres of mutual influence," whose natures are exhausted by dispositions not further analyzable, is not too high for Shoemaker to pay. On the other hand, surrendering Hume's doctrine commits Shoemaker to something like Harré's "distinctive doctrine." For if the regress of explanations is to be ended and can only be ended at entities with causal powers, powers ungrounded in occurrent or manifest properties of the fundamental entities, then these entities will be as Harré describes them. Is this too high a price to pay for the denial of Hume's thesis?

Well, it would be too high for Shoemaker if the rationalist theory is really properly so called. That is, if the knowledge that there is such a stopping place in inquiry really does provide the epistemological pay-off: the conclusion that we can recognize this stopping place, recognize that the connections between objects at it are necessary and from this level build up the logical structure of the rest of science as a body of metaphysical necessities—necessary but synthetic truths known a priori. It is only this payoff that gives content and significance to the rationalist's speculation about an intelligible stopping place in scientific inquiry. Otherwise all talk of "ultimate entities" that are "centres of power" is but idle speculation, only terminologically at variance with the Humean conviction that the regress of explanations ends at mere 'hap', at regularities about nondispositional properties that have no explanation. (In *Enquiry Concerning Human Understanding*, section 26, Hume writes:

But as to the causes of . . . general causes, we should in vain attempt their discovery, nor shall we ever be able to satisfy ourselves, by any particular explication of them. These ultimate springs and principles are totally shut up from human curiosity and inquiry. . . . The most perfect philosophy of the natural kind only staves off our ignorance a little longer.)

It is largely in order to forestall the prospects of a rationalist epistemology that both Hume and Mackie attack the metaphysical rationalism of ultimate causal powers. Consider Mackie's attack on the explanatory pretensions of the rationalist view of dispositions:

> [I]f some one postulated the dormative virtue in accordance with what I have called the rationalist view of dispositions, that is as something whose intrinsic nature, adequately described, would entail that if anyone consumes a fair amount of it he falls asleep, then this is wrong. . . . There are no such intrinsically dispositional properties as this is supposed to be. The explanation given by postulating this one would not be empty, but too good. It does not merely restate what is to be explained, it is not merely the promise of a detailed explanation that has still to be discovered; it is an all-too-perfect explanation which usurps the place of a merely contingent one. What would be the point of showing that opium contains morphine which (despite its name) is only contingently related to sleep, if we knew already that opium contained an intrinsic power whose presence entailed the production of sleep (pp. 143-44)

As I shall argue below, a thesis without such entailments known a priori differs only conventionally from the Humean view that Mackie endorses. It is the epistemic dividends that justify the label "rationalist" theory of dispositionals, and they are the only ones that make it worth embracing.

Of course, Shoemaker explicitly repudiates any epistemic dividends from his "reactionary" conclusion that properties are causal powers and the laws of nature are necessary truths. For he avails himself of Kripke's doctrine that there can be necessary truths knowable only a posteriori, and all the laws of nature, from the most derived to the most fundamental, are of this sort.

III

Shoemaker's unwillingness to draw epistemological conclusion from his argument about the identity conditions for properties threatens to make the dispute between him and Mackie, as well as other Humeans, altogether too easy to reconcile. If the chief concern of the empiricist is to underwrite the empirical, contingent character of our causal knowledge, then there is little in Shoemaker's decision he cannot accept. On the other hand, once having accepted it, all the same old questions that the empiricist faces about our knowledge of causal laws, of the properties manifested by particular objects and of the nature of causal powers, are raised again in new forms.

On Mackie's behalf we may accept the thesis that the identity criteria for a kind give the essences of its members, that they express necessary truths about the kind and its members.[5] We may also accept that the causal powers of objects give the identity criteria for properties they manifest. And since these causal powers reflect the causal laws, it follows (on some further premises we may grant) that whatever the causal laws are, they hold necessarily because the causal powers of a property are the same in all possible worlds. But now the question arises, how do we discover what properties there are and what are the causal laws true at every possible world? The answer to this question both Hume and Mackie on one side, and Shoemaker and Kripke on the other, tell us is a matter of empirical enquiry. There is no other way to determine whether our predicates express properties and whether our lawlike sentences express laws. And once we have found some lawlike statements that seem to be laws and have sharpened our predicates in accordance with them, we may have some confidence that we are on the way to discovering this set of necessary truths. But we must always bear in mind the epistemological possibility that we may be mistaken, that the lawlike propositions we have stumbled on are not after all necessarily true because they may not be true at all. Naturally, if we adopt Shoemaker's and Kripke's view, we forswear the metaphysical possibility that the true laws of nature might be false, but we retain the epistemological possibility that what we have hit upon may be false.

Thus, the empiricist trades in his conviction that the laws of nature are merely contingent for the alternative that they are necessarily true, though it is logically impossible for us to have sufficient grounds to identify them, just because their metaphysical necessity is undetectable by us, the denizens of only one possible world, the actual one. But this leaves the empiricist pretty well where he was before Kripke advanced the doctrine of necessary truths known only a posteriori. The position is rather like that facing one who must choose between treating Euclidean geometry as a body of necessary truths and as an empirical theory about spatial relations. If one adopts the first alternative, it becomes a pressing question, not whether the axioms of geometry are true, but whether there are, in the actual world, any points, lines, triangles, or circles. If one adopts the latter view, then the pressing question is whether the empirical theory geometry constitutes is confirmed by the points, lines, circles, and triangles that exist in the world.

Other things being equal, the choice one faces in this case is not very significant; no difference is made by the choice, nothing is put out of reach so far as explanatory power is concerned by taking either alternative. The same seems true of the alternative of holding that the laws of nature are contingent and might as a matter of metaphysical possibility be false and of holding that they are necessary though there is no way of identifying any candidate for nomological status as such a necessary truth. Similarly, the choice between holding that all properties are causal powers but that we can never tell whether any predicate expresses a property (because we cannot identify the necessary truths about causal powers as such) and holding that we know of at least some properties though we cannot tell a priori whether they figure in any general laws or not, does not seem very significant. Either choice leaves all the hard questions about our knowledge of the world on the same footing.

In the only extended discussion Mackie ever broached on the account of necessity and identity due to Kripke, he wrote that:

> these *de re* modalities are, in a very broad sense, *de dicto* after all. Though these necessities apply to individual things and natural kinds . . . that they do so is primarily a feature of the way we think and speak, of how we handle identity in association with counter-factual possibility. They reflect implicit rules for the ascription of identity, for the recognition of the same person, or thing, or stuff or species, in neutrally described merely possible situations. . . . If this is correct, then these *de re* modalities need not in themselves offend empiricists. But . . . there may be metaphysical assumptions that underlie our ways of handling identity, and these of course may be open to dispute.[6]

The application of these conditions to the present issue I understand as follows. We may accept Kripke's account of our implicit rules for the ascription of identity, "in association with counter-factual possibility." This acceptance will commit us to certain conditionals: for example, if we have knowledge of the existence and identity of properties, and the same set of causal laws gives their identity conditions across all possible worlds, then these laws are logically necessary and all properties are after all dispositional. However, under these circumstances, it is a contingent matter whether any predicate of our languages expresses any property, a matter that depends on the degree of our acquaintance with the causal laws true at every possible world.

Furthermore, empirical considerations on the basis of which we credit hypotheses about what the laws of nature are provide no assurance that they are necessary; this assurance stems from our rules for the identification of properties and the treatment of counterfactual possibility. To accommodate these disclosures about our conceptual scheme, we must restate our claims about dispositions (and doubtless a great deal else). But we can do so in a way that preserves what is correct in the Humean thesis that there can be no necessary connection between distinct existences. This thesis has been widely understood as a restriction on metaphysical as well as epistemic connections. The divergence between the former sort and the latter that Kripke, Plantinga, and others have proclaimed leads us to treat as adequate, for the empiricist's purpose, a restriction of Hume's dictum to epistemologically necessary connections only: There is no epistemologically necessary connection between distinct existences, i.e., there are no synthetic truths known a priori.

Thus, the identification of, say, crystal structure as a property may be metaphysically connected with very many laws that we employ to attribute it and that therefore govern the cluster of causal powers that determine its identity. But for any particular causal power, like defracting X-rays, or any law that governs it, it is epistemologically possible that crystal structure lacks that power or that the putative law governing it is false. Furthermore, the predicates that we believe (on various grounds, some good, some bad) to express properties are connected to one another with only epistemological contingency at most. Perhaps every predicate is lexicographically introduced in what Mackie calls a dispositional style; some are explicitly or literally dispositional, like 'electrical impedance'; they entail conditionals, not just metaphysically, but epistemologically. That is, we can actually identify a priori the general statements that must be true if something has the property they purport to express. But others are epistemologically nondispositional: they come equipped with no such a priori, identifiable, general statement (even though if Shoemaker is correct about identity, there are, as a matter of epistemologically irrelevant, metaphysical necessity, laws associated with the properties expressed by nondispositional predicates—that is, if they express any property at all).

But those predicates without associated conditionals known a priori, even when dispositionally introduced, by the citation of a priori conditionals, are crucially different from predicates that we know a priori to be dispositional. To insist that they too are metaphysically disposition will not after all be tantamount to indulging in the unnecessary fiction that Mackie accuses the rationalist of, but it will be very close. For one may well pose the parallel of Mackie's rhetorical question, "Why should we insert this extra element of metaphysical dispositionality between the epistemologically nondispositional predicate and the causal behavior?" When we assert the epistemologically contingent claim that "metal oxides release gases on heating," what further is added if we qualify this claim with the proviso that "the statement, *if true*, is necessarily true because it will reflect the causal power of releasing gases on heating, which is of the essence of being a metal oxide." Since we can never transcend the epistemological limits on establishing the antecedent of the proviso, the conditional remains forever idle and can do no work in the advancement of our knowledge of properties or of the laws that relate them.

Both Shoemaker and Mackie agree that predicates are introduced dispositionally or causally. As Mackie says, the properties they are taken to express are known "only or mainly by way of the effects they have or would have in such-and-such circumstances." (p. 153) But Mackie's firm denial that all properties are dispositional, and his assertion that every dispositional property has an occurrent categorical base in manifest, nondispositional properties, is reflection of his epistemological conviction that there is no a priori entailment between distinct existences, between the instantiation of a property we recognize and the exemplification of the particular properties we identify as the causes and effects of this instantiation. Here too, Shoemaker agrees, holding that our knowledge of causal relations is never a priori. The disagreements between them arise from issues independent of these two. The disagreements seem to arise from what Mackie conspicuously fails to provide in "Dispositions and Powers," a statement of the identity conditions for properties. The one that Shoemaker provides, together with widely accepted exigencies on criteria of identity, generates the circle of internal relations among concepts like property, causal power, event, similarity, persisting substance, and, we may add, causal law. But as with all circles of concepts into which we cannot break, the question always remains whether there are items in the world that answer to them. And this question is itself one that can be given only at best a contingently true answer.

Mackie's repudiation of the rationalist view of dispositions, and his defense of the realist view, requires nothing more.[7]

Notes

1. *Truth, Probability and Paradox* (Oxford, 1973), 142-43. Further page references to Mackie in the text are to this work.

2. "Causality and Properties," *Time and Cause*, edited by P. van Inwagen (Dordrecht, 1980), 109-35, and "Identity, Properties and Causality," *Midwest Studies in Philosophy* IV (1979):321-42. Further page references to Shoemaker in the text are to the first of these two papers.

3. See "Naming and Necessity," in *Semantics of Natural Language*, edited by D. Davidson and G. Harman (Dordrecht, 1972), 253-355.

4. Rom Harré, *The Principles of Scientific Thinking* (London, 1970); see especially p. 208. Shoemaker cites Rom Harré and E. H. Madden, *Causal Powers* (Oxford, 1975), which elaborates the thesis of the work that Mackie cites.

5. In "De What Re is De Re Modality," *Journal of Philosophy* 71(1974):551-61, Mackie seemed tentatively to accept these claims, subject to empiricist interpretations of them.

6. Ibid., 560-61.

7. I owe thanks to Peter van Inwagen, Jonathan Bennett, and Terrance Tomkow for comments and especially to the last for an argument that I have adapted to my own purposes.

Laws and Causal Relations

MICHAEL TOOLEY

How are causal relations between particular states of affairs related to causal laws? There appear to be three main answers to this question, and the choice among those three alternatives would seem to be crucial for any account of causation. In spite of this fact, the question of which view is correct has been all but totally neglected in present-day discussions. Indeed, since the time of Hume, one answer has more or less dominated philosophical thinking about causation. In this paper I shall attempt to show that the view in question is exposed to decisive objections.

1. THE THREE ALTERNATIVES

There are three views that might be advanced concerning the relation between causal laws and causal relations. Two of the alternatives are quite familiar; the third less so. In this first section I shall briefly describe the three views. I shall then go on, in later sections, to consider which alternative is most plausible.

1.1 The Supervenience View

According to the first view, which is currently accepted by the vast majority of philosophers, causal laws are primary and causal relations are secondary. There are different ways of attempting to make this claim more precise. One way of doing so is in terms of the following general thesis:

> *The Thesis of the Humean Supervienience of Causal Relations*
> The truth values of singular causal statements are logically determined by the truth values of statements of causal laws together with the truth values of noncausal statements about particulars.

This formulation seems perfectly satisfactory, and I believe that it has the merit of being the most modest statement of the basic claim. It says, in effect, only that it is in principle possible to analyze singular causal statements in terms of non-causal statements together with statements of causal laws. It does not indicate, even in outline, the form that such an analysis would take.

But on the other hand, if this claim is to be rendered plausible, it seems likely that one needs at least a sketch of how such an analysis might run. As a consequence, a more common approach is to put forward the general supervenience claim by advancing some specific account of how statements concerning causal relations between particular states of affairs can be analyzed in terms of statements of causal laws together with noncausal statements. A typical suggestion is this:

State of affairs a causes state of affairs b

means the same as:

There are noncausal properties P and Q, and a noncausal relation R, such that a has property P, b has property Q, b is the only state of affairs with property Q standing in relation R to a, and it is causal law that any state of affairs with property P is always accompanied by a state of affairs with property Q that stands in relation R to it.

This analysis has the defect, however, of implying that the underlying laws must be nonprobabilistic. It might seem that this defect is easily corrected: simply replace the clause 'it is a causal law that any state of affairs with property P is always accompanied by a state of affairs with property Q that stands in relation R to it' by something like 'there is some number p such that it is a causal law that for any state of affairs with property P, the probability that there is some state of affairs with property Q that stands in relation R to it is equal to p'. The resulting analysis only works, however, in the case of *immediate* causation. For suppose that the reason that it is a causal law that any state of affairs with property P is accompanied, with probability p, by a state of affairs with property Q that stands in relation R to it, is that there are the following two causal laws:

A state of affairs with property P is accompanied, with probability p_1, by a state of affairs with property S that stands in relation R_1 to it

A state of affairs with property S is accompanied, with probability p_2, by a state of affairs with property Q that stands in relation R_2 to it

where p is equal to $(p_1 \times p_2)$, where R is the logical product of R_1 and R_2, and where there are no other relevant laws. If this were so, one could have a case where there is a state of affairs with property P that does not give rise to one with property S, and so does not give rise to one with property Q, but where something else causes there to be a state of affairs with property Q that just happens to stand in relation R to the state of affairs with property P. The above analysis would then imply the false claim that the state of affairs with property P caused the state of affairs with property Q that stands in relation R to it.

It might seem, however, that this defect could also be easily corrected. One could view the above analysis as giving an account of direct or immediate causation, and then define indirect causation as the ancestral of that relation. To say that state of affairs a causes state of affairs b would thus be to say that either a is the immediate cause of b, or there is some chain of events $c_1, c_2, \ldots c_i, \ldots c_n$ such that a is the immediate cause of c_1, c_n is the immediate cause of b, and each c_i (other than c_n) is the immediate cause of c_{i+1}, the next element in the causal chain.

But this approach involves an assumption that can be seen to be unacceptable. For it is being assumed that if a causes b by means of an intervening causal process, then there must be some state of affairs, c_1, that is causally intermediate between a and b and that is such that there is *no* state of affairs that is causally intermediate between a and c_1. But why should this be the case? Why might it not be that all causal processes are infinitely divisible, so that for any two causally related states of affairs, there are causal intermediaries? As a consequence, it would seem that the relation of causation cannot be analyzed in terms of that of immediate causation.

It is not, therefore, a trivial matter to set out an adequate and completely general analysis of singular causal statements, even given the notion of a causal law. Fortunately, the difficulties involved are not germane to the present issue. Accordingly, it will be both sufficient, and simplest, to work with a formulation of the thesis of Humean supervenience that, rather than offering an analysis of singular causal statements, is along the more modest lines of the formulation set out at the beginning of this section.

It will be useful, however, to offer a slightly more explicit version of that formulation, and also to distinguish between the cases of immediate causation and mediate causation:

The Thesis of Humean Supervenience: Immediate Causation
There are meaning postulates for causal expressions such that a statement of the form 'State of affairs a is the *immediate* cause of state of affairs b' is true if and only if that statement is entailed by the set of statements that consists of:
(1) the relevant meaning postulates;
(2) all true statements of causal laws;
(3) all true statements concerning the noncausal, nonrelational properties of states of affairs a and b;
(4) all true statements concerning noncausal relations between states of affairs a and b.

The Thesis of Humean Supervenience: Mediate Causation
There are meaning postulates for causal expressions such that a statement of the form 'State of affairs a is the *mediate* cause of state of affairs b' is true if and only if state of affairs a is not the immediate cause of b, but there is some nonempty, and possibly uncountably infinite set, S, of states of affairs, other than a and b, such that the above statement is entailed by the set of statements that consists of:
(1) the relevant meaning postulates;
(2) all true statements of causal laws;

(3) all true statements concerning the noncausal, nonrelational properties of states of affairs *a*, *b*, and those belonging to set S;

(4) all true statements concerning the noncausal relations among states of affairs *a, b*, and those belonging to set S.

The introduction of the reference to what may be an uncountably infinite set, S, enables one to deal with the case in which *a* is the cause of *b*, but not the immediate cause, and where, moreover, there is no chain of intervening states of affairs that are tied together by the relation of immediate causation.

One final comment. Many, and perhaps most, philosophers who accept the thesis that causal relations are logically supervenient upon noncausal facts together with causal laws would also accept the following claim regarding causal laws:

The Thesis of the Humean Supervenience of Causal Laws
The truth values of all statements of causal laws are logically determined by the truth values of all noncausal statements about the properties of, and relations among, particulars.

When this thesis is also accepted, one is led to the following, stronger claim regarding the supervenience of causal relations.

The Strong Thesis of the Humean Supervenience of Causal Relations
The truth values of singular causal statements are logically determined by the truth values of noncausal statements about the properties of, and relations among, particulars.

I shall not be discussing this stronger thesis. It seems to me that the only way to support it is by appealing both to the weaker thesis of the Humean supervenience of causal relations and to the thesis of the Humean supervenience of causal laws. The former thesis will be considered here; the latter I have argued against elsewhere.[1]

1.2 The Singularist View

A second and radically different view is that it is causal relations between states of affairs that are primary and that causal laws are secondary. This view is forcefully expressed by C. J. Ducasse in the following passage:

The supposition of recurrence is thus wholly irrelevant to the meaning of cause; that supposition is relevant only to the meaning of law. And recurrence becomes related at all to causation only when a law is considered which happens to be a generalization of facts themselves individually causal to begin with. A general proposition concerning such facts is, indeed, a causal law, but it is not causal because it is general. It is general, i.e., a law, only because it is about a class of resembling facts; and it is causal only because each of them already happens to be a causal fact individually and in its own right (instead of, as Hume would have it, by right of its co-membership with others in a class of pairs of successive events). The causal relation is essentially a relation between concrete individual events. . . .[2]

Ducasse's formulation of this second view involves a Humean account of laws, according to which they are to be equated with certain sorts of regularities. The singularist view can be combined, however, with radically different accounts of the nature of laws. One could, for example, adopt the view that laws, rather than being mere regularities, involve certain genuine relations between universals.

A second point is that the singularist claim that it is causal relations that are primary, rather than causal laws, is compatible with different views concerning whether causal relations can be analyzed in terms of noncausal properties and relations Ducasse maintained that such an analysis is possible.[3] Other advocates of this second position have held that causal concepts must be taken as primitive.

Another philosopher who appears to accept a singularist account of causation is Elizabeth Anscombe. Her essay "Causality and Determination" is admittedly not entirely explicit on this matter. Consider, for example, the following passage, from very near the end of her essay:

> Meanwhile in non-experimental philosophy it is clear enough what are the dogmatic slumbers of the day. It is over and over again assumed that any singular causal proposition implies a universal statement running "Always when this, then that"; often assumed that true singular causal statements are derived from such 'inductively believed' universalities. Examples indeed are recalcitrant, but that does not seem to disturb. Even a philosopher acute enough to be conscious of this, such as Davidson, will say, without offering any reason at all for saying it, that a singular causal statement implies *that there is* such a true universal proposition – though perhaps we can never have knowledge of it. Such a thesis needs some reason for believing it![4]

In this passage, Anscombe is explicitly calling into question only the proposition that causal relations presuppose underlying *nonprobabilistic* laws. Moreover, the discussion throughout her essay is focused upon the claims, first, that causal relations must be instances of exceptionless generalizations, and secondly, that causes must necessitate their effects, and someone who holds that there can be probabilistic laws could agree that those claims should be rejected, without thereby being forced to conclude that causal relations do not presuppose *any* laws – either probabilistic or nonprobabilistic.

Nonetheless, I think it is reasonably clear that Anscombe does wish to accept the singularist view. For consider one of her central lines of argument. It rests upon the following intuition concerning the nature of causality:

> . . . causality consists in the derivativeness of an effect from its causes. This is the core, the common feature, of causality in its various kinds. Effects derive from, arise out of, come of, their causes.[5]

Given this intuition, she goes on to say:

> Now analysis in terms of necessity or universality does not tell us of this derivedness of the effect; rather it forgets about that. For the necessity will be that of laws of nature; through it *we* shall be able to derive knowledge of

the effect from knowledge of the cause, or vice versa, but that does not shew us the cause as source of the effect. Causation, then, is not to be identified with necessitation.

If A comes from B, this does not imply that every A-like thing comes from some B-like thing or set-up or that every B-like thing or set-up has an A-like thing coming from it; or that given B, A had to come from it, or that given A, there had to be B for it to come from. Any of these may be true, but if any is, that will be an additional fact, not comprised in A's coming from B.[6]

As an argument, this does not seem to have much force because everything turns upon the notion of an effect's deriving from, arising out of, its cause, and no analysis of this crucial notion is offered. My point here, however, is simply that the above line of thought does strongly suggest a singularist view of causation. For why does Anscombe maintain that A's coming from B does not imply either that every A-like thing comes from some B-like thing or set-up or that every B-like thing or set-up has an A-like thing coming from it? The answer, I think, is that Anscombe believes that causation is just a relation between concrete individuals, such as A and B, rather than, as Hume thought, something involving at least an implicit reference to corresponding *types* of individuals. But if this view is right, then A's coming from B equally fails to imply either that there is some probability p that any A-like thing comes from some B-like thing, or that there is some probability p that a B-like thing will give rise to an A-like thing. Singular causal statements will not imply the existence of any laws, either probabilistic or nonprobabilistic.

1.3 A Third Alternative

At first glance, the supervenience view and the singularist view might seem to exhaust the alternatives. But this is not the case. An advocate of the supervenience view affirms what a proponent of the singularist view denies: that all causal connections between states of affairs presuppose underlying causal laws. However, the supervenience view involves a further claim to the effect that what causal relations obtain is logically determined by the causal laws together with the totality of noncausal facts. This means that it is possible to reject both the singularist view and the supervenience view. Perhaps singular causal facts are not logically determined by causal laws in conjunction with noncausal facts, but nonetheless, it is impossible for there to be singular causal facts for which there are no corresponding causal laws.

I am not aware of any philosopher who has advanced this third view. This suggests that the third alternative is, perhaps, prima facie implausible. That may well be so. For the nature of the relation between causal laws and causal relations does seem rather more puzzling on this third view than on either the supervenience view or the singularist view. If one finds plausible the idea that causal relations presuppose causal laws, it is natural to be drawn to the clear account of that connection that is provided by the supervenience view of causation. But on the other hand, if it turns out, as I shall attempt to show, that the supervenience account is exposed to very serious objections, this third view may then be an important alternative to the singularist position.

2. THREE RELATED ARGUMENTS AGAINST THE SUPERVENIENCE VIEW

In this section, and the next two, I shall set out five arguments against the view that causal relations between states of affairs are logically supervenient upon causal laws plus noncausal facts. Three of the arguments are very closely related, having essentially the same logical structure. They will be dealt with in the present section.

2.1 Mental Events and Physical Events

The first argument deals with the question of whether mental events have spatial locations. I shall attempt to show that if the thesis of the Humean supervenience of causal relations is correct, then there is a plausible argument for the conclusion that, regardless of whether a materialist view of the mind is correct, mental events *must* have spatial locations.

Some nonmaterialists are, of course, prepared to *assign* spatial locations to mental events. For if one holds, as at least some do, that for every mental event there is some corresponding physical event that is its cause, one can always adopt the convention of assigning to a mental event the same spatial location as the underlying physical event. But the argument here is not concerned with the possibility of a conventional assignment of locations to mental events. The claim is rather that if Humean supervenience obtains, then mental events must have spatial locations *independently* of any convention relating them to physical events with which they are causally connected. To the extent that this conclusion is unacceptable, the argument provides one with a reason for rejecting the supervenience account of the relation between causal laws and causal relations.

The argument runs as follows. In the first place, it is empirically possible, albeit extraordinarily unlikely, that the world contains two human bodies that are, at every moment in time, qualitatively indistinguishable. If all mental events are causally determined by physical events in the relevant body, it would then follow that the minds associated with those two bodies would also have to be qualitatively indistinguishable at every moment at which they existed. But even if mental events are not thus determined, it could still be the case, as a matter of accident, that the two associated minds were qualitatively indistinguishable. So let us assume that such is the case.

Let P_1 be some physical event in the one body that does cause some mental event, M_1. Let P_2 be the corresponding, simultaneous, qualitatively indistinguishable physical event in the other body, and M_2 the corresponding simultaneous qualitatively indistinguishable mental event in the other mind. What happens when the thesis of Humean supervenience is applied to this situation?

The argument is simplest in the case where P_1 is the *immediate* cause of M_1, so let us begin by considering that case. Given the thesis of Humean supervenience, it can be the case that P_1 immediately causes M_1 only if that statement is entailed by the set of statements, call it T, that contains:

(1) the relevant meaning postulates;
(2) all true statements of causal laws;
(3) all true statements concerning the noncausal, nonrelational properties of events P_1 and M_1;
(4) all true statements concerning the noncausal relations between events P_1 and M_1.

Next, P_1 is not the immediate cause of M_2. The thesis of Humean supervenience implies that this condition will obtain only if the statement that P_1 immediately causes M_2 is not entailed by the set of statements, call it U, that contains:

(1) all true meaning postulates;
(2) all true statements of causal laws;
(3) all true statements concerning the noncausal, nonrelational properties of events P_1 and M_2;
(4) all true statements concerning the noncausal relations between P_1 and M_2.

How can it be the case that T entails the statement that P_1 immediately causes M_1, whereas U does not entail the statement that P_1 immediately causes M_2? For this to be the case, T must contain some statement about M_1 such that U does not contain a corresponding statement about M_2. This statement cannot be one of the meaning postulates, nor one of the causal laws, since neither sort of statement, we can assume, will contain any reference to particular events. Nor can the difference be a matter of statements attributing noncausal, nonrelational properties to M_1 and M_2 respectively, since they are, by hypothesis, qualitatively indistinguishable. The only possible difference, therefore, is that there is some noncausal relation that holds between P_1 and M_1, but not between P_1 and M_2.

What might this relation be? Relations may be classified, following a traditional distinction, into internal and external ones—an internal relation being one tht holds by virtue of the nature, or properties, of the relata.[7] Since M_1 and M_2 do not differ with respect to any of their noncausal, nonrelational properties, there cannot be any internal, noncausal relation that holds between P_1 and M_1, but not between P_1 and M_2. The only possibility, then, is that there is some external relation that holds between P_1 and M_1, but not between P_1 and M_2.

What external relations are there? Here I can offer only a hypothesis, not an argument. The hypothesis is that all external relations are of three types: spatiotemporal, causal, and nomological. Since the relations in question must be noncausal ones, the second possibility is immediately ruled out. Accordingly, there must either be some spatiotemporal relation or some nomological relation that holds between P_1 and M_2, but not between P_1 and M_2.

It would seem, however, very implausible to accept the thesis of the Humean supervenience of causal relations without also accepting the parallel thesis with respect to nomological relations:

The Thesis of the Humean Supervenience of Nomological Relations
The truth values of singular, noncausal, nomological statements are logically determined by the truth values of statements of laws together with the truth values of nonnomological statements about particulars.

But given the latter thesis, one can parallel the present line of argument, thereby showing that P_1 can stand in some nomological relation to M_1 in which it does not stand to M_2 only if there is either some spatiotemporal relation or some causal relation that holds between P_1 and M_1, but not between P_1 and M_2.

From this it follows that P_1 can be the immediate cause of M_1, but not of M_2, only if there is some spatiotemporal relation that holds between P_1 and M_1, but not between P_1 and M_2. For differences in nomological relations are either grounded in differences in causal relations or they are not. Suppose, then, that differences in nomological relations are grounded in differences in causal relations. In that case, differences in causal relations cannot be grounded in differences in nomological relations. They must instead be grounded in differences in spatiotemporal relations. So it would have to be by virtue of some spatiotemporal relation obtaining between P_1 and M_1, but not between P_1 and M_2, that P_1 is the immediate cause of M_1, but not of M_2. The other alternative is that differences in nomological relations are not grounded in differences in causal relations. In that case, differences in causal relations could be grounded in differences in nomological relations. The latter, however, would then have to rest upon differences in spatiotemporal relations. So once again, P_1 could be the immediate cause of M_1, but not the immediate cause of M_2, only if there were some spatiotemporal relation holding between P_1 and M_1, but not between P_1 and M_2.

But M_1 and M_2 are, by hypothesis, simultaneous. Therefore, there can be a spatiotemporal relation that obtains between P_1 and M_1, but not between P_1 and M_2, only if there is some *spatial* relation that holds between P_1 and M_1, but not between P_1 and M_2. Hence M_1 must have spatial location.

There are two questions that now need to be considered. First, the argument just sketched started from the assumption that P_1 is the immediate cuase of M_1. What happens when this is replaced by the assumption that P_1 causes M_1 either directly, or by means of a causal process?

The answer is that the argument is not fundamentally altered. If P_1 causes M_1 by means of some causal process, then the thesis of Humean supervenience with respect to mediate causation implies that there is some set, S, of states of affairs, such that P_1's causing M_1 is supervenient upon certain sorts of noncausal facts about P_1, M_1, and the states of affairs in S, together with the causal laws. The question then becomes how the corresponding noncausal facts about P_1, M_2, and the states of affairs in S, together with the causal laws, can fail to make it the case that P_1 also causes M_2. And one can show, by means of the same basic argument, that the only way this can be the case is if M_1 stands in some spatial relation, either to P_1 or to elements in the set S, that M_2 does not. So once again M_1 must have spatial location.

The second question concerns the fact that the argument involves the assumption that M_1 is a mental event that is caused by some physical event, P_1, in the relevant body. Given that this is so, how does the argument establish anything about mental events that *lack* such causes?

The answer is that the argument does not really need the assumption in question. The argument goes through equally well if one assumes, instead, that M_1 causes some physical event, P_1, in the relevant body. Or if the one assumes that there is some other mental event, N_1, belonging to the same mind, such that M_1 causes N_1, or vice versa. The argument only requires the assumption that M_1 is *not causally isolated* both from all mental events in the same mind and from all physical events in the relevant body. And since it seems very plausible to say that any mental event that was thus isolated would not belong to any mind, the qualification of the overall conclusion that is required is a minor one.

This brings me to the final step in the argument. So far I have dealt with a very special case in which there is an exact replica of a given person. How does it follow from this special case that *all* mental events belonging to minds must have spatial locations? The line of thought is this. Let M be any mental event belonging to some mind, and let us assume that M is not causally isolated from all other events. It would seem that it would always be empirically possible for there to be another mental event, M^*, that stands in precisely the same relation to M as M_2 does to M_1 in the case considered above. If this possibility were realized, it would follow, by the above argument, that M has spatial location. But surely it cannot be the case that whether M has spatial location depends upon whether there happens to exist some other mental event, M^*, that is related to M in the same way that M_2 is related to M_1. If mental events in my mind would have spatial location if there were an exact replica of me, say, out near Alpha Centauri, then surely mental events in my mind have spatial location even if no such replica exists. And in general, if it is true that M would have spatial location if there were an appropriate M^*, the reason it is true is that M has spatial location even in the absence of such an M^*. This establishes the desired conclusion: if the thesis of the Humean supervenience of causal relations is true, then every mental event belonging to a mind must have spatial location.

Can this argument be resisted? The most promising way of attempting to do so would seem to be to claim that external relations are not exhausted by spatio-temporal, causal, and nomological relations. What other external relations might there be? David Lewis has suggested that a philosopher who rejects a materialist view of the mind might well want to hold that the relation of *ownership* is another external relation. There are two possibilities that need to be considered here. The first is that of ownership as a relation between a mind and the corresponding body. If there were such an additional, external relation, it is clear that the present argument would be undercut. But is it reasonable to think that if materialism is false, then there is such a relation? It does not seem to me that it is. For if ownership were some additional, external relation, then it would seem that my mind could stand in the relation of ownership to a body that is now in New Zealand, *and could do so even though there are no causal connections* between this mind and the body in New Zealand. A much more plausible view, surely, is that ownership of a body by a mind is a complex relation that can be resolved into a number of types of causal connections. My mind is able to control, in a rather direct fashion, the movement of various parts of my body. Stimulation of different parts of this body typically gives rise to various experiences that I enjoy. Certain types of injuries to my body affect the sorts of mental activities that I can engage in. It seems to me that it is facts such as these that make it the case that my mind owns this body, and that, in general, it is certain causal relations that are constitutive of the relation of ownership between a mind and a body.

Another possibility, urged by Leonard Carrier, is that the nonmaterialist may want to treat the relation of ownership that obtains between a mind and its mental states as an additional external relation. If there is such a relation, then the nonmaterialist can avoid the conclusion that all mental events belonging to minds have spatial location, though a variant of the above argument will show that any mind that is not causally isolated must have a spatial location. But is it really plausible to think that if materialism is false, there is such a relation? It seems to me that postulation of such a relation leads to an unsatisfactory view of the unity of the mind. For if ownership were some additional, primitive, external relation between a mind and its states, two mental events would belong to the same mind if and only if there were some mind that stood in the relation of ownership to each event. This, in turn, would have two consequences. First, there could be minds in which there were no causal connections at all, of even the most indirect sorts, among any of the events belonging to each individual mind. Secondly, there could be mental events entering into direct causal relations, and which formed complex causal networks, but which nevertheless belonged to different minds. Both possibilities seem problematic. It seems to me that a much more plausible view is that it is precisely the presence of certain sorts of causal connections that is constitutive of the unity of a mind.

Neither of the possible ownership relations appears, then, upon reflection, to be a plausible candidate for the role of an additional, external relation that could serve to ground causal relations involving mental events. If this is right, it is hard to see how a nonmaterialist can resist the conclusion that if the thesis of Humean supervenience with respect to causal relations is true, then every mental event that belongs to a mind must have spatial location. Therefore, to the extent that it is reasonable to believe that it is logically possible for there to be mental events that do not have spatial location, but that belong to minds, it is also reasonable to reject the supervenience view of causal relations.

2.2 The Causal Theory of Time

The second argument concerns the possibility of a causal theory of time. The basic thrust of the argument is that it is logically possible that the universe might be in precisely the same state at different times and that this possibility, when conjoined with the thesis of the Humean supervenience of causal relations, leads to the conclusion that a causal analysis of temporal concepts is logically impossible.

The argument can be stated very briefly, since its structure parallels the argument just considered. Let P_1, M_1, and M_2 now be complete temporal slices of the universe—either instantaneous or extended—where P_1 occurs before M_1, but after M_2, and where M_1 and M_2 are qualitatively indistinguishable. It might be a case of a deterministic universe where conditions are such that there is an endless repetition of every type of state that exists at any time. Alternatively, it might be an indeterministic universe in which, by accident, the state of the universe at one time is qualitatively indistinguishable from its state at some other time. The question now is this. Can one give an account of temporal concepts, in causal terms, that will allow it to be the case that P_1 is before M_1, but not before M_2? If the thesis of the Humean supervenience of causal relations is true, the answer would seem to be no, since that thesis, when conjoined with a causal analysis of temporal concepts, seems to imply that P_1 must stand in precisely the same causal relations to M_2 and to M_1. For if one parallels the argument advanced in the previous subsection, one is led once more to the conclusion that P_1 can stand in some causal relation to M_1 in which it does not stand to M_2 only if there is some external relation that holds between P_1 and M_1, but not between P_1 and M_2.

At this point the argument is, if anything, stronger, since rather than raising the general question of what external relations exist, one can ask what external relations can obtain between different complete temporal slices of the world. And here it seems clear that there are only three possibilities: temporal relations, causal relations, and nomological relations. The thesis of the Humean supervenience of causal relations therefore implies that causal relations between complete temporal slices of the universe must be grounded either upon temporal relations or upon nomological relations. The possibility of nomological relations can then be excluded, as before, on the ground that the thesis of the Humean supervenience of causal relations is only plausible if the thesis of the Humean supervenience of nomological relations is also plausible, and the latter thesis forces one to find some nonnomological relation as a basis for nomological relations. The conclusion, therefore, is that if the thesis of the Humean supervenience of causal relations is true, P_1 can be causally related to M_1 in some way in which it is not causally related to M_2 only if there is some temporal relation that obtains between P_1 and M_1, but not between P_1 and M_2. But if one is to be able to analyze temporal relations in causal terms, one cannot appeal to temporal relations to provide that by virtue of which P_1 stands in a certain causal relation to M_1, but not to M_2. Accordingly, a complete causal analysis of temporal concepts is precluded by the supervenience view of causal relations.

2.3 Identity over Time in Rotationally Symmetrical Universes

The third argument is concerned with what account is to be given of the identity of elementary physical objects over time. A rather plausible view is that identity over time in such a case is to be analyzed in terms of causal relations between different temporal parts of the enduring entity. The thrust of this argument is that such an analysis is impossible if causal relations are supervenient.

The argument turns upon the possibility of rotationally symmetrical universes. Consider an extremely simple universe that is governed by Newtonian laws and that contains nothing except two neutrons. Assume further that those neutrons are moving towards each other, along the same line, with velocities that are, at each instant, equal in magnitude but opposite in direction. This universe would be rotationally symmetrical at every instant, since rotation through 180 degrees about any axis passing through the center of gravity of the two particles and perpendicular to any plane containing them would give rise to a qualitatively indistinguishable state of affairs.

Such a universe would also possess bilateral symmetry. It is, however, rotational symmetry that is required in the following argument. Thus, the argument would apply equally well to a slightly different universe in which the two particles were also spinning in a right-handed direction, with equal angular velocities, since such a universe would exhibit rotational symmetry, although not bilateral symmetry. In contrast, given a universe in which the particles were spinning in opposite directions, so that the universe possessed bilateral but not rotational symmetry, the argument would not be applicable.

Let P_1 be the total temporal part of one neutron before some time t, and M_1 the total temporal part of that same neutron from time t onwards. Similarly, let P_2 and M_2 be the corresponding parts of the other neutron. What makes it the case that P_1 and M_1 are temporal parts of a single enduring entity, while P_1 and M_2 are not? A very plausible view is that it is the fact that M_1 is causally dependent upon P_1, while M_2 is not, that makes it the case that P_1 and M_1 are temporal parts of the same enduring thing, while P_1 and M_2 are not.

But now suppose that the thesis of the Humean supervenience of causal relations is true. If M_1 is causally dependent upon P_1, while M_2 is not, there must be some noncausal fact about M_1, or its relation to P_1, such that there is no corresponding fact about M_2, or its relation to P_1. It may seem that such a fact is readily at hand. For is it not true that the end of the one temporal part, P_1, has the same location as the beginning of M_1, and a different location from the beginning of M_2? A problem arises, however, when one asks what meaning is to be assigned to statements concerning the locations of objects at different times. What does it mean to say that the end of P_1 has the same location as the beginning of M_1?

Suppose that one adopts a relational view of space. Then possible coordinate systems at a given time will be defined in terms of objects existing at that time. But in order to make sense of comparisons of the locations of objects at different times, one has to be able to explain what it is for coordinate systems existing at different times to be identical. Now if all the coordinate systems existing at a given time were qualitatively distinguishable by virtue of their relations to different sorts of objects, one might try to solve the problem by appealing to the idea that a requirement of continuity over time can serve to determine when coordinate systems existing at different times are temporal parts of a single enduring coordinate system. But even if this approach will work in such cases, it is not available in the case of the simple universe we are considering here, since for every coordinate system that exists at a given time, there is another one, with axes that are differently oriented, that is qualitatively indistinguishable from it. As a consequence, the only way of sorting out which of a pair of qualitatively indistinguishable coordinate systems existing at a given time is the same coordinate system as some coordinate system existing at an earlier time is by being able to identify the individuals existing at different times. This, however, lands one in a vicious circle. Identity of elementary entities over time rests upon causal relations, and these, in turn, must be grounded upon noncausal facts, if the thesis of the Humean supervenience of causal relations is true. Moreover, we have seen that the noncausal facts in question must include ones concerning the locations of different temporal parts of the relevant elementary entities. But if a relational view of space is correct, then, in the universe containing just the two neutrons, comparisons of locations at different times presuppose the identification of objects over time.

The upshot is that the possibility of rotationally symmetrical universes shows that one cannot accept both the Humean supervenience of causal relations and a relational view of space. Suppose, then, that one adopts an absolute view. Is the problem solved? It seems clear that it is not. To say that the end of P_1 has the same location as the beginning of M_1 will be to say that the end of P_1 is located in the same region as the beginning of M_1. But one now needs some account of what makes it the case that two regions existing at different times are identical. It does not seem acceptable to treat this relation as primitive and unanalyzable.

Yet if it is to be analyzed, what alternative is there to appealing to causal relations? But then, if the identification of spatial regions over time rests upon causal relations, one can consider a universe in which absolute space exhibits rotational symmetry, and simply repeat the above argument—applying it to regions of absolute space, rather than to physical objects. Thus, let Q_1 be the region of space containing the end of P_1, and let N_1 and N_2 be the regions of space containing respectively, the beginning of M_1 and the beginning of M_2. If Q_1 is to be the same region of absolute space as N_1, but a different region from N_2, then it must be the case that there is some causal relation that obtains between Q_1 and N_1, but not between Q_1 and N_2. If the thesis of the Humean supervenience of causal relations is true, this causal difference must be grounded in some noncausal difference between N_1 and N_2. If one were dealing with an absolute space that was not rotationally symmetric about the relevant axis, there might be no problem about the existence of such a noncausal difference. But if one assumes that the universe is one that does possess the relevant rotational symmetry, in what could such a noncausal difference between N_1 and N_2 consist? There does not appear to be any satisfactory answer to this question.

If this is correct, we have arrived at the following conclusion. Regardless of whether a relational view of space or an absolute view is correct, the supervenience view of causal relations implies that either the existence of a rotationally symmetrical universe is impossible, or the relation of identity over time cannot be analyzed in causal terms.

To sum up, I have argued in this section that the view that causal relations between states of affairs are logically supervenient upon causal laws together with noncausal facts has three consequences that seem unwelcome and that therefore constitute at least prima facie objections to that view. The first consequence is that mental events belonging to minds must have spatial locations. The second is that it is impossible to give a causal analysis of temporal concepts. The third is that either the existence of a rotationally symmetrical universe is logically impossible, or else it is impossible to give an account, in causal terms, of the identification over time of either physical objects or regions of space.

3. A FOURTH ARGUMENT: THE CASE OF INVERTED UNIVERSES

The second argument discussed above was directed to showing that the supervenience view of causal relations precludes offering an analysis of temporal concepts in causal terms. In this section I shall set out an argument for a closely related conclusion – to the effect that if the supervenience view is correct, it is impossible to explain the direction of time in terms of the direction of causal processes.

The argument may be put as follows. Imagine that our world was actually created by a cosmic Laplace in the year two billion B.C. and that its laws are both completely deterministic, and symmetrical with respect to time. Before creating this universe, however, the Laplacean-style deity calculated that, given the intended laws and initial distribution of matter and energy, the universe would collapse completely in four billion years. Then, having noted the position and velocity that every particle would have just before the final collapse, at the very instant that he created this universe, he created another, a great distance away, with the same laws, but otherwise inverted with respect to this one. That is to say, the initial relative positions of the particles in the other universe correspond exactly to the relative positions of particles in this universe just before the final collapse, but the velocities are all reversed.

Since the two universes have the same laws, and those laws are deterministic, and symmetrical with respect to time, the result will be a universe just like ours but running, so to speak, in reverse. Thus, for example, a temporal cross section of this universe at some point in the year 2000 A.D. will be just like a cross section of the other universe at a corresponding time in the year 2000 B.C., except that all the velocities will be reversed.

Let A_1 and A_2 be complete temporal slices of our universe in the years 2000 A.D. and 2001 A.D. respectively, and let B_1 and B_2 be the corresponding slices of the inverted universe, from the years 2000 B.C. and 2001 B.C., respectively. A_1 causally gives rise to A_2, but B_1 does not give rise to B_2. The question, now, is whether it is possible for this to be the case if the supervenience view is true.

If causal relations are supervenient, the above causal difference between the two universes can obtain only if there is also a difference either with respect to causal laws, or with respect to noncausal facts concerning the relevant states of affairs. By hypothesis, the laws are the same in the two universes. So the difference must be with respect to noncausal facts.

What differences are there, aside from explicitly causal ones? The only ones are with respect to the direction of time, and with respect to properties and relations that depend upon the direction of time. Thus, while A_1 is temporally prior to A_2, B_1 occurs after B_2, rather than before. And as a consequence, A_1 is not qualitatively indistinguishable from B_1, nor A_2 from B_2. For while the relative positions of the particles in A_1 agree exactly with the relative positions of those in B_1, and do so regardless of whether the slices are instantaneous, or have some temporal thickness, all the velocities are reversed.

But are such differences really noncausal? The answer will depend upon what account is to be given of the direction of time. If the direction of time is to be defined in terms of the direction of causal processes, then the above differences will not be noncausal. This in turn will imply that if Humean supervenience does hold for causal relations, then the world described above cannot really be logically possible, since it could not be the case that A_1 gives rise to A_2 while B_1 does not give rise to B_2. Yet surely the world described above is logically possible. Hence, if the direction of time is to be defined in terms of the direction of causation, the supervenience view of causal relations must be rejected.

The difference between this argument and the second argument, set out in the previous section, is perhaps worth underlining, and it may be put as follows. Some philosophers hold that while a complete account of all temporal concepts in causal terms is impossible, causal concepts do play a role in the analysis of at least some temporal notions. In particular, one might hold, first, that there is a concept of temporal betweenness, which does not have any direction associated with it, and which cannot be analyzed in causal terms, and secondly, that this concept must then be combined with that of the direction of causation to give analyses of those temporal concepts that do involve a reference to the direction of time. For a philosopher who adopted this view, the fourth argument would have force, while the second would not.

4. A FIFTH ARGUMENT: INDETERMINISTIC LAWS

In this section I want to offer a final, somewhat more direct argument against the supervenience view. The argument turns upon certain possibilities of causal relations in worlds that are partly indeterministic. One way of stating the argument involves probabilistic causal laws, and may be put as follows. Suppose that it is a causal law that whenever there is a state of affairs, x, with property P, this always gives rise to a state of affairs, y, with property Q, where y is located in a small region of space that stands either in relation R to x, or in relation S to x, the probability of each outcome being 50 percent. Now given certain choices of property P, and relations R and S, it will be possible for there to be two states of affairs with property P, say x_1 and x_2, such that a region stands in relation R to x_1 if and only if it also stands in relation R to x_2, and similarly for relation S. If, for example, P were the property of having a certain triangular shape, and relations R and S were defined in terms of distances along the extensions of specified sides, the accompanying figure would provide an example of the sort of situation that I have in mind. In the situation depicted, it turns out that there is a y_1 that has property Q

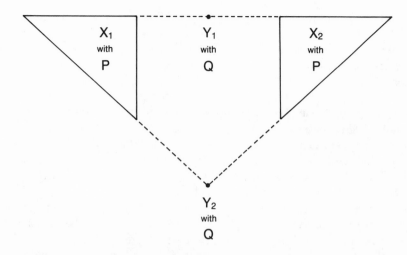

and that stands in relation R to both x_1 and x_2, and similarly, that there is a y_2 that has property Q and that stands in relation S to both x_1 and x_2. How should such a situation be described in causal terms, given the probabilistic law stated earlier? One possibility is this:

> x_1's having property P caused y_1 to have property Q, and
> x_2's having property P caused y_2 to have property Q.

But the correct description might equally well be:

> x_1's having property P caused y_2 to have property Q, and
> x_2's having property P caused y_1 to have property Q.

So the problem is this. What would make one of these things the case, rather than the other?

One answer is that there might be an intervening causal process linking x_1's having P to y_1's having Q, but none linking x_1's having P to y_2's having Q, and similarly, an intervening causal process linking x_2's having P to y_2's having Q, but none linking x_2's having P to y_1's having Q. If this were so, the ontological situation would be sorted out. But why need this be the case? Might not the probabilistic law in question be one that describes *immediate* causal relations? In the case described above, that would involve causal connections over gaps. Some philosophers believe that the idea of a gappy causal process is ultimately incoherent. I believe that that view can be shown to be mistaken. But in any case, the example can easily be re-formulated to avoid that problem, as David Armstrong has pointed out. For example, one can imagine that one is dealing instead with causal laws that say:

> For any x, if x has property P, then x has either property Q or property R;
> For any x, if x has property S, then x has either property Q or property R.

Imagine, then, that a has both property P and property S, and also both property Q and property R. Does a's having P cause it to have property Q? Or is this caused by a's having property S? Here there is no possibility of appealing to an intervening causal process to sort out the ontological situation.

The upshot is that if the thesis of the Humean supervenience of causal relations is true, it follows that in this situation it cannot be the case either that a's having property P caused it to have property Q, or that a's having property S caused it to have property Q. One must rest content with its being the case *only* that a's having property P caused it to be the case that a had either property Q or property R, and similarly for a's having property S. So if one asks, "What *would* have been the case if a *had* had property P, but not property S," the answer is that there is no truth of the matter. For there is nothing that could possibly serve as the truth-maker for a counterfactual such as "If a had had property P, but not property S, then a would have had property Q, but not property R."

How might a proponent of the supervenience view respond to this argument? There seem to be three possibilities. First, one might argue that the notion of indeterministic laws – upon which the argument rests – is in the final analysis incoherent. Secondly, one might attempt to show that even if there can be indeterministic laws, there cannot be causal ones – perhaps on the ground that the notion of cause is only intelligible if it can be unpacked in terms of the notion of a condition that is causally sufficient to ensure that a certain type of effect will occur. Thirdly, one might contend that there is nothing unacceptable about the 'ontological indeterminacy' that, if causal relations are supervenient, is involved in the above situation.

The first response does not seem very promising. In the first place, given the nature of quantum physics, it would be very surprising if it turned out that there was no satisfactory account of probabilistic laws. In the second place, it is important to notice that the argument does not really need the notion of probabilistic laws. As the second formulation illustrates, all that is required is the notion of indeterministic laws. Scepticism regarding probability or probabilistic laws is therefore not sufficient. One must also offer some reason for thinking that indeterministic laws of a nonprobabilistic sort are also logically impossible.

The second response seems equally problematic. Once again, quantum physics poses a serious objection since it certainly seems to contain laws that are both causal and probabilistic. And in the second place, given an account of nonprobabilistic causal laws, there does not appear to be any problem about extending and generalizing that account in a natural way to arrive at one that covers probabilistic laws as well.

What about the third response? It is not clear, perhaps, that ontological indeterminacy of the sort in question is unacceptable. But it does seem clear that, other things being equal, one would prefer an account that did not give rise to such ontological determinacy. The crucial question, therefore, is whether one can set out an account of causation that will enable one to avoid the indeterminacy. If one can offer such an account, and it is not otherwise problematic, then one has a good reason for rejecting the supervenience view. I believe that it is possible to offer such an account. This is not, however, an issue that can be pursued in the present paper.

5. THE THIRD ALTERNATIVE

I have outlined five arguments against the view that causal relations are supervenient upon causal laws together with noncausal facts. I believe that these arguments constitute a very strong case against the supervenience view. If that is so, which of the re-remaining views should be adopted? The singularist view? Or the view that while causal relations presuppose underlying causal laws, what causal relations obtain is not necessarily determined by the causal laws together with the relevant noncausal facts?

The latter alternative has a certain attractiveness, since, on the one hand, it allows one to admit the force of the above arguments against the supervenience view, and, on the other hand, it enables one to avoid the idea, which may seem rather unpalatable, that there could be a world full of causally related events, yet utterly devoid of any laws.

But this third alternative is not without its own problems. On the one hand, it is claimed that underlying laws are necessary if there are to be causal relations. On the other, that laws together with relevant noncausal facts are not always sufficient to determine what causal relations obtain. The combination of these two claims appears to generate a puzzle. Given the second claim, it would seem that a proponent of this third view must hold that there is some special relation, C, that obtains between any two causally related states of affairs. The question, then, is what account is to be given of the first claim. Why are underlying laws necessary if there are to be causal relations? The answer will depend upon whether it is logically possible for there to be states of affairs that stand in relation C, but that do not fall under any law. If this is possible, the reason that underlying laws are necessary if there are to be causal relations will be a very superficial one: our use of causal terms happens to be such that we do not say that two states of affairs are causally related unless it is the case both that they stand in the special relation C and that they fall under some law of the appropriate form. On this view of the matter, the difference between the third position and the singularist position would seem to be merely verbal: a proponent of the singularist approach says that two states of affairs are causally related if they stand in the special relation C; an advocate of the third view says that they are causally related only if they also fall under some law.

The alternative is to maintain that it is logically impossible for two states of affairs to stand in relation C unless they fall under some relevant law. This does give one a philosophically distinctive position. But now one is confronted with the problem of explaining how a relation between first-order states of affairs can possibly entail the existence of some law under which those states of affairs fall. This is puzzling on any view of laws, but it is perhaps especially so if one adopts the view, which I believe to be correct, that laws are relations between universals.

6. SUMMING UP

Where does this leave the issue? What does seem clear is that the supervenience view, which has dominated philosophical thinking about causation since the time of Hume, must be abandoned. Which of the two remaining views should be adopted, however, may seem much less clear. Neither view is without its difficulties. On the one hand, if one opts for the singularist view, one is confronted with the possibility, which many would judge to be counterintuitive, of worlds full of causally related states of affairs but devoid of laws. On the other hand, if one adopts the third view, one is confronted with the obscurity of the logical entailment between the standing of states of affairs in the special relation C, and the existence of an appropriate under-lying law—an entailment that it seems that an advocate of the third view must postulate if the position is to be other than merely a verbal variant of the singularist account. Depending upon which of these difficulties seems more serious, one will give the edge to one view or the other. I myself am rather more impressed by the obscurity of the entailment than by the counterintuitiveness of anomic causal worlds, since it seems to me that the latter is an illusion generated by the deeply en-trenched, supervenience account. But regardless of what view one takes of the rela-tive seriousness of these difficulties, it seems clear that neither amounts to anything remotely resembling a decisive argument in support of the other alternative.

How, then, is the issue to be settled? I suspect that it can only be done by setting out an analysis of the relevant causal concepts. This must be done in any case, since anyone who wishes to adopt either the singularist view, or the third view, must counter what appears to be the crucial argument in support of the super-venience view, namely, that in the end one cannot really make sense of the appar-ent alternatives to the supervenience account.

What happens when this is done? The answer, I believe, is that there is an ex-tremely plausible general approach to the analysis of causal concepts that can be used to formulate both a supervenience account and a singularist account but that cannot be used to formulate an account of the third sort. If this is right, there would seem to be good reason for thinking that the third view *is* unintelligible. The prob-lem of giving an analysis of causal concepts therefore narrows the field to the super-venience and the singularist views. The arguments set out above then show that it is the singularist account that must be accepted.

Notes

1. "The Nature of Laws," *Canadian Journal of Philosophy* 7 (1977):667-98. See also Fred I. Dretske, "Laws of Nature," *Philosophy of Science* 44 (1977):248-68, and, for a much more extended discussion, David M. Armstrong, *What Is a Law of Nature?* (Cambridge, 1983).

2. C. J. Ducasse, "On the Nature and the Observability of the Causal Relation," *Journal of Philosophy* 23 (1926):57-68, and reprinted in *Causation and Conditionals*, edited by Ernest Sosa (Oxford, 1975), 114-25. See 118.

3. Ibid., 116 and 120 ff.

4. G. E. M. Anscombe, "Causality and Determination," in Sosa, *Causation and Condition-als*, 63-81. See 81.

5. Ibid., 67.

6. Ibid., 67-68.

7. David M. Armstrong, *Universals and Scientific Realism*, vol. 2 (Cambridge, 1978), 172.

Causation and Induction[1]

EVAN FALES

The connection between views about causation and attempts to justify inductive reasoning is sufficiently close that some philosophers[2] have taken success at the latter as a litmus test for the truth of the former. I do not agree with this approach. Like Hume, I believe that the nature of causal connections must be understood prior to, and independently of, solutions to the problem of induction. Like Hume, I also hold that the problem of induction cannot be solved if Hume's analysis of causal connections is correct. But unlike Hume, I believe that that analysis is incorrect. However, I shall not attempt to establish this crucial thesis here. I mention it because this paper presupposes it. Hume's difficulty about causation must—and can—be faced head-on. There are phenomenological grounds for affirming that we sometimes directly experience nonlogical, necessary connections between events. I shall only briefly summarize these grounds, which will be argued for in detail elsewhere. The purpose of this paper is to explore the extent to which a necessitarian theory of causation can bring the problem of induction closer to solution.

NATURAL NECESSITY

The phenomenological grounds for our concept of natural necessity are, primarily, our tactile and kinesthetic experiences of pushes and pulls. This is not a novel suggestion, of course; it is interesting that Hume himself considered it and so quickly dismissed it.[3] To be given their philosophical due, these experiences must instead be subjected to a detailed phenomenological analysis. Such an analysis reveals, among other things, that pushes and pulls are sometimes directly perceived, have a magnitude, have a spatial direction, and can combine with other pushes and pulls to form a "total push." For our purposes, the most important feature of the perception of pushes and pulls is the recognition of a nonaccidental connection between the characteristics of a total push and the motions of the objects whose interaction occasions (or is constituted by) that push.[4]

A way of bringing out this latter point is to perform an imaginary thought-experiment. Hume held that the repeated experience of conjoined event-types was a necessary precondition for the formation of expectations concerning the future, and of beliefs as to what laws nature is governed by. The thought experiment in question seeks to refute this claim. To perform it, one must imagine a human being who has experienced *no* previous pushings or pullings. This subject is now to be given his first experience of a push—say, by the exertion of pressure upon his forehead. He is allowed to observe what happens (the resulting motion of the head). Let us suppose, too, that he is able to attend to the feeling of pressure itself, and to understand that this feeling is being referred to by the term 'pressure'. He is asked: "If one minute from now you experience an exactly similar pressure, what, if anything, do you guess will happen next?" The point of this imaginary exercise is that *we* must try to guess what the subject's answer would be.

There are a number of complications, into most of which I shall not enter here. I shall only mention that *one* type of objection to this thought-experiment (having to do with the possibility of dispositions formed on the basis of a single experience) can be deflected by the following modification of the experiment. The naive subject is simultaneously subject to *two* cranial pressures. One of these, however, he cannot feel; it is applied to an anesthetized area on the skull. He feels the other pressure, and observes the motion of his head. He is told that two pressures, one unfelt by him, were exerted upon his head. He is asked: "If only the pressure you actually felt had been exerted, what do you think would have happened?" Now it is conceivable that a correct response even here could be explained in terms of some innate disposition of the human psyche. But it is not easy to imagine an explanation, perhaps in biological terms, as to why *this* sort of disposition should come to be part of the genetic endowment of human beings. Even harder to explain is why we, in imagining such an experiment, should be inclined to predict that the subject would guess in one way rather than another. This would require the postulation of the existence, in *us*, of a "second-order" disposition of a most peculiar sort. It seems obvious that our inclination, if we have one, to make such a prediction is somehow founded in our own direct experience with pushes and pulls. Appeal to hidden dispositions here ought to be eschewed, except as a recourse of last resort.

An objection to the philosophical use of such a thought experiment is that its preconditions are so strange, so foreign to our own experience, that no reliable guess whatever can be made as to its outcome. I am somewhat sympathetic to this objection. But it is not one that could be offered by a consistent Humean. For Hume's position *entails* that the experimental subject can form *no expectations whatever* as to the correct answer to the question he has been posed. I believe, however, that some reasonable guesses can be made as to what a thoughtful subject would say under the above circumstances. Among the things he would affirm is that his head will/would have move(d) in the same direction as the direction of the felt force. I shall not try to defend this guess here—it is tendered as an unargued intuition, nothing more. But I *suspect* that most of us—even committed Humeans—have exactly the same intuition regarding this experiment.

These hints will have to serve as indicating the direction of the argument with which I think Hume ought to be confronted. There are two essential steps in the argument, and two conclusions. The first step—condensed above—attempts to establish that causal necessitation forms part of the content of sense experience. The second (not yet mentioned) tries to show that causal relations are "primary qualities"—that is, can characterize interactions not experienced by any conscious observer. When these considerations are combined with a realist position concerning universals, they can, in my opinion, be used to support a view of causation advocated in recent years by Armstrong, Dretske, and Tooley.[5] According to that view, causation is to be understood in terms of a second-order relation. This relation takes as its relata a complex property or universal instantiated by the (total) cause and the universal that characterizes the effect. This is the view I shall adopt. *If* these conclusions can be established, we can turn to the main concern of this paper. What about induction?

POST-HUMEAN APPROACHES

Not everyone, of course, is convinced that Hume's analysis renders the problem of induction insoluble. Some, such as Ayer and Goodman, adopt modernized versions of Hume's own solution. This is the We-Do-It-Anyway view. Perhaps one can formulate rules, as Goodman has valiantly striven to do, that govern the entrenchment of predicates. But why should entrenchment bear on justified projectibility? In reality, justification is abandoned in favor of human psychology and practice. Or rather, the former is seen as inseparable from, or reducible to, the latter. But this does not mesh well with the conception of justification that we in fact have, one that is linked to a realistic conception of truth.

A second approach is to admit that the problem is insoluble, but to cheerfully claim that it does not need to be solved—at least not for the purposes of scientific inquiry. Popper introduced this line of thought, which I call the Sour-Grapes view. It has at least three defects. First: most of us want to know how it *is* with the world, not merely lots of ways it isn't. Second, even falsifying observation-statements are in Popper's own view not certain. They require—and can supposedly achieve—corroboration. An inspection of the ways in which observation-statements are justified and confirmed easily reveals, I think, that their confirmation involves inductive reasoning. Third, even Popperians admit the need, from a practical or action-guiding standpoint, of inductive predictions.

Finally, we have the The-Buck-Stops-Here position of Strawson, Russell, and others. According to it, the principles of inductive reasoning (or some subset of them) are such that a search for justification is inappropriate. Like the fundamental rules of deduction, they can be appealed to in justifying other inferences but cannot themselves be justified by reduction to any more elementary reasoning. In Strawson's views, these principles appear to be analytic; Russell seems to hold that they are synthetic a priori truths. But in either case, to sustain this line of argument, one needs at least to show that the validity of basic inductive principles is as self-evident as that of, say, modus ponens. This has not been done.[6]

Finally, there is a different strategy that is worthy of mention, although I cannot name any philosopher who explicitly makes use of it. The Inflationist Strategy, as I shall call it, is inspired by a maneuver that is aimed at another problem, the problem of distinguishing laws from accidental generalizations. But clearly the solution of that problem might be taken to invite a solution to the problem of induction. To ascertain that a generalization is a law, or lawlike, and not accidental, is arguably, to ascertain that its instances stand in the sort of evidential relation to it that warrants projection.

The maneuver proceeds by attempting to subsume low-level generalizations under an ascending hierarchy of higher-level generalizations embracing wider and wider classes of instances. The model for such subsumptions is the use of reductive explanation in the sciences (e.g., biochemical explanations of biological phenomena). A candidate generalization is deemed lawlike if, roughly, it has a position in such a hierarchy of generalizations, and no member of the hierarchy has been falsified by disconfirming instances. The upshot of this maneuver is that a generalization can be regarded accidental if it finds no home in such a hierarchy.[7] Because other members of the hierarchy must have positive instances and no negative ones, the field of phenomena among which relevant observations can be obtained is vastly broadened.

It is true enough that we think of laws of nature as joined together in a systematic way, whereas accidental generalizations ought to be only accidentally associated with one another. But there is another natural motive that undoubtedly informs this way of construing the distinction. If a generalization is merely accidental, then "the odds are" that it will at some point be violated. But perhaps a generalization has very few instances, and all of these are positive instances. Here an argument from "the odds" is of little help—unless the field of relevant observable events can be broadened. This is what the Inflationist Strategy achieves. If a whole system of generalizations receives confirmation and no disconfirmation, then its members "must be" lawlike, for the odds against this are vanishingly small. Unfortunately this strategy is powerless against Humean skepticism. Hume's argument shows that any regular pattern of events, no matter how wide-ranging, may be destroyed tomorrow, and that we can have no reason for thinking that it will not be. As we shall see, however, reasoning similar to that which underlies the Inflationist Strategy can legitimately be employed by those who do not accept Hume's theory of causation.

Perhaps some radically new approach to induction, compatible with the Regularity Theory of causation, will yet emerge; but I think it is reasonable to say that the problem cannot be solved within that framework. The consequences of a failure to solve the problem may well extend far beyond its universally recognized implications for practical action and scientific theorizing. Consider the causal theory of perception, as well as other causal theories of more recent vintage (of reference, knowledge, and so forth) that have begun to receive wide attention. If such theories are coupled with a Humean account of causation, the problem of induction is of paramount importance. For any singular causal assertion to be known to be true, it must be established that every circumstance that has and will satisfy the antecedent conditions relevant to that assertion is followed by a similar outcome. In consequence, the truth of a singular causal claim cannot be known unless it is known either that all other instances of the law that covers that claim have been observed or that the law can be inductively supported. Lacking a solution to the problem of induction, one has no rational grounds for belief in singular causal assertions.

Causal theories make it a necessary condition for the existence of a certain state of affairs that some appropriate causally linked chain of events has occurred. The causal theory of perception, for example, requires that for a perceiver P to perceive an object O, it is necessary that certain sensory experiences of P be caused, via a suitable causal sequence, by O. But for it to be the case that O's presence caused P's experience, it must be the case that in every future circumstance in which a P-like observer and O-like object are brought together under identical conditions, the observer has a qualitatively identical experience. The Humean can give no reasons whatever for expecting this condition to be satisfied. Hence if he adheres to a causal theory of perception, he has no reasons for believing—at least prior to the end of human existence—that anyone has ever perceived any object. This I take to be an intolerable consequence. Parallel consequences are entailed, mutatis mutandis, for other causal theories. The tentacles of the problem of induction reach far. Can it be solved, however, even by those philosophers willing to embrace natural necessities?

A NECESSITARIAN APPROACH

It is not my intention to attempt a full solution of the problem of induction or of all the problems involved in using inductive reasoning. For example, the application of inductive reasoning requires the use of premises concerning past events. Thus justifying inductive inferences requires in part justifying other forms of nondeductive reasoning: notably, solving the problem of justifying knowledge of the past. This amounts to the problem of justifying inferences from observed effects to unobserved causes, and I shall only touch upon that problem.

Most of what has been written about the problem of induction has been written by empiricists under the sway of Hume, and very little by philosophers who have thought that causal relations involve a kind of objective necessity.[8] Clearly this is not due to the fact that there is no problem of induction for a philosophy of the latter sort; it is due rather to the fact that advocates of such a philosophy are in short supply. For although there can be little doubt about the tremendous dialectical advantage that acquaintance with causal relations bestows, the achievement of an adequate account of inductive procedure from this perspective is by no means a trivial task.

The problem of induction can be usefully subdivided into four problems. These are:

1. Isolating and identifying significant patterns of regular recurrence from the complex welter of actual experience.
2. Isolating all those factors that are causally relevant to what will happen in a given circumstance.
3. Justifying the prediction of single future occurrences.
4. Justifying generalizations based on finite evidence.

In some favored cases, a philosophy that accepts direct acquaintance with causal relations can solve these problems in relatively straightforward fashion. The favored cases are those in which one is directly acquainted with a causing event and with all of the causal relations of which it constitutes a relatum. In certain such cases, I have suggested that it is in principle possible to predict, at least roughly, what the effect will be even in the absence of any relevant previous experience. Clearly where this is possible the first problem becomes irrelevant and the third and fourth are solved provided the second one can be. Even in the most favored cases, however, the second problem raises difficulties. What is in any case clear is that many—doubtless most—of the inductions we actually perform are not ones whose foundation rests upon such favored circumstances. Either we are not directly acquainted with the cause(s) of an event, or we are not acquainted with the causal relation(s) present, or we are acquainted with neither. In such instances, it is evident that one's inductive inferences must rely upon observed regularities—i.e., upon enumerative induction, upon the method of difference, and upon the panoply of statistical procedures that science and common experience alike employ. Of what significant advantage, then, is it to have had experience of causal relations? My answer to this question will focus on three central inductive procedures: Mill's methods, enumerative induction, and Bayes' method.

I shall discuss a particular one of Mill's inductive methods—the method he calls the Indirect Method of Difference or the Joint Method of Agreement and Difference. This method enables one to eliminate from the antecedent circumstances of an event those that are causally irrelevant to it. It does this by varying, or eliminating, one component of those circumstances while holding the others fixed. If C is a complex event consisting of $C_1, \ldots,$ and C_n, antecedent to E, we ascertain whether C_1 is causally related to E by examining the consequences that follow an event C' similar in all respects to C, save for the absence of an event corresponding to C_1. If C' is followed by an event E' exactly similar to E, then C_1 is not causally related to E.

This reasoning depends, as Mill realized[9], on the assumption that on the second occasion, there is no event beyond those included in C' that is causally relevant to E'. For otherwise, the causal contribution of C_1 to E, lacking in C', might be replaced by an unknown causal influence outside of C'. To eliminate this possibility, it is at the very least necessary to rule out (significant) influence from events spatially and/or temporally distant from E'. What grounds are there for ruling out nonlocal causal influences? Unless these can be ruled out a priori—which seems doubtful—one must rely on inductive grounds. Such grounds are available, but only if enumerative or Bayesian inductive procedures can be justified. In that case, it will be possible to argue from past experience that known types of action at a distance, mediated by force-fields, have effects that can be calculated and that fall off asymptotically with increasing spatiotemporal separation. Hence it is necessary to examine enumerative induction and Bayes' method if we are to justify applications of the Indirect Method of Difference.

If there is no real causal connectedness in nature, if nature consists of nothing over and above a sequence of events, then no inductive procedure can help us achieve true belief. The reason is simple. No matter what patterns observation of the world has revealed to us, and no matter how striking these patterns may be, the structure of the set of as-yet unobserved events remains entirely open. There cannot be any question of *explaining* the existence of such patterns, except perhaps in the trivial sense of showing them to form parts of bigger patterns among the set of observed events. That sort of explanation, however, would have no evidential weight concerning the continuation of such patterns in the as-yet unobserved events. If we think of the universe as being constituted by a single sequence of (global) events, then by Humean lights any coherently imaginable event can occur equally well anywhere in the sequence. The Humean envisages the set of available hypotheses concerning the world to consist of, or at least to entail, a set of propositions, each of which specifies one of the logically possible event-histories that can be constructed from the totality of consistently imaginable events. Even if the set of consistently imaginable event-types were not infinite, the number of infinite event-sequences that can be constructed by permuting these events would clearly be infinite. The past history of the world has "eliminated" many of these sequences; but there are infinitely many distinct sequences whose beginnings exactly match the past history of the world and whose future continuations diverge in every way conceivable. Each of these sequences corresponds to a world-hypothesis, and each must be accorded equal weight on Humean grounds, since each is equally well-confirmed by past events. Which is to say that the past does not confirm any of these hypotheses at all insofar as they pertain to events not yet observed; it is merely logically compatible with each of them. How then does the supposition that a past or presently observed pattern among events can reflect the operation of a necessary causal relation, help us to escape the Humean impasse?

One thing is clear. If a causal relation (in our sense) ever does obtain between observable events, then some sort of pattern or regularity will appear in our experience, on the assumption that we witness repeated instances of these event-types. For if causal relations connect universals, then whenever the universals that characterize the causal event are instantiated, those characterizing the effect will also be. A causal relation between universals entails the corresponding universal generalization. But the converse inference cannot be made; and thus from a finite patterned sample, or even from a total sample that encompasses every existing instance of the relevant event-types, one cannot deduce the corresponding causal relation. Can we, then, have inductive grounds for such an inference? Can we, in other words, have inductive grounds for distinguishing between accidental generalizations and laws of nature? I think we can.

ENUMERATIVE INDUCTON AND BAYES' METHOD

There are arguments that suggest that, sometimes at least, Bayesian and enumerative induction are at odds. Burks and Salmon, following Reichenbach, support the fundamentality of enumerative induction. R. D. Rosenkrantz, on the other side, would jettison enumerative induction in favor of a Bayesian policy.[10] Rosenkrantz's rejection of enumerative induction leans heavily on the problems generated by the confirmation paradoxes of Hempel and Goodman. Secondly, he tries to show that in cases of conflict, the Bayesian strategy wins out over enumerative induction.

The natural necessitarian's attitude toward these questions cannot be worked out in full detail here. Only the main outlines of a solution will be attempted. But, to anticipate a bit, we can say that this solution incorporates both Bayesian and enumerative forms of reasoning, with each assigned a rather different role. The main role of enumerative induction is in guiding the formulation of plausible hypotheses—that is, it has a role in what is sometimes called "the logic of discovery." The main role of Bayesian reasoning lies in its application to the testing and confirmation of hypothesis—i.e., in the "logic of verification." As for the various paradoxes of confirmation, no explicit treatment of them will be offered. It is worth stating, therefore, that I believe the necessitarian has the resources to solve these problems in a rather intuitively natural way. It will be part of the burden of the present discussion to show that, by contrast, neither enumerative induction nor Bayesian arguments can hope to overcome Goodman-type difficulties for those who avail themselves of a Humean ontology: on this point Rosenkrantz is in error. I shall begin with a general difficulty about enumerative induction.

A. J. Ayer has argued that if natural laws have modal strength, they would be even harder to confirm than if they are taken to be generalizations. A generalization embraces all the actual instances of a law; but a modal law, in effect, generalizes over possible instances as well. Thus it is a stronger generalization, and hence more weakly supported by any finite sample of instances. Natural necessitarians argue against Ayer that the admission of modal concepts makes the solution of the problem of induction *easier*, not more difficult. One way to show this would be to show that modal laws permit us to make use of a conception of explanation—and hence, of arguments to the best explanation—of which the Humean cannot avail himself. What is required is an explanatory hypothesis that, if true, renders an observed sequence of events more "probable" than it would be on any competing hypothesis. Indeed, natural necessitarians all make use of some form of the argument from inverse probability—that is, of a Bayesian argument. I shall present my own version of this argument, which is perhaps more general than others that have appeared.

Let us consider a possibly infinite sequence of events, a sequence that may or may not display a patterned order. By an event-sequence I shall mean, in what follows, a chronologically ordered set of event-pairs such that the antecedent event (or cause) of each pair is of the same type. The consequent events may all be similar or not. (We can think of the sequence, if we like, as being generated by all the repeated performances of some experiment: the flipping of a coin, or the colliding of two billiard balls.) Now *any* such sequence, having occurred, is equally deserving of an explanation—if there is an explanation to be had. On the Humean view of nature (and setting aside the essentially irrelevant possibility of deriving the course of a sequence from some more general set of generalizations), the role of laws is to do nothing more than to summarize the facts; thus no such sequence is intrinsically more explainable than any other, there being no fact about the world that renders any sequence intrinsically more likely than any other one. 'Explanation' consists, essentially, of a recitation of the actual facts. If a sequence is regular, then we may give the appearance of providing something more powerful by way of an explanation by virtue of the facts being summarizable in a particularly simple and elegant form—a universal generalization. But the impression of greater explanatory power is an illusion, fostered perhaps by the fact that a universal generalization typically—and thus far unjustifiably—embraces cases that have not yet been examined. At any rate, we should agree with the Humean that *any* sequence calls equally for an explanation, if one can be found. Our point is that, by Humean lights, the sort of explanation available to explain a regular sequence is in no material sense *better* than the sort of explanation that can be given a random sequence.

Richard Fumerton has argued, correctly in my opinion, that for a consistent Humean, arguments to the best explanation are to be understood as just disguised inductive arguments.[11] Leaving aside questions of simplicity, an explanation is "good" just in case we have inductive grounds for believing that it correctly summarizes the facts and correctly predicts the future. We think, for example, that the molecular theory of gases gives us good explanations of gas behavior only because, on inductive grounds, we have reason to believe that small particles such as the postulated "molecules" have behaved and will behave somewhat like colliding billiard balls on a smaller scale. If we had no evidence that molecules (and billiard balls) regularly behave in the required ways, the explanation in question would have the status of empty speculation.

At this point we are in a position to state the contrast between the Humean and the necessitarian, as follows. For the Humean, *no* conceivable sequence is intrinsically more explanable, or better explainable, than any other. But for the necessitarian, regular sequences are candidates for significant explanation, whereas irreduceably chaotic sequences are not. He has available to him a much more full-blooded conception of explanation; but it is one that only admits sequences in some sense regular. (This is not to say that the necessitarian can never hope to explain apparently chaotic sequences. It may be possible to break up a chaotic sequence into disconnected parts and to show how each part is an element in some other regular sequence.)[12]

The fact that, for a Humean, every conceivable sequence is "on a par" generates, as we have seen, the problem of induction. In its Bayesian form, this problem is reflected in the fact that the degree to which a piece of information confirms any hypothesis is proportional to the product of the previous degree of confirmation of that hypothesis and the degree of expectation that the hypothesis confers upon the information in question. Now because, prior to the collection of any empirical information, all the Humean hypotheses are on a par, this means that they should all receive the same initial "weight" or epistemic probability. That is, it is reasonable to make use of a Principle of Indifference: as between any two consistent hypotheses, when one has no more evidence for or against the one than for or against the other, one must assign them equal epistemic probabilities. Secondly, if the available hypotheses are exhaustive and mutually exclusive, then the sum of their probabilities must always sum to one. That is the Normalization Principle. But for a Humean, the number of conceivable event-sequences is clearly infinite. Thus, by the Principle of Indifference, and the Normalization Principle, each sequence must be assigned a prior probability of $1/\infty$, or effectively, zero. But in that case, since the degree to which further information is made probable by any hypothesis is always finite, the posterior epistemic probability of a Humean hypothesis can never be raised; it is always $1/\infty$, or zero. Thus inductive confirmation of a hypothesis is impossible, since initially each hypothesis is itself essentially "impossible," having a prior probability indistinguishable from zero. This is the so-called problem of the priors.

The inductive strategy of the necessitarian makes use, as Bayesians do, of an inverse probability argument. Schematically, the argument runs as follows. We observe an event-sequence that exhibits a regular, repetitive pattern. Intuitively, and in the absence of any auxiliary information, such a sequence is remarkable. The (a priori) odds are against it. Of course, the odds are equally great against any other particular sequence. But *if* the sequence is a regular one, then there is a hypothesis, the truth of which would render the objective probability of the observed sequence very high and the probability of any alternative sequence very low. There is such a hypothesis: namely, that there is a necessary connection between the constantly conjoined event-types.[13] So the existence of the regular sequence enhances the chances that this hypothesis is true.

That is the heart of necessitarian reasoning. Obviously, there are a multitude of complications in its application. When an apparent regularity is violated, for example, it may yet be possible to show that regularity still obtains, only of a more complexly articulated sort. Hence talk of "other things being equal." The necessitarian strategy can also be applied in ways I shall not explore, e.g. to the problem of justifying the reduction of low-level laws to deeper, more general theory.

What is more central is that the necessitarian argument involves two maneuvers that may initially appear to cancel each other. On the one hand, the strategy depends upon the fact that the prior probability of regular event-sequences is very low; it is this fact that prompts the search for an explanatory hypothesis. The longer the sequence, the more surprising its regularity, in the absence of an explanation. The longer—hence initially less probable—a regular sequence is, the stronger the case for an underlying explanation. But on the other hand, the more powerful an explanation is, the lower *its* intrinsic probability. Such, at least, is the case if explanatory power is understood in terms of degree of generality, provided generality (for finite ranges) is measured by the number of instances a hypothesis covers. The more instances a hypothesis projects over, the lower its prior probability. So the more it can explain, the less it is (by Bayesian reasoning) confirmed by its positive instances. The necessitarian strategy depends *both* on the low prior probability of long, regular sequences, and on the existence of explanatory hypotheses that project over infinitely long sequences of this type. How then, can the strategy succeed?

For the Humean, as has been shown, these two aspects of Bayesian strategy do indeed conflict. The prior probability of a hypothesis that postulates a specific regular sequence of events is just equal to the prior probability of any random sequence of events of the same length. This probability is effectively zero even for sequences of *finite* length (given an infinite variety of possible event-types); and it is certainly zero (or $1/\infty$) for infinite sequences. Thus the confirming power of regular sequences of increasing length is always cancelled by the decreasing prior probability of hypotheses strong enough to project over those sequences—certainly if the hypothesis projects beyond to an infinity of cases. From the standpoint of confirmability, there is no distinction here between a hypothesis that predicts a universal regularity and a self-contradictory hypothesis.

These considerations help to clarify what the necessitarian's strategy must be. He begins with a finite (but fairly long) sequence of events that display a patterned structure or regularity. He argues that the intrinsic probability of that sequence is, on pure chance, exceedingly small (as would be the chance probability of any particular random sequence). Next he argues that, since the sequence is regular, there is available to us a hypothesis that, if true, would make that sequence inevitable—give it objective probability of 1. That hypothesis can be shown to have the following features: (1) it is intelligible and consistent, provided that, as I have argued, empirical content can be given to the notion of natural necessity; (b) it is powerful enough to warrant projection over an open class of unexamined cases; (c) it is genuinely explanatory; and (d) its form enables the problem of zero priors to be outflanked. To formulate the relevant hypothesis, the necessitarian uses, in the simplest sort of case, enumerative induction. Thus one hypothesis that will explain the regular association of A-events with B-events is that there is a causal relation between A-hood and B-hood.[14] Bayesian reasoning can be used, in a manner to be explained, to gain confirmation for this hypothesis.

A simple and rather artificial example will bring out the central features of the contrasting epistemic situations in which the Humean and the necessitarian find themselves. For the purposes of this example, suppose that someone is given a large number of boxes. Each of these boxes contains n marbles, and the marbles can be any one of m distinct colors. Each box is so rigged that each time a button on it is pushed, a marble of a given color comes out; the sequence of colors ejected when its button is pushed n times is unique for each box. There is, in fact, one box for each possible n-membered sequence of colors. Therefore, there are m^n boxes. A box is picked *at random* by the experimenter from this set. His task is to guess, on the basis of a sample of k marbles ($k < n$), the color composition of the full sequence of n marbles for that box. Suppose that each of the k marbles drawn on a given trial is blue. What is the probability that he has chosen the box all of whose marbles are blue? Suppose the experimenter knows about the nature of the boxes, or at least, that the uniform color of his k marbles in no way disfavors the above story about them. Then, clearly, he is in the Humean predicament. Intuitively, the probability that the next marble from his box will also be blue is $1/m$; and a Bayesian calculation easily shows that the probability of all $n-k$ of the remaining marbles being blue is $P(H_i, k\ g) = 1/m^{n-k} = m^k/m^n$, where H_i is the hypothesis that the box in question contains the all-blue sequence and g is the condition of picking that box at random from the set of m^n boxes, constructed as specified. Obviously, this probability is exactly equal to that of any *other* box having been picked, from among that subset of m^{n-k} boxes whose first k marbles are all blue. A randomly colored k-membered sequence gives as much information about the future as this uniformly colored sequence does. Furthermore,

$$\lim_{n\to\infty} P\left(H_i, k\ g\right) = 0 \quad \text{and} \quad \lim_{m\to\infty} P\left(H_i, k\ g\right) = 0$$

for any fixed and finite value of k. Hence, in the real world, where the values of m and n are typically infinite, a finite sequence of k constant conjunctions does nothing to improve the posterior epistemic probability of any hypothesis.

Now the preceding Humean predicament may be contrasted to the following situation. An experimenter is given a single box that contains, he is informed, some mechanism for ejecting marbles. This is activated by a button the experimenter can push. Prior to any such trial, the experimenter entertains the following two available hypotheses:

(i) The box is so constructed that it cannot but eject marbles of a single color; and

(ii) The box is so constructed as to pick marbles at random from m internal bins, each containing marbles of a different color.

Hypothesis (i) subdivides into the m initial hypothesis that the box is so constructed that all the marbles are blue, that all are green, etc. It might be thought that hypothesis (ii) similarly subdivides into m^n initial hypotheses, one corresponding to each possible sequence of n marbles. But this is not so. There is but a single hypothesis expressed by (ii)—namely, that the machine be such that its mechanism randomizes marble colors. That single hypothesis accounts—in whatever relevant sense of explanation there may be—for any sequence such a box may actually produce in a trial.

Again, this point may be put as follows. What a hypothesis predicts is a set of observations or data. Its predictive "riskiness" prior to experimental confirmation is a function of the number of logically possible sequences of outcomes, confirmatory and disconfirmatory, that experimental tests of it could produce. Thus the chances that the results of a series of experimental tests will match the predicted ones becomes, a priori, vanishingly small as the number of tests goes to infinity. The degree of riskiness of a hypothesis, in that sense, is often infinitely high. But its prior probability, in the sense relevant to a Bayesian calculation, is a function of the number of explanatory hypotheses that can be formulated. (Not the number we happen to think of—the number that could, in principle, be formulated.[15]) The Humean, because he takes hypotheses to be essentially summaries of the data, identifies the number of possible hypotheses with the number of possible sequences of test results. Thus, by the Principle of Indifference, he assigns each hypothesis a vanishingly small prior probability. The necessitarian does not proceed in this way. For him, a summary of the data does not explain that data at all. He need not, however, subscribe to a Principle of Sufficient Reason. He need not rule out the possibility that the data literally have no explanation; but for him, this possibility amounts to just a *single* hypothesis, a hypothesis that is, by the way, compatible with any possible sequence of data. Though compatible with any sequence, it cannot be highly confirmed by any data sequence, and hence not by one that is sufficiently "nonrandom" to be compatible with the predictions of some causal hypothesis. (This is so even if the causal hypothesis is one that, like the laws of quantum theory, permits some statistical lattitude in the data. In that case, of course, confirmation requires longer runs of data.) For the necessitarian, then, the acausal or random hypothesis counts as a *single* hypothesis, one compatible with any set of outcomes, and hence one that has no predictive power.

Since this claim is crucial to the argument, it must be emphasized that it involves a certain conception of what an empirical hypothesis is and does. According to this conception, a hypothesis is *not* to be identified with—nor is it logically equivalent to—those states of affairs that it predicts. From a necessitarian point of view, a hypothesis is a conjecture about the existence (or nonexistence) of some stable underlying structure that explains what has happened and what will happen. It is only from the Humean perspective—a perspective that does not really admit this notion of explanation at all—that it seems natural to collapse the notion of a hypothesis into the notion of a proposition about a sequence of happenings. From the Humean point of view, the happenings are "all there is," so that it makes no sense to distinguish a hypothesis that predicts a given list of happenings from a hypothesis that predicts the same list of happenings, but as nonrandom, grounded in some causal principle. Conversely, a Humean might distinguish one list of (random) happenings from another, as corresponding to distinct hypotheses, simply on the grounds that different event-types are listed, or that their order differs. If we discard the Humean perspective, we must still of course admit that the Humeans have *a* genuine hypothesis—namely, that the world is so constituted as to have *no* causal structure. From the point of view of that hypothesis, *any* sequence of events —including any highly regular one—is equally possible; but each is also—under this hypothesis—*equally* a manifestation of what that hypothesis asserts concerning the nature of the world. This one hypothesis is compatible with many distinct experimental outcomes. Some of those outcomes—the "regular" ones—are also compatible with—and predicted by—distinct, non-Humean hypotheses. The induction we want to perform is not one to predicted outcomes—though it depends in part on the fulfillment of predicted outcomes; it is an induction to the existence of a structure that will explain those outcomes (except in the degenerate, but admissible, case of randomness). It is only via an induction that favors one explanatory hypothesis and disfavors competing ones, that we can justifiably move to predictions of single future events.

This view of the matter is corroborated by scientific practice. Perhaps arguments that appeal to inductive procedures that are actually used ought not to carry much weight in philosophical discourse. Still, it bears pointing out that induction does not proceed in the Humean manner in that area of science that approximates most closely to the study of random phenomena. In a quantum mechanical system, many distinct sequences of events are compatible with a given hypothesis as to the mechanisms operating in that system. But hypotheses are not individuated by counting the number of alternative conceivable event-sequences compatible with the theory as a whole; nor is a hypothesis that is compatible with a statistical distribution of outcomes weighted initially in proportion to the number of event-sequences or the number of consequent event-types with which it is compatible. Indeed, competing hypotheses may permit the *same* observed event-sequence. Arguments that select among competing quantum mechanical hypotheses are always arguments that employ reasoning from inverse probabilities, counting as *single* alternative hypotheses, laws or theories that predict a *spread* of possible experimental outcomes. Since quantum hypotheses place some nonlogical constraints upon possible outcomes, and the Humean hypothesis does not, one can view the latter as a kind of limiting case. But by parity of reasoning, it is to be counted as just one hypothesis. Now it may be that the necessitarian still confronts an infinite number of *causal* hypotheses, a priori, so that the prior probability of each will be given, by the Principle of Indifference and the Normalization requirement, as vanishingly small. That is an issue to which I shall return. But if the number of causal hypotheses is initially m, and if each of these must be assigned equal weight, then the prior probability of each hypothesis (including the acausal or no-explanation hypothesis) is $1/m + 1$.

It is now apparent why Ayer is mistaken in supposing the necessitarian's inductive task to be more difficult than the Humean's. In Humean fashion, Ayer judges the prior probability of necessitarian hypotheses as an inverse function of the number of their instances—and these include not only actual, but potential instances. But the necessitarian judges prior probability in terms of the number of alternative explanations available, not in terms of the number of actual or possible instances that a hypothesis is able to explain. Each hypothesis (except the degenerate Humean one, postulates a causal structure.

To return to our experiment, suppose the experimenter depresses the button one time and receives a blue marble. This automatically eliminates all but one of the subhypotheses of (i). The remaining hypotheses are (i') that the box must eject only blue marbles, and (ii) that its ejection-policy is random. If this exhausts the possibilities, it is reasonable to assign each of these hypotheses a prior of $1/2$.[16] Suppose now the experimenter depresses the button $(k - 1)$ times more, and each time receives a blue marble. Should he bet on hypothesis (i') or on hypothesis (ii)? The answer here is obvious. Quantitatively, we can say that, if the colors of the marbles were determined by chance, the probability of such a sequence occurring is $1/m^k$, and (see above) the posterior probability that the first n marbles will all be blue $(n > k)$ is given by m^k/m^n. The first fraction becomes small very rapidly as either m or k increases; which is to say that the probability of a uniform "chance" sequence is very small. Conversely, the probability, on hypothesis (i'), that the k marbles are all blue is 1; as indeed is the probability that the first n marbles will be blue, for any value of n. In fact, the posterior probability of hypothesis (i) is given by Bayes' Theorem as $P (i, k\ g) = 1/(1 + 1/m^{k-1})$; and this tends rapidly to 1, as either m or k gets larger. Moreover, it is independent of n, the total number of marbles, past and future, ejected by the box.

Now the above example was brought forward to illustrate the difference between the epistemic situations faced by the Humean and the necessitarian. But like so many examples used by those concerned with the theory of confirmation, it is highly artificial; and this artificiality generates the worry that it may be of little help in showing us how to solve the inductive problems we face in real life. The essential shortcoming of this example, in particular, is that it is implausible to suppose that the hypotheses (i) and (ii) are really exhaustive. Perhaps, for example, the box we are given contains a causal mechanism, but one that is so constructed that the first k marbles ejected are blue, the second k are green, and so on. Or . . . clearly we can imagine an infinity of such hypotheses. Are we not then directly back in the same boat with the Humeans? Would nature be so cruel as to present us with boxes of such prankish sorts? My response to this difficulty has several parts.

HOW MANY HYPOTHESES FOR THE NECESSITARIAN?

"Cruel" boxes, such as the one just envisaged, have causal mechanisms, all right; it is just that they are especially cunning mechanisms. The cunning feature of these boxes, in fact, is that they have mechanisms that enable them to measure time, or to keep track of how many times their button has been pushed.[17] The hypothesis that a box is of some such sort is as genuinely explanatory as is hypothesis (i). The trouble here is that, with respect to every box, the pushing of the button does not constitute the total cause of the ejection of a marble. There are other causally relevant features, which are internal to the box. A box that is able to count the number of times it has been triggered is such that its antecedent state can change, in a hidden way, during successive trials.

It seems clear that, if we are not allowed to pry into a box, we are not going to be able, simply by collecting more marbles, to eliminate any but a finite number of unwanted hypotheses. What if we are allowed to pry apart the box, as nature evidently permits us to pry into her contents?[18] If the mechanism inside is a causal one, perhaps we shall be able to discover its workings, and thus make correct projections concerning future marble ejections. But: what does "discovering its workings" consist in—except the making of further inductions about the behavior of the components in the box, on the basis of our observation of them? Might not some of them, in turn, be little black boxes, as pernicious as—and perhaps responsible for—the perniciousness of the original box? Well, then, we must tear *them* apart. What are the prospects of an infinite regress?

Let us pause here for a moment. Thus far, we have pursued the strategy of trying to render the number of initial hypotheses finite. Perhaps, in spite of the threat posed by "Goodmanian" hypotheses, this danger can be overcome. But before looking further in that direction, we should examine an argument due to Ewing that may obviate the difficulty. Ewing considers the problem of zero priors from a different angle. His response to the problem is to regard the notion of a quantitative probability as meaningless unless relativized to a body of data.[19] Hence assignments of epistemic probabilities can only be made a posteriori; prior probabilities are meaningless. It does not follow, according to Ewing, that the problem of induction cannot be solved at all (due to the inapplicability of Bayesian reasoning to hypotheses that have no assignable epistemic probability). For although the notion of quantitative priors is meaningless, Ewing believes that a qualitative notion of probability is applicable to untested hypotheses.[20] Ewing does not explain this notion, however. I should agree with Ewing that it is unrealistic to suppose that our probability estimates typically are or can be made quantitative. But on the other hand, I believe that the principles of Indifference and Normalization are a priori principles that give a reasonable, if perhaps idealized, model of rational procedure.[21] Nor can I think of any other principles that could serve (with one qualification mentioned in the preceding footnote). If initially there are infinitely many candidate hypotheses, then no restriction to qualitative probabilities can help us. Thus I believe that Ewing's tactic does not succeed.

Hence we arrive at the following position. The fundamental processes that underlie the history of the world are either random or causal.[22] That they are purely random is, we have seen, something we can have Bayesian grounds for dismissing. If we are right about the nature of causation, moreover, a *fundamental* causal process must be such as to be both time-independent and independent of the number of its previous instantiations. This follows from the fact that universals, whether they are atemporal entities or exist in time, are such that their natures are invariable. If the causal relation is a second-order relation between such relata, then its nature cannot depend upon purely temporal facts—e.g., what time it is, or how many times previously it has been instantiated, or how many of its instances have previously been observed by us. Our problem, therefore, comes to this: how do we know when we have succeeded in analyzing a natural mechanism or process into its "basic" causal components?

The answer to this last question is, unfortunately, not easy to give. But there are some things that can be said about it, in the relatively short compass that I shall allow myself.

FUNDAMENTAL THEORIES AND
ANTECEDENT CONDITIONS

Thus far I have largely ignored a fact that is of fundamental importance to the solution of the problem of induction. It is that, among the sorts of causal relations of which we are *directly* aware in experience, are ones that relate event-types whose properties are among those we count as primary properties, properties that are not only presented in sense experience but that are possessed by the objects studied by science. These properties include spatiotemporal properties (position, velocity), solidity, and mass or inertia.[23] In those cases where we directly experience a causal relation, we have noninductive or direct grounds for asserting that properties or event-types are causally related. It makes no difference whether all instances of these event-types are observed by us or not. Since the causal relation is perceived to relate the events themselves (or their properties), and not to be a feature of our subjective awareness of them, anything that instantiates those very properties will a fortiori instantiate the associated causal relations. If, therefore, we can have grounds for believing that some event (whether directly perceived by us or not) instantiates the properties of the antecedent of a known causal relation, we can have the required grounds for predicting what will follow. To illustrate: when we visually apprehend the collision between two billiard balls, we do not perceive the forces they exert upon each other. Nevertheless, we perceive that they instantiate certain kinematic properties — relative position and velocity; and we can discover, by colliding with them ourselves, that they possess mass and solidity. There is, to be sure, the possibility that something will secretly cause a change in the mass or solidity of either billiard ball, or of both; so that their next collision exhibits unanticipated behavior. That is the problem of ensuring that the antecedent conditions are really the same. Often enough, we cannot guarantee the absence of unknown causal factors; and sometimes, we cannot *even in principle* predict their arrival — e.g., the arrival of a light signal into an open system. But, if we can have good grounds under such circumstances to believe that the system is suitably isolated, then we can have good grounds for extending our own direct experience of collision phenomena to the billiard balls.

Let me now summarize and take stock of where we are. I began by distinguishing four inductive problems. They were:

(1) Isolating and identifying significant patterns of regular recurrence;
(2) Isolating all those factors that are causally relevant to what will happen in a given circumstance;
(3) Justifying the prediction of single future occurrences; and
(4) Justifying generalizations and law-statements based on finite evidence.

Next, I contrasted the epistemic situation of the Humean and the necessitarian with respect to problem (4). I showed that, at least for certain artificial cases, the necessitarian can solve this problem whereas the Humean cannot. But these cases relied upon the fact that the causal hypotheses with which we began were particularly docile, or else finite in number. When we dropped that assumption, we were faced with an inductive problem paralleling, to all appearances, the original Humean one — for our wild hypotheses, the "Goodmanian" ones, are neither docile nor finite in number.

Nevertheless there is a fundamental difference. Goodman's own hypotheses involve performing a test (observing the color of emeralds) and obtaining one kind of result (green color) up until some future time when the same test produces a different result (blue color). Thus Goodman's problematic hypotheses present a challenge to inductive reasoning by embodying the possibility that the same type of antecedent condition will in the future be followed by a novel consequent condition. One might describe the sequence of test/result event-pairs generated by such a hypothesis as a consequent-cruel sequence. For Humeans, the fact that the number of consequent-cruel sequences is infinite reflects the infinitude of Goodmanian hypotheses, and results in the problem of zero priors. But not for the necessitarian. For him, consequent-cruel sequences must be admitted as possible, but they all fall under a single hypothesis.

By contrast, the hypotheses I have just been considering are not consequent-cruel. There is no such thing as a genuinely causal hypothesis that generates a consequent-cruel sequence, and the behavior of the sorts of "cruel" boxes I have been considering is governed by causal laws. If novel things begin to happen, this can only be because the antecedent conditions have changed in some (perhaps undetected) way. If this change is hidden and unanticipated, we might say that the test/result sequence is antecedent-cruel. I have put the description 'Goodmanian' in scarequotes to reflect this fundamental difference. It is fundamental because the problem created by "Goodmanian" hypotheses is not the problem of zero priors at all, but rather the problem of ascertaining that one set of antecedent conditions is qualitatively identical to another set.

Causal laws – fundamental causal laws, at any rate – are grounded in relations among universals. Hence the "indexical" character of our "Goodmanian" laws – the fact, e.g., that they predict new behavior after some definite time period or some determinate number of experimental trials – shows that they are not basic laws and that their antecedents do not account for all of the relevant antecedent conditions. For we are supposing that those laws do not by themselves allow us to predict everything about the internal evolution of a system, and that they do not enable us to do so even when taken in conjunction with other well-established laws. Otherwise there would be no inductive problem here.

This means that the problem we are now addressing is no longer problem (4). It is instead a twofold problem: that of ascertaining antecedent conditions (problem (2)), and that of knowing when theory has reached the level at which its laws are basic in the sense of not being further reducible.

These two problems are related, inasmuch as one way in which a dissimilarity between antecedent conditions can be hidden is if it occurs at a level of structure below that which current science has probed. In fact, the problem posed by cruel boxes is just a special case of the problem of inferring causes from known effects. The observations by means of which antecedent conditions are compared may fail to register a relevant difference, for two sets of antecedent conditions may appear qualitatively identical by virtue of affecting measuring instruments identically. Yet they may produce distinct effects elsewhere – e.g., in the domain of our prognostications. I shall not attempt here any general solution to the nondeductive problem of inferring causes from effects. Instead I shall confine myself to a few sketchy remarks concerning the question of whether it would be possible to ascertain whether physical investigation has reached the terminus of the reductive process. If physics ever reaches, or comes close to, a level of structure below which no further structure exists, are there signs by means of which we can determine the advent of this stage?

This is a difficult and little-investigated problem. Undoubtedly most philosophers feel that speculations as to the form of fundamental theories in physics lie outside the proper domain of philosophy. Yet, it may be that there are certain special formal or quasi-formal constraints that a theory must satisfy to qualify for candidature as explanatorily fundamental. One such constraint, I believe, is that all of the laws of such a theory must be strictly exceptionless. Unlike the laws of a derivative theory, they cannot admit of exceptions or approximations due to incomplete description.[24] Unfortunately, the requirement of nondefeasibility is a merely necessary condition, and not a sufficient one. Moreover, a law that is defeasible may not be known to be so, because none of the difficult cases falling under it have been encountered.

A second sort of reason for holding that the limit of structure has been reached is the discovery of particles that give evidence of being indivisible. If, for example, a particle behaves as if it were a point-mass, this would constitute grounds for holding that it cannot be composed of anything smaller. Such an argument has been suggested for the view that electrons (which behave like point-masses) are elementary. The argument seems to involve an a priori principle to the effect that a point cannot be subdivided. However, I am not at all sure how to evaluate the strength of an argument in which that principle is applied to entities in physical space.

There is a different sort of strategy that bears mentioning. Science has delved more and more deeply into the constitution of matter. In so doing, it has revealed many complexities, but few structures that behave as mechanisms that suddenly undergo a major transformation after a certain period of time. So far, we have found few mechanisms that behave as "cruel" boxes do. Is there any inductive reasoning that justifies, on this basis, the expectation that the universe is not filled with "cruel" boxes? "Cruel" boxes are rare at the microscopic level. Molecules, atoms, and subatomic particles do not, so far as is known, contain mechanisms that would cause them to behave cruelly. Is it not unlikely that still finer levels of structure contain "cruel" boxes?

Unfortunately there does not seem to be any sound basis for this bit of inductive reasoning. For one thing, it involves reasoning from the character of entities at previously investigated levels of structure to the character of their unknown constituents. But this means reasoning from the nature of entities of one type to that of entities of (possibly) quite different types. Such reasoning is bound to be weak. It seems entirely conceivable that structures below the finest levels penetrated by current science are marking the time elapsed since the inception of the universe (the "Big Bang") and are destined to surprise us, through sudden changes in the microscopic behavior of the world, at some future date. Moreover there is no a priori guarantee that structure does not descend from level to level ad infinitum. If it does so, then the preceding argument is entirely inconclusive.

I have argued that the natural necessitarian is able to solve one major aspect of the problem of induction, for which no plausible Humean solution exists. That is the problem of projectibility, our problem (4). However, the solutions to other aspects of the problem remain outstanding. Until the remaining work is done, even those of us who count ourselves natural necessitarians cannot claim to have solved the problem of justifying inductive reasoning.

Notes

1. I wish to thank Professors Richard Fumerton, Panayot Butchvarov, and Colin Howson for their helpful comments on an earlier draft of this paper.

2. E.g., A. C. Ewing, *The Fundamental Questions of Philosophy* (London, 1951), 173.

3. Hume's only discussion of this component of experience, so far as I know, appears in two footnotes to Sec. 7, Part I of *An Enquiry Concerning Human Understanding*; see, e.g., pp. 72 and 84 of the Open Court edition (LaSalle, Ill., 1963). Contemporary philosophers who have advocated the view in one form or another include William James and A. C. Ewing.

4. Such a nonaccidental relation or genus of relations underlies, I would maintain, even laws (such as those of quantum mechanics) that are irreducibly probabilistic. Here one might say the relation is one of natural probabilification (or possibilification) rather than natural necessity—although this is merely to give it a name. Like natural necessity, it is a relation that I believe must be understood as a second-order relation between universals (see below). Perhaps we are never immediately aware of instances of this kindred relation. But the existence of such a relation distinguishes probabilistic laws from (partial) accidental correlations, and hence bears on inductive inferences that involve the positing of an underlying structure to explain a statistical regularity. I shall return briefly to this issue below, but in the main I shall ignore the special complications associated with inductive inference using probabilistic laws.

5. See David M. Armstrong, *A Theory of Universals*, Vol. II. (Cambridge, 1978), chap. 24; Fred Dretske, "Laws of Nature," *Philosophy of Science* 44 (1977):248-68; and Michael Tooley, "The Nature of Laws," *Canadian Journal of Philosophy* 7 (1977):667-98. Questions can be raised about the sense in which a singular statement concerning universals [e.g., '$C (F, G)$'] can be said to entail a general statement about individuals [e.g., '$(\forall^x(Fx \supset Gx)$')]: see Herbert Hochberg, "Natural Necessity and Laws of Nature," *Philosophy of Science* 48 (1981):386-99. I shall, however, not address that issue here.

6. See Wesley Salmon, "Inductive Inference," in *Philosophy of Science: The Delaware Seminar* II, edited by Bernard Baumrin (New York, 1962-63), 341-70. An argument of J. L. Mackie's can perhaps be classified as belonging to the Strawsonian camp: see Mackie, "A Defence of Induction," in *Perception and Identity: Essays Presented to A. J. Ayer with His Replies*, edited by Graham F. MacDonald (Ithaca, N.Y., 1979), 113-30. Mackie begins with an inductive inference that seems to be both valid and a priori. One hundred balls, identical except that one is white and the rest black, are placed in an urn and well mixed. The inference is that one that has been drawn at random will be black. Mackie says, rightly, that his inference does not depend upon previous urn drawings; it depends rather upon an epistemic Principle of Indifference that, I should agree, is a priori (see below). However, the form of this inference requires further comment. It is clear, I think, that the only judgment necessary to justify *betting* on black is: "Probably$_e$ (the drawn ball is black)," where 'Probably$_e$' represents epistemic probability. That judgment follows deductively from the description of the experiment, the Principle of Indifference, and the meaning of 'is epistemically probable'. But we might take the conclusion to be: 'The drawn ball is black'. What about the inductive inference from "Probably$_e$ (P)" to "P"? Perhaps questions can be raised here. Yet if such inferences are rational, it seems to me that the rule of inference involved is also a priori. It is not here, in any event, that Hume would put pressure. Rather, he would attack Mackie's attempt to use the Principle of Indifference, coupled to a Bayesian argument, to justify a principle of uniformity of nature. I shall discuss

below the problem of assigning prior probabilities, which it seems to me Mackie does not succeed in solving. (Mackie's solution relies upon the assignment of finite priors to hypotheses predicting long runs of orderly events, but I do not think Mackie has managed to justify this move.)

7. R. B. Braithwaite has been a prominent exponent of this account of laws, although his attempt to solve the problem of induction does not follow the line suggested here. See Richard Braithwaite, *Scientific Explanation: A Study of the Function of Theory, Probability and Law in Science* (London, 1963).

8. Relatively recent attempts of the latter sort have been presented by A. C. Ewing, "Causality and Induction," *Philosophy and Phenomenological Research* 12 (1962):465-85, reprinted in Ewing, *Non-Linguistic Philosophy* (London, 1968); John Foster, "Induction, Explanation and Necessity," *Proceedings of the Aristotelian Society* (1982-83), forthcoming; Michael Tooley, "The Nature of Laws," and Fred Dretske, "Laws of Nature."

9. J. S. Mill, *A System of Logic*, 8th ed. (New York, 1881), 284.

10. R. D. Rosenberg, "Does the Philosophy of Induction Rest upon a Mistake?" *Journal of Philosophy* 79 (1982):78-97.

11. Richard Fumerton, "Induction and Reasoning to the Best Explanation," *Philosophy of Science* 47 (1980):589-600.

12. There is, to be sure, the question of how regular sequences are to be distinguished from random ones. A general criterion of randomness is by no means easy to formulate, and I am skeptical of efforts to do this in terms of the definability of a rule by means of recursive functions. Ultimately a solution to this problem will require the formulation of identity criteria for universals. Short of tackling that problem, it can be said that there must *be* a distinction between random and regular sequences, if Hume's account of causation (or for that matter, mine) is not to be trivialized. For the feature of constant conjunction becomes vacuous if every sequence were to count as regular under some rule.

13. I ignore for the moment the complication that this hypothesis may in turn split up into a number of alternate subhypotheses.

14. Clearly this is not the *only* sort of causal hypothesis available. It may be that an event of type C regularly causes both A-type and B-type events. More complex inductive procedures must be employed to discriminate between such causal alternatives. But that complication need not concern us here.

15. This amounts in effect to dissociating the notion of prior probabilities from a purely subjective or psychological notion of probability. For the Principles of Indifference and Normalization have, it seems to me, the same epistemic status as the truths of pure mathematics. And our inability to think of an explanatory hypothesis in no way affects its initial candidacy. Thus I view prior probabilities, though epistemic, as objective in a sense. They are not the actual probabilities of the alternative hypotheses, of course, but neither are they the degree of confidence that any agent might happen to assign to them. We can think of them as the degrees of confidence that are dictated by the Principles of Indifference and Normalization under circumstances in which no relevant empirical data can be utilized, and in which all of the logically consistent hypotheses that could explain some set of outcomes of as-yet-to-be-performed experiments have been enumerated.

16. This assignment is *"slightly"* posterior, since one marble has already been ejected, but obviously if the experiment can be carried out at all, it can be carried out *this* far. This eliminates the difficulty that, where the number of colors m is infinite, the priors of each of the subhypothesis of (i) become infinitely small. In other words, a single experiment is sufficient to obviate that difficulty. The (very real) worry that the set of hypotheses [(i'), (ii)] is artificially restricted and not exhaustive will be discussed below.

17. These perverse examples come courtesy of Nelson Goodman, but with a twist: the patterns exhibited by the behavior of "cruel" boxes have a causal explanation. Any such sequence could be produced by a randomizing box; but the supposition that a box is genuinely random is a distinct hypothesis and has already been discussed. The distinction is an important one; see below.

18. It does, at least, if we can solve the problem of inferring causes from their effects—the problem of perception, given a causal theory of perception.

19. A. C. Ewing, "Causality and Induction."

20. This does not exclude the possibility of making quantitative estimates of a posteriori probabilities for hypotheses, in virtue of the fact that in many cases the value of the prior probability is swamped by the effect of confirming or disconfirming evidence.

21. Perhaps a certain class of a priori criteria of which relative simplicity is an example ought to temper the application of the Principle of Indifference. More generally, it may be that some kinds of explanations—especially at the level of reductively fundamental explanations (if such a level there be) are intrinsically more satisfying, more illuminating, than competing candidate explanations. This topic deserves closer investigation than it has yet received: it is a necessary propaedeutic to the articulation of an adequate theory of the nature of arguments to the best explanation. Such maneuvers may legitimate assignment of uneven a priori weights to hypotheses. In the present context, however, this is of secondary importance.

22. Twentieth-century developments in physics make us aware of a third possibility: limited randomness underlying an appearance of rigid order. I shall not pursue here the complexities that this possibility introduces into the inductive project.

23. I am setting aside the problem of predicting behavior in open system. This is a problem that cannot be solved inductively or in any other way. According to Special Relativity, for example, electromagnetic radiation may arrive from a distant source and influence a system at any time. There is in principle no way to predict when this will happen.

24. For a fuller exposition of the relation between fundamentality and nondefeasibility, see Evan Fales, "Theoretical Simplicity and Defeasibility," *Philosophy of Science* 45 (1978):273-88. Further discussions of the formal requirements of fundamental theory appear in Evan Fales, "Relative Essentialism," *British Journal for the Philosophy of Science* 30 (1979):349-70, and in Rom Harré and E. H. Madden, *Causal Powers: A Theory of Natural Necessity* (Totowa, N.J., 1975), chap. 9; and other works by Harré.

Hume Was Right, Almost;
and Where He Wasn't, Kant Was[1]

D. S. SHWAYDER

1

Hume denied that causation is a "quality" in pretty much the sense of Berkeley's previous denial that it is an "idea," that is, a sensible phenomenon.[2] *Causation*, Hume held, is an idea applicable to happenings, in or out of the mind; happenings that are qualified as causes and effects are, he thought, indeed subject to observable constraints of contiguity and successiveness; still, maintained Hume, causation is not the idea of a phenomenon wholly resident in or among those qualified happenings. I agree with the negative side of this doctrine, that causation is not a kind of phenomenon wholly resident in or among happenings that may truly be said to be the causes or effects of happenings.

2

Hume, in the *Treatise*, twice over at least, offered consecutive pairs of definitions of causation. I quote:

> We may define a CAUSE to be 'An object precedent and contiguous to another, and where all the objects resembling the former are plac'd in like relations of precedency and contiguity to those objects, that resemble the latter.' If this definition be esteem'd defective, because drawn from objects foreign to the cause, we may substitute this other definition in its place, *viz.* 'A CAUSE is an object precedent and contiguous to another, and so united with it, that the idea of the one determines the mind to form the idea of the other, and the impression of the one to form a more lively idea of the other.'[3]

The two definitions are clearly different. While recent authors favor the message of the first, which has to do with constant conjunction and "covering laws", Hume, in the *Treatise*, must have fancied the second. The allusion in the first definition to "all objects" bespeaks a main interest in happenings of *kinds* and (Hume noticed) brings in matters foreign to the particularities of the singular case. Obviously, no one has ever had an observational impression of constant conjunction. Constant conjunction cannot be an observable phenomenal feature of the relationship between a cause and its effect; it can contribute nothing to the "original" of the idea of causation. The second definition complements the negative thesis—that causation cannot be a kind of phenomenon wholly resident in or among the related happenings—with the positive thesis that our idea of causation derives in part from an "impression of reflection" produced "in the mind" that is of a "determination to pass from one object to its usual attendant" (*Treatise*, p. 165). The fact of this determination owes (causally, of course) to a repeated conjunction of impressions. That's offered up by Hume simply as a bit of natural history, failing which humankind would not have survived to speculate about causation. So the two definitions, if true at all, are true together in this world. The idea of "necessary connection", which (according to Hume) is part of our idea of causation, is the idea of a transition of belief or of inference from an impression of one of the happenings to a belief that the other also occurs. Causation resembles that other Humean relation of ideas of which the perception is an impression of "logical" or "Leibnizian" necessity and, derivatively, a warrant for logical inference. This thought, that *necessity* of any kind depends upon a relation of ideas, will stay to haunt my criticism of Hume.

Hume's two phenomenal constraints upon a cause and its effect jar a little. An impression of contiguity, after all, can be only "at a time". He weaseled by arguing that no cause can be "perfectly co-temporary" with its effect (*Treatise*, p. 76). It's fairly obvious, I guess, that, as Hume saw the matter, the happenings at question are all of them stretches, where some substretch of the cause precedes all substretches of the effect and some substretch of the effect follows all substretches of the cause; the contiguity of something or other is then observed "at a time" at the boundary separating the two happenings in question. Hume didn't include boundary happenings such as impacts among his causes and effects, and he scarcely considered those interactions Kant discussed in his "Third Analogy." Still, Hume saw that something had to be said here, and his anxiety about the matter led him into a curious speculation. He argued that the admission of perfectly "co-temporary" causation would eventuate in "no less than the destruction of that succession of causes, which we observe in the world; and indeed, the utter annihilation of time. For if one cause were co-temporary with its effect, and this effect with its effect, and so on, 'tis plain there wou'd be no such thing as succession, and all objects must be co-existent" (ibid.). This is doubtfully compatible with what Hume elsewhere wrote about both identity and causation, and it verges upon the dubious doctrine that our idea of succession derives from the idea of causation.[4] I dispute the exclusion of "co-temporary" causation and also doubt that Hume's impression of determination to make a transition of belief is the original of the idea of *necessary connection*. For right now, however, I want only to repeat my qualified endorsement of Hume's thesis that causation is not to be taken as an idea of phenomena wholly resident in or among those happenings truly said to be, the one cause and the other effect, and that the idea of *causation* (though perhaps not that of *necessary connection*) does indeed include the idea of a kind of transition of belief in regard to the occurrence of those happenings.

3

The traditional literature of philosophy does not, as it seems to me, stand in so evident an opposition to Hume's thoughts about causation as he himself fancied. Certainly Hume disliked the easy notion that our idea of causation originates from a sense of our own activity.[5] He treated the impression as only one case, and argued that an impression of activity would be cast as of a cause only if of a kind regularly experienced in conjunction with kinds of effects. "We learn the inference of our will from experience alone" (*Enquiry*, p. 66; also *Treatise*, pp. 632f.). While, for Hume, the idea of necessary connection originates from an impression of reflection, it needn't have its primary application to active will as cause. I suspect that Hume would have agreed (as I do) with D. G. Brown that inanimate causation is "primitive" (*Action* [London, 1968], chap. 3).

Hume's opinions about the causal powers of sensible phenomena, including ideas of inner sense, were altogether Berkeleyan. But Hume rejected that other doctrine espoused by Berkeley and other theologues that the unperceivable activity of spirit is an authentic cause of perceivable phenomena (*Enquiry*, pp. 69-73). So there is indeed some opposition to be found in things one may happen to read about causation.

It is apposite to notice that Hume's difference with Berkeley over actual, real causation does not so far bring him into conflict with the Leibniz-Berkeley opinion that only active spirits qualify as genuine substances. Leibniz actually denied "real physical influence or dependence" (e.g., at. p. 134 of the Open Court edition of the correspondence with Arnauld). Neither Leibniz' "parallelism" nor any thoroughgoing (nontheological) occasionalism is incompatible with this part of Hume's philosophy.

Hume mentioned Locke on "power" as an opposed doctrine. Now Locke certainly didn't consider the matter in a Humean way; still, what Locke actually said about the idea of power being an idea of both sensation and reflection is more an amorphous confusion of indistinction than a distinct opposition.

Now I move to something more serious. Kant held that causation was a "category" affiliated (via the "metaphysical deduction") with the hypothetical form of judgment and (via the "transcendental deduction") constitutive of our conception of substance. Since causation, by this, is representative of something in substance, it looks as if Kant must be mustered among the opposition. I think that's right, but not quite obvious. Start with this matter of hypothetical judgment: Mill and such contemporary writers as Mackie and David Lewis stress the connection between the fact of causation and the truth of a strong conditional. The kernel of this kind of doctrine seems to be that C causes E only if the conditional that *if C had not occurred then E would not have either* is true. Let it be so. It needn't yet injure Hume.[6]

We are trafficking in unactualized possibilities. There is a respected body of opinion—even Leibniz endorsed Arnauld on this—that such possibilities exist only in the mind. There is, furthermore, a reputable "analysis" of strong conditionals according to which such a conditional is true only if the truth of what is conveyed by the protasis clause would give reason for believing that what is conveyed by the apodosis clause is also true. What could be more Humean than that? (I argue only that there are ways to go with these issues that are right with Hume, not that these ways are right.)

Now about the "category" of causation as a constituent of our conception of substance: How can such a constituent be anything other than representative of a phenomenal factor latent in substances, conceived of as changeable but perduring identifiable objects of reference, to which various things happen? Interestingly, when we turn to examine what may be the main application Kant made of the causation category, in the "Second Analogy," it is very hard to find anything other than the thought that causation implicates the identifiability of substances over time. We passingly recalled that Hume was poorly positioned to deal with substantial identity over time and noticed that this distresses the sense of his claim that causes are temporally prior to their effects. Kant was right, I think, in holding that identifiability of substances over time is no less essential to our idea of causation than is (say) contiguity. Kant, so far as I know, never invoked a transition of belief as another part of our idea of causation. Still, the connection he makes between causation and hypothetical judgment suggests that he *might* have done so. *If* that is indeed what he had in mind (and Melnick tells me that there isn't a passage in the *First Critique* that suggests he did), he wasn't yet opposed to Hume. On the other hand, if the thesis that substantial identity is the whole essence of causation holds up, then Hume was indeed wrong. We shall find reason to think that substantial identity may be whole essence of *necessary connection*; but before that, we shall find stronger reasons to think that a Humean determination of mind factors into the full conception of *causation*. The two philosophers were certainly opposed, but (I submit) not irreconcilably. We may reconcile the two doctrines by mating them, adding substantial identity, as a further "phenomenal" constraint, onto Hume's impression of a determined transition of belief. Examples suffice to show that the two components are independent. The question of to which of these two factors, if either, we are to assign the *necessary connection* is so far still open. I have, however, anticipated that it should be lodged with identity.

4

Hume didn't so much argue as *notice* that we have no impression of what he called "necessary connection" as a quality or a relationship in or among those happenings truly called causes and effects, no more so for acts of mind than for the actions of bodies (*Treatise*, p. 77, but especially at pp. 64-73 of the *Enquiry*). This is unsatisfying and probably wrong. If the idea of connection did indeed arise from a determination of mind, then causation would be so far undistinguished from statistical and superstitious inferences in regard to contiguous and successive happenings—such inferences are certainly "Humean" and biologically utile in the bargain. But we *do* distinguish causation from superstition; so something must be missing from Hume's picture of causation. I think it is a *connection* and a connection of identifications of the kind which caught Kant's attention. Hume simply didn't look hard enough; but then, of course, he was not disposed to see identity.

5

Since Hume did not actually argue that our idea of causation implicates a determination of mind, it could seem that the Kantian connection he didn't notice, demonstrated by identifications, would be enough. I shall presently offer an argument on Hume's behalf; but first I would like to observe that there is a Kantian example that suggests that something more than connection is also wanted.

Take a clockwise-moving gear wheel, g. A movement of tooth C from c_1 to c_2 might or might not properly be said to be the cause of the movement of E from e_1 to e_2, depending upon other things. Suppose, for example, g were made to move by the action of a clockwise-moving belt strung to its hub; the rotation of the hub is the cause of both tooth movements, and neither of those is the cause of the other. Differently, if g were moved by the action of a counterclockwise-moving pinion meshed at C, then part of C's movement causes part of E's. A movement of C, in the latter sense, is not disqualified as a cause of E's movement just because it wouldn't be a cause unless something else also were. Not all causes are "first". The Kantian connection in this example is in g itself, and is mediated by an identification of that thing across the time of the movement. However, the assignment of causes also depends upon the external drive, hence not on the movement of the gear wheel alone. It depends (I shall suggest) upon our fitting of that movement into a familiar pattern of explanation; and that does sound like a determination of mind induced by a regularity of experience.

6

Passingly: Unless (what is most implausible) our idea of causation is incompatible with the mere possibility of rigid body movements, then the gear wheel example also argues that causes may indeed by "co-temporal" with their effects. Better to replace Hume's two conditions of contiguity and succession with a single Kantian condition of identity: happenings connected as causes and effects, themselves nothing other than changes in identifiable objects, are parts of another happening, that is a change in an aggregation of the identifiable objects. Thus, in the gear wheel example, the two happenings are fixed as movements of the respective gear teeth. Both teeth are parts of g. When the movement of C causes the movement of E, those movements are parts of the movement of g.

7

It now seems that, while both Hume and Kant spoke truth about causation, neither said enough. Kant did argue, especially in the "First Analogy," that causal connections depend upon the existence of identifiable substances. Hume did not argue that causality depends upon a determination of mind, and his side of the story is so far less supported than Kant's. There is a well-known "modern" style of argument we can use to support Hume's thesis that our idea of *causation* implicates a determination of mind, where *that* thesis may have nothing to do with *connection*. If an idea, I, of a phenomenon is such that instances of that phenomenon are identified with reference to other things, but where the phenomenon is not invariant over interchanges of the identifications of those other things, then I is such that its phenomenon should not be thought of as either constituted of or as resident in those other things. Frege argued that our idea of *belief* is that way: Beliefs are identified with reference both to believers and to what the beliefs are about; they are invariant over interchanges of identifications of their "bearers", in whom they are properly held to be resident; but they are not invariant over interchanges of identifications of what they are about, hence beliefs are neither resident in nor are they constituted of those things. Hume, we have seen, held that causation is an idea applicable to pairs of happenings, but yet does not represent a phenomenon wholly resident in or among those happenings. Frege's argument, we all know, was from "opacity". Hume's thesis *predicts* "opacity" and would be confirmed by the fulfillment of that prediction for the context ". . . causes———". I believe that the prediction is borne out. To argue that I shall eventually cite an example Hume could not have used himself.

8

Causes are nothing if not "explanatory factors" and are usually mentioned for purposes of explaining their observed effects. Recent writers on *explanation* are generally though not quite unanimously agreed that the context ". . . explains———" is "opaque". Since the terms of the agreement are unclear and the relation of *causation* to *explanation* just a little intricate, I must tarry a bit over *explanation* before returning to my quest for an example to illustrate the "opacity" of the context ". . . causes———". The asseverations which now follow want support by arguments I'll not give.

A first point to notice about explanation is that it cannot even so much as be attempted unless some (actual) fact (the *"explicandum"*) stands in need of explanation. A condition for the success of the explanation is that something true is said that reports a fact. These two observations eventuate in the double conclusion that *explaining* is itself not to be elucidated simply as a "use of language", e.g., as *generalization, prediction,* or *description,* and, secondly, that there is no "use of language", e.g., *generalization,* which is to be elucidated solely in terms of explaining things. *Explaining,* to be sure, is done *by* use of language, and "fact-stating language" in the bargain; but then (like *persuading* and *informing*) it won't succeed unless it achieves some further nonlinguistic purpose. *Explaining,* in Austin's terminology, is a kind of *perlocutionary* action.

We now have the task of describing the "further purpose" in some not uselessly general way. Explanations are of many kinds. A body falls, and we explain that occurrence by saying that the thing broke loose from a bracket. That is one thing to explain, and one kind of explanation. The equivalence of gravitational and inertial mass is quite another order of fact wanting quite another type of explanation. Now within any such *kind* of explanation there are various kinds of fact properly adducible as *explicantia.* The bell rang, we explain, because the circuit was rigged *or* because the power was on (we didn't expect it to be) *or* because someone broke the circuit ("There must be someone there"). Yet, in particular cases, one particular *explicans* is "enough". An *explicandum,* it seems from this, is a fact in connection with various possible explanatory factors, but where those possibilities for explanation are restricted by some inquirer's knowledge and ignorance of these facts.

We noticed that a condition for attempting an explanation is that something stands in need of explanation. That can mean only that there is something here an inquirer doesn't understand. Now understanding can sometimes be achieved otherwise than by saying something: some dogs, for example, come to understand cats, this, no doubt, by an accustomed Humean transition of belief. So, it seems, "achieving understanding" is a first description of that problematic nonlinguistic "further purpose." As a first half-step toward making that less useless, I suggest that understanding is achieved by "making familiar". Take a classic case: Normally no explanation is needed for a ball falling to the ground when dropped, or for its not falling if it's caught in a chair. We are all familiar with that sort of thing. If, contrastingly, in the course of theorizing, we wonder why things don't fly off in random directions or simply stay where they are, we may look for and find an explanation of that general circumstance, and then use it to explain the motions of the planets as a kind of falling, at which point different orders of phenomena begin to look alike. Now, of course, we are coming into areas of accustomed experience, "constant conjunction" and "generalization". Some writers on explanation have seemed to hold that explanatory "making familiars" must always be a matter of derivation from some general law or, perhaps, from an Aristotelian "definition". I won't dispute whether there is any successful explanation that could not be *recast* as a "derivation", but that word does not give an obvious description of the general case. Our observation that the *explicandum* is a fact seen as standing in connection with other factors suggests a truer if vaguer description, which I hope is not utterly useless: explanation is a kind of action that succeeds by establishing a correspondence between a phenomenon and a known pattern of various sorts of factors, including (e.g.) happenings, states, and presences.

Such a "correspondence" is commonly established by finding some feature of the *explicandum* that answers to one strand of the pattern, e.g., the circuit is energized, or the cell is in place, etc. The explaining may succeed by mention of merely one such factor because others are given in place as soon as we see the phenomenon as an instance of the kind of thing that might be fitted into the familiar pattern.

Differently, one may impose the pattern as a whole on the phenomenon and then, to test for success, look for factors in the phenomenon corresponding to strands in the pattern (e.g., I say "Regard a planet as a body falling into the sun").

Now we need to add only that explaining is achieved by saying something true: it is a kind of perlocutionary action that seeks either to fit a phenomenon into a pattern by finding some factor in the phenomenon to correspond to a strand in the pattern or to fit the pattern onto the phenomenon.

The linguistic means by which an explanation is attempted incorporate "contexts" which may or may not be "opaque"; but then the explanation can contain nothing more of that kind. Explanation itself is not the sort of thing that can be said to be either "opaque" or "transparent" in Quine's technical usage of those terms.

9

If explaining isn't purely linguistic, something else is, namely *saying* that C explains E; such sayings, if successful, produce true-or-false statements of explanation. Our examination of *explaining* suggests that such a statement of explanation exists only if the entries at C and E identify actual facts, where E stands in need of explanation; the statement would then be verified by exhibiting a correspondence between E (or a containing phenomenon) and an explanatory pattern either for C or incorporating a factor type corresponding to C.

That puts us in position to argue that the "context", ". . . explains———" is "opaque". "Why is *he* here?", I ask; you reply, "Because he is the building inspector." If that is correct, then it would be true to say "The fact of his being the building inspector explains the fact of his being here." But if he is the building inspector, which is a condition for the existence of the statement of explanation, then, under plausible assumptions for the sameness of facts, the fact of his being here is the same as the fact of the building inspector's being here; but it is clear that this statement, *the fact of his being the building inspector explains the fact of the building inspector's being here*, is not true in the same circumstances as would be the original one. Also, if the building inspector is the man who just arrived, then the fact of his being the building inspector is no different from the fact of his being the man who just arrived; but it is not true that his being the man who just arrived explains his being here. Again, but more abstractly, if it is true to say "C is the explanation of E", an utterance "The explanation of E is the explanation of E" fails to produce a statement of explanation, for its sense forfeits the possibility of verifying a statement of explanation by establishing a correspondence between pattern and *explicandum*. Here coreferential substitution in the C-place yields nothing at all. ". . . explains — — —", though grammatically a predicate, should not be thought of as used to ascribe a relation to pairs of things; in this respect, it is like such locutions as ". . . is to the left of — — —" and ". . . knows that — — —".

<h2 style="text-align:center">10</h2>

We come, at last, to the question whether the context ". . . causes — — —" is "opaque." The issue has been much in the air of late. Davidson, notably, in seeming opposition to such other notables as Anscombe, M. Beardsley, and Føllesdal, holds that it is not.[7]

A single proven example of nonsubstitutivity of identicals is sufficient to establish the "opacity" of a context. Let me see if I can formulate the opposed opinion, that ". . . causes — — —" is "transparent", before looking for that example. Take, for analogy, an opaquely asserted fact of the *a is to the left of b* sort; that very same fact could also be transparently asserted by saying "a is north of b," which may be taken to ascribe a genuine relation to the pair (a,b). So too, "C explains E" may opaquely assert a fact, which same fact could be otherwise but transparently asserted by ascribing a genuine relation to the pair (C,E). A candidate statement of this latter kind would be that *C caused E to happen*. We have, in this transition, moved away from "explained" to a specification of explanatory factor. Generally, we hypothesize that any fact of explanation would also be a relationship between a specific explanatory factor and the *explicandum*. Of course, the reverse conclusion would not hold, since (e.g.) although C caused E to happen, C may not explain E, perhaps because something else does or because E needs no explanation. Explanatory factors may be present and operative when not appropriate as explanations. An argument for this is that, while to say "The explanation of E (which may be the cause of E) explains E" scarcely makes any sense at all, "The cause of E caused E" seems unexceptionally true. Also this: If the dissolution of the sugar = The sugar's dissolving at such and such a rate, then dropping the sugar into the water may cause that happening under either specification; but surely dropping the sugar into the water does not *explain* its dissolving at such and such a rate; so, sometimes anyway, when a = b and where the explanation of a is not the explanation of b, it may still be that the cause of a is the cause of b.

The example illustrates a proposal; it doesn't prove it. One may demur that explanatory factors such as causes, dispositions and beliefs are selected and classified as such because of their explanatory roles and argue thence that the concept of (e.g.) a *cause* is a concept of explanation. I find that unconvincing: The conception of gravitation was first introduced in connection with the explanation of the trajectories of neighboring bodies; but surely bodies have the gravitational potentials they do without that necessarily explaining anything at all. Causes may be like sortals: while the introduction of specific sortal characterizations is a reflection of human interests and concerns, still an animal may be said to be of the sort it is without the speaker having any particular interest in that sort of thing at all; the speaker identifies a robin for what it is even though he doesn't care a tweet about robins.

I have been trying to formulate my own onetime thought that ". . . causes –––" is transparent.

Davidson, in the cited paper, doesn't actually expatiate on this distinction between "cause" and "explains" as I have just done; so I won't insist that that is what he had in mind. He simply argues the matter on its own terms, using the seeminly unexceptional truth of *The cause of E caused E*, among other data. He holds that happenings ("events") are authentic identifiable objects of reference; I won't dispute that, for, while I think it matters a lot that happenings are not "primary beings", I allow that they may be identifiable individuals of a subordinate category. Davidson holds that "cause" signifies a genuine dyadic predicable of happenings. He argues from examples that the truth values of statements of causation about changes are not altered by switches of coreferences to those things which change. I won't dispute that either. But there are other kinds of references to causes and effects, actually suggested by Davidson's remark about the cause of E being the cause of E, which I don't think he considered.

We need examples, which Hume would disapprove, where the cause and the effect are the same one change. *Action* may provide cases in point: *My successfully raising my arm* causes *the rising of my arm*; but these are one and the same happening, noninterchangeably fixed as *cause* under the first characterization and as *effect* under the second.

Fixing on the fundamental case of causation by contact, I prefer examples of punctual boundary-changes of the kind Hume consequentially disregarded. We saw that his demand for contiguity could not be satisfied without them, and their existence is implied by ancient maxims of the cause reaching to the effect and of there being no action at a distance. Now I certainly do not believe that all causes and effects are punctual boundary changes; indeed, I agree with Kant that these happenings find their place in a causal nexus *only* as boundaries separating stretches that are causes from stretches that are effects. Still, such changes sometimes figure as causes and effects and then, commonly, as both together. Take two classically colliding billiard balls: the movement of the one causes the other to move; those certainly are distinct movements; but of course there is no causation here unless the one ball collides with the other. So, the movement of the first ball, *C*, causes the movement of the second, E, but only if there is a collision or an "impact". E would not have been caused by C unless it were also "proximately" caused by the second ball's being impacted upon by the first; similarly, C would not have been the cause of E unless the proximate effect of C was that the first ball impacted upon the second. The impact is a boundary change separating the movements C and E. Whatever "criterion of identity" you may prefer for other "events", it's clear that boundary changes are unique to the pairs of stretches they separate. That same one impact may be differently and inequivalently described both as the proximate cause of E and as the proximate effect of C. But now (I urge) C would not have caused E unless the proximate effect of C caused the proximate cause of E; to say the opposite would tell a different and competing story about the exchange of movement. The first ball impacting upon the second causes the second ball to be impacted upon by the first, not the reverse; but the "two things" are the same. Here, then, if I am right, we have a happening that is noninterchangeably described as its own cause and effect.

If my description of collisions holds up, then we have, to confirm the prediction we drew from Hume's thesis that causation implicates a determination of mind, noticed a most common kind of example to establish the opacity of ". . . causes
– – –". It strikes a right note. The assignment of an impact as cause or as effect depends upon whether it is "taken" to be the end of one movement or the start of another.

11

This "taking" surely (i.e., "I can't prove it"!) is in relation to some accustomed pattern of causal explanation. Causation, unlike gravity or belief, cannot stand free of explanation. This "Humean" thesis does not imply that there were no causes before minds, for cosmologists right now are trying to provide causal explanations of early cosmic episodes. It does, I believe, imply that a perfected intellect who perceived the cosmos for what it is, in all its continuances and connections and who accordingly never suffered the need for explanations, would never perceive causes.

12

Causal explanation, while common, is distinctive. Not all explanation is causal in the "efficient" sense. We want a description of the causal pattern. Stipulations of contiguity, successiveness, and identity are accordingly in order. My own words on the pattern of efficient causation have been vague and won't become much less so in what now follows. The phenomenon in question is always a happening consisting of changes in an aggregation of bodies or other identifiable substances; the pattern resolves that happening into parts; these parts are connected by the continuance, coalescense and separation of those substances. A break in those connections throws causality into doubt. The connections may be tested for and observed, by tracking and separating. So causation implicates identity. Hume of course drew a blank on identity. Kant didn't, and he understood that identification is indeed a requirement of causation, as is well attested by his demand for perduring substances. What Kant may not have seen is that no amount of tracking and tracing of connections among identifiable bodies will verify the fact of causation until these various phenomena are actually fitted into some accustomed pattern of causal explanation. What Kant lacked Hume supplied, and conversely. That's my conclusion and pretty much a paraphrase of my title.

13

I tail off (where I'd rather have begun) with a reservation and a speculation, both occasioned by the haunting question: Whence our sense of causal "compulsion"? This query revives the thought (section 2) that there is no kind of compulsion that doesn't derive from a relation of ideas. That bothers my criticism of Hume, for it suggests that he may, after all, have been right about necessary connection.

Or perhaps a necessity no less than "logical" may reside in the phenomena? If genuine true statements of identity and distinctness were always necessary (as Wittgenstein and Kripke have seemed to hold) and if statements of the fact of body identity of the kind we have been considering are authentic statements of identity, then causation does indeed involve *necessity* in a more fashionable "logical" sense. I myself believe that the connections we have used as examples are indeed formulable in authentic statements of identity and that such statements, when true, are "quasi-necessary". The compulsion of causation may indeed be the "logical necessity" of identity. The impacting first ball could not have been any other than the one that moved in, nor could the one that moved out have been any other than the one that was impacted upon. Moreover, though the two balls were, for a scant instant, parts of another larger thing, they were separable throughout, hence "logically" distinct; but now the two movements of the respective balls could not have been other than they are either, and they could not have been connected and separated by any other boundary change than the impact. So, on the assumption that all true statements of identity are necessary, it begins to look as if no connection of cause and effect by contact could be other than it is. That if right would support the thesis (which Mackie and Davidson, among others, seem to have endorsed) that the occurrence of a particular cause in particular circumstances is indeed both necessary and sufficient for the occurrence of any particular effect it may have. But this also: Were logical necessity, as Hume held, always exclusively a matter of relations of ideas, then his doctrine of causality and Kant's could collapse into each other in a rather satisfying "Spinozistic" sort of way. A full knowledge of what the object-bearers of changes are would always be enough also to know where lay the cause and its effect.

Speculations these, and a tale for another day.

APPENDIX: ON THE PRIORITY OF CAUSES

The foregoing thoughts about causation may be used to resolve Michael Dummett's question about the priority of causes ("Can the Effect Precede Its Cause," *Arist. Proc. Soc. Suppl.*, 1954, pp. 27-54). We noticed some cases where a cause and its effect are simultaneous (sections 6 and 9). But we are disposed to think that, whenever the two happenings are distinct and successive, the cause must precede its effect. There are, however, various counterexamples. I suspect that most everyone will sense that these are incidental and adventitious, to say the best for them. What now follows will try to explain that common sense of the matter.

I doubt, what was intimated by Hume and argued for by Reichenbach, that the order of causes defines the order of time (section 2 and n. 4 sup.). I have elsewhere[8] tried to show that our most primitive sense of temporal succession is based on the procedure of (presently) identifying a body from where it was; this procedure is a kind of "objectivization" of that kind of self-knowledge a subject has of what it has been doing in knowing what it does, e.g., in standing up or in terminating a five-count. I appeal to that in what follows. I shall additionally use what was prepared above, that causes and effects are registered as such by reference to an explanatory pattern that a phenomenon fits into only if a connection can be traced through a sequence of body (or other constituent) identifications and separations. Starting from there, we can state the problem as follows: Causes and effects are happenings that are connected in space and time. These happenings may be the same or distinct; when distinct, they may or may not be successive. Cases of prior causation are legion, e.g., when we explain yesterday's flood in the lowlands as being caused by a cloudburst in the mountains on the day before. Why then shouldn't there also be cases of posterior causation?

There are! Most everyone, I think, would allow for the possibility of a referee's later ruling to have caused a team to have won the game. Again, I can imagine cases at law in which accused's failure to go for a doctor caused him to have committed manslaughter. "But here the later happening or inaction is a cause only in a 'conventional sense'." Allowed. Here, however, are three different "nonconventional" instances. *First*, there is the rebuttal to Moliere's cock, who fancied his crowing brought the sun to rise. Unless we wish to empower him with a cosmic force commensurate with his vanity, we would more naturally suppose that it is the later rising of the sun that causes him to crow. What explains the noise now is the onset of later light.

Again, we can causally explain the people moving their boats to deep water and shuttering the windows by mention of the fact that a hurricane *will* blow over at midnight.

Finally, the day before writing the first version of this note, I was, when golfing, stung by what I think was a bee. I *then* became aware that I *had* heard something buzzing. The sting caused me to have heard the buzzing of the bee. (A beekeeper who wished to cause me to *have heard* his bees might incite one to sting me.)

Most readers will protest that what *really* caused the rooster to crow was the first, faint, humanly invisible glimmerings of the sun; that what caused the people to shutter their windows was the news that the hurricane was coming; and that really I heard the bee all right, but wasn't aware that I had until stung. Perhaps: But this talk of unseen light is a bit of theory. And suppose I wasn't stung: How would you show me or anyone that I had heard the buzzing of the bee? Resistance is natural, however. In all these instances, the alleged effect is incidental to the cause, and we could never understand the cases unless we saw both cause and effect as ensuing upon other weightier conditions prior to both. We can post the effect only within a nexus that reaches back to an earlier time.

We now look for something in the causal nexus that at once allows for such possibilities and accounts for our sense that they must be abnormal, incomplete, and incidental.

Patterns of causal explanation represent both the cause and effect as happenings, same or different, that are connected into a larger happening. The explanation traces how they are connected within the whole. Now (following Kant) an identification of a happening requires the identification of bodies or other substances; causal explanation therefore requires the identification of substances. Suppose now that the cause and effect occur at different times. The explanation traces between the two. We cannot trace connections between these happenings except by tracking substances. In the simplest cases, where only a single body figures, we must be able to assure ourselves that we have got the same body in both happenings. Further (I would argue), the identifying test must proceed from the context of the earlier happening to the later. The consequence is that the very identification of the later happening depends upon our proceeding from a given individuation of the body in the earlier happening. Assuming that we explain the effect by reference to the cause: then, in the simplest kind of case, we trace the connection from the cause to effect only by tracking from the earlier to the later happening. The order of causes presupposes the order of body identifications that is definitive upon the relation of earlier and later. In more complicated transactions, where several bodies interact, some coalescing while others separate, it remains necessary to establish conditions of body identity; only now we may presuppose staged and staggered sequences of successful identifications. These transactions can always be regarded as processes, and the definition of the process presupposes a sequence of body identifications, which also defines a (partial) order of earlier and later. My conclusion is that we cannot trace a process from cause to effect without being able to fix the identity of bodies or other substances from earlier positions to later ones. The priority of causes in cases of body transactions is due to the dominating requirement for the temporal identification of bodies.

Prior effects are only incidental to the train of identifications by which the nexus is bound. Why the exceptions? In every such case I can think of, we suppose that the identification proceeded from an unobserved earlier cause that trenched more decisively into the later observed cause than to the intermediate observed effect. It is of the very nature of dawn and of hurricanes to come on in continuous stages so as incidentally to envelop crowing cocks and scurrying proprietors, who find their lesser rationale only within the larger nexus of a sunrise or a storm. The connection between the bees proximity and its sting matters more than the sound: the sting ruefully recalls a warning unnoticed at the time. More generally: the pattern of causal explanation, which is spanned by earlier-to later-identifications of substances, does not disallow the after-the-fact identification of intermediate effects.

Notes

1. Almost everything I have to offer by way of interpretations of both Hume and Kant derives from conversations with Arthur Melnick, to whom I am grateful also for suggestions about doctrine and presentation. I benefited from the chance to give the paper to a colloquium of the Department of Philosophy at Urbana, and I must particularly acknowledge the comments and suggestions of Hugh Chandler, Wright Neely, and F. L. Will.

2. *Treatise*, edited by Selby-Bigge, e.g. pp. 75 and 161, and *Principles*, e.g. sec. 25, 64f. I use the *Treatise* as my main text for Hume. I had, when drafting this paper, not even considered the more urbane but looser discussion of *causation* found at Section VII of the *First Enquiry*. Subsequent reading of that passage confirmed predictions I had made about how Hume would have argued against several opposing doctrines.

3. *Treatise*, p. 170, also p. 172. The *Enquiry* version runs as follows: ". . . we may define a cause to be *an object, followed by another, and where all the objects similar to the first and followed by objects similar to the second*. Or in other words *where, if the first object had not been, the second never had existed*. The appearance of a cause always conveys the mind by a customary transition, to the idea of the effect. Of this also we have experience. We may, therefore suitably to this experience, form another definition of cause, and call it, *an object followed by another, and whose appearance always conveys the thought to that other*." (Selby-Bigge ed., pp. 76f.) This statement is notable, not only for the breathtaking addition of "other words", but also both for the conspicuous absence of any mention of *contiguity* and (despite the "other words") for favoring inferences from causes to effects over the equally likely inferences from effects to causes.

4. Kant seems to have had similar thoughts; but, as we shall see, *his* category of causation may cover nothing more than phenomenal identity, upon which (I believe) our sense of temporal succession is indeed based.

An intimation of the opinion that our sense of time depends upon our sense of cause is found in #32 of Reichenbach's book *The Philosophy of Space and Time* (New York, 1958). The Lorentz Transformations, according to this argument, allow us to interchange the order of time for events outside the "cone" of a reference event. Such an interchange could be represented by an appropriate "rotation" of space-time coordinates. If two frames were in fact moving at a relative velocity greater than the speed of light, then either would receive a signal originating in the other at a time earlier than its emission. But in fact we find no such thing. Reichenbach held that we would not treat this as having genuine physical significance unless we allowed that the speed of the signal, which fixes the "cone", is causally determinant upon the temporal order. One must wonder how anyone could get into position to observe supposed causal relationships wihtout a well-entrenched sense of time.

5. Hume went on about this at great length in the *Enquiry*, pp. 64-75; I suspect that someone must have put a bug in his ear. Mackie subscribed to the opposed opinion, e.g., at pp. 56, 170f of *The Cement of the Universe* (Oxford, 1974).

6. See those notorious "other words" of the *Enquiry* passage quoted in n.3. Better, though, that he had tied these words to "customary transition" rather than to constant conjunction.

7. Davidson, "Causal Relations," *Journal of Philosophy* 64 (1967):691-703; Anscombe, "Causality and Extensionality," *Journal of Philosophy* 66 (1969):152-59; Beardsley, "Actions and Events: The Problem of Individuation," *Amer. Phils. Quart.* 12 (1975):263-76; Føllesdal, "Quantification into Causal Contexts," *Boston Studies in the Philosophy of Science*, v. II. Fred I. Dretske's "Referring to Events," *Midwest Studies in Philosophy* II, 90-99, which I reread together with Jaegwon Kim's following remarks after this paper was done, reminds me of how heavily trod the path has been for many years now. I would convert Dretske's argument, by a simple application of *modus tollens*, into collateral support for my own conclusion that ". . . causes – – –" is "opaque."

8. "The Temporal Order," *Philos. Quart.* 7 (1957):32-43, and in recent unpublished work.

Conflicting Intuitions about Causality[1]

PATRICK SUPPES

In this article I examine five kinds of conflicting intuitions about the nature of causality. The viewpoint is that of a probabilistic theory of causality, which I think is the right general framework for examining causal questions. It is not the purpose of this article to defend the general thesis in any depth but many of the particular points I make are meant to offer new lines of defense of such a probabilistic theory. To provide a conceptual framework for the analysis, I review briefly the more systematic aspects of the sort of probabilistic theory of causality I advocate. I first define the three notions of prima facie cause, spurious cause, and genuine cause. The technical details are worked out in an earlier monograph (Suppes 1970) and are not repeated.

> Definition 1. *An event B is a prima facie cause of an event A if and only if (i) B occurs earlier than A, and (ii) the conditional probability of A occurring when B occurs is greater than the unconditional probability of A occurring.*

Here is a simple example of the application of Definition 1 to the study of the efficacy of inoculation against cholera (Greenwood & Yule 1915, cited in Kendall & Stuart 1961). I also discussed this example in my 1970 monograph. The data from the 818 cases studied are given in the accompanying tabulation.

	Not attacked	*Attacked*	*Totals*
Inoculated	276	3	279
Not inoculated	473	66	539
Totals	749	69	818

The data clearly show the prima facie efficacy of inoculation, for the mean probability of not being attacked is 749/818 = 0.912, whereas the conditional probability of not being attacked, given that an individual was inoculated, is 276/279 = 0.989.

Here A is the event of not being attacked by cholera and B the event of being inoculated.

In many areas of active scientific investigation the probabilistic data are not so clear-cut, although they may be scientifically and statistically significant. I have selected one example concerning vitamin A intake and lung cancer to illustrate the point. The results are taken from Bjelke (1975). The sample of Norwegian males 45-75 years of age was drawn from the general population of Norway but included a special roster of men who had siblings that had migrated to the United States. In 1964, the sample reported their cigarette smoking habits. More than 90 percent of those surviving in 1967 completed a dietary questionnaire sufficiently detailed to permit an estimate of vitamin A intake. On January 1, 1968, of the original sample, 8,278 were alive. Their records were computer-matched against the records of the Cancer Registry of Norway as of March 1, 1973.

The sample was classified into two groups according to an index of vitamin A intake as inferred from the dietary questionnaire, with 2,642 classified as having low intake and 5,636 as not low—I am ignoring in this recapitulation many details about this index. There were for the sample, as of March 1, 1973, 19 proven cases of carcinomas other than adenocarcinomas, which we ignore for reasons too detailed to go into here. Of the 19 proven cases, 14, i.e., 74 percent occurred among the 32 percent of the sample—the 2,642, who had a low intake of vitamin A. Only 5 cases, i.e., 26 percent, occurred among the 68 percent of the sample who had a high intake of vitamin A. Let C be the event of having a lung carcinoma and let L be low intake of vitamin A. Then for the sample in question

$$P(C) = .0023 < P(C|L) = .0053.$$

Using Definition 1 we infer that low intake of vitamin A is a prima facie cause of lung cancer. The probabilities in question are small but the results suggest further scientific investigation of the proposition that high intake of vitamin A may help prevent lung cancer.

It is now widely accepted that cigarette smoking causes lung cancer, but as the present data show, the incidence of lung cancer in the general population is so small that it is a primary medical puzzle to explain why so few smokers do get lung cancer. This study is meant to be a contribution to solving this puzzle.

An important feature of this study is that the results are fragile enough to warrant much further investigation before any practical conclusion is drawn—such as the admonition to heavy smokers to eat lots of carrots. In my view, perhaps a majority of scientific studies of causal connections have a similar tentative character. It is mainly science far from the frontiers, much worked over and highly selected, that has clear and decisive results.

A common argument of those who oppose a probabilistic analysis of causality is to claim that it is not possible to distinguish genuine prima facie causes from spurious ones. This view is mistaken. Because in my sense spuriousness and genuineness are opposites, it will be sufficient to define spurious causes, and then to characterize *genuine* causes as prima facie causes that are not spurious.

For the definition of spurious causes, I introduce the concept of a partition at a given time of the possible space of events. A partition is just a collection of incompatible and exhaustive events. In the case where we have an explicit sample space, it is a collection of pairwise disjoint, nonempty sets whose union is the whole space. The intuitive idea is that a prima facie cause is spurious if there exists an earlier partition of events such that no matter which event of the partition occurs the joint occurrence of B and the element of the partition yields the same conditional probability for the event A as does the occurrence of the element of the partition alone. To repeat this idea in slightly different language, we have:

Definition 2. *An event B is a spurious cause of A if and only if B is a prima facie cause of A, and there is a partition of events earlier than B such that the conditional probability of A, given B and any element of the partition, is the same as the conditional probability of A, given just the element of the partition.*

The history of human folly is replete with belief in spurious causes. One of the most enduring is the belief in astrology. The better ancient defenses of astrology begin on sound empirical grounds, but they quickly wander into extrapolations that are unwarranted and that would provide upon deeper investigation excellent examples of spurious causes. Ptolemy's treatise on astrology, *Tetrabiblos*, begins with a sensible discussion of how the seasons, the weather, and the tides are influenced by the motions of the sun and the moon. But he then moves rapidly to the examination of what may be determined about the temperament and fortunes of a given individual. He proceeds to give genuinely fantastic explanations of the cultural characteristics of entire nations on the basis of their relation to the stars. Consider, for example, this passage:

Of these same countries Britain, (Transalpine) Gaul, Germany, and Bastarnia are in closer familiarity with Aries and Mars. Therefore for the most part their inhabitants are fiercer, more headstrong, and bestial. But Italy, Apulia, (Cisalpine) Gaul, and Sicily have their familiarity with Leo and the sun; wherefore these peoples are more masterful, benevolent, and co-operative (63, Loeb edition).

Ptolemy is not an isolated example. It is worth remembering that Kepler was court astrologer in Prague, and Newton wrote more about theology than physics. In historical perspective, their fantasies about spurious causes are easy enough to perceive. It is a different matter when we ask ourselves about future attitudes toward such beliefs current in our own time.

The concept of causality has so many different kinds of applications and is at the same time such a universal part of the apparatus we use to analyze both scientific and ordinary experience that it is not surprising to have a variety of conflicting intuitions about its nature. I examine five examples of such conflict, but the list is in no sense inclusive. It would be easy to generate another dozen just from the literature of the last ten years.

1. SIMPSON'S PARADOX

Simpson (1951) showed that probability relationships of the kind exemplified by Definition 1 for prima facie causes can be reversed when a finer analysis of the data is considered. From the standpoint of the framework of this article, this is just a procedure for showing that a prima facie cause is a spurious cause, at least in the cases where the time ordering follows the definitions given. In Simpson's discussion of these matters and in the related literature, there has not been an explicit attention to temporal order, and I shall ignore it in my comments on the 'paradox'. There is an intuitively clear and much discussed example of sex bias in graduate admissions at Berkeley (Bickel, Hammel, & O'Connell 1975). When data from the university as a whole were considered, there seemed to be good evidence that being male was a prima facie cause for being admitted to graduate school. In other words, there was a positive bias toward the admission of males and a negative bias toward the admission of females. On the other hand, when the data were examined department by department it turned out that a majority of the departments did not show such a bias and in fact had a very weak bias toward female admission. The conflict in the data arose from the large number of female applications to departments that had a large number of rejections independent of the sex of the applicant. As is clear from this example, there is no genuine paradox in the problem posed by Simpson. There is nothing inconsistent, or in fact even close to inconsistent, in the results described, which are characteristic of the phenomenon.

Cartwright (1979) proposes to meet the Simpson problem by imposing further conditions on the concept of one event being a cause of another. In particular, she wants to require that the increase in probability characteristic of prima facie causes defined above is considered only in situations that are "otherwise causally homogeneous with respect to" the effect. I am skeptical that we can know when situations are causally homogeneous. In the kind of example considered earlier concerning high intake of vitamin A being a potential inhibitor of lung cancer, it is certainly not possible to know or even to consider causally homogeneous situations. This is true of most applications of causal notions in nonexperimental settings and even in many experimental situations. I am also skeptical at a conceptual or philosophical level that we have any well-defined notion of homogeneity. Consider, for example, the data from Berkeley just described. There is no reason that we could not also pursue additional hypotheses. We might want to look at partial data from each department where the data were restricted just to the borderline cases. We might test the hypothesis that the female applicants were more able than the males but that at the borderline there was bias against the females. So far as I know, such a more refined analysis of the data has not been performed but there is no reason conceptually that we might not find something by entertaining such additional questions. My point is that there is no end to the analysis of data in a practical sense. We can, of course, exhaust finite data theoretically by considering all possible combinations, but this is only of mathematical significance.

A conflict of intuition can arise as to when to stop the refinement of data analysis. From a practical standpoint, many professional situations require detailed rules about such matters. The most obvious example is in the definition of classes for actuarial tables. What should be the variables relevant to fixing the rates on insurance policies? I have in mind here not only life insurance but also automobile insurance, property insurance, etc. I see a conflict at the most fundamental level between those who think there is some ultimate stopping point that can be determined in the analysis and those who do not.

There is another point to be mentioned about the Simpson problem. It is that if we can look at the data after they have been collected and if the probabilities in question are neither zero nor one, it is then easy to define artificially events that render any prima facie cause spurious. Of course, in ordinary statistical methodology it would be regarded as a scandal to construct such an event after looking at the data, but from a scientific standpoint the matter is not so simple. Certainly, looking at data that do not fit desired hypotheses or favorite theories is one of the best ways to get ideas about new hypotheses or new theories. But without further investigation we do not take seriously the ex post facto artificial construction of concepts. What is needed is another experiment or another set of data to determine whether the hypotheses in question are of serious interest. There is, however, another point to be made about such artificial concepts constructed solely by looking at the data and counting the outcomes. It is that somehow we need to exclude such concepts to avoid the undesirable outcome of every prima facie cause being spurious, at least every naturally hypothesized prima facie cause. One way to do this of course is to characterize the notion of genuine cause relative to a given set of concepts that may be used to define events considered as causes. Such an emendation and explicit restriction on the definition given above of genuine cause seems appropriate.[2]

2. MACROSCOPIC DETERMINISM

Even if one accepts the general argument that there is randomness in nature at the microscopic level, there continues to be a line of thought that in analysis of causality in ordinary experience it is useful and, in fact, in some cases almost mandatory to assume determinism. I will not try to summarize all the literature here but will concentrate on the arguments given in Hesslow (1976, 1981), which attempt to give a deep-running argument against probabilistic causality, not just my particular version of it. (In addition to these articles of Hesslow, the reader is also referred to Rosen [1978] and for a particularly thorough critique of deterministic causality, Rosen [1982].)

As a formulation of determinism that avoids the global character of Laplace's, both Hesslow and Rosen cite Anscombe's (1975, p. 63) principle of relevant difference, "If an effect occurs in one case and a similar effect does not occur in an apparently similar case, then there must be a relevant further difference." Although statistical or probabilistic techniques are employed in testing hypotheses in the biological and social sciences, Hesslow claims that "there is nothing that shows that these hypotheses *themselves* are probabilistic in nature. In fact one can argue that the opposite is true, for statistics are commonly used in a way that presupposes determinism, namely, in various kinds of eliminative arguments."

Hesslow's intuitions here are very different from mine, so there is a basic conflict that could best be resolved by extensive review of the biological, medical, and social science literature. I shall not attempt that here but state what I think is wrong with one of Hesslow's ideal examples. He says that these kinds of eliminative arguments all have a simple structure. He takes the case of Jones, who had a fatal disease but was given a newly discovered medicine and recovered. We conclude, he says, that the cause of his recovery was M, the event of taking medicine. Now he says at the beginning that Jones had a "universally fatal disease." The first thing to challenge is the use of the adverb *universally*. This is not true of all the diseases of interest. Almost no diseases that are the subject for analysis and study by doctors are universally fatal. It is a familiar fact that when medicine is given we certainly like to attribute the recovery to medicine. But ordinarily the evidence is not overwhelming, because in the case of almost all diseases there is evidence of recovery of individuals who were not treated by the medicine. This is true of all kinds of diseases, from the plague to pneumonia. In making this statement, I am certainly not asserting that medicine is not without efficacy but only that Hesslow's claim is far too simple. The actual data do not support what he says.

Hesslow's claim that this is a case of determinism is puzzling because in his own explicit formulation of the argument he says, "Thus, (probably) M caused R," where R is the event of recovery. He himself explicitly introduces the caveat of probability. What he states is that "because something caused the recovery and, other causes apparently being scarce, M is the most likely candidate." Determinism comes in the use of *something*, but the conclusion he draws is probabilistic in character and could just as well have been drawn if he had started with the view that in most cases an identifiable agent caused the recovery but that in the remaining cases the recovery was spontaneous. Moreover, I would claim that there is no powerful argument for the determinism of the kind Hesslow was trying to give. One could look from one end of the medical literature to the other and simply not find the kind of need for the premises he talks about.

There is a point to be clear about on this matter. Because one is not endorsing determinism as a necessary way of life for biological and social scientists, it does not mean that the first identification of a probabilistic cause brings a scientific investigation of a given phenomenon to an end. It is a difficult and delicate matter to determine when no further causes can be identified. I am not offering any algorithms for making this determination. I am just making a strong claim that we do get along in practice with probabilistic results and we do not fill them out in an interesting deterministic fashion.

3. TYPES AND TOKENS

There are a host of conflicting intuitions about whether causality should mainly be discussed in terms of event types or event tokens, and also how the two levels are related. I restrict myself here to two issues, both of which are fundamental. One is whether cases of individual causation must inevitably be subsumable under general laws. The second is whether we can make inferences about individual causes when the general laws are merely probabilistic.

A good review of the first issue on subsumption of individual causal relations under general laws is given by Rosen (1982), and I shall not try to duplicate her excellent discussion of the many different views on this matter. Certainly, nowadays probably no one asserts the strong position that if a person holds that a singular causal statement is true then the person must hold that a certain appropriate covering law is true. One way out, perhaps most ably defended by Horgan (1980), is to admit that direct covering laws are not possible but that there are at work underneath precise laws, formulated in terms of precise properties that do give us the appropriate account in terms of general laws. But execution of this program certainly is at present, and in my own view will forever be, at best a pious hope. In many cases we shall not be able to supply the desired analysis.

There is a kind of psychological investigation that would throw interesting light on actual beliefs about these matters. Epistemological or philosophical arguments of the kind given by Horgan do not seem to me to be supportable. It would be enlightening to know if most people believe that there is such an underlying theory of events and if somehow it gives them comfort to believe that such a theory exists. The second and more particular psychological investigation would deal with the kinds of beliefs individuals hold and the responses they give to questions about individual causation. Is there a general tendency to subsume our causal accounts of individual events under proto-covering laws? It should be evident what I am saying about this first issue. The defense that there are laws either of a covering or a foundational nature cannot be defended on philosophical grounds, but it would be useful to transform the issue into a number of psychological questions as to what people actually do believe.

The second issue is in a way more surprising. It has mainly been emphasized by Hesslow. It is the claim that inferences from generic statistical relations to individual causal relations are necessarily invalid. Thus, he concludes that "if all generic causal relations are statistical, then we must either accept invalid inferences or refrain from talking about individual causation at all" (1981, 598). It seems to me that this line of argument is definitely mistaken and I would like to try to say why as clearly as I can. First of all, I agree that one does not make a logically or a mathematically valid argument from generic statistical relations to individual causal relations. It is in the nature of probability theory and its applications that the inference from the general to the particular is not in itself a mathematically valid inference. The absence of such validity, however, in no way prohibits using generic causal relations that are clearly statistical in character to make inferences about individual causation. It is just that those inferences are not mathematically valid inferences— they are inferences made in the context of probability and uncertainty. I mention as an aside that there is a large literature by advocates of a relative frequency theory of probability about how to make inferences from relative frequencies to single cases. Since I come closer to being a Bayesian than a relative frequentist, I shall not review these arguments, but many of the discussions are relevant in arguing from a different viewpoint than mine about Hesslow's claims.

First, though, let me distinguish sharply between the generic relations and the individual relations and what I think is the appropriate terminology for making this distinction. The language I prefer is that the generic relations are average or mean relations. The individual relations at their fullest and best depend upon individual sample paths known in great detail. An individual sample path is the continuous temporal and spatial path of development of an individual's history. There is in this history ordinarily a great deal of information not available in simple mean data. I can say briefly and simply what the expected or mean life span is of an adult male who is now forty-five years old and is living in the United States, but if I consider some single individual and examine him in terms of his past history, his ancestors, his current state of health, his employment, etc., I may come to a very different view of his expected number of remaining years. Certainly it would be ludicrous to think that there is a logically valid inference from the mean data to the individual data.

But for a Bayesian or near Bayesian like myself, the matter has a rather straightforward solution. First of all, probabilities as matters of belief are directly given to individual events and their individual relationships. Second, by the standard theorem on total probability, when I say that a given individual has an expected lifetime of twenty years, I have already taken account of all the knowledge that I have about him. Of course, if I learn something new, the probability can change, just on the basis of the theorem on total probability. Now the central point is that ordinarily much of what I know about individuals is based upon generic causal relations. I simply do not know enough to go very much beyond generic relations, and thus my probabilistic estimate of an individual's expected remaining lifetime will very much depend on a few generic causal relations and not much else. The absence of logical validity in relating the generic in the individual in no way keeps me from talking about individual causation, contrary to Hesslow's claim. In fact, I would say that what I have said is just the right account of how we do talk about individual causation in the cases where we know something about generic probabilistic causal relations. We know, for example, that heavy clouds are a good sign of rain, and when accompanied by a drop in atmospheric pressure an even better sign. We know that these two conditions alone will not cause rain with probability one, but there is a strong probabilistic causal relation. We go on to say, well, rain is likely sometime this afternoon. We are quite happy with our causal views of the matter based on a couple of generic causal relations. Intimate details of the kind available to meteorologists with the professional responsibility to predict the weather are not available, let us say, in the instance being discussed. The meteorologist faced with a similar problem uses a much more complex theory of generic relations in order finally to issue his prediction for the afternoon. It is also important to note, of course, that on the kind of Bayesian view I am describing here there is no algorithm or simple calculus for passing by probability from generic causal relationships to individual ones, even for the trained meteorologist. It is a matter of judgment as to how the knowledge one has is used and assessed. The use of the theorem on total probability mentioned above depends on both conditional and unconditional probabilities, which in general depend on judgment. In the case where there is very fine scientific knowledge of the laws in question it might be on occasion that the conditional probabilities are known from extensive scientific experimentation, but then another aspect of the problem related to the application to the individual event will not be known from such scientific experimentation except in very unusual cases, and judgment will enter necessarily.

4. PHYSICAL FLOW OF CAUSES

In his excellent review article on probabilistic causality, Salmon (1980) puts his finger on one of the most important conflicting intuitions about causality. The derivations of the fundamental differential equations of classical physics give in most cases a very satisfying physical analysis of the flow of causes in a system, but there is no mention of probability. It is characteristic of the areas in which probabilistic analysis is used to a very large extent that a detailed theory of the phenomena in question is missing. The examples from medicine given earlier are typical. We may have some general ideas about how a vaccine works or about the mechanisms for absorbing vitamin A, but we do not have anything like an adequate detailed theory of these matters. We are presently very far from being able to make any kind of detailed theoretical predictions derived from fundamental assumptions about molecular structure, for example. Concerning these or related questions we have a very poor understanding in comparison with the kinds of models successful in various parts of classical physics about the detailed flow of causes. I think Salmon is quite right in pointing out that the absence of being able to give such an analysis is the source of the air of paradox of some of the counterexamples that have been given. The core argument is to challenge the claim that the occurrence of a cause should increase the probability of the occurrence of its effect.

Salmon uses as a good example of this phenomenon the hypothetical case made up by Deborah Rosen and reported in my 1970 monograph. A golfer makes a birdie by hitting a limb of a tree at just the right angle, not certainly something that he planned to do. The disturbing aspect is that if we estimated the probability of his making a birdie prior to his making the shot and we added the condition that the ball hit the branch, we would ordinarily estimate the probability as being definitely lower than that he would have made a birdie without this given condition. On the other hand, when we see the event happen we have an immediate physical recognition that the exact angle that he hit the branch played a crucial role in the ball's going into the cup. In my 1970 discussion of this example, I did not take sufficient account of the conflict of intuition between the general probabilistic view and the highly structured physical view. I now think it is important to do so and I very much agree with Salmon that the issues here are central to a general acceptability of a probabilistic theory of causality. I therefore want to make a revised response.

There are at least three different kinds of cases in which what seem for other reasons to be prima facie causes in fact turn out to be negative causes, i.e., the conditional probability of the effect's occurring is lowered given the cause. One sort of case involves situations in which we know a great deal about the classical physics. A second kind of case is where an artificial example can be constructed and we may want to make claims about observing a causal chain. Salmon gives a succinct and useful example of this kind, which I discuss. Third, there are the cases in which we attribute without any grounds some surprising event as a cause of some significant effect. In certain respects the ancient predilection for omens falls under this category, but I shall not expand upon this view further.

In the first kind of case there is a natural description of the event after the fact that makes everything come out right. Using the golf ball example as typical, we now describe the event as that of the golf ball's hitting the branch at exactly the right angle to fall into the cup. Given such a description we would of course make the conditional probability close to one, but it is only after the fact that we could describe the event in this fashion. On the other hand, it is certainly too general to expect much to come out of the event described simply as the golf ball's hitting the limb of the tree. It is not really feasible to aim before the event at a detailed description of the event adequate to make a good physical prediction. We will not be given the values of parameters sufficiently precisely to predict that the golf ball will hit the limb of the tree at an angle just right for bouncing into the cup. Consequently, in such cases we cannot hope to predict the effects of such surprising causes, but based upon physical theories that are accurate to a high degree of approximation we understand that this is what happened after we have observed the sequence of events. Another way of putting the matter is that there is a whole range of cases in which we do not have much hope of applying in an interesting scientific or commonsense way probabilistic analysis, because the causes will be surprising. Even in cases of extraordinary conceptual simplicity, e.g., the N-body problem with only forces of gravitation acting between the bodies, extended prediction of behavior for any length of time is not in general possible. Thus, although a Bayesian in such matters, I confess to being unable to make good probabilistic causal analyses of many kinds of individual events. In the same fashion, I cannot apply to such events, in advance of their happening, detailed physical theories. The possibilities of application in both cases seem hopeless as a matter of prediction. This may not be the way we want the world to be but this is the way it is.

Salmon also gives an example that has a much simpler physical description than the golf ball example. It involves the eight ball and the cue ball on a pool table with the player having a 50-50 chance of sinking the eight ball with the cue ball when he tries. Moreover, the eight ball goes into the corner pocket, as Salmon says, "if and almost only if his cue ball goes into the other far corner pocket." Let event A be the player's attempting the shot, B the dropping of the eight ball in the corner pocket, and C the dropping of the cue ball into the other corner pocket. Under the hypotheses given, B is a prima facie cause of C, and Salmon is concerned about the fact that A does not screen B off from C, i.e., render B a spurious cause of C. Salmon expresses his concern by saying that we should have appropriate causal relations among A, B, and C without having to enter into more detailed physical theory. But it seems to me that this example illustrates a very widespread phenomenon. The physical analysis, which we regard as correct, namely, the genuine cause of C, i.e., the cue ball going into the pocket, is in terms of the impact forces and the direction of motion of the cue ball at the time of impact. We certainly believe that such specification can give us a detailed and correct account of the cue ball's motion. On the other hand, there is an important feature of this detailed physical analysis. We must engage in meticulous investigations; we are not able to make in a commonsense way the appropriate observations of these earlier events of motion and impact. In contrast, the events A, B, and C are obvious and directly observable. I do not find it surprising that we must go beyond these three events for a proper causal account, and yet at the same time we are not able to do so by the use of obvious commonsense events. Aristotle would not have had such an explanation, from all that we know about his physics. Why should we expect it of untutored common sense?

The second class of example, of which Salmon furnishes a very good instance, is when we know only probability transitions. The example he considers concerns an atom in an excited state. In particular, it is in the fourth energy level. The probability is one that it will necessarily decay to the zeroeth level, i.e., the ground state. The only question is whether the transitions will be through all the intermediate states three, two, and one, or whether some states will be jumped over. The probability of going directly from the fourth to the third state is 3/4 and from the fourth to the second state is 1/4. The probability of going from the third state to the first state is 3/4 and from the third state to the ground state 1/4. Finally, the probability of going from the second state to the first state is 1/4 and from the second state directly to the ground state 3/4. It is required also, of course, that the probability of going from the first state to the ground state is one. The paradox arises because of the fact that if a decaying atom occupies the second state in the process of decay, then the probability of its occupying the first state is 1/4, but the mean probability whatever the route taken of occupying the first state is the much higher probability of 10/16. Thus, on the probabilistic definitions given earlier of prima facie causes, occupying the second state is a negative prima facie cause of occupying the first state.

On the other hand, as Salmon emphasizes, after the events occur of the atom going from the fourth to the second to the first state, many would say that this sequence constitutes a causal chain. My own answer to this class of examples is to meet the problem head-on and to deny that we want to call such sequences causal sequences. If all we know about the process is just the transition probabilities given, then occupancy of the second state remains a negative prima facie cause of occupying the first state. The fact of the actual sequence does not change this characterization. In my own constructive work on causality, I have not given a formal definition of causal chains, and for good reason. I think it is difficult to decide which of various conflicting intuitions should govern the definition.

We may also examine how our view of this example might change if the probabilities were made more extreme, i.e., if the mean probability of occupying the first energy state comes close to one and the probability of a transition from the second to the first state is close to zero. In such cases when we observe the sequence of transitions from the fourth to the second to the first state, we might be inclined to say that the atom decayed to the first state in spite of occupying the second state. By using such phrases as *in spite of* we indicate our skepticism that what we have observed is a genuine causal chain.

5. COMMON CAUSES

It was a virtue of Reichenbach to have recognized that a natural principle of causality is to expect events that are simultaneous, spatially separated, and strongly correlated, to depend upon some common cause to generate the correlation. There are a variety of controversial questions about the principle of common cause, and the source of the controversy is the absence of clear and widely accepted intuitions about what we should expect of such causes. Should we expect such causes to exist? Thus, when we observe phenomenologically simultaneous events strongly correlated, should we always be able to find a common cause that eliminates this phenomenological correlation in the sense that, when we condition on the common cause, the new conditional correlation is zero? Another question concerns the determinism of common causes. Ought we to expect such causes to be deterministic, or can we find common causes that are strictly probabilistic? In a recent essay, Van Fraassen (1982) expresses the view that the causes must be deterministic in the following way.

> But a belief in the principle of the common cause implies a belief that there is in the relevant cases not merely a compatibility (so that deterministic hidden variables could be introduced into models for the theory) but that all those hidden events which are the common causes, are real, and therefore, that the world is really deterministic (208).

Salmon (1982) in his reply to Van Fraassen suggests that the principle of common cause is sometimes used as an explanatory principle and sometimes as a principle of inference. Also he implicitly suggests a third and different use as a maxim of rationality, which is a use also considered by Van Fraassen. The maxim is: search for a common cause whenever feasible to explain simultaneous events that are strongly correlated. Using the principle as a maxim does not guarantee any explanations nor any inferences but can be important in the strategy of research. The dialogue between Salmon and Van Fraassen in the two articles mentioned contains a number of useful points about common causes, but rather than consider in detail their examples, counterexamples, arguments, and counterarguments to each other, I want to suggest what I think is a reasonable view of the principle of common cause. In doing so I shall avoid references to quantum mechanics except in one instance. I shall also generalize the discussion to more than two events, because in many scientific applications it is not adequate to consider the correlations of only two events.

First let me say more explicitly what I shall mean by common cause. The exposition here will be rather sketchy. The technical details of many of the points made are given in the Appendix.

Let A and B be events that are approximately simultaneous and let

$$P(AB) \neq P(A)P(B);$$

i.e., A and B are not independent but correlated. Then the event C is a *common cause* of A and B if

(i) C occurs earlier than A and B;
(ii) $P(AB|C) = P(A|C)P(B|C)$;
(iii) $P(AB|\bar{C}) = P(A|\bar{C})P(B|\bar{C})$.

In other words, C renders A and B conditionally independent, and so does $\bar{C}$, the complement of C. When the correlation between A and B is positive, i.e., when

$$P(AB) > P(A)P(B),$$

we may also want to require:

(iv) C is a prima facie cause of A and of B.

I shall not assume (iv) in what follows. I state in informal language a number of propositions that are meant to clarify some of the controversy about common causes. The first two propositions follow from a theorem about common causes proved in Suppes and Zanotti (1981).

> Proposition I. *Let events A_1, A_2, . . . , A_n be given with any two of the events correlated. Then a necessary and sufficient condition for it to be possible to construct a common cause of these events is that the events A_1, A_2, . . . , A_n have a joint probability distribution compatible with the given pairwise correlations.*

An important point to emphasize about this proposition is its generality and at the same time its weakness. There are no restrictions placed on the nature of the common causes. Once any sorts of restrictions of a physical or other empirical kind are imposed, then the common cause might not exist. If we simply want to know whether a common cause can be found as a matter of principle as an underlying cause of the observed correlations between events, then the answer is not one that has been much discussed in the literature. All that is required is the existence of a joint probability distribution of the phenomenological variables. It is obvious that if the candidates for common causes are restricted in advance, then it is a simple matter to give artificial examples that show that among possible causes given in advance no common cause can be found. The ease with which such artificial examples are constructed makes it obvious that the same holds true in significant scientific investigations. When the possible causes of diseases are restricted, for example, it is often difficult for physicians to be able to find a common cause among the given set of candidates.

> Proposition II. *The common cause of Proposition I can always be constructed so as to be deterministic.*

Again, without restriction, determinism is always open to us. On the other hand, it is easy to impose some natural principles of symmetry that exclude deterministic causes when the correlations are strictly probabilistic, i.e., the correlations between the events at the phenomenological level are not themselves deterministic. Explicit formulations of these principles of symmetry are given in the Appendix.

> Proposition III. *Conditions of symmetry can easily be found such that strictly probabilistic correlations between phenomenologically observed events have as a common cause one that is strictly probabilistic.*

This last proposition is special in nature, of course. It refers to principles of symmetry discussed in the Appendix. The conditions are sufficient but not necessary. It would be desirable to find significant necessary and sufficient conditions that require the common cause to be probabilistic rather than deterministic in character.

Finally, I state one application to quantum mechanics.

> Proposition IV. *There are correlated phenomenological data that cannot have a common cause that is theoretically consistent with quantum mechanics, because there can be no joint probability distribution of the data, as described in Proposition I.*

APPENDIX ON COMMON CAUSES

In this Appendix I present a number of theorems about inferences from phenomenological correlations to common causes. In the framework of quantum mechanics, the theorems are mainly theorems about hidden variables. Most of the proofs will not be given, but references will be cited where they may be found. The content of this Appendix follows closely the first part of Suppes and Zanotti (1984).

To emphasize conceptual matters and to keep technical simplicity in the forefront, I consider only two-valued random variables taking the values ± 1. We shall also assume symmetry for these random variables in that their expectations will be zero and thus they will each have a positive variance of one. For emphasis we state:

> GENERAL ASSUMPTION. *The phenomenological random variables X_1, . . . , X_N have possible values ± 1, with means $E(X_i) = 0$, $1 \leqslant i \leqslant N$.*

We also use the notion X, Y and Z for phenomenological random variables. We use the notation $E(XY)$ for covariance, which for these symmetric random variables is also the same as their correlation $\rho(X,Y)$.

The basic meaning of *common cause* that we shall assume is that when two random variables, say X and Y, are given, then in order for a hidden variable λ to be labeled a common cause, it must render the random variables conditionally independent, that is,

(1) $$E(XY|\lambda) = E(X|\lambda)E(Y|\lambda).$$

Two Deterministic Theorems

We begin with a theorem asserting a deterministic result. It says that if two random variables have a strictly negative correlation, then any cause in the sense of (1) must be deterministic, that is, the conditional variances of the two random variables, given the hidden variable λ, must be zero. We use the notation $\sigma(X|\lambda)$ for the conditional standard deviation of X given λ, and its square is, of course, the conditional variance.

THEOREM 1   (Suppes and Zanotti, 1976). *If*
$(i)\ E(XY|\lambda) = E(X|\lambda)E(Y|\lambda)$
$(ii)\ \rho(X,Y) = -1$
then
$$\sigma(X|\lambda) = \sigma(Y|\lambda) = 0.$$

The second theorem asserts that the only thing required to have a common cause for N random variables is that they have a joint probability distribution. This theorem is conceptually important in relation to the long history of hidden variable theorems in quantum mechanics. For example, in the original proof of Bell's inequalities, Bell (1964) assumed a causal hidden variable in the sense of (1) and derived from this assumption his inequalities. What Theorem 2 shows is that the assumption of a hidden variable is not necessary in such discussions—it is sufficient to remain at the phenomenological level. Once we know that there exists a joint probability distribution then there must be a causal hidden variable, and in fact this hidden variable may be constructed so as to be deterministic.

THEOREM 2   (Suppes and Zanotti, 1981). *Given phenomenological random variables* $X_1, \ldots, X_N$, *then there exists a hidden variable* λ, *a common cause such that*
$$E(X_1, \ldots, X_N|\lambda) = E(X_1|\lambda) \ldots E(X_N|\lambda)$$
if and only if there exists a joint probability distribution of $X_1, \ldots, X_N$. *Moreover,* λ *may be constructed as a deterministic cause, i.e., for* $1 \leqslant i \leqslant N$
$$\sigma(X_i|\lambda) = 0.$$

Exchangeability

We now turn to imposing some natural symmetry conditions both at a phenomenological and at a theoretical level. The main principle of symmetry we shall use is that of exchangeability. Two random variables X and Y of the class we are studying are said to be exchangeable if the following probabilistic equality is satisfied.

(2) $P(X = 1, Y = -1) = P(X = -1, Y = 1).$

The first theorem we state shows that if two random variables are exchangeable at the phenomenological level then there exists a hidden causal variable satisfying the additional restriction that they have the same conditional expectation if and only if their correlation is not negative.

THEOREM 3 (Suppes and Zanotti, 1980). *If X and Y are exchangeable, then there exists a hidden variable* λ *such that*

(i) λ *is a common cause of X and Y,*

(ii) $E(X|\lambda) = E(Y|\lambda)$

if and only if

$$\rho(X,Y) \geq 0.$$

There are several remarks to be made about this theorem. First, the phenomenological principle of symmetry, namely, the principle of exchangeability, has not been used in physics as explicitly as one might expect. In the context of the kinds of experiments ordinarily used to test hidden variable theories, the requirement of phenomenological exchangeability is uncontroversial. On the other hand, the theoretical requirement of identity of conditional distributions does not have the same status. We emphasize that we refer here to the expected causal effect of λ. Obviously the actual causal effects will in general be quite different. We certainly would concede that in many physical situations this principle may be too strong. The point of our theorems about it is to show that once such a strong theoretical principle of symmetry is required then exchangeable and negatively correlated random variables cannot satisfy it.

Theorem 4 strengthens Theorem 3 to show that when the correlations are strictly between zero and one then the common cause cannot be deterministic.

THEOREM 4 (Suppes and Zanotti, 1984). *Given the conditions of Theorem 3, if* $0 < \rho(X,Y) < 1$ *then* λ *cannot be deterministic, i.e.,* $\sigma(X|\lambda)$, $\sigma(Y|\lambda) \neq 0$.

PROOF. We first observe that under the assumptions we have made:

$$\text{Min}\{P(X = 1, Y = -1), P(X = 1, Y = 1), P(X = -1, Y = -1)\} > 0.$$

Now, let Ω be the probability space on which all random variables are defined. Let $\mathfrak{a} = \{A_i\}$, $1 \leq i \leq N$ and $\mathfrak{K} = \{H_j\}$, $1 \leq j \leq M$ be two partitions of Ω. We say that $\mathfrak{K}$ *is a refinement of* $\mathfrak{a}$ *in probability* if and only if for all i's and j's we have:

$$\text{If } P(A_i \cap H_j) > 0 \text{ then } P(A_i \cap H_j) = P(H_j).$$

Now let λ be a causal random variable for X and Y in the sense of Theorem 3, and let λ have induced parition $\mathfrak{K} = \{H_j\}$, which without loss of generality may be assumed finite. Then λ is deterministic if $\mathfrak{K}$ is a refinement in probability of the partition $\mathfrak{a} = \{A_i\}$ generated by X and Y, for assume, by way of contradiction, that this is not the case. Then there must exist i and j such that $P(A_i \cap H_j) > 0$ and

$$P(A_i \cap H_j) < P(H_j),$$

but then $0 < P(A_i|H_j) < 1$.

We next show that if λ is deterministic then $E(X|\lambda) \neq E(Y|\lambda)$, which will complete the proof.

Let, as before, $\mathfrak{K} = \{H_j\}$ be the partition generated by λ. Since we know that

$$\Sigma_j P(X = 1, Y = -1, H_j) = P(X = 1, Y = -1) > 0$$

there must be an H_j such that

$$P(X = 1, Y = -1, H_j) > 0,$$

but since λ is deterministic, $\mathcal{H}$ must be a refinement of $\mathcal{C}$ and thus as already proved

$$P(X = 1, Y = -1|H_j) = 1,$$

whence

$$P(X = 1, Y = 1|H_j) = 0$$
$$P(X = -1, Y = 1|H_j) = 0$$
$$P(X = -1, Y = -1|H_j) = 0,$$

and consequently we have

(3)
$$P(X = 1|H_j) = P(Y = -1|H_j) = 1$$

$$P(X = -1|H_j) = P(Y = 1|H_j) = 0$$

Remembering that $E(X|\lambda)$ is a function of λ and thus of the partition $\mathcal{H}$, we have from (3) at once that

$$E(X|\lambda) \neq E(Y|\lambda).$$

Notes

1. This article is excerpted from chapter 3 of my *Probabilistic Metaphysics*, which is in press.

2. As Cartwright (1979) points out, it is a historical mistake to attribute Simpson's paradox to Simpson. The problem posed was already discussed in Cohen and Nagel's well-known textbook (1934), and according to Cartwright, Nagel believes that he learned about the problem from Yule's classic textbook of 1911. There has also been a substantial recent discussion of the paradox in the psychological literature (Hintzman 1980; Martin 1981).

References

Anscombe, G. E. M. 1975. "Causality and Determination." In *Causation and Conditionals*, edited by E. Sosa. London.

Bell, J. S. 1964. "On the Einstein-Podolsky-Rosen Paradox." *Physics* 1:195-200.

Bickel, P. J., E. A. Hammel and J. W. O'Connell. 1975. "Sex Bias in Graduate Admissions: Data from Berkeley." *Science* 187:398-404.

Bjelke, E. 1975. "Dietary Vitamin A and Human Lung Cancer." *International Journal of Cancer* 15:561-65.

Cartwright, N. 1979. "Causal Laws and Effective Strategies." *Nous* 13:419-37.

Cohen, M. R., and E. Nagel. 1934. *An Introduction to Logic and Scientific Method*. New York.

Greenwood, M., and G. U. Yule. 1915. "The Statistics of Anti-typhoid and Anti-cholera Inoculations, and the Interpretation of Such Statistics in General." *Proceedings of the Royal Society of Medicine* 8:113-90.

Hesslow, G.. 1976. "Two Notes on the Probabilistic Approach to Causality." *Philosophy of Science* 43:290-92.

Hesslow, G. 1981. "Causality and Determinism." *Philosophy of Science* 48:591-605.

Hintzman, D. L. 1980. "Simpson's Paradox and the Analysis of Memory Retrieval." *Psychological Review* 87:398-410.

Horgan, T. 1980. "Humean Causation and Kim's Theory of Events." *Canadian Journal of Philosophy* 10:663-79.

Kendall, M. G., and A. Stuart. 1961. *The Advanced Theory of Statistics.* Vol. 2, *Inference and Relationship.* London.

Martin, E. 1981. "Simpson's Paradox Resolved: A Reply to Hintzman." *Psychological Review* 88:372-74.

Rosen, D. 1978. "In Defence of a Probabilistic Theory of Causality." *Philosophy of Science* 45: 604-13.

Rosen, D. 1982. "A Critique of Deterministic Causality." *Philosophical Forum* 14(2):101-30.

Salmon, W. C. 1980. "Probabilistic Causality." *Pacific Philosophical Quarterly* 61:50-74.

Salmon, W. C. 1982. "Further Reflections." In *What? Where? When? Why?* edited by R. McLaughlin, 231-80. Dordrecht.

Simpson, E. H. 1951. "The Interpretation of Interaction in Contingency Tables." *Journal of the Royal Statistical Society,* Ser. B, 13:238-41.

Suppes, P. 1970. *A Probabilistic Theory of Causality.* Amsterdam.

Suppes, P., and M. Zanotti. 1976. "On the Determinism of Hidden Variable Theories with Strict Correlation and Conditional Statistical Independence of Variables." In *Logic and Probability in Quantum Mechanics,* edited by P. Suppes, 445-55. Dordrecht.

Suppes, P., and M. Zanotti. 1980. "A New Proof of the Impossibility of Hidden Variables Using the Principles of Exchangeability and Identity of Conditional Distributions." In *Studies in the Foundations of Quantum Mechanics,* edited by P. Suppes, 173-91. East Lansing, Michigan.

Suppes, P., and M. Zanotti. 1981. "When Are Probabilistic Explanations Possible?" *Synthese* 48:191-99.

Suppes, P., and M. Zanotti. 1984. Causality and Symmetry." In *The Wave-particle Dualism,* edited by S. Diner, G. Lochak, and W. Selleri, 331-40. Dordrecht.

Van Fraassen, B. C. 1982. "Rational Belief and the Common Cause Principle." In *What? Where? When? Why?* edited by R. McLaughlin, 193-209. Dordrecht.

Yule, G. U. 1911. *An Introduction to the Theory of Statistics.* London.

MIDWEST STUDIES IN PHILOSOPHY, IX (1984)

Probabilistic Causality Emancipated

JOHN DUPRÉ

INTRODUCTION

Probabilistic accounts of causality concern relations between types of events, states, or processes. Very roughly, the idea is that a cause should raise the probability of the effect; or in other words, that an instance of the type taken to be the cause should increase the probability that an instance of the effect type will occur. A very general problem with such theories is that particular cases in which these types are instantiated will certainly differ one from another. And frequently they will differ in respects that are causally relevant to the production of the effect. The problem, then, is how these causally significant variations are to be accommodated in probabilistic causal generalizations that abstract from such respects of difference.

Two such modes of causally significant variation may be distinguished. First, the cause may occur in many different contexts, and aspects of those contexts may themselves be causally relevant to the effect. Hence the probability of the effect may be influenced by more than just the occurrence of the cause. And second, the cause may affect the probability of the effect in more than one way. The cause may have various possible intermediate effects that have differing and even opposing influences on the probability of the final effect. Another way of stating this problem is to note that there may be different causal routes linking the cause to the effect.

The first of these problems has been widely recognized in formulations of probabilistic theories of causation, and an orthodox response has emerged. The second problem, while it has been noticed, has not, with one notable recent exception,[1] been much discussed. In what follows I shall briefly elaborate and illustrate these problems, and outline both the orthodox solution to the first problem and the solution that has been proposed to the second. I shall then show that there is a considerable tension, if not an outright incompatibility, between these solutions. In resolution of this dilemma, I shall attempt to motivate the rejection of the orthodox solution to the first problem. Finally, I shall suggest that this solution embodies a prejudice imported from the deterministic theories against which these probabilistic accounts were a reaction. The rejection of this prejudice is what I mean by the emancipation of probabilistic causality.

CAUSAL CONTEXTS AND CAUSAL INTERMEDIARIES

As I mentioned above, the basic idea behind probabilistic theories of causality is just that the cause should raise the probability of the effect.[2] A familiar complication arises from cases such as the following. Suppose that smoking causes heart disease, but that smoking is also highly correlated with a tendency to exercise regularly, perhaps because both this disposition and the disposition to smoke are caused by the same genetic factor. The tendency to exercise, we assume, discourages heart attacks, and to such an extent that smokers actually get fewer heart attacks than nonsmokers. It might nevertheless be true that smoking causes heart attacks. This possibility could be demonstrated if we were to partition the population into those that do, and those that do not, exercise regularly, and were then to find that in *each* of these classes the smokers were more likely to have heart attacks.

This kind of example motivates what I referred to as the orthodox solution to the problem of different contexts. The solution is a generalization of the procedure indicated at the end of the last paragraph. It is concluded that a factor is a cause only if it raises the probability of its effect in every possible context of other factors causally relevant to that effect. As this view is generally expressed, we must partition the data with respect to all possible combinations of causally relevant factors, and determine for each such partition that the cause raises the probability of the effect. Brian Skyrms[3] allows a slightly weaker condition, that in some context the cause must raise the probability of its effect, and in no context must it lower that probability. If there is some context in which the probability of the effect is lowered, then, according to Ellery Eells and Elliott Sober, "there will be no such thing as *the* causal role of smoking with respect to heart attacks in the population as a whole."[4]

The same claim is argued in more detail by Nancy Cartwright.[5] She observes that if a cause fails to raise the probability of its effect there must be a reason. Either the reason is a correlation of the kind illustrated by the previous example, or the cause should be treated as interacting with some feature of the context. Two causes are interactive if in combination "they act like a causal factor whose effects are different from at least one of the two acting separately." Hence the interactive cause should be treated as a distinct case from the cause in noninteractive cases, and presumably Cartwright would agree with the conclusion quoted above from Eells and Sober. I shall call this condition on probabilistic causes the requirement of contextual unanimity.

We can use the same example to illustrate the second problem. Suppose we want to raise the question whether the genetic factor responsible for both smoking and exercising is a cause of heart attacks. The problem is just that the genetic factor has two effects, one of which tends to cause heart attacks, and one of which tends to prevent them. This question has, as I mentioned, been addressed in a recent paper by Eells and Sober. The question with which they are explicitly concerned is that of stating the circumstances under which probabilistic causes are transitive. For example, given that the genetic factor causes smoking, and smoking causes heart attacks, does it follow that the genetic factor causes heart attacks? The reason that this is problematic is precisely that the genetic factor might have other effects that have an opposite effect on the likelihood of heart attacks. So the question they address turns out to be the same as the one with which I am now concerned.

The answer they give is quite complex in detail, but simple in principle. First they develop a sufficient condition for such transitivity. This they call unanimity, and it is the condition that all the effects of the initial cause should increase the probability of the final effect. I shall call this unanimity of intermediaries, to distinguish it from the previous case of contextual unanimity. They then go on to claim that this condition is nevertheless not necessary. All that is necessary is that the influence of those intermediaries that increase the probability of the effect should outweigh the influence of those that decrease that probability. Thus in the example, the question whether the genetic factor causes heart attacks turns in the end simply on whether the probability of having a heart attack is increased, on average, by the presence of this genetic factor.

As a matter of fact, I find this account quite plausible. What is curious, however, is the contrast between the roles of these two unanimity conditions. Eells and Sober discuss the first problem at some length and, as we have seen, endorse the requirement of contextual unanimity. "Average effect," they write, "is a sorry excuse for a causal concept."[6] But average effect seems to be exactly what they propose as a solution to the second problem.

What might seem no more than a mildly suspicious asymmetry in the treatments of these problems can be seen to constitute a much more serious dilemma with a little development of the example. Suppose that statistics for the United States indicate that possession of the relevant gene in fact increases one's chance of having a heart attack. In other words, the effect of the increased tendency to smoke outweighs the effect of the greater propensity to exercise. Then the account by Eells and Sober indicates that the gene does indeed cause heart attacks. But then suppose that we were to collect statistics in some part of the world where tobacco is unavailable. Presumably we would find there that the effect of exercising would predominate, and thus that the gene caused one to be less likely to have a heart attack. This transforms the issue into one of different contexts. The availability of tobacco is surely a contextual factor causally relevant to the occurrence of heart attacks, and thus it appears that the gene does not exhibit contextual unanimity in causing heart attacks. And so, according to the orthodox doctrine, it does not cause them.

This problem will surely be quite general. Whenever there are different routes by which a factor may influence its supposed effect, the relative significance of these different routes is extremely likely to depend on independent aspects of the context in which the cause occurs. Whenever there are causal intermediaries some of which increase and some of which decrease the probability of the final effect, it is likely that there will be some contexts in which each type of effect predominates.[7] To the extent that this is so, the requirement of contextual unanimity will force us to accept unanimity of intermediaries as not only a sufficient, but also a necessary condition of causality.

Widely accepted though the requirement of contextual unanimity may be, I shall argue that its rejection is the correct resolution of this dilemma. We should reject the partitioning requirement for causal contexts, I suggest, and accept that average effect over different contexts is the most we can demand in establishing causal connections. Suppose that scientists employed by the tobacco industry were to discover some rare physiological condition the beneficiaries of which were less likely to get lung cancer if they smoked than if they didn't. Contrary to what the orthodox analysis implies, I do not think that they would thereby have discovered that smoking did not, after all, cause lung cancer. Had this condition been the rule rather than the exception, we would rightly have concluded, from statistical investigation, that smoking was a prophylactic against lung cancer. And neither would this conclusion have been refuted by the discovery that those abnormal and unfortunate individuals who lacked this physiological advantage were actually more likely to get lung cancer if they smoked. If this is correct it seems to suggest that causes should be assessed in terms of average effect not only across different causal routes, but also across varying causal contexts.

If my intuition on the preceding example is correct, we must take another look at the example that motivated the requirement of contextual unanimity. For what this example shows, and what I certainly do not mean to deny, is that there can be cases in which a prima facie correlation reverses the actual causal facts. In that example, smokers were statistically less likely to have heart attacks even though smoking was a cause of heart attacks. However, not only does the conclusion drawn from the case seem too strong, for the reasons I have just given, but it is also much stronger than the kind of example to which it is a response requires.

The problem arises in this example because when we take a sample of smokers we do not, because of the (indirect) causal connection between smoking and exercising, get anything like a representative sample of the population. And the sample is biased precisely with respect to a factor that has a strong causal influence on the probability of having a heart attack. The point of partitioning is to remedy this defect in the sample. But all that is really needed is that we get a sample of smokers in which exercisers are fairly represented. The demand for unanimity of causal direction then seems quite redundant. Suppose, for example, that we have such a sample. Suppose also that in such a sample the smokers are significantly more likely to get heart attacks, but that this derives from the fact that the smoking nonexercisers are much more likely to have heart attacks than the nonsmoking nonexercisers whereas the smoking exercisers are actually slightly less likely to have heart attacks than the nonsmoking exercisers. Certainly this would be a very significant *supplementation* of the information that smoking caused heart attacks, but I fail to see why it should be a *refutation* of it. At any rate, all that *follows* from the example is that correlations between factors may come about as a result of a systematic bias in the sample rather than form a direct causal connection between them. No requirement of consistency of the correlation within subpopulations is forced on us.

My conclusion, then, is that a probabilistic causal connection need amount to no more than a statistical correlation in a fair sample. I concede that the notion of a fair sample may present some problems. The crucial respect of fairness required is lack of bias with respect to independent causally relevant factors. It is thus apparent that the fairness of a sample might be no easier to establish conclusively than the condition that the correlation hold in every causally distinguishable context. Nonetheless, it is certainly a weaker requirement than contextual unanimity, and perhaps also one whose satisfaction we would frequently have less reason to doubt.

I shall end this section by admitting one consequence of my view that might be seen as a serious problem. This is the fact that it reverses a very standard assumption that the laws are independent of the facts. For instance, one of my earlier examples implies that a certain gene might have come to cause heart attacks only when tobacco was discovered. Thus the truth of a law will depend on the obtaining of a particular fact. (This is also a consequence of the account by Eells and Sober of causal transitivity.) I can only say that this consequence does not disturb me. Since Hume, most philosophers have come to accept that the truth of laws is contingent. If the laws are probabilistic, then what happens is contingent even relative to the laws. It does not seem too large a step to accept that the laws themselves may be contingent on what happens.

A BROADER PERSPECTIVE ON THEORIES OF CAUSALITY

The increasing interest in probabilistic theories of causality presumably, and I am sure correctly, betokens an increasing dissatisfaction with determinism. Although I shall certainly not attempt here to give either a detailed account or a detailed critique of determinism, I do want to point out one important contrast between deterministic and probabilistic theories of causality. The relevant aspect of determinism for my present purposes is the view that every instance of causality instantiates some precise and exceptionless law. Since there are two very different conceptions of the form such laws might take, I shall first briefly distinguish these.

I shall call these two strategies for arriving at deterministic laws 'elaborationist' and 'reductionist'. The elaborationist approach is embodied in the traditional post-Humean account of causation. No one thinks (though Hume occasionally reads as if he had) that everyday causal statements must be straightforwardly generalizable as they stand. For instance, the claim that a thrown brick caused the window to break does not entail that every thrown brick breaks some window. The traditional approach, exemplified by J. S. Mill, and developed recently to a considerable degree of sophistication by J. L. Mackie,[8] is to provide extremely complex elaborations of the descriptions of the events concerned. Thus one might say that what was strictly the cause was the projection of a brick of a certain mass at a certain velocity, towards a window of a certain thickness and structural constitution, together with the absence of all kinds of factors that might have intervened between the projection of the brick and the impact with the window, etc.

The reductionist approach, developed particularly by Davidson, does not assume that there is any exceptionless generalization to be formulated in commonsense terms. Rather, his idea is that the commonsense descriptions of the cause and effect pick out events that in fact satisfy some highly theoretical descriptions that in turn instantiate causal laws.[9] Since a discussion of reductionism would be beyond the scope of this paper, and since I have argued elsewhere and at some length against its plausibility,[10] I shall here concern myself only with elaborationist conceptions of causal laws.

We may distinguish two crucial aspects of such laws: the generation of unambiguous and certain predictions, and completeness. It is clear that the move to probabilistic laws involves rejection of the former. It is just what it is for a law to be probabilistic that the predictions it gives are only more or less probable, never certain. By completeness, I mean that every factor relevant to the outcome must be mentioned, positively or negatively, in the full formulation of the law. It is obvious that this is a precondition of the possibility of an absolutely certain prediction, since any relevant factor omitted from the law could defeat the prediction. This aspect of traditional deterministic laws resurfaces in probabilistic theories in the demand that data be partitioned with respect to all causally relevant factors, or in what I have called the requirement of contextual unanimity. My suggestion is that emancipation from determinism will not be complete without rejection of this feature also. Another way to put the point would be to say that from the fact that we do not know, or choose to specify, all the factors relevant to the occurrence of a certain kind of event, it does not follow that a probabilistic law pertaining to the production of such events is *in*complete, still less false.

One of the main implausibilities in traditional deterministic accounts was precisely the implication that there must be some specification, presumably finite, of every factor that could conceivably affect the outcome in question. And this implausibility carries over unchanged into the suggestion that there should be some complete specification of all the possible sets of causally relevant factors, as required by orthodox probabilistic theories. The demand for deterministic laws that give certain predictions did, as I indicated above, require the acceptance of this implausibility. But given that the demand is inapplicable to probabilistic laws anyway, this motivation for accepting the demand for completeness is removed. If my previous arguments that the theory does not require it were correct, then perhaps the present considerations will help to indicate that it is also better off without it.

In conclusion, I shall make one further comment on Cartwright's remark, mentioned above, that "whenever a cause fails to raise the probability of its effect, there must be a reason."[11] It is, of course, a consequence of a probabilistic conception of causality that sufficient reasons cannot generally be found for the occurrence of particular events. For example, there might be no explanation of why one smoker but not another gets lung cancer, or of why one radioactive atom decays but another doesn't. What Cartwright here denies is that we should accept the same possibility for generalizations. Part of what I am suggesting is that such an extension may very well be correct. Why should not the efficacy of a cause in different contexts vary in a way that is no more explicable than the behavior of particular radioactive atoms? If this possibility were realized, it would be as misguided to insist on contextual unanimity as to insist on formulating a deterministic law to cover every event.[12]

Notes

1. Ellery Eells and Elliott Sober, "Probabilistic Causality and the Question of Transitivity," *Philosophy of Science* 50 (1983):35-57.

2. For more details, see P. Suppes, *A Probabilistic Theory of Causality* (Amsterdam, 1970); and N. Cartwright, "Causal Laws and Effective Strategies," *Nous* 13 (1979):419-37. For more problems, see W. Salmon, "Probabilistic Causality," *Pacific Philosophical Quarterly* 61 (1980): 50-74.

3. *Causal Necessity* (New Haven, 1980).

4. "Probabilistic Causality and the Question of Transitivity," 37. Emphasis in original.

5. "Causal Laws," 427-28.

6. "Probabilistic Causality and the Question of Transitivity," 54.

7. One example for which this is surely the case is the biological one that Eells and Sober use to illustrate their views. They discuss two possible difficulties with the controversial thesis of genic selectionism, or more specifically, with the claim that single genes may cause the reproductive success of the organisms that possess them. Polygenic effects, in which the effect of a gene depends crucially on the genetic context, are seen as a genuine difficulty on the basis of the requirement of contextual unanimity; pleiotropy, when a gene has more than one effect on the organism, turns out not to be a problem in view of their position on causal transitivity. But certainly the relative influence of such effects will typically depend on peculiarities of the environment in which a particular organism finds itself, so that pleiotropy would generally be just as much of a problem for the view in question. On my view, as should be apparent, neither of these circumstances will present a genuine objection to genic selectionism.

8. *The Cement of the Universe* (Oxford, 1974), chap. 3. It should be noted, however, that Mackie does not consider himself to be providing an analysis of singular causal statements at this point.

9. For Davidson's account of causality, see "Causal Relations," in *Essays on Actions and Events* (Oxford, 1980). The reductionist aspect of his view is more explicit in "Mental Events," ibid.

10. "The Disunity of Science," *Mind* (1983):321-46.

11. "Causal Laws," 427.

12. I am most grateful to Michael Bratman for major assistance in extracting a coherent theme from a rather disorderly collection of ideas on this topic.

Nomic Probability

JOHN L. POLLOCK

1. INTRODUCTION

There are two kinds of physical laws–statistical and nonstatistical. Statistical laws are probabilistic. It is generally recognized that existing theories of probability do not provide us with an account of a kind of probability adequate for the formulation of probabilistic laws. The purpose of this paper is to describe a kind of probability that is adequate for the formulation of probabilistic laws. I will call this *nomic probability*.[1] The theory of nomic probability is of considerable philosophical significance. Among other things, it provides a solution to the problem of induction. Unfortunately, the details of the theory are highly complex, and pursuing them is more apt to obscure the philosophical ideas underlying the theory than to facilitate understanding. I have presented most of the details elsewhere.[2] What I will try to do here is give the reader a philosophical overview of the theory of nomic probability without the encumbrance of all of the logical and mathematical details.

The best way to understand nomic probability is to begin by considering nonstatistical physical laws. The logical positivists popularized the Humean view that there is no necessity in nature and hence that physical laws are just material generalizations of the form $\ulcorner(\forall x)(Fx \rightarrow Gx)\urcorner$. Such a view has profoundly influenced contemporary philosophy of science, but in the end I think that it must be forsaken. A consequence of the rejection of necessity in nature was the rejection of counterfactual conditionals. Counterfactuals appear to involve a kind of neccessary connection–at least a connection stronger than truth functional–and so philosophers were moved to deny their intelligibility. But, of course, counterfactuals are intelligible. We use them all the time, and we understand each other when we do use them. It has proven very difficult to construct a satisfactory theory of counterfactuals, but they are now a topic of major concern in the philosophy of science, and few would any longer deny their intelligibility. If the natural necessity of laws is no more heinous than the natural necessity of counterfactuals, then there is no reason to be wary of it. Instead, we should be trying to understand it.

Despite their Humean inclinations, philosophers of science have always known that there was a good reason for distinguishing between physical laws and material generalizations. Such a distinction is required by the possibility of accidental generalizations. For example, it might be true, purely by chance, that no one named 'Lisa' has ever been stricken by Valley Fever. We would not regard such a true generalization as a law of nature. Laws entail material generalizations, but there must be something more to them than that. I call nonstatistical laws *nomic generalizations*.[3] This reflects the fact that such laws are not just about actual objects–they are also about "physically possible objects." Nomic generalizations can be expressed in English using the locution $\ulcorner$Any F would be a $G\urcorner$. I will symbolize this nomic generalization as $\ulcorner F \Rightarrow G \urcorner$. What this means, roughly, is that any physically possible F would be a G.[4]

Nonstatistical laws are expressed by nomic generalizations. Statistical laws, on the other hand, are probabilistic. Analogous to $\ulcorner F \Rightarrow G \urcorner$ saying that any physically possible F would be a G, we can think of the statistical law $\ulcorner$prob$(G/F) = r\urcorner$ as telling ua that the proportion of physically possible F's that would be G is r. Nomic generalizations can be regarded as the limiting case of nomic probability. To illustrate nomic probability, consider a physical description D of a coin, and suppose there is just one coin of that description and it is never flipped. On the basis of the description D together with our knowledge of physics, we might conclude that a coin of this description would tend to land heads half the time. We might express this by saying that the probability of a flip of a coin of description D landing heads is $1/2$. In saying this, we are not talking about relative frequencies. As there are no flips of coins of description D, the relative frequency does not exist. Or suppose instead that the single coin of description D is flipped just once, landing heads, and then destroyed. In that case the relative frequency is 1, but we would still say that the probability of a coin of that description landing heads is $1/2$.

The reason for the difference between the relative frequency and the probability is that the probability statement is in some sense subjunctive or counterfactual. It is not just about actual flips, but about possible flips as well. In saying that the probability is $1/2$, we are saying that out of all physically possible flips of coins of description D, $1/2$ of them would land heads. To illustrate nomic probability with a more realistic example, in physics we often want to talk about the probability of some event in simplified circumstances that have never occurred. For example, the typical problem given students in a quantum mechanics class is of this character. The relative frequency does not exist, but the nomic probability does and that is what the students are calculating.

The history of the philsophical theory of probability has consisted in large measure of philosophers attempting to construct philosophically unobjectionable *definitions* of 'probability'. This has led to numerous attempts to define 'probability' in terms of relative frequencies. But none of the definitions that have been proposed have constituted reasonable analyses of the probability concepts employed either by the man in the street or by working scientists. It is also obvious that nothing I have said above constitutes a philosophically adequate definition of 'nomic probability'. I have made a number of remarks aimed at giving the reader some grasp of the concept I am talking about, but those remarks constitute no more than a heuristic explanation of that concept. The inability to find definitions for philosophically important concepts is, in fact, the normal state of affairs in philosophy. Until as late as 1960, most attempts to solve philosophical problems proceeded by seeking definitions of concepts like *physical object*, *person*, *red*, but all such attempts failed. The lesson to be learned from this is that philosophically interesting concepts are rarely *definable* in any interesting way.

The standard view in philosophical logic is that concepts are characterized by their truth conditions, but it is not at all clear what this comes to. There is a trivial sense in which every concept is characterized by its truth condition. For example, the concept *red* has as its truth condition the condition of *being red,* and this, presumably, is characteristic of the concept *red.*[5] But the fact that a concept is characterized by its truth condition *in this sense* is no reason to think that concepts can always be analyzed by giving philsophically interesting definitions of them. That requires not only that concepts are characterized by their truth conditions, but also that those truth conditions can always be formulated in terms of concepts that are somehow simpler. We get the picture of concepts forming a logical hierarchy with any concept above the lowest level being definable in terms of concepts below it in the hierarchy. This is the doctrine of *reductive analyses*. The recent history of philosophy gives us ample reason to reject this doctrine. It just does not seem to be true that concepts can always be defined in terms of simpler concepts.

If a concept cannot be defined in terms of simpler concepts, then what kind of informative analysis can be given for it? The essence of a concept is the role it plays in thought. Concepts are categories for use in thinking about the world. When we speak of thought in this context, we mean not just idle and unconnected reflection, but rational thought. Rational thought is the subject of epistemology. My proposal is that concepts can be given informative characterizations in terms of their role in rational thought. The role a concept plays in rational thought is determined by two things: (1) what constitutes a good reason for thinking that something exemplifies the concept or its negation; (2) what we can conclude from reasonably held beliefs involving the concept. In other words, the concept is characterized by its role in reasoning, or more simply, by its *justification conditions.*[6]

There was a time when philosophers tended to suppose that good reasons had to logically entail what they are reasons for. Upon reflection, such a view is really quite preposterous. It has the consequence that every knowable proposition must be entailed by propositions that are "epistemologically basic" in the sense of being knowable without having reasons for believing them. But if there is anything epistemologists have learned in the last century, it is that such entailments do not exist. It has become generally accepted that not all reasons are entailments. We must acknowledge the existence of reasons that are only prima facie. Prima facie reasons are 'defeasible"–they only provide justification in the absence of defeaters. Prima facie reasons constitute a category of reasons in their own right, and they cannot be reduced to entailments. Accordingly, they play an ineliminable role in the specification of the justification conditions of concepts.

To illustrate my general points, consider the problem of perception. That is the problem of explaining how it is possible for us to acquire knowledge of the physical world on the basis of perception. Philosophers tried valiantly to solve this problem by defining various physical object concepts like *red* in terms of concepts describing our perceptual states (like the concept of *looking red*). The resulting theories were versions of phenomenalism. But in the end, all of the phenomenalist theories collapsed in the face of the argument from perceptual relativity.[7] Once it is recognized that concepts can be characterized by their justification conditions, the problem of perception has a relatively trivial solution. It is part of the justification conditions of the concept *red* that something's looking red to a person gives him a prima facie reason for thinking that it is red. This prima facie reason is a brute epistemic fact, partly constitutive of the concept *red* and not derivable from anything more basic. Thus the problem of perception is solved (or perhaps "resolved") by giving a description of the structure of the reasoning involved in perceptual knowledge. It is a mistake to suppose that that reasoning must itself be justified on the basis of something deeper, because there is nothing deeper. That reasoning is itself constitutive of our perceptual concepts.

The conclusion I want to draw from all of this is that there is good reason to resist the insistence that the theory of probability must be founded upon an informative *definition of* 'probability'. A reasonable theory of probability must provide an analysis of the probability concepts in terms of which it proceeds, but we should not automatically expect such an analysis to take the form of a definition. If such a definition could actually be found, that would be all to the good, but there is reason to doubt that that is possible. An attractive alternative is to seek characterizations of our probability concepts in terms of their justification conditions, i.e., in terms of their role in reasoning. Nomic probability is a kind of empirical probability. Our knowledge of empirical probabilities is based upon relative frequencies. Thus an adequate analysis of nomic probability will consist of three elements. First, we must provide an account of how we can ascertain the numerical values of probabilities on the basis of relative frequencies. Second, we must provide an account of the kinds of "computational" inferences that allow us to compute the values of some probabilities on the basis of others. Finally, we require an account of how we can use nomic probability to draw conclusions about other matters.

The first element of this analysis will consist largely of an account of statistical induction. In statistical induction, we observe the relative frequency of F's in a sample of G's and infer that $\text{prob}(F/G)$ is approximately equal to that relative frequency. Ordinary enumerative induction, wherein we observe that all the G's in the sample are F's and infer that any G would be an F, is intimately related to statistical induction. Hume's problem of induction was the problem of justifying induction by deriving it from something more fundamental. The most common view in contemporary philosophy is that that is impossible. Instead, principles of induction are regarded as basic epistemic principles partly constitutive of rationality and not derivable from anything else. But one of the most remarkable features of the theory of nomic probability is that it entails that this common view is mistaken. Principles of induction turn out to be derivable from more fundamental principles concerning nomic probability, thus providing a solution of sorts to the traditional problem of induction.

The second element of the analysis of nomic probability is an account of how nomic probabilities are derivable from one another. To a large extent, these derivations consist of computations in accordance with the probability calculus, but I will suggest below that the standard probability calculus must be augmented in some important ways.

The final element of the analysis of nomic probability is an account of how non-probabilistic conclusions can be drawn from premises about nomic probability. Intuitively it seems clear that, under some circumstances, knowing that certain nomic probabilities are high can justify us in holding related beliefs. For example, I know that it is highly probable that the date appearing on this morning's newspaper is in fact today's date. (I do not know that this is always the case–typographical errors do occur). On this basis, I can arrive at a justified belief regarding today's date. The epistemic rules describing when high probability can justify belief are called *acceptance rules*. The acceptance rules endorsed by the theory of nomic probability constitute the principal philosophical novelty of that theory. The other fundamental principles that will be adopted as primitive assumptions about probability are all of a computational nature, and in effect amount to nothing more than an embellishment of the standard probability calculus. It is the acceptance rules that give the theory its unique flavor and comprise the main epistemic assumptions that make the theory run.

There is an important distinction between "definite" probabilities and "indefinite" probabilities. A definite probability is the probability that a particular proposition is true. Indefinite probabilities, on the other hand, concern properties rather than propositions.[8] For example, the probability of a horse being a palomino is not about any particular horse. Rather, it relates the property of being a horse and the property of being a palomino. Nomic probabilities are indefinite probabilities. But for most practical purposes, the probabilities we are really interested in are definite probabilities. We want to know how probable it is that it will rain, that Bluenose will win the third race, that Sally will have a heart attack, etc. It is probabilities of this sort that are involved in practical reasoning. Thus the first two elements of our analysis must be augmented by a third element. That is a theory telling us how to get from indefinite probabilities to definite probabilities. We judge that there is a 20 percent probability of rain today, because the indefinite probability of its raining in similar circumstances is believed to be about .2. We think it unlikely that Bluenose will win the third race because he has never finished above seventh in his life. We judge that Sally is more likely than her sister to have a heart attack because Sally smokes like a furnace and drinks like a fish, whereas her sister is a nun who jogs and lifts weights. We take these facts about Sally and her sister to be relevant because we know that they affect the indefinite probability of a person having a heart attack. That is, the indefinite probability of a person who smokes and drinks having a heart attack is much greater than the indefinite probability for a person who does not smoke or drink and is in good physical condition. Inferences from indefinite probabilities to definite probabilities are called *direct inferences*. A satisfactory theory of nomic probability must include an account of direct inference.

To summarize, the analysis of nomic probability will consist of (1) a theory of statistical induction, (2) an augmented probability calculus, (3) a set of acceptance rules, and (4) a theory of direct inference. These four elements are precisely the components that make up the theory of nomic probability. Consequenctly, the analysis and the theory are inseparable. To give an analysis of nomic probability is the same thing as constructing a theory of probability that accommodates statistical induction, direct inference, and acceptance rules.

2. NOMIC PROBABILITY AND PHYSICAL POSSIBILITIES

I introduced the nomic probability prob(F/G) as a measure of "the proportion of physically possible G's that would be F." This explanation is heuristically useful in understanding nomic probability, but we must put meat on its bones if it is to be of any help in generating a concrete theory. I suggest that the real content of this heuristic explanation lies in a group of computational principles enabling us to derive nomic probabilities from one another.

To say that all physically possible G's would be F's is elliptical for saying that it is physically necessary that all actual G's are F's, i.e., in every physically possible world it is true that all G's are F's. (A physically possible world is a world having the same laws–both statistical and nonstatistical–as the actual world.) Similarly, talk about the proportion of physically possible G's that would be F must somehow be cashed out in terms of the proportions of actual G's that are F in different physically possible worlds. What we need for this purpose are some principles relating nomic probability to relative frequencies. We can begin with a seemingly uncontroversial principle. There are cases in which the relative frequency is fixed as a matter of logic. For example, it is necessarily true that

$$\text{freq}[x = a \mid x \epsilon \{a,b,c\} \ \& \ a \neq b \ \& \ a \neq c \ \& \ b \neq c] = 1/3.$$

In such cases, the nomic probabillity is the same as the relative frequency:

(2.1) $(\forall r)$ if $\square(\text{freq}[F/G] = r)$ then prob(F/G) $= r$.

This is a minimal principle relating probabilities and relative frequencies, but it will not get us very far by itself. We need some more substantial principles to give content to the idea that prob(F/G) is the proportion of physically possible G's that would be F.

I suggest that the key to our problem lies in the initially appealing idea that probability is the limit of relative frequencies. Given an ω-sequence σ (an infinite sequence of the same length as the sequence of all natural numbers), let σ'n be the sequence of the first n members of σ, and let freq[$F/σ'n$] be the fraction of places in σ 'n occupied by F's. This need not be the same thing as the fraction of objects in the sequence σ'n that are $F's$, because the same object may recur a number of times. The limit of the relative frequency of a property F in the sequence σ is then $\lim_{n\to\infty}$freq[$F/σ'n$]. We cannot endorse the definition of prob(F/G) as $\lim_{n\to\infty}$freq[$F/σ'n$] where σ consists of the set of all G' s arranged in some particular order, because if there are infinitely many G's then the set of all G's can be arranged into different sequences with different limits.[9] Still, limits of relative frequencies seem to have something to do with probability. I suggest that the actual connection between these two concepts can be seen most easily by reflecting upon a theorem of set theory. If X is a finite set and freq[F/X] = r, it does not follow that the frequency of F' s in an arbitrary n-tuple of members of X will *always* be approximately equal to r, but it does follow that the frequency of F's in n-tuples of members of X will *tend* to be approximately equal to r. More precisely, where X^n is the set of all n-tuples of members of X, the following can be proven by standard combinatorial methods:

(2.2)   For every γ, δ > 0 there is an n such that for every finite set X, if freq[F/X] = r then freq[$|$freq[$F/σ$]-$r| < δ / σ\epsilon X^n$] > 1-γ.

prob(F/G) is supposed to be analogous to freq[F/X] in that is is a measure of the proportion of F's among all physically possible G's. To make this precise, we must first consider what we mean by "physically possible G." We cannot mean just a possible object that is G in some physically possible world, because the same object can be G in one physically possible world and non-G in another. I propose to understand a *physically possible G* to be an ordered pair ‹ x, w › such that w is a physically possible world and x is G at w. The proportion of F's among physically possible G's cannot usually be represented by a frequency, because there will almost invariably be infinitely many physically possible G's.[10] Consequently, (2.2) is not directly applicable to talk of the proportion of F's among physically possible G's. But we can instead employ a kind of "logical limit" of the above principle. If we consider longer and longer finite sequences of physically possible G's, the frequency of F's in those sequences should tend to approximate prob(F/G), the approximation getting better and the tendency to approximate getting stronger as the sequences get longer, and in the limiting case in which we consider ω-sequences of physically possible G's, the approximation should tend to become perfect. More accurately, if we consider ω-sequences of physically possible G's, the limit of the frequency of F's in virtually all of them ought to be the same as prob(F/G). But what does it mean to say "in virtually all of them"? In the case of finite sets, that is cashed out in terms of frequencies, but it cannot be done in that way for infinite sets. Instead, we must talk about the *proportion* of ω-sequences of physically possible G's whose limits are equal to prob(F/G), and such proportions are precisely what is measured by probability itself. Thus, taking $\ulcorner \overset{\diamond}{p} \urcorner$ to symbolize physical possibility and letting G^ω be the set of all ω-sequences of physically possible G's, I propose the following analogue of (2.2) as a way of making sense of the notion of prob(F/G) as the proportion of physically possible G's that are F:

(2.3)   If $\underset{p}{\Diamond}(\exists x)Gx$ then prob(F/G) $= r$ iff prob[$\lim_{n\to\infty}$freq[$F/\sigma'n$] $= r$ / $\sigma\epsilon G^\omega$] $= 1$.

Less formally, prob(F/G) $= r$ iff the frequency of F's in "almost all" ω-sequences of G's is r. Obviously, (2.3) cannot serve as a *definition* of 'prob', but it can be adopted as a useful axiom giving content to the heuristic idea upon which the theory of nomic probability is based. It is a way of saying that probabilities act like relative frequencies in the limit.

If G is counterlegal then $\ulcorner G \Rightarrow F\urcorner$ does not really say that any physically possible G would be an F. Instead, it says that *if* it were physically possible for there to be G's *then* any physically possible G would be an F, i.e., $\ulcorner \Diamond \exists G >\underset{p}{\Box}\forall(G \to F)\urcorner$. (Where G is a property, I take $\ulcorner \exists G\urcorner$ to abbreviate $\ulcorner(\exists x)Gx\urcorner$. Similarly, where ϕ is an open formula, I take $\ulcorner \exists\phi\urcorner$ to be its existential closure and $\ulcorner \forall\phi\urcorner$ to be its universal closure.) Similarly, (2.3) only characterizes nomic probability when G is not counterlegal. If it is physically impossible for there to be G's, then rather than being the proportion of physically possible G's that are F, prob(F/G) should be a measure of what that proportion *would be if* it were physically possible for there to be G's. For each possible world w, let prob$_w$ (F/G) be the value of prob(F/G) at w. If w and w^* have the same laws (both statistical and nonstatistical) then prob$_w$(F/G) $=$ prob$_{w*}$(F/G). If G is counterlegal at the actual world w then we should look at the various worlds w^* that result from making minimal deletions to the laws of w to make them consistent with $\exists G$. Let $\mathbf{M}_w(\underset{p}{\Diamond}\exists G)$ be the set of all such worlds. Assuming that there are just finitely many ways of doing that, let $r_1, \ldots, r_k$ be the values of prob$_{w*}$(F/G) at the different worlds in $\mathbf{M}_w(\underset{p}{\Diamond}\exists G)$. prob($F/G$) should then be a weighted average of the r_i's, the weight of each reflecting how likely it is to be the value of prob(F/G) given that one of the r_i's is. This latter likelihood is the second-order probability

prob[prob$_x$(F/G) $= r_i /x\epsilon\mathbf{M}_w(\underset{p}{\Diamond}\exists G)$].

The proposal is then:

(2.4)   prob$_w$(F/G) $= \sum_{i=1}^{n}[r_i$ prob(prob$_x$(F/G) $= r_i / x\epsilon\mathbf{M}_w(\underset{p}{\Diamond}\exists G))]$.

This reduces counterlegal nomic probabilities to non-counterlegal nomic probabilities.

Most calculations of probabilities from one another proceed via the probability calculus. Where F, G, and H are (possibly multiplace) properties, the following comprise an obvious set of axioms for nomic probabilities:

(2.5) $0 \leqslant$ prob(F/G) $\leqslant 1$.

(2.6)   If $F = H$ and $G = J$ then $\mathrm{prob}(F/G) = \mathrm{prob}(G/J)$

(2.7) $\mathrm{prob}(F\&G/H) = \mathrm{prob}(F/H)\cdot \mathrm{prob}(G/F\&H)$.

(2.8)   If $(G \Rightarrow F)$ then $\mathrm{prob}(F/G) = 1$.

(2.9)   If $(G \Leftrightarrow H)$ then $\mathrm{prob}(F/G) = \mathrm{prob}(F/H)$.

(2.10)   If $[(F\&G) \Rightarrow H]$ then $\mathrm{prob}(F/G) \leq \mathrm{prob}(H/G)$.

(2.11)   If $\Diamond \exists H$ and $[H \Rightarrow \sim (F\&G)]$ then $\mathrm{prob}(FvG/H) = \mathrm{prob}(F/H) + \mathrm{prob}(G/H)$.

These axioms amount to saying that prob is an additive measure function on sets of physically possible objects.

Some very useful principles that follow from (2.1)-(2.11) are as follows:

(2.12) $(\underset{p}{\Diamond} \exists G \, \& \, \underset{p}{\Box} P) \to \mathrm{prob}(F/G\&P) = \mathrm{prob}(F/G)$.

(2.13) $(\forall r)$ if $\Diamond \exists (G \, \& \, \mathrm{prob}(F/G) = r$ then $\mathrm{prob}\big[F \,/\, G \, \& \, \mathrm{prob}(F/G) = r\big] = r$.

The probability calculus is usually formulated in a language devoid of modal operators or nomic generalizations, and to that extent (2.5)-(2.11) constitute an extension of the classical probability calculus. But this extension is a minor one. What I want to suggest now is that a much more radical departure from the classical probability calculus is required for a complete theory of nomic probability. Historically, the probability calculus was designed with nonconditional definite probabilities in mind. Thus it has become customary to handle conditional probabilities derivatively by defining $\mathrm{prob}(F/G)$ to be $\mathrm{prob}(F\&G) \div \mathrm{prob}(G)$. Furthermore, no special provisions are made for indefinite probabilities—it is simply assumed that indefinite probabilities satisfy the same axioms as definite probabilities. Both of these aspects of the traditional treatment of probability make standard versions of the probability calculus inadequate when it is applied to nomic probabilities. That additional axioms must be adopted for indefinite probabilities becomes obvious when we reflect that even such an evident principle as:

(2.14) $\mathrm{prob}(Fxy/Gxy) = \mathrm{prob}(Fyx/ Gyx)$

is not a consequence of the standard probability calculus as applied to indefinite probabilities. In general, some new principles are required to handle the behavior of variables in indefinite probabilities. The relationship between the calculus of indefinite probabilities and the calculus of definite probabilities is a bit like the relationship between the predicate calculus and the propositional calculus.

The question of how best to extend the probability calculus to make it a reasonable axiomatization of nomic probabilities is a technically complex one, but we need not pursue the details here. Let me simply assert that a reasonable axiomatization will make the following principle true:

(2.15) $\mathrm{prob}(Axy/Rxy \, \& \, y = b) = \mathrm{prob}(Axb/Rxb)$.

I have only stated (2.15) for binary relations, but it holds in general for relations of arbitrarily many places.[11]

The purpose of this section has been to develop the "computational" properties of nomic probability. Although this has involved a number of departures from standard treatments, the end result is still just a calculus of probabilities. From a philosophical point of view, the axioms we have adopted are not particularly weighty. It will be rather remarkable, then, that we need no assumptions specifically about probability beyond these axioms and the acceptance rule described in section 3 to found our entire theory of nomic probability, including the derivation of principles of induction

3. AN ACCEPTANCE RULE

Rules telling us when it is rational to believe something on the basis of probability are called *acceptance rules*. The simplest and initially most appealing acceptance rule is *The Simple Rule*:

> (3.1)   A person is justified in believing P iff he is justified in believing that it is sufficiently probable that P is true.

It is now generally recognized that The Simple Rule runs afoul of the lottery paradox. In "Epistemology and Probability," I showed that the lottery paradox can be handled properly by adopting the following acceptance rule:

> (A1)   If F is projectible with respect to G, then $\ulcorner Gc \,\&\, \text{prob}(F/G) > r \urcorner$ is a prima facie reason for believing $\ulcorner Fc \urcorner$, the strength of the reason depending upon the value of r.

Projectibility, as it is used in (A1), is the standard notion of projectibility that occurs in discussions of induction. It is defined precisely as follows:

> (3.2)   A property F is *projectible with respect to* a property G iff observation of a sample of G's all of which are F's gives us a prima facie reason for believing that any G would be an F, and this prima facie reason would not be defeated by learning that there are non-F's.

To illustrate how (A1) handles the lottery paradox, suppose we have a fair lottery consisting of one million tickets. The probability that a draw in such a lottery will be a draw of ticket n is .000001, so we have a prima facie reason for believing of each ticket that it will not be drawn. But the collection of all such conclusions is incompatible with what we already know, viz., that some ticket will be drawn. Thus we do not want to be able to conclude of each ticket that it will not be drawn, and as there is nothing to favor one ticket over any of the others, we do not want to be able to conclude of any ticket that it will not be drawn. (A1) handles this properly by virtue of the fact that the reason it provides is only prima facie. For each n, we have a prima facie reason for believing that ticket n will not be drawn. But for each $m \neq n$, we have an equally good prima facie reason for believing that ticket m will not be drawn. This provides us with the following counterargument supporting the conclusion that ticket n will be drawn:

> Ticket 1 will not be drawn.
> Ticket 2 will not be drawn.
>
> .
>
> .
>
> .
>
> Ticket $n - 1$ will not be drawn.
> Ticket $n + 1$ will not be drawn.
>
> .
>
> .
>
> .
>
> Some ticket will be drawn.
> Therefore, ticket n will be drawn.

For each of the premises of this argument, our reason for believing it is as good as our reason for believing that ticket n will not be drawn, and an argument is as good as its weakest link,[12] so this argument provides us with a reason for believing that ticket n will be drawn that is as good as our reason for believing that ticket n will not be drawn. Both reasons are prima facie reasons, so they simply defeat one another, leaving us with no justified conclusion about whether ticket n will be drawn.

In "Epistemology and Probability," I showed that without the projectibility constraint in (A1), all cases of high probability could be given the structure of the lottery paradox, with the result that every use of (A1) would be defeated and the rule would be useless. Basically, the projectibility constraint is required to rule out arbitrary disjunctions. But it is a bit surprising that the required constraint should be one of projectibility. Projectibility has to do with induction. Why should it have anything to do with acceptance rules? As I have indicated, I will propose a solution to the problem of induction. This solution will take the form of deriving principles of induction from our theory of nomic probability. Our acceptance rule will play a central role in that derivation. The derivation will be such that the constraints on the acceptance rule will be inherited by the principles of induction. By definition, the proper constraint on induction is projectibility (that is how I defined projectibility), so that must also be the constraint on our acceptance rule. In other words, the role of projectibility in induction is entirely derivative. Projectibility has first and foremost to do with probabilistic acceptance rules, and it is only because of its role there that it becomes a constraint on induction.

The reason provided by (A1) is only a prima facie reason, and as such it is defeasible. As with any prima facie reason, it can be defeated by having a stronger reason for denying the conclusion. A reason for denying the conclusion constitutes a *rebutting defeater*. But prima facie reasons can also be defeated by defeaters attacking the connection between the reason and the conclusion rather than attacking the conclusion itself. I have called these *undercutting defeaters*. There is an important kind of under-cutting defeater for (A1). In (A1), we infer the truth of $\ulcorner Fc\urcorner$ on the basis of probabilities conditional on a limited set of facts about c (i.e., the facts expressed by $\ulcorner Gc\urcorner$). But if we know additional facts about c that lower the probability, that defeats the prima facie reason:

> (D1)   If H is such that F is projectible with respect to $(G\&H)$ then $\ulcorner Hc$ & $\mathrm{prob}(F/G\&H) < \mathrm{prob}(F/G)\urcorner$ is an undercutting defeater for (A1).

This amounts to a kind of "total evidence requirement." It requires us to make our inference on the basis of the most comprehensive facts regarding which we know the requisite probabilities.

(A1) is not the only defensible acceptance rule. There is another acceptance rule that is related to (A1), rather like modus tollens is related to modus ponens:

> (A2)   If F is projectible with respect to G then $\ulcorner \mathrm{prob}(F/G) > r$ & $\sim Fc\urcorner$ is a prima facie reason for $\ulcorner \sim Gc\urcorner$, the strength of the reason depending upon the value of r.

(A2) is easily illustrated. For example, on the basis of quantum mechanics, we can calculate that it is highly probable that an energetic electron will be deflected if it passes within a certain distance of a uranium atom. We observe that a particular electron was not deflected, and so conclude that it did not pass within the critical distance. Reasoning in this way with regard to the electrons used in a scattering experiment, we arrive at conclusions about the diameter of a uranium atom.

In applications of (A2), G will typically be a conjunction of properties. To illustrate, in the above example what we know is that $\mathrm{prob}(D/E\&S)$ is high where D is the property of being deflected, E is the property of being an electron with a certain kinetic energy, and S is the property of passing within a certain distance of a uranium atom. Upon learning that the electron is not deflected, we conclude that $\ulcorner Ec\&Sc\urcorner$ is false, and as we know that $\ulcorner Ec\urcorner$ is true we conclude that $\ulcorner Sc\urcorner$ is false.

It seems clear that (A1) and (A2) are closely related. I suggest that they are consequences of a single stronger principle:

> (A3)   If F is projectible with respect to G then $\ulcorner \mathrm{prob}(F/G) > r\urcorner$ is a prima facie reason for the conditional $\ulcorner Gc \rightarrow Fc\urcorner$, the strength of the reason depending upon the value of r.

(A1) can then be replaced by an instance of (A3) and modus ponens, and (A2) by an instance of (A3) and modus tollens. Accordingly, I will regard (A3) as the fundamental probabilistic acceptance rule. Just as in the case of (A1), when we use (A3) we are making an inference on the basis of a limited set of facts about c. That inference should be defeated if the probability can be lowered by taking more facts into account. This indicates that the defeater for (A3) should be the same as for (A1):

> (D2)   If F is projectible with respect to $(G\&H)$ then $\ulcorner Hc$ & $\mathrm{prob}(F/G\&H) < \mathrm{prob}(F/G)\urcorner$ is an undercutting defeater for (A2).

I take it that (A3) is actually quite an intuitive acceptance rule. It amounts to a rule saying that, when F is projectible with respect to G, if we know that most G's are F, that gives us a reason for thinking of any particular object that it is an F if it is a G. The only surprising feature of this rule is the projectibility constraint. (A3) will turn out to be the basic epistemic principle from which all the rest of the theory of nomic probability is derived.

4. DIRECT INFERENCE

The basic idea behind what I will call 'classical direct inference' was first articulated by Hans Reichenbach: In determining the probability that an individual c has a property F, we find the narrowest reference class X regarding which we have reliable statistics and then infer that $PROB(Fc) = prob(Fx/x \in X)$. For example, insurance rates are calculated in this way. There is almost universal agreement that direct inference is based upon some such principle as this, although there is little agreement about the precise form the theory should take. In "A Theory of Direct Inference," I argued that classical direct inference should be regarded as proceeding in accordance with the following two epistemic rules (where $\ulcorner \mathbf{W}\phi \urcorner$ abbreviates $\ulcorner$We are warranted[13] in believing $\phi \urcorner$):

(4.1)   If F is projectible with respect to G then $\ulcorner$prob$(F/G) = r$ & $\mathbf{W}(Gc)$ & $\mathbf{W}(P \leftrightarrow Fc) \urcorner$ is a prima facie reason for $\ulcorner PROB(P) = r \urcorner$.

(4.2)   If F is projectible with respect to H then $\ulcorner$prob$(F/H) \neq$ prob(F/G) & $\mathbf{W}(Hc)$ & $\Box \forall (H \rightarrow G) \urcorner$ is an undercutting defeater for (4.1).[14]

Principle (4.2) is called "the principle of subset defeat" because it says that probabilities based upon more specific information take precedence over those based upon less specific information. Note the projectibility constraint in these rules. That constraint is required to avoid various paradoxes of direct inference, but just as in the case of our acceptance rules, it is initially puzzling that there should be such a constraint.

To illustrate this account of direct inference, suppose we know that Herman is a 40-year-old resident of the United States who smokes. Suppose we also know that the probability of a 40-year-old resident of the United States having lung cancer is .1, but the probability of a 40-year-old smoker who resides in the United States having lung cancer is .3. Intuitively, if we know nothing else that is relevant we will infer that the probability of Herman having lung cancer is .3. Principle (4.1) provides us with one prima facie reason for inferring that the probability is .1 and a second prima facie reason for inferring that the probability is .3. However, the latter prima facie reason is based upon more specific information, and so by (4.2) it takes precedence, defeating the first prima facie reason and leaving us justified in inferring that the probability is .3.

I believe that (4.1) and (4.2) are correct rules of classical direct inference, but I also believe that the nature of direct inference has been fundamentally misunderstood. Direct inference is taken to govern inferences from indefinite probabilities to definite probabilities, but it is my contention that such "classical" direct inference rests upon parallel inferences from indefinite probabilities to indefinite probabilities. The basic rule of classical direct inference is that if F is projectible with respect to G and we know $\ulcorner\mathrm{prob}(F/G) = r\ \&\ \mathbf{W}(Gc)\urcorner$ but do not know anything else about c that is relevant, this gives us a reason to believe that $\mathrm{PROB}(Fc) = r$. Typically, we will know c to have other projectible properties H but not know anything about the value of $\mathrm{prob}(F/G\&H)$ and so be unable to use the latter in direct inference. But if the direct inference from $\ulcorner\mathrm{prob}(F/G) = r\urcorner$ to $\ulcorner\mathrm{PROB}(Fc) = r\urcorner$ is to be reasonable, there must be a presumption to the effect that $\mathrm{prob}(F/G\&H) = r$. If there were no such presumption then we would have to regard it as virtually certain that $\mathrm{prob}(F/G\&H) \neq r$ (after all, there are infinitely many possible values that $\mathrm{prob}(F/G\&H)$ could have), and so virtually certain that there is a true subset defeater for the direct inference. This would make the direct inference to $\ulcorner\mathrm{PROB}(Fc) = r\urcorner$ unreasonable.

Perhaps the best way to argue for this presumption is to consider the relationship between definite and indefinite probabilities. It has frequently been observed that an analysis of sorts can be given for indefinite probabilities in terms of definite probabilities. To say that $\mathrm{prob}(F/G) = r$ is tantamount to saying that if b is an object that we know to have the property G, but we do not know anything else relevant about b, then $\mathrm{PROB}(Fb) = r$. Applying this observation to the preceding example, to say that $\mathrm{prob}(F/G\&H) = r$ is tantamount of saying that if c is an object that we know to have the property $G\&H$, but we do not know anything else relevant about c, then $\mathrm{PROB}(Fc) = r$. This is precisely the conclusion we obtain from (4.1) given the assumption that $\mathrm{prob}(F/G) = r$. Thus classical direct inference not only presupposes but provides direct support for the following principles regarding indefinite probabilities:

(4.3)   If F is projectible with respect to G then $\ulcorner\underset{p}{\diamond}\,\exists(G\&H)\ \&\ \mathrm{prob}(F/G) = r\urcorner$ is a prima facie reason for believing $\ulcorner\mathrm{prob}(F/G\&H) = r\urcorner$.

Equivalently:

(4.4)   If F is projectible with respect to G then $\ulcorner\underset{p}{\diamond}\,\exists H\ \&\ (H \Rightarrow G)\ \&\ \mathrm{prob}(F/G) = r\urcorner$ is a prima facie reason for $\ulcorner\mathrm{prob}(F/H) = r\urcorner$.

It will be important in the discussion of induction that (4.4) can be strengthened as follows:

(4.5)   If F is projectible with respect to G then $\ulcorner\Box\forall(H \rightarrow G)\ \&\ (\underset{p}{\diamond}\,\exists G > \underset{p}{\diamond}\,\exists H)\urcorner$ is a prima facie reason for $\ulcorner\mathrm{prob}(F/H) = \mathrm{prob}(F/G)\urcorner$.

The derivation of (4.5) from (4.4) proceeds primarily from (2.4), but I will not give the details here.

Principles (4.3)-(4.5) license inferences from indefinite probabilities to indefinite probabilities. Such inferences comprise *nonclassical direct inference*. Principles (4.3)-(4.5) amount to a kind of principle of insufficient reason; (4.3) tells us that if we have no reason to think otherwise, it is reasonable for us to anticipate that conjoining

H to G will not affect the probability of F. Once it has been pointed out, it seems obvious that this is what is presupposed by classical direct inference. In determining the probability that c will have the property F, we make use of those indefinite probabilities whose values are known to us, and we assume that those whose values are unknown to us would not upset the inference if they were known.

I will adopt principle (4.4) as my basic principle of nonclassical direct inference. I have found that a common reaction to this principle is that it is absurd—perhaps trivially inconsistent. This reaction arises from the observation that in a large number of cases, (4.4) will provide us with prima facie reasons for conflicting inferences or even prima facie reasons for inferences to logically impossible conclusions. For example, since in a standard deck of cards a spade is necessarily black and the probability of a black card being a club is one-half, (4.4) gives us a prima facie reason to conclude that the probability of a spade being a club is one-half, which is absurd. But this betrays an insensitivity to the functioning of prima facie reasons. A prima facie reason for an absurd conclusion is automatically defeated by the considerations that lead us to regard the conclusion as absurd. Similarly, prima facie reasons for conflicting inferences defeat one another. If P is a prima facie reason for Q and R is a prima facie reason for $\sim Q$, then P and R rebut one another and both prima facie inferences are defeated. No inconsistency results. That this sort of case occurs with some frequency in nonclassical direct inference should not be surprising, because it also occurs with some frequency in classical direct inference. In classical direct inference we very often find ourselves in the position of knowing that c has two logically independent properties G and H, where $\mathrm{prob}(F/G) \neq \mathrm{prob}(F/H)$. When that happens, classical direct inferences from these two probabilities conflict with one another, and so each prima facie reason is a defeater for the other, with the result that we are left without an undefeated direct inference to make.

The connection between definite and indefinite probability that was utilized in the defense of (4.4) can also be used to derive the following subset defeaters for (4.4) from subset defeaters for classical direct inference:

(4.6)   If F is projectible with respect to J then $\ulcorner (H \Rightarrow J)\ \&\ (J \Rightarrow G)$
& $\mathrm{prob}(F/J) \neq \mathrm{prob}(F/G)\urcorner$ is an undercutting defeater for (4.4).

We now have two kinds of direct inference—classical and nonclassical. Direct inference has traditionally been identified with classical direct inference, but I believe that it is most fundamentally nonclassical direct inference. The details of classical direct inference are all reflected in nonclassical direct inference. If we could identify definite probabilities with certain indefinite probabilities, we could derive the theory of classical direct inference from the theory of nonclassical direct inference, and perhaps throw considerable light on the nature of direct inference. This can be done as follows.

Suppose that the only thing we know about c is that it has the properties G, H, and K, and we want to ascertain the value of $\mathrm{PROB}(Fc)$. Suppose we know the values of prob(F/G), prob(F/H), and prob(F/K). The moves we would make in classical direct inference are precisely the same as the moves we would make in attempting to ascertain the value of prob($F/G \& H \& K$). For example, if we know that prob(F/G) = prob(F/H) = prob(F/K) = r, then we will infer both that PROB(Fc) = r and that prob($F/G \& H \& K$) = r. If we know that prob(F/G) $\neq$ r but prob(F/H) = prob(F/K) = r, and we do not know anything else relevant, then we will refrain from concluding that PROB(Fc) = r and we will also refrain from concluding that prob($F/G \& H \& K$) = r. If we know the above and also know that H entails G, then we will again infer both that PROB(Fc) = r and that prob($F/G \& H \& K$) = r. And so on. This suggests that what we are really attempting to ascertain in direct inference is the value of prob(F/π) where π is the conjunction of all the properties we are warranted in believing c to possess. More accurately, if we let K be the conjunction of all the propositions we are warranted in believing, my proposal is that PROB(Fc) can be defined as:

(4.7)   PROB(Fc) = prob($Fx/x = c \& K$).

Principle (4.7) consitutes a precise formulation of the elusive "total evidence" requirement. Philosophers have resisted formulating it in this simple manner because they have supposed probabilities like prob($Fx/x = c \& K$) to be illegitimate on the ground either that they must be 1 or 0 (which is to confuse probabilities with relative frequencies) or else that there is no way we could know their values. The objection that they must be either 1 or 0 is dispelled by taking direct inference to pertain to nomic probabilities rather than relative frequencies. The objection that there is no way we could know the value of prob($Fx/x = c \& K$) is more interesting. Our basic way of knowing the values of indefinite probabilities is by statistical induction. It is only possible to ascertain the value of prob(F/G) inductively if the extension of G is large so that we can compile reliable statistics about the proportion of G's that are F. On the supposition that the only way to ascertain the value of an indefinite probability is inductively, it follows that there is no way to ascertain the value of prob($Fx/x = c \& K$). However, that supposition is mistaken. Nonclassical direct inference provides another way of ascertaining the values of indefinite probabilities. Induction and direct inference jointly provide the logical or epistemological machinery for dealing with nomic probabilities. By induction, we learn the values of certain indefinite probabilities, and then by direct inference we infer the values of others. Without direct inference we would be unable to evaluate many probabilities that everyone agrees shoud be respectable. For example, there are no redheaded mathematicians who were born in Kintyre, North Dakota (population 7), but barring evidence to the contrary we would regard being redheaded, a mathematician, and having been born in Kintyre as irrelevant to the likelihood of having lung cancer, and would take the probability of a redheaded mathematician born in Kintyre, North Dakota, having lung cancer to be the same as that for a resident of North Dakota in general. It is direct inference that allows this. If direct inference legitimates such evaluations, it also allows us to evaluate probabilities like prob($Fx/x = c \& K$).

There is a useful way of getting definite probabilities that accord with (4.7). The following is a consequence of the axioms we adopted in section 2 for nomic probabilities:

(4.8)   If $\Box(Q \leftrightarrow Sa_1 \ldots a_n)$ and $\Box(Q \leftrightarrow Bb_1 \ldots b_m)$ and $\Box[Q \to (P \leftrightarrow Ra_1 \ldots a_n)]$ and $\Box[Q \to (P \leftrightarrow Ab_1 \ldots b_m)]$, then prob $(Rx_1 \ldots x_n / Sx_1 \ldots x_n \ \& \ x_1 = a_1 \ \& \ldots \& \ x_n = a_n) =$ prob$(Ay_1 \ldots y_m / By_1 \ldots y_m \ \& \ y_1 = b_1 \ \& \ldots \& \ y_m = b_m)$.

This allows us to define a kind of definite probability as follows:

(4.9)   prob$(P/Q) = r$ iff for some n, there are n-place properties R and S and objects $a_1, \ldots, a_n$ such that $\Box(Q \leftrightarrow Sa_1 \ldots a_n)$ and $\Box[Q \to (P \leftrightarrow Ra_1 \ldots a_n)]$ and prob$(Rx_1 \ldots x_n / Sx_1 \ldots x_n \ \& \ x_1 = a_1 \ \& \ldots \& \ x_n = a_n) = r$.

prob(P/Q) is an *objective* definite probability. It reflects the state of the world, not the state of our knowledge. The definite probabilities at which we arrive by classical direct inference are not those defined by (4.9). Instead, it follows from (4.7) that:

(4.10)   PROB$(Fc) =$ prob(Fc/K)

where K is the conjunction of all our warranted beliefs. I propose that we generalize this and define:

(4.11)   PROB$(P) =$ prob(P/K)

(4.12)   PROB$(P/Q) =$ prob$(P/Q \& K)$.

These are *epistemic* definite probabilities.

The initial defense of nonclassical direct inference appealed to classical direct inference, but now we can turn the tables. Given the reduction of definite probabilities to indefinite probabilities, it becomes possible to derive principles (4.1) and (4.2) of classical direct inference from our principles of nonclassical direct inference. The upshot of all this is that classical direct inference can be explained in terms of nonclassical direct inference, and definite probabilities can be defined in terms of nomic probabilities.

We must still ask what justifies nonclassical direct inference. It turns out that principles (4.3) and (4.4) can be derived from our acceptance rule (A3) together with computational principles governing nomic probability. Let us say that a property H is a *subproperty* of another property G iff $(\genfrac{}{}{0pt}{}{\diamond}{p} \exists G > \genfrac{}{}{0pt}{}{\diamond}{p} \exists H)$ and $(H \Rightarrow G)$, and let us say that *H agrees* with G (relative to a third property F) iff prob$(F/H) =$ prob(F/G). The basic idea behind the derivation of (4.3) is that direct inference would not be reasonable unless it were true that most subproperties of a noncounterlegal projectible property agree with it relative to any other projectible property. The immediate problem is how to understand the 'most' in this requirement. There are infinitely many subproperties of any given property, so this cannot be understood in terms of ratios. It can only be understood in terms of some measure on the set of all properties. What measure could this be? The only reasonable measure is probability itself. It must be extremely probable that a noncounterlegal property agree with its subproperties relative to any other projectible property. More accurately, the following *Principle of Agreement* must hold in order for direct inference to be reasonable:

(4.13)   For any properties F and G such that F is projectible with respect to G, if G is not counterlegal then:
prob$[$prob$(F/G) = $ prob$(F/X) / X$ is a subproperty of $G] = 1$.

I will return to the defense of (4.13), but first I want to show that if we can establish (4.13), our principles of nonclassical direct inference can be derived from it with the help of the acceptance rule (A3). This is very simple. We have the following instance of (A1):

(4.14)   If $\ulcorner$prob$(F/X) = r\urcorner$ is projectible with respect to $\ulcorner X \Rightarrow G\urcorner$ then $\ulcorner H$ is a subproperty of G and prob$[$prob$(F/X) = r / X$ is a subproperty of $G]$ $= 1\urcorner$ is a prima facie reason for $\ulcorner$prob$(F/H) = r\urcorner$.

Principle (4.4) is an immediate consequence of this if we make the reasonable assumption that $\ulcorner$prob$(F/X) = r\urcorner$ is projectible with respect to $\ulcorner X$ is a subproperty of $G\urcorner$ whenever F is projectible with respect to G.

Principle (4.6) (the rule of subset defeat) follows with the help of (D3). According to the present account, the direct inference from $\ulcorner$prob$(F/G) = r\urcorner$ to $\ulcorner$prob(F/H) $= r\urcorner$ proceeds via the instance (4.14) of (A3), and hence it will be defeated by any defeater for that instance of (A3). By (D3) and our assumptions about projectibility, the following is such a defeater:

(4.15)   If F is projectible with respect to J then $\ulcorner H$ is a subproperty of J prob$[$prob$(F/M) = r / M$ is a subproperty of G and M is a subproperty of $J] < 1\urcorner$ constitutes an undercutting defeater for (4.14).

If we are warranted in believing that prob$(F/H) \neq r$, that in itself defeats our direct inference, so suppose instead that we are not warranted in believing that prob$(F/H) \neq r$. To establish (4.6), suppose we are warranted in believing $\ulcorner (H \Rightarrow J)$ & $(J \Rightarrow G)$ & prob$(F/J) \neq$ prob$(F/G)\urcorner$. If $(J \Rightarrow G)$ then any subproperty of J is a subproperty of G, and so

prob$($prob$(F/M) = r / M$ is a subproperty of G and M is a subproperty of $J)$
$= $ prob$[$prob$(F/M) = r / M$ is a subproperty of $J]$.

As we are warranted in believing that prob$(F/J) \neq$ prob(F/G), we are warranted in believing that there is an s such that $s \neq r$ and prob$(F/J) = s$. It follows that we are warranted in believing that for some such s,

prob$[$prob$(F/M) = s / M$ is a subproperty of $J] = 1$

and therefore that

prob[prob(F/M) = s/M is a subproperty of G and M is a subproperty of J]
= 1.

But then we are warranted in believing that

prob[prob(F/M) = r/M is a subproperty of G and M is a subproperty of J] < 1.

Thus we have a defeater of the form of (4.15). Consequently, the Rule of Subset Defeat follows from this account of direct inference.

What has been shown is that given the principle of agreement, we can derive our entire theory of direct inference from the acceptance rule (A3) together with "computational" assumptions about nomic probability. This derivation explains the projectibility constraints in (4.5) and (4.6). They arise directly out of the projectibility constraint in (A3). What remains is to defend (4.13), the principle of agreement. Principle (4.13) can be defended by appealing to our explanation of nomic probability as a measure of proportions among physically possible objects. If G is not counterlegal, to say that prob(F/G) = r is to say that the proportion of physically possible G's that would be F is r. Given this conception of probability, an intuitive defense of (4.13) can be mounted as follows. We begin by noting a simple combinatorial fact. Consider the relative frequency of a property F in a set X. Subsets of X need not exhibit the same relative frequency of F's, but it is a striking fact of set theory that subsets of X *tend* to exhibit *approximately* the same relative frequency of F's as X, and both the strength of the tendency and the degree of approximation improve as the size of X increases. More precisely, the following is a theorem of set theory:

(4.16) For every δ, $\gamma > 0$, there is an n such that if X is a finite set containing at least n members and freq[F/X] = r then:

$$\text{freq}\big[\ |\text{freq}[F/Y]\text{-}r| < \delta\ /\ Y \neq \varnothing \text{ and } Y \subseteq X\big] > 1 - \gamma.$$

It was noted in section 2 [principle (2.2)] that the frequency of F's in a set is approximated by the frequency of F's in sequences of elements of the set. Combining (4.16) with principle (2.2), we obtain the result that different sequences of elements of a set tend to have approximately the same frequencies of F's, with the tendency getting stronger and the approximation getting better as the sequences get longer and the set gets bigger:

(4.17) For every δ, $\gamma > 0$ there are m, n such that if X is a finite set containing at least n members then:

$$\text{freq}\big[\ |\text{freq}[F/\sigma] - \text{freq}[F/\eta]| < \delta\ /\ \sigma \epsilon X^m\ \&\ \eta \epsilon Y^m\ \&\ Y \subseteq X\big] > 1 - \gamma.\text{[15]}$$

In the limit (where X becomes infinite and the sequences become ω-sequences), we would expect the proportion of sequences whose frequencies agree with X within any degree of approximation to become 1. When X is infinite, we can no longer talk about proportions in terms of relative frequencies. Talk about proportions must instead be formulated in terms of probability. Thus the following generalization of (4.17) should hold:

(4.18)   If X is an infinite class then:

$$\text{prob}\big[\lim_{m\to\infty}|\text{freq}[F/\sigma\text{'}m] - \text{freq}[F/\eta\text{'}m]| = 0 \;/\; \sigma\epsilon X^w \;\&\; \eta\epsilon Y^w \;\&\; Y \subseteq X\big] = 1.$$

For any properties G and H, let **G** be the class of all physically possible G's and let **H** be the class of all physically possible H's. Recalling that the class of all physically possible G's is the class of all ordered pairs $\langle x,w\rangle$ such that x is a possible object and w is a physically possible world at which x is G, it follows that $\mathbf{H} \subseteq \mathbf{G}$ iff $\underset{p}{\Box}(\forall x)(Hx \to Gx)$. Thus (4.18) implies:

(4.19)   If G is a property and **G** is infinite then:

$$\text{prob}\big[\lim_{m\to\infty}|\text{freq}[F/\sigma\text{'}m] - \text{freq}[F/\eta\text{'}m]| = 0 \;/\sigma\epsilon\mathbf{G}^\omega \;\&\; \eta\epsilon X^\omega \;\&\; X \subseteq \mathbf{G}\big] = 1.$$

Now observe that $X \subseteq \mathbf{G}$ iff $X = \mathbf{H}$ for some property H such that $\underset{p}{\Box}(\forall x)(Hx \to Gx)$. Futhermore, in order to have $\eta\epsilon X^\omega$, X must be non-empty, which is just to say that $\underset{p}{\Diamond}(\exists x)Hx$. Given that $\underset{p}{\Diamond}(\exists x)Hx$, it follows that $\underset{p}{\Diamond}(\forall x)(Hx \to Gx)$ iff $(H \Rightarrow G)$. Consequently, $X \subseteq \mathbf{G}$ iff $X = \mathbf{H}$ for some subproperty H of G. Note also that $\mathbf{G}^\omega = G^\omega$. Combining these observations, and abbreviating $\ulcorner X$ is a subproperty of $G\urcorner$ as $\ulcorner X \subseteq G\urcorner$, we should be able to rewrite (4.19) as follows:

(4.20)   If G is a property and there are infinitely many physically possible G's then $\text{prob}\big[\lim_{m\to\infty}\text{freq}[F/\sigma\text{'}m] = \lim_{m\to\infty}\text{freq}[F/\eta\text{'}m] \;/\sigma\epsilon G^\omega \; \eta\epsilon X^\omega \;\&$ $X \subseteq G)\big] = 1.$

Despite their intuitive connection, there is no way to formally derive (4.20) from (4.19). I will instead adopt (4.20) as our final computational axiom for nomic probabilities. It tells us that the probability is 1 that the limit of the frequency in an ω-sequence of a subproperty of G will be the same as the limit of the frequency in an ω-sequence of G's. This axiom describes another respect in which probabilities act like frequencies in the limit.

Principle (2.3) was supposed to lend substance to the explanation of nomic probability as measuring proportions among physically possible objects. According to (2.3):

If $\underset{p}{\Diamond}\exists G$ then $\text{prob}(F/G) = r$ iff $\text{prob}\big[\lim_{m\to\infty}\text{freq}[F/\sigma\text{'}m] = r \;/\; \sigma\epsilon G^\omega\big] = 1.$

Intuitively, it seems clear that given (2.3), (4.20) should imply that the probability is 1 that the limit of the frequency of F's in an ω-sequence of a subproperty of G equals $\text{prob}(F/G)$, and hence the probability is 1 that a subproperty X of G will be such that

$\text{prob}(F/X) = \text{prob}(F/G)$. More precisely:

(4.21)   If $\underset{p}{\diamond} \exists G$ and there are infinitely many physically possible G's then:

$$\text{prob}\left[\text{prob}(F/G) = \text{prob}(F/X) / X \subseteq G\right] = 1.$$

This can be turned into a precise derivation. With the help of (2.17) and (2.18), it can be shown that (4.21) is implied by (2.3) and (4.20).

Finally, I want to argue that if (4.21) is true then (4.13) (the principle of agreement) is also true. For this purpose, it suffices to argue that if G is projectible and not counterlegal then there are infinitely many physically possible G's. Recalling that a physically possible G is an ordered pair $\langle x, w \rangle$ such that w is a physically possible world and x is a G at w, it will be true for almost any noncounterlegal property G that there will be infinitely many physically possible G's. A sufficient condition for this is that there be infinitely many physically possible worlds at which there are G's. The latter is very hard to avoid. As I pointed out above, even if G is a property like that of *being Bertrand Russell* which can only be possessed by a single object, there are infinitely many physically possible G's because there are infinitely many physically possible worlds at which Bertrand Russell has the property of being Bertrand Russell. It appears that the only way there can fail to be infinitely many physically possible G's is when G is a very contrived property. For example, picking some particular possible world α, we might consider the property of *being Bertrand Russell and such that α is the actual world*. This peculiar property can only be possessed by Bertrand Russell, and it can only be possessed by him at the possible world α. But such contrived properties are not projectible. Projectible properties are always, in some sense, general or qualitative. Part of what this means is that objects can have these properties at infinitely many different possible worlds. Accordingly, I think it must be acknowledged that (4.13) is true.

5. INDUCTION

Our most fundamental source of knowledge regarding the values of nomic probabilities is *statistical induction*. In statistical induction, we observe the relative frequency of F's in a sample of G's, and then infer that $\text{prob}(F/G)$ is approximately equal to that relative frequency. This is closely related to ordinary *enumerative induction* wherein we observe that *all* of the G's in our sample are F's and infer that any G would be an F.[16]

There are two different philosophical stances that could be taken with respect to statistical and enumerative induction. We could try to derive them from more basic epistemic principles, or it could be maintained that principles of induction are themselves basic epistemic principles. These two stances reflect what have come to be regarded as two different problems of induction. The traditional problem of induction was that of justifying induction. But most contemporary philosophers have forsaken that for Goodman's "New Riddle of Induction," which I will construe here as the problem of giving an accurate account of correct principles of induction.[17] This change in orientation reflects the view that principles of induction are basic epistemic principles, partly constitutive of rationality, and not reducible to or justifiable on the basis of anything more fundamental. The latter was my view until recently, but now I am convinced that it is false. In this section I will address both problems of induction, arguing that precise principles of induction can be derived from (and hence justified on the basis of) the various principles regarding probability that we have already endorsed. This leads simultaneously to a solution to the new riddle of induction and a solution to the traditional problem of induction.

The justification of statistical induction proceeds in terms of what I call *the statistical induction argument*. The details of this argument are complicated, but they are presented fully in "A Solution to the Problem of Induction." My purpose here is just to give the reader a basic understanding of how the argument goes, and the simplest way to do that is to consider a special case of statistical induction. In a normal case, $prob(A/B)$ could have any value from 0 to 1. The fact that there are infinitely many possible values makes the argument complicated. For present purposes, let us suppose that we know somehow that $prob(A/B)$ has one of a finite set of values $p_1, \ldots, p_k$. Suppose we have observed a sample $X = \{a_1, \ldots, a_n\}$ of B's and noted that only $a_1, \ldots, a_r$ are A's (where A, $\sim A$, and B are projectible properties). Then the relative frequency f_X of A's in X is r/n. From this we want to infer that $prob(A/B)$ is approximately r/n. Our reasoning proceeds in two stages, the first stage employing our theory of direct inference and the second stage employing our acceptance rule.

Stage I

Let us abbreviate $\ulcorner x_1, \ldots, x_n$ are distinct $\& Bx_1 \& \ldots \& Bx_n \& prob(Ax/Bx) = p \urcorner$ as $\ulcorner \Theta_p \urcorner$. When $r \leq n$, we have by the probability calculus:

(5.1) $prob[Ax_1 \& \ldots \& Ax_r \& \sim Ax_{r+1} \& \ldots \& \sim Ax_n \& \Theta_p]$

$= prob[Ax_1 / Ax_2 \& \ldots \& Ax_r \& \sim Ax_{r+1} \& \ldots \& \sim Ax_n \& \Theta_p]$

$\times \ldots \times prob[Ax_r / \sim Ax_{r+1} \& \ldots \& \sim Ax_n \& \Theta_p]$

$\times prob[\sim Ax_{r+1} / \sim Ax_{r+2} \& \ldots \& \sim Ax_n \& \Theta_p] \times \ldots \times$

$prob[\sim Ax_n / \Theta_p]$.

Making Θ_p explicit:

(5.2) $prob[Ax_i / Ax_{i+1} \& \ldots \& Ax_r \& \sim Ax_{r+1} \& \ldots \& \sim Ax_n \& \Theta_p]$

$= prob[Ax_i / x_1, \ldots, x_n$ are distinct $\& Bx_1 \& \ldots \& Bx_n \& Ax_{n+1}$

$\& \ldots \& Ax_r \& \sim Ax_{r+1} \& \ldots \& \sim Ax_n \& prob(A/B) = p]$.

Projectibility is closed under conjunction, so $\ulcorner Bx_1 \& \ldots \& Bx_n \& x_1, \ldots, x_n$ are distinct & Ax_1 & . . . & Ax_r & $\sim Ax_{r+1}$ & . . . & $\sim Ax_n$⌐ is projectible. Given principles we have already endorsed, it can be proven that whenever ⌐Fx⌐ is projectible, so is ⌐Fx & prob$(Ax/Bx) = p$⌐. Consequently, the reference property of (5.2) is projectible. Thus a nonclassical direct inference gives us a reason for believing that:

$$\text{prob}\big[Ax_i \,/\, Ax_{i+1} \& \ \ . \ . \ . \ \& \ Ax_r \& \sim Ax_{r+1} \& \ \ . \ . \ . \ \& \sim Ax_n \& \Theta_p\big] =$$

$$\text{prob}\big[Ax_i \,/\, Bx_i \& \text{prob}(A/B) = p\big],$$

which by principle (2.13) equals p. Similarly, nonclassical direct inference gives us a reason for believing that if $r < i < n$ then

(5.3) $\text{prob}\big[\sim Ax_i \,/\, \sim Ax_{i+1} \& \ \ . \ . \ . \ \& \sim Ax_n \& \Theta_p\big] = 1\text{-}p$.

Then from (5.1) we have:

(5.4) $\text{prob}\big[Ax_1 \& \ \ . \ . \ . \ \& \ Ax_r \& \sim Ax_{r+1} \& \ \ . \ . \ . \ \& \sim Ax_n \,/\, \Theta_p\big] =$
$\quad\quad p^r(1-p)^{n\text{-}r}$

The equation ⌐$f\{x_1, \ . \ . \ ., x_n\} = r/n$⌐ is equivalent to a disjunction of $\frac{n!}{r!(n-r)!}$ pairwise incompatible disjuncts of the form ⌐$Ax_i \& \ \ . \ . \ . \ \& Ax_r \& \sim Ax_{r+1} \& \ \ . \ . \ . \ \& \sim Ax_n$⌐, so by the probability calculus:

(5.5) $\text{prob}\big[f\{x_1, \ . \ . \ . , x_n\}\big] = \frac{r}{n} \,/\, \Theta_p\big] = \frac{n!p^r(1-p)^{n\text{-}r}}{r!(n-r)!}$.

This is the formula for the binomial distribution. Ths completes stage I of the argument.

Stage II

I assume at this point that if A is a projectible property and ⌐$f_x = r/n$⌐ reports the relative frequencies of A's in a set X, then ⌐$f_x \neq r/n$⌐ is a projectible property of X. Thus the following conditional probability, derived from (5.5), satisfies the projectibility constraint of our various acceptance rules:

(5.6) $\text{prob}\big[f\{x_1, \ . \ . \ . , x_n\} \neq \frac{r}{n} \,/\, \Theta_p\big] = 1 - \frac{n!p^r(1-p)^{n\text{-}r}}{r!(n-r)!}$.

Let $b(n,r,p) = \frac{n!p^r(1-p)^{n\text{-}r}}{r!(n-r)!}$. For sizable n, $b(n,r,p)$ is almost always quite small. E.g., $b(50,20,.5) = .04$. Thus by (A2) and (5.6), for each choice of p we have a prima facie reason for believing that $\langle a_1, \ . \ . \ . , a_n \rangle$ does not satisfy Θ_p, i.e., for believing ⌐$\sim(a_1, \ . \ . \ . , a_n$ are distinct & $Ba_1 \& \ \ . \ . \ . \ \& Ba_n \& \text{prob}(A/B) = p)$⌐. As we know that ⌐$a_1, \ . \ . \ . , a_n$ are distinct & $Ba_1 \& \ \ . \ . \ . \ \& Ba_n$⌐ is true, this gives us a prima facie reason for believing that $\text{prob}(A/B) \neq p$. But we know that for some one of $p_1, \ . \ . \ . , p_k$, $\text{prob}(A/B) = p_i$. This case is much like the case of the lottery paradox. For each i we have a prima facie reason for believing that $\text{prob}(A/B) \neq p_i$, but we also have a counterargument for the conclusion that $\text{prob}(A/B) = p_i$, viz:

$$\text{prob}(A/B) \neq p_1$$
$$\text{prob}(A/B) \neq p_2$$
.
.
.
$$\text{prob}(A/B) \neq p_{i-1}$$
$$\text{prob}(A/B) \neq p_{i+1}$$
.
.
.
$$\text{prob}(A/B) \neq p_k$$
For some j between 1 and k, $\text{prob}(A/B) = p_j$.
Therefore, $\text{prob}(A/B) = p_i$.

There is, however, an important difference between the present case and the case of a fair lottery. For each i, we have a prima facie reason for believing that $\text{prob}(A/B) \neq p_i$, but these reasons are not all of the same strength because the probabilities assigned by (5.6) differ for the different p_i's. The counterargument is only as good as its weakest link, so the possibility arises that for some of the p_i's, the counterargument will not be strong enough to defeat the prima facie reason for believing that $\text{prob}(A/B) \neq p_i$. Thus there may be a subset R (the *rejection class*) of $\{p_1, \ldots, p_k\}$ such that we will be justified in concluding that for each $p \in R$, $\text{prob}(A/B) \neq p$, and hence $\text{prob}(A/B) \notin R$. Let A (the *acceptance class*) be $\{p_1, \ldots, p_k\} - R$. It follows that we are justified in believing that $\text{prob}(A/B) \in A$. A will consist of those p_i's closest in value of r/n. Thus we can think of A as an interval around the observed frequency such that we are justifed in believing that $\text{prob}(A/B)$ lies in that interval.

This argument can be filled out a bit more fully as follows. Let us make the simplifying assumption that for some i, $p_i = r/n$. $b(n,r,p)$ will always be highest for this value of p, which means that (5.6) provides us with a weaker reason for believing that $\text{prob}(A/B) \neq r/n$ than it does for believing that $\text{prob}(A/B) \neq p_j$ for any of the other p_j's. It follows that r/n cannot be in the rejection class, because each step of the counterargument is better than the reason for believing that $\text{prob}(A/B) \neq r/n$. On the other hand, $\ulcorner\text{prob}(A/B) \neq r/n\urcorner$ will be the weakest step of the counterargument for every other p_j. Thus what determines whether p_j is in the rejection class is simply the comparison of $b(n,r,p_j)$ to $b(n,r,n/r)$. A convenient way to encode this comparison is by considering the ratio:

$$(5.7) \quad L(n,r,p) = \frac{\text{prob}(f_{\{x_1, \ldots, x_n\}} = r/n / \Theta_p)}{\text{prob}(f_{\{x_1, \ldots, x_n\}} = r/n / \Theta_{r/n})}$$
$$= \frac{b(n,r,p)}{b(n,r,r/n)} = \left(\frac{np}{r}\right)^{nf} \times \left(\frac{n(1-p)}{n-r}\right)^{(n-r)/n}.$$

$L(n,r,p)$ is the *likelihood ratio* of $\ulcorner\text{prob}(A/B) = p\urcorner$ to $\ulcorner\text{prob}(A/B) = r/n\urcorner$. The greater the likelihood ratio, the stronger is our overall reason for believing (despite the counterargument) that prob(A/B) $\neq p$, and hence the more justified we are in believing that prob(A/B) $\neq p$. The likelihood ratio can be regarded as a measure of the degree of justification. For each likelihood ratio α we obtain the α-*rejection class* R_α and the α-*acceptance class* A_α:

(5.8) $R_\alpha = \{p_i | L(n,r,p_i) \leq \alpha\}$

(5.9) $A_\alpha = \{p_i | L(n,r,p_i) > \alpha\}$

We are justified to degree α in rejecting the members of R_α, and hence we are justified to degree α in believing that prob(A/B) is a member of A_α.

I have only considered the discrete case in which we know that prob(A/B) has one of a finite set of values, but the argument can be generalized to apply to the continuous case as well. In the continuous case, A_α is an interval, so the argument provides us with justification for believing that prob(A/B) lies in a precisely defined interval around the observed relative frequency, the width of the interval being a function of the degree of justification. For illustration, some typical values of the acceptance interval are listed in table 1.

Table 1. Values of $A_\alpha(r/n,n)$

$A_\alpha(.5,n)$

n

α	10	10^2	10^3	10^4	10^5	10^6
.1	[.196,.804]	[.393,.607]	[.466,.534]	[.489,.511]	[.496,.504]	[.498,.502]
.01	[.112,.888]	[.351,.649]	[.452,.548]	[.484,.516]	[.495,.505]	[.498,.502]
.001	[.068,.932]	[.320,.680]	[.441,.559]	[.481,.519]	[.494,.506]	[.498,.502]

$A_\alpha(.9,n)$

n

α	10	10^2	10^3	10^4	10^5	10^6
.1	[.596,.996]	[.823,.953]	[.878,.907]	[.893,.907]	[.897,.903]	[.899,.901]
.01	[.446,1.00]	[.785,.967]	[.868,.927]	[.890,.909]	[.897,.903]	[.899,.901]
.001	[.338,1.00]	[.754,.976]	[.861,.932]	[.888,.911]	[.897,.903]	[.899,.901]

This completes the statistical induction argument. This argument makes precise the way in which observation of the relative frequency of A's in our sample justifies us in thinking that prob(A/B) is approximately the same as that relative frequency. We have derived this conclusion from our general theory of nomic probability, thus justifying statistical induction on the basis of that more general theory. The conclusions reached by this reasoning bear obvious similarities to the conclusions of orthodox statistical reasoning regarding confidence intervals or significance testing (although there will be differences regarding precisely what intervals are proposed as estimates).

Several writers have suggested general theories of statistical inference that are based on likelihood ratios and that agree closely with the present account when applied to the special case of statistical induction. However, such theories have been based merely on statistical intuition, without an underlying rationale of the sort given here. What is novel about the present account is not so much the conclusions drawn as the arguments advanced on their behalf. In addition, those general theories of statistical inference are all subject to counterexamples having to do with projectibility.[18]

Enumerative induction differs from statistical induction in that our inductive sample must consist of B's *all of which are A*'s and our conclusion is the generalization $(B \Rightarrow A)$. For familiar reasons, $\ulcorner$prob$(A/B) = 1\urcorner$ does not entail $\ulcorner(B \Rightarrow A)\urcorner$, so enumerative induction cannot be regarded as just a special case of statistical induction. Nevertheless, it is shown in "A solution to the Problem of Induction" that in the special case in which the observed realtive frequency is 1, our theory of nomic probability allows us to extend the statistical induction argument to obtain an argument for the conclusion $\ulcorner B \Rightarrow A \urcorner$. Thus enumerative induction can also be justified on the basis of nomic probability.

6. CONCLUSIONS

This completes my sketch of the theory of nomic probability. Let us step back and ask what has been accomplished. Having urged that no previous theory of probability provides an adequate analysis, I now claim to have given a satisfactory analysis of nomic probability. To some extent, I have done that by changing the rules of the game. I have forsaken any attempt to analyze probability by *defining* it in terms of something more basic. Instead, I have proposed an analysis that purports to describe the concept of nomic probability by describing its justification conditions. This change in orientation is not unmotivated. There are general epistemological reasons for believing that this is the only kind of analysis possible for many philosophically interesting concepts. Elsewhere, I have utilized this approach to propose solutions to a number of traditional epistemological problems, and all I have done here is extend the general approach to the analysis of probability.

As I indicated in section 1, a description of the justification conditions for nomic probability can be regarded as having four elements. First, there must be an account of statistical induction to enable us to acquire knowledge of indefinite probabilities from nonprobabilistic premises. Last, there must be an account of probabilistic acceptance rules that enable us to draw nonprobabilistic conclusions from probabilistic premises. In between, there must be an account of the kinds of inferences that can lead us from probabilities to probabilities. These are of two kinds. On the one hand, there are those purely computational inferences of the sort exemplified by the probability calculus. On the other hand, there are those prima facie inferences mediated by the theory of nonclassical direct inference.

The classical probability calculus provides one source of computational inferences, but I have maintained that it must be augmented in various ways by principles pertaining specifically to indefinite probabilities. Some of these principles are new, but the resulting theory is still only an extended version of the probability calculus. It is important, but not philosophically revolutionary.

The acceptance rules constitute the most important assumptions of the theory. I have maintained that there is one basic acceptance rule, namely (A3). Principle (A3) (and the description of its defeaters) can be regarded as the sole noncomputational principle upon which the theory of nomic probability is based. One of the most interesting features of (A3) is the projectibility constraint. Initially, that constraint is apt to seem out of place, but it has turned out that (A3) provides the ultimate source for projectibility constraints in other areas. Given (A3) and our computational principles, the theory of direct inference becomes derivable, and when the theory of direct inference is combined with (A3), principles of induction become derivable. Thus (A3) can be regarded as carrying most of the philosophical burden in the theory of nomic probability.

Notes

1. I introduced the concept of nomic probability in *Subjunctive Reasoning* (Reidel, 1976) (although I called it "subjunctive indefinite probability"). It also bears important similarities to the concept of probability discussed in van Fraassen's recent book *The Scientific Image* (Oxford, 1980).

2. In "Epistemology and Probability," *Synthese* 55 (1982), 231-52; "A Theory of Direct Inference," *Theory and Decision* 15 (1983), 29-96; and " A Solution to the Problem of Induction," forthcoming.

3. I first discussed nomic generalizations in *Subjunctive Reasoning* , where I called them "subjunctive generalizations."

4. More accurately, symbolizing physical possibility and physical necessity by '$\Diamond$'and '$\Box$'and the counterfactual conditional by '$>$', $\ulcorner F \Rightarrow G \urcorner$ is equivalent to $\ulcorner \underset{p}{\Diamond} (\exists x)Fx > \underset{p}{\Box}(\forall x)(Fx \to Gx) \urcorner$.

5. This requires that we individuate truth conditions sufficiently narrowly that logically equivalent truth conditions can be distinct.

6. For a much fuller discussion of this view of the specification of concepts and its application to a wide range of philosophical problems, see my *Knowledge and Justification* (Princeton, 1974).

7. See *Knowledge and Justification* , chap. 3, for a more careful discussion of all this.

8. Properties can be taken to be functions from objects or n-tuples of objects to states of affairs, where states of affairs are identified with the sets of possible worlds at which they obtain. For instance, the property of being red is identified with the function that to each object x assigns the state of affairs x's being red.

9. This is a familiar difficulty for theories that attempt to define probabilities as limits of relative frequencies.

10. There will be only a very few properties G such that there are only finitely many physically possible G's. Even a property like that of *being Bertrand Russell* will be infinite in this sense. It is true that there is only one thing that ever has that property (namely, Bertrand Russell), but the "physically possible things" having this property are pairs $\langle x, w \rangle$ where x has the property at w, and presumably there are infinitely many possible worlds at which Bertrand Russell has the property of being Bertrand Russell.

11. In "A Theory of Direct Inference," I erroneously endorsed the false principle $\ulcorner prob(Ax/Rxy) = prob(Ax/(\exists y)Rxy) \urcorner$. Fortunately, most of the purposes for which I used that principle can be served equally by (2.17)-(2.19).

12. See "Epistemology and Probability" for a discussion of the "weakest link" principle.

13. To say that S is warranted in believing φ is to say that if S were an ideal reasoner possessing his present evidence, he would be justified in believing φ. Warrant has the important property of being closed under deductive consequence.

14. In "A Theory of Direct Inference," I argued that these rules must be supplemented with a complex array of additional principles concerning defeaters for (4.1). I have since discovered that those additional principles can all be derived from (4.2) given a sufficiently sophisticated account of the way in which prima facie reasons interact in determining when a belief is justified.

15. X^m is the set of all m-tuples (sequences of length m) of members of X.

16. The precise connection between statistical induction and enumerative induction is more complicated than might be supposed. It is sorted out in "A Solution to the Problem of Induction."

17. Goodman took this more narrowly to be the problem of characterizing the class of projectible predicates. See *Fact, Fiction, and Forecast* (Cambridge, Mass., 1955).

18. See particularly Hacking's *Logic of Statistical Inference* (Cambridge, 1965), Gillie's *An Objective Theory of Probability* (Methuen, 1973), and A. W. F. Edwards' *Likelihood* (Cambridge, 1972). See also R.A. Fisher, "On the 'Probable Error' of a Coefficient of Correlation Deduced from a Small Sample," *Metreon* I, part 4, 3-32, and "On the Mathematical Foundations of Theoretical Statistics," *Phil. Trans. Roy. Soc.* A, 222 (1922):309-69; and G. A. Barnard, "Statistical Inference," *J. Royal Statistical Society* B, II (1949):115-49, "The Use of the Likelihood Function in Statistical Practice," *Proceedings V Berkley Symposium of Mathematical Statistics and Probability* I (1966):27-40, and "The Bayesian Controversy in Statistical Inference," *J. Inst. Actuar.* 93 (1967):229:69.

Two Ideals of Explanation in Natural Science[1]

ERNAN McMULLIN

1. TWO IDEALS

Within the empiricist tradition in the philosophy of science, the tendency has always been to conceive of explanation in the natural sciences in terms of observed regularities, of fitting the event to be explained into a pattern of lawlikeness.[2] Yet even at the very beginnings of this tradition in Bacon and Locke, there were intimations of a quite different ideal which sought intelligibility in unobserved entities and processes that "underlay" the phenomena and were causally responsible for them.

An illustration of this duality may be found in C. G. Hempel's *Philosophy of Natural Science*, which has served as the epitome of logical empiricism for several generations of beginning students in the philosophy of science. Hempel first develops the deductive-nomological (DN) model of explanation that he himself originally formulated in the 1940s, according to which to explain is "to fit the phenomenon to be explained into a pattern of regularities."[3] To explain E, it is necessary and sufficient that it be deductively derivable from one or more laws, together with a statement of initial conditions; in other words, it must be shown to be "lawlike" in its occurrence. This is all that is needed to make it intelligible.

Towards the end of the book, however, Hempel goes on to describe what appears to be a significantly different type of explanation that he calls "theoretical." When a set of empirical regularities ("laws") has been discovered in some domain, a theory is introduced

> to explain those regularities and generally, to afford a deeper and more accurate understanding of the phenomenon in question. To this end, a theory construes those phenomena as manifestations of entities and processes that lie behind or beneath them, as it were. These are assumed to be governed by characteristic theoretical laws, or theoretical principles, by means of which

the theory then explains the empirical uniformities that have been previously discovered and predicts new (ones).[4]

Here the regularities themselves are explained, and a "deeper and more accurate understanding" is thereby obtained. What constitutes this as explanatory is not the inclusion of these regularities into yet other regularities so much as the introduction of theoretical entities, that is, entities the warrant for whose relevance to this context (and often, for whose very existence) is their effectiveness in accounting for the observed regularities. Though there is a deductive element in this, the pattern here is nomological only in a secondary sense. The explanans is not primarily a set of laws but a postulated structure of entities, relations, processes.

Theoretical explanation is not, then, to be understood as a special case of DN explanation.[5] True, the postulated entities are "governed by characteristic laws," as Hempel remarks.[6] But the primary explanatory elements are not these "laws," which are no longer reports of empirical regularities; they are the postulated structures that suggest these "laws" and many others. "Explaining" here involves relating the explanandum to a structure that "goes beyond" the original experience in a much stronger sense than does an empirical generalization.

The ambiguity of this term, 'law', is what gives the attempt to assimilate theoretical to DN explanation much of whatever plausibility it possesses. If the term be taken in the broadest possible way, it is correct to say that theoretical explanations involve lawlike propositions. But the status of an empirical "law" differs in important respects from that of a theoretical "law." The former purports to describe, with some degree of idealization, an observed regularity; it is warranted in the first place on the basis of observation or experiment. To "explain" in terms of it is no more than to find the explanandum to be an instance of a known regularity, under a specific description of that regularity. A theoretical law, on the other hand, is a consequence of the postulated structure, the model, that constitutes the theory as theory. It does not report directly on observation; its function is to help "explain," usually at several removes, the empirical behavior of bodies by showing it to be derivable in an approximate way from certain assumptions about the intrinsic structure of the bodies.

One cannot decide merely on the basis of the syntactical form of such expressions as $PV = RT$ (Boyle-Charles' Law) whether it is an empirical or a theoretical "law." If it is asserted as a generalization from a set of observations of correlated values of P, V, and T, it is empirical; if it is derived from a theoretical account of an underlying (in this case molecular) structure, it is theoretical. The warrant for the first is inductive and (relatively) direct. The warrant for the second is retroductive and often quite indirect; it rests upon the success of the theory as a whole in accounting for as wide a range of empirical laws as possible.

2. THEORY AND OBSERVATION

But surely (the reader may now be objecting) this way of distinguishing between theoretical and empirical laws and, ultimately, between theoretical and DN explanations, presupposes the sort of sharp distinction between the "theoretical" and the "observational" that philosophers of science have been at such pains to deny in recent years. Have I not assumed above that the inductive generalizations on which DN explanation rests are themselves theory-neutral? This would have been a safe assumption for the logical empiricst (who nevertheless did not, for other reasons, feel inclined to accept the distinction we have just drawn between two levels of explanation). But what if one *denies* that a pure observation-language is possible? If inductive generalizations are theory-laden, if they have to be warranted on a broader basis than the restricted sets of observations from which they were originally derived, would their use in explanation not shade into properly theoretical explanation? To answer, we shall have to retrace our steps some way, and look a little more closely at the manner in which each type of explanation is defined.

What is meant by the claim that the typical empirical law is, despite appearances to the contrary, "theory-laden"? If measurements are involved, it is easy to see that a "theory" of the measure instrument is presupposed. The theory here may be a well-developed one; think of the "reading" on a mass spectrometer. Or it may be no more than a set of unexamined assumptions; think of length measurement before Einstein formulated his first theory of relativity. Or at the very lowest level, it can simply be an accepted way of structuring the world; a generalization like "mules are sterile" depends not only on the "facts" about mules, in the conventional sense, but also on what *counts* as a "mule" and as "sterile." Under the pressure of anomalies (think of what happened with "whales are fish"), even terms as fixed as these could shift, depending on the choice of generalizations one wants to preserve.[7] There is thus a level of assumption lying well under the surface here, one that rarely manifests itself directly.

The arguments here are, of course, familiar, and derive from many independent sources:[8] elementary considerations regarding the nature of measurement; the "network" model of language associated with the names of Duhem, Quine, and Hesse;[9] the inability of the logical positivists to find a satisfactory way of distinguishing between the "observational" and the "theoretical";[10] and the influence of prior knowledge upon perception.[11] The aim of these arguments is to refute the empiricist assumption that a "pure" language of observation is available to serve as a secure and unchanging foundation for scientific theory. The cliché of "theory-ladenness" is evidently an unfortunate one, since it extends the notion of theory to near vacuity.[12] It would have been much better to use a more general term like 'presupposition' or 'assumption'. 'Theory' was chosen presumably as a direct challenge to the then-prevailing belief in a sharp observational/theoretical distinction.

Inductive generalizations cannot, then, be regarded as foundational in the way that logical empiricism required them to be. But this does not mean that they are not reliable and relatively stable against theory-inspired change. Kuhn himself concedes that low-level empirical laws (of which a science like inorganic chemistry can claim literally thousands) are cumulative, "progressive" in that they tend to be retained across the divide of major theory-change. Even when changes in definition or assumption occur, the laws still hold good under the original definitions or assumptions and at the original level of accuracy. The immense amount we now know about the behavior of gases, the precisions that have been wrought since then on the language of measurement do not affect Boyle's Law, within its original terms of reference. Such laws still hold good in the sense that they pick out regularities of nature sufficiently well to enable predictions to be made.

The case of Newtonian mechanics is particularly interesting—and particularly complex. Despite the fact that Newton's theory has been replaced by Einstein's, at the level of empirical law it is for the most part as though nothing had happened. No one uses relativistic formulae to calculate the periods of pendulums or planets. No one worries about changes in the definition of mass or length when applying Hooke's Law to describe the extension of a loaded spring. The classical concepts are still used to describe the basic measure-quantities of mass, length, and time. And the empirical laws can still be (roughly) derived (that is, a corresponding set of theoretical laws can be deduced) by taking classical mechanics to be a limiting case, for low velocities and small masses, of relativistic mechanics.

Feyerabend and others have queries the principle of continuity implied in this notion of a "limiting case." Yet they do not deny that at the practical level of predictable regularity, the classical system still *works*, just as Ptolemy's would (at a less adequate level) in planetary astronomy. Where it fails is as *explanation*. What Einstein showed was that Newton's concepts did not organize the world well; there were inadequacies, even inconsistencies. Thus if one wants to *explain* an instance of planetary motion today, one should not appeal to a law couched in Newtonian concepts, because this would imply a commitment to a system whose explanatory shortcomings have been shown.

There is, however, a notorious ambiguity about what it is to "explain" in mechanics, an ambiguity that goes back to Newton's *Principia*, and beyond. Does one "explain" a motion by merely describing, in kinematic terms, a regularity under which it can be comprised? Or does one postulate an agency (attraction, force) that is causally responsible for the motion? Newton could see the difficulties with which the latter alternative faced him; in the *Principia* he backs away from these and chooses the other approach. But then, his critics were quick to point out, did he really have an *explanation* in the proper sense at all? Throughout much of his later career, he attempted unsuccessfully to find a *theoretical* explanation of gravitational motion in terms of causal agency.[13]

The ambiguities of this issue can be illustrated by recalling an example of scientific change given by Paul Feyerabend:

> The law of inertia of the so-called impetus theory of the later Middle Ages and Newton's own law of inertia are in perfect quantitative agreement. Both assert that an object that is not under the influence of any outer force will proceed along in a straight line with constant speed. Yet despite this fact, the adoption of Newton's theory entails a conceptual revision that forces us to abandon the inertial law of the impetus theory, not because it is quantitatively incorrect but because it achieves the correct predictions with the help of inadequate concepts.[14]

What makes these concepts inadequate is that they suggest that an internal force, impetus, has to act to maintain the uniform speed of the body. Newton, on the other hand, showed that uniform speed did not require an agent cause. Buridan's impetus "law" is theoretical in form because it infers (either explicitly or implicitly, depending on how it is stated) to a cause, itself not directly observed. It is because Newton undermined this inference that the earlier law no longer serves as a proper explanation, even though it is still (as Feyerabend notes) quantitatively correct. More generally, it is where *causes* have been misassigned that the earlier formula will be repudiated. Where no assignment of cause, explicit or implicit, is involved, the empirical formulation (which retains its original operational significance) is unlikely to be challenged as explanation. But then, as we shall see, an empirical law of this noncausal kind, Boyle's law, for example, furnishes only the weakest sort of explanation in the first place.

3. NOMOTHETIC AND RETRODUCTIVE

In the light of this clarification of the relation between the observational and the theoretical, let us return to the task of deciding whether a significant distinction can be drawn between two correlative forms of explanation. A *nomothetic* explanation we can define as one that appeals to an empirical regularity, or combination of such regularities. The explanandum is discovered to be an instance of such a regularity or a combination thereof, taken under some specific description. The language of the explanandum need not be the same as that of the law used to explain; one could for example explain the length extension of a loaded spring by appealing to the most general form of Hooke's Law, which asserts the proportionality of stress and strain in elastic media. Even though a theory may underlie the language adopted for the descriptions used, a nomothetic explanation does not appeal directly to the theory; it takes the presuppositions of the language for granted in order to draw attention to an empirical regularity that the language allows to be characterized in a particular way.

Nomothetic explanation may be causal or noncausal, or undeclared in status between the two alternatives. Some empirical laws are explicitly causal in form, e.g., heating iron causes it to expand. Most are noncausal, e.g., molluscs of this variety have a better chance of survival than others do in heavily silted water; the emission spectrum of iron is of the following kind. Some suggest the possibility of a direct causal connection, while leaving open the possibility of another factor as common cause, e.g., heavy coffee-drinkers are more likely to develop gastric ulcers. Some assert a negative causal relationship, e.g., scurvy is caused by a deficiency of vitamin C in the diet. Laws asserting concomitant variation in two or more parameters do not ordinarily single out one of the parameters as cause. Changes in an independent variable are often said to "bring about" the changes in other parameters, although a proper specification of *cause* in such cases will usually require a further theoretical analysis, e.g., pressure varies with depth in a fluid medium; the angle of refraction at an optical interface between two media depends upon the relationship between the speed of light in one to that in the other.

To explain an empirical regularity, one may either move to a higher-order empirical regularity, or else try to explain the regularity in terms of a theory. Theory explains by suggesting what might bring about the explananda. It postulates entities, properties, processes, relations, themselves unobserved, that are held to be causally responsible for the empirical regularities to be explained. It is thus ampliative, in a strong sense. It opens up a new domain, and it is precisely *this* that constitutes it as explanatory. Concepts are needed that were not required for the description of the explanandum. They may be genuinely novel (as has often been the case in atomic physics); they may be analogical extensions of familiar concepts. Or they may be quite familiar (think of Galileo's postulation of lunar mountains as responsible for certain of the shadows on the lunar surface). In this last case, they would still be "novel" in the sense that they are in no way involved in the original observation report, so that an act of imagination is required.

This kind of explanation may be called *retroductive* because it leads backwards from observed effect to postulated causes.[15] The term is, of course, Peirce's, although he used it primarily for a form of inference. (He also used the terms 'abduction', 'presumption', and 'hypothesis' as rough synonyms.) Peirce noted: "A retroductive conclusion is only justified by its explaining an observed fact."[16] In retroduction, "a theory is suggested which would explain that which is surprising."[17] The strength of the justification given the theory is proportional to the quality of the explanation given; the two go hand in hand, as Aristotle long ago remarked of hypothetical reasoning generally.[18] This is a distinctive quality of retroduction that marks it off from both deduction and induction, as Peirce frequently emphasized.

The search for hypothetical causes of observed effects is necessarily theoretical in form. But it is probably better to avoid the phrase 'theoretical explanation', because of the ambiguities discussed in the last section. What happens in retroductive explanation is that lawlike consequences ("theoretical laws") are inferred from the postulated structure, the "model" as it is usually called. (Note that this is *not* the usage of the term 'model' in the "model theory" of the logician; a failure to appreciate this difference has occasionally led to serious ambiguity in recent philosophy of science.) The theoretical laws are deductive consequences of the theoretical model; they are tested against the empirical laws of the domain to be explained. Usually there will not be a perfect fit because of the various idealizations involved in the model (apart, of course, from actual deficiencies in it). If the fit is reasonably close, the empirical law is said to be "explained" by the theory.

Retroductive explanation is often described as reaching "behind" or "beneath" the phenomena, as in the passage quoted from Hempel in section 1 above. This language must not be taken to imply a Kantian distinction between appearance and thing-in-itself. (It is this supposed implication that has led some philosophers, like Putnam and Fine, to express their uneasiness about taking basic explanation in natural science to involve hidden agency.)[19] No distinction of "reality" is proposed between effect and cause. The suggestion that the "really real" is the hidden cause (in Eddington's famous metaphor, the set of atoms in motion that constitute the table) is not part of the understanding of retroductive explanation per se. It is the further metaphysical interpretation of retroduction characteristic of ancient Pythagoreans and modern reductionists. The postulated causes of a retroductive explanation are not necessarily unobservable; they are only in this context *unobserved*, and thus require a different, *theoretical* warrant. The geologist who explains the earth's magnetic field in terms of a core of iron within the earth is not implying either that this core is what is "really real" about the earth or that it is in principle unobservable. In the context of *these* explananda, it is of course unobserved.

The classical Greek ideal of demonstration excluded retroductive explanation, because of its provisional character, from among the finished products of "science" in the strict sense. But even before the extension of the domains of inquiry of the natural sciences by the telescope and the microscope in the seventeenth century, this exclusion caused many problems.[20] Over the past three centuries, retroductive explanation has gradually become accepted as the basic form of explanation in most parts of the natural sciences.[21] It incorporates not only the structural explanations of physics, astrophysics, chemistry, and genetics, but also the genetic explanations characteristic of geology and evolutionary biology. The hypothetical past states of the world are theoretical entities, removed from the possibility of direct observation by the passage of time, but causally linked to phenomena we can observe.

Retroductive explanation has always encountered difficulties, as already noted, in the field of mechanics. Are the "forces" of classical mechanics causal entities in their own right or are they (as Berkeley and Mach urged) only shorthand ways of describing the products of mass and acceleration, both of these respectable measured quantities? In other words, is explanation in classical mechanics truly retroductive or is it properly nomothetic, with only a misleading appearance of a retroductive character? This became a matter of intensive debate in the nineteenth century. Lagrange and Hamilton reformulated the Newtonian equations of motion in such a way as to eliminate any direct reference to force. The primary concept becomes *energy* instead, a concept which simply describes motion without explicitly assigning a cause for it. Yet an ontology still seemed to be needed in order to understand the communication of action. Thus ethers of various sorts were postulated, in the context of both optical and electromagnetic phenomena. Maxwell united these under a single set of equations, using as support the concept of a field located in an ether of a Newtonian sort. Like Newton before him, he worried about the ontology underlying the conception of electromagnetic transmission, but, again like Newton, he was convinced that the validity of his new mechanics did not depend on his being able to work out a means of specifying this ontology in a more traditional way. The ontology becomes even more indefinite in general relativity theory; though the concept of a field is central, and though the field can in some sense be taken to "cause" the motions described by the equations, it seems to reduce to a set of counterfactuals specifying what would happen if something of a certain sort were to be placed at various points of the space-time manifold "occupied" (or perhaps constituted?) by it.

In elementary-particle physics, the matter gets even more complicated. "Particles" are not reidentifiable individuals. "Forces" are constituted by the exchange of particles, so that particles come to be postulated as a way of explaining forces rather than forces postulated to explain the motions of particles. The tangle of theoretical entities is so dismaying that some physicists, like Heisenberg and Chew, recently proposed a return to a more ascetic science (which Heisenberg dubbed "Pythagorean" to contrast it with the "Democritean" model of science which explains causally in terms of constituent entities).[22] Their S-matrix approach, after some initial success, has not prospered, and the currently fashionable quark model in quantum field theory makes constant use of what sounds like retroductive explanation.

But is it really retroductive? It would seem that there is a third pattern, *dynamic* explanation, which shares features of both nomothetic and retroductive explanation but is in the end irreducible to either. Because we are trying to account for the motions of basic entities, there is nothing further we can appeal to; we cannot specify the forces or fields or energies in terms of a *further* type of entity. We seem to be forced back to a complex set of counterfactuals (which may be taken to express causal powers or basic tendencies or the like), specifying what *would* happen if a particular dynamic state of affairs were to be realized. But the *causal* words introduced to make the explanation conform to conventional causal patterns must be taken with great caution.

Much more would need to be said about the peculiarities of dynamic explanation, but there is not space for that here. What *is* clear, however, is that this mode of explanation is limited to physics and ultimately to mechanics. Though other parts of the natural sciences utilize mechanics, their own patterns of explanation are not simply dynamic in form. They involve postulated elements of more complex sorts, and hence a form of explanation which is properly retroductive. Though we have identified a third pattern of explanation, then, besides the nomothetic and the retroductive, and though this pattern may be called a basic one because of the fundamental character of mechanics itself, we shall focus here on the two types of explanation which may be said to characterize natural science as a *whole*.

4. RETRODUCTIVE EXPLANATION AND SCIENTIFIC REALISM

It is obvious that retroductive explanation is in some way associated with the doctrine of scientific realism, i.e., the view that the entities postulated by successful scientific theories are not just fictions utilized for the practical purposes of more effective prediction but agencies that play a causal role in the physical world. Both of the main types of argument for scientific realism rely on an analysis of retroduction. One seeks an explanation for the striking (and, so far as one can tell, contingent) success of this mode of explanation in the recent history of science.[23] The other uses the causal aspect of retroduction to argue that this will work only if the causes are taken to be active (i.e., existing) entities.

It may be helpful to give an illustration of how this latter argument goes, drawn from a paper by Wesley Salmon.[24] Brownian motion can be explained retroductively by postulating the existence of microentities (molecules), the number of which per mole of gas ($6.0225.10^{23}$), Avogadro's number, can be estimated with the aid of some quantitative data concerning the motion. One can by means of the same postulate account for a multitude of other phenomena of quite disparate sorts, such as electrolysis and alpha decay. The postulated microentities come out in each case to exactly the same number per mole. The number is so large and so precisely known that it seems altogether unlikely that different sorts of entities could be involved; a single kind of entity, the molecule, exerting several different kinds of causal agency, seems to be the only reasonable explanation. The instrumentalist ploy fails here because it can assign no plausible reason why the theoretical construct invoked to explain Brownian motion should turn out to be conceptually identical with the entity that explains electrolysis.

Suppose, however, that someone were to reject scientific realism. Would this imply that the distinction proposed above between retroductive and nomothetic explanation would collapse? I think not. Even if the causal aspect of retroduction were to be so interpreted as not to require any real agency as cause, one would still have to contend with the conceptual enlargement that we have seen to be characteristic of retroductive explanation, and the awkward problem (for the empiricist) about what to do with the resultant nonreferring concepts. The logical positivists, who were keenly aware of this difficulty, tried various devices like correspondence rules to give these concepts empirical respectability. The modern-day nonrealist would still be faced with the same problem and would, at the very least, have to acknowledge that from the empiricist standpoint, there is a significant difference between explanation which does employ this special cateogry of terms and explanation which does not. The nonrealist is likely to feel more comfortable with the latter.

The consequences of the distinction between the two forms of explanation are thus very different for the realist and the nonrealist. Though both will admit the distinction, the realist is likely to regard retroductive explanation as basic and nomothetic explanation as preliminary. The nonrealist, on the other hand, will emphasize the primacy of nomothetic explanation and may tend to treat retroductive explanation as in some way suspect.

5. THE INADEQUACY OF THE NOMOTHETIC IDEAL

It is time to look more closely at the issue just posed: which, if any, of the two forms of explanation ought be regarded as basic in natural science, excluding mechanics as a special case. Admittedly, both are needed in the course of scientific work. But can one or the other of them be taken to be primary? From Hume to Goodman, nomothetic explanation (i.e., explanation in terms of observed lawlikeness) has been proposed as the proper goal of science by a variety of philosophers: empiricists, phenomenalists, positivists, nominalists, seem to agree on this if not on much else. One argument against this could be based, obviously, on the thesis of scientific realism. But there are other arguments too. Two are worth noting.

The first of these has often been pointed out before. Consider one of Hempel's examples of explanation: "The slush on the sidewalk remained liquid during the frost because it had been sprinkled with salt."[25] Note that this explanans will serve to explain the condition of the sidewalk only if (1) the person seeking the explanation[26] did not know that salt had been sprinkled there, or if (2) he did not know the effect of sprinkling salt on snow. If someone who knowingly sprinkled salt on snow, which then proceeded to melt, were to seek an explanation for this, it would be a rather weak response to say that under these conditions, salt always does this! This would function as an explanation only in the sense that the questioner learns under which of the possible descriptions of natural regularity the explanandum is to be classed.

More generally, it must be emphasized that the inclusion of an explanandum under a regularity, even a causal regularity, is not ordinarily sufficient to count as explanation in science. Someone notes that a piece of iron being heated is expanding slightly. It will not help to inform that person that this is what iron regularly does. What the questioner will usually want to know is *why* iron does that. And this is explained, not as a rule by invoking higher-order regularities (such as "*all* metals expand when heated"), but by postulating a molecular structure for iron and then relating temperature to molecular motion, i.e., by producing a proper retroductive explanation.

In a DN-type explanation, one can, of course, invoke more than one law, and the combination of these often can be explanatory. Consider another example of Hempel's: the radiator of a car cracked after it was left out in the cold.[27] To explain this requires a reference to the temperature behavior of both water and metal as well as to the actual construction of the radiator. Someone who knew each of these items quite well might still find it explanatory to be told that the radiator crack was due to the freezing temperatures of the night. The manner of *combining* the laws and the initial conditions may be quite complex, and to that extent a nomothetic explanation may be helpful.

But there is a more serious weakness in the nomothetic ideal, and it is illustrated rather well in the two examples cited from Hempel. Each of the explananda here is a singular historical occurrence: the slush that didn't freeze and the radiator that did. The scientist is here being asked to explain singular events that have taken place in all the uncontrolled causal complexity of the natural world. But single-case explanations of this sort are *not* the norm in natural science. It is the engineer, the applied physicist, the architect, the historian, who is faced with puzzling singulars and who draws on as much science as is needed (or as he can find) in order to explain them. In these circumstances, a nomothetic explanation could well suffice.

The physicist or the chemist however, is concerned to discover *repeatable* explananda, that is, events whose causal environment is as fully controlled as possible.

Explanation in the natural sciences is not of raw singulars but of regularities. Even a single measurement, claimed to be repeatable, is implicitly a regularity. Of course, there is idealization at work here, a move away from the complex world to which explanation must ultimately return. But it is this sort of idealization that has made science of the Galilean style possible. What the theories of the scientist explain are empirical laws that are already at one remove of idealization; the theories are usually at several more removes, and the "idealizations" here are of different sorts. It is sufficient for our purposes here to note that the historical contingencies, the causal unknowns that are not included in the explicit specification of the problem situation, are screened out before the theorist goes to work. What theoretical scientists are trying to explain is not, in one step, the buzzing confusion of the world around them. Rather, they aim to explain an orderly, controlled, laboratory simplification of that world, teased out as far as possible into its single components. It is their *success* in doing this that provides the warrant (the only possible warrant) for their theories. But the application of these theories and laws to the unordered world of history is a delicate affair of approximations and imperfect understanding, and the task of application will not usually fall to the natural scientists themselves; it is the specialty of others.

It was, in part, a misconstrual of the explanatory aims of the scientist that led in the 1950s to such confusion in the sometimes acrimonious debates that went on regarding the relationship between explanation in science and explanation in history. If the scientist is thought to be primarily concerned with historical singulars, like a particular car radiator cracking on a particular night, then indeed science and history *can* be assimilated to one another, as far as their explanatory goals are concerned at least. But these are *not*, in fact, the explananda that scientists actually deal with. The aim of the laboratory environment is to make quite sure of this.

Nomothetic explanation has traditionally been presented as single-case explanation, as the inclusion of singulars under a law. When it is realized, however, that explanation in science is basically *not* of this type, that what scientists ordinarily attempt to explain are idealized (though still empirical) laws, a more complex form than the nomothetic is clearly called for, one in which the basic explanatory elements are not laws but model-structures from which these laws and others may be derived. To say that the retroductive pattern carries with it a greater explanatory power than does the nomothetic would be misleading if one were to think of explanatory power in a purely extensional way as, say, effectively organizing the data in hand. The term is used here in a broader sense to convey that the model *suggests* new lines of enquiry or appropriate responses to anomaly. The fertility that is the mark of a good model is not just a matter of predicting new data; it is a much more extended resource for suggesting (not predicting) new lines of development. This sort of fertility is characteristic of a model, not of a set of empirical laws.[28]

Furthermore, retroductive explanation carries us into new realms; it opens hitherto unknown domains, domains inaccessible to the nomothetic imagination. This is, in the end, why retroduction *is* the basic form of explanation in science. There could well be a universe, of course, in which *only* nomothetic explanation would be possible. But the history of science since Hume's day has shown that in *this* universe, we can do better. The basic patterns of explanation in theoretical natural science, especially since the early nineteenth century, have not been nomothetic.

6. THE THEORETICAL AND THE CAUSAL

I am inclined to believe that a misconstrual in one respect similar to the "single case" one above may lurk under the controversial thesis conveyed by the title of Nancy Cartwright's new book, *How the Laws of Physics Lie.*[29] She argues that the theoretical (unlike the phenomenological) laws of science "do not get the facts right," "do not tell the truth":

> If the fundamental laws are true, they should give a correct account of what happens when they are applied in specific circumstances. But they do not. If we follow out their consequences, we generally find that the fundamental laws go wrong; they are put right by the judicious corrections of the applied physicist or the research engineer.[30]

Note who it is who gets it *right* here. The failure of the theoretical laws (and also of the theoretical physicists and chemists?) is that these laws are not true of complicated real-life situations, like helium-neon lasers or intricate amplifier circuits. They are true only "of objects in the model," not of the "substance" of things.[31] But *is* this in fact a failure? Are we entitled to use words like 'lie' here? Only if the laws *purport* to be true, and really aren't. Some people (whom Cartwright calls "realists," using the label in rather a different sense to that of our section 4 above) tend to attribute a fundamental sort of truth to theoretical laws, and regard any approximations or "tricks" that have to be used to apply them to concrete problems as simply due to the complexity of the situation, not to possible defects in the laws themselves. This is the view that Cartwright opposes. But to oppose this, it would be sufficient to speak of the laws as "idealizations."

The Galilean model of idealization to which the natural sciences have been committed since the seventeenth century implies an initial separation of theory from the causally complex "natural" situation. It is, of course, ultimately the ability of theory to explain (classes of) "natural" situations, whether simple or complex, that warrants the theory. But the inability of a theory to describe the behavior of a causally complex system may or may not be held against the theory. It is often (as Cartwright's case histories illustrate) extremely difficult to tell where the blame is to be laid. That is precisely why the causally simpler systems have to come first. If a theory does well with these, it will give a presumption (though not, of course, an infallible one) in its favor.

The danger of downgrading the theoretical as a source of truth is that it suggests a sort of instrumentalism. Yet Cartwright (unlike most critics of "realism," in her sense of the term) *is* a realist; she is happy to admit the existence of theoretical entities. But theory, which is suspect in her eyes, naturally cannot be the warrant for their existence. So she relies on the "causal tracing" approach discussed in section 4 above. The existence of unobserved entities is asserted to the extent that a causal line can be traced back to them. By detaching the realist issue from the explanatory one, she is able to play down the existential implications of successful retroductive explanation without falling into the instrumentalist alternative, as van Fraassen and others who agree with her on explanation do.

The trouble is that causal tracing can only be done through theory: the causal agencies can be defined (and thus identified in different experimental contexts) only *through* theory. Though one may prefer the "causal" argument for realism to the "explanation" one, one cannot separate them as sharply as Cartwright does. One cannot challenge retroductive explanation as a source of ontological insight without (I think) undermining the causal argument too. The causal and the theoretical are indissolubly part of the same basic retroductive mode of explanation. But this is a large issue, more appropriate for another occasion.

7. POSTSCRIPT: EXORCISING A GHOST

One final moral is worth drawing from this analysis of explanation. Even though Hume's account of causation has been rather generally repudiated, it is striking how Humean notions still influence the formulation of problems regarding explanation in the philosophy of science. Take the "new riddle of induction" with its attendant train of "grue" predicates, the Rubik's Cube of philosophers of science in the 1960s. The assumption underlying it was that expectations are formed, predictions are justified (if indeed they *can* be justified) by referring simply to invariable associations (emerald, green) in the past. But since the past can be *explained* (so it was alleged) in terms of the "grue" predicates just as well as by the more familiar "green" ones, how is one to warrant an expectation in terms of the former in preference to a future of "grue"? The assumption evidently is that explanation is nomothetic in form, that observed regularities are all we have to go on. Goodman's suggested answer to the "riddle," that some predicates are more entrenched than others, comes as a new light if one accepts his nomothetic starting point as a given. But if explanation in natural science is understood to be normally *retroductive* in form, the notion that some predicates are more "entrenched," i.e., theoretically fruitful, would have been obvious from the beginning, and the "riddle" might not have been thought so threatening.

The ghost of Hume has still not been laid in philosophy of science. It may be worth summarizing very briefly the successive stages in the critique of the Humean account. Invariable correlations of the sort Hume describes cannot be regarded as the norm for a causal relationship. Often one has to be satisfied with statistically significant correlations. It may indeed be that only one in a hundred of those who take a particular antibiotic suffers a debilitating side effect, yet the administration of the drug in such cases would still be accounted the main "cause." The term no longer refers to a single event but to a cluster of conditions, each of a different weight (depending in part on the pragmatic context of the original demand for explanation). And this cluster can, in principle, be extended indefinitely outward and backward.

A second inadequacy of the Humean schema, one that has been exhaustively discussed, is its inability to handle counterfactual and other modal contexts, normal to causal assertions. A richer notion of agency is needed to sustain the modal claims we commonly make. The extensionalist language of the Humean tradition is too sparse and the devices required to make it work too ad hoc to make the effort seem worthwhile. So far, however, the critique has not touched the nomothetic model of explanation that Hume takes for granted.

But the next line of criticism bears on this model. The familiar argument, developed by Reichenbach and Salmon, recalls that the relatively regular succession between falling mercury in a barometer and rain is not enough to demonstrate a direct causal relationship. What is indicated, rather, in such cases is a common cause, itself not part of the observed regularity. It is inferred to by means of a retroductive explanation, which asks what would bring about such a regularity. This is incompatible with the Humean doctrine because one is appealing to an agency that is itself not part of the observed sequence.

A different sort of "common cause" argument, also developed by Salmon, we have already noted in another context. The significance is sought of the fact that the theoretical analysis of so many quite disparate classes of phenomena seems to terminate in the same theoretical entity, the molecule. Molecules are the *cause* of these varied effects, but they are discovered not by arguing from a statistically significant relationship between type A events and type B events to a common cause of both. Rather, the different sets of effects occur in totally different physical contexts, each of which yields a separate retroductive argument to molecules as the cause responsible. The indirect causal relationships between the events of the different types in no way require any patterns of regularity to hold between them. None of the Humean requirements still holds good.

And yet one still finds Salmon hoping that he can "provide an explication of causality without violating Hume's strictures against hidden powers and necessary connections."[32] The ghost refuses to be laid! Salmon has argued to the existence of entities that (from Hume's point of view, certainly) are in principle unobservable. He has made such entities the causes of a variety of apparently unrelated effects. It is difficult to see at this point why he should still give Hume's strictures much force in this domain.

It is a mistake to think that one can abandon the nomothetic ideal of explanation in the natural sciences, with its attendant notion of causality as a regularity relation between observed event-types, without at the same time repudiating the spirit of the entire Humean enterprise in natural philosophy. One can make excuses for Hume himself in this regard. One can recall that the only developed science of his day, mechanics, is the one science in which (as we have seen) the nomothetic ideal can be made to seem plausible.

But there can, in the end, be no compromise between Hume's notion of explanation in terms of observed lawlikeness and the retroductive ideal of explanation that the experience of working science appears to have validated long since. The logical positivists did their best to revive the nomothetic ideal and failed. There is no longer any incentive to continue their efforts to reduce cause and explanation within the categories of event succession. The task, rather, is to characterize the sort of ontology that the successes of retroductive explanation should lead us to expect.

Notes

1. The first version of this paper (for an abstract, see *Proceedings, Seventh International Congress of Logic, Methodology and Philosophy of Science*, edited by P. Weingartner and G. Dorn, vol. 3 [Salzburg 1983], 145-48) was ambiguous in several important respects. I am grateful to Henk Zandvoort, George Gale, Pascal Gorman, Nancy Cartwright, Hugh Mellor, Gerd Buchdahl, and Howard Wettstein for asking the right questions.

2. One can construe the earlier Aristotelian ideal also in terms of lawlikeness, of observable regularity. There were, however, important differences between it and the later empiricist account: The explanandum was the inherence of a property in a subject rather than the occurrence of an event; the connections were seen as necessary and as rooted in potentialities; there was an overarching teleological principle according to which nature acts for the "good," either of the particular nature or of the cosmic order as a whole. See McMullin, "Cosmic Order in Plato and Aristotle," in *The Concept of Order*, edited by P. Kuntz (Seattle, 1968), 63-76.

3. *Philosophy of Natural Science* (Englewood Cliffs, N.J., 1966), 50.

4. Ibid., 70.

5. This is Hempel's suggestion, ibid., 51.

6. Ibid., 52.

7. Since rare cases of fertility among female mules *have*, in fact, been reported without any change in the definition of the two terms, it would seem that this "law" is not one that would be preserved at the cost of definitional shifts.

8. For a review and bibliography, see R. Causey, "Theory and Observation," in *Current Issues in the Philosophy of Science*, edited by P. Asquith and H. Kyburg (East Lansing, Mich., 1979), 187-206.

9. See M. Hesse, "Theory and Observation," in *The Structure of Scientific Inference* (London, 1974), 9-44.

10. See P. Achinstein, "Theoretical Terms," chap. 6 of *Concepts of Science* (Baltimore, 1968).

11. Though this last line of argument, developed originally by Hanson and Kuhn, had a considerable influence on the early formulation of the issue, two serious objections have been raised against it. The integrative properties of perception play a relatively small role in science where *measurement* is the norm; in fact, one of the reasons why pointer readings are preferred, where possible, to skilled pattern recognitions, is precisely to avoid the subjectivity of which Hanson spoke. (See *Patterns of Discovery* [Cambridge, 1958].) More important, perhaps, is that developments in cognitive psychology would challenge the rather quick assumptions Hanson made in regard to the influence of knowledge upon perceptual judgment. This is not to say that such an influence does not exist, but only that it operates in a more complex way than Hanson realized, a way that is by no means yet fully understood. See A. Shimony, "Is Observation Theory-laden? A Problem in Naturalistic Epistemology," in *Logic, Laws and Life*, edited by R. Colodny (Pittsburgh, 1977), 185-208.

12. Achinstein, in "Theoretical Terms," reviews a dozen or more of the possible senses of 'theory' in the context of this controversy.

13. See McMullin, *Newton on Matter and Activity* (Notre Dame, 1978).

14. "How to Be a Good Empiricist," *Philosophy of Science: The Delaware Seminar*, vol. 2 (New York, 1963), 3-40; see sec. 7.

15. In an earlier paper, I used the term 'structural' for it to designate one common feature in the retroductive explanations of the natural sciences. See "Structural Explanation," *American Philosophical Quarterly* 15 (1978):139-47.

220 **ERNAN MCMULLIN**

16. *Collected Papers*, edited by C. Hartshorne and P. Weiss (Cambridge, Mass., 1932), I, 89.

17. Ibid., II, 776. See also 777: retroduction (presumption) "is the only kind of reasoning which supplies new ideas."

18. *Posterior Analytics*, I, 13.

19. See McMullin, "A Case for Scientific Realism," in *Essays on Scientific Realism*, edited by J. Leplin (Berkeley, in press).

20. See McMullin, "The Conception of Science in Galileo's Work," in *New Perspectives on Galileo*, edited by R. Butts and J. Pitt (Dordrecht, 1978), 209-57.

21. See L. Laudan, *Science and Hypothesis* (Dordrecht, 1981).

22. W. Heisenberg, "Tradition in Science," in *The Nature of Scientific Discovery*, edited by O. Gingerich (Washington, D.C., 1975), 219-36. In his earlier work (for references, see P. Heelan, *Quantum Mechanics and Objectivity* [The Hague, 1965], 144-48), Heisenberg often argued that the "idealism" of Plato (as he understood it) is superior to the "materialism" of Democritus as a framework for quantum mechanics. In his later references to this dualism, his emphasis is rather more on the mathematicism of Pythagoras.

23. For a review, see McMullin, "A Case for Scientific Realism."

24. "Why Ask 'Why'?" *Proceedings American Philosophical Association* 51 (1978):683-705.

25. *Philosophy of Natural Science*, 52.

26. *Explanation* is, of course, a pragmatic notion, unlike *cause*. In this essay, to simplify matters it has been assumed that explanation is being offered to a standard group proficient in the science, since the focus is on two general explanation-types. But in other contexts, the pragmatic aspect would have to be stressed very much more.

27. "The Function of General Laws in History" (1942), in C. G. Hempel, in *Aspects of Scientific Explanation* (New York, 1965), 232.

28. See McMullin, "The Fertility of Theory and the Unit for Appraisal in Science," *Boston Studies in the Philosophy of Science* 38 (1977):395-432.

29. New York, 1983. This section was added after the rest of this essay had been completed.

30. Ibid., 13.

31. Ibid., 17.

32. "A Third Dogma of Empiricism," in *Basic Problems in Methodology and Linguistics*, edited by R. Butts and J. Pitt (Dordrecht, 1977), 149-66; see 162. See also "Why Ask 'Why'?" 69.

A Type of Non-Causal Explanation[1]

PETER ACHINSTEIN

There is a type of explanation frequently employed in the sciences, particularly the quantitative ones, that I intend to focus on. It seeks to understand some phenomenon or regularity that occurs in a type of system S by deriving an equation describing that phenomenon or regularity from a set of equations that govern S. I want to propose a way of understanding such explanations.

1. AN EXAMPLE: THE COMPTON EFFECT

A. H. Compton showed in experiments in 1923 that when a beam of X rays of known frequency strikes weakly bound electrons the frequency of the scattered X rays is less than that of the incident rays, and hence their wavelength is greater. Compton offered both a qualitative and a quantitative explanation of this phenomenon (the "Compton effect"). My interest is with the quantitative one, but let me briefly note the qualitative one. Compton wrote:

> From the point of view of the quantum theory, we may suppose that any particular quantum of X rays is not scattered by all the electrons in the radiator, but spends all of its energy upon some particular electron. This electron will in turn scatter the ray in some definite direction, at an angle with the incident beam. This bending of the path of the quantum of radiation results in a change in its momentum. As a consequence, the scattering electron will recoil with a momentum equal to the change in momentum of the X ray. The energy in the scattered ray will be equal to that in the incident ray minus the kinetic energy of the recoil of the scattering electron; and since the scattered ray must be a complete quantum, the frequency will be reduced in the same ratio as is the energy. Thus on the quantum theory we should expect the wave-length of the scattered X rays to be greater than that of the incident rays.[2]

Compton is assuming here that the incident X rays are composed of particles (photons) whose energy is equal to Planck's constant h times the frequency of the radiation v. He can then treat the scattering as a problem involving a system in which there is an elastic collision between a photon and an electron. After the collision the electron and photon recoil at different angles. The phenomenon is shown in the accompanying diagram, which is very similar to the one Compton used in his original paper.

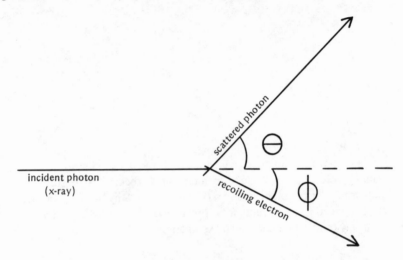

The system in which such a collision occurs is subject to two of the most fundamental laws of physics, the law of conservation of momentum and the law of conservation of energy. Compton applies the former law by assuming that the electron after collision recoils with a momentum equal to the change in momentum of the X ray. He applies the latter law by assuming that the energy of the scattered X ray is equal to the energy of the incident ray minus the kinetic energy of the recoil electron. The frequency of the photon after collision is less than that before collision because some of the energy has been transferred to the electron, and according to the quantum hypothesis, energy is proportional to frequency.

After presenting these remarks Compton proceeds to offer a quantitative explanation, which I shall reformulate as follows. Consider a system consisting of an incident X ray (photon) of frequency v and an electron that scatters the X ray. Let E_0 = the energy of the incident X ray, E_θ = the energy of the X ray scattered at an angle θ, and E_m = the energy of the recoil electron. According to the law of conservation of energy, the total energy of a system of particles before an elastic collision is the same as the total energy afterwards. Accordingly, for the system in question,

(1) $E_0 = E_\theta + E_m$.

Now, according to a law of Planck, energy is radiated or absorbed in whole quanta in such a way that $E = h\nu$, where h is Planck's constant and ν is the frequency of the radiation. In the system in question, then,

(2) $E_0 = h\nu_0$ (where ν_0 is the frequency of the incident X ray)

(3) $E_\Theta = h\nu_\Theta$ (ν_Θ is the frequency of the X ray scattered at angle Θ)

The energy E_m, the energy of the recoil electron, is assumed to be kinetic energy. Using the kinetic energy relationship from special relativity we obtain

(4) $E_m = mc^2(\frac{1}{\sqrt{1-B^2}} - 1)$, $B = v/c$

where v is the velocity of the electron after collision, c is the velocity of light, and m is the mass of the electron. Combining (1), (2), (3), and (4), we obtain

(5) $h\nu_0 = h\nu_\Theta + mc^2(\frac{1}{\sqrt{1-B^2}} - 1)$,

which represents the application of the law of conservation of energy to the system in question.

Let p_0 = the momentum of the incident X ray, p_Θ = the momentum of the X ray scattered at angle Θ, and P_m = the momentum of the recoil electron. According to the law of conservation of momentum, the total momentum of a system of particles before collision is the same as the total momentum afterwards. For our system this means that (in vector notation)

(6) $\bar{p}_0 = \bar{p}_\Theta + \bar{P}_m$.

From Einstein's special theory of relativity and Planck's hypothesis, we derive the result that the momentum of a photon of frequency ν is $h\nu/c$ where c is the velocity of light. And from special relativity we also obtain the result that the relativistic momentum of a particle of mass m and velocity v is $mv/\sqrt{1-B^2}$. Accordingly, for our particular system

(7) $p_0 = \dfrac{h\nu_0}{c}$

(8) $p_\Theta = \dfrac{h\nu_\Theta}{c}$

(9) $P_m = \dfrac{mv}{\sqrt{1-B^2}} = \dfrac{mBc}{\sqrt{1-B^2}}$

We combine (6)–(9) by analyzing the momentum vectors in (6) into two components, one giving the component of momentum in the direction of the propagation of the incident X ray, and the other at right angles to it:

(10) $\dfrac{h\nu_0}{c} = \dfrac{h\nu_\Theta}{c} \cos\Theta + \dfrac{mBc}{\sqrt{1-B^2}} \cos\phi$

(11) $0 = \dfrac{h\nu_\Theta}{c} \sin\Theta - \dfrac{mBc}{\sqrt{1-B^2}} \sin\phi$

where ϕ is the angle of deflection of the electron after collision. Now wavelength λ of radiation is related to the frequency v by the equation $\lambda = c/v$, where c is the velocity of light. Therefore, for the wavelengths of the incident and scattered X ray we obtain

(12) $\lambda_0 = c/v_0$

(13) $\lambda_\Theta = c/v_\Theta$

Substituting (12) and (13) into (10) and (11) and transposing, we obtain

$$\frac{h}{\lambda_0} - \frac{h}{\lambda_\Theta} \cos \Theta = \frac{mBc}{\sqrt{1-B^2}} \cos \phi$$

$$\frac{h}{\lambda_\Theta} \sin \Theta = \frac{mBc}{\sqrt{1-B^2}} \sin \phi$$

We then square these two equations and add them, yielding

$$\frac{h^2}{\lambda_0^2} + \frac{h^2}{\lambda_\Theta^2} - \frac{2h^2}{\lambda_0\lambda_\Theta} \cos \Theta = \frac{m^2B^2c^2}{1-B^2} = \frac{m^2c^2}{1-B^2} - m^2c^2$$

Now dividing (5) through by c and combining this with (12) and (13), we obtain

$$\frac{h}{\lambda_0} - \frac{h}{\lambda_\Theta} + mc = \frac{mc}{\sqrt{1-B^2}}$$

Squaring both sides of this equation, subtracting the result from the previous equation, and rearranging terms we get

(14) $\lambda_\Theta - \lambda_0 = \frac{h}{mc} (1 - \cos \Theta)$.

This states that the wavelength λ_Θ of the scattered X ray is greater than the wavelength λ_0 of the incident ray by the amount given on the right side of the equation, where Θ is the angle of deflection of the X ray. Equation (14) describes in quantitative terms the Compton effect, which is the phenomenon to be explained.

2. A PRELIMINARY ANALYSIS OF THIS EXPLANATION

There is a discernable strategy behind this explanation of the Compton effect, which is common to many quantitative explanations. First, general laws or principles are given that govern a variety of systems, including the one in question. In the present case appeal is made to the laws of conservation of energy and momentum, Planck's relationship $E = hv$, laws giving the kinetic energy and momentum of a relativistic particle, and a principle relating wavelength and frequency of radiation. Second, these general laws and principles are written as equations *for the particular kind of system in question,* i.e., for a system in which there is an incident X ray colliding with an electron. For example, equation (1) expresses the law of conservation of energy for that system;

equations (2) and (3) express Planck's radiation law as applied to the incident and scattered X ray; equation (4) expresses the relativistic kinetic energy for the recoil electron; similarly for equations (6), (7), (8), (9), (12), and (13). Third, from the general laws written as equations for the particular system in question, a new equation is derived mathematically that describes the phenomenon or fact to be explained. Thus, equation (14), which quantitatively describes the Compton effect, is derived mathematically from equations (1)–(13).

I want to propose a way of viewing the explanation of the Compton effect that reflects this strategy. To do so I shall utilize a general conception of explanation developed in *The Nature of Explanation* (hereafter NE). On this conception (for reasons we need not explore here) an explanation can be treated as an ordered pair

$(p; \text{explaining } q)$

whose second member, explaining q, is a type of explaining act in which q is an indirect question expressing what is to be explained. The first member p is a (certain type of) proposition that constitutes an answer to q. (My theory imposes various constraints on the proposition p and the question q; it also provides general conditions for the concept of an explaining act.) Suppose, e.g., that in explaining why this litmus turned red our favorite chemist says:

The reason this litmus turned red is that it was put into sulfuric acid, and any acid turns litmus red.

The chemist's explanation would then be the ordered pair

(The reason this litmus turned red is that it was put into sulfuric acid and any acid turns litmus red; explaining why this litmus turned red).

The first member of this ordered pair is an answer to the indirect question contained in the second member, viz., why this litmus turned red. I am not claiming here that the explanation is necessarily a good one, or that it is correct, but only that it is the explanation the chemist gave. Any explanation—good or bad, correct or incorrect—can be represented in this way. (The theory also gives general conditions for evaluating explanations, but these are not germane to the present concern. I simply want a scheme that can be used to represent the quantitative Compton effect explanation given in section 1—whatever the merits of that explanation.)

I suggest now that the quantitative explanation in section 1 is usefully thought of as comprising not one but three explanations, each corresponding to an element in the strategy noted in the beginning of this section. Corresponding to that part of the explanatory strategy in which general laws are written as equations for the particular system S (in which an incident X ray collides with an electron) is an explanation of why S satisfies (14) that appeals to the fact that it satisfies those equations. (Call this set of equations E_c for Compton. It comprises equations [1]-[4], [6]-[9], [12], and [13]. These equations express general laws written for the particular system S; the remaining equations [5], [10], and [11] are mathematically derivable from them.) Using the ordered pair representation:

(I)   (The reason that system S satisfies equation [14] is that it satisfies equations in the set E_c; explaining why S satisfies equation [14]).

This explains the Compton effect occurring within system S by invoking a set of equations governing S from which that effect is derivable. (The conditions under which such an explanation can be regarded as correct will be discussed later.) But this leaves two questions in need of an answer: Why is S governed by these equations, and how does one get from equations in the set E_c to (14)?

Corresponding to the part of the explanatory strategy in which general laws are given that govern a variety of systems including S, the first question is answered by appeal to these general laws. Using the ordered pair theory, this can be represented as a set of explanations each having the general form

(II)   (The reason that system S satisfies equation E is that it is a law that L; explaining why S satisfies E),

in which equation E is a formulation of law L for the particular system S.
For example,

(The reason that S satisfies equation [1] is that it is a law that the total energy of a system of particles before an elastic collision is the same as the total energy after; explaining why S satisfies equation [1])

(The reason that S satisfies equation [2] is that it is a law that energy is radiated or absorbed in whole quanta according to the relationship $E = h\nu$; explaining why S satisfies [2])

and so forth.

Finally, corresponding to the explanatory strategy in which from the set of particular equations governing S a new equation is derived mathematically that describes the phenomenon to be explained, we have

(III)   (Equation [14] is derivable from equations in the set E_c in the following manner [here follows the mathematical reasoning given in section 1]; explaining how equation [14] is derivable from equations in the set E_c).

To distinguish three explanations here, as I have done, is not to deny or minimize the fact that they are related. Explanation I—which indicates what equations govern the particular system S in virtue of which S satisfies (14)—immediately suggests the questions answered by (II) and (III) (viz., why these equations hold, and how [14] is derivable from them). However, by my criteria for explanations—the ordered pair view—all three are explanations. Each contains an explanatory question and a proposition purporting to provide a correct answer to it. Moreover, the explanations are not identical. The question asked and the answer given is different in each case.

In what follows I want to characterize the types of explanations represented by (I), (II), and (III) by asking under what conditions they are correct and whether or not they are causal.

3. SPECIAL-CASE-OF-A-LAW EXPLANATIONS

I begin with explanations of type (II) that (in NE) I call special-case-of-a-law explanations. They can be given the form

(1)   (The reason that p is that it is a law that L; explaining why p),

in which the sentence replacing "p" describes some regularity or fact that is a special case of law L. Here is a simple example:

(2)   (The reason that bullets when fired horizontally from a gun fall toward the earth with uniform acceleration is that it is a law that all unsupported bodies fall toward the earth with uniform acceleration; explaining why bullets when fired horizontally from a gun fall toward the earth with uniform acceleration.)

The regularity described by the sentence "bullets when fired horizontally from a gun fall toward the earth with uniform acceleration" is a special case of the law cited in the explanation. In the Compton explanation, system S's satisfying the equation $E_0 = E_\theta + E_m$ is a special case of the law of conservation of energy. The regularities are special cases of the law in an obvious way: they are what the law prescribes for one particular system (of many) to which the law applies.

Let me make the latter idea more precise by supplying a pair of sufficient conditions. Consider sentences of the form

(i)   (All) S is P

(ii)   All A's are B's.

Case 1: where the predicate P in (i) has the form "satisfies equation E." If (ii) entails (i), and if S and A are the same predicate or S denotes a subclass of the class denoted by A, and if (ii) expresses a law, then (i) describes something that is a special case of the law expressed by (ii). Thus,

(Any) system of type S (any mechanical system in which there is an elastic collision between a photon and an electron) satisfies the equation $E_0 = E_\theta + E_m$

is entailed by the law

In any mechanical system the total energy before an elastic collision is the same as the total energy afterwards.

Since the remaining conditions are satisfied, the former sentence describes something that is a special case of the law expressed by the latter sentence.

Case 2: where the predicate *P* in (i) does not contain an expression of the form "satisfies equation *E*." If *P* in (i) is the same predicate as *B* in (ii), and *S* in (i) denotes a proper subclass of the class denoted by *A* in (ii), and (ii) expresses a law, then (i) describes something that is a special case of the law expressed by (ii). By this criterion the sentence

> All bullets when fired horizontally from a gun fall toward the earth with uniform acceleration

describes something that is a special case of the law

> All unsupported bodies fall toward the earth with uniform acceleration.

There are two questions I propose to raise about special-case-of-a-law explanations. First, are they causal? Second, under what conditions can they be regarded as correct? The first question may be of interest to those who claim that (or wonder whether) all explanations in the sciences are, and must be, causal. Wesley Salmon, for example, defends such a view as being one of two "quite sound" intuitions about scientific explanations (the other being that they involve subsumption under laws).[3] The thesis that scientific explanations are causal has also been supported quite recently by Nancy Cartwright,[4] Robert Causey,[5] and David Lewis.[6] Of course, the plausibility of this view depends on what concept of causal explanation is being employed. In NE I develop a general definition of causal explanation that is too complex to reproduce here. For present purposes, let me propose a simple, and I believe, intuitive idea, viz., that an explanation of an event, or regularity, or phenomenon, or fact is causal only if it provides, or at least purports to provide, a cause for that event, regularity, phenomenon, or fact. Using the ordered pair theory, I shall assume that an explanation of the form

(3)   (The reason that *p* is that *r*; explaining why it is the case that *p*)

is causal only if the truth of the proposition "the reason that *p* is that *r*" requires the fact that *r* to cause it to be the case that *p*. Accordingly, an explanation of form (1) is causal only if the truth of its constituent proposition ("the reason that *p* is that it is a law that *L*") requires that the existence of the law that *L* cause it to be the case that *p*. Now (following NE) I take the following principle to express a general feature of causation:

(A)   The existence of a regularity or fact is not caused by the existence of a law of which that regularity or fact is a special case.

Therefore, a special-case-of-a-law explanation of form (1)—in which *p* describes some regularity or fact that is a special case of law *L*—is not causal. More precisely, given (A) no *correct* "special-case" explanation of type (1)—no explanation of this type in which the proposition "the reason that *p* is that it is a law that *L*" is true—is a causal explanation.

Can (A) be defended by appeal to a more general feature of causation? On some views (including the one I shall espouse), cause and effect must be distinct in a sense that precludes the effect from being "included in " the cause:

Principle of non-inclusion: If *Y* is included in *X* then *X* does not cause *Y*.

To make this idea precise as well as plausible what is needed is a criterion of inclusion. Let me propose a sufficient condition.

Consider sentences of the form

(a)   (All) *S* is *P* (*S* may be a type or an individual)

(b)   All *A*'s are *B*'s (or, it is a law that all *A*'s are *B*'s)

Suppose that *S* is *A*, and that "*S* is *A* and *A*'s are *B*'s" entails "*S* is *P*." Then the state of affairs described by (a) is included in that described by (b).[7] By this criterion the state of affairs described by

> All bullets when fired horizontally from a gun fall toward the earth with uniform acceleration

is included in that described by

> It is a law that all unsupported bodies fall toward the earth with uniform acceleration.

This obtains because bullets fired horizontally from a gun are unsupported bodies, and "bullets when fired horizontally from a gun are unsupported bodies and unsupported bodies fall toward the earth with uniform acceleration" entails "bullets when fired horizontally from a gun fall toward the earth with uniform acceleration." By the principle of non-inclusion, therefore, the existence of the regularity involving bullets is not caused by the existence of the law governing unsupported bodies.

Similarly, by the above criterion the state of affairs described by

> System *S* (in which a photon collides elastically with an electron) satisfies equation (1) ($E_0 = E_\Theta + E_m$)

is included in that described by

> It is a law that any mechanical system of particles involving elastic collisions is such that the total energy at any time is the same as at any other.

Therefore, by the principle of non-inclusion the latter state of affairs does not cause the former.

More generally, it can be shown that if a sentence of form (a) above satisfies either of the sufficient conditions given earlier for expressing something that is a *special case* of a law expressed by (b), then the state described by (a) is included in that described by (b). Accordingly, if (a) expresses something that is a special case of law (b), then the existence of the law (b) does not cause the state of affairs (a).

It is a consequence of this analysis that an explanation that contains a law involving causal concepts need not be a causal explanation. Newton's law of gravitation—that any body exerts a gravitational force on any other body that is inversely proportional to the square of the distance between them—invokes the concept of a gravitational force, which is surely causal. Indeed, this concept can be used to construct causal explanations, e.g.,

> (The reason that projectiles fall to the earth is that the earth exerts a gravitational force on projectiles that is inversely proportional to the square of the distance between the earth and the projectile; explaining why projectiles fall to the earth).

This explanation is causal because the inverse square gravitational force exerted by the earth is what causes projectiles to fall to the earth. Yet it does not follow that every explanation invoking the concept of gravitational force is causal. Consider

> (The reason the earth exerts a gravitational force on a projectile that is inversely proportional to the square of the distance between them is that it is a law that any body exerts a gravitational force on any other body that is inversely proportional to the square of the distance between them; explaining why the earth exerts a gravitational force on a projectile that is inversely proportional to the square of the distance between them).

This special-case-of-a-law explanation, although it contains a law utilizing causal concepts, is not itself causal because it does not supply a cause of the fact to be explained.

Under what conditions is a special-case-of-a-law explanation of form (1) correct? If $(p$; explaining $q)$ is an explanation, it is a correct explanation if and only if p is a correct answer to the question q. In NE the concept of a correct answer to an explanatory question q is defined in such a way that it follows that if $(p$; explaining $q)$ is an explanation, it is correct if and only if the proposition p is true. (A correct explanation need not be the best one possible, or a good one to give on a particular occasion. But it does provide an answer to the question that can be a good one to give in an appropriate situation. General criteria for goodness of explanations are proposed in NE.) Accordingly, for special-case-of-a-law explanations of form (1) in which p purports to describe some regularity or fact that is a special case of a law L, we must ask for the conditions under which "the reason that p is that it is a law that L" is true.

Here is a set that is almost sufficient:

1. p is true;
2. It is a law that L;
3. p describes a regularity or fact that is a special case of the law that L.

The reason this is not sufficient is that causes are possible that make p true but not for the reason that law L obtains, although L does obtain and p describes a special case of L. There are several such possibilities.[8]

Consider first a case involving a single individual that behaves in accordance with a law but not because the law obtains. Suppose it is a law that any headache sufferer who takes medicine M is relieved of the headache. Suppose that a particular headache sufferer (always) takes medicine M and gets relief. Even though this case involves just one individual, I shall say that

(p)   This headache sufferer who takes medicine M obtains relief (understood to mean that whenever he takes M he gets relief)

is a special case of the law that

(L) Any headache sufferer who takes medicine M obtains relief.

Proposition p satisfies the condition for being a special case of law L given earlier; p gives what law L prescribes for the particular person in question. But suppose that in addition to taking medicine M our headache sufferer also takes medicine N, which not only relieves headaches but when taken in conjunction with M renders M ineffective. When they are taken together it is N, not M (or their conjunction), that causes the headache to disappear. Then, I suggest, the explanation which claims that the reason that p is true is that it is a law that L is incorrect. The reason that p is true is that medicine N intervenes to make p true. Yet conditions 1-3 above are satisfied: p is true; it is a law that L; p describes a fact that is a special case of L. In such a case the law, although it obtains, has no explanatory efficacy.

Let us add a causal condition to 1-3 above. Suppose that S_1 (e.g., being a headache sufferer who takes medicine M) is a property the having of which in the absence of S_2 (e.g., being a headache sufferer who takes medicine N) causes P (e.g., relief from headache); but when something has both S_1 and S_2 then (the having of) S_2 causes P but S_1 does not. Under these conditions let us call S_2 *an intervening cause of P with respect to S_1.*[9] Then where p is of the form

This S_1 is P

and law L is of the form

All S_1's are P's

a special-case-of-a-law explanation is correct only if

4a.   There is no property S_2 that this S_1 also has that is an intervening cause of P with respect to S_1.

In our example there is a property that this S_1 (this headache sufferer who takes medicine M) also has (viz., being a headache sufferer who takes medicine N) that is an intervening cause of P (relief from headache) with respect to S_1.

Condition 4a does not preclude there being something that causes p to be true. To change our example a bit, suppose the headache sufferer in question takes medicine M but not N or anything else (other than M) that causes his headaches to disappear. Then p remains true, and condition 4a is satisfied (since there is no property that the headache sufferer also has that is an intervening cause of headache relief with respect to taking medicine M). Yet this does not mean that p has no cause. The fact that he takes medicine M is what causes it to be true that p.

Earlier, I argued that a special-case-of-a-law explanation such as

(The reason this headache sufferer who takes medicine M obtains relief is that it is a law that any headache sufferer who takes medicine M obtains relief; explaining why this headache sufferer, etc.)

is non-causal. Note that this is so even if (a) there is a cause of the fact that p; even if (b) the law cited in the explanation is a causal law (in the sense that its antecedent cites a condition that under appropriate circumstances is sufficient to cause its consequent); and even if (c) the cause of the fact that p would not be a cause unless the law obtained. This is not a causal explanation precisely because the fact or state of affairs being explained is not caused by the fact that the law obtains. (And this is so because one fact is included in the other.)

The next two causal cases I shall consider may involve either a single individual or general regularities that are special cases of (even more general) laws.

Suppose (as stated above) that medicines M and N are each by themselves sufficient to cure headaches but that when both are taken N causes the headache to disappear and M does not. Let

p = Any (or, this) headache sufferer who takes medicine M and also takes medicine N will be relieved of the headache

L = Any headache sufferer who takes medicine M will be relieved of the headache.

By our previous criterion, p describes a regularity that is a special case of law L. Yet although p is true and it is a law that L, it is, I think, incorrect to say that the reason that p is true is that it is a law that L. The reason that any (or, this) headache sufferer who takes both medicines M and N will be relieved of the headache is that in such a case medicine N will be effective.

We can generalize this by saying that where p is of the form

Any (or, this) S_1 which is S_2 is P

and law L is of the form

Any S_1 is P,

a special-case-of-a-law explanation of form (1) is correct only if

4b. S_2 is not an intervening cause of P with respect to S_1.

A third type of causal case can be illustrated as follows. Suppose that medicine M and medicine O are each by themselves sufficient to cure headaches, but that when both are taken they enhance each other's power and both together cause the headache to disappear. Let

p = Any (or, this) headache sufferer who takes medicine M and also takes medicine O will be relieved of the headache

L = Any headache sufferer who takes medicine M will be relieved of the headache.

Under these circumstances it does not seem (quite) correct to say that the reason that p is that it is a law that L. L is part of the reason; the other part is that any headache sufferer who takes medicine O will obtain relief and M and O enhance each other.

To generalize this case, suppose that S_1 and S_2 are properties each of which in the absence of the other is sufficient to cause P; and when something has both S_1 and S_2 then both properties together cause P. Under these conditions call S_1 and S_2 *joint* causes of P. Then, where p is of the form

Any (or, this) S_1 that is S_2 is P

and law L is of the form

Any S_1 is P,

a special-case-of-a-law explanation of form (1) is correct only if

4c. It is not the case that S_1 and S_2 are joint causes of P.

We might wonder about the case in which two medicines, say M and Q, are each sufficient to relieve a headache, but when taken together cancel each other so as to prevent the headache from being relieved. This case will not present a problem for our correctness conditions because, under these circumstances, the p-statement

Any headache sufferer who takes medicine M and also takes medicine Q will be relieved of the headache

is false. (The p-statement must be true for the explanation to be correct.)

Are there other causal cases that need to be included in condition 4 as well? Let me mention two possibilities.

Suppose that something causes it to be true that law L obtains but does not cause it to be true that p, even though p is a special case of L. To concoct an example, Descartes believed that God preserves the totality of motion in the universe. Let us understand this to mean that God causes the law of conservation of momentum to hold in all (closed) systems of particles. However, suppose Descartes is wrong about one type of sytem, viz., Compton systems in which a photon collides with a weakly bound electron. Let us suppose that it is the Devil, not God, that causes such systems to satisfy conservation of momentum, although God causes all other systems to do so. Let

p = Compton systems S are such that the momentum of the incident photon = the momentum of photon scattered at angle θ + momentum of recoil electron

L = any (closed) system of particles is such that the total momentum of the system before a collision is the same afterwards.

We are supposing that what cause it to be true that L are independent acts of willing of God and the Devil. But what cause p to be true are only acts of willing of the Devil. The question is whether, under these circumstances, the special case explanation

(The reason that p is that it is a law that L; explaining why p)

is correct. If not, then we need an additional causal principle that might say that a speical-case-of-a-law explanation is correct only if whatever causes it to be the case that L causes it to be the case that p.

I am inclined to resist this condition. If conservation of momentum is a genuine law in our universe—through the independent workings of God and the Devil—then the reason Compton systems behave in the manner described by p is that such a law operates universally. This can be so even if it is possible to give different supernatural causal explanations for why the law holds universally and for why it holds in Compton systems. One thing that may be clouding the issue in this example is that if the Devil, not God, is causing p to be true, then given the capriciousness of the Devil there could well be changes in the behavior of Compton systems that would make p and hence L false. (L is not necessarily true.) If so, L is not a genuine law for all systems. If it is, I am saying, then it is explanatorily efficacious in the present example.

The final causal case I shall mention is one in which there is nothing that causes p (or L) to be true. If so can a special-case-of-a-law explanation of form (1) be correct? My answer is: definitely yes. Stephen Toulmin has claimed that in Newtonian mechanics the law of inertia is an "ideal of natural order."[10] It describes the natural motion of bodies and is not subject to explanation. Only deviations from the law—only accelerations—are explainable. Suppose this is correct (I don't want to argue the point). Then nothing causes it to be the case that the law of inertia (L) holds. Now consider a particular case of the law:

p = a moving spaceship in outer space that is not under the action of (unbalanced) forces will continue to move in a straight line with constant speed.

There is a reason that p is true, viz., that it is a law that (L) any body not under the action of (unbalanced) forces will continue at rest or in a straight line with constant speed. This is a correct special-case-of-a-law explanation even if nothing causes p to be true. (In particular the existence of the law L does not cause this since p is a special case of L.)

Conditions 4a-c cover cases involving certain intervening and multiple causes that prevent a special-case-of-a-law explanation from being correct. Perhaps there are other causal cases that need to be included in condition 4 as well. (I am not able to suggest any further ones.) What I will assume, then, is that in the absence of such intervening and multiple causes, the law L of which the fact that p is a special case is explanatorily efficacious: it is the reason that p is true. Accordingly, I propose that 1-4 constitute a set of necessary and sufficient conditions for *correct* special-case-of-a-law explanations. As noted earlier, an explanation may be correct without being what is wanted or needed on a particular occasion. Thus, although explanation (2) at the beginning of this section is correct, one who asks why bullets when fired horizontally from a gun fall to the earth with uniform acceleration may be seeking a cause of this phenomenon, not the law of free fall of which it is a special case. If so, explanation (2), although correct, is not appropriate for the occasion.

4. SPECIFIC EQUATION EXPLANATIONS

In section 2, one of the explanations distinguished had the form:

(I)   (The reason that system S satisfies equation E_1 is that it satisfies equations $E_2, \ldots, E_n$; explaining why S satisfies equation E_1),

where the equations $E_2, \ldots, E_n$ are special cases for the system S of general laws. Let me call these specific equation explanations. I suggest that such explanations are correct only if

1. System S satisfies equation E_1.
2. System S satisfies equations $E_2, \ldots, E_n$.
3. Equations $E_2, \ldots, E_n$ are special cases for the system S of general laws. They are legitimate formulations of the laws for that type of system; and these laws govern system S.
4. Equation E_1 is mathematically derivable from equations $E_2, \ldots, E_n$.
5. A causal condition is satisfied similar to the one for special-case-of-a-law explanations.

The fifth condition is needed to exclude certain intervening and multiple causes that would otherwise prevent a specific equation explanation from being correct. Before trying to formulate such a condition let me invoke the headache cases of section 3 to construct some examples. Here we will need to invent equations. Suppose that for any headache sufferer who takes medicine M the duration of the headache after taking the medicine is (within certain bounds) inversely proportional to the quantity of medicine taken:

(a) $T \alpha \dfrac{1}{Q(M)}$,

where T is the duration of the headache after taking the medicine and $Q(M)$ is the quantity of M taken. Let us also suppose that it is a law that for any headache sufferer who takes medicine M, the headache will disappear in accordance with the equation

(b) $T = k\dfrac{I}{Q(M)}$,

where I is a measure of the intensity of the headache at the time the medicine is taken and k is some constant of proportionality. (Note that [a] is mathematically derivable from [b].) Suppose there are similar equations for medicine N:

(a)′ $T \alpha \dfrac{1}{Q(N)}$

(b)′ $T = k\dfrac{I}{Q(N)}$,

where the k in both sets of equations is the same.

Let the "system" S be a particular headache sufferer who always takes medicine M to relieve headaches. We can then say that

(i)   This headache sufferer who takes medicine M satisfies the equation (a) $T \propto 1/Q(M)$.

Assume further that this headache sufferer who takes M always takes an equal quantity of medicine N, and that, under these conditions, only N is effective. It (not M) causes the headaches to disappear and to do so in such a way that equations (a)' and (b)' are satisfied by S. In such a case (I am supposing) (a) and (b) are also satisfied. But is the reason that (a) is satisfied by S—is the reason that (i) above is true—that (b) is satisfied, i.e., that

(ii)   This headache sufferer who takes medicine M satisfies the equation (b) $T = kI/Q(M)$

is true? I think not. The reason that (a) is satisfied is that this headache sufferer who takes a quantity of medicine M always takes the same quantity of medicine N, that under these conditions only N is effective, and that equation (a)' is satisfied; therefore, so is (a) because $Q(N) = Q(M)$ and $T \propto 1/Q(N)$. More briefly, we can say that the reason that (a) is satisfied by our headache sufferer who takes M is that medicine N intervenes to cause this to be the case.

Let the property of being S (e.g., being a headache sufferer who takes medicine M) be such that the having of this property in the absence of S' (e.g., being a headache sufferer who takes medicine N) causes something with this property to satisfy equation E [e.g., $T \propto 1/Q(M)$]. But suppose that when something has both S and S' then the having of S', rather than S or their conjunction, causes that which has it to satisfy equation E. Then (following section 3) I shall call (the having of property) S' an intervening cause of satisfying equation E with respect to (the having of) S. We can now write the following by way of spelling out the causal condition 5 above:

There is no property that S has that is an intervening cause of S's satisfying equation E_1 with respect to the property of being S.

In the example above our headache sufferer who takes medicine M has the property: being a headache sufferer who takes medicine N. Since the having of this property is an intervening cause of satisfying equation (a) with respect to being a headache sufferer who takes medicine M, our causal condition is violated.

To help formulate another causal condition, let us change the system S to be headache sufferers who take equal quantities of medicines M and N. Again only N is effective when taken in conjunction with M. We can still say

Headache sufferers in S satisfy equation (a) $T \propto 1/Q(M)$.

But is the reason for this that such headache sufferers satisfy equation (b)? No, the reason that (a) is satisfied is that the headache sufferers in S take medicine N in addition to M, that under these conditions only N is effective, and that equation (a)' is satisfied (and therefore so is [a]). In short, medicine N is an intervening cause of satisfying equation (a) with respect to medicine M. We need to exclude such an intervening cause.

Let S be a system of F's and G's (e.g, headache sufferers who take M and also take N). Let there be quantities in equation E_1 associated with the property F but not with G. [For example, the quantity $Q(M)$ in equation (a) is associated only with medicine M, not with medicine N; it is the quantity of M taken, not the quantity of N.] Then G is not an intervening cause of system S's satisfying equation E_1 with respect to F. Nor (to further extend this condition in the manner of section 3) are F and G joint causes of S's satisfying equation 1. So much for the causal condition 5.

Are conditions 1-5 sufficient? One type of explanation we surely want to disallow is self-explanation: explaining why S satisfies equation E by appeal to the fact that it satisfies E. This is precluded by the requirement in condition 4 that the derivation be mathematical. (Mere logical entailment is not sufficient.)[11] But this won't rule out cases that are dangerously close to being self-explanations. Suppose we want to explain why a bullet fired horizontally from a gun falls toward the earth in such a way that

(1) $y = 1/2gt^2$

is satisfied, where y is the vertical distance fallen, t is the time of the fall, and g is a constant. Equation (1) is mathematically derivable from equations obtained from (1) by adding the same constant to both sides, e.g.,

(2) $y + 100 = 1/2gt^2 + 100$.

Yet it seems incorrect to say that the reason the falling bullet satisfies equation (1) is that it satisfies equation (2). How can such a case be precluded?

Equation (1) is a formulation of Galileo's law of falling bodies for the system in question (indeed, for any system in which a particle is falling toward the earth). And equation (1) is mathematically equivalent to equation (2). Yet—I want to say—equation (2) is not a *legitimate* formulation of Galileo's law. (Condition 3 for correct explanations requires legitimate formulations.) Unfortunately, I have no general criterion of legitimacy to offer. Intuitively, in the present case there is no physical reason to add 100 to both sides of the equation. (Any number could have been added, subtracted, divided, or multiplied, provided the same is done for both sides.) This is not to deny that two mathematically equivalent equations can both be legitimate formulations of a law. Another equation representing Galileo's law is

(3) $a = \ddot{y} = g$

where a is vertical acceleration, $\ddot{y}$ is the second derivative of y with respect to time, and g is the constant in (1). Equation (3) is obtainable mathematically from (1) by taking the second derivative of y; (1) is obtainable from (3) by integration (assuming the body starts from rest so that constants of integration are zero). Equation (1) expresses the idea that the distance fallen is proportional to the square of the time, whereas (3) expresses the idea that the acceleration of a falling body is constant. According to conditions 1-5, then, an explanation of the following form could be correct:

(The reason that S satisfies equation [1] is that it satisfies equation [3]; explaining why S satisfies equation [1]).

Indeed, texts in physics frequently employ just such an explanation. Similarly, the following is correct:

(The reason that S satisfies equation [3] is that it satisfies equation [1]; explaining why S satisfies equation [3]).

Which explanation a text uses depends on which mathematical formulation of Galileo's law—(1) or (3)—it starts with. (The fact that both explanations are correct doesn't by itself settle which, if either, it is best to use on a given occasion; here "pragmatic"considerations become important. See NE.)

I suggest that conditions 1-5 are sufficient as well as necessary for correctness in specific equation explanations.

Are such explanations causal? I will argue that they are not. Consider once again the following general principle of causation introduced in section 3:

Principle of non-inclusion: If Y is included in X then X does not cause Y.

In an intuitive sense, I suggest, if an equation E_1 is mathematically derivable from a set of equations $E_2, \ldots, E_n$, then the state of affairs described by

(a)   System S satisfies equation E_1

is included in the state of affairs described by

(b)   System S satisfies equations $E_2, \ldots, E_n$.

By the principle of non-inclusion, therefore, the latter state of affairs does not cause the former. Accordingly, a specific equation explanation of type (I) that appeals to (b) as the reason for (a) is not causal. (It would be causal only if the truth of "the reason that S satisfies equation E_1 is that it satisfies equations $E_2, \ldots, E_n$" requires the state of affairs described by [b] to cause that described by [a].) To buttress this argument some criterion of inclusion of states is needed that dictates that (a) is included in (b).

For this purpose, the criterion introduced in the previous section can be used. In accordance with this, if S is A, and if "S is A, and A is B" entails "S is P," then the state of affairs described by "S is P" is included in that described by "A is B." If equation E_1 is mathematically derivable from equations $E_2, \ldots, E_n$, then "System S satisfies equations $E_2, \ldots, E_n$" entails "System S satisfies equation E_1," and the above criterion of inclusion can be shown to be satisfied.

One might be tempted to suggest an even simpler criterion of inclusion for such cases. One might suppose that if a sentence p_1 is entailed by a sentence p_2, then the state of affairs described by p_1 is included in that described by p_2. But if we want to retain the principle of non-inclusion, then this concept of inclusion is too broad. Consider

p_1: John took a fatal dose of aspirin
p_2: John died.

Using the simple entailment criterion of inclusion, the state of affairs described by p_2 is included in that described by p_1; therefore, by the principle of non-inclusion the state of affairs described by p_2 cannot be caused by that described by p_1. Yet the latter conclusion is too strong. John's death could certainly be caused by his taking a fatal dose of aspirin. Can the simple entailment criterion be modified?

Let us say that a predicate P_1 is a definitional causal predicate with respect to a predicate P_2 if by definition something's having (the property designated by) P_1 causes it to have P_2. For example, "takes a fatal dose of aspirin" is a definitional causal predicate with respect to "dies," since by definition (by the definition of "fatal" as something like "sufficient to cause death") a persons's taking a fatal dose of aspirin causes that person to die. Now consider two sentences of the form

(i) S has P_1
(ii) S has P_2.

If (i) entails (ii) and P_1 is not a definitional causal predicate with respect to P_2, then the state of affairs described by (ii) is included in that described by (i). In the example above, although p_1 entails p_2, the predicate "takes a fatal dose of aspirin" is a definitional causal predicate with respect to "dies." Therefore, on the present criterion we cannot conclude that the state described by p_2 is included in that described by p_1. So we cannot use the principle of non-inclusion to infer that the state described by p_2 cannot be caused by that described by p_1.[12]

Contrast this with the following example. Let

P_1 = is fat and bald
P_2 = is fat.

P_1 is not a definitional causal predicate with respect to P_2. (It is not true that by definition a person's being fat and bald causes that person to be fat.) Since "S has P_1" entails "S has P_2," it follows that the state of affairs described by the latter is included in that described by the former. Therefore, by the principle of non-inclusion, a person's being fat and bald does not cause that person to be fat.

With this modification of the simple entailment criterion of inclusion, we can return to specific equation explanations. Here we must consider sentences of the form

(a)   System S satisfies equation E_1
(b)   System S satisfies equations $E_2, \ldots, E_n$

where (b) (mathematically) entails (a). In such cases a predicate of the form "satisfies equations $E_2, \ldots, E_n$" is not a definitional causal predicate with respect to "satisfies equation E_1." For example, the predicate "satisfies the equation $s = 1/2$

gt^2'' is not *defined* in such a way that something's satisfying this equation causes it to satisfy the equation a $=$ g. (It might be argued that it is defined in such a way that anything satisfying this equation sa..sfies $a = g$; but it is not defined in terms requiring a causal relationship between the one and the other.) In general, predicates of the form "satisfies equation E," unlike terms such as "fatal," are not defined by reference to their causal effects. (To be sure, something's satisfying equation E may have certain causal consequences, but this is not in general true by definition.)

Since (b) entails (a) and "satisfies equations E_2, . . . , E_n" is not a definitional causal predicate with respect to "satisfies equation E_1," the state of affairs described by (a) is included in that described in (b). (This is so on the present criterion of inclusion as well as on the one in section 3.) Therefore, by the principle of non-inclusion the former state is not caused by the latter. So a specific equation explanation that appeals to state (b) in explaining state (a) is not a causal explanation.

5. DERIVATION EXPLANATIONS

The third explanation distinguished in section 2 is this:

(III)   (Equation [14] is derivable from equations in the set E_c in the following manner [here follows the mathematical reasoning given in section 1]; explaining how equation [14] is derivable from equations in the set E_c).

More generally, such derivation explanations have the form

(1)   (Proposition p_1 is derivable from a set of propositions p_2 in such and such a way; explaining how p_1 is derivable from p_2).

They explain how a conclusion follows from a set of premises. In the quantitative sciences to explain why a system satisfies an equation describing a certain regularity it is frequently not enough to cite other regularities that the system satisfies that are expressible by means of equations. It may not be enough because the relationship between these equations may not be obvious. What is needed is not simply an "argument" containing a set of equations as premises and the equations to be explained as conclusion, but an explanation of how one can get from the premises to the conclusion.

There is a simple correctness condition for derivation explanations: An explanation of form (1) is correct if and only if proposition p_1 is derivable from p_2 in the manner specified in the explanation. So if the mathematical steps used in the derivation of equation (14) from equations in the set E_c are legitimate, then explanation (III) is correct. It is not required that the set of propositions p_2 be true (or probable), or that the derivation be elegant or intuitive. The latter criteria would be relevant in a more general evaluation of an explanation as a good one. Nor is it required that p_2 be better known or more fundamental than p_1. The point of a derivation explanation is not to explain why p_1 is true but simply how it is derivable from p_2.

Is explanation (III) a causal explanation? It is only if it is supplying a cause of the fact that equation (14) is derivable from equations in the set E_c. What could such a cause be? Is it the existence of the mathematical rules and principles (e.g., rules of algebra)? This seems the likeliest candidate. If so, then we can say that the state of affairs described by

(2)   Such and such rules of mathematics exist

causes it to be the case that

(3)   Equation (14) is derivable from equations in the set E_c.

I want to suggest that such a claim is unjustified because the state of affairs described by (3) is included in that described in (2). If so, then by the principle of non-inclusion state (2) cannot cause state (3). To use this argument I shall extend the entailment criterion of inclusion given in section 4 in a natural way.

Suppose that a sentence p_1 entails p_2, and that no predicate in p_1 is a definitional causal predicate with respect to any predicate in p_2. Then I shall say that the state of affairs described by p_2 is included in that described by p_1. Now (2) above—when suitably fleshed out to include the mathematical rules used in deriving equation (14) from equations in E_c—entails (3). It entails that if we assume equations in E_c then equation (14) is derivable. By analogy, in logic the fact that

The rule modus ponens exists

entails that

"I am happy" is derivable from "if the sun is shining then I am happy" and "the sun is shining."

Furthermore, no predicate in (2) is by definition something the having of which causes something to have a predicate in (3). So by the extended entailment criterion of inclusion, state (3) is included in state (2) and cannot be caused by it.

More generally, the existence of a set of rules used in the derivation of a proposition p_2 from p_1 does not cause p_2 to be derivable from p_1.

6. DETERMINATION

I have analyzed the quantitative explanation of the Compton effect into three explanations and have argued that none of these is causal. Miss Anscombe distinguishes the concept of cause from that of determination:

> . . . a thing hasn't been caused until it has happened; but it may be determined before it happens . . . . When we call a result determined we are implicitly relating it to an antecedent range of possibilities and saying that all but one of these is disallowed. What disallows them is not the result itself but something antecedent to the result. The antecedences may be logical or temporal or in the order of knowledge. Of the many—antecedent—possibilities, *now* only one is—antecedently—possible.[13]

For example, in a game of chess, given the position of the pieces on the board, the next move may be determined by the rules. The antecedent possibilities are the powers of pieces, and given the present situation the rules exclude all but one move. The rules determine, but do not cause, the move. Similarly, laws of nature may determine what happens in a particular system without causing it. Consider a system S in a given state at time t, and a law L governing that system. With respect to a later time t' the "antecedent possibilities" can be taken to be all states of S at t' that are logically possible (or perhaps that are not excluded by laws other than L). If L excludes all but one of these possibilities then L determines the state of S at t'.

This idea of determination can be broadened. The existence of a regularity in a system S may be determined by a law or set of laws governing that system. For example, the fact that the system in the Compton effect satisfies equation (1) ($E_0 = E_\Theta + E_m$) is determined by the law of conservation of energy. (The law can be thought of as excluding all but one possible energy equation for this system.) But equally, the existence of a regularity in a system S may be determined by the existence of other regularities exhibited by the system. The fact that the Compton system S satisfies equation (14) (describing the Compton effect) is determined by the fact that S satisfies equations in the set E_c. Determination in such cases depends on the existence of laws (which exclude possibilities). Where laws are involved the concept of *inclusion* can be invoked to provide the following sufficient condition for determination.

Suppose the state of affairs described by a sentence p_1 is included in that described by p_2 but not conversely. Suppose, further, that p_2 expresses a law or a special case of a law (or a set of these) for a particular system described in p_1. Then the state of affairs described by p_1 is determined by that described by p_2. By this condition the fact that the Compton system S satisfies equation (1) is determined by the law of conservation of energy. And the fact that S satisfies equation (14) is determined by the fact that S satisfies equations in the set E_c. (The equations in E_c formulate special cases of laws for S.)

In such cases we can see why determination of one state of affairs by another precludes the determining state from causing the determined one. One state of affairs determines another only if the latter is included in the former. But then by the principle of non-inclusion, the included state is not caused by the including one. This, of course, does not preclude the determined state from being caused. The state of affairs described by (p) "This headache sufferer who takes medicine M obtains relief" is determined (not caused) by the state of affairs described by the law that any headache sufferer who takes medicine M obtains relief. This is so even though the former state is caused by the fact that the headache sufferer takes medicine M (or N). (If N is the cause then the law determines the fact that p—it excludes all possibilities but p—even though the law does not correctly explain why p is the case.)

7. CONCLUSIONS

Finally, the following very general question might be asked: What makes it possible to (correctly) explain by means of the three kinds of explanations we have distinguished?

How are such explanations possible in science? My answer is a simple one that appeals to "pragmatic" and "nonpragmatic" considerations. The nonpragmatic ones are these: There are general laws of nature that govern a multitude of systems. There are special cases of these laws for individual systems. The latter mathematically entail equations that govern the behavior of items comprising these systems. Turning to pragmatic considerations, scientists may not understand a regularity exhibited by a particular system for one or more of these reasons: they do not know what general laws govern the system; even if they do they may not know how to formulate these laws for that particular system; and even if they know these things they may not know how to derive an equation describing the behavior of the system they seek to understand from the laws as written for that system. For such lacunae in their knowledge the three types of explanations I have distinguished provide a remedy. If the facts mentioned among the nonpragmatic considerations obtain—if there are general laws, and these do govern the system, and there is a legitimate derivation of the behavior in question from them—then it is possible for explanations of forms (I)-(III) to be correct. If they are correct, and if there are scientists with the epistemic lacunae mentioned above, then it is possible to explain to them by providing the information in these explanations.[14]

Notes

1. This paper is an extension of some ideas in my recent book *The Nature of Explanation* (New York, 1983).

2. A. H. Compton, *Physical Review* 21 (1923), 485.

3. Wesley Salmon, "Why Ask, 'Why'?" *Proceedings and Addresses of the American Philosophical Association* 51 (1978), 685.

4. Nancy Cartwright, "Causal Laws and Effective Strategies," *Nous* 13 (1979), 424.

5. Robert Causey, *Unity of Science* (Dordrecht, 1977).

6. David Lewis, "Causal Explanation" (mimeograph of Howison Lectures).

7. A restriction that will be given later might be imposed.

8. The examples that follow are fictitious. It would be interesting to know whether there are actual causal phenomena of this kind and in what systems they operate.

9. Human behavior may provide more realistic examples of this. Thus, an order from a captain will cause a sergeant to obey, and the same order from a general will also cause this; but if both a captain and a general issue the same order at the same time what may cause the sergeant to obey is that a general has issued the order, not that a captain has or that both have.

10. Stephen Toulmin, *Foresight and Understanding* (London, 1961).

11. Similarly, this will preclude a case in which some irrelevant equation E' satisfied by S is tacked on to the set $E_2, \ldots, E_n$. Of course, I am not here defining "mathematical derivation," and admittedly the distinction between this and "(purely) logical entailment" is not always crystal clear.

12. A similar restriction might be imposed on the sufficient condition for inclusion given in section 3. Thus we might say that the state of affairs described by "S is P" is included in that described by "all A's are B's" if S is A, "S is A and A's are B's" entails "S is P," and B is not a definitional causal predicate with respect to P. With this restriction we would not be precluded from saying that the state of affairs described by "anyone who takes 50 aspirins dies" is caused by the state described by "anyone who takes 50 aspirins takes a fatal dose."

13. G. E. M. Anscombe, *Metaphysics and the Philosophy of Mind* (Minneapolis, 1981), 140-41.

14. This paper was written as part of a project on explanation supported by the National Science Foundation. I am indebted to Gary Hatfield, David Zaret, George Wilson, and Mark Wilson for helpful criticisms.

EPR: Lessons for Metaphysics

BRIAN SKYRMS

By now everyone knows that the thought experiment of Einstein-Podolsky-Rosen (1935) has something to teach us about the structure of quantum mechanics and about the world. The premise of this paper is that it has something to teach metaphysicians about causation.

I. SEVEN THEORIES OF CAUSATION MEET EPR

Here is a list of seven familiar metaphysical theories of causation:

1. A cause is a ceteris paribus sufficient condition for the effect.
2. A cause is a ceteris paribus necessary condition for the effect.
   2a. Sine qua non (counterfactual version of 2): the effect would not have occurred without the cause.
3. Statistical causation: a cause is positively statistically relevant to the effect conditional on the relevant background factors.
4. Causality as explanation: a cause explains the effect.
5. Causation as transfer of energy-momentum (or some other quantity for which there is a conservation law for closed systems).
6. Manipulability: wiggle the causal variable experimentally and the effect variable wiggles.
7. Causation is a primitive physical relation. In some accounts it is directly observable.

The foregoing is meant neither to be exhaustive nor precise in formulation, but merely a way to jog the memory. (For further help see Sosa [1975].)

Now consider this simple version of the EPR: Two particles are created by a certain process and rush off in opposite directions. When they are widely separated in space, they each encounter a measuring apparatus oriented in the vertical direction.

The measuring apparatus consists of a magnetic field that either deflects the particle up or down and counters in the two respective paths. The measurements of the two distant particles take place simultaneously in the reference frame of the observer (although there are perfectly good reference frames in which the left measurement precedes the right one and conversely). Our best physical theory tells us that given the state of the system prior to measurement, the probability of getting an up measurement on a given side is $1/2$, but the probability of getting an up measurement on a side *conditional on getting a down measurement on the other side* is 1. (Likewise with up and down interchanged.)

Now consider a trial of this experiment where you get *down* on the left and *up* on the right. It appears that on the first three theories of causation listed (1-3) (including Lewis's [1973] version of theory 2a), we must say that the measurement results *down on left* and *up on right* caused each other, forming a rather odd, closed causal chain consisting of two spacelike-separated events. Our theory resolves the vagueness of 'ceteris paribus' and 'relevant background factors' in this context by specifying a concept of state for the system. Then conditional on the antecedent state, *down on left* is necessary and sufficient for and positively statistically relevant to *up on right.*[1]

With regard to the fourth theory, causation as explanation, it depends on whether we have a version that allows us to say that *up on left* and *down on right* explain each other. They appear to do so in the sense of *deductive-nomological* explanation (Hempel [1965]) and statistical explanation (Salmon [1971]) for the reasons just given.

With the fifth theory of causation, the situation begins to change in a subtle way. Our theory for the particles tells us that there is a conserved quantity (total spin in vertical direction) that is operative here, but we cannot say that there is a *transfer* of spin between the particles because the theory does not attribute *any* up-down spin to the particles prior to the measurement. The theory also regards the two particles as forming one system rather than two despite their separation in space. So we do not have causation between spacelike-separated events on this sort of theory, although it fails in a rather novel way.

The sixth theory, the manipulability theory, does not apply directly to the experiment as described because there is nothing that the experimenter manipulates. Mother Nature throws the dice and decides whether we get up-on-left-down-on-right or down-on-left-up-on-right. The experimenter can only manipulate the measuring apparatus. She *could* choose to orient the measuring apparatus in a different direction and thus make a different measurement. Then if "wiggling" the measuring apparatus on one side corresponded to a difference in measuring results on the other side, the manipulability theory would affirm causation. We shall see later that these considerations are of some importance and how, indeed, there is *no* causation in the manipulability sense just given.

Finally, we have the position that causation is a primitive, unanalyzable physical relation. How do such theories stand on whether we have mutual causation in the EPR? It is difficult to see, given what is usually said, how one would even attempt to find out. Serious proponents of such theories owe us an answer, or at least some direction as to how one would go about finding one.

We now have a preliminary sketch of the situation. Theories 1 through 3 and several versions of 4 say we have a rather odd instance of reciprocal causation at a distance; 5 and 6 say we do not; 7 is mum.

II. EINSTEIN-PODOLSKY-ROSEN

The story that I told in the last section might naturally raise suspicions that "our best physical theory" is not telling the whole story; that the particles carry with them a hidden property that determines whether they will go up or down from the time of their creation onward; that the correlation of measurement results can be explained by a common cause. This is what Einstein suspected, and it is the point of the Einstein-Podolsky-Rosen paradox. (The version given above with spin 1/2 particles created in a singlet state and Stern-Gerlack magnets as detectors is a simplified version due to Bohm [1951]. It has the conceptual virtues that each experiment must give one of two possible results and that the spin measurements can be thought of as also determining the positions of the particles without engendering any theoretical difficulties. An analogous experiment is possible with photons and polarizers.)

That is, Einstein thought that the EPR established the disjunction: *Either the principle of locality of causation is false or quantum mechanics is incomplete.* He says so, in slightly different ways, in a number of places. For instance, in his reply (1949) to criticisms in Schilpp:

> And now just a remark concerning the discussions of the Einstein-Podolsky-Rosen Paradox. I do not think that Margenau's defense of the "orthodox" ("orthodox" refers to the thesis that the ψ-function characterizes the individual system *exhaustively*) quantum position hits the essential [aspects]. Of the "orthodox" quantum theoreticians whose position I know, Neils Bohr's seems to me to come closest to doing justice to the problem. Translated into my own way of putting it, he argues as follows:
>
> If the partial systems, A and B form a total system which is described by its ψ-function, $\psi/(AB)$, there is no reason why any independent existence (state of reality) should be ascribed to the partial systems A and B viewed separately, *Not even if the partial systems are spatially separated from each other at the particular time under consideration.* The assertion that, in this latter case, the real situation of B could not be (directly) influenced by any measurement taken on A is therefore, within the framework of the quantum theory, unfounded and (as the paradox shows) unacceptable.

By this way of looking at the matter it becomes evident that the paradox forces us to relinquish one of the following two assertions:

(1) The description by means of the ψ-function is complete.

(2) The real states of spatially separated objects are independent of each other.

[Einstein sets out the same argument in "Quantum Mechanics and Reality," a manuscript printed with the 88th item in the Einstein-Born correspondence, Born (1971), and published in *Dialectica* (1948)].

Einstein's view of the matter was that he would stick with locality of causation while "orthodox" quantum theorists took the other alternative. Thus, in a letter to Born on 3 March 1947 (Born [1971]):

I cannot make a case for my attitude in physics which you would think at all reasonable. I admit, of course, that there is a considerable amount of validity in the statistical approach which you were the first to recognize clearly as necessary given the framework of the existing formalism. I cannot seriously believe in it because the theory cannot be reconciled with the idea that physics should represent a reality in time and space free from spooky actions-at-a-distance.

and again in "Quantum Mechanics and Reality," Section II (Born [1971]):

An essential aspect of this arrangement of things is that they lay claim, at a certain time, to an existence independent of each other, provided that these objects are 'situated in different parts of space'. Unless one makes this kind of assumption about the independence of the existence (the 'being thus') of objects which are far apart from one another in space . . . physical thinking in the familiar sense would not be possible. It is also hard to see any way of formulating and testing the laws of physics unless one makes a clear distinction of this kind. . . .

The following idea characterizes the relative independence of objects far apart in space (A and B): external influence on A has no direct influence on B; this is known as the 'principle of contiguity', which is used consistently only in field theory. If this axiom were to be completely abolished, the idea of quasi-enclosed systems, and thereby the postulation of laws which can be checked empirically in the accepted sense, would be impossible.

Einstein concludes that quantum mechanics is incomplete; that there must be some deeper description of reality in terms of which there emerges a "common cause" that saves the "principle of contiguity." That is, he believed that there must be a local hidden variable theory for quantum mechanics.

I quoted Einstein at some length to provide the reader with text relevant to this question: What sense, or senses, of causation are involved in Einstein's conception of locality?

III. BELL'S ANALYSIS

Let us begin by asking whether there could be a hidden variable theory that restores locality in the sense of theory 3, statistical causation, to the EPR as described. That is, can there be a theory that makes the same predictions as our theory and in which the concept of state, as determined by the hidden variables, is such that the outcomes of the measurements are independent conditional on the state? That is:

$$Pr\,(R_R\,\&\,R_L\,/\lambda) = Pr\,(R_R\,/\lambda)\,Pr\,(R_L\,/\lambda)$$

Where R_R is the result on the right and R_L is the result on the left and λ the hidden state.

The answer is trivially "Yes"! We need only to have two hidden states: λ_1 in which the right particle carries with it instructions to go up and the left instructions to go down, and λ_2 in which the right carries instructions to go down and the left instructions to go up. Our theory will say that given our preparation of the system in the given macrostate, the probability that each hidden state is the true one is one-half. Then the predictions of the original theory are reproduced and *conditional on the hidden state* λ, the probabilities of measurement results are zero or one and the results on the left and right are trivially independent.

Notice that the *deterministic* character of this theory—that the hidden state λ determines with probability one what the results of measurements are to be—is *required* to restore independence of the measurement results conditional on λ, because of the strict anticorrelation of the measurement results (Bell [1964]; Suppes and Zanotti [1976]). Determinism is both necessary and sufficient for conditional independence.

So far, the requirement that the probabilities specified by the theory admit of an explanation by local hidden variables is no requirement at all. But, remembering considerations of manipulability, we may want to consider variations in the measurements we choose to make. In our example, this variation can be accomplished by rotating the detectors. Let us consider four possible settings of the detectors, with the quantum mechanical probabilities of the results for each setting (from Stapp [1980]).

Setting 1 (parallel) ‖		
↑↑ 0	↑↓ 1/2	
↓↑ 1/2	↓↓ 0	

Setting 2 (perpendicular) ⊥	
↑→ 1/4	↑← 1/4
↓→ 1/4	↓← 1/4

Setting 3 \\		
↘↑ 1/4 + $\sqrt{2}$/8	↘↓ 1/4 − $\sqrt{2}$/8	
↖↑ 1/4 + $\sqrt{2}$/8	↖↓ 1/4 − $\sqrt{2}$/8	

Setting 4 \\	
↘→ 1/4 − $\sqrt{2}$/8	↘← 1/4 + $\sqrt{2}$/8
↖→ 1/4 + 2/8	↖← 1/4 − $\sqrt{2}$/8

Notice that we could *still* have trivial independence of the results conditional on λ provided that we could make the hidden state depend on the setting of the detectors. Let $\lambda^1 - \lambda^4$ be compatible with setting 1, $\lambda^5 - \lambda^8$ with setting 2, $\lambda^9 - \lambda^{12}$ with setting 3, $\lambda^{13} - \lambda^{16}$ with setting 4. Let each value of λ be deterministic for the settings for which it is compatible, e.g., λ^{13} determines ↘→, λ^{14} determines ↘←, λ^{15} determines ↖→, λ^{16} determines ↖←. Then let the probability of λ conditional on the setting equal the desired probability of outcome: $Pr\,(\lambda^{13}$ given setting 4) = 1/4 − $\sqrt{2}$/8; $Pr\,(\lambda^{14}$ given setting 4) = 1/4 + $\sqrt{2}$/8; etc.

The problem with this strategy is that it buys independence of results conditional on λ at the price of giving up a locality requirement more plausible than the one being maintained. The choice of settings of the detectors can be made at random, while the particles are already in flight. Theoretically, it could be made by another quantum system that we have every reason to believe *is* independent from one under consideration, e.g., by a radioactive decay. If λ is supposed to characterize information that the particles are already carrying about how to react, how can the particles already know how the detectors will be set? It seems reasonable to assume that the sort of locality that Einstein wanted should also require that the state λ be independent of the settings of the detectors. [Note that this additional requirement now gives us the result that each value of λ must determine the results of measurement for every setting. For each value of λ must now be compatible with every setting. For any setting on the right the left could be set parallel, so $Pr(R_R/M_R$ & λ) must equal zero or one as noted before. Likewise for the left.]

This finally puts teeth in the requirement that the theory admit of a local hidden variable explanation. Under it, we can't simply glue together trivial hidden variable theories tailored to each setting of the detectors. Rather, it is required that the probability of the hidden states, independent of the setting, account for the probabilities of results for all settings. That is to say that our Bell-local theory must supply a probability distribution ρ, independent of the settings of the measuring apparatus, such that the quantum mechanical probabilities of results given measurement settings are recoverable thus:

$$Pr(R_L \text{ \& } R_R/M_L \text{ \& } M_R) = \int Pr(R_L/M_L \text{ \& } \lambda) \, Pr(R_R/M_R \text{ \& } \lambda) \, \rho(\lambda) \, d\lambda$$

Bell (1964) showed that no theory could, in this sense, locally reproduce the quantum mechanical statistics.

One whose intuitions strongly favor this sort of locality might perhaps hope that quantum mechanics is not just incomplete, but also wrong. The evidence, however, favors quantum theory. A number of experiments have been undertaken to test the predictions of quantum mechanics against the inequalities that Bell-local theories must satisfy. The evidence is impressively in favor of quantum mechanics. (Experimental test was first suggested in Clauser, Horne, Shimony, and Holt [1969]. There is an extensive reivew of both theory and evidence to that data in Clauser and Shimony [1978]. Aspect [1982] reports the results of later experiments, the most decisive of which, given that the observations are a fair sample, confirms quantum mechanics against Bell locality by more than twenty standard deviations.) According to our best evidence, nature is not Bell-local.

IV. COUNTERFACTUAL DEFINITENESS

Quantum mechanics gives us probabilities that are, in a certain sense, subjunctive and sometimes counterfactual. That is, the quantum mechanical state grounds statements about the probabilities of results *if* certain measurements were made (even if those measurements are incompatible with others that are actually made).

This subjunctive character of the quantum mechanical probabilities and perhaps of the probabilities in stochastic hidden variable theories for quantum mechanics has been an item of some concern in the literature. (Stapp [1971]; Herbert and Karush [1978]; Eberhard [1978]). Perhaps we can only legitimately reason about the situation in terms of subjunctive conditionals with chance consequents instead of conditional probabilities.

It is worth reformulating the question of statistical locality in this way in order to see that under the assumptions relevant to Bell's theorem, the reformulation really makes no difference. We will not assume any special philosophical theory of subjunctive conditionals here. We will assume that *modus ponens*—from "If M then $Pr(R) = a$" and "M" you can conclude that "$Pr(R) = a$" is valid for them. Now let me show how to move between the sort of formulation familiar to physicists and the formulation in terms of subjunctive conditionals with chance consequents.

Let λ determine the concept of state for the theory. If λ together determines R, we shall state that λ grounds the truth of the conditional "If M then R," i.e., the conditional is true in state λ. Conversely, if "If M then R" is true in state λ, then if we have λ together with M we have (If M then R) & M and by validity of *modus ponens* we have R. In this way, the concept of state for a deterministic theory corresponds to a bundle of subjunctive conditionals with measurement performed as antecedent and measurement result as consequent.

For stochastic theories, corresponding to each pair (λ, M) there is a determinate probability distribution, $Pr_{\lambda \& M}(R)$. We shall say that each λ grounds conditionals with probabilistic consequents so that "If M then $Pr(R) = a$ is true in state λ if $Pr_{\lambda \& M}(R) = a$. Conversely, if "If M then $Pr(R) = a$ is true in state λ, then if we have $\lambda \& M$, we have M & [If M then $Pr(R) = a$] and, by *modus ponens*, $Pr(R) = a$ [i.e., $Pr_{\lambda \& M}(R) = a$]. In this way the concept of state for a stochastic theory corresponds to a bundle of conditionals with measurement performed as antecedent and chance of measurement results as consequent.

Now let us consider stochastic hidden variable theories for quantum mechanics. I assume that these are theories for which $Pr_{\lambda \& M}(R)$ is always well defined. (Note that this means that for these theories we have conditional excluded middle: Either [If M then $Pr(R) = a$] or [If M then $Pr(R) \neq a$]. This is a principle of logic in some theories of subjunctive conditionals but not in others.) For any such theory we can formulate statistical locality and conservation of spin subjunctively as follows (where the subscripts indicate left or right, the superscripts on "M" indicate the orientation of the measuring apparatus, and the superscripts on "R" are -1 for up and $+1$ for down.)

Locality:
If a value of λ makes the following subjunctive true:
$$\text{If } M_L^h \ \& \ M_R^i \text{ then } Pr(R_R^n / R_L^m) = a$$
then it makes the following true:
$$\text{If } M_R^i \text{ then } Pr(R_R^n) = a$$
And likewise going the other way with "L" and "R" interchanged.)

Conservation:
    Any value of λ that makes:
$$\text{If } M_L^i \ \& \ M_R^i \text{ then } Pr(R_L^{-1}) \neq 0$$
    true, also makes:
$$\text{If } M_L^i \ \& \ M_R^i \text{ then } Pr(R_R^1/R_L^{-1}) = 1$$
    true.
    And likewise with the superscripts 1 and -1 interchanged.)

It is easy to show (A) that any such theory satisfying locality and conservation must be deterministic and (B) for any deterministic hidden variable theory where the state λ is independent of the measurement made we have the probability of the conditional, Pr (If M then R) equal to the conditional probability $Pr(R/M)$. (For more details see Skyrms [1982].)

The formulation in terms of subjunctive conditionals with chance consequents reduces, under the conditions for Bell's theorem, to the familiar conditional probability formulation. The distinctions between conditional probabilities, probabilities of conditionals, and expectations of the consequent in conditional with chance consequent mark real differences in general, but the special case salient to our concerns is one in which those distinctions collapse. There was really nothing to worry about after all.

V. SIGNAL LOCALITY

Few metaphysicians hold the manipulability theory in high regard. It is generally thought to be too closely tied to human powers, and perhaps to be circular. Nevertheless, we will see that manipulability considerations have an important role to play in discussions of locality.

We would have causation in the manipulability sense at the manifest level if changing the setting of the measuring apparatus on one side (say the left) changed the probability of getting a result of a given measurement on the right. If we had manipulability causation in this sense, an experimenter on the left could signal to a colleague on the right by manipulating the left-most measuring apparatus. That is, he could convey *information* in the sense of Shannon and Weaver. It is appropriate, then, to call the principle that the result of a measurement on one side be statistically independent of the setting on the other side, *signal locality*.

It is possible for a theory to be *signal-local* even if it is not *Bell-local*. That is, it is possible for the probability of a *result* of a measurement on the right-hand side to be independent of the *setting* on the left, even though it is not independent of the measurement results on the left either unconditionally or conditional on λ. Our quantum mechanical example is a case in point. Consider settings 2 and 4, which have the same setting on the right-hand side but different settings on the left. The probability of getting UP on the right is independent of the setting on the left; it is 1/2 in both settings 2 and 4. In setting 2 it is 1/4 + 1/4 = 1/2; in setting 4 it is $(1/4 - \sqrt{2}/8) + (1/4 + \sqrt{2}/8) = 1/2$.

This is not an accidental feature of our example. The requirement of signal locality is, in fact, built into the structure of local relativistic quantum field theory in the requirement that the operators that correspond to physically measurable quantities commute for spacelike-separated space-time points. (See Streater and Wightman [1964] or Sakurai [1967]). This requirement of local commutativity is something over and above Lorentz invariance, and it is motivated precisely by the fact that it guarantees signal locality.

Indeed, my friends in physics tell me that signal locality is a principle that is generally regarded as empirically well confirmed. It leads to predictions regarding dispersion relations that are in close agreement with experiment. (There is a review of some of this experimental evidence in Lindenbaum [1969].)

The leading idea of manipulability causation can, after all, lead to something of fundamental theoretical importance: *signal locality*. According to our best evidence, nature is signal-local. The status of signal locality is so dramatically different from that of Bell locality that it is essential that we mark well the differences between them.

VI. CAUSATION 5: MOTIVATION FOR
HIDDEN VARIABLES?

Einstein's motivation for hidden variables was the desire for locality. From what we have seen, there is not much left of that motivation. *Bell locality* can't be delivered by hidden variable theories that reproduce the quantum mechanical statistics. *Signal locality* we have already with quantum mechanics.

Perhaps we should look for locality of causation in some other sense of cause. The eligible candidate that we have not yet discussed is number 5: causation as the transfer of energy-momentum (or some other quantity for which we have a conservation law for normally closed systems). This gives, in fact, a sense of causal chain that appears to capture the paradigm examples in relativity theory. (See Havas [1969] and the discussion in Skyrms [1980], sec. IIB2.)

EPR experiments do not violate the principle of local causes in this sense of causation, because according to the theory the conserved quantity is not *had* prior to the measurement. This is however a rather curious way in which to avoid violation of the principle. One motivation for hidden variable theories has been the desire to say that each particle always has a definite energy-momentum, spin in each direction, or whatever; exactly the value that was determined to show up if a measurement were made. And we would have a stronger version of the principle of local causes if it was respected by particles for whom the quantities in question were always well defined.

No motivation could be more ill fated. Since the appropriate hidden variable theory is conceived of as deterministic in the sense of section III, if the measurements are carried out so that the state is independent of the measurement made, we will have a Bell-local theory and by Bell's result the hypothesized theory will be unable to account for the quantum mechanical probabilities. (Worse things could be said about such a theory, if we were willing to go beyond EPR-type considerations.

Such a theory could not account for well-known phenomena such as *tunneling* without violating conservation of energy-momentum.)

With regard to locality in the sense corresponding to theory 5 of causation, the introduction of hidden variables makes things *worse* than they are in the quantum theory. The curious way in which quantum theory respects locality in the sense of theory 5 may be the maximum that nature will allow.

VII. LESSONS FOR METAPHYSICS

In section I of this paper, I recalled seven theories of causation, three of which for various reasons came to occupy center stage. These are (3) statistical causation, (5) causation as a transfer of energy-momentum, etc., and (6) manipulability causation, which in the form salient to our concerns is signaling.

These are sometimes thought of as competitors for the title: "The True Theory of Causation," but I would like to suggest that we look at the matter in a slightly different way. I think that our ordinary, everyday conception of causation is an amiably confused jumble of all three, with the principles of locality of causation and temporal priority of cause to effect and perhaps a few other things thrown in for good measure.

It is an *amiable* confusion, one with real heuristic value, because in the noisy macroworld of everyday life they often go together (especially when their application is guided by principles of locality and temporal priority). Manipulation is by a transfer of mass or energy that propagates locally; messages so carried in a sea of noise are randomly degraded in a way consistent with statistical causation (Skyrms [1980], sec. IIB2). Statistical causation when examined more closely often discloses an underlying deterministic causation. There is no real point in drawing the sharp distinctions we have made in such an environment. It is better to stick with the amiable jumble. Anything else will seem inadequate.

The game has been altered by the progress of science. The notion of temporal precedence was qualified by relativity; that of constant conjunction made obsolescent by quantum mechanics. When we ask whether causes operate locally in the quantum domain, the old cluster concept loses its heuristic value and becomes positively misleading.

A metaphysician might decide on the basis of general relativity that an adequate theory of causation should allow for closed causal chains. We saw in section II that theories 1-3 give closed causal chains consisting of two spacelike-separated events. These were hardly the kind of closed causal chains that were desired. A metaphysician might decide that the success of special relativity gives us good reason to believe that causation operates locally. As we have seen, this means something quite different for causation 3, causation 5, and causation 6. And, according to our best experimental evidence, these distinctions are physically significant. Metaphysics must take lessons in philosophical analysis from Mother Nature.

Notes

1. The result could be avoided by requiring that the cause be in the backward light cone of the effect; i.e., by ruling out superluminal causation by stipulative definition.

And, as Lewis points out in correspondence, the result could be avoided if the underlying theory of events does not recognize the measurement results *down on left; up on right* as distinct events but regards them rather as aspects of a single, indivisible nonlocal event – the collapse of the wave packet. In connection with this idea the differences between the frameworks of classical quantum theory and quantum field theory become important.

References

Aspect, A. 1982. "Experimental Tests of Bell's Inequalities." In *Mathematical Problems in Theoretical Physics* (Lecture Notes in Physics 153), edited by J. Ehlers et al., 162-67. Berlin.

Bell, J. S. 1964. "On the Einstein-Podolsky-Rosen Paradox." *Physics* 1 (October):195-200.

Bell, J. S. 1971. "Introduction to the Hidden Variable Question." In *Foundations of Quantum Mechanics*, edited by B. d'Espagnat. New York.

Bohm, D. 1951. *Quantum Theory*. Englewood Cliffs, N. J.

Born, M., ed. 1971. *The Correspondence Between A. Einstein and Max and Hedwig Born.* Translated by Irene Born. New York.

Clauser, J. F., and M. A. Horn. 1974. "Experimental Consequences of Objective Local Theories." *Physical Review* D10:526-35.

Clauser, J. F., M. A. Horne, A. Shimony, and R. Holt. 1969. "Proposed Experiment to Test Local Hidden Variable Theories." *Physical Review Letters* 23 (October):880-84.

Clauser, J. F., and A. Shimony. 1978. "Bell's Theorem: Experimental Tests and Implications." *Reports on Progress in Physics* 41 (December):1881-1927.

P. Eberhard, 1970. "Bell's Theorem and the Different Concepts of Locality." *Il Nuovo Climento* 46B (August):392-419.

Einstein, A. 1949. "Reply to Critics." In *Albert Einstein: Philosopher-Scientist*, edited by P. A. Schilpp. La Salle, Ill.

Einstein, A., B. Podolsky, and N. Rosen. 1935. "Can the Quantum Mechanical Description of Reality Be Considered Complete?" *Physical Review* 47:777-80.

Havas, P. 1969. "Causality Requirements in the Theory of Relativity." In *Boston Studies in the Philosophy of Science* 5, edited by R. Cohen and M. W. Wartofsky. Dordrecht.

Hempel, C. G. 1965. *Aspects of Scientific Explanation and Other Essays in the Philosophy of Science*. New York.

Herbert, N., and J. Karush. 1978. "Generalization of Bell's Theorem." *Foundations of Physics* 8:313-17.

Lewis, D. K., 1973. "Causation." *Journal of Philosophy* 70:556-67.

Lindenbaum, S. J. 1969. "Forward Dispersion Relations: Their Validity and Predictions." In *Pion-Nucleon Scattering*, edited by G. L. Shaw and D. Y. Wong. New York.

Sakurai, J. J. 1967. *Advanced Quantum Mechanics*. Reading, Mass.

Salmon, W. 1971. *Statistical Explanation and Statistical Relevance*. Pittsburgh, Pa.

Skyrms, B. 1980. *Causal Necessity*. New Haven.

Skyrms, B. 1982. "Counterfactual Definiteness and Local Causation," *Philosophy of Science* 49:43-50.

Sosa, E., ed. 1975. *Causation and Conditionals*. London.

Stapp, H. P. 1971. "S-Matrix Interpretation of Quantum Theory." *Physical Review* D3:1303-20.

Stapp, H. P. 1980. "Locality and Reality." *Foundations of Physics* 10:767-95.

Streater, R. F. and A. S. Wightman. 1964. *PCT, Spin and Statistics, and All That*. Reading, Mass.

Suppes, P., and M. Zanotti. 1976. "On the Determinism of Hidden Variable Theories with Strict Correlation and Conditional Statistical Dependence of Observables." In *Logic and Probability in Quantum Mechanics*, edited by P. Suppes.

Epiphenomenal
and Supervenient Causation

JAEGWON KIM

1. EPIPHENOMENAL CAUSATION

Jonathan Edwards held the doctrine that ordinary material things do not persist through time but are at each moment created, and recreated, by God ex nihilo. He writes:

> If the existence of created *substance*, in each successive moment, be wholly the effect of God's immediate power, in *that* moment, without any dependence on prior existence, as much as the first creation out of *nothing*, then what exists at this moment, by this power, is a *new effect*, and simply and absolutely considered, not the same with any past existence, though it be like it, and follows it according to a certain established method.[1]

Thus, the present "time slice" of this table, although it is very much like the one preceding it, has no causal connection with it; for each slice is a wholly distinct creation by God. The temporal parts of this table are successive effects of an underlying persisting cause, God's creative activity. In arguing for this doctrine, Edwards offers the following striking analogy:

> The *images* of things in a glass, as we keep our eye upon them, seem to remain precisely the same, with a continuing, perfect identity. But it is known to be otherwise. Philosophers well know that these images are constantly *renewed*, by the impression and reflection of *new* rays of light; so that the image impressed by the former rays is constantly vanishing, and a *new* image impressed by *new* rays every moment, both on the glass and on the eye. . . . And the new images being put on *immediately* or *instantly*, do not make them the same, any more than if it were done with the intermission of an *hour* or a *day*. The image that exists at this moment is not at all *derived* from the image which existed at the last preceding moment. As may be seen, because if the succession of new *rays* be intercepted, by something interposed

between the object and the glass, the image immediately ceases; the *past ex-ixtence* of the image has no influence to uphold it, so much as for a moment.[2]

Two successive mirror reflections of an object are not directly causally linked to each other; in particular, the earlier one is not a cause of the later one, even though the usual requirements of "Humean causation," including that of spatiotemporal contiguity, may be met. If all we ever observed were mirror images, like the shadows in Plato's cave, we might very well be misled into ascribing a cause-effect relation to the two images; but we know better, as Edwards says. The succession of images is only a reflection of the real causal process at the level of the objects reflected.

Edwards's example anticipates one that Wesley Salmon has recently used to illustrate the difference between "causal processes" and "pseudoprocesses":[3] consider a rotating spotlight, located at the center of a circular room, casting a spot of light on the wall. According to Salmon, a light ray traveling from the spotlight to the wall is a *causal process*, whereas the motion of the spot of light on the wall is only a *pseudoprocess*. Each spot of light on the wall is caused by a light ray traveling from the spotlight; however, it is not the cause of the spot of light appearing on the wall at an instant later. Two successive spots of light on the wall are related to each other as two successive mirror images are related. Both pairs mimic causal processes and are apt to be mistaken for such. Neither, however, is a process involving a real causal chain.

By "epiphenomenal causation" I have in mind *roughly* the sort of apparant causal relation in the examples of Edwards and Salmon. I say "roughly" because, as will become clear later, they are somewhat less central cases of epiphenomenal causation, as this notion will be used in this paper; these examples are helpful, however, in the initial fixing of the concept that I have in mind. In any event, Edwards's contention was that *all* causal relations holding for material bodies, events, and processes are cases of epiphenomenal causation, the only true causation being limited to God's own creative actions. The world is constantly created anew by God; we may think that fire causes smoke, but it is only that God creates fire at one instant and then smoke an instant later. There is no direct causal connection between the fire and the smoke. The relation between them is one of epiphenomenal causation.

Another case of epiphenomenal causation, familiar in daily life, is the succession of symptoms associated with a disease: the symptoms are not mutually related in the cause-effect relationship, although to the medically naive they may appear to be so related. The appearance of a causal connection here merely points to the real causal process underlying the symptoms.

It should be clear that by saying that two events are related in an epiphenomenal causal relation I do not mean to suggest that the events themselves are "epiphenomena." The standard current use of this term comes from discussions of epiphenomenalism as a theory of the mind-body relation, and to call an event an "epiphenomenon" in this context is taken to mean that though it is a causal effect of other events, it has no causal potency of its own: it can be the cause of no other event, being the absolute terminal link of a causal chain. It is dubious that this notion of an epiphenomenon makes sense—for example, it is doubtful how such events could be known to exist.[4] In this paper I use the modifier "epiphenomenal" in "epiphenomenal causation" to qualify the causal relation, not the events standing in that relation.

One might object at this point that these examples of the so-called epiphenomenal causation are not cases of causation at all and that it is misleading to label them as such, because "epiphenomenal causation" sounds as though it is a *kind* of causal relation. In reply, I shall say two things: first, even though it is true that an earlier mirror image is not a cause of a later one, it is also true that there *is* a causal relation between the two—the two are successive effects of the same underlying causal process. To leave the matter where we have simply denied that the first is the cause of the second would be to ignore an important causal fact about the relation between the two events. Second, I shall argue that the central cases of epiphenomenal causation that will interest us will be seen to involve "real" causal relations and that epiphenomenal causal relations of this kind are pervasively present all around us.

What is common to these cases and the earlier examples, such as Edwards's mirror images, which do not seem to involve real causal relations, is just this: they all involve at least *apparent* causal relations that are *grounded* in some underlying causal processes. These causal relations, whether only apparent or real, *are reducible to more fundamental causal relations*. If one takes the view that reducibility entails eliminability, there perhaps is no significant difference between the two types of cases. But then there also is the apparently opposed view: to be reduced is to be legitimatized. I believe in any case that my use of the term "epiphenomenon" is entirely consistent with the standard dictionary definition of "epiphenomenon" as "secondary symptom," "secondary phenomenon," or "something that happens in addition"; the idea that an epiphenomenon is causally inert is best taken as a philosophical doctrine of epiphenomenalism as a theory about the nature of the mental, not as something that merely arises out of the meaning of the term "epiphenomenon."

The principal claims that I want to defend in this paper are the following: that macrocausation should be viewed as a kind of epiphenomenal causation in the broad sense sketched above; that macrocausation as epiphenomenal causation should be explained as "supervenient causation" in the sense to be explained below; and that psychological causation, that is causation involving psychological events, is plausibly assimilated to macrocausation—that is, it is to be construed as supervenient epiphenomenal causation.

2. MACROCAUSATION AS SUPERVENIENT CAUSATION

By "macrocausation" I have in mind causal relations involving macroevents and states, where a macroevent or state is understood as the exemplification of a macroproperty by an object at a time (this characterization can be generalized to macro-*relations* in obvious ways). The micro-macro distinction is of course relative: temperature is macro relative to molecular motion; properties of molecules are macro

relative to properties and relationships characterizing atoms and more basic particles, and so on. For our present discussion, however, the paradigmatic examples of
macroobjects and properties are medium-sized material bodies around us and their
observable properties. Thus, fire causing smoke would be a case of macrocausation;
so is the rising temperature causing a metallic object to expand. All observable phenomena are macrophenomena in relation to the familiar theoretical objects of
physics; hence, our first claim entails that all causal relations involving observable
phenomena—all causal relations familiar from daily experience—are cases of epiphenomenal causation.

My defense of this claim is two-pronged. The first prong consists in a general
argument to the effect that a certain familiar and plausible reductionist perspective
requires us to view macrocausation as epiphenomenal causation. The second prong
consists in the observation that modern theoretical science treats macrocausation as
reducible epiphenomenal causation and that this has proved to be an extremely successful explanatory and predictive research strategy.

First, the general argument: philosophers have observed, in connection with
the mind-body problem, that a thoroughgoing physicalism can no more readily tolerate the existence of irreducible psychological features or properties than irreducible psychological objects (e.g., Cartesian souls, visual images).[5] The thought behind
this may be something like this: if F is an irreducible psychical feature, then its
existence implies that something is F. (If F is never exemplified, being a mere "concept" of something psychical, the physicalist has nothing to worry about.) This
means that there would be a physically irreducible event or state of this thing's
being F, or a physically irreducible fact, namely the fact that the thing is F. So the
world remains bifurcated: the physical domain and a distinct, irreducible psychical
domain; and physical theory fails as a complete and comprehensive theory of the
world. Moreover, we might want to inquire into the *cause* of something's being F.
This gives rise to three possibilities, none of them palatable to the physicalist: first,
the cause of the psychical event is a mystery not accessible to scientific inquiry; second, an autonomous psychical science emerges; third, physical theory provides a
causal account of the psychical phenomena. The last possibility may be the worst,
from the physicalist point of view: given the irreducibility of the psychical phenomena, this could only mean that physical theory would lose its *closed* character, by
countenancing within its domain irreducibly nonphysical events and properties.

Parallel considerations should motivate the rejection of macrocausation as an
irreducible feature of the world. It seems to be a fundamental methodological pre-
cept of theoretical physical science that we ought to formulate *microstructural
theories* of objects and their properties—that is, to try to understand the behavior
and properties of objects and processes in terms of the properties and relationships
characterizing their microconstituents. The philosophical supposition that grounds
this research strategy seems to be the belief that macroproperties are determined
by, or supervenient upon, microproperties. This Democritean doctrine of mereological supervenience, or microdeterminism, forms the metaphysical backbone of
the method of microreduction,[6] somewhat in the way that the principle of causal

determinism constitutes the objective basis of the method of causal explanation. (I shall return to these themes below.)

In this global microdeterministic picture there is no place for irreducible macrocausal relations. We expect any causal relation between two macroevents (x's being F and y's being G, where F and G are macroproperties) to be micro-reductively explainable in terms of more fundamental causal processes, like any other facts involving macroproperties and events. If the causal relation is backed up by a law relating F and G, we would expect this macrolaw to be microreducible. A standard example: the rising temperature of a gas confined within a rigid chamber causes its pressure to rise. This macrocausal relation is subsumed under a macrolaw (the gas law), which in turn is microreduced by kinetic theory of gases. This explains, and reduces, the macrocausal relation. If the causal relation is at bottom just some sort of counterfactual dependency, then the macrocounterfactual "If x had not been F, y would not have been G" should be grounded in some lawlike connection involving microproperties associated with x and y in relation to F and G; or else, there should be some more basic counterfactual dependencies involving microconstituents of x and y that can explain the counterfactual dependency between F and G. It would be difficult to believe that this macrocounterfactual is a fundamental and irreducible fact about the world. At least, that should be our attitude if we accept the universal thesis of mereological supervenience and the validity of microreductive research strategy.

What is the general form of the reduction of a macrocausal relation to a microcausal process? The following model is attractively simple: if the macrocausal relation to be reduced is one from an instance of property F to an instance of property G, we need to correlate F with some microproperty m(F), and also G with m(G), and then show that m(F) and m(G) are appropriately causally connected. Showing the latter may take the form of exhibiting a precise law that connects the two microproperties, or a causal mechanism whereby an instance of F leads to an instance of G. How is the correlation between F and m(F) to be understood? The strongest claim defended by some philosophers is that F and m(F) are one and the same property.[7] The thought is that such property identities are necessary for the required microreduction to go through. Taking this identity approach, however, would force a reconstrual of the notions of microproperty and macroproperty; how could one and the same property be both a microproperty and a macroproperty? But a more serious problem is this: in the given instance under consideration, the macroproperty may be "realized" or "grounded" in m(F), but in another instance F may be realized or grounded in a different microproperty m*(F), and there may be many other microproperties that can realize F, in that if anything has one of them, then necessarily it also exhibits F as a result. And it may well be that from the explanatory-causal point of view, the possibly infinite disjunction of these underlying microproperties could hardly be considered as a unitary property suitable as a reductive base.

The foregoing is a point often made in connection with the mind-body problem and used sometimes to support the "functionalist" view of the mental.[8] The multiple realizability of a state relative to a more basic level of analysis, or a richer descriptive vocabulary, appears to hold, with equal plausibility, for macrophysical characteristics in relation to microphysical properties and processes; perhaps this is a pervasive feature of mereological reduction. For these reasons, among others, I suggest the use of the concept of *supervenience*, which allows for the possibility of *alternative supervenience bases* for a given supervenient property, as particularly well suited for the purposes on hand. The core idea of supervenience as a relation between two families of properties is that the supervenient properties are in some sense *determined by,* or *dependent on*, the properties on which they supervene. More formally, *the supervenience of a family A of properties on another family B* can be explained as follows: necessarily, for any property F in A, if any object x has F, then there exists a property G in B such that x has G, and necessarily anything having G has F.[9] When properties F and G are related as specified in the definition, we may say that F is *supervenient* on G, and that G is a *superveneince base* of F. On this account, it is clear that a property in the supervenient family can have multiple supervenience bases: an object x has F, and for x the supervenience base of F is G; however, another object y that also has F does not have G, but rather has G^*, as *its* supervenience base for F; and so on. Thus, if we think of macroproperties as supervenient on microproperties, the account allows for a given macroproperty F to be supervenient on a number of microproperties; that is, an object has a certain macroproperty (e.g., fragility) in virtue of having a certain microproperty (e.g., a certain crystalline structure) on which the macroproperty supervenes; another object has the same macroproperty in virtue of having a different microproperty (another kind of crystalline structure); and so on.

The notion of *event supervenience* is easily explained on the basis of property supervenience: an event, x's having F, supervenes on the event, x's having G, just in case x has G and G is a supervenience base of F.

So the general schema for reducing a macrocausal relation between two events, x's having F and y's having G, where F and G are macroproperties, is this: x's having F supervenes on x's having m(F), y's having G supervenes on y's having m(G), where m(F) and m(G) are microproperties relative to F and G, and there is an appropriate causal connection between x's having m(F) and y's having m(G).

Any causal relation conforming to the pattern set forth above will be called a "supervenient causal relation." For the pattern can be taken to show the causal relation itself to be supervenient upon an underlying causal process through the supervenience of its relata upon the events involved in the underlying process.

I have left the causal relation between the two microevents unspecified; for it is not part of my present aim to advocate a particular analysis of causation. Generally, however, we would expect it to be mediated by laws, whether deterministic or statistical, and in favorable cases we may even have an account in terms of a mechanism by which one microstate evolves into another. But the kind of position I want to advocate here concerning macrocausation is largely independent of the particular views concerning the anlaysis of causation. Moreover, I do not wish to tie the fate of my general views about macrocausation too closely to the fate of my proposal regarding a proper construal of the relation between macroproperties and the microproperties on which they "depend." Although the use of mereological supervenience is an integral part of the total account being sketched here, the main points of the general picture of macrocausation I am advancing are independent of the question of what particular account is to be accepted for the macro-micro relation. What are these points? There are two: (1) macrocausal relations should be viewed as in general reducible to microcausal relations, and (2) the mechanism of the reduction involves identifying the microstates on which the macrostates in question depend, or with which they are correlated, and showing that a proper causal relation obtains for these microstates. Thus, to affirm (1) is to accept the view that macrocausation is to be viewed as epiphenomenal causation. To affirm that macro-causation is supervenient causation is to accept a particular account of the mechanism of reduction referred to in (2).

The sort of account I have given should be found attractive by those philosophers who believe that precise laws are rare—perhaps nonexistent—for macro-properties and states, at least those that are routinely referred to in ordinary causal talk, and that they must be "redescribed" at a more basic level before precise laws could be brought to bear on them.[10] My account in essence adds two things to this view: first, that *whether or not* there are macro-lawlike connections, macrocausal relations ought to be viewed as reducible to microcausal relations, and second, that what sanctions a given microredescription of a macrostate can be taken as a super-venience relation—that is to say, the relation between a macrodescription and a corresponding microredescription can be understood in terms of supervenience.

The broad metaphysical conviction that underlies these proposals is the belief that ultimately the world—at least, the physical world—is the way it is because the microworld is the way it is—because there are so many of just these sorts of micro-entities (elementary particles, atoms, or what not), and they behave in accordance with just these laws. As Terence Horgan has put it, worlds that are microphysically identical are one and the same world.[11] Even those who would reject this universal thesis of microdeterminism might find the following more restricted thesis plausible: worlds that are microphysically identical are one world from the physical point of view. This doctrine urges us to see macrocausal relations as emerging out of properties and relations holding for microentities, and this naturally leads to a search of microreductive accounts of macrocausal relations as well as other macroproperties, states, and facts. In fact, causal relations pervade our very conceptions of physical properties, states, and events (consider, for example, heat, magnetic, gene), and the reduction of causal relations, which often takes the form of exhibiting the micro-mechanisms underlying macrocausal relations, is probably the most important part of microreductive research. Causal relations that resist microreduction must be considered "causal danglers," which, like the notorious "nomological danglers," are an acute embarrassment to the physicalist view of the world.

There is ample evidence that the method of microreduction has been extremely successful in modern science, and it seems evident that much of the reduction that has been accomplished involves the reduction of macrocausal laws and relations.[12]

The reduction of gas laws within kinetic theory of gases is of course a case in point; such examples are legion. Given our interest in identifying and understanding causal connections, it is not surprising that a predominant part of the reductive efforts in scientific research is directed toward the microreduction of macrocausal laws and relations. These last few remarks constitute the promised second prong of my defense of the claim that macrocausation ought to be viewed as epiphenomenal causation—and, more specifically, as supervenient causation.

3. MEREOLOGICAL SUPERVENIENCE AND MICRODETERMINISM

The foregoing discussion moved fairly freely among such doctrines and concepts as microreduction, microexplanation, mereological supervenience, and microdeterminism, and I think it may be helpful to set forth their relationships more precisely. First of all, I am taking mereological supervenience and microdeterminism as a thesis concerning the objective features of the world—a metaphysical doctrine— roughly, as I said, to the effect that the macroworld is the way it is because the microworld is the way it is. The two doctrines can of course be sharpened and separated from each other. Mereological supervenience is usefully taken to be a general thesis affirming the supervenience of the characteristics of wholes on the properties and relationships characterizing their proper parts. Here, "characteristics" is understood to include relations, such as causal relations, among wholes. Mereological supervenience (in the sense of supervenience explained in the preceding section) requires that each (exemplified) macrocharacteristic be grounded in some specific microcharacteristics, and in this way it goes beyond the less specific thesis, earlier mentioned, that worlds that are microphysically identical are one and the same (physical) world. It may be convenient to reserve the term "microdeterminism" for this less specific thesis. It is plausible to think that under some reasonable assumptions, mereological supervenience as applied to the physical world entails microdeterminism; I am inclined to believe that, again under some reasonable assumptions, the converse entailment also holds.

In any event, it is useful to think of mereological supervenience and microdeterminism as constituting the metaphysical basis of the method of microreduction and microexplanation. By this I mean that the metaphysical doctrine rationalizes our microreductive proclivities by legitimatizing microreduction as a paradigm of scientific understanding and helping to explain why the microreductive method works as well as it does. Underlying this remark is the view that explanatory or reductive connections, as essentially epistemological connections, must themselves be grounded in the objective determinative connections holding for the events in the world. The root idea of causal determinism is the belief that the existence and properties of an event are determined by its temporally antecedent conditions. The metaphysical thesis of causal determinism can be thought of as the objective basis of the method of causal explanation—the method of seeking "laws of succession" and formulating explanations of events in terms of their antecedent conditions.

Mereological supervenience views the world as determined along the part-whole dimension, whereas the causal determinism views it as determined along the temporal dimension; they respectively provide a metaphysical basis for the method of microreduction and that of causal explanation.

These are rather speculative and bald remarks; they are intended only to give a rough picture of the metaphysical terrain within which my more specific remarks concerning macrocausal relations can be located.

4. MENTAL CAUSATION AS SUPERVENIENT CAUSATION

To say that the causal relation between two macroevents is a case of epiphenomenal causation is not to be understood to mean that the relation is illusory or unreal. In this respect, Jonathan Edwards's case of mirror images, Salmon's moving spot of light, and the case of successive symptoms of a disease differ from our central cases of macrocausal relations. For in those cases, the causal relations are indeed only apparent: although the events are causally *related* in a broad sense, there is no direct causal relation *from* one event *to* the other—that is to say, one event is not the cause of the other. On the other hand, the causal relation between rising temperatures and increasing pressures of gases is no less "real" for being microreducible. To take microreducibility as impugning the reality of what is being reduced would make all of our observable world unreal. However, one reason for bundling the two types of cases together under "epiphenomenal causation" is the existence of another sense of "real" in which reduction does make what is reduced "less real," a sense in which modern physics is sometimes thought to have shown the unreality of ordinary material objects or a sense in which secondary qualities are sometimes thought to be "less real" than primary qualities. As I alluded earlier, reducibility is often taken to imply eliminability; but this is a complex and unfruitful question to pursue here. There is, however, another more concrete reason for viewing these two kinds of cases under the same rubric; in both there is present an *apparent* causal relation that is explained, or explained away, at a more fundamental level. The difference between the two cases is this: macrocausal relations are *supervenient causal relations* —supervenient upon microcausal relations—whereas cases like Edwards's mirror images are not. This can be seen by reflecting on the fact that in a perfectly straightforward sense, mirror images, symptoms if a disease, and so on are causal effects of the underlying processes—they are not mereologically supervenient upon those processes. This is the theoretical difference between the two cases: some epiphenomenal causal relations are supervenient causal relations, and these are among the ones that are "real"; there are also cases of epiphenomenal causation that do not involve direct causal connections, and these include ones in which the events involved are successive causal effects of some underlying process.

What of causal relations involving mental events? Consider a typical case in which we would say a mental event causes a physical event: a sharp pain in my thumb causes a jerky withdrawal of my hand. It is hardly conceivable that the pain sensation qua mental event acts directly on the muscles of my arm, causing them to contract. I assume we have by now a fairly detailed story of what goes on at the physiological level when a limb movement takes place, and no amount of intuitive conviction or philosophical argument about the reality of psychophysical causation is going to preempt that story. If the pain is to play a causal role in the withdrawal of my hand, it must do so by somehow *making use of* the usual physiological causal path to this bodily event; it looks as though the causal path from the pain to the limb motion must *merge* with the physiological path at a certain point. There cannot be two independent, separate causal paths to the limb motion. But at what point does the mental causal path from the pain "merge" with the physiological path? If there is such a point, that must be where psychophysical causal action takes place. The trouble, of course, is that it is difficult to conceive the possibility of some nonphysical event causally influencing the course of physical processes.[13] Apart from the sheer impossibility of coherently imagining the details of what might have to be the case if some nonphysical agency is going to affect the course of purely physical events, there is a deeper problem that any such nonphysical intervention in a physical system would jeopardize the closed character of physical theory. It would force us to accept a conception of the physical in which to give a causal account of, say, the motion of a physical particle, it is sometimes necessary to go outside the physical system and appeal to some nonphysical agency and invoke some irreducible psychophysical law. Many will find this just not credible.

The difficulty of accounting for the possibility of psychophysical causation is simply resolved if one is willing to accept psychophysical identity: the pain *is* in fact a certain neural state, and the problem of accounting for the psychophysical causal relation is nothing but that of accounting for the causal relation between two physical states. On the other hand, if, for various reasons, one is averse to accepting a straightforward identity thesis, as many philosophers are, then the problem of accounting for psychophysical causation confronts us as a difficult problem, indeed.[14] The classical form of epiphenomenalism fails to provide a satisfactory solution, for it denies that mental-to-physical causal action ever takes place: mental phenomena are totally causally inert. And this is what many thinkers find so difficult to accept. If our reasons and desires have no causal efficacy at all in influencing our bodily actions, then perhaps no one has ever performed a single intentional action![15]

It seems to me that what is being advocated as "new" epiphenomenalism is not much help either. According to Keith Campbell, mental states are in fact brain states, but they have residual irreducible phenomenal properties as well; however, these phenomenal properties are causally impotent.[16] This position is akin to one of the two characterizations of epiphenomenalism offered by C. D. Broad some decades ago:

> Epiphenomenalism may be taken to assert one of two things. (a) That certain events which have physiological characteristics have *also* mental characteristics, and that no events which lack physiological characteristics have mental characteristics. That many events which have physiological characteristics are not known to have mental characteristics. And that an event which has mental

characteristics never causes another event in virtue of its mental characteristics, but only in virtue of its physiological characteristics. Or (b) that no event has both mental and physiological characteristics; but that the complete cause of any event which has mental characteristics is an event or set of events which has physiological characteristics. And that no event which has mental characteristics is a cause-factor in the causation of any other event whatever, whether mental or physiological.[17]

The only significant difference between Broad's (a) and Campbell's epiphenomenalism seems to be that Broad's epiphenomenalism is formulated for all *mental* characteristics, presumably including intentional states such as belief and desire as well as phenomenal states, whereas Campbell is happy to take a straight physicalist approach with regard to mental states not involving phenomenal qualia. It is interesting to note that some versions of the currently popular "token identity" thesis are also strikingly similar to Broad's epiphenomenalism. Consider, for example, the influential "anomalous monism" of Donald Davidson.[18] According to this account, there are no type-type correlations between the mental and the physical; however, each individual mental event is in fact a physical event in the following sense: any event that has a mental description has also a physical description. Further, it is only under its physical description that a mental event can be seen to enter into a causal relation with a physical event (or any other event) by being subsumed under a causal law. If we read "mental characteristic" for "mental description" and "physiological characteristic" for "physical description," then something very much like Broad's (a) above emerges from Davidson's anomalous monism.

Broad's epiphenomenalism, however, did not satisfy philosophers who looked for a place for our commonsense conviction in the reality of psychophysical causation. Thus, William Kneale refers to "the great paradox of epiphenomenalism," which arises from "the suggestion that we are necessarily mistaken in all our ordinary thought about human action."[19] It seems to me that, for similar reasons, Davidson's anomalous monism fails to do full justice to psychophysical causation—that is, it fails to provide an account of psychophysical causation in which the mental *qua mental* has any real causal role to play. Consider Davidson's account: whether or not a given event has a mental description (optional reading: whether it has a mental characteristic) seems entirely irrelevant to what causal relations it enters into. Its causal powers are wholly determined by the physical description or characteristic that holds for it; for it is under its physical description that it may be subsumed under a causal law. And Davidson explicitly denies any possibility of a nomological connection between an event's mental description and its physical description that could bring the mental into the causal picture.[20]

The delicate task is to find an account that will give the mental a substantial enough causal role to let us avoid "the great paradox of epiphenomenalism" without infringing upon the closedness of physical causal systems. I suggest that we view psychophysical causal relations—in fact, all causal relations involving psychological events—as epiphenomenal supervenient causal relations. More specifically, when a mental event M causes a physical event P, this is so because M is supervenient upon a physical event, P^*, and P^* causes P. This latter may itself be a supervenient causal relation, but that is no matter: what is important is that, at some point, purely physical causal processes take over. Similarly, when mental event M causes another mental event M^*, this is so because M supervenes on a physical state P, and similarly M^* on P^*, and P causes P^*.

Thus, if a pain causes the sensation of fear an instant later, this account tells the following story: the pain is supervenient on a brain state, this brain state causes another appropriate brain state, and given this second brain state, the fear sensation must occur, for it is supervenient upon that brain state. I think this is a plausible picture that, among other things, nicely accounts for the temporal gaps and discontinuities in the series of causally related mental events. Returning to the case of a pain causing a hand to withdraw, we should note that, on the present account, no causal path from the pain "merges" with the physiological causal chain at any point. For there is no separate path from the pain to the limb withdrawal; there is only one causal path in this situation, namely the one from the neural state upon which the pain supervenes to the movement of the hand.

Does this proposal satisfy the desiderata we set for an adequate account of psychophysical causation? It would be foolish to pretend that the proposed account accords to the mental the full causal potency we accord to fundamental physical processes. On the other hand, it does not treat mental phenomena as causally inert epiphenomena; nor does it reduce mental causation to the status of a mere chimera. Mental causation does take place; it is only that it is epiphenomenal causation, that is, a causal relation that is reducible to, or explainable by, the causal processes taking place at a more basic physical level. And this, according to the present account, is also precisely what happens with macrophysical causation relations. *Epiphenomenal causal relations involving psychological events, therefore, are no less real or substantial than those involving macrophysical events. They are both supervenient causal relations.* It seems to me that this is sufficient to redeem the causal powers we ordinarily attribute to mental events. Does the account meet the other desideratum of respecting the closed character of physical theory? It evidently does; for supervenient epiphenomenal causation does not place the supervenient events at the level of the underlying causal processes to which it is reduced. Mental events do not become part of the fundamental physical causal chains any more than macrophysical events become part of the microphysical causal chains that underlie them.

One remaining question is whether psychological events do supervene on physical events and processes. If psychological states are conceived as some sort of inner theoretical states posited to explain the observable behavior of organisms, there is little doubt that they will be supervenient on physical states.[21] However, there are serious questions as to whether that is a satisfactory conception of the mental; and I believe these questions lead to a serious doubt as to whether *intentional* mental states, namely those with propositional content such as beliefs and desires, are determined wholly by the physical details of the organism or even by the total physical environment that includes the organism. However, this need not be taken as casting doubt on the account of psychological causation offered here; I think we may more appropriately take it as an occasion for reconsidering whether, and in what way, intentional psychological states enter into causal relations—especially with physical events. I think that the two questions, whether intentional psychological states are supervenient on the physical and whether they enter into *law-based* causal relations with physical processes, are arguably equivalent questions. Psychophysical supervenience is a good deal more plausible, I believe, with regard to phenomenal mental states, and I am prepared to let the account of psychological causation proposed here stand for all psychological events and states that are physically supervenient.

Notes

1. Jonathan Edwards, *Doctrine of Original Sin Defended* (1758), Part IV, Chap. II. The quotation is taken from *Jonathan Edwards*, edited by C. H. Faust and T. H. Johnson (New York, 1935), 335. I owe this interesting reference to Roderick M. Chisholm's discussion of Edwards's views in connection with the "Doctrine of Temporal Parts," in *Person and Object* (La Salle, Ill., 1976), 138ff.

2. Faust and Johnson, *Jonathan Edwards*, 336.

3. Wesley C. Salmon, "An 'At-At' Theory of Causal Influence," *Philosophy of Science* 44 (1977):215-24.

4. For a discussion of the issues see John Lachs, "Epiphenomenalism and the Notion of Cause," *Journal of Philosophy* 60 (1963):141-45.

5. For example, see J. J. C. Smart, "Sensations and Brain Processes," *Philosophical Review* 68 (1958):141-56.

6. The thesis of mereological supervenience itself need not carry a commitment to atomism.

7. There is a large literature on this and related issues concerning microreduction; see, e.g., Lawrence Sklar, "Types of Inter-Theoretic Reductions," *British Journal for the Philosophy of Science* 18 (1967):109-24; Robert L. Causey, *Unity of Science* (Dordrecht, 1977).

8. See, e.g., Hilary Putnam, "The Nature of Mental States," and Ned Block and J. A. Fodor, "What Psychological States Are Not," both in *Readings in Philosophy of Psychology* vol. 1, edited by Ned Block (Cambridge, Mass., 1980).

9. This corresponds to "strong supervenience" as characterized in my "Concepts of Supervenience" (forthcoming); for a general discussion of supervenience see also my "Supervenience and Nomological Incommensurables," *American Philosophical Quarterly* 15 (1978):149-56.

10. For an influential view of this kind see Donald Davidson, "Causal Relations," *Journal of Philosophy* 64 (1967):691-703.

11. See Terence Horgan, "Supervenience and Microphysics," *Pacific Philosophical Quarterly* 63 (1982):29-43; see also David Lewis, "New Work for a Theory of Universals" (forthcoming).

12. See the somewhat dated but still useful "Unity of Science as a Working Hypothesis" by Paul Oppenheim and Hilary Putnam, in *Minnesota Studies in the Philosophy of Science*, vol. 2, edited by Herbert Feigl et al. (Minneapolis, 1958).

13. For an effective description of the difficulty see Richard Taylor, *Metaphysics*, 3d ed. (Englewood Cliffs, N.J., 1983), chap. 3.

14. For some arguments against the identity thesis see Putnam, "Nature of Mental States"; Saul Kripke, *Naming and Necessity* (Cambridge, Mass., 1980), 144-55. For discussions of the problem of psychophysical causation see, e.g., J. L. Mackie, "Mind, Brain, and Causation," *Midwest Studies in Philosophy* 4 (1979):19-30; and my "Causality, Identity and Supervenience in the Mind-Body Problem," *Midwest Studies in Philosophy* 4 (1979):31-49.

15. See, e.g., Norman Malcolm, "The Conceivability of Mechanism," *Philosophical Review* 77 (1968):45-72.

16. *Body and Mind* (New York, 1970), chap. 6.

17. *The Mind and Its Place in Nature* (London, 1925), 472.

18. In "Mental Events" reprinted in Davidson, *Essays on Actions and Events* (New York, 1980).

19. William Kneale, "Broad on Mental Events and Epiphenomenalism," in *The Philosophy of C. D. Broad*, edited by P. A. Schilpp (New York, 1959), 453. See also Jerome A. Shaffer, *Philosophy of Mind* (Englewood Cliffs, N.J., 1968), 68-71; Taylor, *Metaphysics*, chap. 4.

20. See his "Mental Events" for an extended argument against psychophysical lawlike connections. I give an analysis, and a partial defense, of Davidson's argument in "Psychophysical Laws" (forthcoming).

21. For details see my "Psychophysical Supervenience," *Philosophical Studies* 41 (1982): 51-70.

Mind-Body Interaction
and Supervenient Causation

ERNEST SOSA

T he mind-body problem arises because of our status as double agents apparently en rapport both with the mental and with the physical. We think, desire,
decide, plan, suffer passions, fall into moods, are subject to sensory experiences,
ostensibly perceive, intend, reason, make believe, and so on. We also move, have
a certain geographical position, a certain height and weight, and we are sometimes
hit or cut or burned. In other words, human beings have both minds and bodies.
What is the relation between these? Religion often tells us that we are really embodied souls released at death from our bodily prisons. Could this be right?

It is said that our supposed problem is nothing more than a pseudoquestion
and a waste of time, that we should admit only what is verifiable by means of perceptual observation; and hence that any supposed thought, desire, or experience
not reducible to bodily behavior is a meaningless delusion. But these sayings are un-
philosophical. We will not be bullied into blocking out a whole dimension of intellectual experience for the sake of a neat fit between some preconceived physicalist
theory and the data left in view. We are mental beings at least as surely as we are
physical beings, and if our mental lives are not reducible to the physical, then so
much the worse for any preconceived physicalism.

Whether or not the mental is reducible to the physical, or for that matter the
other way around, one thing stands out for its plausibility on the relation between
the two. The body is often a puppet of the mind and the stream of consciousness
often moves in a physical bed. Desires, beliefs, and decisions appear for all the world
to affect our physical movements, at least now and then: pains, tickles, and sensory
experiences derive from cuts, feathers, and open eyes, at least on some occasions.

Concerning the difficulty "pointed out since the days of Descartes in seeing
how two such diverse things as matter and mind could possible affect each other,"
J. B. Pratt once complained that "the a priori denial of the possibility of such causal
relation is pure dogma."[1] Thirty-eight years later, C. J. Ducasse was to lodge a very
similar complaint as follows:

271

[Contrary] to what is sometimes alleged, causation of a physical by a psychical event, or of a psychical event by stimulation of a physical sense organ, is
not in the least paradoxical. The causality relation . . . does not presuppose
at all that its cause-term and its effect-term both belong to the same ontological category, but only that both of them be *events*. . . . Moreover, the objection that we cannot understand how a psychical event could cause a physical one (or vice-versa) has no basis other than blindness to the fact that the
"how" of causation is capable at all of being either mysterious or understood
only in cases of *remote* causation, never in cases of *proximate* causation.[2]

What we have in view so far is hence entirely receptive to the religious conception of people as embodied souls quite possibly immortal despite the dissolution
of their bodies. But other conceptions of people are equally compatible with the
data in view. Thus people may simply be identical with their bodies. Bodies do
move, and who says they cannot think? Is there any way to decide between these?

Four key notions figure prominently within the data in view: the notions of
body, of mind or soul, of spatial location, and of causation. Now whatever else may
be true of bodies, at least they are lodged in space and in time, for they have height
and they move. As for minds or souls, at least they are subjects of consciousness
and they are also in time, since for one thing their desires wax and wane. Now according to tradition a soul is substantially simple, since complexity would tend to
show mortality through eventual dissolution into parts. But if a soul is simple and
immortal then it cannot be lodged in space, for anything lodged in space must have
distinct subparts: a left half and a right half, say, or a bottom half and a top half.
So we reach the conclusion that whereas bodies endure through time while filling
space, souls endure without such extension.

What of our third key notion, that of spatial location? It is not true that only
three-dimensional bodies are located in space, since shadows, smiles, and surfaces
are so located. It does seem true, however, or at least much more plausible, that
nothing is *fundamentally* located in space unless it has three-dimensional volume.
Thus a smile is located on a face, and a shadow on the surface upon which it is
cast. As for surfaces, their location would seem to derive from the location of outermost shells of the objects whose surface they are (shells that preserve relations
among parts unchanged from the way they in fact are at the time when a certain
location is attributed to the surface).

In keeping with these reflections and in view of numerous pro examples and
none counter, let us assume the following at least provisionally as a general principle concerning location in space.

TFLS   That Three-Dimensionality is Fundamental for Location in Space:
         Anything, x, not three-dimensional but located in space must be lo-
         cated superveniently on the location in space of something y such
         that (a) y is three-dimensional and (b) (the existence of) x supervenes
         on (the existence of) y.

Thus nothing is fundamentally located in space unless it is three-dimensional and three dimensionally located in space. It accords with this that a smile is derivative from a smiling face, and that the location of a smile is derivative from the location of the smiling face from which it derives; also, that a surface is derivative from a surfaced solid, and that the location of a surface is derivative from the location of the surfaced solid from which it derives; and also, finally, that a shadow is derivative from a shadowed solid, and that the location of a shadow is derivative from the location of the shadowed solid from which it derives. And so on. (Our principle can be made more precise, and more can be done in support of it by appeal to further pro examples. But here I wish to argue only that it does deserve such attention, by showing how it serves crucially in an interesting argument for a philosophically important conclusion. So we assume it provisionally and continue our argument.)

What of our fourth key notion, finally, that of causation? Can we bring it into sharper focus, with greater definition of detail? To begin, consider an example. Someone takes a picture of you, a photograph. Your image is imprinted on a piece of film. The film is imprinted with an image of a face that looks a certain way *because* you have a certain physiognomy. But your physiognomy causes the image on the film only in virtue of the fact that certain conditions hold at a given time with respect to you and the piece of film. The film is in a camera aimed in your direction, and you and the camera are not too far apart, there are no obstacles obstructing the line of sight, you are facing the camera at the time, and there is enough light, and so on; and it is only in virtue of the fact that these conditions all hold that your facial appearance causes the image on the film.

It seems quite evident, moreover, that if any twin of yours is ever noncausally related to a twin of that piece of film in just the way you are now noncausally related to that piece of film, and in exactly similar noncausal conditions, then once again an image will appear on the film as a causal result of the physiognomy of the man.[3]

Take another example. A karate expert hits a board and splits it in two. The board splits in two *because* of the blow by the man. And if this is so it is presumably in virtue of certain noncausal conditions that hold at the time, including the board's thickness; its composition; the angle, speed, and force of the blow; etc. And it seems quite evident, moreover, that if anything noncausally a perfect twin of that board, is hit by anyone noncausally a perfect twin of that man, with a blow exactly like that blow in all noncausal respects, then that new board must also split just as did the old, because of the blow.

When causation ties together a pair of particular things like a piece of film and a human being, or a wood board and a karate chop, it is always in virtue of certain noncausal properties or relations holding of the members of the pair, so that any pair equally propertied and related would be equally tied together by causation. This principle is encapsulated in the saying that causal relations among particulars derive from causal relations among their properties and relations. Any other set of particulars with just the same (noncausal) properties and relations must also be linked by causal relations in just the same way.

Consider now someone in pain because his body is in contact with a flame. If distress is a mental state, then the one in distress is a simple, unextended, and immortal soul, or so we are told. So we have two things, the soul in distress and the body in the fire, and somehow the distress in the soul is caused by the flames on the body. But if that is so, then there must be certain noncausal properties of that particular soul, and certain noncausal properties of that particular body, and certain noncausal relations between the two, such that when any soul with such properties of that soul and any body with such properties of that body are related by such relations between that soul and that body, the new soul will be in just the same distress once again because of flames licking the new body. But just what properties or relations could these be?

There are many bodies and many souls, or so we are told. What makes the events in a given body causally relevant to a given soul, or the events in a given soul causally relevant to a given body?

Could it be a special relation of embodiment or of ownership, so that direct causal interactions take place between a soul and a body only if that soul is embodied in that body, or only if that soul owns that body in the sense that it is its body? But neither this embodiment nor this ownership is clear enough to be illuminating. A soul is not in its body the way a pilot is in his ship. Just how then is it embodied in that body? And if a soul does own its body in just the sense in which a pilot owns his ship, i.e., legally and even morally, that only moves the question to a deeper level. For if you own something legally or morally, there must be something about its relation to you other than your ownership of it that makes you its owner. Thus it may be that you inherited it, or that it is a fruit of your labors, or the like. If a given soul does own a certain body, then, what relation can there be between them that makes that soul the owner of that body? It won't do now to reply that it is just the moral or legal ownership of that body by that soul. But if it is not moral or legal ownership, then what kind of ownership is it that permits a soul to interact directly with a given body?

If embodiment and ownership are not to be explained by reference to the spatial inclusion of a pilot in his ship or to the moral or legal ownership of a ship by its pilot, perhaps they are explicable by reference to a notion of direct causal effects. Thus we might say that x has a direct causal effect on y iff an event in x has an effect on y without first having an effect on anything that is not a part of y. A soul then would have direct causal effects exclusively or for the most part only on a given body, and that body would then have direct causal effects exclusively or for the most part only on that soul, all of which would signify the embodiment of that soul in that body and the ownership of that body by that soul.

That seems indeed a promising analysis of embodiment or ownership until we reflect on our goal in introducing these notions. What we wanted from these notions, after all, was some way of specifying what relation it is that makes a given body subject to the direct causal action of a given soul, and what it is that makes a given soul subject to the direct causal action of a given body. From this point of view the notions of embodiment and of ownership turn out to be useless under analysis. For it is useless to be told that what makes something subject to direct causal interaction with something else is that it is indeed subject to direct causal interaction with it. And that is precisely what the answer by reference to ownership or embodiment resolves to under analysis.

Our picture begins to look bleak for immortal souls. What pairs physical objects as proper mates for causal interaction is in general their places in the all-encompassing spatial framework of physical reality. It is their spatial relations that pair the piece of film with the man photographed, and distinguishes him as the cause from the billions of other men in existence including his exact look-alikes.

We are told that each of the billions of men in existence has his own immortal soul. What framework serves to sustain the one-one pairing of souls and bodies in the way that the spatial framework sustains the pairing of photographic images of people and the people whose images they are? What noncausal relation between souls and bodies might possibly marry a particular soul to a particular body as its proper mate for a certain causal interaction at a certain time? We have found no plausible answer for this question.

Even if for that reason we reject the supposed causal interaction between body and soul, nevertheless, there remains the possibility of interaction between the mental and the physical, of interaction not between substances but only between events, between mental events and physical events. Two sorts of monism, both the neutral and the anomalous, offer to buttress the possibility of such interaction.

In introducing his anomalous monism, Donald Davidson introduces also a concept of supervenience into the recent literature on the mind-body problem:

> Although the position I describe denies there are psychophysical laws, it is consistent with the view that mental characteristics are in some sense dependent, or supervenient, on physical characteristics. Such supervenience might be taken to mean that there cannot be two events alike in all physical respects but differing in some mental respect, or that an object cannot alter in some mental respect without altering in some physical respect. Dependence or supervenience of this kind does not entail reducibility through law or definition. . . .[4]

Supervenience has long been known in axiology and ethical theory, where values are said to supervene upon facts. And values do seem to supervene thus at least in Davidson's sense that it is not possible for two things to be exactly alike in all nonevaluative respects but unlike in some evaluative respect.

Such *supervenience* of evaluative properties is linked closely to the *universalizability* of value judgments and their special dependence on *reasons* and *principles*. If an apple is a good apple it must be so in virtue of certain reasons: perhaps because it is large, sweet, and juicy. There must be some such reasons that make the good apple good. If so, and if these are *all* the reasons in virtue of which that particular apple is a good apple, then (a) *all* apples that are large, sweet, and juicy are also equally good apples (universalizability to a principle governing the goodness of apples); and (b) the property of being a good apple exemplified by that apple *supervenes* on its properties of being large, sweet, and juicy (in that particular case: depends on, is derived from such properties).

Supervenience would seem to pertain in fact not only to evaluative properties but also, for example, to any "determinable," which would always supervene on one or another of its corresponding "determinates." For example, if our apple is chromatically colored (colored but not white, black, or grey), it surely will be so in virtue of some reason: perhaps because it is red, or because it is yellow. If so, and if what makes it chromatically colored is that it is red, then (a) *all* red apples are equally chromatically colored; and (b) the property of being chromatically colored exemplified by that apple *supervenes* on its property of being red (depends on, or is derived from that property).

Although the supervenience of main interest to us here is that of properties, there is a concept of ontological supervenience or derivation with much wider scope. As we have seen, smiles derive from smiling faces, shadows from shadowed surfaces, and surfaces in turn from the existence of outermost layers of the things whose surfaces they are. And so on.

Supervenience is moreover a key concept of ontology and metaphysics. From the Greeks on, our tradition perennially seeks an underlying reality on which all intellectual appearance may be seen to supervene. The underlying reality may be found in ethereal forms, in material atoms, in monads, or in spirits and their ideas. But in each case there is much else that derives from the fundamental by ontological supervenience.

Restricting ourselves once more to the supervenience of properties from other properties: How more exactly are we to conceive of such supervenience?

We have first Davidson's suggestion:

WS   Weak Supervenience: A set of properties A supervenes on a set of properties B iff indiscernibility in respect of B necessitates (necessarily implies) indiscernibility in respect of A, and change in respect of A necessitates change in respect of B.

Compare such weak supervenience with the following stronger variety:

SS   Strong Supervenience: A set of properties A supervenes on a set of properties B iff nothing can have any property in A without also having certain properties in B such that anything that ever had such properties in B, necessarily would also have the property in A.

Note that strong supervenience necessitates weak supervenience, but not conversely.[5]

James Cornman's "neutral monism" is rather similar to Davidson's anomalous monism.[6] And this similarity of doctrine brings with it also similarity of arguments.

In each case we are told that there are mental events in human beings that are both causes and effects. But mental properties (predicates) have no place in any network of psychophysical laws—on pain, so Cornman argues, of violating certain principles of conservation (such as the principle of the conservation of momentum). Only physical properties fit into laws of nature. All the same, if an event x causes an event y, there must be a law that relates x to y on the basis of their properties and relations (predicates). Therefore, any mental event that is cause or effect of any other event must have physical properties lawfully connected with some physical properties of its cause or effect.

Regarding principles of conservation, in the first place, these involve isolated systems. But to suppose that physical nature, as we know it, is an isolated system is to suppose that the known physical forces—for example, electricity and gravitation—are *all* the forces that ever act on anything physical. And it is doubtful that we have the right to feel sure of any such assumption. Too much remains unexplained: about people, for example, their actions and their thoughts. That being so, it would be a mere physicalist pretension to claim knowledge of all forces affecting human thought and action, and to suppose that full explanation awaits only the filling of details.

Davidson develops his anomalous monism to show, like Kant, that though apparently incompatible, certain independently attractive principles are after all compatible.

> The first principle asserts that at least some mental events interact causally with physical events. . . . The second principle is that where there is causality, there must be a law: events related as cause and effect fall under strict deterministic laws. . . . The third principle is that there are no strict deterministic laws on the basis of which mental events can be predicted and explained. . . .[7]

The key to his proposed solution for this three-pronged paradox is the idea that mental events enter into causal relations *not* as mental but only as physical. (I try to convey the main idea here very briefly in my words, though I doubt Davidson would himself accept these words; so far as I know, he does not recognize the terminology of an event causing something or being caused by something "*as* such-and-such.")

Does that key really unlock a resolution to Davidson's Paradox? I cannot believe that it does, as I can't see that it does justice to the full meaning of his first principle. Some examples may convey my doubt.

A gun goes off, a shot is fired, and it kills someone. The loud noise is the shot. Thus, if the victim is killed by the shot, it's the loud noise that kills the victim.

Compare this. I extend my hand because of a certain neurological event. That event is my sudden desire to quench my thirst. Thus, if my grasping is caused by that neurological event, it's my sudden desire that causes my grasping.

We have considered a case of causality directed from the mind to the body. Let us turn to one in reverse direction.

First an analogous case. The tenor misses a very high note as the entire roof caves in. His miss is the end of that concert. Thus, if his miss is caused by the slipping of his wig, it's the slipping of his wig that causes the end of the concert.

Compare this. A certain physical event (which is in fact my catching sight of some water) causes a certain neurological event (which is in fact my sudden desire to quench my thirst). Thus, if the neurological event is caused by the physical event, it's the physical event that causes my sudden desire.

Yes, in a certain sense the victim is killed by the loud noise; not by the loud noise as a loud noise, however, but only by the loud noise as a shot, or the like. Similarly, assuming the anomalism of the mental, though my extending my hand is, in a certain sense, caused by my sudden desire to quench my thirst, it is not caused by my desire qua desire but only by my desire qua *neurological* event of a certain sort. Besides, the loudness of the shot has no causal relevance to the death of the victim: had the gun been equipped with a silencer, the shot would have killed the victim just the same. Similarly, the being a desire of my desire has no causal relevance to my extending my hand (if the mental is indeed anomalous): if the event that is in fact my desire had not been my desire but had remained a neurological event of a certain sort, then it would have caused by extending my hand just the same.

In parallel fashion, it is true that the slipping of the tenor's wig causes the end of the concert, but it does not cause the end of the concert *to be* the end of the concert. That is caused by the cave-in of the roof. In the same way, if we accept the anomalism of the mental, then *although* it is true that my sudden desire to quench my thirst is caused by a certain physical event (which is in fact identical to my catching sight of water), *still* that physical event does not cause my sudden desire *to be* my sudden desire. That, apparently, for anomalous and for neutral monism, has *no* cause or causal explanation.

I conclude that neither neutral monism nor anomalous monism is really compatible with the full content of our deep and firm conviction that mind and body each acts causally on the other.

And what shall we say to the second principle, of the three that jointly yield the paradox? According to that principle, ". . . where there is causality, there must be a law: events related as cause and effect fall under strict deterministic laws." But why must there always be a law to cover any causal relation linking events x and y? What enables us to assume such a general truth?

Our plan has been: first, to reflect briefly and generally on our nature as persons; second, to formulate the principle of the supervenience of causality; and then, third, to draw certain consequences from that principle for two doctrines about our nature: (a) interactionism; and (b) neutral or anomalous monism.

One consequence for interactionism is that there can be no interaction between an immaterial soul and a material body. That of course has been the view of so many, since Gassendi to the present, that it is firmly settled as a platitude of introductory philosophy. What may perhaps be novel in our inference from the supervenience of causation is an *explanation* of why such interaction is impossible or at least implausible.

Though we reject substantial interaction, however, that leaves standing the possibility of interaction between the physical and the mental; not interaction between body and soul, of course, but only interaction between mental events and physical events. Both neutral and anomalous monism offer to buttress the possibility of such interaction, but we have found the offer empty. According to such monism, the various ways of being mental are all absurd and barren. Their presence is caused by nothing and causes nothing; it can never be explained and can explain nothing.

The supervenience of causation requires that we reject substantial interaction. But far from requiring also the rejection of interaction between mental and physical properties, it offers support for the hypothesis of such interaction. When told that a burn causes a pain, we may understand and accept what we are told as the claim that the burn *as such* causes the pain *as such*: in other words, that the burn's *being* a burn causes the pain *to be* a pain. (Recall the similar claim that the cave-in of the roof causes the end of the concert. And note the contrast with the claim that the slipping of the tenor's wig causes the end of the concert. Even though the tenor's miss is indeed the end of the concert – the last note – the slipping of his wig causes his miss to be a miss but it does not cause his miss to be the end of the concert. That is caused by the cave-in of the roof.) But if we understand the statement that the burn causes the pain as the statement that the burn's being a burn causes the pain to be a pain, then that causal relation between events supervenes on certain properties of that burn and certain properties of that pain, and certain relations between the two, such that, if ever there be a pair of events like that pair in all such respects, the being a burn of one member of the pair would cause the being a pain of the other. And such supervenience of the causal relation may now be explained as something required by its very analysis, provided we can accept the following proposed analysis:

> The having of property P by event x, $<P, x>$, causes event y to have property Q, $<Q, y>$, iff there are properties of x, including P, and properties of y, and a relation R between x and y, such that it is nomologically necessary that whenever an event has such properties of x and bears relation R to some other event with such properties of y, then that other event also has Q.

If this analysis, or one like it, is right, we may easily understand why the causal relation between events x and y supervenes without fail on noncausal properties and relations of x and y. For the notion that x causes y may then be understood as the notion that x, qua possessor of some property P, causes y, qua possessor of some property Q. In other words, we understand

> Event x causes event y

as

> There are properties P and Q such that $<P, x>$ causes $<Q, y>$.

And this last, according to its very analysis, requires that there be properties of x, including P, and properties of y, as well as a relation R between x and y, such that by law of nature whenever an event turns out to have such properties of x and to be related by that relation R to have some event with such properties of y, then that other event also has Q.[8]

In this way we *explain* (a) the fact that where there is causality there must be a law, and also (b) the fact that the causal relation among particular things or events supervenes on noncausal properties and relations of such things or events. This double explanatory power of such an analysis seems a weighty reason in its favor – or at least in favor of the view that some such analysis is bound to be right.

Note finally that if that analysis or one like it is in fact correct, and if we believe that burns cause pains to be painful, it follows that the mental property of being painful cannot be causally unconnected with the physical. Accordingly, combining an analysis like ours with the belief that burns cause pains to be painful yields an interactionism of mental and physical properties.[9]

What shall we conclude about the person? If the mental life of a person interacts with his physical career, the person cannot be fundamentally immaterial. One must then be either one's body (or part of it) or something that supervenes on one's body (or a part of it).

A person passes away without the vanishing of his body, since it's his body we bury. It follows that the person is never identical to his body. There remains then only the other possibility: that the person supervenes on a live body with certain abilities and capacities. When a body loses life, it no longer constitutes a person. Thus the person is not identical with any body, but is constituted by some body when that body has the properties required for such constitution. Supervening as a person always does on his body (or a part), the person is superveniently located where his body (or a part) is located; it is this spatial relation with his body that enables the causal interaction between them.[10]

Notes

1. J. B. Pratt, *Matter and Spirit* (New York, 1922).

2. C. J. Ducasse, "In Defense of Dualism," in *Dimensions of Mind*, edited by Sidney Hook (New York, 1960), 85-90; 88.

3. A relation or condition is causal if and only if it includes the relation of causation – of X causing Y – as a logical constituent.

4. Donald Davidson, "Mental Events," in *Experience and Theory*, edited by L. Foster and J. W. Swanson (Amherst, 1978), 88.

5. Jaegwon Kim defines and compares such concepts in "Psychological Supervenience as a Mind-Body Theory," in *Cognition and Brain Theory* V (1982). He has moreover pointed out to me (in correspondence) that dropping the last clause in the definition of weak supervenience yields a concept of supervenience that is even weaker. And we agree also (in conversation) in recognizing stronger forms of supervenience that involve a kind of formal causation (a by-virtue-of relation) apparently not definable by the modal notions.

6. James Cornman, "A Nonreductive Identity Theory about Mind and Body," in *Reason and Responsibility*, edited by Joel Feinberg (Belmont, Ca., 1981).

7. Davidson, "Mental Events," 80-81. James Van Cleve showed me the need to look here at the wider context, which makes it clear that the first principle involves causation in both directions, and that the third principle is based on an assumption that there are no psychophysical laws whatever, in either direction.

8. Davidson's suggestion in "Causal Relations" (in *Causation and Conditionals*, edited by E. Sosa [Oxford, 1975]) about the logical form of causal laws – according to which the causal relation between events is an inseparable constituent of such laws – seems incompatible on pain of circularity with our notion that the causal relation between events has an analysis on the basis of a proposition affirming the existence of a causal law that links properties and relations of these events. If that is so, it closes our avenue to an explanation for the principle that where

there is causality, there must be a law. Closing that avenue incurs some obligation to try to open another, for such a principle stands in need of explanation.

9. So far we have raised doubts about a proposed resolution to Davidson's Paradox that focuses on the first of its three prongs. But closing an avenue to the resolution of a paradox leaves some obligation to try to open another. Our reflections so far imply focusing on the third rather than the first of the three prongs. They imply rejecting the principle that "there are no strict deterministic laws on the basis of which mental events can be predicted and explained." In fact, it seems to me that our assumptions can be weakened in such a way that all three principles may be retained. The main steps involved would include these: (i) introducing a strict and restrictive sense of "law" to serve in principle three; and (ii) revising our analysis of causation in such a way that $<P, x>$ may cause $<Q, y>$ even though there is no (strict) law connecting P and Q themselves but only properties P' and Q' related in some (to-be-specified) way to P and Q. (Thus for the cave-in of the concert hall to cause the death of fifteen people, it is not required that there be a strict law connecting the property of being the cave-in of the concert hall with the property of being the death of fifteen people. What is required, rather, is perhaps something closer to this: that there be a (very complex) property P' of a certain event on which the property of that event of being the cave-in of the concert hall supervenes, and a property Q' of another event on which the property of that event of being the death of fifteen people supervenes, such that $<P', x>$ does cause $<Q', y>$ according to our analysis of causation as it presently stands.) But there would also be a third important step: (iii) recognizing that the expression 'X causes Y' is context-dependent (in ways some of which have been much discussed).

10. Beside the problem of the supervenience of causation, at least two further problems challenge the soul as innermost seat of a person's psychology: (a) Since diversity and its deductive progeny (e.g., diversity-or-loving) cannot stand as the *sole* relations between two intrinsically indistinguishable entities, and since souls are not spatially related and presumably can be intrinsically indistinguishable entities, what relation can it be (or what relations can they be) that would accompany the diversity of souls? (b) Since capacities, skills, abilities, virtues, and vices are dispositional properties or potentialities, and since these require a ground in intrinsic properties of their bearers, what sorts of intrinsic properties could provide it in immaterial souls? What to say in answer seems in each case occult.

Mind and Anti-Mind:
Why Thinking Has No Functional Definition

GEORGE BEALER

Functionalism is perhaps the most prominent theory of mind today. The central thesis of functionalism is that the standard mental relations (or properties or states) are uniquely determined by their causal roles in functioning organisms. That is, the principles of psychology specify the characteristic way that (behavioral or physiological) input, the standard mental relations such as belief and desire, and (behavioral or physiological) output are causally arranged; and the central idea of functionalism is that, e.g., belief's characteristic causal role can be fulfilled by exactly one relation–namely, belief itself. Clearly, then, the most direct way to refute functionalism would be to show that there are relations that demonstrably differ from the standard mental relations and that, nevertheless, could fulfill the same causal role as those mental relations.

However, it is unsatisfactory to leave the discussion couched in these imprecise terms: imprecise positions are difficult to defend or to refute. What exactly are causal roles? What exactly are their identity conditions? What sorts of things have them? Is it mental types or tokens that are uniquely determined? It is for good reason, therefore, that the imprecise functionalist thesis is often reformulated more precisely as follows: the principles of psychology, taken together, implicitly define the standard mental relations. That is, these relations–and no others–make the principles of psychology true when we hold constant the interpretation of the physical and logical constants contained in these principles. There are well-known techniques for converting implicit definitions into direct definitions,[2] and thus many functionalists also put their central thesis as follows: the standard mental relations have direct functional definitions based on the principles of psychology.[3] So when functionalism is formulated in one of these precise ways, the most direct way to refute it is to show that, in addition to the standard mental relations, there exists a demonstrably different system of deviant relations that make the principles of psychology come out true when we hold constant the interpretation of their physical and logical constants. The purpose of this paper is to construct just such a system of deviant relations. This new system of relations in effect comprises an ''anti-mind''–a system causally and functionally indistinguishable from the system of familiar relations that comprises the true mind. The existence of anti-mind simultaneously refutes all versions of functionalism whether behavioral, physiological, or computer-theoretic in emphasis.

What makes the construction possible is, in a word, *intensionality,* specifically, those ''fine-grained'' distinctions that can exist among our intentional states. There are some well-known arguments showing that no elementary behavioral or physiological reduction can capture this aspect of those states. A generalized version of these arguments provides the key to the construction of anti-mind.[4]

THE NECESSITY FOR A GLOBAL REFUTATION

To understand more clearly the conditions that a refutation of functionalism must meet, let us begin with a brief survey of the currently popular criticisms of functionalism.[5] Although these criticisms abound, I believe that either they miss our target–namely functionalism's central thesis–or they are inconclusive. I will briefly sketch why I believe this. To minimize controversy, I will try to avoid taking issue with the assumptions upon which a given criticism is based.

Consider first the criticism given by some eliminative materialists.[6] According to this criticism, functionalism is just unscientific: with the progress of science, the standard mental notions will join the company of the unscientific notions belonging to such theories as alchemy and astrology. However, this criticism has no bearing on the thesis that our mental notions have functional definitions. Even if mental notions are destined to play no role in the science of the future, nevertheless, the functionalist's definitions of mental notions could be logically correct. A functional definition could specify logically necessary and sufficient conditions for belief or desire, for example, regardless of whether these notions are needed in the prediction or explanation of our behavior. Indeed, the correctness of such a definition is a *modal* fact which holds independently of whether any extant beings happen to have beliefs or desires. Furthermore, philosophers will continue to be interested in the correctness of such definitions regardless of the course of future science. For it is one of the jobs of philosophy to determine what it *would* take for a being to have beliefs or desires. And surely it is logically possible for some being to have a belief or a desire.

The remaining criticisms may all be viewed as counterexamples to the kind of definitions posited by functionalists. The first one derives from recent attacks on individualism.[7] Individualism is the doctrine that the identity of a person's mental states depends exclusively upon the ''internal'' state of the individual at the moment; social factors are entirely incidental. However, according to the recent anti-individualist doctrine, two individuals who are in qualitatively the same internal states but different social situations can be in different mental states. One of the arguments goes as follows. Suppose that we have doppelgängers on ''Twin Earth'' who use the term 'water' to refer to a water-like stuff XYZ on occasions otherwise just like those on which we refer to the stuff water. Suppose that a linguistically competent Earthling and his doppelgänger are in qualitatively the same internal states, and suppose that each of them sincerely utters the sentence 'Water is wet'. Then, the critic asserts, the Earthling would believe that water is wet but the Twin Earthling would believe that XYZ is wet. If the critic is right, this would be a counterexample to individualism. And to the extent that functionalism is committed to individualism, it would be a counterexample to functionalism. However, even if this attack on individualism is right, it does not clearly damage functionalism. First, the functionalist can deny that he is committed to individualism. He might relax his criteria for what counts as an "input condition" upon an individual; specifically, he might count as an input condition any physical feature in the individual's extended environment. Since water is found in the Earthling's extended environment where XYX is found in that of his doppelgänger, their input conditions differ, and this suffices to explain why their mental states differ. Second, the functionalist is free to invoke a more sophisticated theory of our psychological make-up. According to this theory, in the psychological make-up of every person there is an "individualist core," i.e., a body of mental states that conform to all the traditional individualist doctrines and that are immune to all the anti-individualist arguments.[8] (A person's purely qualitative self-presenting states are one example of the sort of state typically belonging to his individualist core.) Although the identity of some mental states may be determined *in part* by social factors, the identity of a mental state is never determined *exclusively* by social factors; the mental states in the persons's individualist core are always a factor in determining the identity of his non-individualistic mental states. If some such theory of psychological make-up is right, then functionalists can circumvent the anti-individualist attack by restricting functionalism to mental states of the type belonging to individualist cores. Accordingly, the functionalist's central thesis would be that all mental states of this basic type are uniquely determined by their causal roles in functioning organisms. Though more restricted, this thesis still would be very important philosophically.

The next type of counterexample is that of a system that is in significant respects functionally isomorphic to a human being and yet does not strike us as having genuine mental states. Counterexamples of this type range from everyday digital computers to Ned Block's China example, which goes as follows.[9] The number of people in China is about the same as the number of cells in a human brain. Block suggests that the Chinese people could be so coordinated that China, taken as a whole, could be functionally isomorphic to a human brain. He holds, however, that China would nevertheless have no genuine mental states. Unfortunately, examples of this type are inconclusive. To begin with, the functionalist can challenge Block's assumption that China's physical states could ever possess physical causal roles isomorphic to those possessed by the states of a functioning person's brain. Second, even if China's *physical* states could be like this, more is needed for a genuine counterexample: China must also be in states possessing causal roles isomorphic to those possessed by the *mental* states of the person whose brain it is. But what guarantees that this second isomorphism would hold? On the one hand, since not all versions of functionalism are committed to the mind/body identity theory, Block is not free to assume that the second isomorphism follows directly (by Leibniz's law) from the supposed physical isomorphism. On the other hand, perhaps Block would say that the second isomorphism follows from the physical isomorphism indirectly via some special new kind of supervenience principle. However, it is hard to think of any credible supervenience principle that would do the job. After all, China and the person whose brain we are considering are in very different physical states. Finally, if this gap in Block's reasoning is not enough to undermine his example, the functionalist can always just assert that entities like China would be in genuine mental states; for example, Douglas Hofstadter holds, ". . . there could be a 'big person' built out of ordinary people–but probably it would take many trillions of people, not just hundreds of millions, on the assumption that one ordinary person is simulating the function of a single cell in the giant person."[10] Maybe the functionalist would be wrong, but how is the critic to *show* that he is? We need a counterexample that is *demonstrably* immune to this easy dodge on the part of the functionalist.

Another candidate counterexample, which is far more threatening to functionalism, derives from the prospect of an inverted spectrum.[11] The following is a forceful way to formulate this counterexample.[12] Let a function f map the shades from one end of the color spectrum onto shades from the other end and conversely. Consider the relation sensing*: x senses* y iff$_{df}$ x senses $f(y)$) if y is a shade and x senses y if y is not a shade. The worry is that the relation sensing* satisfies all the principles in the psychology of sensation that are satisfied by the genuine sensing relation. Therefore, these psychological principles do not implicitly define the sensing relation and, hence, do not form the basis for a direct functional definition of sensing. However, this line of criticism is inconclusive. First, the possibility that sense experience is "uninterpreted" or "raw" might mean that sensing is not an intentional relation. If so, the inverted-spectrum example would leave untouched the functional definability of intentional relations, which is perhaps the most interesting aspect of functionalism. Second, there are principles of traditional philosophical psychology and epistemology that sensing* cannot satisfy, namely, those concerning introspective intentional states and states involving direct experience of the conscious operations of mind themselves. (See pp. 300-304 for a fuller discussion of such principles.) According to one such principle, for example, although a person can introspect that he is sensing red, no one could introspect that he is sensing* red. For whereas sensing is a conscious operation of mind, the *ad hoc* relation sensing* is not, and thus, unlike the genuine conscious operations of mind, it is not open to direct introspective scrutiny. In this connection, a person's knowledge that he is sensing red need not be inferential in any sense, but his knowledge that he is sensing* red is always inferential in some sense. Or consider another example. According to traditional empiricist psychology (such as that of John Locke), a person can in acts of reflection actually experience his own conscious operations of mind (sensing, feeling, thinking, craving, introspecting, and experiencing itself), but he cannot in any way experience such *ad hoc* operations as sensing*. The point here is not that principles such as these are right; the point is that they might be right. So unless the critic can *show* once and for all that they are not, he has not refuted functionalism. Since this is out of the question, the only way for the critic to block a response based on principles such as these is to extend the "inversion" strategy *globally* to all other mental relations. That is, the critic must construct, not only the sensing* relation, but also the relations feeling*, thinking*, craving*, introspecting*, experiencing*, etc., which are synchronized with sensing*, and then he must show that, taken together, these relations satisfy the full body of psychological principles contemplated by the sophisticated functionalist. For example, he must show that a person can introspect* that he is sensing* red and that a person can experience* such things as sensing*, feeling*, thinking*, introspecting*, and even experiencing*. Until now no critics have attempted this kind of global counterexample, but only this will suffice.[13]

The final type of counterexample I will consider is more or less parallel to the inverted-spectrum example except that it is aimed at intentional relations rather than the sensing relation. Searle's Chinese-room example falls into this type of criticism.[14] According to Searle, someone who is locked in a room and who knows no Chinese could, by following appropriate instructions written in English, instantiate a computer program for "speaking Chinese" and yet fail to be speaking Chinese. Searle concludes that a certain narrow version of functionalism, namely, Turing-machine functionalism, must be mistaken. (Like more liberal versions of functionalism, Turing-machine functionalism–or AI functionalism–holds that the standard mental relations are implicitly defined by the principles of psychology. But it goes further, requiring that the principles of psychology are, in effect, no more than a Turing-machine table, i.e., an abstract characterization of a purely mechanical computational process.) Perhaps, when suitably refined, the Chinese-room example can refute certain forms of Turing-machine functionalism, but can it refute functionalism per se? After all, there are many forms of Turing-machine functionalism, and there are many versions of functionalism besides Turing-machine functionalism.[15]

To be a counterexample to functionalism per se, the activity of the person in the Chinese room would have to be functionally indistinguishable from the activity of speaking Chinese. But a functionalist has excellent grounds for denying that it is. For example, the functionalist can hold, à la Grice and Searle, that speaking Chinese is a complex intentional activity, namely, an activity performed with the intention to impart beliefs to hearers who are intended to recognize that original intention via a certain inference route involving a certain mutually agreed upon system of rules (i.e., the semantics and pragmatics for Chinese). Now in order for the Chinese-room activity to be functionally indistinguishable from this complex intentional activity, it is not enough that the phonetic or orthographic input/output functions should match. The inner states must be functionally isomorphic as well. How might we fill out the Chinese-room example to meet this essential further condition? There are really only two alternatives. First, we could simply specify that the Chinese-room activity be performed with all the standard Gricean intentions. However, in that case the activity would be just one more instance of speaking Chinese (though admittedly a recherché one), so it would be no counterexample. The second alternative would be to try to construct new relations (intending*, believing*, recognizing*, inferring*, mutually agreeing*) that are distinct from, but functionally isomorphic to, the standard intentional relations (intending, believing, recognizing, etc). And then we might specify that the Chinese-room activity be performed with the intention* to impart beliefs* to hearers who are intended* to recognize* that original intention* via a certain inference* route involving a certain mutually agreed* upon system of rules (i.e., the semantics and pragmatics for Chinese). In this case, the requisite isomorphism would be insured, and yet the Chinese-room activity would not qualify as speaking Chinese. But filling out the counterexample in this way would require establishing the existence of the new relations intending*, believing*, recognizing*, etc., which are functionally isomorphic to the standard relations of intending, believing, recognizing, etc. Notice, however, that these standard relations participate in a wide variety of psychological principles, principles that involve in one way or another *every* basic mental relation, including even introspecting and experiencing (discussed above in connection with sensing). Moreover, these psychological principles are thought by many (especially by traditional philosophical psychologists) to have a strong modal value. (For example, some think that these principles hold, not just in all actual situations, but in all causally possible counterfactual situations as well. Others think that the basic psychological principles are constitutive of rationality and, therefore, that, for all normal beings in all normal circumstances, these principles are metaphysically necessary; and others inclined to strict essentialism about the mind think that the basic principles are metaphysically necessary with no qualification vis-à-vis normality.) Therefore, to fill out the Chinese-room example, we must establish the existence of a *global* system of relations–intending*, believing*, recognizing*, sensing*, feeling*, craving*, introspecting*, experiencing*, etc.–that satisfies the *whole* body of psychological principles, perhaps with a strong modal value. If we could do this, though, we would thereby already have succeeded in refuting functionalism, and the Chinese room would drop out of picture. Furthermore, if true psychological principles really do have strong modal values, it is just not plausible that artificial, contingent set-ups such as the Chinese room or ones patterned after it could yield a global system of deviant relations that could satisfy such modally qualified principles. Moreover, this conclusion would hold even if these principles stipulate that all mental processes must be computational in nature.

There are clear flaws, then, in all the current candidate counterexamples. They all fall short of a refutation of functionalism because they fail to provide a global system of relations that uncontroversially can be shown to differ from the standard mental relations and that satisfy the whole body of psychological principles, principles that might well possess strong modal values. So how are we to go about constructing the requisite global system of deviant relations, intending*, thinking*, etc.? The example that is heuristically useful for this purpose is the inverted spectrum. Recall that the function f that inverts the color spectrum by mapping it onto itself can be used to define a nonstandard relation sensing* which functions (at least locally) rather like the standard sensing relation. On analogy, suppose we can find a way to "invert" our total conceptual scheme, i.e., a function that maps our total conceptual scheme onto itself. Then, this function can be used to define a system of "inverted" relations–intending*, thinking*, etc.–that correspond to the system of standard mental relations–intending, desiring, etc. If these definitions are suitably constructed, the system of inverted relations will satisfy the body of psychological principles that, according to functionalism, implicitly defines the standard mental relations. However, if there are two systems of relations–the standard mental relations and their inverted counterparts–that satisfy this body of principles, then these principles cannot implicitly define the standard mental relations, and, hence, they cannot provide the basis for direct functional definitions of the standard mental relations. Thus, the existence of these two systems of relations–that is, the existence of mind and anti-mind–will lead to a formal disproof of the central thesis of functionalism; the principles of psychology will be blind to the distinction between mind and anti-mind.

THE ELEMENTARY BELIEF/DESIRE MODEL

When one thinks of inversions of the conceptual scheme, Quine's thesis of the indeterminacy of translation springs to mind. Quine's indeterminacy thesis derives ultimately from the insight that speakers of a radically alien language could think–or could be interpreted as thinking–in a way that is systematically different from ours and yet that is fully as rational. And this insight inspires Quine's premise that there exists more than one fully adequate translation manual for each radically foreign language. Now Quine uses this premise to support his conclusion that there is no objective fact of the matter concerning which translation manual is correct, and, by parity of reasoning, Quine would use the original insight to support the conclusion that there is no objective fact of the matter concerning which way the foreigners really think, our way or the systematically different way. But these two conclusions need not concern us now (though I will return to them later). What matters at present are the Quinean premises that speakers of a radically alien language could think–or could be interpreted as thinking–in a way systematically different from, but fully as rational as, the way we think and, relatedly, that there exists more than one fully adequate translation manual for their language.

Let L be a radically alien language for which there are two fully adequate translation manuals, and let g_1 and g_2 be the functions, generated by these manuals, that map sentences of L onto their English "translations." For example, perhaps g_1('Gavagai gua') = 'There exists a rabbit' and g_2('Gavagai gua') = 'Rabbithood is manifest'. (N.B. For ease of presentation I will use this particular/universal example in my preliminary remarks about Quinean transformations. Later in this section I will also use a certain left/right transformation, which was inspired by conversation with Donald Davidson and with George Myro.) Let the function g, which maps English sentences onto English sentences, be defined as follows: $g(A) =_{df} g_2(g_1^{-1}(A))$. That is, the value of g when applied to the English sentence A is the English sentence that results when g_2 is applied to the L-sentence whose g_1-value is A. For example, $g('There\ exists\ a\ rabbit') = 'Rabbithood\ is\ manifest'$. And if g_1 and g_2 have been suitably constructed, $g('Rabbithood\ is\ manifest') = 'There\ exists\ a\ rabbit'$. Indeed, if g_1 and g_2 have been suitably constructed, the following will hold for all English sentences A: $g(g(A)) = A$. Now let m be the function that maps English sentences onto their meanings, i.e., onto the propositions they express. For example, since 'There exists a rabbit' means that there exists a rabbit, $m('There\ exists\ a\ rabbit') =$ the proposition that there exists a rabbit. Then we define a function t that maps propositions onto propositions: $t(p) =_{df} m(g(m^{-1}(p)))$. That is, the value of t when applied to proposition p is the proposition that is expressed by the sentence that is the g-value of the sentence that expresses p. For example, t (the proposition that there exists a rabbit) $=$ the proposition that rabbithood is manifest. And if g_1 and g_2 have been suitably constructed, t(the proposition that rabbithood is manifest) $=$ the proposition that there exists a rabbit. Indeed, for any proposition p expressible in both English and L, $t(t(p))$ $= p$. That is, t maps each proposition expressible in both English and L to an inverted counterpart, and each inverted counterpart, right back to the original.

The function t has been constructed in a linguistic setting, and accordingly t is defined only on propositions expressible in both English and the alien language. This restriction can easily be removed, however, by skipping the linguistic detour and constructing t directly within a theory of properties, relations, and propositions. In this construction t would be defined on everything in the domain of discourse–individuals, properties, relations, and propositions. Further, $t(t(x)) = x$ would hold for all x in the domain. This function t would thus invert the conceptual scheme in the way we are seeking. In what follows I will call functions of this kind *Quinean transformations*. (Incidentally, our construction would go through substantially unchanged if, as David Lewis suggests in ''General Semantics,'' we were to identify the objects of the propositional attitudes with a certain kind of abstract tree rather than with propositions.)

We can use a Quinean transformation t to define an inverted relation for each of the standard propositional attitudes:

x thinks* p iff$_{df}$ x thinks $t(p)$.[16]

x wants* p iff$_{df}$ x wants $t(p)$.

. . . .

With these inverted relations in hand, we can now return to functionalism. In this section I will assess the adequacy of functionalism relative to a certain set of psychological principles, viz., the elementary belief/desire model of action (described below). (I do the same for a more sophisticated set of principles in the next section.) My assessment follows from two theses. First, the system of inverted relations (thinks*, etc.) resulting from the above definitions satisfies all the principles in the elementary belief/desire model of action. Second, (at least some of) these inverted relations are significantly different from their standard counterparts; indeed, they are typically not even co-extensive with them. Given these two theses, it follows that the elementary belief/desire model of action does not implicitly define (all of) the standard propositional attitudes and, therefore, that this model does not provide the basis for direct functional definitions of them either. This conclusion is of interest for two reasons. First, many cognitive psychologists and philosophical functionalists are content with this model. And second, though the model might not reflect all of the distinctive features of a sophisticated mental life, if "lower" creatures (and perhaps also computers) have minds, their minds might be adequately described by a model with this degree of complexity.

I begin with a defense of the first thesis. My strategy shall be to present an idealization of the elementary belief/desire model of action and then to prove that, if the standard propositional attitudes satisfy this idealized model, then so do their inverted counterparts. Then I will indicate why this result can be extended to richer versions of the elementary belief/desire model.

When I speak of the elementary belief/desire model of action, I mean the psychological theory consisting of all elementary principles for the standard propositional attitudes. A principle for the attitudes is elementary if it is not concerned with the behavior of the attitudes in connection with multiple embeddings. Thus, principles such as the following are *not* elementary: (Infallibility) If x is thinking that x is thinking p, then x is thinking p. I will deal with psychological models that include non-elementary principles in the next section.

The following will be our idealization of the elementary belief/desire model. I will take the liberty to simplify significantly the principles contained in it, but nothing substantive should ride on this. For all x, p, q, and F:

> *Input*.   If p is true and it is causally necessary at the moment that x entertains p if and only if p is true, then x thinks p.[17]
>
> *Pure Reason*.   If x thinks that if p then q and x thinks p and x entertains q, then x thinks q.
>
> *Practical Reason*.   If x thinks that if p then q and x wants q and x does not want not p and x entertains p, then x wants p.
>
> *Intention*.   If x wants that Fx and x thinks that x can F at the moment, then x intends that Fx.
>
> *Output*.   If x intends that Fx and it is causally possible at the moment that Fx, then Fx.

The thesis that the system of inverted relations–thinking*, wanting*, etc.–satisfies these principles naturally depends on our choice of Quinean transformation t. I will suggest two transformations that easily fill the bill (though there are many others). The first, which I used in my illustrations earlier, is a function that maps existential propositions (e.g., that there exists a rabbit) to propositions concerning the manifestation of associated universals (e.g., that rabbithood is manifest) and propositions concerning the manifestation of universals back to associated existential propositions. I call this the *particular/universal transformation*. Since it is fairly obvious how to define this transformation rigorously, I will suppress technicalities until the next section when they are unavoidable. Suffice it to say that, aside from converting existential propositions into propositions concerning the manifestation of associated universals (and conversely), the particular/universal transformation leaves everything else about a proposition unchanged. That is, this transformation leaves intact all the "nonformal" features of a proposition. For example, it does not alter any proposition that is embedded as a subject within a given proposition upon which it is acting.

The second transformation, which I call the *left/right transformation*, is constructed as follows. (The construction invokes a certain kind of artificial object that is a logical construct out of ordinary physical objects. Such artificial objects could be avoided by complicating the construction in certain ways.)[18] Let $l(x)$ be the infinite moving plane that always follows x around dividing his body (and the universe) into a left half and a right half. Let the function h_x be defined as follows. If $v = x$ or v is not located in space, then $h_x(v) =_{df} v$. Otherwise, $h_x(v) =_{df}$ the object u such that, necessarily, if x exists, u is located at the same distance d ($d \geqslant 0$) from the plane $l(x)$ as v but on the opposite side, and if x does not exist, u has the same location as v. Thus, if x exists, $v \neq x$, and v is located in space, then $h_x(v)$ is v's "logical shadow" on the other side of the plane $l(x)$.[19] Let us extend h_x to properties and i-ary relations as follows: $h_x(F) =$ the property of being a v such that $F(h_x(v))$ and $h_x(R) =$ the relation holding among $v_1,\ldots, v_i$ such that $R(h_x(v_1),\ldots, h_x(v_i))$. Then the transformation t_x may be defined inductively. To illustrate, I will state the definition for the case of atomic propositions: if $h_x(F) = F'$, $h_x(R) = R'$, and $h_x(a_k) = a_k'$, $k \geqslant 1$, then $t_x(F(a_1)) = F'(a_1')$ and $t_x(R(a_1,\ldots, a_i)) = R'(a_1',\ldots, a_i')$. More complex cases are handled analogously. (Naturally, our definitions of the inverted relations are to be understood as having the following form: x thinks* p iff$_{df}$ x thinks $t_x(p)$. That is, a person thinks* p if and only if he thinks the proposition that arises from p via the left/right transformation that is defined in terms of the infinite plane that always moves around with his own body dividing it left and right. Incidentally, when the context permits, I will often write t instead of t_x in order to simplify things notationally.) To get a better idea of how the left/right transformation works, consider the proposition that this (i.e., my left hand) moves. Let $h_{me}(\text{this}) = \text{this}'$ [i.e., my left hand's "logical shadow" on the other side of the plane $l(me)$]. Let $h_{me}(\text{moving}) = \text{moving}'$ [roughly, the property of being the "logical shadow" of something that moves on the other side of the plane $l(me)$]. Then, $t_{me}(\text{the proposition that this moves}) = \text{the proposition that this}' \text{ moves}'$.

The particular/universal transformation and the left/right transformation are defined so that this lemma follows directly: for any proposition p, p and $t(p)$ are necessarily equivalent. Given this lemma, it is straightforward to prove that the system of inverted relations based on either Quinean transformation satisfies the principles in our idealization of the elementary belief/desire model. For example, consider the Input principle. We wish to show that the inverted relations thinking* and entertaining* satisfy this principle. It will suffice to show that the following inverted counterpart of the original principle holds for arbitrary p:

> If p is true and it is causally necessary at the moment that x entertains* p if and only if p is true, then x thinks* p.

Suppose that $t(p) = q$. Then, given the definitions of 'thinks*' and 'entertains*', this principle is necessarily equivalent to the following:

> If p is true and it is causally necessary at the moment that
> x entertains q if and only if p is true, then x thinks q.

Notice that 'p' now occurs only in contexts in which necessary equivalents can be validly substituted *salva veritate*. However, by our lemma, we know that p and q are necessarily equivalent. So 'q' may be validly substituted for 'p' *salva veritate*. Therefore, the last formula–and, in turn, the inverted counterpart of the original Input principle–is necessarily equivalent to the following:

> If q is true and it is causally necessary at the moment that
> x entertains q if and only if q is true, then x thinks q.

But this is just an instance of the original Input principle. Therefore, since the original Input principle holds, it follows that the inverted counterpart of this principle holds too. In the case of the Intention and Output principles the proofs are much the same except that, when dealing with the particular/universal transformation, they make use of the facts that t (the proposition that Fx) = the proposition that Fx and t (the proposition that x can F at the moment) = the proposition that x can F at the moment. And when dealing with the left/right transformation, they make use of the facts that t_x (the proposition that Fx) = the proposition that $F'x$ and t_x (the proposition that x can F at the moment) = the proposition that x can F' at the moment. Finally, in the case of the Pure Reason and Practical Reason principles, the proofs are again much the same except that they make use of the fact that t (the proposition that if p then q) = the proposition that if r then s, where $r = t(p)$ and $s = t(q)$.

So, therefore, the systems of inverted relations based on our two Quinean transformations satisfy our idealization of the elementary belief/desire model of action. Moreover, this conclusion generalizes. For example, let T be any elementary principle for the standard propositional attitudes such that (1) every formula within the scope of a propositional-attitude predicate in T is built up out of propositional variables and propositional connectives, and (2) except for propositional-attitude predicates, each constant in T is either a predicate of individuals or a logical operator for which the principle of the substitutivity of necessary equivalents is valid.[20] (These operators may include, e.g., modal, causal, probability, and even counterfactual operators as long as the substitutivity principle is valid for them.) Let T^* arise from T by replacing all predicates for the standard propositional attitudes with predicates for their inverted counterparts. Then our generalization is this: T and T^* are necessarily equivalent, and, hence, if P is any infinite class of T-like principles and P^* the associated class of T^*-like principles, P and P^* are necessarily equivalent. This generalization is proved by a straightforward inductive argument.

Stronger generalizations are also possible. In proofs of these further generalizations the following resources are used. First, if t is the particular/universal transformation, all the nonformal "constituents" in $t(p)$ are the same as those in p, and since p and $t(p)$ arise from one another by a mechanical logical manipulation, they are not just necessarily equivalent but are provably equivalent (in a theory of properties, relations, and propositions). Second, if t is the left/right transformation, p and $t(p)$ always have the same logical form. Third, consider the Quinean premise discussed at the outset of this section, i.e., the premise that there could be beings who think (or can be interpreted as thinking) in systematically different, yet equally rational, ways. When this premise is rigorously formulated, it entails that, for every principle characterizing some feature of one way of thinking (e.g., "particularese"), there exists a complementary principle characterizing an analogous feature of a corresponding way of thinking (e.g., "universalese"). Take as an example the following "particularese" principle:

If x clearly and distinctly understands the proposition that (Fa only if something is F), then x will think that (Fa only if something is F).

The complementary "universalese" principle is this:

If x clearly and distinctly understands the proposition that (Fa only if F-ness is manifest), then x will think that (Fa only if F-ness is manifest).

Clearly, if the original principle is true, so is the complementary principle. To show that the inverted relations satisfy the first principle, replace 'understands' with 'understands*' and 'think' with 'think*'. Then, expand 'understands*' and 'think*' in accordance with their definitions. After that, replace 't(that Fa only if something is F)' with the necessarily equivalent expression 'that Fa only if F-ness is manifest'. The result is none other than the complementary principle. Since the latter principle is true and since our substitutions are equivalence preserving, it follows that the inverted relations satisfy the original principle. Moreover, by analogous argument, we can employ the original principle to show that the inverted relations also satisfy the complementary principle. More generally, if the standard psychological attitudes satisfy any universal psychological principle–i.e., any psychological principle that is neither species-dependent nor particular-dependent (see below)–then this fact can be used to show that the inverted relations satisfy the complementary principle, and conversely.[21] This special complementarity, together with the earlier two facts, entail much stronger generalizations on our previous results. Indeed, these generalizations extend to all universally applicable elementary psychological principles, i.e., to all elementary principles that concern the *general* nature of the mind rather than only the mental idiosyncrasies true of isolated species or of isolated individuals.

Granted that the inverted relations satisfy all true universal elementary principles, there are, nevertheless, true species-dependent and particular-dependent principles that the inverted relations do not satisfy.[22] However, this fact can do nothing at all to save functionalism. First, given that there is an open-ended list of possible species and possible thinking beings, species-dependent and particular-dependent principles have no place in the philosophical analysis of a universally applicable concept such as thinking. In this connection, one of the fundamental goals of functionalism is to provide a *general explanation* of why psychological concepts are true of some entities and not of others. If species-dependent or particular-dependent principles are invoked in the functional definitions of psychological concepts, this fundamental goal of functionalism is completely undermined. Second, consider any set of species-dependent (or particular-dependent) principles there might be for any given list of possible species (or particulars). Even if such principles are used as the basis for a functional definition of, e.g., thinking, this functional definition will always fail, for such principles will always be satisfied by some new "inverted" relation (e.g., thinking**) which we can construct by adapting the formal technique sketched at the close of this section.

So our overall conclusion is this. Any system of universal (i.e., non-species-dependent and non-particular-dependent) elementary principles is satisfied by the standard psychological attitudes only if it is also satisfied by one of our systems of inverted relations; moreover, any system of elementary principles containing possibly the non-universal principles for any list of possible species (or particulars) is satisfied by the standard psychological attitudes only if it is also satisfied by some new system of inverted relations constructed in accordance with the technique mentioned just above.

A functionalist who is content to work with the elementary belief/desire model of action might hope to avoid this conclusion by emphasizing the notion of causal role.[23] Even if the inverted relations and the standard relations satisfy the same causal laws, perhaps they do not have the same causal roles. However, relations, just on their own, have no causal efficacy at all. Events cause events; phenomena cause phenomena. Relations cause neither. Now it is true by *definition* that xS^*p if and only if $xSt(p)$, for any standard propositional attitude S and its inverted counterpart S^*. For example, it is true by *definition* that you are thinking* p if and only if you are thinking $t(p)$. Therefore, the event of someone's thinking* p must be identical to the event of that person's thinking $t(p)$. In general, every event of thinking* must be identical to an event of thinking. Furthermore, it is *provable* that, for every proposition q, there is a p such that, necessarily, $q = t(p)$ and, hence, necessarily, x thinks q if and only if x thinks $t(p)$.[24] Therefore, even on extremely strict criteria of event identity (criteria much stronger than those used in arguments for the token/token identity thesis), for every q, there is a p such that the event of someone's thinking q is identical to the event of that person's thinking $t(p)$. However, we have just seen that the event of someone's thinking $t(p)$ is identical to the event of that person's thinking* p. It follows, therefore, that for every proposition q, there is a p such that the event of someone's thinking q is identical to the event of that person's thinking* p. Thus, every event of thinking is identical to an event of thinking*. So, in summary, every event of thinking* is an event of thinking, and every event of thinking is an event of thinking*. It follows that any event of thinking* possesses exactly the same causal role as an event of thinking and any event of thinking possesses exactly the same causal role as an event of thinking*. It is implausible, therefore, that the usual notion of causal role could help save functionalism from the line of criticism developed in this section.

Let us turn finally to my second thesis, namely, that (at least some of) the inverted relations thinking*, wanting*, etc. are significantly different from their standard counterparts thinking, wanting, etc. There is compelling evidence for this thesis. Consider thinking, for example. It is clearly possible for a person to be thinking that there exists a rabbit and to fail to be thinking that rabbithood is manifest. For that matter, most people who are right now thinking that there exists a rabbit are not also thinking that rabbithood is manifest. Indeed, many people who have thought the former have never thought the latter, and some are not disposed even to *understand* the latter.[25] However, the latter proposition is the result of applying the particular/universal transformation to the former proposition. Therefore, there is a proposition p such that someone thinks p but does not think $t(p)$, i.e., such that someone thinks p but does not think* p. So, when thinking* is defined in terms of the particular/universal transformation, thinking and thinking* are not even materially equivalent. (For further justification of this conclusion, see below.)

Next consider the case where thinking* is defined in terms of the left/right transformation. Take the proposition that this (i.e., my left hand) moves. Let h_{me}(this) = this$'$ [i.e., my left hand's "logical shadow" on the other side of the plane l(me)]. Let h_{me}(moving) = moving$'$. Then t_{me}(the proposition that this moves) = the proposition that this$'$ moves$'$. Plainly, it is possible for me to think that this moves without thinking that this$'$ moves$'$. Moreover, I never thought that this$'$ moves$'$ until today even though I have numerous times thought that this moves. Indeed, I confess to having some difficulty understanding with clarity and distinctness the proposition that this$'$ moves$'$. Thus, there is plainly a proposition p such that I have thought p and not thought $t_{me}(p)$. Therefore, when thinking* is defined in terms of the left/right transformation, thinking and thinking* again are not even materially equivalent. So, with either of our two Quinean transformations, thinking and thinking* are significantly different.

Are there any grounds on which a functionalist might resist this conclusion? There are three that I can think of, and I will discuss them in turn. First, there is a theory according to which all intensional entities, including propositions, are identical if necessarily equivalent. (The familiar possible-worlds treatment is committed to this theory.) However, our Quinean transformations have been constructed so that, for any proposition p, $t(p)$ and p are necessarily equivalent. Therefore, according to the above theory of the identity conditions for propositions, $t(p) = p$. Hence, it would follow that, if we use these transformations in our definitions, thinking = thinking*, desiring = desiring*, etc. And this would defeat my argument.

However, most people today acknowledge the striking inadequacy of this theory of the identity conditions for propositions. For example, if the theory is right, then whoever knows a trivial necessary truth knows every necessary truth, and this is plainly false. Or consider an argument involving ontological commitment. Take the proposition that there exists a rabbit and the proposition that rabbithood is manifest. If the theory is right, these two propositions would have the same ontological commitments. But clearly they do not. The former proposition is not committed to the existence of any universals, but the latter proposition is. This point can be dramatized as follows. An extensionalist philosopher who, like Quine, believes that universals do not exist would deny the latter proposition and yet affirm the former. If the above theory were correct, such a philosopher would be guilty of explicit contradiction. But obviously this is not the case. Finally, the best functional explanations of certain kinds of verbal behavior invoke fine-grained intensional distinctions. Suppose that I am a normal, sincere English speaker. Then the most straightforward functional explanation of my assertion of the sentence 'Awhile ago I was thinking that there exists a rabbit but was not thinking that rabbithood is manifest' requires that there be a distinction between thinking that there exists a rabbit and thinking that rabbithood is manifest. Do those who are realists about the propositional attitudes have any good reason not to accept such an explanation?

For these sorts of reasons, we may safely conclude that the standard propositional attitudes characteristically are sensitive to distinctions cut more finely than necessary equivalence. Those who do not honor such distinctions might be interested in relations having certain gross resemblance to the standard propositional attitudes, but they certainly are not interested in these relations themselves.

The second reason someone might object to our conclusion that thinking $\neq$ thinking* goes as follows. Quine uses his indeterminacy argument to urge that there exists no objective difference between an alien's meaning p and his meaning $t(p)$ and that there exists no objective difference between an alien's thinking p and his thinking $t(p)$. Therefore, it is improper for us to use a Quinean transformation to define the relation thinking*–thinking* $p =_{df}$ thinking $t(p)$–and then to go on to claim that there is an objective difference between thinking and thinking*. One way to reply to this objection is to challenge Quine's conclusion. That is, we could accept Quine's premise that it is impossible for us to determine whether an alien means p rather than $t(p)$ and that it is impossible for us to determine whether an alien is thinking p rather than $t(p)$; and at the same time, we could deny that it follows from this that there is no objective difference between an alien's meaning p and his meaning $t(p)$ or between his thinking p and his thinking $t(p)$. However, each of us on his own can avoid this head-on challenge to Quine's conclusion simply by shifting to the *first person*.[26] For example, *I* know that thinking $\neq$ thinking* if any of the following holds. At least once

I have been thinking that there is a rabbit and have failed at that time also to have been thinking that rabbithood is manifest. Or at least once I have been thinking that something hits something and have failed at that time also to have been thinking that the property of being something x such that the property of being hit by x is manifest is itself a manifest property. (See note 25.) Or at least once I have been thinking that this (i.e., my left hand) moves and have failed at that time also to have been thinking that this' moves'. And I know I have. So I know that thinking $\neq$ thinking*. Therefore, I may confidently conclude that no elementary psychological principles can implicitly define what it is for me to be thinking p rather than to be thinking* p. Likewise, each of you can go through an analogous chain of reasoning, at the end of which you can conclude that no elementary psychological principles can implicitly define what it is for you to be thinking p rather than to be thinking* p.

The third possible objection to the conclusion that thinking $\neq$ thinking* is that the construction of thinking* presupposes that thinking is a relation holding between individuals and propositions; functionalists who believe that the thinking relation holds between individuals and pure syntactic entities such as sentences in Mentalese ("the language of thought") might make this sort of objection. However, this whole issue can be side-stepped by re-defining our Quinean transformation t so that it maps, e.g., sentences in Mentalese onto corresponding necessarily equivalent, non-synonymous sentences in Mentalese. (Our function g from the beginning of this section is just like this re-defined function t except that it maps English sentences onto necessarily equivalent, non-synonymous English sentences.) Once t is re-defined in this way, the rest of the above argument goes through substantially unchanged.

The "syntactic functionalist" might believe, however, that this re-definition of t gives him a special advantage not available to the "propositional functionalist." The reason is that, since syntactic entities are pure abstract shapes, they can have physical inscriptions in such materials as brain cells; propositions cannot. (To assist the syntactic functionalist, I will use the term 'pure abstract shape' in a liberal way so that quite dissimilar physical objects may, if desired, be counted as having the same pure abstract shape. However, the use of this term should not be so liberal that a sentence and its Quinean transform are counted as being the same pure abstract shape, for that would undermine the syntactic functionalist's ability to preserve the sort of fine-grained distinctions that are characteristic of intentionality.) So, for example, since a given Mentalese sentence S differs in pure abstract shape from its transform $t(S)$, the inscriptions of S and of $t(S)$ in the brain will differ physically. Now, the syntactic functionalist might think that such physical differences will in turn help to distinguish the standard mental relations from their inverted counterparts. However, as I will show, this is not so.

Suppose for the sake of argument that the objects of the standard psychological attitudes are not propositions but sentences in Mentalese and that t has been re-defined so that it maps Mentalese sentences onto appropriate necessarily equivalent, non-synonymous Mentalese sentences. Now functionalism is based on the insight that functionally indistinguishable structures can have quite different physical realizations. The only thing that two such realizations must have in common is the following: (1) there must be a structural isomorphism between the components of one and the components of the other, and (2) the components of one must interact causally with one another and their outside environment in the same way as the components of the other interact with one another and their outside environment. Beyond this it makes no difference what the components are like. In particular, it makes no difference just which syntactic entities (i.e., which pure abstract shapes) are physically inscribed in which realization. All that is required is that each syntactic entity physically inscribed in one realization have a structural isomorphism to the corresponding syntactic entity physically inscribed in the other realization and that the causal role played by inscriptions of the former within the first realization is the same as the causal role played by inscriptions of the latter within the second realization. However, physical inscriptions of sentences that are Quinean transforms of one another could easily have such a structural and causal isomorphism to one another. After all, sentences that arise from one another via the left/right transformation are identical in syntactic form, and sentences that arise from one another via the particular/universal transformation differ only by a syntactic manipulation that, from a mechanical point of view, has no more significance than a difference in punctuation convention.

To dramatize the point, consider the following rather fanciful hypothetical example.[27] According to functionalism, it should be possible that each being of type-a thinks the Mentalese sentence S if and only if an actual inscription of, say, the English sentence A occurs in a certain region of its brain and that it thinks $t(S)$ if and only if an inscription of $g(A)$ occurs in that region. And according to functionalism, since A and $g(A)$ have a direct structural isomorphism to one another (i.e., the function g itself), it should also be possible that each being of type-b (perhaps a type of being made of quite different materials) thinks S if and only if an inscription of $g(A)$ occurs in an analogous region of its brain and that it thinks $t(S)$ if and only if an inscription of A occurs in that region of its brain. Now according to functionalism, since A and $g(A)$ have a direct structural isomorphism to one another (i.e., function g itself), the causal role of inscriptions of A within type-a beings would be identical to the causal role of inscriptions of $g(A)$ within type-b beings, and the causal role of inscriptions of $g(A)$ within type-a beings would be identical to the causal role of inscriptions of A within type-b beings. Thus, according to functionalism, beings of type-a would be functionally indistinguishable from beings of type-b. Therefore, the mere existence of A-inscriptions or of $g(A)$-inscriptions in a being's "thinking center" does nothing in itself to indicate whether a being is thinking S or whether it is thinking $t(S)$ instead; i.e., it does not indicate whether the being is thinking S or whether it is thinking* S. Generalizing on this, we may conclude that the fact that syntactic entities can have physical instances in brains does nothing to reduce the threat that thinking* satisfies all the principles of functional psychology that are satisfied by thinking.

The functionalist might hope to avoid this conclusion by retreating from pure functionalism and by moving back toward naive physiological reductionism. To do this, he would add to his set of psychological principles a list of species-dependent psycho-physiological correlations, for example:

the type-a-being-thinks-S/A-inscription correlation;

the type-a-being-thinks-$t(S)/g(A)$-inscription correlation;

the type-b-being-thinks-$S/g(A)$-inscription correlation;

the type-b-being-thinks-$t(S)/A$-inscription correlation.

But even this will not help. We can show that the enriched set of principles does not implicitly define thinking, desiring, etc. by defining a new system of inverted relations thinking**, desiring**, etc. that are tailored to the enriched set. For example, x thinks** S iff$_{df}x$ thinks S if x is type-a or type-b and otherwise x thinks* S. So defined, thinking** and thinking, desiring** and desiring, etc. are significantly different; indeed, they can fail to be co-extensive. For according to functionalism, there is an *open-ended* list of different possible physical realizations of the same functional structure; type-a and type-b beings are only two of a potentially infinite number of such realizations. Although the extension of thinking** and the extension of thinking are the same concerning beings of type-a and type-b, concerning all these other types of beings they will differ. But do thinking**, desiring**, etc., satisfy the enriched set of principles? Since thinking*, desiring*, etc., satisfy the original set of principles (and we have already shown that they do), thinking**, desiring**, etc. satisfy the enriched set. For thinking and thinking** must have the same extensions over type-a and type-b beings, and thinking* and thinking** must have the same extensions over all other types of beings.[28]

In this way, we can always keep one step ahead of the functionalist who would add psycho-physiological correlations to his other psychological principles: for any enriched set of principles satisfied by the standard propositional attitudes, we can define a system of inverted relations that also satisfies them. Therefore, invoking the "language of thought" or other syntactical constructs does nothing to ward off the line of attack we have mounted against functionalism. Thus, as far as the truth of functionalism is concerned, we might as well identify propositions as the objects of the standard propositional attitudes; the syntactical alternatives offer no advantage.[29]

This completes my discussion of possible objections to my argument. The overall conclusion is that the elementary belief/desire model of action cannot implicitly define the standard propositional attitudes and, hence, cannot serve as the basis of direct functional definitions of them either. However, we have not shown that stronger psychological principles cannot validate functionalism. To show this, we must turn to the principles that characterize the self-conscious rational mind.

THE SELF-CONSCIOUS RATIONAL MIND

The elementary belief/desire model contains no principles concerned with the behavior of the propositional attitudes in connection with multiple embeddings and no

principles concerned with the behavior of psychological relations that are not propositional attitudes. When such principles are added to the elementary belief/desire
model, we approximate a theory adequate for characterizing the self-conscious rational mind. Perhaps this enriched theory–or a perfected version of it–is sufficiently
strong to define implicitly the standard psychological relations and, in turn, to provide
a basis for direct functional definitions of them. Our previous construction, at any rate,
does not rule out this possibility, for the system of inverted relations (thinking*, etc.)
turns out not to satisfy many of the principles that might be added when we enrich the
belief/desire model. What we shall discover is this. Intensionality–the very phenomenon that made our previous ''Quinean'' construction succeed in the elementary
setting–leads to its downfall in the more sophisticated setting of the self-conscious rational mind. Specifically, there are intensional distinctions that show up in the way the
mind gains access to information about itself–to the *contents* of its own conscious intentional states and to its own conscious *operations*–and our ''Quinean'' construction
is insensitive to these distinctions. Thus, the prospect of a successful functionalism is
still alive.

Consider the matter of the contents of one's own conscious intentional states.
Each of our Quinean transformations–and each Quinean transformation known in the
philosophical literature–is ''superficial'' in the sense that it transforms only the ''uppermost'' level of any proposition upon which it is operating; it leaves intact the
propositions embedded as subjects within those propositions. (For example, the par-
ticular/universal transformation simply alters the uppermost quantificational structure
of a proposition p; it does not alter the quantificational structure of propositions embedded within p.) However, non-elementary principles that characterize the mind's
access to the contents of its own intentional states typically ''mix levels.'' That is,
they describe direct internal links between, e.g., x's thinking a proposition p and x's
thinking the proposition that x is thinking p. (It is crucial that p be the same in each
case.) When a Quinean transformation t is applied to a proposition p, often the result
q is significantly different. However, when t is applied to the proposition that x is
thinking p, the embedded proposition p is left intact; the new proposition q does not
take its place. (For example, the result of applying the particular/universal transformation to the proposition that x is thinking p just is the proposition that x is thinking p.
This is so because this proposition is ''atomic'' and has no quantificational structure.
The fact that p might itself have a complex quantificational structure is beside the
point.) Now although p and q are necessarily equivalent, there is always a significant
fine-grained intensional information gap between propositions in which p is embedded and those in which q is embedded. Therefore, the familiar ''superficial'' Quinean
transformations break the direct internal link between x's thinking p and x's thinking
that x is thinking p. And since our inverted relations thinking*, etc. are defined in
terms of such Quinean transformations, they too fail to preserve the direct internal
links that typify the self-conscious rational mind. Indeed, to restore this kind of direct
internal link, we will be forced to construct an entirely new system of inverted relations.

I will illustrate the breakdown in our earlier construction by examining in more detail some principles that have played an important role in the history of philosophical psychology and epistemology. For convenience, I will formulate these principles in a simplified–and, no doubt, overly strong–way, and I will employ the traditional idiom.

The first example is the doctrine of the infallibility of a person's thoughts about his own present thoughts. According to this doctrine, the following is a necessary truth:

Infallibility. If x is thinking that x is thinking p, then x is thinking p.

To test whether the inverted relation thinking* satisfies this principle, let us substitute 'thinking*', for 'thinking':

If x is thinking* that x is thinking* p, then x is thinking* p.

Next let us expand the occurrences of 'thinking*' in accordance with the definition. [30] We obtain:

If x is thinking t(that x is thinking $t(p)$), then x is thinking $t(p)$.

To simplify this further, let us determine the identity of t(that x is thinking $t(p)$). Suppose that t is the particular/universal transformation. Consider an analogy: the proposition that $x < f(y)$. This proposition has no quantificational structure; i.e., it is not an existential generalization,[31] nor is it the result of predicating the property of being manifested of some universal. Therefore, t does not alter this proposition at all: t(that $x < f(y)$) = that $x < f(y)$. Now for exactly the same reason, t does not alter the proposition that x is thinking $t(p)$. That is, because this proposition has no quantificational structure, t(that x is thinking $t(p)$) = that x is thinking $t(p)$. Substituting this identity in the above principle, we obtain:

If x is thinking that x is thinking $t(p)$, then x is thinking $t(p)$.

Now suppose that p is some proposition with a complex quantificational structure; then $p \neq t(p)$. Let $q = t(p)$. Is the proposition that x is thinking $t(p)$ identical to the proposition that x is thinking q? Not at all. In fact, this is what we learned in our first lesson on the failure of substitutivity of co-referential expressions in intensional contexts. For example, the proposition that $7 <$ the number of planets is not identical to the proposition that $7 < 9$. Since 'the proposition that $7 <$ the number of planets' generates an intensional context and since 'the number of planets' is a descriptive phrase having narrow scope, it cannot be replaced by the co-referential expression '7' without changing the reference of the whole expression. Analogously, since 'the proposition that x is thinking $t(p)$' generates an intensional context and since '$t(p)$' is a descriptive expression having narrow scope (recall n. 16), it cannot be replaced by the co-referential expression 'q' without changing the reference of the whole expression. Thus, the proposition that x is thinking $t(p) \neq$ the proposition that x is thinking q. And, therefore, it is possible to think one and not the other. It is exactly this possibility that creates a host of counterexamples to the last principle, proving that the inverted relation thinking* does not satisfy the original Infallibility principle.

Here is one such counterexample. Let p = the proposition that the property of hitting something is manifest, and let q = the proposition that something is such that the property of being hit by it is manifest, then $q = t(p)$. (Recall n. 25.) Suppose that x is not thinking q, i.e., that x is not thinking $t(p)$. Suppose, however, that x is thinking that something hits something, and suppose that x therefore thinks that he is thinking that something hits something. And suppose, finally, that, given the general human susceptibility to occasional logical errors, x mistakenly thinks that t (that hitting something is manifest) = that something hits something. Then, x might easily infer that he is thinking t (that hitting something is manifest). The resulting situation would be this: x would be thinking that x is thinking $t(p)$ and yet x would not be thinking $t(p)$. Hence, we have a counterexample to the principle that arises from the Infallibility principle when 'thinking*' is substituted for 'thinking'. Therefore, thinking* does not satisfy the Infallibility principle.

Moreover, this kind of breakdown is not an isolated phenomenon. Quinean constructions suffer analogous breakdowns in connection with a large range of principles concerning the mind's access to the contents of its own conscious intentional states. The following are two further examples, each of which has had an important role in the history of epistemology and philosophical psychology:

> Privileged Access. If x is thinking p and x is entertaining the proposition that x is thinking p, then x knows that x is thinking p.
>
> Introspection. If x is thinking p and x is entertaining the proposition that x is thinking p, then x introspects that x is thinking p.[32]

Using the previous example as a guide, one can easily show that the inverted relations thinking*, etc. do not satisfy these principles. And this conclusion holds regardless of which familiar Quinean transformation is used to define the inverted relations.

So far I have been discussing obstacles to our Quinean construction that arise in connection with the mind's access to the *contents* of its own conscious intentional states. I should now say a few words about obstacles that arise in connection with the mind's access to its own conscious *operations*. Consider the above Introspection principle. Let us follow our usual test procedure by putting in 'think*' for 'think', 'entertain*' for 'entertain', and 'introspect*' for 'introspect':

> If x is thinking* p and x is entertaining* the proposition that x is thinking* p, then x introspects* that x is thinking* p.

Expanding 'entertain*', 'introspect*', and the unembedded occurrence of 'think*', we obtain:

> If x is thinking $t(p)$ and x is entertaining the proposition t (that x is thinking* p), then x introspects t (that x is thinking* p).

Suppose for illustrative purposes that t is the particular/universal transformation.

Then, by considerations like those above, t(that x is thinking* p) = that x is thinking* p. Plugging in this identity, we obtain:

> If x is thinking $t(p)$ and x is entertaining the proposition that x is thinking* p, then x introspects that x is thinking* p.

This principle is plainly unacceptable for the sort of reasons discussed above. But there is a new defect as well. Let $q = t(p)$. Suppose x knows by introspection that he is thinking q. And suppose he knows the logical truth that he is thinking q if and only if he is thinking* p. In this situation, x could know by *inference* that he is thinking* p. However, that he is thinking* p is *in principle* simply not the sort of thing x (or anyone) can *directly* introspect; it is not the sort of thing someone can be aware of directly without the aid of some form of inference. The reason is that thinking* is not a conscious operation of mind, and the only relational propositions a person can directly introspect are those comprised of a conscious operation of mind and its immediate object. [For the same reason, a person x cannot directly introspect that x is thinking $t(p)$. True, x can directly introspect that x is thinking q, where $q = t(p)$. But, as we have seen, even though the descriptive proposition that x is thinking $t(p)$ and the purely relational proposition that x is thinking q are necessarily equivalent, they are quite distinct. Though x can know the descriptive proposition by inference via his introspective knowledge that he is thinking q and his logical knowledge that $q = t(p)$, it is impossible for him to introspect it. Only the purely relational proposition is a candidate for direct introspection.] The point, then, is that the range of the introspecting relation is necessarily restricted in something like the following way:

> x can introspect that xRy iff R is a conscious-operation-of-mind and it is possible that xRy.

That is, x can introspect that xRy if and only if R is either sensing, thinking, desiring, intending,..., or introspecting itself and it is possible that xRy. Thus, introspection defines a "hermetically sealed" circle of mutually tuned relations: all and only genuine conscious operations of mind are permitted entry. No system of relations thinking*, desiring*,..., introspecting* generated by our Quinean procedure can have this hermetically sealed character. On all such constructions, it is *impossible* for someone to introspect* that he is thinking* p. And on many of these constructions (e.g., the one based on the particular/universal transformation) it is *possible* for someone to introspect* propositions involving relations from outside the circle thinking*, desiring*,..., introspecting*; e.g., it is possible for someone to introspect* that he is thinking p.

A closely related theory about the interdependent structure of the conscious operations of mind is found in traditional empiricist psychology of experience (such as the theory propounded by John Locke). According to this theory, a person can in acts of reflection actually experience his own conscious operations of mind. So, for example, it is possible to experience thinking, desiring, deciding, introspecting, etc., and, indeed, it is possible to experience experiencing itself. However, according to the theory, it would be impossible to experience such things as thinking*, desiring*, etc. just because they are not conscious operations of mind. Our system of inverted relations clearly cannot satisfy this traditional empiricist theory.[33] What we need is an entirely new system of relations, one that mimics the behavior of the standard psychological relations "all they way down," even in their roles as constituents in the contents of conscious intentional states and as immediate objects of psychological relations themselves.

Of course, the foregoing are only examples of the kinds of principles for the self-conscious rational mind that we should take into account; there are many more. One especially worth mentioning arises in connection with the fact that rational beings can know a priori a great number of necessary truths. We may approximate this fact with the following principle:

A Priori Knowledge. If p is necessary and x clearly and distinctly understands p, then x knows p.[34]

(To understand a proposition clearly and distinctly is, roughly, to "grasp its full significance." This is far stronger than merely entertaining the proposition.) Since this general principle of a priori knowledge is elementary, our inverted relations knowing* and clear and distinct understanding* do satisfy it. However, there are infinitely many specific principles of a priori knowledge that are not satisfied by the inverted relations, namely, non-elementary knowledge principles concerning specific logical relationships holding between the standard psychological relations and their inverted counterparts.[35]

Now let P be our best theory for the self-conscious rational mind. Suppose P includes the sorts of principles we have been discussing. This makes it much harder for a system of relations to satisfy P. Therefore, it is much more likely that P will be satisfied by only one system of relations–namely, the standard psychological relations–and, in turn, it is much more likely that P will serve as the basis for adequate functional definitions of the standard psychological relations. Now the principles that we have considered in this section might be controversial. However, to refute functionalism once and for all, either we must exclude all such principles or we must construct a new system of inverted relations that satisfies P. It is out of the question to dispute all such principles; surely at least some versions of some of these principles are sound. Therefore, one must adopt the second strategy, i.e., one must give a construction that works even when P contains such principles.

The difficulty of giving such a construction is magnified because we must allow for the possibility that P attributes a very strong modal value (indeed, even metaphysical necessity) to each of its constituent principles, including those of the sorts we have considered in this section. As I indicated earlier, none of the currently popular criticisms of functionalism comes close to providing a construction that fills this requirement. The goal of this section is to give such a construction. In effect, the construction is a global generalization of the construction given in the previous section. Specifically, I will define a new system of inverted relations that, like the earlier one, may be thought of as comprising an "anti-mind." This time, however, even the totality of principles for the self-conscious rational mind will be blind to the distinction between anti-mind and the true mind.

Before I launch into the construction it might be helpful for me to say something about the logical form of the kind of sentences that are used to express non-elementary principles for the propositional attitudes. Recall our first example, 'Whenever some-one thinks that he thinks something, then he in fact thinks it'. On its intended reading, this sentence imposes the following condition on the thinking relation T: for any x and p, if x stands in relation T to the result of applying T to x and p, then x stands in relation T to p. Thus, a canonical representation of (this reading of) the sentence would be something like this:

$$(\forall x)\,(\forall p)\,(xT[xTp] \rightarrow xTp)$$

where all *three* occurrences of 'T' express the same relation, namely, thinking. Only then will we capture the condition imposed on the thinking relation by the original (reading of the) sentence.

To appreciate better the significance of this point, notice that a strict "language-of-thought" theory allows for no natural way to represent the original (reading of the) sentence or others like it. For on a strict "language-of-thought" theory, pure syntactic entities are the only objects of thought. Therefore, the closest one could come to the original sentence would be something like this:

$$(\forall x)\,(\forall p)\,(xT\text{'}xTp\text{'} \rightarrow xTp).$$

This fails to capture the condition imposed on thinking by the original sentence, for the second occurrence of 'T' does not stand for the thinking relation but rather for the symbol 'T' itself. (Moreover, the second occurrences of 'x' and 'p' do not serve as variables ranging over persons and objects of thought but rather as names for the symbols 'x' and 'p' themselves.) There are certain rather artificial techniques for avoiding this outcome. But each of these methods, in effect, permits selected non-linguistic entities–e.g., real psychological relations such as the thinking relation–right into the objects of thought. Now anti-representational realists may accept this feature, but strict language-of-thought theorists may not. For this feature violates the basic philosophical tenet of their position, namely, that every constituent in an object of thought is a mere representation, i.e., an expression in the language of thought. But psychological relations are not expressions in the language of thought; rather they are what relate people to expressions in the language of thought (or so the language-of-thought theory goes)![36]

I begin the construction with an informal characterization. The construction is based on two intuitive ideas, the first of which is this. Suppose that, for every standard psychological relation, there is a distinct relation (called the "counterpart") that is necessarily like the original in two significant ways. I will illustrate with the example of thinking and its counterpart, which I will call thinking*. (This relation should not be confused with the one constructed in the previous section.) First, the extensions of thinking and thinking* are necessarily the same when it comes to propositions that do not "involve" the standard mental relations or their counterparts. So, for example, if q is a proposition concerning only individuals, necessarily, x thinks q iff x thinks* q. Second, when it comes to propositions that do "involve" mental relations or their counterparts, the extensions of the two relations are connected as follows: necessarily, for any such proposition p, x thinks p iff x thinks* p^*, where p^* arises from p by "substituting" mental relations for their counterparts and counterparts of mental relations for their originals wherever they "occur" in p. (For example, if p is the proposition that x thinks something, then p^* is the proposition that x thinks* something. Thus, necessarily, x thinks that x thinks something iff x thinks* that x thinks* something.) Now given that these relationships hold necessarily, thinking and thinking* will, I submit, be functionally indistinguishable. Nevertheless, they will be significantly different. After all, the type of proposition that is the characteristic object of the thinking relation is very "fine-grained." Therefore, if p and p^* are as specified in the example, p and p^* must be distinct, for p "contains" thinking where p^* "contains" thinking*. Yet for any two distinct propositions, it is at least possible that someone x thinks one and not the other. Therefore, suppose that x thinks p, then it is at least possible that x does not at that moment also think p^*. However, necessarily, x thinks p iff x thinks* p^*. Hence, it is at least possible that thinking and thinking* are not co-extensive, and this constitutes a significant difference between them. Thus, the mere distinctness of two relations (such as thinking and thinking*) that are otherwise indistinguishable can actually generate a distinction in their extensions when it comes to higher-level propositions that "contain" them as "constituents." This fact about the "fine-grained" intensionality of the standard propositional attitudes leads directly to model-theoretic proofs of the following: the standard psychological relations cannot be implicitly defined by any of a wide variety of psychological theories.[37]

My goal, however, is to *define explicitly* a system of new relations that comprises an anti-mind. To carry out this construction, we must incorporate our second intuitive idea. The function of this idea will be to guarantee that, when defined, our new relations thinking*, desiring*, etc. truly are distinct from the standard psychological relations. The idea is once again that of a Quinean "inversion" of our conceptual scheme, except that this time the inversion will be more radical. Recall that in our first construction the Quinean transformation t leaves intact every embedded proposition that is a constituent of the proposition upon which t is operating. By contrast, in its new, more radical role, t would, in effect, be applied over and over again to transform every embedded proposition "all the way down." Thus, in the new construction all the following will hold:

x thinks* that rabbithood is manifest iff x thinks that there exists a rabbit.

x thinks* that x thinks* that rabbithood is manifest iff x thinks that x thinks that there exists a rabbit.

x thinks* that x thinks* that x thinks* that rabbithood is manifest iff x thinks that x thinks that x thinks that there exists a rabbit.

. . . .

Observe that t is applied to every embedded proposition "all the way down" and also that every occurrence of thinking* is replaced by an occurrence of thinking. The aim of the new construction is to generalize this inversion procedure. That is, we will apply t "all the way down" to all fine-grained intensions–concepts as well as propositions. Moreover, for every property or relation F, we will define an inverted counterpart F^* such that F^* will play F's role and F will play F^*'s role at every occurrence in every fine-grained intension. (Of course, F and F^* will be identical in certain key cases, namely, where F is a physical property or relation, or F is one of the familiar logical relations such as identity or necessary equivalence.) The way this generalized inversion procedure will be achieved is by the definition of an operation $*$ which turns every property or relation F into an inverted counterpart F^* and which turns F^* right back into the original property or relation F. That is, $*(*(F)) = F$.

In defining this operation, we will use some relatively powerful logical machinery. Let me explain why. If we were dealing with specific versions of functionalism that invoke only some kinds of non-elementary psychological principles, a less powerful construction might suffice. For example, consider a version of functionalism that invokes only non-elementary principles of the kind that can be expressed within a strict theory of types (such as that of Russell or of Church); we could then construct an operation $*$ by straightforward inductive means. However, the kinds of non-elementary principles we have been discussing in this section require a type-free logical setting so that a psychological relation (e.g., thinking) can occur as a constituent of propositions that fall within its very own range. This special form of impredicativity appears to undermine an inductive approach to the definition of $*$ and of the $*$-counterparts of the standard psychological relations. There are two reasons why this is so. The first is this. Suppose that we have a candidate inductive characterization of some relation. Then, we can transform such a characterization into a direct definition of the relation simply by taking either the intersection or the union of all relations that satisfy the characterization. However, for any relation that exhibits the special kind of impredicativity that the $*$-relations must exhibit, these familiar methods appear to be of no use. For, if there should happen to exist more than one relation satisfying the inductive characterization of, e.g., thinking*, then, given the special impredicativity these relations would have, their intersection would be too "small" and their union would be too "large." And there appears to be no reason why there could not in fact exist *several* distinct relations satisfying any candidate inductive characterization of thinking*. The second problem, which is really far more serious, is that an inductive approach seems unable to provide any guarantee that there exists even *one* relation satisfying an inductive characterization of, say, thinking*. When we try to use an in-ductive rationale to prove the existence of such a relation, we seem simply to go round in a circle: given its special impredicativity, we must in effect already know that think-ing* exists in order to be in a position to prove its existence by building up its extension in inductive stages. It appears, therefore, that something more powerful than an induc-tive construction is needed to break out of such circles. What I will show is that a new kind of diagonalization does the job. Moreover, this diagonalization, which is based upon the construction of a special kind of substitution function, will lead to a *direct* definition of the operation * and, in turn, to direct definitions of all the *-counterparts of the standard psychological relations.

The construction is formulated within the framework of informal intensional logic.[38] However, many of the ideas used are borrowed from the formal intensional logic developed in *Quality and Concept*. (This is a convenience; there are alternate, but more cumbersome, terms in which to formulate the construction.) According to this formal theory, each fine-grained intension–i.e., each concept and each proposi-tion–has a unique logical form that is determined by decomposing the intension under the inverses of certain fundamental logical operations (called *proposition-forming op-erations*), e.g., existential generalization, negation, conjunction, singular predica-tion, relativized predication, etc. I call the outcome of this type of decomposition procedure the *decomposition tree* for the original fine-grained intension. Some of the nodes in a decomposition tree may be terminal; others are not terminal. A *terminal node* is one occupied by an entity that cannot be decomposed further under the inverses of the fundamental proposition-forming operations. Such entities, then, are simple with respect to logical form. In each decomposition tree, a node can play one of two roles–formal or substantive. For each application of the inverse of one of the funda-mental proposition-forming operations, there is a corresponding node occupied by that operation. Such nodes are called *formal nodes*. All others are called *substantive*. Among the substantive nodes there is a special kind called *subject nodes*. These nodes are distinguished by the fact that the entities occupying them are the subjects of associ-ated predications. (For example, a occupies a subject node in the decomposition tree of the proposition $[Fa]$ since this proposition results from a singular predication of the property F of the item a.) Every substantive node that is not a subject node is called a *predicate node*. (Thus, the property F occupies a predicate node in the decomposition trees of the propositions $[Fa]$, $[(\exists x)Fx]$, etc.)

I will call a fine-grained intension *purely particular* if its decomposition tree contains no predicate node occupied by the property of being manifested. A fine-grained intension is then called *pure* if its decomposition tree can be obtained from that of some purely particular intension by the following procedure. Working up from ter-minal nodes, we may whenever we wish replace an existential generalization with an associated predication whose predicate node is occupied by the property of being man-ifest, but if we do then all the nodes from which the altered one descends must be adjusted accordingly. For example, if M is the property of being manifest, then

$[(\exists x)\,(\exists y)Rxy]$, $[(\exists x)M\,[Rxy]_y]$, $[M\,[(\exists y)Rxy]_x]$, and $[M\,[M\,[Rxy]_y]_x]$ are the pure propositions that arise via this procedure from the purely particular proposition $[(\exists x)\,(\exists y)Rxy]$. The intuitive idea here is this. A fine-grained intension is pure if each predicative occurrence of M in its decomposition tree is, in effect, a "quasi-formal" node. Specifically, taken together with its adjacent predication operation, each such occurrence of M behaves much the same way as a genuine formal node occupied by the operation of existential generalization. With this in mind, I will as a terminological convenience extend my use of the term 'formal node' so that, whenever the property M occupies a predicate node in the decomposition tree of a pure fine-grained intension, I will also call that node a *formal node*. No confusion should result from this liberalization.

We come now to the generalized Quinean transformation T, which is like the particular/universal transformation t used earlier except that it transforms fine-grained intensions "all the way down." Stated in intuitive terms, the definition of T is this. If x is not a pure fine-grained intension, $T(x) =_{df} x$, and if x is a pure fine-grained intension, then $T(x) =_{df}$ the pure fine-grained intension whose decomposition tree can be obtained from that of x by the following procedure. Working up from the terminal nodes in x's tree, (1) we replace every existential generalization with a suitably associated predication whose predicate node is occupied by M, (2) we replace every predication whose predicate node is occupied by M with an associated existential generalization, and (3) we make corresponding adjustments at every node from which any altered node descends. So, for example:

$$T([(\exists x)\,(\exists y)Rxy]) = [M\,[M\,[Rxy]_y]_x]$$
$$T([M\,[M\,[Rxy]_y]_x]) = [(\exists x)\,(\exists y)Rxy]$$
$$T([(\exists x)M\,[Rxy]_y]) = [M\,[(\exists y)Rxy]_x]$$
$$T([M\,[(\exists y)Rxy]_x]) = [(\exists x)M\,[Rxy]_y]$$
$$T([(\exists u)Ru\,[(\exists x)\,(\exists y)Rxy]]) = [M\,[Ru\,[M\,[M\,[Rxy]_y]_x]]_u].$$

Now let us extend T to finite sequences. If β is a sequence $\beta_1,\ldots,\beta_n$ then we define $T(\beta)$ to be the sequence β' that is just like β except that, for any fine-grained intension β_i that is an element in β, $T(\beta_i)$ is the corresponding element in β'.

So far I have been discussing fine-grained intensions–concepts and propositions. I must now say a word about "coarse-grained" intensions–i.e., properties, relations, and conditions. These intensions are coarse-grained in the sense that their identity conditions are less strict than those of fine-grained intensions. Specifically, coarse-grained intensions are identical if they are necessarily equivalent. Now just as fine-grained intensions are the values of the fundamental proposition-forming operations, coarse-grained intensions are values of fundamental logical operations of a corresponding type; I call these *condition-forming operations*. Of course, since coarse-grained intensions have much weaker identity conditions, the inverses of the condition-forming operations never determine unique decomposition trees for any coarse-grained intension; indeed, each coarse-grained intension has infinitely many such trees. These trees, however, have nothing to do with logical form since coarse-grained intensions are simple with respect to logical form.

In light of the distinction between condition-forming and proposition-forming operations, a terminological stipulation is now in order. Henceforth, when I speak of the singular predication operation, I will always mean the condition-forming operation of singular predication; I will never mean the proposition-forming operation. (Both operations are discussed at length in *Quality and Concept*.) In this connection a few examples of how this operation works might be helpful. The condition that I think, for example, is the result of predicating of me the property thinking; symbolically, $[I \text{ think}] = \text{Pred}([x \text{ thinks}]_x, \text{me})$. Consider next the property of loving Mary. This is the result of predicating of Mary the relation loving; symbolically, $[x \text{ loves Mary}]_x = \text{Pred}([x \text{ loves } y]_{xy}, \text{Mary})$. Consider, finally, an example of self-predication: the property of being identical to the identity relation. This property is the result of predicating the identity relation of the identity relation itself; symbolically, $[x = [x = y]_{xy}]_x = \text{Pred}([x = y]_{xy}, [x = y]_{xy})$.[39]

Next a word on notation is needed. In what follows (and in the previous paragraph) I use the bracket notation to denote coarse-grained intensions. Specifically, I use $[A]$ to denote the condition that A; $[A(v)]_v$ to denote the property of being a v such that $A(v)$; and $[A(v_1, \ldots, v_n)]_{v_1 \ldots v_n}$ to denote the relation among $v_1, \ldots, v_n$ such that $A(v_1, \ldots, v_n)$. I will not use this notation for denoting fine-grained intensions (concepts or propositions). For the sake of readability I will use lower-case Greek letters $\alpha, \beta, \gamma, \delta$ as variables that range over finite sequences. These same letters numerically subscripted will be used as variables that range over the relevant elements of the associated sequences; thus, α_i will indicate the i-th element of the sequence α. (I identify finite sequences, not with set-theoretic entities, but with appropriate properties.)[40] Notice that, although for readability I use several sorts of variables, the definition of $*$ and the ensuing theorems about it will be set forth so that they can be easily written out in a first-order language with a single sort of variable. This is important philosophically, for it guarantees that the construction will have maximum generality.[41]

Let c be any function, and let α be any sequence $\alpha_1, \ldots, \alpha_k$ for $k \geq 1$. I define a substitution function $\alpha(G/c(G))$ on sequences α as follows. Suppose that c always maps properties to properties and i-ary relations to i-ary relations, for each $i \geq 2$. Then $\alpha(G/c(G))$ is the new sequence β whose elements $\beta_1, \ldots, \beta_k$ arise from those of α as a result of the following substitutions. There are three cases. First, an element α_i in α might be an individual or condition. In this case, $\beta_i = \alpha_i$. Second, α_i might be a property or relation. In this case, if $\alpha_i = c(c(\alpha_i))$, then $\beta_i = c(\alpha_i)$, but if $\alpha_i \neq c(c(\alpha_i))$, then $\beta_i = \alpha_i$. Third, α_i might be a fine-grained intension. In this case, β_i is the fine-grained intension whose decomposition tree is just like that of α_i except for the following. Consider any property or relation G that occurs at a nonformal terminal node n in α_i's decomposition tree. If $G = c(c(G))$, then $c(G)$ occurs at node n in β_i's decomposition tree (and corresponding adjustments are then made at all nodes from which n descends), but if $G \neq c(c(G))$, then G itself occurs at node n in β_i's decomposition tree. On the other hand, suppose c does not always map properties to properties and i-ary relations to i-ary relations, for each $i \geqslant 2$; then $\alpha(G/c(G))$ is just α itself.

Consider an example. Suppose that c always maps properties to properties and i-ary relations to i-ary relations, for each $i \geqslant 2$. Let the sequence α consist of three elements: an individual x, the relation believing, and the proposition that someone believes something. Finally, let believing* $= c$(believing). Then, if believing $=$ $c(c$(believing)), $\alpha(G/c(G))$ consists of: x, believing*, and the proposition that someone believes* something. On the other hand, if believing $\neq c(c$(believing)), then $\alpha(G/c(G))$ is simply α itself. Of course, if c does not always map properties to properties and i-ary relations to i-ary relations, for each $i \geqslant 2$, then $\alpha(G/c(G))$ is once again α itself.

I next introduce an operation d on properties and relations. Again there are three cases. First, for $i \geqslant 2$, if F is an i-ary relation that is not necessarily null, then $d(F) =_{df}$ $[\alpha$ satisfies $F]_\alpha$, i.e., the property of being a sequence α that satisfies F. Second, if F is a property that is not necessarily null, then $d(F) =_{df} [(\exists x) (x$ has F & $v = [u = x]_u)]_v$, i.e., the property of being identical to the property of being identical to some item x that has F. Finally, in the degenerate case where F is a necessarily null i-ary relation, $i \geqslant 1$, $d(F) =_{df} [v = i]_v$, i.e., the property of being the natural number i, which is F's degree. Since d is a one-one function, we may define a related one-one function e which takes any property in the range of d back to the property or relation that this property came from: $e(F) =_{df} d^{-1}(F)$ if F is in the range of d; otherwise $e(F)$ $=_{df} F$. The effect of d is to provide a unique property that acts as a "code" for any given property or relation, and the effect of e is to "decode" any such property by turning it back into the original uncoded property or relation it came from.

Let S be some binary relation. Then, given the above definitions, the complex S-based substitution function $\alpha(G/e(\text{Pred}(S,G)))$ is defined on all sequences α, and hence, so is the substitution function $T(\alpha(G/e(\text{Pred}(S,G))))$. Let us call the latter the S-inversion of α. Using this notion, I will now define 'β arises from an F-satisfier via S-inversion' for all properties and relations F. Once again there are three cases. First, for $i \geqslant 2$, let F be an i-ary relation that is not necessarily null. Suppose that, for some α, α satisfies F and β is the sequence that arises from α via S-inversion, i.e., suppose that

$$(\exists \alpha) \, (\alpha \text{ satisfies } F \, \& \, \beta = T(\alpha(G/e(\text{Pred}(S,G))))).$$

Then, I will say that β *arises from an F-satisfier via S-inversion*. Second, let F be a property that is not necessarily null. Suppose that, for some 1-ary sequence α, α has F and β is the property of being identical to the item that arises from α via S-inversion, i.e., suppose that

$$(\exists \alpha) \, (\alpha \text{ has } F \, \& \, \beta = [v = T(\alpha(G/e(\text{Pred}(S,G))))]_v).$$

Then, I will again say that β *arises from an F-satisfier via S-inversion*. Third, for the degenerate case, let F be a necessarily null i-ary relation, $i \geqslant 1$, and let $\beta = i$. Then,

for convenience, I will again say that β *arises from an F-satisfier via S-inversion*.
Consider the following relation Q:

$$[(\forall S)\,(\mathrm{Pred}(R,R) = S \rightarrow \beta \text{ arises from an } F\text{-satisfier via } S\text{-inversion})]_{\beta FR}.$$

Q holds among sequences β, properties or relations F, and relations R such that, if S is the result of predicating R of R, then β arises from an F-satisfier via S-inversion. Now for the diagonalization. Let Q be predicated of Q. The result is:

$$[(\forall S)\,(\mathrm{Pred}(Q,Q) = S \rightarrow \beta \text{ arises from an } F\text{-satisfier via } S\text{-inversion})]_{\beta F}.$$

Let us abbreviate this as follows: $[\mathrm{S}(\beta,F\,)]_{\beta F}$. Then the following is our definition of the operation $*$ on properties and relations F:

$$*(F) =_{df} e\,([\mathrm{S}(\beta,F\,)]_\beta).$$

In the coming paragraphs I will show that this operation is in fact the one we are seeking; that is, I will show that it meets all the requirements set forth in our informal characterization of $*$.

The first step is to prove the following theorem for all sequences β and all properties and relations F:

β satisfies $*(F)$ iff $(\exists \alpha)\,(\alpha$ satisfies F & $\beta = T\,(\alpha(G/*(G))))$.

There are three cases. The first case is that in which F is an i-ary relation, $i \geqslant 2$, that is not necessarily null. For such relations F the theorem follows by putting together a chain of six biconditionals, which I will now present. By the definition of $*$:

(1) β satisfies $*(F)$ iff β satisfies $e\,([\mathrm{S}(\beta,F\,)]_\beta)$.

Since F is an i-ary relation that is not necessarily null, we can easily check that $[\mathrm{S}(\beta,F\,)]_\beta$ is a non-necessarily-null property of i-ary sequences β. Therefore, by the definition of e,

(2) β satisfies $e\,([\mathrm{S}(\beta,F\,)]_\beta)$ iff β has the property $[\mathrm{S}(\beta,F\,)]_\beta$.

The abstraction principle governing the property $[\mathrm{S}(\beta,F\,)]_\beta$ tells us:

(3) β has the property $[\mathrm{S}(\beta,F\,)]_\beta$ iff $\mathrm{S}(\beta,F\,)$.

By expanding 'S' in accordance with the definition, we obtain:

(4) $\mathrm{S}(\beta,F\,)$ iff
      $(\forall S)\,(\mathrm{Pred}(Q,Q) = S \rightarrow \beta$ arises from an F-satisfier via S-inversion).

Since F is an i-ary relation, $i \geqslant 2$, that is not necessarily null, it follows by the definition of 'β arises from an F-satisfier via S-inversion' that:

(5) $(\forall S)\,(\mathrm{Pred}(Q,Q) = S \rightarrow \beta$ arises from an F-satisfier via S-inversion) iff
      $(\forall S)(\mathrm{Pred}(Q,Q) = S \rightarrow (\exists \alpha)\,(\alpha$ satisfies F & $\beta = T(\alpha(G/$
      $e\,(\mathrm{Pred}(S,G))))))$.

Our sixth biconditional requires a more extended argument. By its definition, $[S(\beta,F)]_{\beta F}$ is the unique outcome of predicating Q of Q. But notice that the condition imposed on S in the antecedent of the expanded version of 'S' is that $\mathrm{Pred}(Q,Q) = S$; i.e., S must be the unique outcome of predicating Q of Q. Therefore, $S = [S(\beta,F)]_{\beta F}$. At the same time, $\mathrm{Pred}([S(\beta,F)]_{\beta F},G) = [S(\beta,G)]_{\beta}$. It follows that $e(\mathrm{Pred}(S,G)) = e([S(\beta,G)]_{\beta})$. But by the definition of $*$, $*(G) = e([S(\beta,G)]_{\beta})$. Hence, $e(\mathrm{Pred}(S,G)) = *(G)$. Thus, $T(\alpha(G/e(\mathrm{Pred}(S,G)))) = T(\alpha(G/*(G)))$. Applying this identity, we obtain our sixth biconditional:

(6) $(\forall S)\,(\mathrm{Pred}(Q,Q) = S \rightarrow (\exists\alpha)\,(\alpha \text{ satisfies } F \,\&\, \beta = T(\alpha(G/$
      $e(\mathrm{Pred}(S,G)))))))$ iff $(\exists\alpha)\,(\alpha \text{ satisfies } F \,\&\, \beta = T(\alpha(G/*(G))))$.

Putting these six biconditionals together, we directly establish our theorem for the case in which F is an i-ary relation, $i \geq 2$, that is not necessarily null. By an analogous argument we can establish the theorem for the case in which F is a property that is not necessarily null. And the theorem holds trivially for the case in which F is a necessarily null property or relation. Thus, the theorem holds for all properties and relations F.

What the theorem says is this. For any sequence β, β satisfies $*(F)$ if and only if, for some sequence α, α satisfies F and β is the outcome of performing the compound substitution $T(\alpha(G/*(G)))$. Hence, for any sequence α, if α satisfies F, then $T(\alpha(G/*(G)))$ satisfies $*(F)$. Now let us assume that the compound substitution $T(\alpha(G/*(G)))$ is one-one. That is, assume that, for all α and δ, $\alpha = \delta$ if $T(\alpha(G/*(G))) = T(\delta(G/*(G)))$. Given this assumption, it also follows that, for all sequences α, if $T(\alpha(G/*(G)))$ satisfies $*(F)$, then α satisfies F. Putting these two conclusions together, we obtain:

$T(\alpha(G7*(G)))$ satisfies $*(F)$ iff α satisfies F

for all sequences α.

Let us assume that $*$ always maps properties to properties and i-ary relations to i-ary relations, for each $i \geq 2$. And let us also assume that $G = *(*(G))$ for all properties and relations G. Then, given the conclusion just reached, the sequences $T(\alpha(G/*(G)))$ that satisfy $*(F)$ will be precisely those stipulated in our original informal characterization of the extension of $*(F)$. For they will be the sequences we obtain from those satisfying F if we perform the compound substitutions stipulated in our informal characterization. Specifically, if an element in α is a property or relation G, then the corresponding element in the new sequence is $*(G)$. And if an element in α is a fine-grained intension, then the corresponding element in the new sequence is the fine-grained intension arising from the original via the following two-step procedure. First, we form an intermediate fine-grained intension whose decomposition tree is like that of the original intension except that, for each property or relation G occupying a nonformal terminal node in the original tree, $*(G)$ takes G's place in the new tree, and, in turn, all appropriate adjustments reflecting these changes are made in the new tree. Second, this intermediate intension is then subjected to the generalized Quinean transformation T.

Therefore, if we can prove our three assumptions–(1) the operation $*$ always maps properties to properties and i-ary relations to i-ary relations, for each $i \geqslant 2$; (2) the compound substitution $T(\alpha(G/*(G)))$ is one-one; and (3) $G = *(*(G))$ for all G–then we will be certain that we have indeed constructed the operation $*$ we have been seeking.

To prove proposition (1), assume its contrary. Then, by the definition of $\alpha(G/*(G))$, we know that $\alpha(G/*(G)) = \alpha$. Given this and the above theorem it is trivial to verify that $*$ always maps properties to properties and i-ary relations to i-ary relations, for each $i \geqslant 2$. Thus, the hypothesis leads to a contradiction, and so proposition (1) must be true.

The generalized Quinean transformation T was expressly constructed as a one-one operation. Thus, to prove proposition (2), we must only prove that $\alpha = \delta$ if $\alpha(G/*(G)) = \delta(G/*(G))$. Suppose that $\alpha(G/*(G)) = \delta(G/*(G)) = \beta$. To show that $\alpha = \delta$, we show that $\alpha_i = \delta_i$ for each element α_i in α and δ_i in δ. Given proposition (1), it is easy to verify that α_i and β_i must be the same type of entity–individual, condition, property, relation, or fine-grained intension. Likewise for δ_i and β_i. Therefore, α_i and δ_i must be the same type of entity, too. Suppose α_i and δ_i are individuals or conditions. Then since the substitution procedure leaves these types of entities unchanged, $\alpha_i = \beta_i$ and $\delta_i = \beta_i$. So $\alpha_i = \delta_i$. Suppose that α_i and δ_i are properties or that they are relations. First, we show that $*(*(\alpha_i)) = \alpha_i$ iff $*(*(\delta_i)) = \delta_i$. Suppose otherwise. For example, suppose $*(*(\alpha_i)) \neq \alpha_i$ and $*(*(\delta_i)) = \delta_i$. Then, given proposition (1) and the definition of $\alpha(G/*(G))$, it follows that $\beta_i = \alpha_i$. And given proposition (1) and the definition of $\delta(G/*(G))$, it follows that $\beta_i = *(\delta_i)$. Given these two conclusions, it follows that $\alpha_i = *(\delta_i)$. Hence, by an application of $*$, $*(\alpha_i) = *(*(\delta_i))$. Then, by our hypothesis that $*(*(\delta_i)) = \delta_i$, it follows that $*(\alpha_i) = \delta_i$. Therefore, by another application of $*$, $*(*(\alpha_i)) = *(\delta_i)$. Thus, by our conclusion that $\alpha_i = *(\delta_i)$, it follows that $*(*(\alpha_i)) = \alpha_i$ contradicting our hypothesis that $*(*(\alpha_i)) \neq \alpha_i$. By an analogous argument we can show that it is impossible that $*(*(\alpha_i)) = \alpha_i$ and $*(*(\delta_i)) \neq \delta_i$. Therefore, there are only two possible cases: (1) $*(*(\alpha_i)) \neq \alpha_i$ and $*(*(\delta_i)) \neq \delta_i$, and (2) $*(*(\alpha_i)) = \alpha_i$ and $*(*(\delta_i)) = \delta_i$. Suppose the former. Then, given proposition (1) and the definition of $\alpha(G/*(G))$, $\beta_i = \alpha_i$. And given proposition (1) and the definition of $\delta(G/*(G))$, $\beta_i = \delta_i$. Hence, $\alpha_i = \delta_i$. Or suppose the latter. Then, given proposition (1) and the definition of $\alpha(G/*(G))$, $\beta_i = *(\alpha_i)$. And given proposition (1) and the definition of $\delta(G/*(G))$, $\beta_i = *(\delta_i)$. Thus, $*(\alpha_i) = *(\delta_i)$. Hence, by an application of $*$, $*(*(\alpha_i)) = *(*(\delta_i))$. Therefore, by the hypothesis that $*(*(\alpha_i)) = \alpha_i$ and $*(*(\delta_i)) = \delta_i$ it follows that $\alpha_i = \delta_i$ once again. Consider, finally, the possibility that α_i and δ_i are fine-grained intensions. We know, by the definition of $*$, that any difference between the decomposition tree of α_i and that of β_i arises from differences in their nonformal terminal nodes resulting from replacing some property or relation G with $*(G)$. Likewise for the decomposition tree of δ_i and that of β_i. Therefore, any difference between the decomposition tree of α_i and that of β_i results from a difference between a property or relation G occupying a nonformal terminal node in the one and a property or relation H occupying the corresponding nonformal terminal node in the other. However, by an argument exactly like that given a moment ago, we can prove that for every such G and H, $G = H$. Therefore, there can be no difference between the decomposition tree of α_i and that of δ_i. Hence, $\alpha_i = \delta_i$ once again. Since this exhausts all possible cases, $\alpha = \delta$. And this completes our proof.

Next we prove that $*(*(F)) = F$ for any property or relation F. For each sequence α, there is a unique sequence β that arises from α via our substitution procedure and there is a unique sequence γ that arises from β via the same procedure; i.e., for each α, there is a unique β and a unique γ such that $\beta = T(\alpha(G/*(G)))$ and $\gamma = T(\beta(G/*(G)))$. We begin by showing that each element α_i in α is identical to the corresponding element γ_i in γ. Let an element α_i in α be an individual (or condition). Then the corresponding element β_i in β–and, in turn, the element γ_i in γ–is just that individual (condition). Thus, $\alpha_i = \gamma_i$. Let α_i be a property or a relation. Suppose that $\alpha_i \neq *(*(\alpha_i))$. Then, given proposition (1) and the definition of $\alpha(G/*(G))$, $\beta_i = \alpha_i$. Therefore, by substitution of β_i for α_i in the hypothesis, $\beta_i \neq *(*(\beta_i))$. Thus, given proposition (1) and the definition of $\beta(G/*(G))$, $\gamma_i = \beta_i$. Hence, by our conclusion that $\beta_i = \alpha_i$, $\alpha_i = \gamma_i$. On the other hand, suppose that $\alpha_i = *(*(\alpha_i))$. Then, given proposition (1) and the definition of $\alpha(G/*(G))$, $\beta_i = *(\alpha_i)$. Hence, by an application of $*$, $*(\beta_i) = *(*(\alpha_i))$. Therefore, by the hypothesis, $*(\beta_i) = \alpha_i$. Hence, by another application of $*$, $*(*(\beta_i)) = *(\alpha_i)$. So, by our conclusion that $\beta_i = *(\alpha_i)$, it follows that $*(*(\beta_i)) = \beta_i$. Therefore, given proposition (1) and the definition of $\beta(G/*(G))$, $\gamma_i = *(\beta_i)$. Hence, by our conclusion that $*(\beta_i) = \alpha_i$, $\gamma_i = \alpha_i$ once again. Finally, let α_i be a fine-grained intension. We know that there is a one-to-one correspondence between the nonformal terminal nodes in α_i's decomposition tree and those in β_i's decomposition tree and between those in β_i's decomposition tree and those in γ_i's decomposition tree. Hence, there is a one-to-one correspondence between the nonformal terminal nodes in α_i's decomposition tree and those in γ_i's. Moreover, our generalized Quinean transformation T is such that $\Theta = T(T(\Theta))$ for every fine-grained intension Θ. Therefore, the formal nodes in α_i's decomposition tree are the same as those in γ_i's decomposition tree. Hence, if there is a difference between α_i's decomposition tree and γ_i's decomposition tree, it must result from a difference between the items occupying the nonformal terminal nodes in α_i's tree and the items occupying the corresponding nonformal terminal nodes in γ_i's tree. However, individuals and conditions are always left alone by the substitution procedure. So if there is a difference between any item G occupying a nonformal terminal node in α_i's tree and the item H occupying the corresponding nonformal terminal node in γ_i's tree, then G and H are properties or they are relations. However, by an argument exactly like that given for properties and relations a moment ago, $G = H$ if G and H are properties or if they are relations. It follows, therefore, that there can be no difference between the decomposition trees of α_i and γ_i. Hence $\alpha_i = \gamma_i$. Since $\alpha_i = \gamma_i$ for all α_i in α and γ_i in γ, $\alpha = \gamma$. And, this holds for all α and γ such that, for some β, $\beta = T(\alpha(G/*(G)))$ and $\gamma = T(\beta(G/*(G)))$. Now given our first theorem and proposition (2), we know that for each such α, β, and γ, α satisfies F iff β satisfies $*(F)$ iff γ satisfies $*(*(F))$. Combining this with our conclusion that $\alpha = \gamma$ for each such α and γ, we obtain the following. For each α, α satisfies F iff α satisfies $*(*(F))$. Since all of the above holds necessarily, it follows, therefore, that F and $*(*(F))$ are necessarily equivalent. But since properties and relations are coarse-grained intensions, they are identical if necessarily equivalent. Thus, $F = *(*(F))$ for all properties and relations F. And this completes the proof.

As a notational convenience, let us extend our usage of $*$ to fine-grained intensions: if Θ is a fine-grained intension, $*(\Theta)$ is defined to be the fine-grained intension that results when the 1-ary sequence Θ is subjected to our substitution procedure for fine-grained intensions; i.e., $*(\Theta) =_{df} T(\Theta(G/*(G)))$. Now when we were dealing with the elementary belief/desire model in the previous section, our argument repeatedly invoked the following lemma: for any proposition p, $p \approx_N t(p)$; i.e., p is necessarily equivalent to $t(p)$. In the present setting, the lemma that would play an analogous role would be this: for any proposition p, $p \approx_N *(p)$.

To facilitate the proof of this lemma, let us also extend our usage of $*$ to cover individuals and conditions: if Θ is an individual or a condition, $*(\Theta)$ is defined to be Θ itself. Given this, $*$ is now defined on all types of things–individuals, properties, relations, conditions, and fine-grained intensions. The first step is to use proposition (3) to prove the following generalization: $\Theta = *(*(\Theta))$ for any item Θ. I will omit the proof since it is straightforward. Next, for any item Θ, if $*(\Theta) = \tau$, let us use the expression Θ^* to denote τ. Also, let us use $[A]$ to denote the proposition that A.

Now for the proof of the lemma. If α is a sequence $\alpha_1,\ldots, \alpha_i$, then by definition $T(\alpha(G/*(G)))$ is the sequence $\alpha_1^*,\ldots, \alpha_i^*$. We have proved that, necessarily, α satisfies F iff $T(\alpha(G/*(G)))$ satisfies F^*. Thus, necessarily, $\alpha_1,\ldots, \alpha_i$ satisfies F iff $\alpha_1^*,\ldots, \alpha_i^*$ satisfies F^*. Therefore, necessarily, $F\alpha_1,\ldots, \alpha_i$ iff $F^*\alpha_1^*,\ldots, \alpha_i^*$.[42] (Call this the *basic equivalence*.) Hence, the atomic proposition $[F\alpha_1,\ldots, \alpha_i]$ is necessarily equivalent to the atomic proposition $[F^*\alpha_1^*,\ldots, \alpha_i^*]$. Suppose that F is not the property of being manifest; i.e., suppose that $F \neq M$. Then, by definition of $*$, $*([F\alpha_1,\ldots,\alpha_i]) = [F^*\alpha_1^*,\ldots, \alpha_i^*]$. Thus $[F\alpha_1,\ldots, \alpha_i] \approx_N *([F\alpha_1,\ldots, \alpha_i])$. For our next case, consider any atomic proposition whose predicate is M and whose subject z is anything that is not a complex 1-ary intension. Suppose that z is a non-property or that $z = M$, then $[Mz]$ is an impure proposition. Therefore, by definition of $*$, $*([Mz]) = [M^*z^*]$. However, by the basic equivalence, we know that $[Mz] \approx_N [M^*z^*]$. So $[Mz] \approx_N *([Mz])$. Or suppose that z is a property G that is distinct from M. Then, $[Mz] = [M[Gx]_x]$. By definition of $*$, $*([M[Gx]_x]) = [(\exists x)G^*x]$. By the basic equivalence, we know that, necessarily, for all x and x^*, Gx iff G^*x^*. Using this, we will show that $[(\exists x)Gx] \approx_N [(\exists x)G^*x]$. Suppose $[(\exists x)Gx]$ holds. Then, for some x, $[Gx]$ holds, and, hence, so does $[G^*x^*]$. And, thus, $[(\exists x)G^*x]$ holds. For the other direction, suppose that $[(\exists x)G^*x]$ holds. Then, for some x, $[G^*x]$ holds. But given our theorem that, for all x, $x = *(*(x))$, we know that $x = *(y)$ where $y = *(x)$ and, therefore, that $x = y^*$. Consequently, $[G^*y^*]$ holds and, hence, so does $[Gy]$. And thus, $[(\exists x)Gx]$

holds. Since these relationships hold necessarily, it follows that, necessarily, $[(\exists x)Gx]$ holds iff $[(\exists x)G^*x]$ holds. Thus, $[(\exists x)Gx] \approx_N [(\exists x)G^*x]$. However, it is a logical truth that $[(\exists x)Gx] \approx_N [M[Gx]_x]$. Hence, $[M[Gx]_x] \approx_N [(\exists x)G^*x]$. But $*([M[Gx]_x]) = [(\exists x)G^*x]$. Therefore, $[M[Gx]_x] \approx_N *([M[Gx]_x])$. Summing up, suppose that p is an atomic proposition whose predicate is either a property other than M or a relation, or suppose that p is an atomic proposition whose predicate is M and whose subject is anything that is not a complex 1-ary intension. Then $p \approx_N *(p)$. Beginning with this conclusion for the above types of atomic propositions, we can argue by induction on the complexity of the remaining types of propositions that $p \approx_N *(p)$ for all p. There are four cases: (1) molecular propositions, (2) general propositions, (3) atomic propositions in which the predicate is M and the subject is a complex 1-ary intension, (4) atomic propositions in which the predicate is a complex i-ary intension, $i \geq 1$. The ideas used in the proofs are straightforward variants of those used in the proofs for the initial atomic cases.

It is easy to check that $*$ leaves all physical properties and relations unchanged, and it leaves a number of logical properties and relations unchanged, e.g., M, necessity, $=$, $\approx_N$, and $*$ itself. But can we be sure that $*$ alters the standard psychological relations; i.e., can we be sure that $R \neq *(R)$ for the standard psychological relations R?[43] (An affirmative answer is required for at least one such R if our construction is to refute functionalism.) To see that the answer is affirmative, consider the standard propositional attitude thinking. The generalized Quinean transformation T insures that $p \neq p^*$ for every pure proposition whose decomposition tree contains a formal node occupied by M or by existential generalization. Consider any such p. We know that, since $p \neq p^*$, it is not necessary that x thinks p iff x thinks p^*. At the same time, we know by the basic equivalence that, necessarily, x thinks p iff x thinks* p^*. It follows, therefore, that thinking and thinking* can have divergent extensions and, hence, that they are significantly distinct relations. Of course, thinking and thinking* can be multiply embedded within propositions that someone might think or think*. Therefore, the fact that thinking and thinking* are distinct produces an explosion in the possible ways the extensions of thinking and thinking* can diverge. And this, in turn, produces a chain reaction, namely, further possible ways in which the extensions of other propositional attitudes and of their $*$-counterparts can diverge. Furthermore, the distinction between thinking and thinking* guarantees that the extensions of introspecting and introspecting* can be distinct. The reason is this. A person x can introspect that xRy only if R is one of the conscious operations of mind (e.g., thinking); however, for suitable y, a person x can introspect* that xRy, where R is one of the $*$-counterparts of a conscious operation of mind (e.g., where R is thinking*). Likewise, the distinction between thinking and thinking* guarantees that, given the traditional empiricist theory of experience, the extensions of experiencing and experiencing* can be distinct. For although a person can experience the conscious operations of mind, he cannot experience their $*$-counterparts; however, a person can experience* the $*$-counterparts of the conscious operations of mind.

The operation $*$ has been constructed so that we can prove that the system of $*$-relations satisfies all the psychological principles we have been discussing in this paper, including even those for the self-conscious rational mind. To begin with, the proofs for the principles in the elementary belief/desire model are virtually identical to those given in the previous section except that (1) we make use of the fact that $p \approx_N *(p)$ where previously we made use of the fact that $p \approx_N t(p)$ and (2) we make use of the fact that xS^*p iff $xS*(p)$ where previously we made use of the fact that xS^*p iff $xSt(p)$. To see how the proofs go for the principles characterizing the self-conscious rational mind, let us start with the Infallibility principle. Given that principle, we wish to derive the following for arbitrary p:

If x thinks* that x thinks* p, then x thinks* p.

But, given our lemma and given that $p^* = q$, for some q, we see that this is actually equivalent to the following instance of the original Infallibility principle:

If x thinks that x thinks q, then x thinks q.

Thus, if the latter conditional is true, so is the former. And this completes the proof. Next consider the Introspection principle. Given this principle, we wish to derive the following for arbitrary p:

If x is thinking* p and x is entertaining* the proposition that x is thinking* p, then x introspects* that x is thinking* p.

However, given our lemma, and given that $p^* = q$, for some q, this is just equivalent to the following instance of the original Introspection principle:

If x is thinking q^* and x is entertaining the proposition that x is thinking q^*, then x introspects that x is thinking q^*.

Hence, if the latter conditional is true, so is the former. For a final example, consider the a priori Knowledge principle. Given this principle, we want to derive the following for arbitrary p:

If p is necessary and x clearly and distinctly understands* p, then x knows* p.

But given our lemma and given that $p^* = q$, for some q, this is just equivalent to the following instance of the original a priori Knowledge principle:

If q is necessary and x clearly and distinctly understands q, then x knows q.

Thus, if the latter conditional is true, the former is too. Furthermore, these results can be generalized in a a variety of ways. Indeed, our situation is quite analogous to the one we were in when we were generalizing our results concerning the elementary belief/desire model. In particular, we may use each of the resources developed in that context in order to obtain generalizations of comparable strength. (We might need to adjust the details to handle certain nonstandard logical or philosophical theories.) The conclusion is that the principles of psychology–even when they include principles for a sophisticated self-conscious rational mind–do not implicitly define the standard mental relations.

Do the *-counterparts of the standard psychological relations have the same causal roles as the standard relations? By an argument like that used in the previous section, we can show that every event of thinking* is an event of thinking and every event of thinking is an event of thinking*. Likewise for every other standard psychological relation and its *-counterpart. Thus, there exists no asymmetry in causal roles.[44] We have a complete system of relations that is functionally indistinguishable from the system of standard psychological relations.

THE STATUS OF MIND

We have a complete system of inverted relations that satisfies all the psychological principles satisfied by the standard psychological relations. It follows, therefore, that the principles of psychology do not implicitly define the standard psychological relations and, hence, do not provide a basis for direct functional definitions of them either. Moreover, because of their special modal ties to the standard psychological relations, these inverted relations cannot be distinguished from the standard relations in terms of causal role. Causally, the inverted relations are completely indistinguishable from the standard relations. Thus, the primary thesis of functionalism is untenable.

Those who are attracted to functionalism have two choices at this juncture. They can *abandon* functionalism and begin anew their search for a satisfactory theory of mind. Or they can *revise* their theory within a more powerful logical and metaphysical framework, namely, one with the ontology of qualities and connections. I will now say a few words on how this revision would go and on the metaphysical picture that results.

Consider the difference between green and blue, on the one hand, and grue and bleen, on the other. We can give logically necessary and sufficient conditions for grue and bleen in terms of green and blue, and we can give logically necessary and sufficient conditions for green and blue in terms of grue and bleen. However, only green and blue are genuine *qualities*. Grue and bleen are not; they are mere "Cambridge properties." Therefore, green and blue are logically and metaphysically prior to grue and bleen. Accordingly, on a logically and metaphysically strict conception of definition, grue and bleen are definable in terms of green and blue, but green and blue are not definable in terms of grue and bleen. In the domain of relations there is an analogous distinction. Many relations are grue-like "Cambridge relations." Others, however, are logically and metaphysically basic. Only these are genuine *connections*. If we are limning the true and ultimate structure of reality, the canonical scheme is that of qualities and connections; Cambridge properties and relations are wholly derivative. Or so this theory goes.

We have stated logically necessary and sufficient conditions for thinking* in terms of thinking, and we have stated logically necessary and sufficient conditions for thinking in terms of thinking[*]. And likewise for the other standard psychological relations and their inverted counterparts. However, it does not follow that on a metaphysically and logically strict conception of definition the standard psychological relations are definable in terms of their inverted counterparts. For just as green and blue are genuine qualities (namely, sensible qualities) and grue and bleen mere Cambridge properties, so the standard psychological relations might be genuine connections and their inverted counterparts mere Cambridge relations. Let us suppose that this is so. Then, by revising the earlier functionalist definitions, one can avoid the threat posed by the inverted relations. The revision consists of adding to the earlier definitions a new clause requiring that all the key relations involved be genuine connections.

This revison has two philosophically significant consequences, however. First, it would commit its proponents to the prospect of a purely logical analysis of intentionality and mind of the sort I have advocated elsewhere.[45] For that analysis begins with the premise that the standard psychological relations–or at least the basic psychological relations in terms of which the others are definable–are genuine connections and, hence, that they are logically and metaphysically basic. Then the analysis attributes to psychological connections certain characteristic logical properties, all of which are entailed by any moderately rich list of psychological principles. Thus, the revised definitions would incorporate both components of this purely logical analysis of intentionality and mind. Second, the revised definitions would rule out the prospect of saving any philosophically interesting form of materialism. (This prospect is what attracted many of the adherents of functionalism in the first place.) The reason philosophically interesting forms of materialism would be ruled out is that, given the revised definitions, the standard psychological relations would form a new category of connections that is logically different from the category of physical connections. For according to those definitions, the standard psychological relations would be identical to (or necessarily included in) connections that can contingently connect an individual to an intension independently of how that intension is realized in the world; as a categorial fact, physical connections can never have this distinctive logical character.[46] Therefore, since mental activity always involves mental connections, there is something essentially non-physical in all mental activity. But this is something that all philosophically interesting forms of materialism deny. In summary, perhaps the revised definitions succeed. But they entail an expanded conception of logic inasmuch as they commit one to the prospect of a purely logical analysis of intentionality and mind. And they entail an elevated, anti-materialist conception of the mind's metaphysical position in the universe.

More refined alterations of functionalism might be possible within this logical framework, but in the end the conclusion of the dialectic is always the same–no revised doctrine can succeed without elevating the mind well beyond any interesting materialist conception.

In informal terms what the existence of mind and anti-mind shows is this. We are in principle unable to identify the standard mental relations from the "outside," except perhaps by invoking a formulation that attributes to the mind a metaphysically basic, non-material character. In spite of this, we are certain that we can already identify these relations even in the absence of such a formulation. The only explanation is that we have access to the mind from the "inside."

Notes

1. George Myro, a brilliant philosopher and generous friend, has helped during each phase of my thinking about this topic. Donald Davidson, Jaegwon Kim, and Brian Loar made valuable points in preliminary conversations. Mark Bedau and David Reeve have contributed important comments and revisions, and Charles Wasson has done a dedicated and expert job editing, typing, and proofreading.

2. To illustrate, let us suppose that $A(S_1,...,S_n)$ is the conjunction of the psychological principles that are supposed to define implicitly the standard mental relations $S_1,...,S_n$. Let $A(R_1,...,R_n)$ be the result of substituting variables 'R_1',..., 'R_n' for the constants 'S_1',..., 'S_n'. Then, the following would be a direct functional definition of the relation S_1 based on the theory A: $S_1 =_{df}$ the unique relation R_1 such that there exist unique relations $R_2,...,R_n$ that, together with R_1, make the theory $A(R_1,...,R_n)$ come out true when we hold constant the interpretation of the physical and logical constants in A. See my paper "An Inconsistency in Functionalism," *Synthese* 38 (1978): 333-72, for a discussion of the various kinds of direct functional definitions.

A word is in order about the identity conditions of properties, relations, and propositions. In this paper I will adopt the standard practice of treating properties as identical if they are necessarily equivalent and of treating relations (of equal degree) as identical if they are necessarily equivalent. However, I will treat propositions as more "fine-grained" than this, for in thought we can cut distinctions more finely than necessary equivalence.

3. Since such functional definitions would contain only physical and logical constants, functionalism is consistent with physicalism of the terminological variety.

4. I should add that the construction can be adapted to refute functional theories and reductionistic theories in any subject area where "fine-grained" intensionality plays a role. Thus, it can be adapted to refute many forms of functionalism and reductionism in linguistics, social and political theory, legal theory, ethics and aesthetics. And it can be adapted to refute many forms of the currently popular "causal theory" of reference, meaning, and mind.

5. There are some damaging technical criticims based upon the results given in my paper "An Inconsistency in Functionalism" and upon those given in S. Thomas, *The Formal Mechanics of Mind* (Ithaca, N.Y., 1978). I will not discuss these criticisms in this paper since they presuppose knowledge of recursive functions. However, I do wish to note that some commentators have failed to grasp the significance of these criticisms, perhaps as a result of their liberal use of mathematical logic. For example, Ned Block ("Introduction: What Is Functionalism?" *Readings in Philosophy of Psychology*, vol. 1 [Cambridge, Mass., 1980], 171-84) erroneously reports that the aim of "An Inconsistency in Functionalism" is to show that functionalism can be made to fit a certain formal definition of behaviorism, and then, without giving any argument, Block concludes that the technical result in the paper is "misguided" because it "blurs the distinctions between functionalism and behaviorism." This is seriously confused. First, my criticism of functionalism is expressly aimed at physiologically oriented functionalism as well as behaviorally oriented functionalism. Second, the aim of the paper is not at all to get functionalism to "fit" a definition of behaviorism; that would be silly. Nor are the distinctions between functionalism and behaviorism blurred. The technical result in the paper is a proof that a functional definition is *adequate* if and only if there also exists an adequate non-functional definition. Now functionalism is based upon a few well-known negative arguments to the effect that the non-functional definitions envisaged by behaviorists and psycho-physiological reductionists must always be inadequate. However, if these arguments are sound, we can easily generalize them so that they will apply to all the non-functional definitions of the kind dealt with in my technical result. (From a formal point of view, it makes absolutely no difference to the success of these negative arguments

that some of these non-functional definitions might be wholly impractical, and it makes no difference that some of these definitions might be more complex than those envisaged by many behaviorists.) Therefore, it follows that, if the functionalist's negative arguments are sound, then his proposed functional definitions can never be adequate. Hence, the inconsistency in functionalism. For some reason Block thinks that this criticism turns on what historically counted as behaviorism; but plainly that question is irrelevant.

6. For example, J. Paul Churchland, "Eliminative Materialism and the Propositional Attitudes," *Journal of Philosophy* 77 (1981):67-90. For a powerful argument against eliminative materialism, see George Myro, "Aspects of Acceptability," *Pacific Philosophical Quarterly* 62 (1981):107-22.

7. For example, Tyler Burge, "Individualism and the Mental," *Midwest Studies in Philosophy* 4 (1979):73-122.

8. Such a theory is developed in sec. 39, "Pragmatics," in my book *Quality and Concept* (Oxford, 1982).

9. Ned Block, "Troubles With Functionalism," in *Perception and Cognition: Issues in the Foundations of Psychology*, edited by C. W. Savage, Minnesota Studies in the Philosophy of Science, vol. 9 (Minneapolis, 1978), 261-325.

10. Douglas R. Hofstadter, "Who Am I Anyway?" *New York Review of Books*, May 29, 1980.

11. See, for example, Ned Block and Jerry Fodor, "What Mental States Are Not," *Philosophical Review* 81 (1972):159-81; Sydney Shoemaker, "The Inverted Spectrum," *Journal of Philosophy* (1982):357-82.

12. There is some confusion over what the functionalist's thesis implies. It does not imply that sensible qualities (e.g., the various shades of red) have functional definitions; nor does it imply that such properties as the property of sensing-red or the property of having-an-experience-of-red are functionally definable. Rather it implies that, given an arbitrary quality F (e.g., a shade of color), the property of sensing F or the property of having an experience of F has a functional definition. This, in turn, implies that the relation of sensing or the relation of experiencing has a functional definition. We can, of course, experience "reflective" qualities (e.g., sadness), which are psychological by nature. The functionalist is committed to the functional definability of these special qualities. But can distinct reflective qualities be perfectly equivalent functionally? Perhaps, but the problem is that no one seems able to give a conclusive argument for this view, and there are some plausible considerations that seem to count against it. See, e.g., David Lewis, "Mad Pain and Martian Pain," in Block, *Readings*, 216-22.

13. Another candidate counterexample, which bears some resemblance to the inverted-spectrum example, is based on the alleged possibility of "absent qualia," i.e., the possibility that there could be a psychological state that is functionally equivalent to one involving, say, sensing red but that does not involve any sensible quality at all. (See Block and Fodor, "What Mental States Are Not"; Sydney Shoemaker, "Functionalism and Qualia," *Philosophical Studies* 22 [1975]:291-315, and "Are Absent Qualia Impossible–A Reply to Block," *Philosophical Review* 90 [1981]: 581-99; Ned Block, "Are Absent Qualia Impossible?" *Philosophical Review* 89 [1980]:257-74.) However, considerations analogous to those just given in connection with the inverted-spectrum example show that this type of counterexample is also inconclusive.

14. John R. Searle, "Minds, Brains, and Programs," *Behavioral and Brain Sciences* 3 (1980):417-24. I have heard of a somewhat related example, namely, that of some computer game software with the following intriguing property. When this software is used with one type of computer hardware, a certain game is "played"; but when it is used with another type of computer hardware, a quite distinct game is "played." Although this example is also very suggestive, it cannot be used to refute functionalism, for it is open to the same kind of rejoinder the functionalist may use against the Chinese-room example. In particular, following a program is not sufficient for *playing* a game. Playing a game requires *knowing* how to play the game and *intending* to do so. Using a chain of reasoning analogous to that used in reply to the Chinese-room example, we are driven to the following conclusion. To use the example in a refutation of functionalism, we must already have established the existence of a global system of new relations–knowing*, intending*, etc.–that is functionally isomorphic to, yet distinct from, the system of standard psychological relations–knowing, intending, etc. But if we could do this, we would already have succeeded in refuting functionalism quite

independently of the present example. So once again we are no closer to a refutation of functionalism.

15. For example, the versions of Lewis, Harman, Shoemaker, Loar, and others. It should also be emphasized that, just as functionalism is not tied to the Turing-machine doctrine, it is not tied to the language-of-thought thesis, i.e., the thesis that the immediate objects of thought are mere syntactic entities. David Lewis, for example, is adamantly opposed to this thesis. Incidentally, if the Chinese-room example were to refute Turing-machine functionalism, would it follow that we intentional beings are not Turing machines? Yes and no. The example would show that being a Turing machine is not a sufficient condition for intentionality, but it would do nothing to show that being a Turing machine is not a necessary condition. Thus, as far as the example is concerned, every intentional being might have to be a species of Turing machine, i.e., a Turing machine with some special additional feature.

16. Two observations are in order. First, in this paper I use 'thinks' to single out a central use of 'believes', viz., the use often conveyed in philosophical discussion by 'occurrently believes'; I do not use 'thinks' in the sense of 'entertains'. Second, in the definitions of the inverted relations, '$t(p)$' is intended to have narrow scope.

17. In symbols, $(p \ \& \ \boxed{c} \ (p \leftrightarrow x \ \text{entertains} \ p)) \to x \ \text{thinks} \ p$. This is a coarse approximation of a causal theory of perceptual belief.

18. For example, we could give the construction in the setting of a "world-relative" and time-relative treatment of identity: accordingly, relative to any given "possible world" and any given time, $h_x(v)$ would be identified with an appropriate ordinary object or region of space. Or we could rephrase the second clause in the definition of h_x thus: $h_x(v) =_{df}$ the object u such that, if x exists, u is the ordinary object (if there is one; otherwise, u is the region) that is located at the same distance d ($d \geqslant 0$) from the plane $l(x)$ as v but on the opposite side, and if x does not exist, $u = v$. Then in the definition of t_x we would treat the notation 'a_i'', $i \geqslant 1$, as a defined descriptive expression: $a_i' =_{df} h_x(a_i)$.

19. Any question about the uniqueness of $h_x(v)$ can be resolved by any of a number of standard techniques. For example, if v is an ordinary physical object, let $h_x(v)$ be the mereological union of the objects satisfying the remainder of the defining condition for $h_x(v)$; and if $v = h_x(v')$ for some ordinary physical object v', let $h_x(v) = v'$.

20. That is, the following principle is valid for all logical operators Θ in T: if it is necessary that A iff B, then $\Theta(A)$ iff $\Theta(B)$.

21. This complementarity neutralizes the functional significance of differences in logical form between, say, particularese propositions and universalese propositions.

22. The following is a principle of this type that fails to be satisfied by thinking*: if x is a *Homo sapiens* (or if x is George Bealer) and x's eyes are focused on x's moving left hand, then, in all probability, x will think that it moves.

23. Another functionalist response would be to restrict the range of the relations over which he quantifies in his candidate functional definitions; specifically, he might restrict the eligible relations to those that are "internal." (See, e.g., Ned Block, "Psychologism and Behaviorism," *Philosophical Review* 90 [1981]:5-43.) However, this response is of no help if 'internal' is intended to mean either physically internal or causally independent of things "outside" (e.g., physically separate from) the individual agent or anything in this vein. For our inverted relations thinking*, etc. are in these respects every bit as internal as the standard propositional attitudes. Like the standard propositional attitudes, the inverted relations are realized "in" us all the time. Indeed, it is necessary that xSp iff $xS^*t(p)$ and $xSt(p)$ iff xS^*p, for every particular x, every proposition p, and every standard propositional attitude S and its inverted counterpart S^*. So, for example, every time you think that there exists a rabbit, you are also thinking* that rabbithood is manifest. And this is so whether or not you realize it. On the other hand, if 'internal' is intended to mean "psychologically internal" in the sense of being present to the mind, the present response only undermines functionalism. For the central thesis of functionalism is that the standard psychological relations are functionally definable without recourse to psychological terms. But 'internal' in the last sense is patently psychological.

24. If t is the particular/universal transformation, something even stronger holds. The following will help to show what it is: for any sentence A, there is a sentence B such that it is provable that, necessarily, the

proposition that $B = t$(that A) and, in turn, it is provable that, necessarily, x thinks that B if and only if x thinks t(that A).

25. Some more complex examples will help to dramatize the point. Thus, t(the proposition that the property of hitting someone is manifest) = the proposition that someone is such that the property of being hit by him is manifest. In symbols, $t([M[(\exists y)Hxy]_x]) = [(\exists x)M[Hxy]_y]$. Or t(the proposition that someone hits someone) = the proposition that the property of being someone such that the property of being hit by him is manifest is itself a manifest property. In symbols, $t([(\exists x)(\exists y)Hxy]) = [M[M[Hxy]_y]_x]$. Or just try the proposition that someone gives something to someone; in symbols, $t([(\exists x)(\exists y)(\exists z)Gxyz]) = [M[M[M[Gxyz]_z]_y]_x]$. Clearly, we can think such particularese propositions without even being able to understand their universalese counterparts. Of course, with practice we could readily think the latter, and no doubt there could be beings who naturally think the latter but have trouble thinking the former.

26. This point was inspired by conversation with Donald Davidson.

27. The following example makes the same point even more directly. Suppose that type-a beings think S iff physical inscriptions of the pure abstract shape S occur in the "thinking centers" in their brains and that they think $t(S)$ iff physical inscriptions of the pure abstract shape $t(S)$ occur there. And suppose that type-b beings think S iff physical inscriptions of the pure abstract shape $t(S)$ occur in their "thinking centers" and that they think $t(S)$ iff physical inscriptions of the pure abstract shape S occur there. According to functionalism, since S and $t(S)$ have a direct structural isomorphism to one another (i.e., the function t itself), the causal role of inscriptions of S in type-a beings would be identical to the causal role of inscriptions of $t(S)$ in type-b beings, and the causal role of inscriptions of $t(S)$ in type-a beings would be identical to the causal role of inscriptions of S in type-b beings. Therefore, according to functionalism, type-a and type-b beings would be functionally indistinguishable. Thus, a physical inscription in a being's "thinking center" of a Mentalese sentence S (i.e., a physical inscription of the pure abstract shape S) is on its own no indication of whether the being is thinking S or whether it is thinking $t(S)$ instead. (Of course, it is far-fetched to think that physical inscriptions of the pure abstract shapes S and $t(S)$ would occur in any more than the smallest fraction of the possible beings who think S or think $t(S)$.)

28. Of course, the fact that actual physical inscriptions of syntactic entities can occur in the brains of these other types of beings is of no help. For just as type-a and type-b form a functionally indistinguishable complementary pair, these other types also come in functionally indistinguishable complementary pairs. For example, type-c beings might think S iff an inscription of the sentence B in langauge L occurs in their "thinking centers," and they might think $t(S)$ iff an inscription of $k(B)$ occurs there. And type-d beings might think S iff an inscription of $k(B)$ occurs in their "thinking centers," and they might think $t(S)$ iff an inscription of B occurs there. (This function k is defined on L in a way analogous to the way g was defined on English.)

29. Incidentally, we are now in a position to identify an inherent defect in the language-of-thought theory itself. I can think that A , that B , that C , and so on. It is certainly possible to hypothesize ideal languages such as Mentalese, and we can easily define some mapping r from the English expressions 'that A ', 'that B ', 'that C ' , etc. onto sentences in Mentalese. However, we can just as easily define an alternative mapping s such that $s(x) = t(r(x))$ always holds. Now with which sentence in Mentalese should we identify the entity denoted by 'that A '? Should it be r('that A ') or s('that A ')? The choice is utterly arbitrary. This arbitrariness is damaging just in its own right. However, I believe that it becomes absolutely fatal when language-of-thought functionalism tries to define the relationships between thought and sensation and between thought and the properties of external objects. To succeed at this, one must reject the representationalism implicit in the language-of-thought theory and adopt instead a form of realism.

30. There is some question about whether it is valid to expand the embedded occurrences of 'thinking[*]'; for example, such expansion overlooks the phenomenon of the paradox of analysis. However, a moment's reflection will show that our original construction is beset with the same problem whether or not we expand these occurrences of 'thinking[*]'. So for simplicity of exposition I will do so in the text.

31. On one treatment of functional constants, 'f' is contextually defined as follows (where 'F' is an appropriate 2-place predicate): $x < f(y)$ iff$_{df}$ $(\exists_1 z)$ $(Fyz \ \& \ x < z)$. On this treatment, therefore, the proposi-

tion that $x < f(y)$ would be an existential proposition. Thus, if we were to adopt this treatment, my argument in the text would need to be complicated somewhat. But the main point would remain the same: t (that $x < f(y)$) would not contain z as a constituent even though $f(y) = z$; on the contrary, it would continue to contain y as a constituent, just as it did prior to being transformed by t. And this is where the problem lies with all the "superficial" Quinean transformations: the embedded propositions remain unchanged.

32. In a comprehensive formulation, the above principles of Introspection should be supplemented with the following companion principle: for any relation R, if x introspects that xRy, then xRy.

33. We should try to construct a new relation experiencing* such that it is possible to experience* such things as thinking*, desiring*, deciding*, etc. but not thinking, desiring, deciding, etc. However, we must do this in such a way that it would be possible to experience* experiencing* itself but not to experience* experiencing. It is a challenge to construct a new relation with this special kind of impredicativity.

34. We should also take into account some version of the following companion principle:

If p is not contingent and x clearly and distinctly understands p and x believes p, then p is necessary.

35. For example:

If x stands in the relation of clear and distinct understanding to the proposition that knowing $\neq a$, then x stands in the relation of knowing to the proposition knowing $\neq a$

where a rigidly designates knowing*. To test whether the inverted relations of clear and distinct understanding* and knowing* satisfy this principle, substitute 'clear and distinct understanding*' for 'clear and distinct understanding' and 'knowing*' for 'knowing'. We obtain:

If x stands in the relation of clear and distinct understanding* to the proposition that knowing* $\neq a$, then x stands in the relation of knowing* to the proposition that knowing* $\neq a$.

(Note that we do not substitute anything for the rigid designator 'a'. The reason is that 'a' refers directly to the relation of knowing* quite independently of the fact that we chose to define knowing* in terms of knowing. For in the present context we are proceeding under the standard assumption that relations are identical if necessarily equivalent and, hence, that each relation has an infinite number of necessarily equivalent definitions, none more basic than another.) Given our definitions of the inverted relations, however, we know that this is equivalent to the following:

If x stands in the relation of clear and distinct understanding to the proposition that knowing* $\neq a$, then x stands in the relation of knowing to the proposition that knowing* $\neq a$.

But this outcome is plainly wrong. No one can know something that is false, and it is certainly false that knowing* $\neq$ a. Thus, we see that, when the inverted relations knowing* and clear and distinct understanding* take the place of knowing and clear and distinct understanding, respectively, they do not satisfy the original principle. It will occur to the reader that we might save our construction from this problem as follows. First, define a third relation knowing**. Then, show that when the three relations clear and distinct understanding*, knowing*, and knowing** take the place of clear and distinct understanding, knowing, and knowing*, respectively, they do succeed in satisfying the original principle. However, when generalized, this strategy forces us to posit an infinite hierarchy of mutually dependent relations: knowing, knowing*, knowing**, knowing***,...; believing, believing*, believing**, believing***,...; and so on. And it turns out to be extremely difficult to construct such a hierarchy. Furthermore, if we are not careful, the identity of the standard psychological relations might be uniquely determined by their "functional roles" (i.e., their ground-level positions) in this hierarchy, thus validating a version of functionalism. These, then, are some further problems a new construction must overcome.

36. See sec. 42, "Realism and Representationalism," *Quality and Concept*, for more on the realism/representationalism controversy.

It takes a special logical framework to treat non-elementary psychological principles. This logic must be equipped to treat liberal forms of quantifying-in. It must cut the "fine-grained" intensional distinctions characteristic of intentional matters, and at the same time it must have an apparatus for treating necessary truths. It must be able to represent relations (e.g., thinking) whose objects are propositions that can "contain" those very same relations as "constituents," and it must be able to represent relations (e.g., identity, thinking of, experiencing, etc.) that can fall within their very own ranges. Finally, it must be able to represent "transcendental" relations, i.e., relations (such as identity, thinking of, introspecting, experiencing) whose ranges span more than one ontological category. As far as I know, *Quality and Concept* provides the only philosophically satisfactory logical framework that has all these special features. So I will take the liberty to allude to it in what follows.

37. For example, consider a psychological theory consisting of the elementary belief/desire model plus all the principles for the self-conscious rational mind listed above. Let this theory be formulated in the intensional logic T2 (see sec. 16, *Quality and Concept*) supplemented with predicates for primitive physical and mathematical relations $O_1, \ldots, O_m$ and primitive psychological relations $S_1, \ldots, S_n$. Let ⟨M, I⟩ be a model for the resulting theory P in which the physical and mathematical predicates are given their intended interpretation. To show that P does not implicitly define $S_1, \ldots, S_n$, we construct an alternate model structure M^* that has two systems of relations $S_1, \ldots, S_n$ and $S_1^*, \ldots, S_n^*$ but that is identical to M in its physical and mathematical components. To do this, adjoin to the domain D of M any new primitive relations $S_1^*, \ldots, S_n^*$, and then close the new domain D^* under the extended logical operations Conj*, Neg*, Exist*, etc. [E.g., Conj* is such that: (1) if $x, y \in D_i$ for $i \geq 0$, then Conj$^*(x,y) = $ Conj(x,y) and (2) if $x, y \in D_i^*$, for $i \geq 0$, and $x \notin D$ or $y \notin D$, then a new element z is added to D_i^* and Conj$^*(x,y) = z$.] Next define the alternate extension functions $H^* \in K^*$ in M^* in terms of the alternate extension functions $H \in K$ in M: (1) $H^*(x) = H(x)$ if x is either an individual or $O_1, \ldots, O_m$ or $S_1, \ldots, S_n$; (2) $H^*(\text{Id}) = \{uv \in D^*: u = v\}$; (3) $H^*(S_i^*) = \{uv: \langle u, *(v)\rangle \in H(S_i)\}$, where $*(v) =_{df}$ the item w in D^* that is just like v except that, for every occurrence of S_i, $1 \leq i \leq n$, in v's decomposition tree, there is an associated occurrence of S_i^* in w's decomposition tree. For each of the remaining items $x \in D^*$, $H^*(x)$ is determined by the standard conditions characterizing the behavior of the fundamental logical operations. Finally, the actual extension function G^* in M^* is the function H^* in K^* that is associated by the above definition with the actual extension function G in M. With M^* so constructed, it is easy to prove a lemma that, for every proposition p in D^*, p and $*(p)$ are necessarily equivalent. Now let I^* be an interpretation that is just like the original interpretation I except that I^* assigns S_i^* to a predicate in P iff I assigns S_i to that predicate. Given the above lemma, it is then simple to show that ⟨M^*, I⟩ and ⟨M^*, I^*⟩ both satisfy P. Hence, P does not implicitly define the standard psychological relations $S_1, \ldots, S_n$ even when the interpretation of its physical and mathematical predicates is held constant. And much stronger results of this general type are also possible.

38. That is, a framework of intensional logic that has not yet been characterized axiomatically. It is well known that in intensional logic, just as in set theory, the use of certain pathological principles leads to paradoxes. No one has yet found a systematic method for weeding out only pathological principles so that the sound ones can be set forth axiomatically. But this does not invalidate arguments that employ sound principles. Recall, moreover, that the reason we find ourselves in this territory is that we are trying to accommodate *the functionalist's* request for a logical framework that can handle the special forms of impredicativity present in his various non-elementary psychological principles.

39. A similair example is the property of being someone who is thinking of the thinking-of relation. This property is the result of predicating the thinking-of relation of itself; symbolically,

[u thinks of [u thinks of v]$_{uv}$]$_u$ = Pred([u thinks of v]$_{uv}$,[u thinks of v]$_{uv}$).

Another example involving self-predication is a psychological property encountered earlier, namely, the property of being someone who experiences experiencing itself. This property is the result of predicating the experiencing relation of the experiencing relation itself; symbolically,

[u experiences [u experiences v]$_{uv}$]$_u$ = Pred([u experiences v]$_{uv}$,[u experiences v]$_{uv}$).

40. The notation for unordered pairs is defined thus:

$$[x,y] =_{df} [v = x \text{ or } v = y]_v.$$

Then the notation for finite sequences is defined as follows:

$$\langle\alpha_1\rangle =_{df} \alpha_1; \quad \langle\alpha_1, \alpha_2\rangle =_{df} [[\alpha_1, \alpha_1], [\alpha_1, \alpha_2]]; \quad \langle\alpha_1,\ldots, \alpha_{i+1}\rangle =_{df} \langle\langle\alpha_1,\ldots, \alpha_i\rangle, \alpha_{i+1}\rangle.$$

For simplicity I often omit the use of the angle brackets in the text.

41. For an explanation of why this is so and for a general defense of first-order constructions, see chap. 5, "Predication," *Quality and Concept*.

42. This step in the proof relies on the intuitive assumption that, for each F and F^*, the following two abstraction principles either are both valid or are both not valid: (a) $F\alpha_1,\ldots, \alpha_i$ iff $\alpha_1,\ldots, \alpha_i$ satisfies F, and (b) $F^*\alpha_1^*,\ldots, \alpha_i^*$ iff $\alpha_1^*,\ldots, \alpha_i^*$ satisfies F^*. Certain instances of these abstraction principles give rise to a familiar problem: for pathological relations F and F^*, (a) and (b) are inconsistent with principles of classical logic. Although we still await an ideal solution to these paradoxes, this does not detract from the soundness of my argument. For my argument assumes only that the validity of (a) and the validity of (b) stand or fall together. A survey of examples indicates that F and F^* are both non-pathological or they are both pathological. If the former, then (a) and (b) would both be unproblematically valid. If the latter, then special steps must be taken. One approach would be to deny the relevant instances of (a) and (b); another approach would be to depart from principles of classical logic, e.g., by permitting truth-value gaps for the relevant pathological propositions. However, whichever approach is taken, symmetry demands that it be taken for both (a) and (b). Thus, whether or not F and F^* are pathological, (a) and (b) would stand or fall together; i.e., they would both be valid or they would both fail to be valid. Therefore, we may expect that this symmetry will be preserved in any ideal solution to the paradoxes. Indeed, when we speak of an ideal solution, we mean one in which symmetries of this sort are preserved. Therefore, even though we do not yet possess an ideal solution, we have good reason to expect that it will validate the assumption used in our proof.

Of course, the whole issue might be avoided simply by weakening our lemma to propositions not dependent on the pathological cases. Since it is implausible that the truth of functionalism could turn on psychological "laws" for how we think about pathological cases, such a weakened lemma should suffice in the remainder of our argument.

43. The sensing relation is one exception, for we have not built into the definition of * a function f that "inverts" some spectrum of sensible qualities. This could be done, but it would invite special controversies that we should be wise to avoid here. After all, our construction already refutes functionalism. Moreover, given the traditional empiricist theory of experience, sensing is only a mode of experiencing, and experiencing has been shown to be quite distinct from its inverted counterpart experiencing*.

44. Are the *-counterparts of the standard psychological relations "internal" relations? By an argument just like the one used in note 23, we can show that, in any sense of "internal" available to the functionalist, these *-relations are internal. Necessarily, you are thinking* p* whenever you are thinking p, and this is so whether or not you realize it!

45. Chap. 10, "Mind," *Quality and Concept*.

46. These claims are examined more thoroughly, ibid.

Parallelism, Interactionism, and Causation

LAIRD ADDIS

One may gather from the arguments of two of the last papers[1] published before his death that J. L. Mackie held the following three theses concerning the mind/body problem:

(1) There is a distinct realm of mental properties, so a dualism of properties at least is true and materialism false.

(2) All bodily movements probably have sufficient causes in physical facts and properties, but mental facts and properties are not causally irrelevant to human action.

(3) At the same time, the view that there are not sufficient causes in the physical realm alone for all bodily movements has no good and adequate empirical or philosophical reasons against it.

In this paper I wish (1) to register my strong agreement with the first thesis by way of simply taking it for granted, (2) to defend the second thesis in greater detail and in a manner somewhat different from Mackie's, and (3) to show the third thesis to be false.

I

If a dualism of properties is true, there are fundamentally three abstract possibilities: the mental properties are related to the crucial physical properties by (1) laws of coexistence, (2) laws of succession, or (3) no laws at all. These views may reasonably be labeled as (1) *parallelism*, (2) *interactionism*, and (3) *fatalism*, respectively. Although there have been people who, crippled by their theological commitments, have thought they believed in fatalism, it is phenomenological absurdity to maintain that what one desires or chooses or values never *makes a difference* to one's behavior; and no one ever acts that way either (whatever it could possibly be to act as if one's mental life made no difference to one's behavior). That leaves only parallelism and interactionism as realistic contenders for the dualist's allegiance.

But are parallelism and interactionism, as characterized above, really exhaustive of the remaining possibilities? What about a theory according to which some mental properties are tied by laws of coexistence while others are tied by laws of succession to the crucial physical properties? My reply is that if any mental properties are tied to the physical world *essentially* by laws of succession, then the view of the interactionist is correct. The reason is that in such a case the physical world is not *causally closed*, and the issue between the parallelist and the interactionist is really just the question of whether or not that is so. So it is time to explain clearly what is meant by saying of a system that it is causally closed.[2]

Assume that determinism is true. Eventually I shall remove the assumption, but it makes it easier to state the basic ideas initially. Determinism is the thesis that for every occurrence or state of affairs in the past and present and future of the universe, there exists some earlier occurrence(s) or state(s) of affairs that is lawfully sufficient for its occurrence at the time at which it in fact occurs. Otherwise put, determinism is the thesis that identical conditions not acted on from without produce of lawful necessity identical consequences. Citing a lawfully sufficient condition for a given occurrence as well as the relevant law(s) is to provide a *full explanation* of that occurrence. (I say this stipulatively and do not thereby rule out other kinds of explanations of occurrences—by *reasons* or *dispositions* or *constituents* or whatever.)

It is evident then that a given occurrence will have more than one full explanation if, for example, the occurrence of either the set of properties *a, b*, and *c* or the set *a, b*, and *d* is lawfully sufficient for that occurrence. This will be so for one reason if *c* and *d* are themselves bound by a law of coexistence such that the occurrence of either lawfully implies the simultaneous occurrence of the other. To put the idea somewhat more informally: the fact that one has found a full explanation for some occurrence in the sense stipulated does not imply that the occurrence or nonoccurrence of anything else is lawfully irrelevant, especially insofar as that something else is itself lawfully related to that which is offered originally in explanation.

A *kind of system* is specified by listing the properties (or variables, as some say) that are taken to characterize the kind of things in the system. A *particular system* is specified by additionally listing the names of or otherwise indicating all the particulars in it. A *state of the system* is specified by describing for an instant the *values* of each of the variables for each of the particulars of the system. A deterministic system is *causally closed* if for every state of the system there exists some earlier state of the system that is lawfully sufficient for its occurrence, that is, that given the laws of the system constitutes its full explanation. If one *must* go "outside" the system to properties[3] that are not part of it (or of its kind) to obtain a full lawful explanation of any occurrence in the system, then the system is not causally closed. Notice here for later reference the use of 'must' rather than 'may' in the last sentence: a system's being causally closed does *not* preclude the possibility of legitimately citing some occurrence "outside" the system as at least part of the full explanation of some occurrence within the system. If *a, b* and *c* are within a system and (some values of them) are advanced correctly as a full explanation of (some value of) *e*, which is also within the system; and if further (the values of) *c* is (are) tied by a strict law of coexistence to (the values of) *d*, which is "outside" the system, then *a, b,* and *d* also constitute a full explanation of *e*. Thus my use of 'must' rather than 'may'.

It will now easily be seen that the general idea of a causally closed system can be captured even when the system is nondeterministic provided that we allow some nonformalized notion of "degree of explanation" into our thinking. If for some occurrences in the system there do not exist any full explanations (that is, these occurrences have no lawfully sufficient antecedent conditions no matter what is taken into account either within or without the system), then the system is causally closed but not deterministic if whatever degree of explanation those occurrences do admit of can be found within the system. This circumstance too does not preclude the possibility of occurrences or properties outside the system being legitimately cited in an explanation of some occurrences within the system.

Before I use these ideas to attempt a precise characterization of parallelism and interactionism, one preliminary remains. Even the dualist, such as myself, agrees that some of the properties that are commonly called mental are (also) physical properties.[4] But since the theses of the parallelist and interactionist apply crucially to ("occurrent") conscious mental states, it is desirable for analytic purposes to treat as mental properties only those that are exemplified by such states and to consider all other properties as physical. So doing, we may now say that contemporary parallelism and interactionism consist of the following propositions, respectively:

Parallelism
  (1) Mental properties and physical properties constitute exclusive and exhaustive sets of the properties of the universe.
  (2) The physical world is causally closed.
  (3) The mental world is *not* causally closed.
  (4) Every mental property is tied to some physical property (or disjunction of physical properties) by a law of coexistence.

Interactionism
  (1') Mental properties and physical properties constitute exclusive and exhaustive sets of the properties of the universe.
  (2') The physical world is *not* causally closed.
  (3') The mental world is *not* causally closed.
  (4') At least some mental properties are tied to physical properties *only* by laws of succession.

Three comments on these characterizations are necessary before I turn to evaluation of the views.

First, probably the most famous parallelist of all, at least on one reasonable interpretation of his words, denied (3) explicitly and possibly (4) as well. In short, this philosopher held that the realm of the mental is also of such a scope that everything that happens in it has a full explanation by some other occurrence(s) in it. Whether Spinoza should really be treated as holding (4) when he explicitly insists that the connection is one of *perception*, we need not bother with. In any case, the contemporary parallelist need not, nor to my knowledge does any, hold that the mental is of such a scope. But (3) of course implies (given also [1], it must be added) the *necessity* of the physical in the explanation of the mental. Since therefore this "parallelism" is by no means a simple, one/one connection (and I shall weaken it further a few sentences hence), one may wish to question the propriety of the label. And further, since this implication of the *asymmetry* of the relation of the mental to the physical in general seems to suggest that the physical *causes* the mental but never the other way around, some may ask why we don't forthrightly admit that parallelism so-called is really epiphenomenalism and be done with it? For the moment, however, I wish to characterize the alternatives of what I shall continue to call parallelism and interactionism only in terms of the kinds of lawful connection that each involves and, despite my use of 'causally closed', reserve all questions of *causation* in the relation of the mental to the physical until later. This way of proceeding, despite its rarity in the literature, is, I am convinced, the more fruitful in grasping clearly what is involved.

Second, it is important to see that my use of 'only' in (4') above is not superfluous: if every mental property is related by a law or coexistence to some physical property, then whatever laws of succession may *also* apply to the system, the physical world is causally closed and parallelism is true. For, at any point at which one might cite some mental occurrence in the explanation of some later physical occurrence, there will always be a lawfully simultaneous physical occurrence that can serve instead. But the interactionist insists that some physical occurrences *require* mention of the mental in their full (or maximally possible) explanations, that there are "gaps" in the physical realm as far as the explanation of some occurrence in it is concerned. Hence the use of 'only'.

Third, I have so far given the impression that the parallelist would hold or even must hold that the lawful correspondence of any given mental property to some physical property is one/one. It is now time to loosen this assumption and to understand clearly that the parallelist is not so bound, consistent with the four propositions that define the position; and that the parallelist can therefore allow for the possibility of different physical grounds for qualitatively identical states of consciousness. Given the asymmetry noted earlier—the physical but not the mental realm is causally closed—all that is required for parallelism is that the laws permit the "deduction" of the mental from the physical but not the other way around. In short, the parallelist may allow a many/one connection from body to mind, but not a one/many from body to mind nor, obviously, a many/many connection. This will always imply that two persons or any things or beings whatsoever that are in qualitatively identical physical states will have qualitatively identical mental states. Indeed, with this idea, the parallelist's position may usefully be contrasted with the interactionist's as follows: *the parallelist affirms and the interactionist denies the lawful impossibility of two persons or other beings or things being in the same physical state but having different mental states.* Putting the matter this way will permit me eventually to formulate a very serious objection to interactionism.

II

"Parallelism implies fatalism, and fatalism is absurd." That is, both historically and analytically, the most serious objection to parallelism. The objection goes that if the physical world is causally closed, as the parallelist claims, then it really makes no difference what goes on in a person's mind, what states of consciousness a person has, including the conscious states of desiring, willing, and so on; and that is fatalism. Surely, it may be said, if we are going to be dualists at all, we must also be interactionists in order, like the central-state materialists, to give the mind its proper explanatory role in human behavior. The materialist, to be sure, holds with the parallelist that the physical world is causally closed; but then, according to the materialist, that world is all the world there is and already includes whatever one may wish to call "mental." What should the parallelist say in response to the charge of holding a position that implies fatalism while surely agreeing that any view that implies fatalism is itself absurd?

Not only does parallelism *not* imply that it makes no difference what goes on in one's mind to one's behavior, but in fact implies just the opposite. If I did not have the mental state I now have, then by the law of coexistence that ties that mental state to some state of my brain, that brain state would not be occurring and so my behavior would be different, and so on. It is lawfully impossible, by the parallelist's very position, for that brain state to occur without that state of consciousness also occurring; and if someone wonders why, on the parallelist's view, the universe couldn't just as well have been exactly as it is physically but without the occurrence of any mental states at all, the answer is that the universe well *could* have been that way in the sense that its laws could have been different from what they are without contradiction, but that is not the way it in fact *is*. The way it *is* makes it lawfully impossible for me to write this essay without thinking about what I am doing, desiring to write it down, and so on, because unless those states of consciousness occur in me, the relevant brain states won't occur either.

None of this, however, contradicts the original assumption that the physical world is causally closed and that those brain states also have a full lawful explanation (or maximum degree of explanation) in the physical world alone. To make use once more of the abstract symbols for the sake of clarity: let a, b, and c be physical properties with c being the relevant brain state; let d be a mental property; and let e also be a physical property, the person's behavior. Then while, by assumption, a, b, and c jointly explain e (a and b perhaps being the state of the rest of the physical universe at the moment), so do a, b, and d. But c lawfully cannot occur unless d occurs since, also by assumption, they are tied together by a law of coexistence. Hence e will not occur (in the particular case: I have not assumed that a, b, and c

are lawfully *necessary* for the occurrence of *e*) unless *d* occurs. This also illustrates how the parallelist may say, at least consistently with what has been said so far, that *the* explanation of a person's behavior lies in his mental state insofar as everyone allows that a particular context permits one to cite but one of the factors of a set that only jointly are sufficient for any given occurrence.

Many other arguments have been made for and against parallelism and interactionism. Many of them, I believe, carry very little weight, such as: *direct* appeals to common sense, calling attention to various facts about evolution, arguments that involve the principle of the conservation of energy, and a priori arguments about the ontological possibility or impossibility of either view. I shall comment briefly on the first and the last of these matters, taking the latter first, however.

Without going into much detail, let it be said here that none of the positions mentioned so far—parallelism, interactionism, fatalism, and even materialism—is *ontologically* impossible. By this I mean that, consistent with the basic principles and findings of *general* ontology, the universe *could* have been as each view says it in fact is. The only amendment I would make to that stark claim concerns materialism: insofar as the materialist says simply that everything is physical, what he says involves no obvious ontological impossibility, Berkeley and some other idealists to the contrary notwithstanding. But insofar as the materialist maintains that mental properties are literally also physical properties, or that no properties exist (and, paradoxically, therefore no mental properties), or that only the basic properties of physics exist in a world that is given to sentient beings in that world as having many other properties as well, he does speak ontological nonsense. Fatalism's absurdity, as I said earlier, is phenomenological and not ontological: there *could* be a world with two lawfully unrelated sets of variables—the mental and the physical—with the noncausal ties of intentionality and time being the only "links" between members of the two sets. But experience shows conclusively that this is not our world. Finally, since I have defined parallelism and interactionism by way of the kinds of *lawful* connections that may hold between mental and physical *properties*, there should not be and is not any *ontological* difficulty with either view. That judgment does indeed presuppose something like a Humean ontological principle that between and among *simple* properties, any lawful connection or lack thereof whatsoever is possible, a principle which, although I shall not argue for it (I really wouldn't know how to argue for such a fundamental principle), I firmly believe is true.[5] So no basis for choosing between parallelism and interactionism is to be found among the principles of ontology themselves.

It is a piece of true common sense, firmly grounded in the phenomenology of the relevant situations, that what happens to and in our bodies affects what goes on in our minds *and* also that what goes on in our minds affects what happens in and to our bodies. Call this, if you will, "commonsense interactionism." But we have already seen that parallelism can account for, and even requires, the fact that some of what happens in each realm make a difference to what happens in the other. Hence, commonsense interactionism is fully consistent with parallelism. So a *direct* appeal to this kind of common sense as an argument for interactionism is simply a mistake. But how then shall we proceed in an evaluation of the relative merits of these two positions, one of which is almost certainly the truth about the relation of mind to body?

When one considers again a certain feature of the interactionist's view and investigates its implications, we find, I believe, good and adequate reasons for rejecting interactionism. Since there are no similarly good reasons for rejecting parallelism (although I still have the crucial matter of *causation* to deal with), we must conclude that it is rational to believe that parallelism is the truth. That feature of interactionism that leads to its difficulties is the fact that on it, any one of a *range*, perhaps an unlimited range, of mental states lawfully may accompany a given physical state whether the latter be a brain state or a behavioral state. Without this feature, which is shared with fatalism, the view is not interactionism but parallelism, that is, if the "range" is one. It is again the question of whether or not two physically identical persons could, lawfully, have different conscious states. What this feature of interactionism entails is that it is *not* calculable by the kinds of laws that the interactionist claims to hold between mental and physical variables what the state of a person's mind is from the states of his body.

To see this idea more clearly, consider the analogy of mechanics in which an interacting set of variables of mass, position, and velocity is such that given (the values of) any one or two of those variables for some object or objects, (the values of) the third remain unknown, and this independent of temporal relations. To apply the laws of succession that are the laws of mechanics, one must *independently* ascertain the values of all three variables at some time in order to calculate the present, past, or future values of any one variable (except, trivially, the value of the same variable in the same object at the same time). When we apply this consequence to the mind/body problem, it has grave consequences for interactionism, as we now shall see.

When anesthesiologists do their job correctly, they and everyone else assume that by putting the brain of the patient in a certain state, that patient's consciousness ceases temporarily. When a suspected criminal is given a lie detector test and it shows a certain pronounced pattern when certain questions are asked, both those involved and most others assume that when the suspect's body is in a certain state as shown by the machine, the suspect has the mental state of intending to deceive. When a parent gives a child a spanking, that parent and everyone else assume that the child has the mental state of feeling pain in its posterior. These facts, and innumerable others like them, are, I submit, incompatible with interactionism and intelligible only on parallelism if the assumptions involved are true. All of them presuppose that when the body is in a certain definite state, the mind is in a certain definite state. This general fact, which we may label as "commonsense parallelism," does support its philosophical namesake, parallelism, for, unlike the relation of commonsense interactionism to parallelism, *commonsense parallelism entails the falsity of interactionism*. Commonsense parallelism is in fact just the vaguely perceived fundamental claim of the parallelist: that it is lawfully impossible for two persons who are in every respect physically alike to have qualitatively different mental states at that same moment. Same body, same mind.

The interactionist may try to avoid these damaging implications by limiting to a very narrow range the lawfully possible mental states that can accompany a given brain or other physical state; by stipulating that the members of the set of possible mental states that accompany a given brain state must be very similar to each other; by allowing that some but not all mental states or features of them are, after all, tied by strict laws of coexistence (which, again, may be many/one from body to mind) to properties of the physical world; or by some combination of the foregoing. Any such move would obviously be a significant step in the direction of parallelism proper.

Can the interactionist leave things there and be left with a defensible position? The answer, I suppose, is that it depends on how closely the interactionist comes to resemble the parallelist. But for an interactionism that remains strong enough to be of any interest and that has any sense of internal coherence (that is, is not modified just to meet every example on an ad hoc basis), there remains a very serious objection which is my fundamental argument against interactionism.

Common sense holds that each of us often knows not only that another person is conscious and awake but what in particular, at least in part, is, as we say, "going on" in that other person's mind. Common sense also realizes that, at nearly any moment, there may be more, even much more, going on in a person's mind than anyone else knows and that sometimes we have no good idea at all what the conscious state of another person at a certain time is. Finally, common sense also acknowledges what science likewise takes for granted, that the only access we have to the mind of another person is through the observation of that other person's body and the physical objects that he or she produces, such as books, works of art, conversations, and so on. Precise formulation of this idea is as difficult as it is unnecessary; however, the description of what we observe may be as sophisticated as and of whatever scope anyone wants, provided that it does not include the properties of conscious mental states as exemplified by anyone other than oneself.

Now ignoring the matter of the very existence of other minds, how on the interactionist's view could anyone ever know or even make a reasonable guess what another person is thinking? For, on this view, the fact that that person is in some particular bodily or behavioral state does not lawfully entail (or in any other way entail) that that person is in any specific mental state. Certainly we cannot *ask* the person what he or she is thinking, for taking the answer seriously would presuppose a connection of the coexistence kind between linguistic behavior and states of mind. (Thus the fact of communication and its presupposition that there is a systematic but not unbendable correlation between what a person *says*—in the sense of what sounds or marks are produced—and what a person *thinks* is another important aspect of commonsense parallelism, although this connection is, of course, not "natural" in the sense that one learns a language with all of its conventional aspects.) In short, nothing I can observe about a person at a moment can give me even a clue as to what that person is thinking, if interactionism is true.

But, it may be said in reply, we don't ordinarily rely only on what we observe at the moment anyway in order to calculate or come to believe what is going on in another person's mind. We rely, varying widely as to the person and the sort of situation we are in and other factors, on shared and unshared cultural traditions, on what we know about human beings in general and what we know of the person's past in particular, and probably much more besides. So if the interactionist is forced to deny that we can simply "read off" what another person is thinking from any observation of only that person's roughly simultaneous physical properties in addition to knowledge of laws or lawlike generalizations, he too only affirms common-sense truth.

The parallelist, in retort, may immediately grant that while, according to his view, there exist laws that would in principle allow a person to calculate anyone's mental state from a full description of his bodily and especially his brain state, in fact we often come to know what other persons are thinking in the manner just described. Not only do we not know all (or perhaps any, strictly speaking) of the relevant laws, but actully determining the precise state of anyone's brain or body is factually impossible. *But*, the parallelist must insist, at certain crucial points and in certain crucial respects, we do know what is going on in another person's mind on the basis alone of simultaneous circumstances and knowledge of or belief in certain generalizations. As to what *causes* us to have such knowledge or beliefs, we may speculate that much of it is part of our genetic endowment; for example, taking certain gestures (bodily motions) as indicative of friendly intentions or of fear or of submission.

As to what *justifies* or could justify such knowledge and belief, something like the so-called argument from analogy *must* suffice. (But I do not argue here that, by some rigorous philosophical standard, we ever do know what is going on in another person's mind. I take for granted that we do, in any ordinary sense of "know", sometimes know what another person is thinking. My point is that interactionism entails the *impossibility* of any such knowledge, or even plausible guess.) I can know that another person is in pain on the basis of his behavior only if (1) I know from my own experience what pain is, and (2) I know from my own experience what behavior typically accompanies pain (which, of course, I may learn to inhibit; but that presupposes a natural accompaniment). Again, it is probable that we are "preprogrammed" to react in certain definite ways to "pain behavior" in others— to regard it with alarm, sympathy, and so on. It is difficult to understand how the species could survive when its newborns need such extended attention if it were otherwise, that is, all "learned." But this is irrelevant to the question of what, if anything, *could* justify the rationality of such reactions even if they are causally impossible not to have. But then *we cannot help but believe* that others have minds, are sometimes in pain, feel desire, and so on.

The reason that the parallelist must insist on the existence of certain crucial situations of the kind in which one does virtually "read off" the other's mental state from his behavior of the moment is in order to be able to avoid the same scepticism that the interactionist is necessarily faced with. Consider again the case of mechanics. Mass, position, and velocity constitute a set of interacting variables (properties). By assumption and in fact, the values of no one of those variables is, by any true law or generalization, calculable even within a certain range from the values of the other two either at the same time or any different time. In short, if I wish to make any reliable predictions about any future states of a system with respect to these properties, I must *independently* ascertain, that is, by separate observation of each, the values of *all three* variables at a time. The interactionist says, in effect, that a person "is" or "has" a set of interacting properties, some mental and some physical. But if another person can neither observe, and thereby independently ascertain, a state of another person's mind at a time nor by any law of coexistence calculate that state from observation of the other person's body (or anything else whatsoever), he could not possibly know or have the slightest good reason to believe that any other person is in any particular state of mind rather than any other, either at this moment or in the future. Nor, by the way, could he ever make any rational prediction about the future behavior of any other person. It would be comparable to trying to predict any of the future positions, velocities, or masses of some bodies on the basis of knowing only the present positions and velocities and the laws of mechanics—a sheer impossibility.

Now it is true that we sometimes, in fields of science that do not involve the mind, come to believe that there are unobservable properties that apparently interact with the properties we do observe and even that we can sometimes calculate the values of those variables. The most obvious example is atomic and subatomic physics. Would my argument, therefore, not be subject to the reductio ad absurdum that if it were sound, it would also prove the impossibility of atomic and subatomic physics?

The correct answer to this objection, probably already apparent to many readers, in fact strengthens my point and my argument. For any time a scientist wishes to *test* an hypothesis about the existence of an entity of a certain kind (that is, as having a certain property or set of properties), he must assume a connection of the *coexistence* kind between that entity as exemplifying certain properties and some feature of the world of everyday experience even if it be only a reading of a dial (with many intermediate steps, of course, each of which assumes a connection of the coexistence kind). Every *difference* that is to be knowable and therefore testable for in the realm of the nonobservable must be *paralleled* by some difference under *some* condition in the realm of the observable. We need not make this a condition of meaningfulness in order to insist that an hypothesis about causes (or apparently so, such as "God wills all") that yields no concrete predictions about what, under any specifiable condition whatsoever, will occur in the realm of the observable is, at least as an *explanatory* account, idle and empty. But this, it now seems clear, is exactly the position each of us would be in, with respect to the contents of everyone else's mind, if interactionism were true. Only parallelism even makes *possible* the knowledge each of us supposes ourself to have about what is going on in the minds of others.

Parallelism therefore appears to be the only position that is in accord with common sense correctly understood, with the experience each of us has of himself or herself, and with any attempt of science to discover as precisely as it can those features of the brain and central nervous system that are correlated with, say, dreaming or doing mental mathematics or willing to wiggle one's ears. In its dualism, parallelism fully accepts the commonsense view confirmed by introspection that there are certain properties of the universe known to us only by introspection, that is, that there is a distinct set of mental properties, while in its parallelism proper, it and only it satisfies the requirements of common sense, inner experience, and science.

III

There remains the matter of causation. I call the reader's attention more fully now to my conscious design to leave this matter until last in a discussion of the present issue in the belief that much contemporary discussion of the matter is flawed by a too hasty and unexamined introduction of causal (as opposed to merely lawful) notions into the argument. How often does one read that parallelism is patently absurd in denying any *causal* role to the mind in behavior and so may be safely and quickly dismissed from further consideration? Is it not, after all, the contention of the parallelist that every physical occurrence has a purely physical *cause*? Now we have already taken notice of the fact that while on the one hand parallelism may imply to some (as in fact Spinoza explicitly held) that each realm has only its own causes, the modern parallelist is certain to deny that the realm of the mental is in fact causally closed and therefore to insist that only the realm of the physical can complete the full explanation of occurrences in the realm of the mental. But since the parallelist also holds that the physical realm is causally closed, the ground is laid for the charge that the modern parallelist is really better called an epiphenomenalist and a believer in one-way causation from the physical to the mental. This is *not* simply to repeat the earlier objection based only on the lawful connections involved, but rather to insist that even granted that it is lawfully impossible for certain brain states to occur without certain mental states also occurring on parallelism, that is not to say that mental states ever *cause* any physical and especially any behavioral state. And what common sense and possibly morality require is just that —that by having certain mental states such as desiring or willing or choosing, we *cause* certain effects in the realm of the physical. Since the parallelist must deny that anything in the realm of the mental ever really causes anything in the realm of the physical, parallelism must be false. So charges the critic.

Causation is lawfulness plus context. That is my formula and my thesis. Clarifying it and defending it to some degree will at the same time allow me to defend parallelism against the charge that it denies some patent fact about the connection between mind and body. (So I do not take the line that some defenders of parallelism have — that is merely an *illusion* that our mental states sometimes cause our behavioral states.)[6] At the same time I do not propose to make an elaborate defense here of any particular account of causation but only to state briefly what the theory of causation involved is and how it can rescue parallelism from the charge.

If we begin by asking what lawfulness itself is, I have no new answer to that question. My view is that it is mere regular connection, understood to mean that a true law of nature is a generalization that does or would survive the tests of Mill's methods. That of course does *not* imply, contrary to the beliefs of some, that for two properties *A* and *B* to be lawfully connected, there must be a true law that connects them alone in some regular fashion, that is, as either "If *A*, then *B*" or "If *B*, then *A*" or "*A* if and only if *B*." *A* and *B* are lawfully connected in a law of the form "If *A* and *C*, then *B*," for example, which implies none of the three previous sentences. That is one qualification to the notion of "regular connection." Another is that since laws are best understood as not having existential import, a law may hold and even be importantly true of our universe even though it has no instantiations. Newton's first law, the law of inertial motion, may be an example. Then the "regular connection" is or may be hypothetical — what *would* occur if certain conditions *were* to obtain rather than what *does* occur when certain conditions *do* obtain. This distinction between the subjunctive and the indicative is the source of many familiar difficulties and disputes which, however, I shall not discuss here. I merely register my agreement with what I take to be the essential insight of Hume — that there is not, in anyone's experience, any additional *entity* such as a "necessary connection" to be included in the proper understanding of lawfulness or, now to move on, *causation*.

If, as the examples of many philosophers might show, we can in a sense "observe" a causal connection in the particular instance, such as when a rolling boulder smashes a hut (to repeat an example from the literature), nothing very important philosophically follows. We may be simply "preprogrammed" to take certain kinds of occurrences as instances of causal connections immediately, so to speak, rather than, as the regularity view might seem to suggest, only by realizing those occurrences to be instances of lawful connections. Indeed, the survival of the species would seem to require such "preprogramming" at least in the behavioral responses to such situations, if not also in their cognitive evaluation. The work of Chomsky, of the so-called sociobiologists, and of others such as the traditional ethologists has made it increasingly plausible to believe that certain beliefs that we have are partially "preprogrammed" in us in the sense that these beliefs, while possibly true and even rationally justifiable, come to be held on the basis of extremely slight evidence which, by the usual canons of induction, and at the time and by the means that they typically come to be held by a particular person, have an entirely inadequate foundation in the justificatory sense. It is easy to see, in the case of beliefs about causal connections, how, provided that it is biologically possible for it to be so, there could be considerable survival value in having the genetically based predisposition to have such beliefs under relatively "weak" circumstances. Observations such as these are in any case, I believe, the proper way to discount the otherwise somewhat perplexing examples of the sort I mentioned. Negatively, these philosophers have as yet failed to make clear what additional entity of an ontologically interesting kind is supposed to be present in such experiences. It is this failure and not any utter lack of difficulty in the regularity view that makes the regularity theory the most plausible account of lawfulness and the ontology of causation.

But causation, I said, is lawfulness *plus context*. For, at least as we speak, not all lawful connections are causal connections. Which ones are, which not, and why? I believe that, despite the attempts of some philosophers to have a "theory" of what additional features must or must not be present in order that a certain lawful connection be a causal one, it is altogether a mistake for the philosopher to attempt any formal or systematic account of these features. Even the most commonly mentioned one of the temporal relation (as a necessary, not a sufficient, condition) of priority of cause to effect is reasonably disputable insofar as specification of contexts is largely a description of linguistic behavior (or, as some philosophers like to call it, "intuitions"). What remains therefore is to specify certain contexts that are relevant to talk about, or allusion to, the relation of mind to body. Specifying such contexts up to a certain point will, if I am successful, achieve the goal of reducing the charge against parallelism to a harmless one that can be lodged, once one sees through it all, against all of its alternatives as well – that the sense of the view seems incongruous with certain ways of speaking and thinking when, in a certain context, some features of the lawful situation are being treated as causal and others not while in a different context, the opposite or something like it might be true. I begin with the easier task, mainly in order to illustrate the idea of specifying contexts, of showing circumstances in which it would be natural to say that the physical is the cause of the mental but not the other way around.

Almost anyone can be caught in a frame of mind in which he or she will readily agree that while there can be lifeless and therefore "mindless" bodies, there cannot be disembodied minds. This view, which simply asserts the primacy of matter, is sometimes called philosophical materialism; but it might reasonably also be called "commonsense materialism," provided that it is clearly seen that commonsense materialism does not entail absolute materialism, the theory that there is nothing nonphysical. More specifically, we do believe (apart from religious and other even more unworthy motives) that while a brain can exist without a mind, a mind cannot exist without a brain or other, somehow comparably complex physical ground. This fact, or one's awareness of it, provides a context for saying that while, on the parallelist's view, a certain brain state lawfully cannot occur unless a certain mental state occurs simultaneously and even while, if the connection is many/one from body to mind, that mental state might occur under different physical conditions, the brain state is the *cause* of the mental state and not the other way around. Another, related context is provided by the fact just mentioned – the probable many/one relation of body to mind – which, given also the relevant laws, makes the mental *calculable* from the physical but not the other way around. And of course a third context has already been mentioned in formulating the objection – the claim of the modern parallelist that the physical realm but not the mental is causally closed with its implication that the full (or maximally possible) lawful explanation of mental phenomena *requires* mention of the physical but not the other way around.

But all of this, while it identifies contexts for saying that on the parallelist's view the physical is sometimes the cause of the mental, is only the less important half of the story as far as most critics of parallelism are concerned. For the great fear as we know, is that if parallelism is true, it is never the case that anything mental *causes* anything physical. How, finally and precisely, should this charge be dealt with?

One may begin by pointing out that it is usually *subsequent behavior* and not simultaneous brain states that anyone is anxious to be able to regard correctly as being sometimes the causal consequences of having certain mental states. Of course, insofar as there is a chain of intermediate physical occurrences between one's choosing to do something and doing it, one may wish to say that the mental state of choosing must also be the cause of those intermediate physical occurrences. But that is, philosophically speaking, irrelevant detail. It may also be noted that any talk about *the* cause of an occurrence, including an instance of human behavior, apart from a specific context sounds a little odd, although perhaps not outright misleading or false. There is, of course, in a different *philosophical* context, a long story to be told about reasons, motives, intentions, and so on in which more subtle distinctions and finely grained contexts would be drawn upon than we need to invoke here.[7]

In a sense, therefore, after all this preparation it remains to point out only the same fact that was earlier stressed when it was alleged that our mental states make no difference to anything physical if parallelism is true, a charge that I was careful to distinguish initially from the one now under examination. The fact is, to remind ourselves, that on parallelism, it is lawfully impossible for certain behaviors to occur at least as constituents of certain patterns of behavior unless certain mental states also occur *and* occur temporally prior to and "in" the same person as the behavior in question. This fact, when combined with the general conception of causation that is the only ultimately intelligible one, gives a sufficient context and a sufficient reason for being entitled to characterize such situations, even on the parallelist's view of the lawful connections involved, as ones in which a mental state *causes* a physical state.

The "particularists" about causation often point to our experience of willing and doing as another and, for some of them, the most important kind of case in which causation is immediately experienced. They may be right. As one strongly committed to the importance of the phenomenology of experience in philosophical musings, I find it difficult to deny the strength of this claim. But if I am also right, this fact is entirely consistent with the regularity account of causation and with parallelism. And *if* I am right about that, then, I submit, we have removed the last and most difficult barrier many have encountered in believing what is surely so —that parallelism is true.

APPENDIX: A SPECULATION

Mental properties are not publicly observable. Yet each of us has observed (by introspection) a sudden remembering, for example. How does any of us know that in observing a sudden remembering he is observing the *same property* as others do? How, for that matter, does any of us know that he is observing the same property on successive occasions of his own sudden rememberings? I am willing to allow a certain force to these Wittgensteinian questions with their implicit answer that "the inner stands in need of an outer criterion" provided that it is also realized that since at some point a person simply does take some property or properties as being the same without a "criterion," there is no reason in principle, that is, by the intrinsic nature of the mental as mental, why that person cannot so take mental properties. Certainly the "privacy" of their particular instantiations is no such reason, but only, if at all, the *causal* fact that one cannot learn to identify them as such without an "outer" criterion and without language. Furthermore, whether the property that is given to me when I am aware of my sudden remembering is the same property that is given to you when you are aware of your sudden remembering is a matter of no greater significance than whether the properties given to me (or otherwise observed by me) when I see a cow or hear someone speak are the same properties observed by you in similar situations. Every experience that involves a cognitive aspect, whether of something "inner" or "outer," requires a judgment or a presupposition or (not to be too intellectualistic about it) a simple taking of some property or properties as the same properties one has experienced before. (And I am *not* talking about culturally determined "family resemblances" but literally the same simple property, such as a particular shade of red or a certain pitch.)

I have already argued that if interactionism were true, we could never know what particular state of mind, if any, another person was in at a particular time. That, of course, is quite a different sort of doubt from the kind that Wittgenstein's musings are supposed to engender. But his are, I believe, entirely misplaced *except* insofar as they may show how very deeply rooted in common sense parallelism really is. If there were not some reasonably systematic connection of the coexistence kind between our inner and our outer lives, we probably would never learn the language of mental life. But that is "merely" a causal fact and goes little deeper than the fact that while most of us learn to identify colors as such, that is, without any "criterion," few of us can do so with pitches. Mental properties, I suggest, are somewhat between colors and pitches in this dimension: we are able at first to identify mental properties, or some among them, *only* by outer "criteria," but eventually we are able to identify them in themselves.

Since we can, one way or another, come to identify at least some mental properties without "criteria," it *is* intelligible for a philosopher, including the empiricist, to hold that mental properties are a distinct set from the physical and to imagine that the world *could have been* such that mental and physical properties interact, that is, that parallelism *could have been* false. My suggestion is that it is only because the physical world is causally closed that we can have, as we do, a conception of a distinct mental realm. For if the physical world were not causally closed, that is, if interactionism were true, then we would never be able to learn the language of mental life and would have no systematic idea of a distinct realm. There would be no outer criteria of inner episodes. So we may be assured that parallelism is true by the simple fact that we can imagine it.

Notes

1. "Mind, Brain, and Causation," *Midwest Studies in Philosophy* VI: *The Foundations of Analytic Philosophy*, edited by P. French, T. Uehling, and H. Wettstein (Minneapolis, 1979); and "The Efficacy of Consciousness: Comments on Honderich's Paper," *Inquiry* 24 (1981).

2. Some of what follows can be found also, but in more detail, in my "Behaviorism and the Philosophy of the Act," *Nous* 16 (1982).

3. One might go "outside" the system also in the sense of having to mention other *particulars*; but this is of no theoretical interest, in science or philosophy.

4. See my "Dispositions, Explanation, and Behavior," *Inquiry* 24 (1981).

5. For some discussion of the principle in the context of the philosophy of the human sciences, see my *Logic of Society* (Minneapolis, 1975), chap. III.

6. See, for example, Ted Honderich, "Psychophysical Lawlike Connections and Their Problem," *Inquiry* 24 (1981).

7. I have told some of this story recently in my "Dispositions, Explanation, and Behavior."

Action, Causality,
and Teleological Explanation

ARTHUR COLLINS

I f, as Melden claims, causal explanations are "wholly irrelevant to the understanding we seek" of human actions then we are without an analysis of the "because" in "he did it because . . . ," where we go on to name a reason.

Donald Davidson[1]

INTRODUCTION

In the fifties and sixties, many analytic philosophers argued that reason-giving explanations of human actions should not be interpreted as causal explanations. Some also thought that actions per se should not be thought caused at all. The concerns of this essay are limited to the first, that is, the lesser claim, that, whether or not actions are caused, reason-giving explanations do not appeal to the causes of the actions they explain. This once-popular view has been challenged, notably by Davidson as in the 1963 essay quoted above. What follows is an argument against views like that of Davidson. I support and explain a noncausal interpretation of reason-giving.

I will consider first teleological explanations of events that are not actions. Such explanations provide a nonmysterious paradigm for explanations of occurrences that do not consist in picking out causes for what is explained. I do not know whether to say that just this much is a controversial claim. In any case, the character of teleological explanations will be examined here with a view to securing agreement on the general proposition that a teleological explanation of phenomena in an organic system of a machine makes essential reference to the effect of the event explained and does not refer to causes. Correct teleological explanations can be given in cases where the causes of what is explained are unknown.

The further point of this discussion is the application of the concept of teleological explanation to the context of reason-giving explanations for actions. I mean

345

to provide an analysis of the "because" in "He did it because . . ." that Davidson finds wanting. *Many* reason-giving explanations fall under the general pattern of teleological explanation and are, as such, not to be interpreted causally. I do not claim to have shown that all reason-giving explanations are teleological. Reason-giving is not a precise concept. Those explanations that Davidson called "rationalizations," the explanations for which he said that "primary reasons" can be given, appear to fit the pattern of teleological explanation quite readily.

1. THE STANDARD VIEW OF ENDS, ENDS-IN-VIEW, AND CAUSALITY

A provisional idea of the thesis to be defended here can be had by focusing on the role of reference to the objectives or goals of actions in reason-giving explanations. One line of thought is so commonly followed that it deserves to be called the *standard view*. Suppose a man explains his action as contributing to some future state of affairs. The standard view regards this as a condensed account wherein what is really intended is the assertion that, prior to acting, the agent had reaching that state of affairs as an objective, or that prior to acting he intended to reach that goal, or desired to reach it, or had reaching the objective as an end-in-view. What I call the standard view depends on the intuitive feeling that, if we fail to convert a reference to a future state into a reference to a prior aim, we will wind up explaining the present in terms of the future. This would be an unacceptable finalism that violates the temporal direction of causality and affronts firm convictions about nature. When we have deleted reference to the goal in favor of reference to *having that goal*, we have moved from the temporal framework later than the action to the temporal framework earlier than and up to the action. This prepares us to entertain the question, Could this item: 'His having such and such an objective,' be thought to have caused a man's action?

Much of the discussion of action and causality in the last few decades has been focused by following this standard line of thought. We are brought to think of having an intention, of wanting to accomplish something, or of setting an objective as eventlike items. We are to regard them as occurrences in the mental life of the agent. The debate centers on the appropriateness of thinking of these alleged prior occurrences as causes of what reason-giving explanations explain. Familiar debates have hinged on the conceptual independence that is required of causes and effects. Can intentions or desires be individuated without essential reference to actions they are supposed to explain? This kind of question becomes relevant only if we accept the move from outcome to aim.

The standard line about reason-giving tends to make conscious functions a prominent element in the understanding of action. Our reason-giving abilities rely on matters such as planning, thinking about what will happen under various circumstances, realizing that particular steps will bring about a particular situation, consciously making an effort, and conceiving of one's situation and prospects in a specific and articulated way. These conscious activities play a role in the standard line of thought about action because one can and one often does think about what one will do prior to acting, and one can decide to try to attain a goal before acting on that decision. Familiar prior conscious activities, therefore, provide illustrations that appear to encourage the view that it is always possible to restate reference to outcomes in terms that substitute prior ends-in-view, so that there is always an element in a reason-giving explanation about which the question, "But isn't this the cause?" is apt.

In what follows, I concede that these conscious functions are connected with the *giving* of explanations of one's own actions, but are not a part of the *substance* of such explanations. The fact that a man can think in advance that he will act to attain a certain goal is another manifestation of the fact that he is able to say, having acted, what the goal of his action was, that is, to what outcome it contributed. When a man thinks over things and forms an intention before acting, he knows what he will do and *he knows why*. He projects his action together with a teleological explanation for it. The fact that he knows the explanation in advance does not convert it into a causal explanation.

The standard view induces a double shift in focus in philosophical discussion of reason-giving explanation. The first shift is from one temporal frame to another. If we accept this shift we agree to consider matters that might, at any rate, be causes of what is explained in that they belong to the temporal frame appropriate for causes. The particular matters to which attention is directed are then such things as desires, intentions, decisions, and beliefs. So the second shift moves us from the question of the temporality of explanatory matters adduced in reason-giving to the question of the causal efficacy of mental things. The standard view thereby trades the problem of finalism for the quandaries of mind-body interaction.

Teleological explanation of organic and machine phenomena is unencumbered by the concept of consciousness. This is a great advantage for philosophical analysis. Isolation from unresolved issues in the philosophy of mind makes it possible to clarify a concept of explanation in terms of outcomes that is not causal explanation. When we have a good grasp of this concept, we are in a position to see the force of reason-giving explanations without being distracted by issues relating to consciousness. If we accept the view that I advance here, we are still entitled to the question, "How is it that men are able to give reasons for their actions?" I do not treat this important question here but rather try to distinguish it from the question, "What does a man say about his action when he gives a reason for having performed it?"

2. TELEOLOGY AND COMPENSATION

I call any explanation that derives its explanatory force from appeal to the outcome, goal, or objective of what is explained a teleological explanation. In physiological contexts where there is no question of intentions, desires, or beliefs, the validity of this type of explanation seems to be intuitively evident, although this appearance is often undermined by philosophical reflection and criticism. In the absence of subtleties, it seems obvious that some teleological explanations are true and others false. It is true to say that sweating occurs to cool the body and false to say that pumping it to the brain occurs to cool the blood. Teleological explanations can have different kinds of objects. Regularities are explained (sweating when it is hot), as are particular events (a rise in the rate of perspiration of an individual on an occasion) and the possession of organs (sweat glands). To further the analogy with explanations of particular actions, I will consider only teleological explanations of particular occurrences. Within this restricted domain, I will not present an analysis that tries to fit all cases but will confine attention to a single kind of illustration, namely, teleological explanation of instances of compensatory activity.

Any study of the human body reveals many compensatory physiological activities; among them (and most useful for our purposes) are instances of homeostasis, of which the maintenance of stable body temperature is an often-discussed example. I choose this illustration because it makes it particularly easy to separate the single issue of the outcome-orientation of explanations from other questions with which this single issue is often mixed up. The concept of compensation gets its footing from facts like these: Things happen in the environment of the human body that would, of themselves, cause significant changes in internal body temperature, but body temperature does not change much. Temperature stability is maintained in the face of destabilizing causal factors. How does this happen?

Although the full physiological story involves complex neural functions and is, as far as I know, not yet fully understood, there is no mystery here. Threats to the stability of body temperature are accompanied by offsetting changes in the body, such as changes in the rate of perspiration. Sweat on the skin evaporates and causes heat loss. The more sweat, the more heat loss. Perspiration is only one of the physiological resources for temperature control. Blood vessels dilate and contract. Various glands secrete various amounts of various substances. Under normal conditions, with the mediation of neural functions, perspiration together with other physiological responses combine to produce a joint causal influence that is precisely suited to the maintenance of stable temperature under the particular environmental conditions that happen to present themselves.

Homeostasis makes the fact of compensation obvious because environmental challenges and physiological responses can be extremely varied, whereas the outcome — stable temperature — remains the same. What is obvious is that a body reacts *in whatever way is required under the circumstances so as to produce the same outcome* vis à vis body temperature. To deny that this is what happens would be to suppose that the constancy of the outcome is somehow an accident or a coincidence. Such a denial would entail a refusal to predict that a given threat to stability will be accompanied by just the needed offsetting changes. The willingness to make that prediction, in turn, is equivalent to the acceptance of the idea of compensation. No one takes seriously the thought that the constant outcome might be an accident or coincidence, and everyone would predict offsetting changes to stability threats. Hence, it is right to say that the physiological changes do, indeed, compensate for environmental changes that would affect stability. The body is so structured that it produces whatever response is needed to secure the stability of internal temperature. The stability of the outcome is the foundation of our predictions and explanations of compensating activities.

This account is oversimplified in a number of ways. Some environmental changes are not offset. If it becomes too hot, temperature stability within the body will be lost. Some possible environmental temperatures, such as $1,000,000°$ F, are so great that they would destroy not only temperature stability but also the very circumstances under which talk of internal temperature is meaningful. But, where we can speak of compensation, there is a range of environmental changes for which compensation does succeed. Again, there are important differences among cases in which a given outcome is not preserved. Fevers sometimes have their own teleological explanation: to eliminate a heat-sensitive, invading microorganism. But fever can also result from the failure of temperature control mechanisms. The detailed structures required for these distinctions are complex but do not introduce anything that challenges the concept of compensation. The same is true of the fact that temperature-controlling responses of the body may compensate not only for environmental threats to temperature stability but also for changes originating within the body itself.

The concept of the outcome preserved by compensating changes may be more or less arbitrarily specified. Three outcomes with respect to which human bodies manifest compensatory activities are these:

O_1: Body temperature in the range 98.1-99.1° F
O_2: Body temperature in the range 98.0-100.0°F
O_3: Body temperature in the range 90.0-100.0°F

The degree of compensatory success ascribed to an organism will depend upon the choice of outcome and the range of environmental change for which that outcome is preserved. In actual investigations of organic systems, we think of outcomes preserved by compensation in terms of the normal functioning, health, and survival of organisms. Then outcomes are easily thought of as goals related to the welfare of th system manifesting compensation. These understandings do not play any part in the concept of compensation and outcome-oriented explanations per se. We could readily identify compensatory behavior whether or not we possess any understanding at all of the outcome preserved and whether or not the preservation of that outcome does contribute anything whatever to the welfare of individuals or species. This point will be significant in discussions to come.

3. COMPENSATION AND CAUSALITY

In physiological illustrations of compensation, the event that compensates for environmental changes is a causal factor for the outcome adduced in a teleological explanation. That it will maintain normal temperature explains a change in perspiration rate, and that change, under the circumstances, causes the temperature to fall in the normal range. So the explanatory factor is the effect of the explained event.

Teleological explanation would be finalistic if it represented the outcome as, somehow, the cause of the changes that produce it. But there is no reason to make such an implausible claim. The outcome is the effect in the ordinary sense and temporal order of things, but it is the effect that is explanatory. This is not at all, as is sometimes suggested, simply a way of bringing out the thought that the cause is a necessary condition for the effect. It is the compensatory structure of the behavior of the system generally that supports the teleological explanation, and not merely the fact that causes are necessary for their effects. It is only because we believe that just the right compensating change needed to cause *this* effect will be the one that occurs that we say of one such change that it occurs in order that the outcome be attained.

Causality bears on the concept of compensation at a second critical juncture. This fact can prompt scepticism about the distinctive character of teleological explanation. We have said that where compensation exists, environmental changes are accompanied by offsetting changes so as to bring about a given outcome. This accompaniment is itself a manifestation of causal relations. Let S be a system that reveals compensatory activity with respect to an outcome O, let F be a particular environmental change that threatens the attainment of O, and let E be the instance of compensatory activity that offsets F and, under the circumstances, causes O. What accounts for the fortunate occurrence of E just when F comes along and threatens the maintenance of the outcome O? No doubt, the occurrence of E is a consequence of a causal link between F and E. In other words, F threatens O and at the same time causes E, which removes the threat, again causally. A teleologically organized system is precisely one that works in a way that guarantees that this will happen for a range of environmental changes. There will be causal explanations for everything that happens in such compensatory mechanisms. Does teleology then reduce to causal explanation? I say that it does not.

Engineers are called upon to construct machines that exhibit compensatory activity, and that means activity that will be teleologically explicable. In building such a machine, an engineer has to exploit causal relationships between the machine, its environment, and possible outcomes. He is not called upon to go beyond such causal relationships nor to build in an occult device that anticipates the future. Outcome-oriented explanation is a feature of events in it because of the organization of his machine, given its environment, and not a further component or peculiar principle operating in it. It is for just this reason that teleological explanation in terms of compensation and outcome-orientation can be both successful and nonmysterious.

We can say that a fully understood compensating change is a causal link between an environmental change and the outcome. F causes E, which causes O. It would be entirely misleading, however, to say that the explanatory force of a teleological explanation comes from a tacit reference to the causes of the event explained. On the contrary, confidence that there is a causal relation between F and E is frequently engendered by acceptance of the teleological explanation itself. Our ideas about the causal history of a teleologically explained event may have no support at all apart from the teleological explanation. We recognize that E compensates for F because E-like responses to F-like threats *actually do attain O*.

The example of homeostasis makes this particularly obvious. This much puts us in the position to assert, "Since E offsets F so that O is attained, there must be a causal connection between F and E, for we do not think that the compensatory activity is a miracle." In actual biological investigations, the discovery of homeostatic phenomena and other end-oriented organization raises the question of the causal relations that underlie compensation. Compensation can be identified and teleological explanations rightly given whether or not we have discovered anything about the causal history of the compensating events.

This point is brought with special force when the demand for teleological explanation includes some causal understanding of the puzzling event: "Why does working in hot weather make us sweat?" This is answered by: "To keep the body temperature from rising." The only causes of E (sweating) that we are familiar with are already incorporated in the explanation-seeking question. Surely they cannot also be presented as the answer. Here we are thinking of explanation for the layman. The conceptual point remains the same in the context of a technical explanation for E. We might know all there is to know about the cause of E but not know the teleological explanation for it. Teleological and causal explanations are independent. When we eat, enzymes are released in the saliva to trigger the secretion of hydrochloric acid in the stomach and facilitate digestion. Who knows what causes the release of the enzymes? Experts surely have a causal account and we could learn it. After reaching a complete causal understanding of E, we might discover that the teleological explanation was wrong to begin with. The enzymes may not be what causes secretion of the acid. Then too, the expert explanation we accept for E may prove to be wrong without threatening the teleological explanation.

It is the structure of the behavior of S in its environment that manifests compensation. This suffices for recognition of instances of compensation and, therefore, for teleological explanation. No causal account of what is teleologically explicable captures what is expressed in the teleological explanation.

4. TELEOLOGY AND BEHAVIORISM

I mean to use the pattern of teleological explanation considered so far as a paradigm for explanations of actions that state reasons for which they were done. A teleological explanation is never restatable as a causal explanation. Reference to an effect or outcome of what is explained is the crux of teleology. The standard view of reason-giving insists on a preliminary shift from outcomes to aims on the ground that appeals to outcomes are finalistic, if they are not heuristic shorthand for appeal to causes. The cases we have examined show that, as a general thesis, this is not true. There are plenty of correct explanations that advert to outcomes and not to causes. I plan to show that many reason-giving explanations of actions fit this pattern so that the preliminary shift is quite without justification.

In his book *Teleology*, Andrew Woodfield follows a line of thinking that is as opposed to what I will argue as is possible.[2] Whereas I argue that nonmentalistic teleological explanations of events that are not actions should be our model for reason-giving, Woodfield argues that mentalistic reason-giving explanations of actions should be our model for all teleological explanation. Woodfield's position is much influenced by his criticism of "the theory of goal-directedness" or of "directive correlation" that was developed by G. Sommerhof, E. Nagel, and others.[3] These accounts of teleology, like my own, which is much indebted to them, try to explicate teleological organization and teleological explanation without introducing anything either finalistic or mental in the contexts where teleological explanations have footing.

According to Woodfield's critique, these efforts to dispel mysteries employ a spurious conception of goals and goal-directedness, and this vitiates their account of teleology. He finds the theories of goal-directedness excessively *behavioristic*. Whereever explanations that invoke goals are legitimate, Woodfield contends, we must be able to say who it is that has the goal and we must be able to posit an inner state that constitutes *the having of that goal* by the organism. This, in turn, means that we must be able to think in terms of desirelike and belieflike states or events in organisms that have goals.[4] At least, Woodfield believes that all this is essential to the core concept of teleology from which usage has been extended more or less figuratively to other contexts that resemble but fall short of core cases. In other words, Woodfield accepts the standard view reconstruction of reason-giving explanations of actions and then he extends that conception to teleological explanations generally. Apparently, even in contexts like temperature homeostasis, Woodfield will insist on one of three alternatives: (a) a posited framework of mental states and events, (b) an analogical similarity to cases where mental states and events are posited, or (c) the rejection of teleological explanations.

I cannot try to do justice to Woodfield's very full and subtle discussions of the problems of teleology in this essay. Some of the questions he raises are matters on which I do not have a view that is satisfactory. At the same time, I am quite confident that the mentalizing of all teleology is a big step in the wrong direction. I will consider only two themes here in the hope of making my antimentalism plausible. The first theme concerns the concept of a goal; the second is the claim that teleological organization and teleologically explicable behavior are manifest and, therefore, cannot be thought dependent upon posited, unobserved states.

In describing compensation and homeostasis in part 3, I intentionally avoided the expression "goal" and the expression "goal-directed behavior." I do not think that we should describe temperature stability as a goal of organisms that exhibit temperature homeostasis. This usage is worth avoiding just because it does give rise to the question, "Who or what is it that has this goal?" and the question, "In what does the possession of this goal by this organism consist?" When these questions go wholly unanswered, the very idea of outcome-oriented explanation comes to seem suspect. But that appearance is mostly the result of the ill-advised use of "goal" for the outcome for which compensation is exhibited in the behavior of the organism. We do not look for an owner of an outcome as we inevitably do look for the owner of a goal. So confinement to "outcome" deletes a mentalizing temptation.

We saw above that where there is compensation, the description of the outcome is arbitrary or, in any case, determined by understandings that are external to the fact of compensatory organization. Just what temperature is it that a human body maintains? There is nothing to be said against any of the three different outcomes formulated in part 3 or against other specifications. Woodfield thinks that, where teleological explanation is truly apt, we ought to be able to point to something answering to the idea of "having the goal G." But is it not extremely doubtful that we should ever find a reason for identifying one of the possible temperature ranges as the goal that the organism actually has? Notice that if we make the outcome range narrow—for example, 98.5-98.7° F—we will not be able to identify changes that keep temperature within wider limits as compensatory at all because they simply fail to maintain temperature in the chosen narrow range. Obviously, many compensatory events will be excluded since normal temperature so often strays from this range. A very wide range, such as 93.6-103.6° F, is no better. Though body temperature rarely escapes it, this range does not capture compensations that offset less extreme threats. With this huge outcome range, an environmental factor that would, by itself, cause a fever of 103° F would not even count as a threat to stability!

Our decision to think of some one range as "normal temperature" does not mean that this is the range the body really cares about. For every choice of ranges, wide, narrow, or medium, there will be compensatory activity that fails to be represented as such given that choice. The recognition that a system exhibits compensation is compatible with this variability in the description of the outcome. Thus the concept of compensation does not require that any outcome be identified as the real goal of the organism.

The fact that we can sometimes explain events teleologically even though they fail to attain the designated outcome is one of the reasons for which it seems tempting to think of the outcome as a goal. A goal, as Woodfield remarks, is an intentional object, and reference to it can explain even if it is not reached. Since this is sometimes true of outcome-explanations, outcomes seem goallike. But to speak of goals is to speak of what an agent has in mind, what he is trying to do, whether or not he succeeds. The concept of an outcome does not support these ideas. We understand that sweating is explicable as producing normal temperature, in the first instance, because it succeeds in compensating for threats to normal temperature. On the basis of that understanding, we will explain an instance of sweating teleologically even though the outcome, normal temperature, is not produced. We may know, for example, that it would have been produced if the ambient temperature had not been so very high.

It is this sort of consideration and not analogies with conscious effort that accounts for teleological explanation in the face of goal-failure. Goals may be intentional objects, outcomes are certainly not. As Woodfield says, analysts of "goal-directedness" do not justify their use of the word "goal." But the concept of goals is simply not required at all for understanding compensation and, with it, teleological explanation.

I say that compensation is manifest in the behavior of an organism. In contrast

Woodfield's requirement of an inner state of having goal G is intended as a condition for the legitimacy of teleological explanation. In the absence of such an inner state, we are supposed to withdraw the use of teleological language or, at best, to regard it as analogically extended usage. This is simply a mark of Woodfield's over-confidence in the standard view that recasts outcome-oriented explanations as causal explanations. It means, for example, that to the extent that we do not believe that the body contains a state roughly describable as "having the goal of keeping temperature normal," we should deny that the body does maintain normal temperature. No one, however, is going to deny this. Will Woodfield want to invoke unconscious mental items here, as he suggests elsewhere?[5] Does temperature homeostasis in lower animals go to show, as Woodfield says, that "Minds may be far *more* widespread than some philosophers have thought?"[6]

It seems clear that whatever scruples we feel about teleological explanations in physiology, nothing will be advanced by ascribing to ourselves unconscious ends-in-view, desires, and beliefs to go with every subtle manifestation of outcome orientation discovered in the body. The blood coagulates to minimize losses through bleeding. If we accept this explanation, it will not help us to express our understanding of the phenomenon to posit an unconscious desire to keep our blood from flowing out. Even if I have such a desire, it will be utterly ineffectual in the absence of the mechanism of coagulation. And with the mechanism of coagulation, blood loss through bleeding will be limited whether I desire it or not.

Woodfield's discussion of teleology are consistently sensitive to conceptual problems, but the direction in which he turns for solutions is faulty because of his reliance on the standard view of reason-giving as the ultimate pattern for all teleological explanation. The misuse of the word "goal" in the tradition that Woodfield calls behaviorist may be largely responsible for the inadequacies of his own thinking about teleology. Essentially, he believes that where one can properly speak of goals, one must be able to speak of the having of goals; goals will inevitably be the intentional objects of desirelike states and thus impose the general format of mentality on any context where goals play a part. A behaviorist analysis like that of Nagel uses the concept of goals but makes no room whatever for any of the required mental states or for any analogs to them. So behaviorism fails.

Woodfield is entirely right in this criticism. The proper response, however, is simply the deletion of the concept of goals from the behaviorist reconstruction of teleological explanation. We can thus retain the insight that teleological organization is something discoverable about a system and its environment that requires no behind-the-scenes functioning of any kind. As I have insisted above, compensatory structure is simply observable in behavior, and homeostasis makes this as obvious as it can be. Of course, it is correct to predict that the very organic changes that will maintain temperature stability are the ones that will occur. Compensation would be ascribable and prediction justified even if we had no idea whatever about either the utility of stable temperature for the organism or the causes of the bodily changes that ensure it.

Many philosophers reflecting on teleology have thought, "To be sure, this homeostasis is a good thing for the organism, but ought we say that changes are teleologically explicable unless we think that the organism, in some sense, wants and tries to secure homeostasis?" The fact is that compensatory behavior would authorize teleological explanation even if we could make out no advantage to the organism in the outcome and even if there were, in fact, no such advantage. Patent compensatory structure of behavior will always inspire speculations and research aimed at providing an understanding of the utility of the outcome and of the cause of the compensatory events. Recognition of the existence of compensation is in no way dependent on our actually attaining some understanding of the utility of the outcome or of the causal history of the events that we can explain teleologically.

5. THEOLOGY AND EVOLUTION

Compensatory behavior motivates investigation of the causal mechanisms that make compensation possible and also motivates the question, "How does the body come to possess these mechanisms?" Just as recognition of compensation does not depend on our understanding the causes of compensatory activity, so too the existence of compensation and its complete causal analysis do not depend on our success in explaining how systems exhibiting teleological organization come to exist.

Familiar theological arguments are relevant here. The body has features that are wonderfully suited to the welfare of the creature. It is as though bodies were designed as devices to secure that welfare. The body of a man, for example, is equipped with sweat glands as though its designer foresaw the need to control temperature in variable environments. Might not God be the designer here? If this were right, we could see through the phenomena to the goals and purposes of God. I am not interested in the merits of theological thinking here but rather in its assumptions concerning teleology and the goals and purposes of designers. Now that we have entered the age of genetic engineering, the format of the argument here is intelligible with or without the theology. We can plausibly, if incorrectly, discern the mentality of a designer through the structure and function of an organic body, just as we can discern the mentality of the designer through the structure and function of a machine made of springs and valves and gears.

There is something like the standard view at work again here in arguments that go from perceived organization to posited designer. Finding a subtly operating, outcome-oriented mechanism, we look for an agent designer to be the owner of the goals that the mechanism *automatically* attains. This way of putting the matter gives rise to the idea that the teleological discourse that comes into play rests on the mentality of the designer, and that the machine or organic body itself is only described in teleological language because it is the concrete embodiment of means to ends that are expressly desired by the designer. We can say that an automobile's carburetor exists in order to mix air with fuel only because this was the designer's reason for including a carburetor in his design. We can say that the human body maintains a constant internal temperature only because God has equipped it with sweat glands and other features so that its temperature should remain constant.

This is the thought that teleology in mechanisms reduces to teleology in the goal-seeking actions of designers of them. The thought is based entirely on conflating explanations of events that occur in mechanisms with explanations of the existence of those mechanisms.

If the reduction in question here were not an error, we would be obliged to say that—in the absence of a designer—teleology in nature is only an illusion to be replaced by straightforward causal explanation. That is, we would say that, if the human body was not designed by God or by anyone else, then it is not a teleologically organized system at all, but only seems to be one. In the heyday of the debate between the mechanists and vitalists, I think that this principle was widely accepted by both sides. Entelechies and vital forces were like self-contained surrogates for a designer. Those who rejected these concepts and proposed a natural etiology for organisms of the sort suggested by the theory of evolution seemed to believe that the advocacy of such a view included opposition to teleological explanation in biology altogether. The hard-headed scientific school wanted to read teleology out of the organic world because science admits no designer for natural things and, therefore, no owner for any goals. Without an owner of goals, there can be no goals. With no goals, there can be no teleology.

I hope the appropriate refutation of this reduction of teleology to the goals of designers is by now familiar to the reader. Since compensation and teleological organization are manifest in behavior, failure to find a designer cannot possibly entail the absence of compensation and teleological organization. It is the irrevocable recognition of compensation that generates the designer argument. The pattern here is, (a) *since there is compensation*, we need an explanation for this fact, and a designer would be a good explanation. The pattern is not, (b) *If there is compensation*, then there must be a designer. Only from the latter would it follow that there is no compensation if there is no designer.

Abandoning the theological designer argument does nothing to cloud our perception and study of compensatory mechanisms in the body. The very existence of evolutionary explanations of the existence of compensatory mechanisms (again, independent of the correctness of those explanations) should make this evident. The main point of evolution-based explanations is that they do not posit anything in the role of a designer, whereas they do accept the demand for some explanation of the existence of mechanisms whose operation is patently teleological.

If this point stands, we are entitled to a further conclusion. In the case of artifact machines where there is a designer, the outcome orientation of the structure of the behavior of the machine is conceptually independent of the thoughts, goals, and purposes of the designer. By hypothesis, a compensating mechanism in a man-made machine exists as a consequence of the purposes and foresight of designers and builders. But that they are compensating mechanisms is simply a fact about the structure of mechanisms in relation to their environment and not an allusion to the mental processes of their designers. A simple thermostat system compensates for changes in the temperature of a room by turning on and off a furnace: To say this is to remain at the level of the activity of the mechanism. Teleological explanation is fully authorized by the fact that these activities are compensatory. The system actually maintains a stable temperature. In the case of an artifact, we are entitled to infer designer goals from machine performance. We are not entitled to reduce teleological explanation to appeals to the goals of the designers of systems that exhibit teleological organization.

6. TELEOLOGY AND ACTION

In "Teleological Explanation and Teleological Systems," Ernest Nagel does not address the question of the bearing of his analysis on human action and reason-giving explanation. In fact, he seems to adopt a conception of reason-giving explanation in passing that would rule out the possibility that teleological explanation might serve as a pattern for reason-giving. Although I do not follow Nagel in this connection at all, I do believe that attention to his apparent line of thought is instructive. Consider this passage:

> Quite apart from their association with the doctrine of final causes, teleological explanations are sometimes suspect in modern natural science because they are assumed to invoke purposes or ends-in-view *as causal factors* in natural processes. Purposes and *deliberate goals* admittedly play important roles in human activities; but there is no basis whatever for assuming them in the study of physico-chemical and most biological phenomena.[7]

Here Nagel is dismissing the charge that teleological explanations are anthropomorphic. (Curiously enough, Woodfield's criticism of Nagel is roughly the claim that they ought to be anthropomorphic.) Nagel thinks teleological explanations would be anthropomorphic if they ascribed "purposes and deliberate goals" to the nonhuman phenomena they explain, but, as his analysis shows, teleological explanations do not require any role for these concepts. In passing, Nagel makes it clear that he regards reason-giving explanations of human actions in much the same way as does Davidson. Purposes and ends-in-view are "causal factors." In its reference to ends-in-view, this passage illustrates what I have called the standard line of thought. A man has an end-in-view before he acts or when he acts, so that "having an end-in-view" could be a candidate causal factor for the explained behavior. A restatement of the explanation that adduced the end or outcome rather than the end-in-view would not make this candidate cause available.

Finally, Nagel's word "deliberate" in "deliberate goals" illustrates the pattern of thinking that appeals to conscious activities as a support for construing the purposiveness of actions in terms of antecedent events in the mind. In this case, the conscious activity would be the deliberate adoption of a goal or the adoption of a goal after conscious deliberation. Actually, the words "deliberate goals" are rather awkward. Why does not Nagel just say "purposes and goals?" The answer is surely that Nagel's account of teleological explanation of nonhuman organic and machine functioning will speak of "goals". He introduces "deliberate" in the context of human action out of the conviction that what is important in the human case is that people consciously think about what they are going to accomplish, weigh considerations, and so on. All this is true. If I am right, however, this is not what gives explanations of actions in terms of objectives and outcomes their force.

The prima facie case for regarding reason-giving as a kind of teleological explanation is strong. Whatever the bearing on action of the cluster of concepts — conscious deliberation, foresight, desire, understanding, planning, trying, and so on — reason-giving explanations obviously refer actions to objectives, outcomes, or end-states that are caused by the explained events. Consider an illustration of Davidson's: "I flipped the switch because I wanted to turn on the light." Ordinarily, in such cases, my flipping the switch certainly does cause the end-state: having the light on. Although Davidson's "I wanted to turn on the light" is perfectly natural, so too is simply "In order to turn on the light." Only the standard view of reason-giving explanation requires that the latter be considered a condensed version of the former.

The straightforward causality involved in the relationship between the switch flipping and the light going on contrasts with the murkiness of the supposed causal account of the act of flipping the switch. I say that, on the surface of it, it seems likely that the accessibility and intelligibility of the reason-giving explanation is a consequence of its reliance on the straightforward relationship between the act and the objective, and not on the precarious system of hypotheses converting reference to the outcome into reference to a prior state of *wanting*, together with the dark speculation that the wanting caused the relevant switch-flipping action.

To move beyond a primitive preference for the teleological interpretation of reason-giving, two analyses are relevant: (1) The context of reason-giving and action must be shown to exhibit structural similarities to the context of teleological explanations of events that are not actions. I believe that the similarities are so full and evident that they strengthen the credentials of the teleological interpretation to such a degree that the superimposition of a further causal claim about the explained action comes to seem entirely gratuitous. Contrary to Davidson's contention we do have a convincing and natural analysis of the "because" in "He did it because . . . ," that is not a causal analysis. Once we agree that the structure of a man's behavior in acting bears detailed similarities to the structure of teleologically explicable activities in organic systems and machines, it becomes very hard to avoid the conclusion that the made-to-order pattern of teleological explanation — outcome-oriented and noncausal — is just what we need in understanding the force of reason-giving.

(2) The standard line of thought must, at last, be expressly evaluated. The pull of the standard line is very strong. In construing reason-giving as teleological explanation, we seem to ignore the thought that the agent may experience pangs of desire before acting, that he may think it all out consciously beforehand, foresee the consequences of his action and deliberately set himself to realize those consequences. The resurgent standard view will insist on a role for these things in reason-giving explanations. Isn't it true that he only did it because he realized beforehand that . . . ? Didn't his gnawing desire finally drive him to do it? In short, the bare appeal to the attainment of an outcome seems to leave out something essential

in reason-giving, however apt it may be for cases of compensation. It isn't just that the light is caused to go on by flipping the switch that makes it appropriate and true to say, "I flipped the switch in order to turn on the lights." Reason-giving involves my recognizing such causal relations and wanting to exploit them. Defense of the teleological interpretation requires either that this appearance of inadequate attention to these ingredients is an illusion or that giving the fullest play to these ingredients is compatible with the teleological interpretation of explanations of actions.

7. ACTION AS COMPENSATION

A satisfactory parallel between events in a teleologically organized system and actions depends upon finding something like compensation in ordinary action. The first thing to be noted on this head is that actions can be patently compensatory behavior for the maintenance of a homeostatic outcome. Given a man in a room with a thermometer, a heater, and an air conditioner, we can construct a perfect analogy for the control of body temperature where the compensating events are not the operations of automatic mechanisms but the actions of the man. A man steering a boat with the help of a compass is a naturally occurring illustration of the same type. The homeostatic outcome is the coincidence of the direction of the motion of the boat and a point of the compass. Whenever currents, swells, or wind would move the boat from the given heading, the helmsman acts so as to maintain the constant outcome-state. Here we find exactly the relationships that obtain in a physiological system with homeostatic compensatory activities, except for one point. In the exposition of physiologically based homeostasis, we required that the environmental event needing to be offset be causally related to the compensating event, which is then explained teleologically as occurring in order that homeostasis be maintained.

In the context of action-based homeostasis, this relationship between the outcome-threat and the compensating occurrence is uncertain. It is an action that does the compensating, and we cannot baldly assert that the helmsman's action is *caused* by the shift in the wind that tends to move the boat off course and thus threatens the heading in a manner for which the helmsman compensates. Insofar as we are in doubt about the relationship of action and causality, we cannot simply claim a causal relationship here. This uncertainty is a significant issue for the teleological interpretation of reason-giving. But uncertainty here does not tell in favor of accounts like that of Davidson.

In this kind of illustration, a man's action is fitted into a context that has exactly the same broad organizational features as a teleologically explicable instance of compensation in a physiological context. We cannot draw the unqualified conclusion that reason-giving (in this kind of case, at least) is teleological explanation because the causal relationship between outcome-threats from the environment and compensatory events is essential to our account of teleology, and it is not clear that it is to be found where compensations are actions. However, if the relationship between outcome-threats and compensating actions were found to be causal, that would tell *against* a causal interpretation of reason-giving, *against* the standard view, and *against* Davidson's account. The discovery (or decision to say) that actions are caused by the events that threaten homeostasis would remove the only scruple standing in the way of saying that the helmsman with compass and boat *constitutes* a teleologically organized system and does not merely resemble such a system. It is precisely in teleological systems, where the relationship in question is certainly causal, that one can give teleological explanations that do not adduce causes of what they explain. We know that it is the heat that somehow causes sweating that offsets it and keeps temperature within the body stable. But the teleological explanation cites the outcome and not the cause of the sweating. Were we satisfied that the shifting wind somehow caused the compensating adjustment at the helm, we would be in a position to say with confidence that the explanation "He moved the wheel in order to stay on course" is teleological and not causal.

Doubts about this causal relationship are not a serious threat to the teleological interpretation of reason-giving in any case. We required a causal relationship in the case of physiological compensatory activity in order to understand how the right compensating event manages to accompany the right threat. Without a causal relation, compensatory behavior would appear either miraculous or coincidental and, in that case, not really compensation at all. That is why we posit a causal connection between environmental changes and compensatory responses though we are ignorant of the details. In the context of action, doubts about the causal character of the relation between environmental changes and compensating actions do not have the same basis at all.

We do not suspect that if a compensating action was not caused by events threatening a goal then it is not compensation. Those who hold that actions are uncaused to not mean that actions do not help to bring about objectives. Whatever the relationship between environmental change and compensating act, that relationship will support counterfactuals such as "Had the wind not shifted as it did, the helmsman would not have done what he did." Even in the setting of physiology it is the support of counterfactuals like this and not an actual causal story that is crucial for the recognition of homeostasis. All we really need know about rises in environmental temperature and sweating is that, had the environment not become hotter, the sweating would not have occurred. Compensation and teleology could be systematically characterized by substituting supporting counterfactuals for causal connection between threat and compensation. We could then distinguish two ways in which this condition could be satisfied, since both activities *caused by* threats to homeostasis and actions *prompted by* threats to homeostasis offer the needed counterfactual support.

We have considered only very special examples of explanation of actions constructed in order to create a systematic resemblance to physiological homeostasis, that is, examples wherein actions plainly compensate for outer influences for the sake of the maintenance of a constant outcome-state. Within the framework of this narrowly conceived set of examples, the basis for rejecting a teleological interpretation for reason-giving explanation seems to shrink to dogmatism. But most human actions do not offer such good analogies to physiological compensatory activities. For the most part, actions are not compensations prompted by the presence of some particular factor that threatens homeostasis. The difficulty, however, in seeing actions as similar to compensation stems largely from the fact that there is nothing in particular to pick out as environmental menace to a given objective and, therefore, nothing for which the action could be viewed as compensating.

The maintenance of body temperature and the steering of a boat are both examples of homeostasis, and homeostasis puts the concept of compensation in high relief just because it draws attention to specific influences that threaten the homeostatic goal. The control mechanism is structured in relation to these influences so as to prevent their having their normal effect and thus protect the "goal." It is not the case that all organic and machine activity that it teleologically explicable is homeostatic. Enzymes are released in the saliva to bring about the secretion of hydrochloric acid, but the release of enzymes does not keep the value of some organic parameter in a constant normal range on the analogy of temperature control.

I have directed attention to homeostasis not because it is essential to teleological explanation, but only because the constancy of the outcome makes the outcome-orientation of our explanations most obvious. For the most part, actions pursue short-term goals that cannot be represented as homeostasis; however, this does not tend to show that reason-giving explanations for actions are not generally teleological.

One might say that any action that is done to bring about something or to reach some objective compensates for the fact that the ordinary course of events does not bring about that something without help. A man wants to see in a dark room. The world being what it is, the light is not going to go on by itself. So a man compensates for this general feature of the world by flipping the switch that turns it on. Looked at in this way, the compensatory character of most actions is masked by the fact that nothing usually stands to bring about the objective except the action itself, and nothing stands to impede the objective if the action is done. Action is a kind of limiting case of compensation. The action compensates for the general failure of the world to produce the objective without intervention from the agent.

Somewhat more naturally, a kind of compensatory character is detectable in the fact that circumstances sometimes do block the success of the undertaken and ordinarily effective action. Reason-giving explanations carry the implication that the failure of the explained action to reach its goal would have prompted other actions as explicit compensation for whatever obstacles it is that have prevented attainment of the objective. A man who wants a lighted room will do various things besides flipping a switch in order to turn on a light, if other actions are needed. He will pull chains, test bulbs, run extension cords, check fuse boxes, and pay overdue electric bills. There is no particular limit to the things that might be relevant and that might be done. The explanation "in order to turn on the light" does not define the lengths to which a man would go rather than let this objective remain unattained. This parallels the fact that the correctness of teleological explanations outside the context of action also implies nothing about the range of variations for which the teleologically organized system will provide compensation, although it does imply that there is such a range.

Intuitively, if we accept a certain reason-giving explanation, we will certainly expect that the agent was prepared to do other things that he recognized as alternative routes to his objective, especially if those alternatives are of equal simplicity and without deterrent side effects. To establish that action is essentially compensatory, however, we have to go beyond appeal to customary expectations. We have to show that reason-giving actually carries the implication that compensatory actions would have been undertaken had the explained action failed.

The required allusion to alternatives and consequent compensatory structure is tacitly incorporated in Davidson's account of reason-giving. According to Davidson, "a primary reason" always involves two elements: "a pro attitude towards actions of a certain kind" and a belief "that [the performed action] is of that kind."[8] The appeal to a class of actions of a certain kind is needed because "we cannot explain why someone did what he did simply by saying that the particular action appealed to him; we must indicate what it was in the action that appealed."[9] This leads us to a general class of actions since any appropriate characterization of the explained action will impute to it something that other actions will also possess. Davidson shows that the particularity of the action: "I turned on the light," is not shared by the pro attitude: "I wanted to turn on the light." The latter does indicate a pro-attitude toward a general class of actions, although grammatical similarities mask the generality:

> If I turned on the light, then I must have done it at a precise moment in a particular way — every detail is fixed. But it makes no sense to demand that my want be directed at an action performed at any one moment in some unique manner. Any one of an indefinitely large number of actions would satisfy the want, and can be considered equally eligible as its object.[10]

Davidson does not say that the members of the class of actions alluded to in a primary reason include alternative actions that would compensate for obstacles to the attainment of an objective. It is certain, however, that the principle of similarity in terms of which actions are "of a certain kind" has to be the fact that they are all thought by the agent to be ways of bringing about the objective. In the quoted passage, Davidson seems to have in mind only trivial differences between actions having the same outcome, such as flipping the switch with my right index finger, flipping the switch with my left index finger, etc. This is all that is needed to show that a general class of actions is involved. But true alternative actions emerge as constituents of the class toward the members of which the agent has a pro attitude in a further example Davidson offers: "If I say I am pulling weeds because I want a beautiful lawn, it would be fatuous to eke out the account with, 'And so I see something desirable in any action that does [make], or has a good chance of making, the lawn beautiful!"[11] Davidson means that it would be fatuous just because this general assertion is obviously implied by the reason-giving explanation.

What is common, then, to all the actions that are equally objects of a pro-attitude involved in reason-giving is that they are all causally relevant to the same outcome, namely, to the objective of the explained action. Upon reflection, we are entitled to say that compensatory actions will be found in any such class of actions, even those that appear to differ only trivially. After all, if my left index finger proves to be too weak, will I not try to flip the switch with another finger, that is, if I really do want to turn on the light? In saying that the generality involved in pro attitudes is equivalent to the ascription of compensatory status to actions, I mean to assert that a man who explains performing one action by saying that it belonged to a class of actions toward each of which he had a pro attitude is, at the same time, committing himself to the assertion that, had the performed action been inefficacious in attaining the goal that defines the class in question, then (in the absence of countervailing reasons) he would have performed one or more other such actions in order to secure the goal.

The number of alternatives that stand to compensate for the failure of an action may be limited, and a man can fend off challenges for failing to employ recognized alternatives rather easily, saying, for example, "I just didn't care about it that much," or "I decided not to bother." He may be ignorant of available alternatives, and he may reject otherwise viable alternatives that he does recognize for countless reasons. But reference to the limited urgency of the objective, or ignorance of alternative means to it, or countervailing reasons against their adoption are all of them pertinent only because of the general implication that alternative courses would be pursued if the one adopted did not produce the objective. Were this implication to fail utterly, were the agent to wholly reject liability for this implication, or to have no explanation at all for not satisfying it, then the reason-giving explanation would itself fail.

Thus, the concept of reason-giving explanations of actions reproduces the essential features of teleological organization that we found to account for the intelligibility of explanations that cite effects rather than causes. An explained action is referred to its objective or goal, and reason-giving explanation implies the kind of compensatory plasticity upon which the analysis of teleology was found to depend. Therefore, noncausal teleological explanation constitutes a natural interpretation for reason-giving. The premise that no noncausal interpretation of the "because" in a reason-giving explanation is available, the premise that motivates Davidson and other causal theorists, is overthrown. As Davidson himself expressed this premise, "Failing a satisfactory alternative the best argument for a [causal] scheme like Aristotle's is that it alone promises to give an account of the mysterious connection between reasons and causes."[12]

This connection is no longer mysterious. Reasons explain actions by referring them to their effects and to the compensatory character of behavior vis a vis those effects. In light of the availability of this interpretation, there is no foundation at all for the expectation that reason-giving explanations may *also* refer to the causes of what they explain. We have seen that, in connection with organic or mechanical outcome-oriented explanation, the question of the causal history of teleologically explained events is always raisable. No answers to this question, however, are contained in teleological explanations themselves.

8. PRO ATTITUDES AND CAUSALITY

In the interpretation of reason-giving put forward here, I press for the elimination of any role for the fact (where it is a fact) that the agent wanted to attain the objective reference to which explains his action. Of course, I do not deny that agents commonly do want to reach the objectives that their actions do reach. The teleological interpretation removes reference to this antecedent desire in favor of reference to the outcome itself. The thesis that I called the standard view of reason-giving earlier in this essay regards antecedent desires and beliefs about their possible satisfaction as the very crux of reason-giving. Can I really mean to assert that the mere outcome of the action can be explanatory without the mental processes of the agent who desired and tried to produce that outcome? I do not assert that the mere fact that an action has a certain outcome will validate an explanation adverting to that outcome. We must believe that the agent was disposed to compensate for some obstacles, at least, had the outcome not occurred. Action has a compensatory aspect that is entailed by reason-giving explanations but is not legible from the outcome alone.

This parallels organic cases closely. Suppose that we know about a creature S that its environment changed in temperature from T_1 to T_2 and that the effect of this on constitution of S produced an internal temperature of T_o. By itself, this outcome does not vouch for any teleological explanation. We have to know about the structure of S and, in particular, its compensatory organization. This means that we have to know what would have happened on other circumstances before we can offer "in order to reach or retain T_o" as an explanation for anything. In the same way, desires and beliefs are relevant to explanations of actions because they are the source of our confidence in the compensatory dispositions of the agent, and not because desires and beliefs cause his actions.

It is worth emphasizing that the teleological structure of reason-giving explanations is independent of the resolution of the question, "Do desires and beliefs cause actions?" We have seen in the setting of organic homeostasis that compensation involves two causal relations. The compensating event in the organism causes the homeostatic outcome (under the threatening environmental conditions), and the threatening environmental conditions cause the compensating event in the organism. We saw that the existence of these two causal relationships cannot be construed as implying a causal reading for teleological explanation. This is brought out by the independence of the teleological and causal explanations of the compensating event. The causal account may be utterly unspelled out, or may be in error and rejected, or may be corrected, without affecting the teleological explanation at all. The causal account may be correct, and the teleological explanation may turn out to be mistaken (in case we are right about what causes perspiration and wrong about what perspiration causes). If we have complete knowledge of the relationships, the causal account of the compensating event cannot be substituted for the teleo-logical explanation.

When we compare these relations with the context of explanations of actions, the question of the causal powers of desires and beliefs is analogous to the question of a causal account for a compensating event in an organic system. We said that the compensatory element in action must support counterfactuals with the form, "Had such and such obstacle arisen, the agent would have taken such and such compensa-tory course." The thought that desires and beliefs cause actions would show up as part of the background of the truth of such counterfactuals. Roughly, the percep-tion of the obstacle would be presumed to engender a belief about the prospects of various courses of action. The desire together with this obstacle-appreciative belief will cause an action that compensates for the obstacle.

I do not endorse any such account of desire, belief, and causality. But that is not at issue. If this causal theory of mental items were fully acceptable, its contri-bution to the understanding of reason-giving explanations would be limited to the auxiliary question "What caused the compensating action?" Insofar as we see com-pensation in action, we cannot substitute the successful account of this auxiliary matter for the teleological explanation of action. By the same token, uncertainty, both empirical and philosophical, about the status of desires and beliefs vis a vis the causes of actions is no more relevant to teleological explanation offered in giv-ing reasons than uncertainty about the causal account of sweating is relevant to the fact that sweating occurs to keep body temperature normal. In sum, whether the claim that certain desires and beliefs caused a given action turns out to be true or false, that causal explanation is not even in the running in the search for the charac-ter of objective-oriented explanations of actions.

This contention faces a formidable objection. I say that prior desires and be-liefs are strictly irrelevant to reason-giving, which should be interpreted teleologi-cal-ly and not in terms of antecedent matters at all. The objection is the plain fact that reason-giving explanations are commonly formulated by simply stating the desires and beliefs that might or might not be causes. "Why did you flip that switch?" Natural answers will include, "Because I wanted the light on" and "Because I thought that would turn the light on." The availability of these formulations undermines the credibility of the analogy of action and compensatory physiological activities. In the physiological framework, "To maintain stable temperature" does not name the cause of sweating on the surface of it. In consequence, it is conceivable that the teleological explanation is not an appeal to causes. But reason-giving explanations explicitly mention desires and beliefs. If these are the causes of the action explained, how can one possibly argue that the explanation that is offered by mentioning these desires and beliefs does not really invoke their causal efficacy?

Part of the difficulty here stems from the use of the verb "want" and its con-nection with desires. There is no denying that, if I flipped the switch in order to turn on the light, it will be proper for me to say, in a sense, "I wanted to turn on the light." "He wanted to . . ." is available in the context of any action that could conceivably be explained by adverting to an outcome or objective. The formula with "want" will always be constructible out of the outcome or objective mentioned. The universal feasibility of "want" formulas is, however, misconstrued as an expression of the presence of something like a prior state of desire for the outcome. On the evidence provided by this misconstruction, the causal picture of reason-giving is encouraged to regard behavior that tries to satisfy a desire as behavior caused by that desire. People do sometimes act in an effort to satisfy desires that they had prior to acting. But I say that the phrase "I wanted to . . ." does not classify an action as one of those to be understood as an effort to satisfy an antecedent desire. The universal availability of "I wanted to . . ." should be evidence against the idea that it alludes to a prior desire, since satisfaction of a desire is one among many alternative backgrounds for action.

There is a sense in which "I wanted the light on" follows immediately from the fact that I acted so as to put it on. In the same way, "I thought that would get the light to go on" will always be feasible if I have acted so as to put on the light. But there is another sense in which the assertions "I wanted the light on" and "I thought that would get the light to go on" contrast with "She wanted the light on" and "She thought that would get the light to go on." I flip the switch and I am asked, "Why did you want the light on?" Cannot I say, "I didn't want it on, she did?" Or, to, "Why did you think that switch would turn on the light?" Cannot I answer, "I didn't think so. I rather doubted it. She thought so." In other words, it seems that, if desires or states of that genre do have a role here, they need not be the desires of the agent. And the same for beliefs. But the desires of others, though they may motivate my switch-flipping, will not seem as plausible as causes of my switch-flipping as my own desires and beliefs. In fact, even in these contexts, we would be ill-advised to move at once to a desire-interpretation of wanting. In placing my action in the setting of what someone else wants, I need not be asserting that the sense in which she wants the light on has anything to do with her desires. I can speak of her wanting the light on, as opposed to my wanting it on, whenever I have turned it on because she was in favor of it, asked me to turn it on, or the like. I am asked, "Would you please turn on the light?" I flip the switch. I am entitled to say, "She wanted the light on." But do I know anything at all about her desires? Maybe a third party asked her. Talk about "wanting" bodes nothing for desire.

The fact that the wants, desires, and beliefs of another can appear in explanatory discourse about my actions helps to dispel the illusion that references to desire and beliefs are especially strong candidates for causes of my actions. Being an agent, if a man has a desire that really is a desire (a state of desire that might exist and be appreciated prior to a satisfaction-seeking act), he can try to gratify that desire. This only manifests the same ability he has to gratify the desire of another. Mention of an agent's desire is explanatory not because the desire caused anything, but simply because it leads us to see what objective the action had, namely, the satisfaction of the desire. When an agent explains his action saying, "She wanted . . . ," he leads us to the goal of his action, namely, the satisfaction of her desire, if the "wanted" really alludes to a desire. Whether the desire was his or hers, reference to it furthers the intelligibility of an action only on the assumption that he acted so as to bring about the satisfaction of a desire. In other words, it is not the case that reference to an outcome in explaining an action presupposes a tacit reference to a desire, but it is the case that reference to a desire in explaining action presupposes tacit reference to an outcome.

Desires play a role in the explanation of actions that parallels reference to contractual obligations, moral principles, promises, the expectations of others, orders, requests, rules, laws, and so on. All these generate reason-giving explanations because reference to them enables us to see the goal of the explained action. Being able to act means being able to bring it about that contractual obligations are met, or to bring it about that a promise is kept, or the expectation of another fulfilled, or an order obeyed, a request acceded to, a rule followed. In just this way, an agent can bring it about that a desire (whether his or not) is satisfied. We are wrong to try to generate a desire to go with every sort of reason: a desire to obey the law, a desire to follow a rule, or a desire to meet a contractual obligation. We are wrong if we say that "in order to turn on the light" only explains in virtue of a tacit "I wanted to turn on the light." In the sense in which "I wanted to . . ." is always available, it is merely another way of saying "In order to . . ." and not a further premise about prior states. In the sense in which "I wanted to . . ." can refer to something like a prior state of desire for something, *wanting* will not enter into all reason-giving explanations, and it will enter only when I have acted so as to satisfy a desire as opposed to acting because it is my job, because I promised, in order to please her, etc.

The thought that there is always a desire or something like a desire involved in actions, as a candidate causal factor, is not suggested in the least by the phenomenology of action. It originates in the requirements of a causal theory of action together with the hope that desires are more plausible as causes than other matters that are equally natural as reasons. Whatever the foundation of this theory of desire and causality, it does not even make much sense when we try to project it into the realities of desire and reason-giving.

Imagine a setting in which a man does have a desire to have a light on. "Oh, if only the light were on," he says, by way of expressing this desire. Then he sees a switch and he forms the belief that flipping that switch would turn the light on. He flips the switch. What does the agent himself understand about his action here, so that he might try to convey that understanding to us by giving a reason for his action? Does he seem to know something about how he brought about his own action? Does he seem to be able to tell us how he got himself to flip the switch? Does he know what caused switch-flipping to take place?

It is hard to assign a clear sense to these questions, much less to suppose that in offering the explanation "I wanted to turn on the light," an agent is relying on an affirmative answer for these questions. In contrast, is it not obvious that what he understands is the end state that his action was chosen to bring about? Flipping a switch is something that a man is able to do, and, in consequence, he is able to bring about whatever can be brought about by flipping switches accessible to him. A man who knows what is caused by flipping switches accessible to him has a range of potential goals. He knows that he can have the light on if he wants (or someone else does), not because he understands that wanting the light on will somehow cause him to move the switch, but because he knows that the switch turns on the light and that he can flip it.

Finally, there are contexts where causal factors are the point of explanatory discussions of actions, and these contexts offer sharp contrasts with reason-giving explanation. We can describe actions in terms of their effects in ways that provoke curiosity satisfiable only by explaining how causal factors were deployed so as to bring about an objective. I tell you that I put the engine block on the workbench and you wonder how I managed to get that state of affairs to come about, because the engine block weighs 900 pounds. Then I explain how I deployed causal factors such as jacks or pulleys in raising the object. Prior to this explanation, you know the goal of my action, but you are left with a question of the form, "That was the goal alright, but how did he get it to come about?"

Causal theorists of pro attitudes construe the explanatory function of wants and desires as though they answer to this kind of curiosity. The standard line about reason-giving insists that it is well and good to say that an action brought about such and such an outcome, but, without reference to a want or other pro attitude, we are entitled to ask, "That was the outcome, but how did he get something with that outcome to come about?" If this were a feasible interpretation for the role of pro attitudes, then "He wanted to turn on the light" would parallel "He put a jack under it." They would be offered as the causes of the motion of the engine and the switch-flipping, respectively. Where an understanding of causes is involved an agent can say, "If I could put a jack under that, I could get it up on the bench." If pro-attitude reasons were offered as causal illumination, they would also generate "I could have the switch flipped in no time, if only I had a cause like wanting the light on." It seems reasonably certain that "I wanted the light on" is never offered as a causal explanation for switch-flipping. If this is so, then there is really no serious competition for the teleological interpretation of reason-giving explanation.

Notes

1. "Actions, Reasons, and Causes," *Journal of Philosophy* 60 (1963); reprinted in David-son's *Essays on Actions and Events* (New York, 1980), 11. The phrase Davidson quotes is from A. I. Melden, *Free Action* (London, 1961), 184.

2. *Teleology* (Cambridge, 1976).

3. G. Sommerhof, *Analytical Biology* (London, 1950); and E. Nagel, "Teleological Expla-nation and Teleological Systems," in *Vision and Action*, edited by S. Ratner (New Brunswick, N. J., 1953).

4. Thus, for example, plants cannot be said to have goals according to Woodfield (*Teleolo-gy*, 33). Chap. 10 of *Teleology* presents Woodfield's frankly mentalist theory of teleology.

5. *Teleology*, 171.

6. *Teleology*, 172.

7. Quoted as reprinted in H. Feigl and M. Brodbeck, *Readings in the Philosophy of Science* (New York, 1953), 540. Emphasis added.

8. *Essays*, 3-4.
9. *Essays*, 3.
10. *Essays*, 6.
11. *Essays*, 7.
12. *Essays*, 11.

Agency and Causation

ZENO VENDLER

I

John broke the window. What he did, the breaking of the window, is clearly an event. Therefore, it seems, some actions at least are events. Hence, since events are the things that are typically caused, actions too may have to be caused by something or other.

This familiar reasoning overlooks the ambiguity in *the breaking of the window* and similar phrases. It may come from the sentence *The window breaks* or *(Somebody or something) breaks the window.* To put it somewhat superficially, the first sentence contains an intransitive and the second a transitive occurrence of the verb *to break.* Later on I shall give a better account of this difference, but for the time being it will do.

Many intransitive verbs, if not most of them, can occur in such transitive disguise: think of *walking the dog, burning the wood, boiling the water,* and so forth. It is obvious that it is the dog that actually walks, the wood that actually burns, and the water that actually boils, and not the agent who makes these things happen in various ways. Notice, incidentally, that whereas such nominalized forms as *the walking of the dog* are ambiguous in this respect, forms like *to walk the dog* and *walking the dog* (e.g., in *Walking the dog is not easy*) demand the transitive sense.

There is, fortunately, a small class of verbs that mark the transitive occurrence with a morphological change in the verb root. Some examples: *rise-raise, fall-fell, sit-set, lie-lay.* Accordingly, the full nominal forms are not ambiguous in these cases: the rising of the flag is not the same thing as the raising of the flag, the falling of the tree is a different thing from the felling of the tree. And the sun rises every day, yet it is not raised at any time.

"But what is the importance of this difference?" you ask. "After all, both the falling of the tree and the felling of the tree are events which take place at a certain time, which can be observed, etc., and which, presumably, can be caused."

Events they may be, I reply, but the last claim does not hold. The falling of the tree can be caused by all sorts of things (wind, earthquake, John's action of cutting the trunk), but the felling of the tree has no causes. It is not something caused, but something *done*: by John or perhaps the wind. Similarly, when John raises his arm, the physical event involved, namely, the *rising* of that arm, is something for which causes can be given: contraction of muscles, firing of neurons, and the like. This event, moreover, is not "done" by anybody; the rising of an arm is not something that can be done—it is not an action. What is an action is the *raising* of the arm: this is done by John, and not caused by anything.

"But cannot John cause the rising of his arm?" Yes he can, by, say, operating a pulley with his other hand. Then, indeed, his action of pulling on the rope causes his arm to rise. In this way, he also can be said to raise that arm. This implication is due to the "accordion effect" peculiar to action talk: what the agent's actions cause often can be attributed to the agent.[1] The result is that although the rising of the arm is caused by John's action (of pulling on the rope), the raising of the arm is not caused but done by him, by means of operating a pulley.

II

Still, it seems that in this case a person is called the cause of an event: "John caused the rising of his arm," we said. Therefore, might not we say in the first case too, namely, when John simply raised his arm, that he caused the rising of his arm, that is to say, that he is the cause of an event?

This reasoning is based on a false move. From the fact that John caused the rising of his arm it does not follow that John is a cause. It is nonsense to say that John was the cause of the rising of his arm. Persons are not causes, but their actions can be. Indeed, his action of pulling on the rope was the cause of that event. We often speak elliptically, however: instead of saying "His action (of pulling on the rope) caused the rising of his arm" or "He caused the rising of his arm by pulling on the rope," we simply say "He caused the rising of his arm." The point is that whenver we ascribe the predicate *cause* . . . to an individual directly, there is always a possibility of completing the sentence by specifying the action (or quality) of that individual which was the real cause: "The second bullet caused Mary's death," i.e., "The impact of the second bullet . . . ," etc.

The leniency of our language in this respect has certain limits. As we move on from the form *N causes* . . . to the form *N is the cause of* . . . , the elliptical forms begin to sound deviant or clumsy: **John was the cause of the rising of his arm. ?The second bullet was the cause of Mary's death.*

Now, clearly, whereas the elliptical form is available in the pulley case, in which the raising of the arm was achieved by John's pulling on a rope, it is certainly not available in the original case of John simply raising his arm. It is, as is called, a "basic" action: he raised his arm directly, not *by* doing something else. Hence, since the sentence *He caused his arm to rise by* . . . is incompletable, the predicate *cause* . . . is disallowed, and, a fortiori, the predicate *is the cause of* . . . John, in simply raising his arm, did not cause the rising of his arm, and he is not the cause of that event. Leave that to the contraction of his muscles and the like. Thus even in the cases in which it makes sense to say that a person caused something or other, this locution presupposes some more basic action by means of which the agent caused that thing, and this action is something done and not caused.

III

But is this "doing" not something like causation? Linguists tell us that, e.g., *raise* is the "causative" form of *rise*, and the occurrence of *walk* in *Sam walked the dog* is a "causative" occurrence. Indeed, these are but instances of a very wide phenomenon in our language.[2] Think of such sentences as *Mary heated the water, Karpov queened his pawn, The workers crated the books*. Without getting into technicalities, what happens in these sentences is quite clear. The speaker's intention to attribute an event to an agent is marked by lifting out the key word of the predicate from the sentence describing the event and ascribing it to the agent directly. The water's becoming hot is attributed to Mary: so we say that she *heated* it; the pawn becomes queen, and this is due to Karpov: so he *queened* the pawn; the books end up in crates, and this is done by the workers: so they *crated* the books. To put it in another way, intuitively, if somewhat clumsily: these agents did something *so that* the water became hot, the pawn a queen, and the books (packed) in crates.

The *so that* is the key phrase, for its use spearates, again on an intuitive level, these "causal" constructions from "instrumental" ones, which are the results of a similar move. For example, *The workers carted the books, Mary axed her husband*. Here, obviously, the key word of an instrumental adverbial *(in carts, with an axe)* is lifted out of the phrase and ascribed to the subject directly.

As we saw, in many instances the causative occurrence shows some morphological alteration *(fall-fell, hot-heat)*. There are even cases in which there is an "original" form acting as causative. Whereas *murder* at least shows an etymological link to dying *(mori)*, *kill* seems to be an original. Yet the causative role is obvious. Compare *He shot her dead* and *?He killed her dead*. The second sentence is redundant.

One can symbolize, in a crude way, the pattern of such causative constructions as follows:

(1) $N_1 c(N_2(\ldots W \ldots)) \rightarrow N_1 V_W N_2 \ldots$

In this formula c marks the "causal" factor, W stands for the key word of the predicate involved, and V_W stands for the causative derivative of that word (with or without a morphological change).

There is a less radical way of forming causative constructions. In many cases the key word in the predicate is not amenable to verbalization, or we just do not opt for the "short" form. A "long" form is always available: "deverbalize" the enclosed sentence and ascribe the leftovers to the agent by means of a causal auxiliary. For example:

Sam *made* the dog walk

Karpov *made* his pawn queen

The workers *put* the books in crates.

Now we see what I meant by "deverbalization": *walk* lost its suffix, and *his pawn queen* and *the books in crates* lack the copula. And, of course, *make* and *put* are instances of a causal auxiliary. These range from such semantically colorless specimens as *make, render*, and *get* to more colorful items like *put, place*, etc. Even instrumentality can be absorbed, as in *Mary painted the window black.*

If we reflect on the fact that in *yes-no* questions the same "deverbalization" occurs (e.g., *Did the dog walk?, Are the books in crates?*), then we come to see that in our cases too it is the copula or the auxiliary *do* that is "stolen" from the enclosed sentence, in much the same way as a whole verb (or adjective) is "stolen" in the move represented by (1). So we can give the formula for the less radical move:

$$(2) \quad N_1 c(N_2 \text{ be/do } (P)) \rightarrow N_1 \text{aux}_c N_2 P$$

where P stands for a predicate string minus *be* or *do*. To put it poetically, whereas (1), the radical move, entails "predicate napping," (2), the milder move, entails only "be/do-napping."

There is an interesting semantic difference between the employment of (1) and the employment of (2).[3] As (1) is a more direct move, we use it to mark more direct, or immediate, influence by the agent. Compare:

Same walked the dog

Mary opened the door

John raised his arm

and

Sam made the dog walk

Mary got the door open

John made his arm rise.

To put it simply: the second group describes doing things in a "roundabout" way. The last sentence, for instance, might very well be a description of what John did by means of that pulley.

IV

Now we are ready to answer the question posed at the beginning of the previous section. What an agent does is normally expressed by a "causative" construction. I shall argue later that this fact corresponds to a basic feature of all actions. Does it follow, then, that agents in acting cause events?

I wish to remark, first, that the term *causative* is a *nom de métier* invented by linguists, so its use, by itself, indicates nothing.

Yet there is an undeniable inclination shared by all of us to think that since agents "make things happen," their influence is something like causation. Why is this so?

One reason is the following. Not only agents but genuine causes can also figure in the subject slot of causative constructions. Consider these examples:

The expansion of the gases raised the roof
The explosion broke the window
The (force of the) wind felled the tree.

Notice, however, that these sentences not only have the transforms

The expansion of the gases caused the roof to rise
The explosion caused the window to break
The (force of the) wind caused the tree to fall,

but also admit such "full-blown" causal forms as

The expansion of the gases caused the rising of the roof
The explosion was the cause of the breaking of the window
The fall of the tree was caused by the (force of the) wind.

Now these transforms are not available in the cases of "agent causation." Except for the "roundabout" situations mentioned above, such claims as

John raised his arm
Mary killed the chicken

cannot be equivalently expressed by sentences like

John caused his arm to rise
Mary caused the chicken to die.

More important, the full-blown causal sentences nearly always fail:

*John was the cause of the rising of his arm
?The death of the chicken was caused by Mary.

(This last one may be tolerated in *very* roundabout situations, but not if Mary just chopped off the poor bird's head.)

Conclusion: As the sentence forms become more and more explicitly causal, they become less and less suitable for expressing what agents do.

Now the other side of the same coin. Agents *do* things, causes don't.[4] What John *did* was to raise his arm, and what Mary *did* was to kill the chicken. On the other hand, it is nonsense to ask questions like *And then what did the force of wind* (or *the expansion of the gases) do*? Sure enough, we often personify natural forces (think of Hurricane Edna) and speculate about what a big earthquake would *do* to Los Angeles, or a renewed inflation to our savings. But this is poetry. Just ask yourself: would it be easy or difficult for earthquakes or inflation to do these things? . . . Yet for John it was easy to raise his arm, and for Mary difficult to kill the chicken.

For these reasons, the most one should admit concerning the relation of agency and causation is a weak family resemblance.

That it is indeed a weak resemblance can also be shown by the following consideration. As events in the world go, John's arm going up, or the chicken's death, following upon some axe swinging, following upon some processes in Mary's body, are by no means exceptional occurrences in the history of the world. They all fit into the causal network of the universe with no gaps letting such "causes" as John and Mary enter the picture. The causal network may be "gappy" here and there (think of some subatomic phenomena), but there are no ghostly "agents" lurking in these holes. *Pace* Descartes and his gland, the domain of agency and the domain of causation are not contiguous.

V

I claimed above that the employment of causative constructions is by no means accidental to action talk. All overt actions at least (I am not talking about "mental" acts) begin with some movements of one's body: raising an arm or leg, bending a finger, closing an eye, turning the head, and the like. Now all the verbs we just used occurred in the causative frame: *raise an arm*, as we know from (1), is *c (arm rises)*, bend a finger is *c (finger bends)*, etc. In general, *move one's body* is *c (one's body moves)*. The rest of the story consists of morphological variations on the same theme (think of killing, breaking, pushing, etc.). In some cases, "adverbial" elements are absorbed in the semantic content of the causative verb, e.g., *winking* (shutting the eye with a certain intention), *murdering* (killing unlawfully, with malice afore-thought), etc. In other cases we give an "integral" description of a structured sequence of more basic actions: playing tennis, climbing a mountain, or even things like walking, eating, and the like. All these actions can be resolved into more basic acts, ultimately, to moving one's body in various ways.

Given this result, and the fact that what the agent *does* is not the bare event (the rising of the arm) but the event in a causative frame (the raising of the arm), we arrive at the following "schema" of an action:

(3) A does $(c(E))$.

To spell it out in words: in the actual performance of a given action, four elements are to be distinguished: the event, the action, the doing of the action, and the agent.

This pie may strike some people as being too rich, having too many layers. But the proof of the pie is in the eating. I am now going to demonstrate that this "enriched" schema can do a few things that other views on the logical form of action sentences cannot.

VI

In the first place, we can make sense of the bane of action descriptions, namely the variety of (mainly adverbial) adjuncts.[5] We all remember Austin's challenge: account for the difference in meaning between sentences like

(4) Clumsily he trod on the snail

(5) He trod on the snail clumsily[6]

or

(6) He deliberately walked out of the room

(7) He walked out of the room deliberately.

Given (3), the solution is readily forthcoming.

Let us move systematically. Formula (3) gives four factors, and each of them can receive added modifications.

Starting with E:

He rang the bell loudly
She threw the ball over the fence.

The ringing of the bell is loud; his ringing it is not. Similarly, the flight of the ball goes over the fence, not her throwing. In other words, the adjuncts attach themselves to the event description.

Then the action, $c(E)$:

He pulled the rope hard.

The movement of the rope is not hard; the pulling of it is. Just compare it with

He pulled the rope tight.

In this case, once more, it is the event description (rope becomes tight), not the action description (pulling), to which *tight* belongs.

Then it is clear that in (5) and (7) above the adverbs modify the action description, $c(E)$: the manner of the treading was clumsy, and the manner of the walk was deliberate (he stepped on the snail with a clumsy tread; he left the room with a deliberate walk).

Now the doing of the action, *does (c(E))*:

He pulled himself up easily
He did the chin-up easily.

These examples speak for themselves. The event of his body's going up is not easy, nor the chin-up (the action) in itself. But he *did* it easily. *For him* it was something easy to *do*. This takes care of (4) and (6). *Clumsily* means roughly: without paying attention to what he was doing; and *deliberately* means roughly: intentionally, on purpose. Both adverbs describe the manner of doing, not the manner of the thing done.

Another pair in which the same adverb is attached now to *does (c(E))* then to $c(e)$ (or perhaps to E alone):

Stupidly, he answered the question
He answered the question stupidly.

In the first case his answer may have been clever, but it was stupid *of* him to answer at all. In the second case his answer (the process or the product?) was stupid.

One more contrast illustrating the same distinction:

Vivisection is a messy thing
Vivisection is a wicked thing.

Both of these sentences are all right. But then consider

?Vivisection is a messy thing to do
Vivisection is a wicked thing to do.

Wicked belongs to the doing, *messy* to the thing done.

Finally, adjuncts to *A*. Consider the following sentence:

He shot the policeman on the street.

Now it is either he who was on the street, or the policeman (the subject of *E*), or both. But such ambiguities are less insidious than the previous ones.

The first bite of the pie has proved to be quite nourishing.

VII

Max shoots the donkey and the poor beast dies. Formula (3) helps us in spelling out the full story:

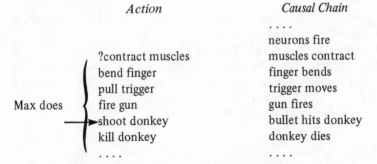

	Action	*Causal Chain*
		. . . .
		neurons fire
	?contract muscles	muscles contract
	bend finger	finger bends
	pull trigger	trigger moves
Max does	fire gun	gun fires
	→shoot donkey	bullet hits donkey
	kill donkey	donkey dies
	. . . .	. . . .

The right column records a causal chain which is open-ended in both directions. This representation is, of course, oversimplified. There are other causes affecting, and effects spinning off, the same sequence. Think of the pressure of gases, chemical reactions, air resistance, movements of donkey, etc., on the one hand, and the scaring of birds and neighbors, convergence of crows, etc., on the other. But, as always in telling a causal story, we have to be selective. In claiming that the explosion of the heater caused the fire, we do not mention oxygen in the atmosphere, and the like. When we speak of a causal chain, what we mean is one thread, the one we are interested in, embedded in the texture of the causal network of the world.

The left column tells us what Max did, with a dubious item at the beginning. True, one can just flex one's muscles (e.g., to display biceps), but in this case it is very unlikely that this is what Max did. Why? Simply because one does not just flex muscles with the finger on the trigger. At any rate, and this is important, Max certainly did not fire his neurons. Again, why? Because one cannot be said to *do* something of which one *cannot* be aware.

This does not mean that we *do* all things occurring in our body of which we are aware. We salivate, shiver, hiccough, move parts of our body as a result of spasms, ticks, neural stimulation, etc. But notice that in all these cases we *become* aware of what is happening by feeling, or even seeing, what is going on. In really doing something, however, we do not have to wait, as it were, for the testimony of the senses to arrive to realize what we are doing. If my arm rises in a muscular spasm (or as a result of stimulation of my brain), I might exclaim: "Good gracious, my arm is going up!" (think of our surprise at the first experience of the knee-jerk reflex); but no such surprise is involved in simply raising my arm: I *know* what I am doing "under a description," as it is said, in advance of the report of the senses.[7] Infelicities may occur, of course: my arm may be partly paralyzed and fail to execute the move. And this (often to my surprise) I come to realize by means of the senses. But at least I *tried* to raise my arm, but it did not quite come off.[8]

Such "involuntary" movements, moreover, are attributed to the subject simply because they occur in his body: when my mouth salivates I salivate, when my body shivers I shiver, and when my leg kicks out I kick out. If I raise my hand intentionally, however, it is not true that I raise my hand because my hand goes up. No, my hand goes up because I raise it. But it would be nonsense to say that the palsied man's hand shakes because he shakes it. . . .

Let us return to Max and his donkey. What did he do? The straightforward anwer is: he shot the donkey. This is so, because most likely this is the description under which he undertook the action. Of course, he may have intended to kill the beast (shoot to kill . . .), but in a normal case, say, in which the donkey is at a distance away, the killing of the beast is better viewed as a result of what he did rather than what he did, because of the uncertainties involved. When the Federal Reserve restricts the money supply to curb inflation, that is what it does (restricting the money supply) and *by* doing so, hopefully, curb inflation. That is to say, they may *succeed* in curbing inflation, as Max *succeeded* in killing the donkey. But, unless one makes it too difficult (donkey is too far, it's dark, etc.), one is less likely to say that Max succeeded in shooting the donkey, let alone in firing the gun or pulling the trigger.

To put it simply, "I am shooting the donkey" is the most likely answer Max might give, and we might give for that matter, when asked what he is doing. To say more (killing the donkey, feeding the vultures) would be too optimistic, to say less (pulling the trigger) too pessimistic. This does not mean that in shooting the beast Max need not be aware of the other possible descriptions of his act: that he is pulling the trigger, or that he might kill the donkey or scare the neighbors. Some of these things he may view as means, others as results (he wants them to happen), others again as consequences (he foresees their possibility and allows for them, i.e., hopes they don't happen, or does not care if they do). After all, as the saying goes, the lucky man gets results, the unlucky ones consequences. . . .

To be more exact: these results and consequences are not actions, but facts and possibilities concerning the events on the right side of our table. For it is the donkey's death, and not his killing the donkey, which is the result of his act, and it is the fact that the neighbors get scared, and not his scaring the neighbors, which is a consequence. Still, by the accordion effect, he killed the ass and might have scared the neighbors. He may claim, of course, that he did not foresee some of the consequences.

Thus we see that it is the causal chain of events (represented on the right side of our table) that holds the accordion together. What the agent does is describable by all the action descriptions that put these events into causative frames (left column). Yet one must not go too far. We already mentioned one limit. The neural processes, which are part of the causal chain, do not generate action descriptions. But there are limits on the other end too: action descriptions derived from events too remote, impossible to foresee, cannot be attributed to the agent. Even if, for instance, one of the scared neighbors suffers a fatal heart attack in consequence, we would not say that Max has killed the victim; he could not be aware of this description of his act. Yet, maybe, some responsibility remains. Here, as expected, we trail off into the foggy regions in which casuists and lawyers ply their trade.

"But," asks the philosopher, "how many things did Max do in shooting the donkey?" My first inclination is to reply: "I'll tell you that if you tell me first how many *things* there are in this room. . . ." I can give a more kindly answer too. Napoleon, notoriously, could do many things at the same time: e.g., eating, playing chess, and dictating letters.[9] Jerry Ford, allegedly, could do no more than one thing at a time. In this sense, Max did only one thing. But we often talk differently; we might say that the Federal Reserve, in restricting the money supply, did many things by one stroke: lowered inflation, reduced interest rates, but also increased unemployment, etc. In this sense, Max may have done many things.

Our table helps us to understand the difference. Napoleon did many things at the same time inasmuch as he actualized several relatively independent causal chains. The Fed did many things inasmuch as the causal chain it actualized has several branches bearing foreseeable sweet or bitter fruits.[10]

An action is an event with a handle: not E, but $c(E)$.[11] But E is a member of a causal chain. So doing $c(E)$ is to grab the handle and pull the whole chain into existence. Max, in shooting the donkey, actualized the whole causal sequence (given on the right side of our table), together with such offshoots as the neighbors' scare, etc. And this is the reason for the accordion effect characteristic of action talk. Real causes, themselves but links in the chain, are "responsible" only for the next member: the trigger's movement caused the firing of the gun, but not the death of the beast. Max, however, is not a cause, not a member of the causal chain; he is an agent determining the whole sequence from the outside as it were. Therefore, within limits, he is responsible for the whole: he *did* it all.[12]

VIII

Max must have had reasons for what he did; shooting a donkey is a grave matter, not to be indulged in on mere whim. But now, while thinking about this business, I am walking up and down in the room. I am *doing* this for sure: my walking is no mere reflex; I am not surprised at it, I know what I am doing. Do I have reasons for walking up and down? *Pace* Freud, in any normal sense of having reasons, I do not. I *just* do it—or to give a trivial answer· I just feel like doing it. Again, do we need reasons to stretch, look out the window, eat soup when served, and so forth?

Philosophers have foisted upon us the notion that whatever we do, we do it for reasons. Why should this be so? Because, they argue, doing something must be the result of a choice, since we are free, i.e., not determined to do or not to do. And choice, lest it be blind, requires reasons. Again I demur: it is not true that choice, or a discernible act of the will for that matter, must precede all of our actions. Think again of the modest activities I mentioned a moment ago: I did not choose to walk, to stretch, or to spoon up my soup. What is true is that I could have done otherwise; I was not constrained, forced, or acting under duress. But this does not entail that I had made a choice.

In certain circumstances, when something worthwhile is at stake, we indeed make choices, often after long deliberation, i.e., weighing reasons pro and con. But this feature is not essential to all actions. What is essential is that the agent is aware of what he is doing, "under a description," that is to say, in conceptual terms, independent of the delivery of the senses. What we really *do* is an action and is free not because it is done for reasons, follows deliberation, and executes an intention, but the other way around. One can have reasons for, deliberate upon, and intend to perform an action *because* it is something that is to be done under a description, that is to say, something that can stand in logical relations to reasons, motives, intentions, and the like. To put it somewhat paradoxically: we are free not because we can choose, but we can choose because in acting we are free.

IX

"But," the philosopher asks again, "are these reasons (and their ingredients, i.e., beliefs, desires, etc.) not causes of action?" Earlier in this paper we confronted the claims of "agent causality" and found them wanting: agents do not cause but do their actions; and the events involved have their proper causes without room left for agents to enter the causal chain. The idea of "event causality" suggested by this question fares no better.

We just saw, to begin with, that reasons, intentions, and the like are by no means essential to actions. But, I grant, we do have reasons and motives for many things we do. And we often say things like: such and such reason, or motive, made him do what he did. . . . Or even: these reasons caused him to do this or that. . . . Thus there seems to be a prima facie case for regarding reasons as causes, as there was a similar case for viewing agents as causes. To call this "event causality," however, puts a further strain on the imagination: reasons are not events. But I shall not argue this point.

Instead I return, once more, to Max and his ill-fated ass. As I mentioned above, Max must have had reasons to shoot the beast. Suppose he was offered a good price for the carcass by the local dog food manufacturer. Thus, to make matters simple, let us say that it was his greed that made him kill the donkey. I even go along with the version: his greed caused him to kill the beast. Is this a case of real causation?

The first question is the following: what is being caused by the greed? The event (E), i.e., the donkey's death? No, that was caused by the bullet going through the heart. There is no room for greed at this point, or at any point in the causal chain.

The action of shooting the donkey $(c(E))$? No, it was not caused by anything; it was *done* by Max. Remember, it is the rising of my arm and not the raising of my arm, which is caused by something or other. Admittedly, genuine causes can precede causative constructions; e.g., the expansion of the gases raised the roof. But this means that the event, i.e., the rising of the roof, was caused by the expansion. Now try:

*Max's greed shot the donkey
*The donkey's getting shot was caused by Max's greed.

Max's performing that action [*does (c(E))*]? This seems to offer a foothold: Max did what he did for that reason. Indeed, greed *made* him *do*, or *caused* him to *do*, the deed. Yet the sentence

?Max's greed caused his shooting (of) the donkey

is marginal at best.

Let us have another example:

The lady caused the butler to ring the bell.

Now what is the force of *cause* in this context? What do we mean by this sentence? Most probably, that the lady has *asked* or *ordered* the butler. Indeed we can complete the sentence: . . . *by asking (begging, ordering, etc.) him*. In other words, the lady has provided a reason for the butler to do as bid. But, of course, the butler may have refused. Consider this, however:

The lady compelled (or forced) the butler to ring the bell.

By doing what? By threatening, or even using physical force. In this case (morally or physically) the butler could not refuse: he acted under duress.

Thus we see that the use of *cause* in this context marks a rather "mild" influence, much weaker than *force* or *compel*; it does not mean determination: it remains up to the butler to comply or refuse. In real cases of causality, however, the cause determines: if we say that the expansion of the gases caused the rising of the roof, then we mean that *in the given situation* (think of all the other "causes" we do not care to mention), the roof could not but rise given that cause.

It is now obvious that Max's greed causes him to shoot the ass in the same way as the lady's request causes the butler to ring the bell: not by necessitating as real causes do but by providing a reason, and not a *compelling* reason at that. There are compelling reasons, which reduce our freedom to choose, and there are compulsions ("irresistible impulses"), which eliminate it altogether. Max's reasons, stemming from his greed, are not likely to amount to such. Most of the time we have no compelling reasons to act; in fact, in many cases, as we mentioned above, we do things for no reason at all.

If some philosophers still want to claim that all our actions are determined by reasons (desires, motives, urges, etc.), that is to say, that we always do things under the influence of reasons which are jointly compelling, then the burden of proof is upon them. The attempt to assimilate agency to the processes of nature by making causes out of reasons is based on a bad paradigm: the agent as a "spiritual automaton," a paramechanical piece of non-clockwork endowed with the freedom of a turnspit.

Of course we can cause things to happen (the lady did), and reasons may cause us to do things (Max's greed did), and explosions can cause fires. The use of *cause* shows a family resemblance. But to argue that the first two claims are to be understood in the manner of the third is like arguing that knowing how to swim is to be explained in terms of knowing what is the case. Fortunately, both with *know* and *cause* (unlike with Wittgenstein's *game*), there are fairly clear grammatical differences between the various uses. As I tried to show, the lady may cause things, but she is not a cause; and Max's greed may cause *him* to do this and that, but the greed is not the cause of what he does. In a similar way, knowing how to swim does not increase one's knowledge.

X

Since neither agents nor their reasons enter the causal chain, we do not have to worry about the problem: at what point they do (pineal gland, cortex).[13] As we said above, agency and causation are not contiguous.

"But then," you ask, "how on earth are we able to make things happen in our body, and by means of that, in the world at large?" We undoubtedly do, I reply, and our view of the world better accommodate this fact. I cannot discuss the "how" in this paper, but I can say a few words on "why not?" What do we have to sacrifice to accommodate agency? Not much: what we have to give up is the idea that a person at any given time—in the manner of Laplace's demon—can foresee the future in all details on the basis of his current representation of the world. We do not have, and no one has, such a picture of the universe. This does not mean that we can do anything: I can raise my arm, but not fly; lift a book, but not a car. But if I raise my arm, I do not have to worry about interfering with nonumenal processes, or messing up a predetermined world representation; in doing so I make my arm's going up, together with all of its antecedents and consequences, part of the actual world, neatly integrated into its causal network. Moreover, if you are so inclined, you may regard the causal order as deterministic. My arm's going up may be determined by its causes. But it is my doing that the universe is such that this event, rather than some alternative, is woven into its texture at this point in space and time.

After all, the present condition of the world, to some extent at least, is certainly due to what Hitler, Stalin, Roosevelt, and other worthies have done in the past.

Notes

1. On this notion see J. Feinberg, "Action and Responsibility," in *Philosophy in America*, edited by M. Black (Ithaca, 1965), 134-60; and D. Davidson, "Agency," reprinted in his *Essays on Actions and Events* (Oxford, 1980), 43-61.

2. I have discussed the details of this matter in "The Structure of Efficacy," in *Contemporary Research in Philosophical Logic and Linguistic Semantics*, edited by D. Hockney, W. Harper, and B. Freed (Dordrecht-Boston, 1975), 119-36.

3. Professor J. R. Ross made me aware of this distinction in a conversation.

4. The following discussion shows the influence of J. R. Ross's "Act," in *Semantics of Natural Language*, edited by D. Davidson and G. Harman (Dordrecht-Boston, 1972), 70-126.

5. Adverbs are important. For example, Professor D. Davidson arrives at his theory of action sentences by considering adverbial phrases. See his "The Logical Form of Action Sentences," reprinted in *Essays on Actions and Events*, 105-22.

6. J. L. Austin, "A Plea for Excuses," in *Philosophical Papers* (Oxford, 1961), 123-52.

7. In more Kantian terms: in the one case, the data of the senses await a schema that fits them; in the other, a schema awaits the data of the senses that fit into it.

8. I do not discuss another kind of infelicity: if, for instance, the "donkey" Max shot turns out to be a mule.

9. By the way, playing chess: the master plays against fifteen opponents simultaneously. Is he doing fifteen things or one?

10. Such forked causal trees explain the possibility of "double effect": the agent aims at the sweet fruit on one branch, and allows for the bitter fruit on another.

11. Accordingly, actions can cause, since they contain E, but cannot be caused, since they contain more than E.

12. This is the reason why such questions as "When exactly did Sirhan kill Kennedy?" (when he fired the gun, when the victim died) have an eery aura about them. The events are datable; but his doing? When did the Fed reduce inflation?

13. Professor R. M. Chisholm seems to hold the view that the agent directly causes a neural event in "Freedom and Action," in *Freedom and Determinism*, edited by K. Lehrer (New York, 1966), 11-44.

MIDWEST STUDIES IN PHILOSOPHY, IX (1984)

Thoughts and Their Ascription[1]

MICHAEL DEVITT

1. INTRODUCTION

Thoughts are one thing, their ascription another. A theory of the former is primarily in the philosophy of the mind: it is primarily a metaphysical/ontological theory. A theory of the latter is primarily in the philosophy of language: it is primarily a semantic theory.

The two sorts of theory are, of course, related. Thoughts have semantic properties. So one cannot give a theory of them without commitment to a semantic theory, which is likely to have implications for a theory of thought ascriptions. On the other hand, one cannot give a theory of thought ascriptions without implying some view of the thoughts ascribed.

The question arises: Which theory should one start with? It is common for philosophers to start with the theory of thought ascription, leaving the theory of thought pretty much to look after itself. I think this is a mistake.

In general, I think it best not to attempt a semantic question that requires an answer to a metaphysical/ontological question until we have answered the latter question.[2] The most plausible semantics, in my view, does not posit new objects but is concerned with certain properties and relations of old objects; in particular, it is concerned with certain intrinsic properties of people and their linguistic output and with the relations of people and output to a reality *that we suppose to exist for reasons quite independent of semantics*. For, it is hard to see how a specially semantic entity can help explain what needs to be explained: the role the output plays in people's dealings with nonsemantic reality. Thus, suppose there are no non-semantic reasons for believing in nonactual possible worlds. The semantic task is then to explain the role of linguistic output in the actual world. How could positing the nonactual help with that?

The general approach of putting metaphysics first is particularly important in handling the problems of thought ascription. These problems seem to encourage the positing of Platonic entities like "propositions." Often these entities are unexplained. They are nearly always dubious, in my view. However, worst of all, they are *irrelevant* to the reality in which thought ascriptions have their role. The special reality that concerns thought ascriptions is a mental one. I suggest that the following is a plausible initial view of that mental reality. A person has a particular thought in virtue of the intrinsic state of that person's head and its extrinsic causal relations with the familiar world of independent physical objects. We need some such picture to explain a person's behavior and our learning from him or her about the familiar world. Our explanatory purposes will certainly require that this picture be enriched, but they can hardly require the including of Platonic entities like "propositions." Insofar as such entities are not represented in the head, they are irrelevant to the explanation. Insofar as they are represented, it is only their representations that are relevant. Either way we have no need of these entities. If they have no role in our metaphysical theory of the mind, they should have no role in our semantic theory of sentences that describe the mind.

Putting metaphysics first has a further advantage. It is not hard to throw sufficient light on the nature of thought to make the problems of thought ascription seem much more tractable than before. It may also make them seem less interesting: nothing of cosmic significance hinges on our choice between various ways of settling them. Some problems may even disappear, because they seem to arise from the positing of propositions, or from a confusion of the semantic with the metaphysical, a confusion fostered by the focus on the semantic.

In an earlier work, *Designation*,[3] I drew on the work of many others to offer theories of thoughts and their ascription. I used a causal theory of reference in both theories. I did not always put metaphysics first. This did not lead me to posit Platonic entities, but it did detract from the presentation of, and argument for, my theory of thought ascription. My first aim in this paper is to correct that mistake. The second aim is to consider some new problems and reconsider some old ones. The first aim leads to a change in emphasis but not theory; the second leads to a change in theory.

In section 2, I describe my theory of thoughts. I think there is a language of thought that, in mature humans, is largely their public language, and that the thoughts we ascribe to people are relations to tokens in their language of thought.[4] In section 3, I describe my theory of thought ascriptions, which involves two distinctions: transparent/opaque and designational/attributive. It offers solutions to various well-known problems: most importantly to failures of substitutivity, of quantifying in, and of exportation from opaque ascriptions to transparent ones.[5] In each of these sections, I take a dim view of the widespread use of the terms 'de dicto' and 'de re'. In the rest of the paper I apply these theories: to the classification of thoughts (sections 4 and 6); to "self-demonstrative" thoughts (often called "de se") and their ascription, taking account of recent papers by John Perry, David Lewis, and Stephen Boër and William Lycan[6] (section 5); to identity thoughts and their ascription (section 7); and to Saul Kripke's "puzzle"[7] (section 8). These applications lead to modifications in the theory of ascriptions. The modifications are made tentatively, for the evidence for one interpretation against another is far from decisive. Further, it may be the case that there are some situations where one interpretation is appropriate, some where another is, and some where there is no determinate matter of fact which is. Nothing important hangs on these issues.

My discussion throughout is informal. However, I attach an Appendix giving more formal statements of the truth conditions of ascriptions. I simplify the main discussion by mostly ignoring "tacit" thoughts (ones held but not entertained); "empty" thoughts (ones containing empty singular terms); general thoughts (ones not containing definite singular terms); and thoughts that are not in a public language. The first two of these are taken account of in the Appendix. I follow the usual custom of always using beliefs as examples of thoughts.

2. A THEORY OF THOUGHTS

Thoughts may differ in two very different ways. First, oversimplifying, some are beliefs and some are desires. This difference is one of functional role within the organism. Second, thoughts differ in that they have different "objects." This difference is in the syntactic and semantic properties of the sentence token involved. If our concerns are only the computational ones of "narrow" psychology, the properties that count are only syntactic ones and such semantic ones as come from a token's relation to sensory input and behavioral output. Differences in these syntactic, and anemically semantic, properties are sufficient to explain the difference thoughts make to the explanation and prediction of the behavior of others.[8] It is hard to see why we need to go beyond this to "wide" psychology, as folk psychology seems to. However, I think we do need to in order to explain learning and teaching.[9] Assume that we do need to. Then the properties of tokens that count include the full-blooded semantic ones: referential and truth-conditional properties.[10] It is the referential properties that give thoughts intentionality.[11]

The anemically semantic properties of a thought token that, with its syntax, determine its role between input and output, must be registered in its form. For, only formal properties of the token can make a computational difference. Thus, tokens of 'a is F' and 'b is G', which are formally different but syntactically alike, might be thoughts with different relations to input and output.[12]

The full-blooded semantics of thought requires truth. Truth is explained in terms of reference, which then itself needs explaining. The theory of (singular) reference I use is a twofold development of the ideas of Kripke and Donnellan. The ideas in question are those of a causal theory of names[13] and of a distinction between referential and attributive uses of descriptions.[14]

The first development is to draw a distinction between descriptions at token level, based on Donnellan's at type level, and then to apply this new distinction across the board, covering names, demonstratives, and pronouns, as well as descriptions. I prefer the term 'designational' to 'referential'. So my distinction is between designational and attributive definite singular-term tokens.

Signs of this distinction are to be found in folk semantics: we distinguish using a singular term "with a particular object in mind" from using it to refer to whatever is the such and such. Donnellan captured this intuitive distinction in a number of examples of confusion and mistake. I argue for my distinction by focusing on the relation between "imperfect" descriptions like 'the man' and demonstratives. It is implausible to see these descriptions as like Russellian descriptions.

The second development is to give a causal theory of designational tokens. These tokens depend for identifying reference on a certain sort of causal chain. Such a chain starts with face-to-face perception of an object, a "grounding," and may run through many people by the device of "reference borrowing." There may be several chains involving the one object and term, all linked together to form a network. A designational token refers to the object, if any, in which the causal network underlying the token is grounded. I call this mode of identifying reference, "designation." An attributive token, in contrast, refers to the object, if any, to which the appropriately related description (sometimes the token itself) uniquely applies. I call this mode of identifying reference, "denotation."

People who are able to use a term designationally to refer to an object are part of the causal network for that term. Their abilities are sets of thoughts, related by identity beliefs, and including tokens of the term that are grounded by the network in the object.[15]

This is *not* a theory of "direct reference" for names, if by that is meant the view that there is nothing more of semantic significance about a name than its referent. I think its underlying causal network, its *mechanism* of reference, is also significant. I do not mostly talk of the "meaning," "sense," or "connotation" of a name. However, if I were to, they would be *abstractions of some sort from the underlying network.*

A qualification to this theory of thought may be called for: people seem to have thoughts that they have never entertained and that cannot plausibly be thought to be tokened in their heads. I think[16] that the correct response to this is to see only "core" or "explicit" thoughts as tokened and to take a dispositional view of "tacit" or "implicit" thoughts: they are obvious (to the people) consequences of core thoughts, so that the people would quickly infer them in appropriate circumstances.[17] I shall ignore the need for this qualification in what follows (but see Appendix).

From this theoretical perspective, there are various things we might truly say about a thought in virtue of the properties of its token: e.g., that it is a one-place predication, or a disjunction; that it includes a natural kind, or an artifactual, general term; that it includes a designational or attributive singular term (and hence, we shall say, is itself designational or attributive); that it includes a token of 'Reagan' or, 'politician'; that it refers to (is about) Reagan or politicians.

Is it appropriate to talk, as almost everyone does, of thoughts and their ascriptions being "*de dicto*" or "*de re*"? I think not. First, it should be noted that the terms in question are seldom clearly explained. Each is used as if it already had one well-known meaning. I don't think it has. Rather, second, the terms are used in many different ways, sometimes by the same person; they have many different definitions, implicit if not explicit. Since there are some real, and useful, distinctions underlying these usages, we could, of course, define the terms to capture one of these. However, third, the terms' common association with other ideas would make the terms still misleading. Fourth, the terms have a common unambiguous, and relatively clear, use to capture a distinction in modalities and their ascriptions, but that distinction is not appropriately analogous to any of the useful distinctions among thoughts and their ascriptions. So, once again, their use to describe thoughts and their ascriptions is misleading. Finally, that use is unnecessary: we have other, relatively clear, and unambiguous, terms to do the required jobs.

It may be uncharitable to take the people who seem to be using these terms of thoughts themselves to be really doing so. For, it is a common practice (to which I have in the past succumbed) to use 'belief', for example, where what one means to refer to is belief *ascription*. My argument in this section is that the application of the terms '*de dicto*' and '*de re*' to thoughts is, *if taken literally*, inappropriate. In the next section I shall criticize the application of these terms to ascriptions.

A puzzle about the application of the terms to thoughts is that it so often arises as if it were an obvious consequence of their application to thought ascriptions.[18] Yet a difference in sorts of thought ascription clearly does not entail a difference in sorts of thought object ascribed. Consider, for example, love ascriptions: particular ones, like 'Tom loves Dick', differ from general ones, like 'Tom loves someone', but this does not entail that there are particular lovers and general lovers.

It is said that a necessity is *de dicto* if it is a property of a "proposition." Analogously, it is usual to say that a thought is *de dicto* if it is a relation (a two-place property) between a person and a proposition.[19] What is a "proposition"? We are often told simply that it is the object of a belief. If so, then the term '*de dicto*' applies trivially to all beliefs and can have no explanatory role when so applied. Sometimes a proposition is said to be the "meaning" of a sentence, or what the sentence "expresses."[20] The key terms here are as mysterious as 'proposition'. Aside from that problem, there is the one of motivation. Why suppose there are such entities as propositions? The few people who join David Lewis in thinking there are good nonsemantic reasons for believing in the nonactual have a solution to both problems: propositions are sets of possible worlds. However, those few seem no better off than the majority with the next problem. Propositions are *irrelevant* to what thoughts explain: behavior and learning (section 1). Further, if they were relevant to some thoughts, why would they not be relevant to all equally? For example, if one sentence token in the head has a "meaning," why would they all not have one? If '*de dicto*' is defined to apply to thoughts that relate a person to a proposition, how could it not apply trivially to all thoughts?[21]

It is said that a necessity is *de re* if it is a property of an object. Analogously, we might expect to say that a thought is *de re* if it is a relation between a person, an object, and something else (a property, perhaps). It sometimes seems as if this is what is being said. It will not do. *All* singular thought tokens refer (or purport to),[22] and so all singular thoughts relate a person to an object.

If we stay close to the application of the terms '*de dicto*' and '*de re*' to modalities in attempting to apply the terms to singular thoughts, they both apply trivially to all thoughts (insofar as they apply at all).

Often the above relational view of *de re* thought is modified, apparently under the influence of a view of *de re* thought ascription: *de re* thought relates a person to an object in a special sort of way, so that he or she has *that particular object in mind*; he or she is en rapport with it.[23] This modification can have no analogy with *de re* necessity where there is no (relevant) person to have anything in mind.

Consider Quine's famous example.[24] Ralph's belief of the man in the brown hat that he is a spy seems to involve Ortcutt in particular, who happens to be that man. In contrast, in Kaplan's example,[25] Ralph's belief that the shortest spy is a spy does not seem to involve Mata Hari in particular, who happens (let us suppose) to be that spy. I think this does reveal a useful distinction between beliefs. I explain a case of the former sort by saying that the belief token contains a designational term referring to the object (e.g., 'the man in the brown hat'): it is in virtue of being causally connected to an object in the way appropriate for a designational term that a person can "have the object in mind" (see above). On the other hand, in a case of the latter sort, the belief token contains an attributive term referring to the object (e.g., 'the shortest spy') that does not enable the believer to have the object in mind. In sum, on the modified view, *de re* thought is designational thought.

We could then define *de dicto* thought as attributive thought. This does come close to a characterization of *de dicto* thought that is different from, and less common than, the one criticized above: it is said to be thought involving a *general* proposition (with *de re* involving a singular one).[26] For, an attributive thought is equivalent to a general one. Once again, however, we have a usage that has no analogy with discussions of modalities.

If we abandon the analogies with modalities, and the ideas associated with '*de dicto*' and '*de re*' reflecting those analogies, we can therefore find a use for the terms in describing thoughts. However, it is a very misleading use because of what we are abandoning. It is also unnecessary: 'designational' and 'attributive' will do the descriptive job.

3. A THEORY OF THOUGHT ASCRIPTIONS

Quine noted that there seemed to be two ways of interpreting a thought ascription like

(1) Ralph believes that Ortcutt is a spy.

On the first, 'Ortcutt' is not "used as a means simply of specifying its object"; it is not in "purely referential position"; it is not subject to the law of substitutivity of identity.[27] On the second, the opposite is the case. He suggested that the second interpretation could be made explicit by a paraphrase along the following lines:

(2) Ortcutt is such that Ralph believes him to be a spy.

In (2), the 'Ortcutt' is outside the scope of 'believes'; that scope is narrow. The importance of having the second interpretation as well as the first was brought home to Quine by the striking difference between

(3) Ralph believes that someone is a spy,

where all he believes is that there are spies, and

(4) Someone is such that Ralph believes him to be a spy,

where Ralph must have a particular person in mind as a spy. In (4), but not (3), we are "quantifying into" the 'belief' construction. Finally Quine conjectured that the "exportation" of a singular term involved in the move from (1), on the first interpretation, to (2) was generally "implicative."

Quine named the context of the definite singular term 'Ortcutt' in (1), on the first interpretation, and the context of the indefinite singular term 'someone' in (3), "opaque." In contrast he named the contexts of those terms in (2) and (4), "transparent." So he used the test of substitutivity for transparency involving definite singular terms, and that of quantifying in for transparency involving indefinite singular terms (or variables). I shall adopt this usage. Note that though an ascription that quantifies in is transparent, one that *licenses* an ascription that quantifies in may not be: if exportation holds, we can infer (2) from the opaque (1) and thence, by existential generalization, (4). Since my focus is almost entirely on definite singular terms, substitutivity is my key test of transparency. I shall follow the common practice of often calling the whole sentence (not just the context of the singular term) opaque or transparent.

Doubt was cast on Quine's observations by cases like that of "the shortest spy."[28] Using the rule of exportation, we can *almost infer* (4) from (3). For it is only a small step from (3) to

(5) Ralph believes that the shortest spy is a spy.

Exporting 'the shortest spy' yields

(6) The shortest spy is such that Ralph believes him to be a spy.

Existentially generalizing, we get (4). To save Quine's observations we need some restriction on exportation.

I have argued for a simple restriction on exportation: *only (nonempty) designational terms may be exported*. The inference from the opaque (1) to (2) is valid, as Quine supposed, because 'Ortcutt' is designational; that from (5) to (4) is not because 'the shortest spy' is attributive. An opaque ascription licenses an inference to a statement that quantifies in only if the opaque ascription is designational.[29] So I make use of *two* distinctions in handling the semantics of thought ascriptions: first, Quine's structural distinction between transparent and opaque contexts; second, my distinction between designational and attributive singular terms (a distinction motivated independently of the problems of thought ascriptions). These two distinctions yield four standard forms of thought ascription: transparent designational, exemplified by (2); transparent attributive, exemplified by (6); opaque designational, exemplified by (1) (on its first interpretation); and opaque attributive, exemplified by

(5).[30] The difference between the first two is of no special interest, but all other differences are.

The restriction on exportation is supported by a theory of the truth conditions of the four standard forms.[31] In general, an ascription of a belief to Ralph is true if and only if Ralph stands in a believing relation to an appropriate sentence token. What is appropriate varies from form to form.

The basic idea of what is appropriate in each case, briefly put, is as follows. If the ascription is transparent, Ralph must have his belief *under some designational term for the object*. If the ascription is opaque, then Ralph must have his belief *under the same term for the object as the ascriber used*. So if that term is designational, so also must Ralph's be; similarly, attributive.

If a person has a belief under a designational term—if he or she has a designational belief—then he or she has a particular object in mind (section 2). On the above account, a transparent ascription requires Ralph to have a designational belief. So I capture the central intuition about that ascription: it requires Ralph to have the object in mind. An opaque designational ascription requires Ralph to have a designational belief involving a certain term. So he has the object in mind in a certain way. So he has it in mind. So exportation is in order.

The theory of designation explains the folk-theoretic idea of having an object in mind: a person has an object in mind in virtue of being causally linked to it in the appropriate way (section 2).

Statement (2) illustrates the transparent designational form. Accepting Quine's story, (2) is true because Ralph has a belief he would express, "The man in the brown hat is a spy," where 'the man in the brown hat' is causally linked to Ortcutt in the appropriate way to be a designational term. In more normal circumstances, on the other hand, (6) is likely to be false because Ralph is unlikely to be causally linked in the right way to whoever happens to be the shortest spy. The only difference between the transparent designational and attributive ascriptions is in the ascriber's mode of identifying the object about which Ralph is alleged to have a designational belief.

In Quine's story, the opaque designational (1) is false, but the opaque designational

(7) Ralph believes that the man in the brown hat is a spy

is true: Ralph has the belief of Ortcutt using the designational term 'the man in the brown hat', not 'Ortcutt'. Exportation is valid in both cases, as Quine surmised (but that from [1] can establish nothing because [1] is false).

An opaque attributive ascription requires Ralph to have an attributive token for the object, and so does not require having the object in mind. So exportation does not hold for it. Statement (5) can be true even though Ralph has nobody in mind as the shortest spy. We cannot infer (6) from (5) because 'the shortest spy' is attributive and hence not open to exportation.

In section 2, I criticized the common application of the terms '*de dicto*' and '*de re*' to thoughts. It is even more common to apply them to thought ascriptions, but hardly more appropriate, in my view.

Consider first their use to describe modal ascriptions. There are two pairs of definitions. The first one is in terms of what is ascribed: a *de re* ascription ascribes a *de re* modality, which is a property of an object; a *de dicto* ascription ascribes a *de dicto* modality, which is a property of a "proposition." The second definition is in terms of the structural characteristics of the ascription: a *de re* ascription is transparent; a *de dicto* ascription is opaque. There is no problem having the two pairs of definitions because they classify ascriptions the same. (Indeed my "second definition" might better be regarded as the *test* for ascriptions fitting the first.)

We find analogies of both these definitions in the classification of thought ascriptions. The second is taken straight over from modal ascriptions, but the first usually appears in a modified form. The problem for thought ascriptions is that the two definitions do not classify ascriptions the same, yet they are commonly used together.

If my earlier criticisms of the use of '*de dicto*' and '*de re*' are sound, they count against any attempt to define *de dicto/de re* thought ascriptions, as the first definition does *de dicto/de re* modal ascriptions, in terms of what is ascribed. We cannot, for example, satisfactorily define *de dicto* ascriptions as those that ascribe to a person a relation to a proposition,[32] nor *de re* as those that ascribe to a person a relation to an object[33] (for each ascription would then be trivially both *de dicto* and *de re*).

In fact, the major definition of a *de re* ascription in terms of what is ascribed seems to modify this one: the ascription relates a person to *a particular object he has in mind* (is en rapport with).[34] So what is ascribed is a designational thought, the *special* relational thought of our earlier discussion. This modification has no analogy with *de re* modal ascriptions: there is no (relevant) person to have anything in mind in the modal case.

The other usual definition of a *de re* thought ascription *is* analogous to the modal case, for it follows the structural second definition: *de re* ascriptions are transparent ascriptions; *de dicto* ones are opaque.[35] Thus (2) is a paradigmatic example of what is usually called a *de re* ascription. It is also, of course, a paradigmatic example of ascribing a designational thought, which doubtless has something to do with the modification that took place when the first definition for modal ascriptions was applied to thought ascriptions.

The two definitions work together in classifying transparent ascriptions, whether designational like (2) or attributive like (6), as *de re*. No obvious problem arises with opaque attributive ascriptions like (5). The second definition clearly classifies them as *de dicto* and the first, insofar as it has any content, *seems* to also, because it would classify *any* ascription as *de dicto* (triviality problem). The problem comes with opaque designational ascriptions like (1) or (7) (under one reading). The two definitions classify these differently. The first classifies them as *de re* because they ascribe designational thoughts, thoughts with a particular object in mind.

The second classifies them as *de dicto* because they are opaque. Note that in Quine's story the very same (designational) belief makes both the opaque (7) and the transparent (2) true.

The two definitions are bound to pull apart if exportation ever holds. For it, together with existential generalization, licenses an inference from an opaque ascription to one that quantifies in, i.e., to one that ascribes a thought about a particular object in mind. (Note that exportation never holds for modal ascriptions.)

The one pair of terms, '*de dicto*' and '*de re*', cannot cope satisfactorily with a reality containing two distinctions: that between ascribing designational and attributive thoughts, and that between transparent and opaque ascriptions.[36] If the terms were restricted to the latter distinction, they would be clear and analogous to their use of modal ascriptions. However, the terms' common association with the other ideas we have mentioned would make this usage still misleading. The terms 'transparent' and 'opaque' do the job better.

My conclusion on the discussion of '*de dicto*' and '*de re*' in this and the last section is as follows. There are a number of real distinctions that seem to underlie the use of these terms. At the level of thoughts, there are the distinctions between designational and attributive, and between singular and general (and between empty and nonempty?).[37] At the level of ascriptions there are distinctions between ascriptions of those different sorts of thought, and between transparent and opaque. The terms are not appropriately applied to any of these distinctions. Much confusion has resulted from using the terms without adequate explanation and from using them at one and the same time to cover more than one distinction.[38]

4. ASCRIPTIONS AND THE CLASSIFICATION OF THOUGHTS

Any two tokens of anything are alike in some respects and different in others. When we classify tokens into types, we focus on certain similarities and ignore differences. Ascriptions of thought classify thought tokens. In considering how we classify thought tokens when we ascribe them—in considering the truth conditions of ascriptions—it helps, as William Lycan emphasizes, to consider *why* we classify beliefs. Lycan identifies two basic concerns: in my terms, those of narrow psychology and those of wide psychology.[39] I think he is right. Partly as a result of this view, Lycan claims further that we use two schemes, the narrow and the wide, to classify tokens when making ascriptions. I think we do mostly use two schemes, but they are not the narrow and the wide. They are the opaque and the transparent, which are both wide.

Transparent belief ascriptions fairly obviously serve wide concerns. These concerns are, roughly, with beliefs as a guide to the way the world is. Suppose we are interested in a certain object x. If we know that x is such that Ralph believes it to be F, and that Ralph is likely to be right in this matter, then we know that x is likely to be F.

Jerry Fodor has claimed[40] that opaque ascriptions are our ordinary (folk-theoretic) way of meeting the needs of narrow psychology. I think that *mostly* they are, but that self-demonstrative ascriptions are exceptions. Ignore these exceptions until section 5 and consider the relation between the opaque and the narrow.

When our concerns are narrow, the only properties of thoughts that count are syntactic ones and such semantic ones, reflected in form, as come from a thought's relation to sensory input and behavioral output (section 2). So it could make no difference to the classification of a thought, according to the narrow scheme, what the thought is *about* or *refers* to. It could make no difference what object in the external world caused the stimulus and is the likely target of the behavior. Yet we find that *none* of our thoughts ascriptions are indifferent to reference. If I say of the recently arrived Twin-Earth-Ralph, "He believes that Reagan is a ham," my statement is false because he has no beliefs about Reagan at all. Yet at the narrow level it is exactly as if he had the required belief, because he does have one about Twin-Earth-Reagan that he tokens "Reagan is a ham." Consider a more down-to-Earth example. I say, demonstrating a certain horse, "Ralph believes that horse is a winner." In fact Ralph has never spotted that horse but has another one, indistinguishable to Ralph from the first horse, about which Ralph tokens a belief, "That horse is a winner." My ascription is false, and yet I am right about those aspects of Ralph's belief that play a role in predicting and explaining his behavior: its links to input and output. Finally, consider my saying, "Ralph believes that Bruce is a philosopher." I have the new Bruce in mind. Ralph has never heard of him but has of one of the other departmental Bruces. Ralph tokens "Bruce is a philosopher," having that Bruce in mind. My ascription is false but I have got Ralph right at the narrow level.

Reference is irrelevant to narrow concerns but is not to opaque ascriptions. On the other hand, some formal differences that are relevant to narrow concerns are not to opaque ascriptions. Thus it does not matter to the truth of, "Ralph believes that you are a spy," whether Ralph tokens his belief, "You are a spy," or "He is a spy."

The above ascriptions, construed opaquely, are examples of the way folk ascribe beliefs to meet narrow concerns. Since we would evidently get better explanations of behavior by making narrow ascriptions, why don't we do so? The question splits in two. (i) Why, when our concerns are narrow, do we make reference relevant? (ii) And why, when our concerns are narrow, do we ignore relevant differences of form?

In answer to (i), I suggest, first, that we make reference relevant partly because our concerns are often wide as well as narrow. *Opaque ascriptions meet wide concerns. Indeed they may meet them more effectively than transparent ones do.* For, they tell us under what term Ralph has his belief of *x*. Though this is irrelevant to *the truth value* of Ralph's belief, it is very relevant to *our assessment of the likelihood of the belief's being true* and hence of *x*'s being as Ralph believes it is: Ralph may be unreliable about a person's spyhood under one mode ('the man seen at the beach') but reliable under another ('the man in the brown hat'). So the opaque form enables us to kill two birds with one stone.

Next, consider what we would have to do if we didn't make reference relevant.

We would need some other way to identify the sort of stimulus and behavior that is related to the belief ascribed. To explain and predict Ralph's behavior, it is not enough to know that Ralph tokens, "Reagan is a ham." We need to tie Ralph's belief to the sort of stimulus President Reagan produces rather than, say, Ralph's neighbor who is also called 'Reagan', and to the type of behavior that is likely to affect the President not the neighbor. Ralph is likely to token many beliefs using 'Reagan', referring to many different Reagans and, for that very reason, related to quite different input and output. These different representations must, of course, be formally different in order to play their different roles (section 2). Adopting a device from the linguists, we might name the different representations: 'Reagan$_1$', Reagan$_2$', ... Suppose that 'Reagan$_1$' refers to President Reagan. So Ralph's 'Reagan$_1$' beliefs are tied to the input and output associated with President Reagan (and his Twin-Earth counterpart, of course). In ascribing a belief to meet our narrow concerns, we need to distinguish that input-output from ones tied to Ralph's other 'Reagan' beliefs. Making the reference of a belief relevant to the ascription is one way to do this. Perhaps it is the only easy way.

Further, we mostly know enough about the context to be mostly right about a believer's reference: problems like those of the wrong Reagan, the wrong horse, and the wrong Bruce are rare. So, we seldom have to pay a price for introducing reference.

Finally, when we *are* right about reference, opaque ascriptions provide a shortcut in a broader explanation or prediction. We are interested not only in a person's behavior but also in the effects of it on the world; we are interested not only in the bodily movements prompted by Ralph's tokening, "That horse is a winner," but also in which horse, as a result, he backs. An opaque ascription, if it's right about reference, explains in one step what would otherwise take two: first, the narrow ascription; and second, an account of what in the world is appropriately related to the input and output to be on the receiving end of the bodily movements. Of course, if we have the information to be right about reference, we have the information for the second step. An opaque ascription simply puts this information together with our information about what a person narrowly believes.

In answer to (ii), I suggest that the loss in power to explain and predict behavior, as a result of overlooking such relatively minor differences as those between 'you' and 'he', are more than compensated for by the other advantages of opaque ascriptions mentioned above.

To talk of classifying thoughts using a narrow, opaque, or transparent scheme is not to talk of classifying thoughts *as* narrow, opaque, or transparent (a fortiori it is not to talk of classifying them as *de dicto* or *de re* because they are opaque or transparent). *All* beliefs have the formal, syntactic, and semantic properties to be classified according to *each* scheme. We can illustrate what the schemes do as follows. Consider the earlier example. Ralph tokens a belief, "Bruce is a philosopher": he has heard of only one Bruce in the department, say, the Head. Then Ralph believes narrowly-that-Bruce-is-a-philosopher, even if I refer here to the new Bruce; he believes opaquely-that-Bruce-is-a-philosopher only if I refer to the Head; he believes transparently-that-the-Head-of-the-Department-is-a-philosopher. 'Narrow', 'opaque', and 'transparent' modify descriptions of "content."

5. SELF-DEMONSTRATIVE THOUGHTS AND THEIR ASCRIPTION

Among people's thoughts are some they have of themselves. So, we might call these thoughts "*de se*." The following story, taken from John Perry, illustrates the special conceptual role that one sort of thought *de se* plays.

> I once followed a trail of sugar on a supermarket floor, pushing my cart down the aisle on one side of a tall counter and back the aisle on the other, seeking the shopper with the torn sack to tell him he was making a mess. With each trip around the corner, the trail became thicker. But I seemed unable to catch up. Finally it dawned on me. I was the shopper I was trying to catch.
>
> I believed at the outset that the shopper with a torn sack was making a mess. And I was right. But I didn't believe that I was making a mess. That seems to be something I came to believe. And when I came to believe that, I stopped following the trail around the counter, and rearranged the torn sack in my cart. My change in beliefs seems to explain my change in behavior.[41]

The dramatic change in Perry's behavior came when he tokened a belief using 'I'. His earlier belief, using the attributive 'the shopper with a torn sack', played a very different role. So, in suitable circumstances, would other beliefs *de se* using 'Perry', or designational tokens of, say, 'that man' (looking in a mirror). The circumstances are ones where Perry does not know that he himself is, for example, that man.

David Lewis, and Stephen Boër and William Lycan,[42] call beliefs of the sort that changed Perry's behavior, "*de se*." I do not restrict the term to these, because people can clearly have beliefs that are *of themselves* that are not of that sort; Perry's initial belief of the shopper with a torn sack is an example.

Perry called beliefs of the sort that changed his behavior, along with others he would express using demonstratives referring to his spatial and temporal location (e.g., 'here' and 'now'), "essentially indexical" and "locating." I shall not follow this usage. (i) *All* beliefs that are indexical are, it seems, essentially so. Consider, for example, the belief that I would express to Perry, "You are making a mess." Any nonindexical replacement (using, e.g., 'the shopper with the torn sack') will not do the same job of explaining my behavior. (ii) Beliefs that involve 'I' may not be locating at all. *Any* belief that refers to a time or place (even by name) is locating.

What is peculiar about the beliefs in question is that they include a "self-demonstrative" like 'I' (another one in English is 'myself'). So I call the beliefs "self-demonstrative."[43] Note that a person's belief might demonstrate himself (via, e.g., 'that person') and yet not be, in my sense, self-demonstrative because it might not *contain* a self-demonstrative. A self-demonstrative belief must be essentially so.

What a story like Perry's shows is that self-demonstrative thoughts have a special explanatory role, a role that is not even the same as that of any other sort of *de se* thought. There is nothing particularly puzzling or exciting about this on the account of thought I am urging. We should *expect* (what are intuitively) syntactic and semantic differences in thought tokens to be explanatorily significant in narrow or wide psychology. Consider some examples. We expect the role of predicational beliefs to be different from that of quantificational ones; designational ones, from attributive ones; ones containing a token of 'Reagan' from ones containing a token of 'Nixon'; ones containing a token of 'you' from ones containing a token of your name. The world of beliefs is full of sorts having special roles. Cognitive psychology faces the formidable task of characterizing all these special roles, but there is no reason to suppose that self-demonstrative beliefs pose any peculiarly difficult problem.

Perry argues that these beliefs pose "a problem for various otherwise plausible accounts of belief."[44] In my view these accounts are otherwise *im*plausible, despite their popularity, because they all talk of "propositions" (sections 1 and 2). Faced with the problem for these accounts, Perry does not drop propositions but rather adds a further sort of abstract entity: "belief states."[45] He posits those to meet the needs of narrow psychology and retains propositions to meet those of wide psychology (in my terms). Concrete sentence tokens will do both jobs just as well.

Lewis rightly urges that we should seek uniform objects of thought. A consideration of self-demonstrative thoughts leads him to prefer properties, defined in terms of possible beings, to propositions, defined in terms of possible worlds, as uniform objects. In doing so, he reduces all thought to self-demonstrative thought.

The theory offered here shares with Lewis' the advantages of assigning uniform objects to thoughts and of allowing for the special role of self-demonstrative thoughts. In my view, it has other advantages that Lewis' lacks: it talks only of actual entities and avoids the implausibility of a person's thoughts all being about himself.

Given that there are self-demonstrative thoughts, a semantic question arises. Is there an ordinary form of words that ascribes such a thought to a person? The question is interesting but not of great importance. We have already noted that there is an ordinary form of words to ascribe, for example, a predicational thought (using a predication), a designational thought about Perry (using a term that refers to Perry in a transparent ascription), or an attributive thought about Perry qua shopper with a torn sack (using 'the shopper with a torn sack' in an opaque ascription). On the other hand, we have noted that we do not have a form of words to ascribe a designational thought about Perry that is not merely about him qua demonstrated object, but about him qua *you* (the person addressed; section 4). Given the special role self-demonstrative thoughts play, and hence our interest in which ones a person has, we should not be surprised to discover that there is a special form of words to ascribe one to a person. Indeed we would *expect* there to be such a form. Thus, everyone concerned with the tidiness of the supermarket is interested in whether the shopper with the torn sack tokens a belief, "I am making the mess."

Hector-Neri Castañeda has argued convincingly that there is a form for ascribing self-demonstrative beliefs:

a believes that he himself is *F*.[46]

In the light of our discussion of these beliefs, the truth conditions of such ascriptions are obvious: *a* must stand in a believing relation to a token including a self-demonstrative.

Ascriptions of self-demonstrative thoughts are strikingly different from the four standard forms of ascription we have previously identified (working the variations on the two distinctions, transparent/opaque and designational/attributive): the statements of truth conditions for these forms do not fit ascriptions of self-demonstrative thoughts; the latter have a distinct "logical form."

In this respect, these ascriptions differ from ascriptions of the other thoughts Perry calls "locating." These thoughts are ones that a person would express by demonstrating his or her spatial or temporal location. Consider one of Perry's examples:[47] a professor comes to token, "The meeting is now beginning." We can ascribe this thought using the standard opaque designational form of ascription with a demonstrative: e.g.,

The professor believed that the meeting started at that time.

Such ascriptions, just like the opaquely construed

Ralph believes that that man (demonstrating Ortcutt) is a spy,

require the alleged believer to token a belief including a demonstrative that is codesignational with the ascriber's demonstrative; the alleged believer's singular term must be "of the same type" as the ascriber's in that respect.[48] (Of course, we may need to ascribe more to the professor to explain his behavior: that he believed he himself was at that time. But this is just an ascription of a self-demonstrative belief of the sort we have been discussing.)

I agree with Castañeda's "Irreducibility Thesis": ascriptions of self-demonstrative thoughts cannot be reduced to another sort of ascription. Boër and Lycan reject this thesis, holding that these sentences simply ascribe "*de re*" a thought about a person to that very person. Indeed, they hold the even more surprising view that self-demonstrative thoughts themselves are reducible: "What we contend is that attitudes *de se* are simply attitudes *de* their owners."[49] Yet it seems obvious, for example, that Perry might, as a result of observing himself in a mirror, token a belief, "That person is making a mess," whilst also without irrationality tokening, "I am not making a mess"; and that we might in these circumstances assert without inconsistency both "That person is such that Perry believes him to be making a mess" and "Perry does not believe he himself is making a mess." Boër and Lycan are convinced by their argument against this obvious point largely, I think, because they overlook the possibility of opaque designational ascriptions of belief.[50]

In section 4 we considered whether transparent and opaque ascriptions met the concerns of narrow and wide psychology. Which concern does an ascription of self-demonstrative thought meet? Alone of ordinary ascriptions of one-place predicational thoughts, it classifies thoughts, so far as their singular terms are concerned, as they would be classified by narrow psychology. Yet it also meets the needs of wide psychology just as an opaque ascription does. What is peculiar about the ascription of a self-demonstrative thought is that the reference of the thought, required by the ascription to meet wide concerns, *must* be determined by information about the belief relevant to narrow psychology: the reference of 'I' is determined by the head it's in.

This peculiarity of self-demonstrative beliefs explains a lot of the interest they have created. It has the consequence that self-demonstrative beliefs cannot be *shared* in the way all other beliefs can. People who are inclined to think that we share beliefs when we believe "the same proposition" (or "content") find here that there can be no such "proposition." That is the problem Perry and Lewis address.[51] My view eschews abstractions like "propositions" as the objects of belief. The objects of belief are sentence tokens, which cannot, of course, be *literally* shared. Nevertheless, we can make sense of people sharing a belief: they do so in virtue of having belief tokens of the same type. Each scheme of classification yields a criterion for being of the same type. Thus, Tom and Ralph share the belief narrowly-that-Bruce-is-a-philosopher because they both believe tokens of "Bruce is a philosopher" that are similarly related to input and output. Should their tokens of 'Bruce' be of the same network, then they share the belief opaquely. Should their tokens of 'Bruce' refer to the Head, then they share a belief transparently with Harry who tokens, "The Head of the Department is a philosopher." Now, the Head and the new Bruce might both token, "I am a philosopher," and hence share a self-demonstrative belief narrowly. But that is not the sort of sharing that normally interests us and that people have in mind in talking of "belief in the same proposition." We are normally interested in sharing opaquely or transparently. This interest requires coreference for sharing. But two people cannot have coreferential self-demonstrative beliefs, for each such belief refers to the person whose head it's in. With self-demonstrative beliefs there can be no "proposition" that the two people believe. So much the worse for the view that what we believe are "propositions." The difficulties in sharing a self-demonstrative belief pose no threat to the view that what we believe are sentence tokens.

6. WIDE-SCOPE TRANSPARENT ASCRIPTIONS

In section 4, I considered the ways transparent and opaque ascriptions classify thoughts but not the ways designational and attributive ascriptions classify them. All the examples were designational.

Consider my theory of ascriptions of a belief "about *x*." (i) A transparent one, whether designational or attributive, ascribes a belief about *x under some designational term*. (ii) An opaque designational one ascribes a belief about *x under a particular designational term*. (iii) An opaque attributive one ascribes a belief about *x under a particular attributive term*. (iv) None ascribes a belief about *x* simply *under some attributive term*, nor (v) a belief about *x* simply *under some term* (whether attributive or designational). There are reasons for thinking this theory of ascriptions is not right. These reasons will concern me for the rest of this paper.

Ascriptions need to serve two basic concerns, narrow and wide. Transparent ascriptions serve only wide. Opaque ascriptions serve both. There is no surprise, given these concerns, that we should have the means to make the ascriptions mentioned in (i) to (iii). But why should we not have the (standard) means to make the ascriptions mentioned in (iv) and (v)? Both ascriptions seem relevant to wide concerns.

I think we may be able to explain the special interest we have in designational belief. This would explain why we have the (standard) means to make the designational ascriptions of (i) but not the attributive ones of (iv). The special interest of a designational belief may be explained by the epistemic significance of being in a position to designate something. If people are in that position, then they are causally related to the object in a way that is apt to lead them to true beliefs about it (which is not to deny that many designational beliefs are false).[52]

I can see no satisfactory answer to the rest of the question. If we are interested in what x is like then we should be interested in any belief a reliable person has about x. An attributive belief is also a guide to reality. If the ascriber wants to be specific about the term under which the attributive belief is held then he or she can, of course, address our interest in that belief using the opaque attributive style. However, surely, the ascriber will not always want to do this. Even if we can explain (as above) our having a nonspecific style of ascription for designational but not for attributive belief, how can we explain our not having a nonspecific style that covers attributive belief (as well as designational belief)? Even if we can explain our having the style of (i) but not (iv), how can we explain our not having the style of (v)?

An example due to Stephen Schiffer[53] suggests we do have that style. Smith is found dead. Ralph, the famous sleuth, suspects murder. Further, the manner of the slaying makes him think that whoever is responsible is insane. The newspapers report this:

(8) Ralph believes that Smith's murder is insane.

The murder was in fact committed by a well-known mobster:

(9) Big Felix is Smith's murderer.

Big Felix's moll knows this. She reads the newspaper and remarks to one of the mob:

(10) Ralph believes that Big Felix is insane.

According to my theory, (10) must be false. It cannot be true construed transparently, since Ralph does not have Big Felix (or anyone else) particularly in mind as the insane murderer: 'Smith's murderer' in (8), and in Ralph's belief, is a paradigmatic attributive term. It cannot be true construed opaquely, since Ralph does not believe insanity of the murderer under the name 'Big Felix'. The problem for my theory is that (10) seems true. Furthermore, it seems a good example of an ascription in the style of (v) and of why we need that style. The mob's wide concerns are strikingly served by (10): insofar as they think Ralph a good judge of insanity, they had better watch out for Big Felix.

Why not then take (10), in the circumstances, as ascribing a belief about Big Felix under some term or other? Because to do so, it seems, is to construe (10) transparently and hence to make it equivalent to the narrow-scope

(11) Big Felix is such that Ralph believes him insane.

Yet Quine's original observation that this requires Ralph to have Big Felix particularly in mind still seems good: (11) seems false (section 3). That is the observation that I have captured in (i): a transparent ascription ascribes a belief under some *designational* term.

Clearly, we have a choice about what we give up: (a) our new way of interpreting (10) to make it true; (b) the Quinean observation about the narrow-scope transparent style that makes (11) false; or (c) the view that our new interpretation of the likes of (10) is equivalent to the narrow-scope transparent style. My reluctance to give up (b) has previously led me to reject (a). But why not reject (c)? One reason might be an Occamist distaste for multiplying styles of belief ascription beyond necessity. Yet if there is a need for a variety of belief ascriptions, as there seems to be to meet our wide and narrow concerns, we should expect to find that need met in our standard styles of ascription.

What I am contemplating is that ascriptions of the form

(12) a believes that b is F

have an interpretation that is not the familiar opaque one and that is nevertheless not equivalent to the explicitly transparent, narrow-scope,

(13) b is such that a believes him to be F.

The new interpretation differs from the opaque one in allowing substitutivity; the moll's inference from (8) and (9) to (10) is a good example. It differs from the opaque also in not allowing the exportation of a designational 'b'. Related to that, it differs from the narrow-scope transparent in not requiring a to have a designational belief of b. It differs from both in not licensing an inference to a statement that quantifies in.

Should we then call this new style of belief ascription "wide-scope transparent"? I think so, but a word of caution is appropriate. We have mostly ignored the fact that 'b' in (12) and (13) could be empty. If it were, the transparent (13) would not be true, but (12), on the usual opaque interpretation, could be true. Could (12) be true on the new interpretation? The fact that substitutivity holds for it does not settle that it is not true (because if 'b' is empty it is plausible to think that any identity statement involving it will not be true). Yet if (12) is properly called "transparent" then the emptiness of 'b' should prevent it being true. I am inclined to think that the emptiness of 'b' does prevent truth. Certainly, if it does not, it is hard to see how this new style of ascription could serve wide concerns: for those concerns are with a's beliefs as a guide to the way the world *really* is. If I am wrong in my inclination then the term "semiopaque" would be a more appropriate name for this new style.[54]

In section 4 I pointed out how opaque ascriptions may meet wide concerns more effectively than transparent ones. Why then do we have transparent ones *as well as* opaque? One reason has just been mentioned: the opaque tolerates emptiness. Schiffer's example illustrates another reason. Suppose that the mobster addressed by Big Felix's moll does not know that Big Felix murdered Smith. If the moll were simply to repeat the newspaper's opaque (8), the mobster could learn nothing of vital interest to him about the world. From (10), in contrast, he can. It is in such circumstances that we need the wide-scope transparent style of (12). Replace 'Smith's murderer' in (8) by some designational term that Ralph, but not the mobster, has for Big Felix, and we similarly illustrate a need for the narrow-scope transparent style of (13).

Trivial beliefs seem to pose a problem for the view that there are wide-scope transparent ascriptions. Suppose:

(5) Ralph believes that the shortest spy is a spy;
(14) Mata Hari is the shortest spy.

If (5) is transparent, we can infer the transparent:

(15) Ralph believes that Mata Hari is a spy.

Yet (15) seems false on any interpretation. Perhaps we should overlook (5), treating it as a degenerate case of the wide-scope transparent. Or perhaps we should restrict the wide-scope interpretation to the ascription of beliefs that are not trivial in this way.

Lack of confidence seems to me an appropriate state in considering many of the semantic issues of thought ascription. First, the evidence for interpreting a particular form one way or another is often far from decisive. Second, perhaps there are more ambiguities than we have noted. Third, perhaps there is no determinate matter of fact which of several possible interpretations is correct on a particular occasion: the differences between interpretations may often be irrelevant to our concerns in making an ascription. These semantic problems do not, however, reflect on our ontology of thought. That ontology seems to provide a basis for giving a semantics for all the plausible possible interpretations of ascriptions.

7. IDENTITY THOUGHTS AND THEIR ASCRIPTION

The ascription of thoughts about identities has bothered semantic theorists ever since Frege's point about "cognitive value"[55] and Russell's about what could "be attributed to the first gentleman of Europe."[56]

(16) Ralph believes that $a = b$

need not ascribe the triviality: belief in the law of identity. Further,

(17) Tom believes that $a \neq b$

need not ascribe the contradiction: rejection of the law of identity. This problem, and others, have led traditionally to description theories of proper names: the solution was thought to lie in the different descriptions associated with 'a' and 'b'. Causal theories of reference were born out of the rejection of description theories: names are not associated with descriptions in the way specified. This rejection has seemed to many to leave 'a' and 'b' identical in "semantic content," "sense," or "connotation" (given that $a = b$) and hence to revive the above problem.[57]

A preliminary point. The rejection of description theories should not be exaggerated. A causal theorist should allow that some names are attributive. There is a good deal of truth in description theories if they are restricted to attributive names.[58] So the old response to the problem of identity ascriptions may work for those names.

A temptation to be resisted here is to suppose that whenever (16) seems not to ascribe a triviality and (17), not a contradiction, this indicates that either 'a' or 'b' (or both) are attributive.[59] (i) It is simply not plausible to suppose that names like 'Hesperus', 'Phosphorus', 'Tully', and 'Cicero', used in classical examples of the problem, are not as designational as any name. (ii) It is ad hoc to suppose that a name that is elsewhere designational is attributive in identity contexts.

The ability to use a term designationally to refer to an object is a set of related thoughts involving the term and grounded in the object (section 2). If a person can have one designational term for an object, he or she can have many. Since the designatum of such a term is determined by a causal chain much of which is outside the person's mind and noncognitive, we should *expect* the person to be unaware of some of the identities consequent upon his or her use of codesignational terms. There should be no surprise that the person may use 'Tully' and 'Cicero' without tokening, "Tully = Cicero." Situations like this do not arise only with names. Ralph, in Quine's example, may use 'the man in the brown hat' and 'the man seen at the beach' designationally, without tokening, "The man in the brown hat = the man seen at the beach." A person, looking at a long ship not all of which is visible to him, may use 'this ship' designationally pointing at the bow, and 'that ship' designationally pointing at the stern, without tokening, "This ship = that ship." There is no mystery about this. The terms in each pair, though codesignational, are formally different in the person's language of thought and are thus able to play different conceptual roles between input and output.[60] Since the two terms 'a' and 'b' are distinct in the person's cognitive life, it is not trivial to entertain the thought, "$a = b$," nor (formally)[61] contradictory to entertain the thought, "$a \neq b$."

If this is right about the ontology of designational identity thoughts, there seems to be no puzzle about their ascription. The standard account for (doubly-) opaque (doubly-) designational ascriptions of two-place predicational thoughts will do. Statement (16) is true if Ralph tokens a belief, "$a = b$," and (17) if Tom tokens one, "$a \neq b$," the tokens of 'a' being part of the same causal network as the ascriber's 'a', and similarly for 'b'. We have seen that there is nothing trivial about what (16) ascribes, or (formally) contradictory about what (17) ascribes.

To explain the contribution a designational term makes to the truth conditions of an opaque thought ascription, we have to talk of more than its role of designating something: we have to talk of the way in which it fulfills this role, "the mode of presentation." This mode is not to be found, as traditionally thought, in associated descriptions, but in the causal mechanisms of reference. That is the respect in which 'a' and 'b' differ in "semantic content."[62] And the talk of mechanisms was required anyway to explain reference. A virtue of the causal theory of reference I urge is that the very same mechanisms needed to explain the notion of reference (needed in turn to explain truth conditions in general, e.g., of predictions like 'Tully is an orator'), can be used to explain the truth conditions of thought ascriptions.

Kripke's "puzzle about belief" poses a problem for this account of the truth conditions of opaque ascriptions. I set that aside until the next section. The problem I shall consider here arises from exportation and the truth conditions of (narrow-scope) transparent ascriptions. (Presumably a similar problem arises for wide-scope ascriptions, but I shall not consider this.) I have accepted the rule that (nonempty) designational terms may be exported from the opaque to the transparent. Applying this to (16), using the fact that $a = b$, and existentially generalizing, we get:

(18) Something is such that Ralph believes it = itself.

This seems to ascribe a triviality. That is no problem: it does not matter that we can derive something that ascribes a triviality from something that does not. The problem comes when we follow the same procedure with (17), yielding:

(19) Something is such that Tom believes it $\neq$ itself.

This seems to ascribe a contradiction. So, from the true (17) we have derived the almost certainly false (19). The rule of exportation must be changed.

The first sign that exportation was in trouble, even when restricted to designational terms, came in Quine's original discussion of his famous example. The true opaque ascriptions

(20) Ralph believes that the man in the brown hat is a spy,
(21) Ralph believes that the man seen at the beach is not a spy,

yield (with appropriate identities):

(22) Ortcutt is such that Ralph believes him to be a spy,
(23) Ortcutt is such that Ralph believes him not to be a spy.

Quine rightly pointed out that this was not to say,

(24) Ortcutt is such that Ralph believes him to be a spy and not a spy,

which ascribes an inconsistency to Ralph.[63] Nevertheless, the suggestion that both (22) and (23) were true in the circumstances seemed a little paradoxical.

The next sign of trouble came, for me at least, with Herbert Heidelberger's criticism[64] of David Kaplan's discussion of suspension of judgment.[65] I thought the criticism misguided, because it rested on an unargued assumption that was inconsistent with the Quinean assumptions about transparent ascription and exportation that guided Kaplan's discussion, and have guided me here. Nevertheless, Heidelberger's assumption had a worrying plausibility. Adapted from suspension of judgment to belief, the assumption is as follows: if a rational person has a belief of an individual that it has a certain property, then he or she does not believe of that individual that it does not have that property. This led me to contemplate a different view of transparent ascription and exportation that would preserve the assumption and avoid the apparent paradox of (22) and (23). The view of transparent ascription I have been urging so far requires Ralph to have a belief about x under *some* designational term he has for it. Call this a "weak" transparent ascription. The view suggested by Heidelberger's assumption is that a transparent ascription requires Ralph to have a belief under *all* the designational terms he has for x. Call this a "strong" transparent ascription. Exportation of a designational term from the opaque to the weak transparent is in order; that to the strong transparent is not. I could see no decisive reason for construing the ordinary transparent form as weak rather than strong (but continued to construe it as weak out of conservatism). I wondered whether we were faced here with ambiguity or indeterminacy.[66]

The problem with identity ascriptions gives a decisive reason for construing at least some ordinary transparent ascriptions as strong, and hence for not allowing exportation. The opaque (17) entitles us to say that Tom has a belief about a under some designational term he has for it, and about b under some designational term he has for it, that the former $\neq$ the latter; we are entitled to the weak transparent ascription. It does not entitle us to say that he has the belief of a and b under all the designational terms he has for them; we are not entitled to the strong transparent ascription. Indeed, we know that the strong ascription is false because

(25) Tom does not believe that $a \neq a$.

If we hold to the view that (19) ascribes a contradiction, we cannot interpret it as weak, but can as strong.

If the ordinary transparent form is strong, exportation does not hold. Why then does it mostly appear to hold? Presumably, because the designational term specified in an opaque ascription is mostly taken to be representative of all the designational terms the person has for the object. We mostly assume that the person knows all the appropriate identity statements about the object. And mostly the person does. Though we expect some cases like the earlier ones about Tully, Ortcutt, or the long ship, these are the exceptions rather than the rule. Not even all ascriptions of negative identities are exceptions: if we believe the negative identity true, then exportation may appear to hold. However if we believe it to be false, there can be no appearance of exportation holding: it is a consequence of what we believe that the designational terms specified by our ascription are not representative.

A consideration of our needs also inclines me to favor the strong interpretation. The transparent form serves wide concerns. It is clear that if it is construed strongly, it gives a more valuable guide to reality than it does if construed weakly. However, this is not a decisive consideration. Perhaps we prefer to have the less informative, but more easily assertable, weak construal.

In sum, the strong interpretation gets powerful support from identity ascriptions; it also gets some support from its dissolution of the apparent paradox, its accord with Heidelberger's assumption, and its better meeting our needs. Is there anything against it?

I once thought that negative ascriptions counted against it. Kaplan argued that just as (22) and (23) do not ascribe an inconsistency to Ralph, (22) and

(26) Ortcutt is such that Ralph does not believe him to be a spy

should not amount to an inconsistency on the ascriber's part. This led Kaplan to distinguish two readings of (26). On one reading, in my terminology, Ralph, under *each* designational term he has for Ortcutt, does not believe him to be a spy. On the other reading, Ralph, under *some* designational term, does not have the belief.[67] The first is a strong negative ascription and is the negation of a weak positive ascription; the second is a weak negative ascription and is the negation of a strong positive ascription. I was bothered by the thought that if ordinary positive ascriptions are interpreted strongly, it would be hard to interpret strongly any negative ascription, particularly:

(27) It is not the case that Ortcutt is such that Ralph believes him to be a spy.[68]

Certainly (27) seems to be the negation of (22), so if (22) is strong, (27) must be weak. However, there seems no reason why (26) could not be interpreted strongly. Intuitively, that seems at least one right way of interpreting it.[69] Indeed, given the well-known scope ambiguities of 'not', we might expect (26) to be open to both a strong and a weak interpretation. In sum, interpreting positive ascriptions strongly does not prevent us making all the distinctions among negative ascriptions that we might need and expect.

In conclusion, I think the evidence, aside from a few uncertain intuitions, favors the strong over the weak interpretation of positive transparent ascriptions. However, perhaps the form is ambiguous.

8. KRIPKE'S PUZZLE

In the last section, I considered semantic problems arising from the fact that a person's designational thoughts about the one object are likely to be associated with many physical[70] types of the spoken or written language; e.g., some thoughts he would express using 'Tully', some 'Cicero'. The problems were ones of thought ascription. It is also a fact that a person's designational thoughts about many objects are likely to be associated with the one physical type. Does this give rise to semantic problems?[71]

Consider the usual situation with the name 'Bruce'. A person has many sets of thoughts he or she would express using 'Bruce', each set, when all goes well, concerning a different person and constituting a different ability with the name. Though all the sets involve tokens of 'Bruce', those in one set are formally different in the language of thought from those in another. I have borrowed (section 4) a device from the linguists to distinguish the way 'Bruce' is tokened in the various sets: 'Bruce$_1$', 'Bruce$_2$', ... This formal difference comes about because the person does not token various identity beliefs (e.g., that Bruce$_1$ = Bruce$_2$). The difference enables thoughts that are otherwise alike—e.g., several that Ralph would express, "Bruce is a philosopher"—to play different conceptual roles between input and output. This fact gives rise to a problem of ambiguity in speech but, when all goes well, no other semantic problem. It poses no *special* problem for thought ascription:

the opaque, "Ralph believes that Bruce is a philosopher," is true if one of Ralph's belief tokens of 'Bruce is a philosopher' includes a token of 'Bruce' that is part of the same network as the ascriber's token of 'Bruce'.

All may not go well at a grounding or reference borrowing, leading to two different sorts of mistake. First, the one set or ability is grounded in more than one object: a person unites as one ability what should be kept distinct as two; there are two conventional meanings but only one speaker meaning. Consider an example. Joe has a number of politically well-informed friends who frequently discuss the history of socialism. They often use the name 'Liebknecht', sometimes to designate Wilhelm, the father, and sometimes Karl, the son. Joe, who knows little of politics, takes all of these uses of the name to be about one person: he misunderstands by wrongly coming to hold a certain identity belief (that $Liebknecht_1 = Liebknecht_2$). He comes to have thoughts that are grounded in both Wilhelm and Karl.

The second mistake is that more than one set or ability (each associated with the one physical type) is grounded in the one object: a person keeps distinct as two abilities what should be united as one; there is one conventional meaning but two speaker meanings. A person might, for example, first hear of Russell in a logic seminar, and later hear of him at a peace rally, but not unify the resulting beliefs involving tokens of 'Russell': the person wrongly fails to hold a certain identity belief (that $Russell_1 = Russell_2$).

The first sort of mistake is serious: it leads to thoughts and statements that do not have determinate reference. In my view, we need to use Hartry Field's notion of partial reference[72] to describe these thoughts and statements. So Joe does not refer to either Wilhelm or Karl by 'Liebknecht', but partially refers to both.

The second sort of mistake, which underlies Kripke's puzzle, is much less serious. In my view, there is nothing especially puzzling about the beliefs this mistake gives rise to, nor is there anything in Kripke's paper, "A Puzzle about Belief,"[73] to show there is anything puzzling about them. What Kripke does show is that there is a puzzle about belief *ascriptions*. The paper is misnamed.

Consider briefly the consequences of the first mistake for thought ascriptions. On the basis of Joe's sincere assertion, "Liebknecht is F," someone states,

(28) Joe believes that Liebknecht is F.

The ascriber is unaware of Joe's confusion and is using 'Liebknecht' to refer, say, to Karl. Is (28), construed opaquely, true? I think that it is not: Joe does not have any beliefs about Karl, though he does have some that are partially about him.[74] Our statement of truth conditions for the opaque style can prevent (28) coming out true by requiring that Joe's token of 'Liebknecht' must be part of the same network as the ascriber's *and part of no other*.

Kripke generates his puzzle with the help of the "disquotational principle": "If a normal English speaker, on reflection, sincerely asserts to 'p', then he believes that p."[75] Statement (28), it seems, is not covered by this principle: either we should say Joe is not normal, because of his confusions; or we should say that the difference between his and the ascriber's use of 'Liebknecht' gives rise to an ambiguity, which Kripke explicitly disallows.

The first mistake is serious, but it gives rise to no interesting new problem for thought ascription. The second mistake is less serious, but it does give rise to such a problem: Kripke's puzzle.

Kripke's main example concerns the bilingual Pierre and his beliefs about London. However, the puzzle can arise in the one language, as Kripke himself notes using the examples of Paderewski.[76] This example has the advantage of not introducing any question of translation. I shall use the similar one above concerning Russell.

Suppose that the ubiquitous Ralph is the person confused about Russell. Ralph is enthusiastic about logic and is moved to demur when another member of the seminar complains about Russell: Ralph asserts, "Russell is not a menace." Ralph is also a bit of a conservative and so responds later to a report of the peace rally by asserting, "Russell is a menace." There is no puzzle at the level of thoughts: Ralph tokens two formally distinct beliefs, "Russell$_1$ is not a menace" and "Russell$_2$ is a menace." Given that we can use the same name for different people, and that reference is not determined by what is in the head, we should expect a few such cases. The puzzle comes when we try, after Ralph's assertions, to describe his beliefs. Even the most precise of the ordinary styles of ascription, the opaque, seems inadequate (and its troubles are inherited by the transparent styles).

The following opaque ascription seems justified by what followed the seminar:

(29) Ralph believes that Russell is not a menace.

Similarly, the following seems justified by what followed the peace rally:

(30) Ralph believes that Russell is a menace.

The plausible disquotational principle captures such intuitions. Yet it seems as if Ralph must have contradictory belief if (29) and (30) are both true, even though his failings are not logical. Worse still, the *ascriber* seems caught in a contradiction because the assertion after the seminar seems to justify

(31) Ralph does not believe that Russell is a menace,

which is inconsistent with (30). Kripke's puzzle is about the truth conditions of opaque ascriptions.[77]

Set aside, for a moment, what we ought to say about this puzzle, and consider what my theory commits me to saying. My account of the truth conditions of (positive) opaque ascriptions makes both (29) and (30) true. According to my account, (29) requires that Ralph belief-tokens, "Russell is not a menace," and that his token of "Russell" is part of the same network as ours. This is the case. Similarly for (30). According to my account of negative opaque ascriptions, not previously mentioned here,[78] (31) requires that Ralph not token, in the appropriate way, "Russell is a menace." Given Ralph's performance after the peace rally, this makes (31) false. So my theory assigns truth values that clear the ascriber of contradiction but not Ralph.

An obvious enough modification to my theory reverses these three assignments of truth values. The theory makes (29) and (30) true, because it only requires that Ralph have his belief under *some* ability he has to use 'Russell' to designate Russell.[79] Borrowing the terminology I used for transparent ascriptions (section 7), we can call this a "weak" positive opaque ascription. The obvious modification makes (29) and (30) false, because it requires that Ralph have his beliefs under *all* abilities he has to use 'Russell' to designate Russell. We can call this a "strong" positive opaque ascription. The negation of the weak positive is the strong negative, which is the way my theory construes (31), thus making it false. The negation of the strong positive is the weak negative, which, assuming (31) is still taken as the contradiction of (30), is the way the modification construes (31), thus making it true. So the modification assigns truth values that clear both Ralph and the ascriber of contradiction.

This alone is a reason to favor that assignment and hence the modification. Intuitions are not strong here, but mine generally favor the results given by the modification over those given by the theory. Further, a consideration of our narrow and wide concerns seems to favor the modification.

Consider our narrow concerns. Construed weakly, as the theory requires, the opaque

(32) *a* believes that *b* is *F*

has a weakness as an explainer or predicter of *a*'s behavior: it is consistent with *a*'s having another belief that would dispose him or her toward opposite behavior. For example, construed opaquely, (29) is true but so is (30). On its own, (32) would be a good guide to behavior only because situations like Ralph's are relatively rare. In the rare ones, it would be very misleading. In contrast, if (32) is construed strongly, as the modification requires, it rules out the opposite disposing belief and so is a better explainer and predicter. The modification leaves us then with no standard way of describing the beliefs of someone in Ralph's rare situation. However, it is better not to describe a situation than to describe it misleadingly. What we need are *finer* descriptions of Ralph's mental life than the ordinary styles of thought ascription make possible. Given that Ralph's situation is rare, it is not surprising that the ordinary styles are not so fine.

Our wide concerns are with *a*'s beliefs as a guide to whether *b* is *F*. To serve these concerns, we must assess how reliable *a* is likely to be about *b* under the mode of presentation '*b*'. Suppose *a* is reliable. Construed weakly, (32) has a weakness as evidence that *b* is *F*: it is consistent with *a*'s having another belief that would be equally good evidence that *b* is not *F*. For example, (29) would give equally good evidence that Russell is not a menace as (30) would give that he is. Once again, (32) would be a good guide only because Ralph's situation is rare; but where there is a rare situation, it would mislead. Construed strongly, in contrast, (32) is a better guide to reality and is not misleading.

So I think we ought to favor the view that (29) and (30) are false and (31) true, and hence ought to favor the modified theory that makes these truth value assignments. However, the evidence is not very decisive. Perhaps (32) is ambiguous between strong and weak. The ontology of belief enables us to state truth conditions whichever way we jump on this matter of interpretation. Kripke's puzzle is interesting but no cause for consternation.

Kripke would object to the assignment I favor. First, it goes against the disquotational principle. I see Kripke's puzzle as showing that this plausible principle is false. However, a related epistemic principle is true: if a normal English speaker, on reflection, sincerely assents to 'p', then that is *very good evidence* that the speaker believes that p. It is very good evidence because Ralph's situation is rare. If this principle *is* true, it is not surprising that the disquotational principle should *seem* true.

Second, it cannot be denied that there was a time, before Ralph heard of the peace rally, at which it would have been correct to describe him as believing that Russell was not a menace. So, Kripke would claim, we must say that Ralph has *"changed his mind, has given up his previous belief."*[80] I don't think we must say that. We can say that, although he still has the belief that would have made that description true, he now has another that makes it not true. An object can change by addition as well as by subtraction.

My solution to the puzzle has the consequence that there is no standard way of describing Ralph's state of tokening both "Russell$_1$ is a menace" and "Russell$_2$ is not a menace." Another of his states is similarly elusive: "Russell$_1 \neq$ Russell$_2$." It is in virtue of this negative identity belief that Ralph has two abilities to designate Russell by 'Russell' instead of one. To ascribe this belief, we have to resort to a contrived form; e.g.,

Ralph believes that *this* Russell $\neq$ *that* Russell,
Ralph believes that Russell qua logician $\neq$ Russell qua peace marcher.

The contrivance is necessary to show that Ralph's problem is not irrationality, but having two uses of the name. (Contrivance is easier in the case of the bilingual Pierre: he believes that London $\neq$ Londres.)[81]

One problem with (29) and (30) both being true was that it seemed incorrectly to make Ralph irrational. We should avoid the opposite error of making Ralph necessarily rational: we should not give truth conditions to (29) and (30) that make it *impossible* for them both to be true. We have not done so. Irrationality is present where Ralph's belief tokens, "Russell is a menace" and "Russell is not a menace," are in the one set or ability, united by identity beliefs. If that is his only ability to designate Russell by 'Russell', then both (29) and (30) come out true when construed strongly.

Kripke draws a moral from his puzzle: that an argument against substitutivity, which he thinks is widely accepted, is dubious.[82] The argument uses the disquotational principle to infer belief ascriptions from Jones' sincere assent to 'Cicero was bald' and 'Tully was not bald'. If substitutivity applied to these ascriptions, we could infer that Jones had inconsistent beliefs. And by strengthening the disquotational principle into a biconditional, we could infer an inconsistency in ourselves. So, the argument runs, substitutivity does not apply. Kripke's doubt arises because his puzzle derives the same inconsistencies in Ralph and ourselves from the disquotational principle alone, without invoking any principle of substitutivity: see (29), (30), and (31). Kripke concludes that

> it is wrong to blame unpalatable conclusions about Jones on substitutivity . . . it would be foolish to draw any conclusion, positive or negative, about substitutivity.[83]

The argument against substitutivity can be revived in a modified form. We replace the disquotational principle with my epistemic one, yielding the conclusion to the argument: we have very good evidence that substitutivity does not apply. This argument is not undermined by Kripke's puzzle, because our explanation of the puzzle is consistent with the epistemic principle.

We have other evidence against substitutivity from our intuitions about the truth values of ascriptions. Most important of all, we have a theory of beliefs, and our concerns in ascribing them, that count against substitutivity, as we have seen throughout this paper. So I draw a negative conclusion on substitutivity.[84]

Kripke claims that Jones' situation with 'Cicero' and 'Tully' is essentially the same as that of someone in his puzzle situation; e.g., that of Ralph with 'Russell'. I agree: Jones and Ralph both have two distinct abilities to designate the one object; there are codesignational speaker references. However *our* positions in describing the two situations are different, for Jones' two abilities are parts of distinct causal networks, but Ralph's two are parts of the one network; Jones' speaker references involve two conventions, Ralph's one. As a result we can readily describe Jones's situation but not Ralph's.

The examples in Kripke's paper are all of opaque *designational* ascriptions. So are those in my discussion of it. I see no reason why the same puzzle would not arise from opaque *attributive* ascriptions. If it does, I expect the same solution would be called for.

9. CONCLUSION

This paper is concerned with thoughts, a topic in the philosophy of mind, and the ascriptions of thought, a topic in the philosophy of language. Most of the "problems" I have tackled have been in the latter topic, but I have always approached them from a perspective on the former. I think we should always give metaphysics priority over semantics.

One way I have used my view of thoughts to help with each problem of their ascription is to ask: Which of the kinds of thought that I have already concluded people have would we be interested in ascribing to them to serve our wide and narrow psychological concerns? For, where we have a major interest in a kind of thought, it is likely that some standard form will enable us to ascribe it.

A consequence of putting metaphysics first is that the semantic problems become more tractable. Many possible interpretations of ascriptions could be based on the theory of thoughts. We are not surprised to find that some of the interpretations fit actual ascriptions and some not, nor that sometimes it is hard to choose between interpretations for an actual ascription. Nothing very significant hinges on our decisions.

My main conclusions were as follows. Two distinctions play crucial roles in the theory of ascriptions: transparent/opaque and designational/attributive (section 3). I argue further for a distinction between the standard narrow-scope transparent ascription, which requires Ralph to have his thought of an object he has particularly in mind, and a wide-scope transparent ascription, which requires only that he have his thought of the object (section 6). A consideration of the ascription of identity thoughts suggests that the (narrow-scope) transparent ascription should be construed strongly and not, as Quine thought, weakly: it requires that Ralph has his thought of the object under all the designational terms he has for it, and not merely under some such term (section 7). A consideration of Kripke's puzzle suggests a similar view of an opaque designational ascription: it should be construed strongly, requiring Ralph to have his thought under all his abilities to use the term for the object. Perhaps a similar view applies also to opaque attributive ascriptions (section 8). Self-demonstrative thoughts play an important role in explaining behavior. Castañeda is right in thinking that we have a special form for ascribing those thoughts (section 5).

My discussion breaks with two customs. First, the custom of positing "propositions" and their like. I follow Quine in thinking such entities creatures of darkness. Worse, they are irrelevant to our topics (section 1). Second, the custom of applying the terms '*de dicto*' and '*de re*' to thoughts and their ascriptions. This application is unnecessary, poorly explained, and confused (sections 2 and 3). Further, I believe (though I have not argued) that these two customs generate pseudo problems.

APPENDIX

To Section 3

A person may have a thought without having entertained it: he is *disposed* to token it; it is *tacit*. Because of this, I take the person having the thought to be related not to a sentence token but to an ordered set of term tokens. Take the opaque (1) as an example. For it to be true, Ralph must be in a believing relation to (roughly) 'Ortcutt' and 'spy'. He might be in this relation in virtue of either already belief-tokening 'Ortcutt is a spy' or belief-tokening other sentences involving 'Ortcutt' and 'spy' that dispose him to belief-token that sentence.

'*Des*' abbreviates 'designates' (which refers to the relation between a designational term and its referent); '*Den*' abbreviates 'denotes' (which refers to the relation between an attributive term and its referent); '*App*' abbreviates 'applies' (which refers to the relation between a predicate, including a thought predicate like 'believes', and its referents). Let 'cotypical', abbreviated '*Cotyp*', refer to the relation between a token and any token "of the same type"; e.g., to the relation between a designational token and any other such token in its causal network; or to the relation between a predicate token and any synonymous token. The truth conditions of thought ascriptions are to be given in terms of these referential notions.[85]

Let 'a' be a variable taking designational terms as its values. Let 'k' be a variable taking attributive terms as its values. Let 'F' be a variable taking predicates as its values. For convenience, I shall always take belief as the example of thought, and Ralph as the alleged believer. A subscript 'o' indicates an opaque construal.

The truth conditions of an opaque designational ascription like (1) are stated as follows:

$\ulcorner$ Ralph believes$_o$ that a is $F \urcorner$ is true if and only if
$(\exists x)(\exists y)(\exists z)($'Ralph' $Des\ x$. $a\ Cotyp\ y$. $F\ Cotyp\ z$.
'believes' $App\ x <y, z>$).[86]

(We ignore the fact that F might have extensional position.) The ascription requires that Ralph be in a believing relation to a set including a designational token in the same causal network as the ascriber's a. The ascription could be true if a were empty; even empty terms have networks.

To state the truth conditions of an opaque attributive ascription like (5), we would replace 'a' by 'k'. The crucial difference from the above would be in what is cotypical with k: a synonymous attributive term rather than a designational term in the same network.

The truth conditions of a transparent designational ascription like (2) are stated as follows:

$\ulcorner a$ is such that Ralph believes it to be $F \urcorner$ is true if and only if
$(\exists x)(\exists y)(\exists z)(\exists w)($'Ralph' $Des\ x$. $a\ Des\ y$. $z\ Des\ y$. F
$Cotyp\ w$. 'believes' $App\ x <z, w>$).

So the ascription requires that Ralph be in a believing relation to a set including a token that is codesignational with a. If a is empty, the ascription is not true. The inference from the opaque designational, together with $\ulcorner a$ exists $\urcorner$, to the transparent designational is valid: it is exportation.

To state the truth conditions of a transparent attributive ascription like (6), we would replace '$a\ Des\ y$' by '$k\ Den\ y$' on the right-hand side. To state those of an ascription like (4), which quantifies in, we delete '$a\ Des\ y$'.

To Section 5

'$Self$-dem' abbreviates 'self-demonstrative' (which refers to tokens like 'I'). Let us follow Castañeda in using 'he*' for the reflexive pronoun in ascriptions of self-demonstrative belief. The truth conditions of such an ascription are stated as follows:

$\ulcorner$ Ralph believes that he* is $F \urcorner$ is true if and only if
$(\exists x)(\exists y)(\exists z)($'Ralph' $Des\ x$. $Self$-$dem\ y$. $F\ Cotyp\ z$.
'believes' $App\ x <y, z>$).[87]

To Section 6

A subscript 't' indicates a transparent reading of a wide-scope ascription, exemplified by (10). This ascription differs from the narrow-scope transparent one above, exemplified by (2), in not requiring Ralph to have his belief under a designational term; it can be under an attributive term. The truth conditions of this wide-scope transparent designational ascription are stated as follows:

⌜ Ralph believes$_t$ that a is F ⌝ is true if and only if
($\exists x$)($\exists y$)($\exists z$)($\exists w$)('Ralph' $Des\ x$. $a\ Des\ y$. ($z\ Des\ y$ v
$z\ Den\ y$) . $F\ Cotyp\ w$. 'believes' $App\ x <z,w>$).

To state the truth conditions of the corresponding attributive ascription like (8), we would replace '$a\ Des\ y$' by '$k\ Den\ y$' on the right-hand side.

To Section 7

The section 3 statement of truth conditions for transparent designational ascriptions like (2) construes it "weakly." Construed "strongly," its truth conditions are:

⌜ a is such that Ralph believes$_s$ it to be F ⌝ is true if and only if
($\exists x$)($\exists y$)($\exists z$)($\exists w$)('Ralph' $Des\ x$. $a\ Des\ y$. $z\ Des\ y$.
$F\ Cotyp\ w$. 'believes' $App\ x <z,w>$. (v)($v\ Des\ y$.
x has $v \supset$ ($\exists u$)($F\ Cotyp\ u$. 'believes' $App\ x <v,u>$))).[88]

The subscript 's' indicates the strong construal. This differs from the statement for the weak construal in the addition of the last clause, which requires Ralph to have his belief under *all* the designational terms he has for what a designates. Because of this additional clause, exportation to the strong transparent ascription is not valid.

To Section 8

The section 3 statement of truth conditions for an opaque designational ascription like (1) construes it "weakly." Construed "strongly," its truth conditions are:

⌜ Ralph believes$_{os}$ that a is F ⌝ is true if and only if
($\exists x$)($\exists y$)($\exists z$)('Ralph' $Des\ x$. $a\ Cotype\ y$. $F\ Cotyp\ z$.
'believes' $App\ x <y,z>$. (v)($a\ Cotyp\ v$. x has v . $v\ Diff\ y$
$\supset$ ($\exists u$)($F\ Cotyp\ u$. 'believes' $App\ x <v,u>$))).

This differs from the statement for the weak construal in the addition of the last clause, which requires Ralph to have his belief under *all* the tokens which are: (i) cotypical with a; (ii) had by Ralph; (iii) in abilities different from that of the original belief (this difference is referred to by '$Diff$', and is necessary to make it *possible* for Ralph to have contradictory beliefs making, for example, both [29] and [30] true).

Notes

1. In writing this paper I have benefited from the comments of John Bacon, Denise Gamble, David Kaplan, Kim Sterelny, and, especially, of Bill Lycan.

2. Devitt (1984) contains a justification of this maxim.

3. Devitt (1981a).

4. Devitt (1981a, 75-80). The commitment to this relational view of thought was not as clear as it should have been because of a confused discussion on p. 238. I claim there that "if belief, in its ordinary sense, is a relationship at all, it is one that holds between people and *sentence types.*" This uncharacteristic devotion to ordinary usage is mistaken. My own account of the truth conditions of belief ascriptions *requires* that these ascriptions relate people to *sentence tokens.*

I failed (out of ignorance) to acknowledge that the contemporary origin of this view of thought is Sellars (1956).

5. Devitt (1981a, chaps. 9-10).

6. Perry (1979); Lewis (1979); Boër and Lycan (1980).

7. Kripke (1979b).

8. A psychology that is narrow is "autonomous" (Stich 1978) and accords with "methodological solipsism" (Fodor 1980). On the distinction between wide and narrow psychology, see also Putnam (1975, 220-22) and Field (1978, 44, 46-47).

9. See Devitt (1984, chap. 6).

10. See Lycan (1981) for a detailed defense of a theory of belief of the type outlined here.

11. Kraut (1979) offers an account of the intentionality of a psychological state. He characterizes a state in narrow functional terms only. If I am right, a state with only those properties has no intentionality.

12. There can be no "ambiguity" within a person's language of thought (cf. Devitt 1981a, 78-79).

13. Kripke (1972) and Donnellan (1972).

14. Donnellan (1966, 1968). Donnellan is equivocal on the significance of his distinction. I take it to be a semantic distinction: a distinction between two conventions for using descriptions. Kripke (1979a) argues that the distinction does not have semantic significance. I reject this argument in Devitt (1981b).

15. This summary of the theory of reference oversimplifies. For more details, and qualifications, see Devitt (1981a, chaps. 2, 5, and 6). For the place of a theory of reference in a theory of truth, see also pp. 68-74 and 118-26, which are based on Field (1972).

16. Devitt (1981a, 78, 237-38). The response is due to Field (1978).

17. Lycan (in preparation) has raised some difficulties for this response. Some of these do not strike me as serious. I am optimistic about removing the others.

18. See, e.g., Boër and Lycan (1980, particularly 427-31); Perry (1979, 9-11); and Sosa (1970, 883-85).

19. Some of the very many places where this view is aired (though not necessarily endorsed): Sosa (1970, 883-84); Chisholm (1976, 1-3); Burge (1977, 340); Lewis (1979, 521); Schiffer (1979, 62); Perry (1979, 9-11); and Ackerman (1980b, 501).

20. For this view of propositions and/or the earlier one, see, e.g.: Chisholm (1976, 6-7); Pastin (1974); Schiffer (1979, 62-63); Perry (1979, 8); Ackerman (1980a, 471-72); and Fitch (1981, 26).

21. David Lewis has argued (1979) that beliefs *de se*, which I consider in sec. 5, cannot be beliefs in propositions taken as sets of possible worlds. So to that (small) extent, *the possible world theorist* has an answer to this question.

22. It is obviously inappropriate (and unnecessary) to use '*de re*' simply to distinguish thoughts involving nonempty singular terms from those involving empty ones.

23. See, e.g., Chisholm (1976, 9-10); Donnellan (1979, 54); Perry (1979, 11); Lewis (1979, 537-42); and Pollock (1980, 480-92). The unmodified view seems to be what Chisholm calls the "latitudinarian" view of *de re* thought: see e.g., Sosa (1970, 883-84); and Pastin (1974). See also Schiffer (1979, 62-65); and Ackerman (1980b, 501).

24. Quine (1966, 185).

25. Kaplan (1969, 220).

26. Schiffer (1979, 62); Heidelberger (1980, 525). Burge (1977) seems to have an extreme version of this view, calling a belief *"de dicto"* only if it is not dependent on context to determine its reference. But all beliefs have their reference determined by context, for reference is a matter for wide psychology that takes in the context, particularly the causal one, in which the mind sits. Even 'the tallest bachelor' is dependent on context for reference.

27. Quine (1960, 142). On this paragraph, and the next, see Quine (1953, 139-59; 1960, 141-51, 166-69; 1966, 183-94).

28. Sleigh (1967, 28); Kaplan (1969, 220).

29. Devitt (1981a, 224-33).

30. These are four forms of ascribing predicational beliefs using a definite singular term to refer to the object the belief is alleged to be about. There are, of course, other forms of ascription: (3) and (4) exemplify two other ones. See section 5 also.

31. Devitt (1981a, 235-50). See the Appendix for a more precise statement of truth conditions.

32. See many of the items cited in note 19 for examples.

33. See, e.g., Chisholm (1976, 4); Sosa (1970, 884-85); Perry (1979, 9-12); Pastin (1974); and Schiffer (1979, 66).

34. See the examples of the modified view in note 23.

35. For signs of this, see, e.g.: Chisholm (1976, 1-4); Burge (1977, 340); Donnellan (1979, 54); Kripke (1979b, 242); Perry (1979, 9-12); Boër and Lycan (1980, 428); and Fitch (1981, 25).

36. The failure to cope is vivid in Boër and Lycan (1980). Both distinctions are important in their argument, but they blur the difference between them by ignoring the possibility of an opaque designational ascription: they write as if a designational ascription *must* be transparent (see particularly pp. 447-49). They call transparent ascriptions *"de re"* and opaque attributive ones *"de dicto."* It helps to avoid this error to start at the ontological level. Even a designational belief must use some referential device to pick out the object (it's not done by magic). An opaque ascription of such a belief is simply one that specifies *which* device is used. Opaque ascriptions are as appropriate with the designational as with the attributive. In subsequent writings (1981), Lycan accepts a construal of belief ascriptions that is close to the opaque designational.

37. See note 22.

38. I have briefly criticized the use of 'de dicto' and 'de re' before: 1981c, 214-15. After writing this present paper I discovered that Dennett (1982) makes some similar criticisms.

39. Lycan (1981, 146). However, I don't think he is right in suggesting that wide psychology is needed to explain personal success. Narrow psychology can explain success (Devitt 1984).

40. Fodor (1980, 66-67). The next two paragraphs draw on these pages.

41. Perry (1979, 3).

42. Lewis (1979); Boër and Lycan (1980).

43. I have discussed such thoughts, and their ascription, in 1981a, 260-63.

44. Perry (1979, 3).

45. Perry (1979, 16-19).

46. Castañeda (1966, 1967a, 1967b, 1968). Sosa has constructed an example that casts doubt on the view that this form is unambiguously an ascription of a self-demonstrative belief (1970, 893). I discuss this in Devitt (1981a, 262-63).

47. Perry (1979, 4-5).

48. In *Designation* I tentatively, but erroneously, supposed that there could not be an opaque belief ascription with a designational demonstrative (1981a, 245).

49. Boër and Lycan (1980, 432).

50. See also notes 36 and 59. A more detailed response to their discussion can be readily inferred from my statements of the truth conditions of various belief ascriptions throughout this paper.

51. See also Lycan (1981, 148-50).

52. Lewis (1979, 541-42) has a similar idea.

53. Schiffer (1979, 67). I have been worried by this example before: 1981a, 273-74; 1981c, 220. Sosa (1970, 890), has an example like Schiffer's. See also Pastin (1974). In effect I am here defending what we might call, following Chisholm (1976, 9-10), a "latitudinarian" ascription of belief about an object.

54. I have used this term before for a different, but related, interpretation of (12): 1981a, 249-50. I doubt now that there is that interpretation.

55. Frege (1952, 56-57).

56. Russell (1956, 47-48).

57. E.G., Loar (1976, [cf. Devitt 1980]); Schiffer (1979); and Ackerman (1979 [cf. Devitt 1981c]). Ackerman (1980a) makes a similar point against causal theories of natural kind terms (cf. Devitt 1983). See also Baker (in press).

58. Devitt (1981a, 40-41).

59. Boër and Lycan (1980, 436-40) surrender to this temptation. So also, in effect, does Marcus (1981, 505).

60. Devitt (1981a, 152-57) contains a discussion of identity beliefs and statements along these lines.

61. Some might say that '$a \neq b$' is contradictory because it is "not true in any possible world." That sort of *semantic* contradictoriness is different from the *formal* contradictoriness of '$a \neq a$'. It is not *irrational* to entertain a thought that is contradictory only in this semantic sense.

62. This is my resolution of Lycan's "paradox of naming" (in press).

63. Quine (1966, 188-89).

64. Heidelberger (1974).

65. Kaplan (1969, 234-35).

66. Devitt (1976; 1981a, 253-57).

67. Kaplan (1969, 234-35).

68. Devitt (1981a, 257).

69. I tentatively suggested the opposite about (26) and (27) in Devitt (1981a, 255-56), under the influence of a weak interpretation of positive ascriptions. So much for theory-laden institutions!

70. I include the word 'physical' to make it explicit that the types I am talking about are defined by intrinsic physical characteristics: they are not "semantic types": 1981a, 9-10.

71. These paragraphs preceding the discussion of Kripke's puzzle draw in Devitt (1981a, 129-57).

72. Field (1973).

73. Kripke (1979b).

74. This may be too strong: refinements in the notion of partial reference suggest that Joe might have some beliefs it is plausible to say are about Karl (Devitt 1981a, 147-48).

75. Kripke (1979b, 248-49).

76. Kripke (1979b, 256-66).

77. Note that Kripke's puzzle arises where what is conventionally one name, is two names for the alleged believer. It is likely to remain, therefore, even if one has solved the standard problems of opacity arising from there being two conventional names like 'Cicero' and 'Tully' for the one object. It remains for my theory, for example. It also remains for Lycan's. So his claim to have solved Kripke's puzzle with his suggestions about the standard problems is mistaken (1981, 145-48; in press).

78. But see 1981a, 252-53.

79. This is not quite right, but accurate enough for our purposes here: the theory actually requires Ralph's 'Russell'-ability to be part of the same network as ours; compare 1981a, 239.

80. Kripke (1979b, 256).

81. Similar contrivances enable us to describe Ralph's views of Russell as a menace. These do not remove Kripke's puzzle, of course, because, as Kripke points out (1979b, 259), it is a puzzle about *ordinary* ascriptions.

82. Kripke (1979b, 253-54, 267-70).

83. Kripke (1979b, 268-69).

84. To be more precise, I think there is one sort of thought ascription – the most common one – for which substitutivity does not hold. It does hold for narrow-scope (section 3) and wide-scope (section 6) transparent ascriptions.

85. Truth is explained in terms of reference that then, in turn, must be explained: Field (1972).

86. These statements in this part of the Appendix are modified, but equivalent, versions of those in Devitt (1981a, 235-50).

87. This statement is a modified, but equivalent, version of that in Devitt (1981a, 260-63).

88. This statement is a modified, and corrected, version of that in Devitt (1981a, 256).

References

Ackerman, Diana. 1979. "Proper Names, Propositional Attitudes and Non-Descriptive Connotations." *Philosophical Studies* 35:55-69.

Ackerman, Diana. 1980a. "Natural Kinds, Concepts, and Propositional Attitudes." *Midwest Studies in Philosophy* 5:469-85.

Ackerman, Diana. 1980b. "Thinking about an Object: Comments on Pollock." *Midwest Studies in Philosophy* 5:501-7.

Baker, L. R. "Underprivileged Access." *Nous* (In press).

Boër, Steven E., and William G. Lycan. 1980. "Who, Me?" *Philosophical Review* 89:427-66.

Burge, Tyler. 1977. "Belief *De Re*." *Journal of Philosophy* 74:338-62.

Castañeda, Hector-Neri. 1966. "'He': A Study in the Logic of Self-Consciousness." *Ratio* 8: 130-57.

Castañeda, Hector-Neri. 1967a. "On the Logic of Self-Knowledge." *Nous* 1:9-21.

Castañeda, Hector-Neri. 1967b. "Indicators and Quasi-indicators." *American Philosophical Quarterly* 4:85-100.

Castañeda, Hector-Neri. 1968. "On the Logic of Attributions of Self-Knowledge to Others." *Journal of Philosophy* 65:439-56.

Chisholm, Roderick. 1976. "Knowledge and Belief: '*De Dicto*' and '*De Re*'." *Philosophical Studies* 29:1-20.

Dennett, Daniel C. 1982. "Beyond Belief." In *Thought and Object: Essays on Intentionality*, edited by Andrew Woodfield. Oxford.

Devitt, Michael. 1976. "Suspension of Judgment: A Response to Heidelberger on Kaplan." *Journal of Philosophical Logic* 5:17-24.

Devitt, Michael. 1980. "Brian Loar on Singular Terms." *Philosophical Studies* 37:271-80.

Devitt, Michael. 1981a. *Designation*. (New York.)

Devitt, Michael. 1981b. "Donnellan's Distinction." *Midwest Studies in Philosophy* 6:511-24.

Devitt, Michael. 1981c. *Critical Notice of Contemporary Perspectives in the Philosophy of Language*, edited by Peter A. French, Theodore E. Uehling, Jr., and Howard K. Wettstein. *Australasian Journal of Philosophy* 59:211-22.

Devitt, Michael. 1983. "Realism and Semantics." Part II of a critical study of *Midwest Studies in Philosophy* 5. *Nous* 17:669-81.

Devitt, Michael. 1984. *Realism and Truth*. Oxford.

Donnellan, Keith S. 1966. "Reference and Definite Descriptions." *Philosophical Review* 75: 218-304.

Donnellan, Keith S. 1968. "Putting Humpty Dumpty Together Again." *Philosophical Review* 77:203-15.

Donnellan, Keith S. 1972. "Proper Names and Identifying Descriptions." In *Semantics of Natural Language*, edited by Donald Davidson and Gilbert Harman, 356-79. Dordrecht.

Donnellan, Keith S. 1979. "The Contingent *A Priori* and Rigid Designators." In *Contemporary*

Perspectives in the Philosophy of Language, edited by Peter A. French, Theodore E. Uehling, Jr., and Howard K. Wettstein, 45-60. Minneapolis.

Field, Hartry H. 1972. "Tarski's Theory of Truth." *Journal of Philosophy* 69:347-75.

Field, Hartry H. 1973. "Theory Change and the Indeterminacy of Reference." *Journal of Philosophy* 70:462-81.

Field, Hartry H. 1978. "Mental Representation." *Erkenntnis* 13:9-61.

Fitch, G. W. 1981. "Names and the *'De Re-De Dicto'* Distinction." *Philosophical Studies* 39:25-34

Fodor, J. A. 1980. "Methodological Solipsism Considered as a Research Strategy in Cognitive Psychology." *Behavioural and Brain Sciences* 3:63-73.

Frege, Gottlob, 1952. *Translations from the Philosophical Writings of Gottlob Frege*, edited by Peter Geach and Max Black. Oxford.

Heidelberger, Herbert. 1974. "Kaplan on Quine and Suspension of Judgment." *Journal of Philosophical Logic* 3:441-43.

Heidelberger, Herbert. 1980. "Beliefs and Propositions: Comments on Clark." *Midwest Studies in Philosophy* 5:525-31.

Kaplan, David. 1969. "Quantifying In." In *Words and Objections: Essays on the Work of W. V. Quine*, edited by Donald Davidson and Jaakko Hintikka, 206-42. Dordrecht.

Kraut, Robert. 1979. "Attitudes and Their Objects." *Journal of Philosophical Logic* 8:197-217.

Kripke, Saul. 1972. "Naming and Necessity." In *Semantics of Natural Language*, edited by Donald Davidson and Gilbert Harman, 253-355, 763-69. Dordrecht.

Kripke, Saul. 1979a. "Speaker's Reference and Semantic Reference." In *Contemporary Perspectives in the Philosophy of Language*, edited by Peter A. French, Theodore E. Uehling, Jr., and Howard K. Wettstein, 6-27. Minneapolis.

Kripke, Saul. 1979b. "A Puzzle about Belief." In *Meaning and Use*, edited by A. Margalit, 239-83. Dordrecht.

Lewis, David. 1979. "Attitudes *De Dicto* and *De Se*." *Philosophical Review* 87:513-43.

Loar, Brian. 1976. "The Semantics of Singular Terms." *Philosophical Studies* 30:353-77.

Lycan, William G. 1981. "Toward a Homuncular Theory of Believing." *Cognition and Brain Theory* 4:139-59.

Lycan, William G. "The Paradox of Naming." In *Analytical Philosophy in Comparative Perspectives*, edited by J. L. Shaw. Dordrecht, in press.

Lycan, William G. "Tacit Beliefs." In preparation.

Marcus, Ruth Barcan. 1981. "A Proposed Solution to a Puzzle about Belief." *Midwest Studies in Philosophy* 6:501-10.

Pastin, Mark. 1974. "About *De Re* Belief." *Philosophy and Phenomenological Research* 24:569-75.

Perry, John. 1979. "The Problem of the Essential Indexical." *Nous* 13:3-21.

Pollock, John L. 1980. "Thinking about an Object." *Midwest Studies in Philosophy* 5:487-99.

Putnam, Hilary. 1975. *Mind, Language and Reality: Philosophical Papers*. Vol. 2 Cambridge.

Quine, W. V. 1953. *From a Logical Point of View*. Cambridge, Mass.

Quine, W. V. 1960. *Word and Object*. Cambridge, Mass.

Quine, W. V. 1966. *The Ways of Paradox and Other Essays*. New York.

Russell, Bertrand. 1956. *Logic and Knowledge*, edited by R. C. Marsh. London.

Schiffer, Stephen. 1979. "Naming and Knowing." In *Contemporary Perspectives in the Philosophy of Language*, edited by Peter A. French, Theodore E. Uehling, Jr., and Howard K. Wettstein, 61-74. Minneapolis.

Sellars, Wilfred. 1956. "Empiricism and the Philosophy of Mind." In *The Foundations of Science and the Concepts of Psychology and Psychoanalysis: Minnesota Studies in the Philosophy of Science, vol. 1*, edited by Herbert Feigl and Michael Scriven, 253-329. Minneapolis.

Sleigh, R. C. 1967. "On Quantifying into Epistemic Contexts." *Nous* 1:23-31.

Sosa, Ernest. 1970. "Propositional Attitudes de Dictu and de Re." *Journal of Philosophy* 67:883-96.

Stich, Stephen P. 1978. "Autonomous Psychology and the Belief-Desire Thesis." *Monist* 61:573-91.

Establishing Causal Connections:
Meta-Analysis and Psychotherapy

EDWARD ERWIN

M eta-analysis is a new quantitative technique for integrating diverse empirical data. It has been used most notably to establish causal connections between psychotherapy and beneficial therapeutic outcomes (Smith, Glass, and Miller 1980), but it has also been applied to a variety of other causal problems, including the effects of drug therapies on psychological disorders; the effects of school class size on attainment; sex differences in conformity; experimenter effects; the effects of self-serving bias; and the relationship between social class and achievement. The technique is also likely to be widely used in the future in a variety of areas of the social sciences; one commentator has already referred to the "meta-analytic revolution" in outcome research (Fiske 1983).

In this paper I intend to concentrate on the conceptual and epistemological issues raised by the use of meta-analysis in assessing the effects of psychotherapy. However, I also want to highlight a causal problem that motivates the use of meta-analysis, one that, I believe, has received too little attention from epistemologists and philosophers of science: the integration problem.

CRUCIAL EXPERIMENTS AND THE
INTEGRATION PROBLEM

Assuming that crucial experiments are possible in principle, which not everyone concedes, it might be feasible to devise such an experiment to test a *singular* causal judgment about psychotherapy, such as: "The use of therapy A by therapist B helped cause the production of therapeutic effect C with client D in situation E." Scriven (1959) came fairly close, I think, to describing such a test for psychoanalysis, although the experiment has never been carried out. If we move along the continuum from singular to more general to extremely abstract causal claims about psychotherapy, it becomes less and less likely that a crucial experiment will be feasible. It is practically impossible, for example, to do one experiment to decide whether or not psychotherapy is generally effective. One reason is that there are too many kinds of psychotherapy (by some counts over 100) and clinical problems, and too many factors that require control. Even if one established that a certain type of psychotherapy produced such and such effects in a very large number of clients, there would still be little warrant for inferring that all other types of psychotherapy would be effective for the same problems, and even less warrant for generalizing to very different types of clinical problems. A second factor that makes a crucial experiment very unlikely, if not impossible, is that too much has already been done. Too many experiments have already been carried out with diverse types of therapies, therapists, clients, and problems. Some of these experiments have had positive results, but some have not. Even if one could succeed in performing what once would have counted as a crucial experiment, the results would now have to be weighed against the existing evidence.

A reviewer of the psychotherapy outcome evidence, then, cannot turn to any one experiment to assess very abstract claims about psychotherapy. Instead, he or she must make sense of a large collection of data, some of which are conflicting, about many different therapies and clinical problems. Adding to the difficulties is the variability in the quality of the studies that produced the data. Some are relatively well designed; others are of moderate quality; and others are almost impossible to interpret. Here, then, we have the "integration problem." If we want to judge the effects of psychotherapy in general, we must have some way of putting together and assessing all of the relevant data, some of which are conflicting. How precisely are we to do this? Are there reliable rules to be followed? Do we rely on the unargued judgment of experts? Is there some other way? Consider one facet of the problem. How do we weigh the evidence from poor studies against that from superior studies? There are at least two standard solutions to this problem. The first is the "box score" solution used by Luborsky, Singer, and Luborsky (1975). The reviewers resolved to consider all studies that compared two or more therapies, but included only studies that were at least passably controlled. Poor studies and superior studies were given equal weight. Scores were then tabulated for each comparison (e.g., behavior therapy vs. psychotherapy; group vs. individual therapy) by counting the number of studies in which treatments did significantly better or worse than their competitors, or were tied with them. Luborsky et al. also included a grading of the studies, using twelve methodological criteria to decide whether a study deserved an "A," "B," "C," or "D." They then compared the results of the superior and poorly designed studies, found no difference in their *trend*, and used this finding to justify giving equal weight to all of the studies.

Several reviewers have objected to the use of the box score method. For example, Smith et al. (1980) point out that use of the method ignores considerations of sample size. Large samples tend to produce more statistically significant findings than small samples. For example, one may find nine small studies that concern a particular clinical hypothesis, none of which quite reaches statistical significance. If one large sample study is significant, then the box score is one for the hypothesis and nine against.

A second approach to the integration problem has been termed the "narrative" solution (Smith et al. 1980, 36). A reviewer will attempt to portray multiple findings in a verbal, nonquantitative report written like a story. To make the story intelligible, the reviewer is forced to cut the body of evidence down to size by ignoring certain studies and by "impeaching" others because of bad design or use of poor outcome measures. Smith et al. (1980) object to the narrative approach for reasons that will be examined later (see Part II).

A third and newer solution to the integration problem, one favored by Smith et al. (1980), is to use meta-analysis. The key feature of this approach is the transformation of different measures of therapeutic effects into a single measure, the *effect size* (ES). ES is calculated for each study by subtracting the average score on the outcome variable for the control group from the average score for the treatment group and dividing the result by the standard deviation for the control group. Thus:

$$ES = \frac{M \text{ (therapy)} - M \text{ (control)}}{S \text{ (control)}}$$

M (therapy) = the average outcome score for the psychotherapy group
M (control) = the average outcome score for the control group
S (control) = the standard deviation for the control group.

Smith et al. (1980) calculated approximately 1,760 effect sizes for 475 controlled studies of psychotherapy and found that the average effect size was .85 (with a standard error of .03). This result is explained as follows: subject to certain qualifications, the average person receiving psychotherapy is better off at the end of it than 80% of those persons who do not undergo psychotherapy (Glass and Kliegl 1983, 29).

By transforming outcome findings into a single metric, Smith et al. were able to perform a wide variety of statistical analyses on the data they evaluated. They then reached four general conclusions (183-89).

1. Psychotherapy is beneficial, consistently so and in many different ways; its benefits are on a par with other expensive and ambitious interventions, such as schooling and medicine.

2. Different types of psychotherapy (verbal or behavioral; psychodynamic, client centered, or systematic desensitization) do not produce different types or degrees of benefit.

3. Differences in how psychotherapy is conducted (whether in groups or individually, by experienced or novice therapists, for long or short periods of time) make very little difference in how beneficial it is.

4. Psychotherapy is scarcely any less effective than drug therapy in the treatment of serious psychological disorders. When the two therapies are combined, the net benefits are less than the sum of their separate benefits.

In addition to the above claims about the effects of psychotherapy, Smith et al. claim that: (1) their use of meta-analysis is sufficient for resolving the integration problem and demonstrating a causal connection between psychotherapy and beneficial therapeutic effects; and (2) other methods of research integration are inadequate. Other writers have endorsed one or both of these claims (Glass and Kliegl 1983; Vanden Bos and Pino 1980; Fiske 1983). Fiske (69) adds that meta-analytic studies are clearly superior to the conventional qualitative reviews of research domains, simply because they are more scientific and because they more closely approximate the ideal in scientific work.

In what follows, I argue that claims (1) and (2) of Smith et al. are both unwarranted.

I. THE ADEQUACY OF THE USE OF META-ANALYSIS BY SMITH ET AL.

Some critics (Eysenck 1978; Rachman and Wilson 1980) have objected that Smith and her colleagues included in their analysis too many studies of poor quality. However, this criticism has been anticipated and answered. Smith et al. (1980) and Glass and Kliegl (1983) make several points in defense of their treatment of weak studies.

First, they contend that many weak studies can support a strong conclusion (Smith et al., 49). On this point, we agree. Suppose that 10 studies of psychotherapy all have positive outcomes, but each has a serious design flaw. If the design flaws are different, the studies might still provide strong support, other evidence aside, that the kind of therapy used was effective. Suppose, for example, that the hypothesis that the therapy was effective, H_1, has only two credible rivals, H_2 and H_3, and that some of the studies rule out H_2 and some H_3. If we combine the data from all 10 studies, then it might be that only H_1 plausibly explains all of the data. This shows, however, only that a number of bad studies *might* yield one good argument for a hypothesis; this does nothing to show that the bad studies in the particular sample by Smith et al. lend support to any of their conclusions. We cannot assume without additional argument that the design flaws in their set are sufficiently different so that collectively the poor studies rule out all but one hypothesis; this assumption is especially risky given the persistent failure of psychotherapy studies to rule out a placebo hypothesis (Prioleau, Murdock, and Brody 1983). To be fair to Smith et al., their point may have been intended to answer only one objection: that the inclusion of poor studies *necessarily* precludes any reasonable causal inferences. On this point, at least, we agree.

A second defense is that meta-analysis was designed to satisfy three basic requirements, one of which is this: studies should not be excluded from consideration on arbitrary and a priori grounds; boundaries must be drawn around fields, but it is better to draw them wide rather than narrow (Smith et al., 39). Why draw the boundaries wide? One reason is to avoid bias. In disputes about psychotherapy, Smith et al. claim (48) that the judgment of quality of design and evidence has usually been made ad hoc in order to impeach the methodology of the studies of one's enemies. A second reason is that, apart from questions of bias, one should not discard useful information from a study merely because it has design flaws.

Several comments are in order. First, it can be agreed that data from weak studies should not be ignored entirely, but this is not justification for any particular treatment of them. One could count such results as being on a par with evidence from a superior study, or count them as weak evidence, or as no evidence at all. Second, Smith et al. did exclude not only some well-controlled studies, as pointed out by Wilson and Rachman (1983), but also a vast number of weak studies, namely those case studies that lack all experimental control. They would presumably reply that this latter exclusion does not violate their first requirement because it is not arbitrary; there are sound reasons for saying that *uncontrolled* case studies generally fail to provide any firm evidence of causal connections. However, the same point can be made about *controlled* studies with serious design flaws. Why, then, is it arbitrary to exclude poorly controlled studies but not arbitrary to exclude uncontrolled case studies? The answer is: it is not. There is no warrant for drawing a general epistemological distinction between uncontrolled and poorly controlled studies in terms of their capacity to provide firm evidence of causal connections. Both sorts of studies generally fail to rule out plausible rivals to the hypothesis that the therapy caused any beneficial therapeutic results. There is a dilemma, then, for Smith et al. If judgments of methodological quality should not be made because they are inevitably arbitrary, then a reviewer should cast the net very wide and include all outcome studies of psychotherapy whether controlled or uncontrolled (in fact, why not consider unpublishable studies and anecdotal oral reports as well?); but if judgments of quality should be made, then some justification is needed for treating evidence from bad studies on a par with evidence from superior studies. Finally, suppose that judgments of methodological quality were generally reliable but only up to the point at which Smith et al. draw their line of demarcation; i.e., reviewers could reliably decide which studies are controlled and which are not, but inevitably bias would set in when a reviewer made more refined judgments. Even if this were true, and Smith et al. provide no evidence that it is, it would stil provide no justification for weighting all controlled studies equally; one possibility that would have to be ruled out is a skeptical conclusion. It might be that research integration of the sort Smith et al. are attempting is inevitably unreliable.

Third, it is not clear that Smith et al. wish to rely on any of the aforementioned defenses of their treatment of low-quality studies. Their main, and possibly only, defense is empirical. Consider the following example used by Smith et al. (1980). Some reviewers tend to dismiss findings of studies where the subjects are volunteers, but one can question this practice. Suppose one does a meta-analysis and finds that the covariance is quite small between the size of experimental effect and whether or not the subjects were volunteers; this would undermine the methodological objection to a certain study that it used volunteers. More generally, whatever methodological criteria are used in judging that a study is poor, one can decide empirically whether poor studies tend to yield different results from good ones. Smith et al.

examined this question and found a negative answer. They then concluded that good and bad studies may be weighted and considered together.

There are two premises to this argument: (1) If the best designed studies do not yield evidence different from more poorly designed studies, then the studies may be weighted equally and considered together; and (2) the best-designed studies do *not* yield evidence different from the more poorly designed studies (64). Both premises need to be examined. I will begin with the second premise.

Premise (2)

Smith et al. argue for premise (2) by dividing all studies in their sample into three groups ("low," "medium," and "high" quality) and then demonstrating that the difference in effect size between the three groups are negligible. The soundness of their argument for premise (2) depends on the soundness of the criteria used for rating the designs. Smith et al. judged a design to be "high" in internal validity if and only if it used random assignment and had low, controlled mortality rates. These criteria are demonstrably inadequate, and this inadequacy seriously weakens their argument for premise (2). Studies that meet their criteria may still be faulted on several grounds. First, they may still be weak with respect to internal validity because the control group is inadequate for ruling out alternative hypotheses.

As is well known, the two main rivals to the hypothesis that beneficial therapeutic effects were caused by the use of psychotherapy are the spontaneous remission and placebo hypotheses. Roughly put, the first says that the therapeutic improvement was caused by events that would have occurred in the absence of formal therapy; the second says that the improvement was caused by events occurring in the therapy setting that are not elements of the therapy (such as therapist's attention or the client's expectation of being helped). Some of the studies rated "high" in quality by Smith et al. used a wait list control, but there is controversy about its power to rule out a spontaneous remission hypothesis. Eysenck (1983) argues that a wait list control is not a true no-treatment control because people in the former group are likely to behave differently than those in the latter group. Clients placed on a waiting list are told that they will soon receive professional help; consequently, they are less likely than those not signing up for therapy to seek help from friends, family members, and others who provide a certain amount of support, reduction of anxiety, relaxation, and who contribute, generally, to an extinction of conditioned emotional responses. On these grounds, then, one should predict that clients in wait list controls would show less improvement than those not seeking professional help. One could also argue the reverse: if expectancy of cure is of major therapeutic importance, then those in the wait list group, given that they expect to have their problems soon resolved, may improve more quickly than those who never contact a therapist (Erwin 1983). What the exact effects are of being placed in a wait list control is an empirical question that has not yet been answered. Nevertheless, the doubts raised by Eysenck and others (e.g., Prioleau et al. 1983) need to be resolved before a wait list control can be safely assumed to be adequate for ruling out a spontaneous remission hypothesis.

Such a control is even more clearly inadequate for ruling out a placebo hypothesis. If clients in the treatment group do better than those in the wait list control, the result may be due entirely to such factors as receiving attention from the therapist or having confidence that the therapy they are receiving will help them; the ingredients that make up the therapy may, either singly or in combination, have no beneficial effects at all. The standard procedure for ruling out placebo factors has been the use of a pseudotherapy, but even this strategy encounters problems. As Kazdin and Wilcoxin (1976) point out, in many of the seemingly well-designed studies of systematic desensitization, the placebo treatments were not as credible as the therapy; so, the possibility was not ruled out that the difference in outcomes was caused by the differences in confidence in the treatments. Ruling out a placebo hypothesis is not impossible, but it is difficult; use of a wait list control is generally insufficient to achieve that end.

Even if a study ranks high on criteria of internal validity, it may be faulted on conceptual grounds. On the causal side, one may object that the therapy studied was not a form of psychotherapy, assuming that its results are being cited as evidence for the effectiveness of psychotherapy. Smith et al. adopted a definition of psychotherapy that in one respect is very narrow; it requires that a technique be derived from *established* psychological principles. Such a test would probably disqualify most of the therapies that they classify as "psychotherapy." If we delete this condition, then the resulting definition is a very wide one and applies to almost any *psychological* form of therapy: in particular, it does not distinguish psychotherapy from behavior therapy. This is not a defect in the definition if one uses the term "psychotherapy" as Smith et al. do. However, many of their critics use the term in a narrower sense to cover only what is sometimes called "insight therapy" or "verbal therapy." In the narrower sense, behavior therapy is not a form of psychotherapy. Hence, these critics would be right to object to the inclusion by Smith et al. of studies comparing behavior therapy with either a placebo or wait list control as part of the "high-quality" group; in the narrower sense of "psychotherapy," such studies provide no test at all of the hypothesis that psychotherapy is generally effective. I do not want to make too much of this issue, given that there is still disagreement as to whether there are general important theoretical differences between traditional psychotherapy and behavior therapy. Nevertheless, there is an issue here that tends to be glossed over when a study ranking high on criteria of internal validity is equated with "good study of psychotherapy." Another conceptual issue concerns the effect side of the therapeutic equation. A study that resolves all problems of internal validity may still be faulted if the effect was not therapeutically beneficial or if the test used to measure the effect (or at least to provide evidence of its occurrence) was faulty. Some of the studies cited by Smith et al. are defective because there are inadequate grounds for believing that the outcome measures (in some cases, projective tests) measure any effect that is therapeutically beneficial.

In sum, the criteria used by Smith et al. were far too lax to allow a decision that a study had a good design. Many of the studies they rated highly either had serious conceptual defects or failed to rule out one or more credible rival hypotheses.

If this criticism is correct, then finding a correlation in effect sizes between studies they rated as "high" and "low" would not establish their second premise: that the best-designed studies do not yield evidence different from the more poorly designed studies. The most such a correlation proves is that studies ranking high in internal validity *using the minimal criteria employed by Smith et al.* do not yield evidence different from poor studies.

Premise (1)

Suppose it were true that the best-designed studies did not yield evidence different from more poorly designed studies. Would it then be true that both sorts of studies might be weighted equally and considered together? Not necessarily. It is crucial to inquire about the hypothesis that the evidence is being enlisted to support. If the hypothesis is that the average effect size is such and such, then the poor studies may be grouped with the good studies; if the average effect size is the same for both sorts of studies, it will be the same for the combination of them. The average effect size, then, will not be inflated by adding in the data from the poor studies. However, the converse also holds: subtracting out data from the poor studies will not reduce the average effect size. What, then, is the justification for adding in the data from the poor studies if doing so makes no difference?

Suppose, however, that the hypothesis being considered is that psychotherapy is generally effective (Smith et al.'s first major conclusion). If this means that each of the kinds of psychotherapy being considered is usually effective in treating typical (nonpsychotic) psychological problems, then it may be impermissible to group the good and bad studies together even if their average effect sizes are identical. It may be that the empirical support of effectiveness for certain sorts of psychotherapy comes mainly or entirely from bad studies. The same objection applies if the hypothesis is that different types of psychotherapy do not produce different types or degrees of benefit (Smith et al.'s second major conclusion). It may be that therapies *A* and *B* show the same effect sizes but that the studies of the *B*-type therapy are mainly inferior studies.

Conclusion

Smith et al. (1980) reach four general conclusions about the effects of psychotherapy. These conclusions are important, are inconsistent with those of certain other reviewers, and, being nontrivial, need to be supported by solid argument. Critics have objected that the argument provided by Smith et al. is deeply flawed because of the equal weighting given to good and bad studies. A detailed documentation for this charge is contained in Rachman and Wilson (1980). Smith et al. and Glass and Kliegl (1983) have anticipated and replied to this criticism; they give several arguments to justify their treatment of the evidence. What I have tried to show is that their attempted justification is a failure; consequently, their argument *is* undermined by the "quality of study objection' made by Rachman and Wilson (1980), Eysenck (1983), and others.

There have been other attempts to defend the inclusion of weak studies in their analysis. Fiske (1983, 67) replies that criticisms concerning criteria of inclusion should carry little weight unless the critic has made additional comparable analyses of published studies based on what the critic believes to be more appropriate criteria. This reply seems mistaken. Any reviewer who purports to establish a nontrivial conclusion about the effects of psychotherapy needs to argue for that conclusion. To explain why a reviewer's argument is flawed, it is not necessary to do an alternative meta-analysis of the data. Suppose, for example, that I claim to show, on the basis of a meta-analysis, that psychotherapy is more effective than lithium in treating manic-depressives. My argument could be shown to fail completely if it were demonstrated that none of the studies analyzed was of psychotherapy, or that none of the patients was a manic-depressive; doing an alternative analysis based on more appropriate criteria would not be necessary. Consider one more example. Glass and Kliegl (1983) acknowledge that there exists in the Smith et al. data base not a single experimental study that would qualify by even the "shoddiest" standards as an outcome evaluation of orthodox psychoanalysis. Suppose, however, that I manage to dredge up twenty such shoddy studies that use some sort of control group, however inadequate, perform a meta-analysis, and then argue that the results show that orthodox psychoanalysis is generally effective. To show that my argument proves nothing of the sort, another meta-analysis is not needed; it would be sufficient to show that *all* of the studies are too flawed to support any causal inferences.

Another defense of the conclusions of Smith et al. is contained in Landman and Dawes recent paper (1982). In their original analysis, Smith and Glass (1977) used a disjunctive criterion for including a study: a study had to have at least one therapy treatment group compared with an untreated group *or* with a different therapy group. This left open the possibility that some unspecified proportion of their studies had no untreated control group, but rather compared two therapies neither of which may have been effective. Landman and Dawes (1982) did a re-analysis of the data, randomly selecting 65 of the studies in the Smith and Glass set. Of these studies, 42 were judged to have used adequate random assignment and to have included a no-treatment control. A meta-analysis of the 42 studies produced results similar to those of Smith and Glass (1978) and, by implication, Smith et al. (1980). Landman and Dawes take their result to be a vindication of Smith and Glass's conclusions. In fact, it is not. Landman and Dawes do show that the inclusion of studies lacking a no-treatment control did not inflate the results of Smith and Glass, but they did not meet the quality of design objection. They concluded that their 42 studies were adequately controlled, but, like Smith et al., they used inadequate criteria of adequacy: inclusion of a no-treatment group and adequate randomization. As argued earlier, studies that meet these conditions may still provide no evidence of causal connections because the outcome measures are inadequate, or because a placebo explanation is not ruled out, or for other reasons. Landman and Dawes (1982) did take up the question of placebo explanations and concluded that the effect of psychotherapy was greater than placebo treatment.

However, this conclusion is based on an examination of only five studies, most of which were studies of behavior therapy. In fact, it is not clear that even one study was found in which a psychotherapy treatment of patients with typical clinical problems exceeded that of a placebo.

Prioleau et al. (1983) also report a reanalysis of Smith and Glass's data, but they use more stringent criteria of inclusion than Smith et al. (1980), and they reach very different conclusions. They focus on the subset of Smith and Glass studies that used psychotherapy rather than behavior therapy, and they include only those studies that contain a placebo comparison. Prioleau et al. conclude that for real patients there is *no* evidence that the benefits of psychotherapy are greater than those of placebo treatment.

The publication of the Prioleau et al. (1983) paper and the responses in the same journal by leading psychotherapy researchers and critics has demonstrated one conclusion beyond doubt: contrary to the suggestions of Smith et al. (1980), the use of meta-analysis has not ended disagreements about the effects of psychotherapy. Instead, as Garfield (1983) points out, its use appears to have raised the level of controversy to new heights.

II. ARE TRADITIONAL REVIEW METHODS ADEQUATE?

Meta-analysis was developed because of dissatisfaction with standard methods of integrating research findings (Glass and Kliegl 1983). As noted earlier, Smith et al. (1980) object to the so-called "box score method" mainly because it ignores consideration of sample size. They also draw an analogy between research reviews and primary research designs, and then use this analogy to criticize the traditional nonquantitative type review (sometimes called the "literary" or "qualitative" or "narrative" review). They point out that the reviewer of studies, like the primary investigator, has a hypothesis concerning certain independent variables (characteristics of the studies) and dependent variables (e.g., rate of improvement or magnitude of effect). To provide an adequate test of the hypothesis, the reviewer must either include all studies in the population of interest (e.g., all studies of client-centered therapy) or include a representative sample. He or she must then use some method of aggregating the data from these studies (e.g., all outcomes might be labeled either "improved" or "not improved") and then use the results to confirm or disconfirm the hypothesis being tested. The conclusions of the reviewer, Smith et al. contend, can be subjected to the same standards for evaluating validity that Campbell and Stanley (1966) and others have developed for evaluating primary studies. That is, we can determine whether the review avoids the typical threats to internal validity posed by selection, instrumentation, history, etc. Using Campbell and Stanley standards, Smith et al. criticize the earlier reviews of psychotherapy outcomes by Eysenck (1952) and Rachman (1971). The Eysenck review, they charge, used a "design" with a nonequivalent comparison group. Viewed this way, the review is deficient with respect to selection, history, and instrumentation; therefore, no conclusions are warranted at all (Smith et al., 14). Smith et al. fault the Rachman

(1971) review partly because of sampling bias. They object that he did not include all studies of psychotherapy and also did not explain his selection criteria. A second objection is that Rachman used an unsupportable strategy of ex post facto impeachment of some studies based on design quality and outcome measurement. This strategy presumes an objectivity and distance from the problem that is rare; any such judgmental strategy permits the introduction of bias. Smith et al. (38) even charge that the true purpose of dismissing studies on methodological grounds has been to eliminate most of the literature; what few studies have survived were consistent, probably because they had been conducted by the reviewer himself, his students, or his friends.

Smith et al.'s criticisms are important if correct; their objections would tell against not merely the Eysenck and Rachman reviews but against all traditional reviews of the psychotherapy literature. If no single experiment is likely to establish causal relations between types of psychotherapy and types of therapeutic effects, and if meta-analysis cannot by itself solve the problems inherent in integrating data from multiple studies, and if traditional methods are doomed to fail, then it is likely that the effects of psychotherapy will remain largely unknown. It is also likely that a skepticism about causal connections would be warranted in other areas in the social sciences and perhaps even in areas in the natural sciences.

Are the Smith et al. criticisms of standard review procedures sound? The first thing that should be questioned is the analogy on which their criticisms rest. Is a review of experiments itself an experiment? If it is, then it can always be faulted using Campbell and Stanley criteria. A review is always ex post facto; there is no prior random assignment to a treatment and control group. However, reviews are not intended to be "experiments," as Campbell and Stanely (1966, 1) use the term. In a review, unlike a primary experimental study, there is no manipulation of variables. Despite this crucial difference, there might also be important similarities, but it has to be demonstrated that the similarities provide grounds for using identical criteria for judging both experiments and reviews. Smith et al. provide no such demonstration.

It is probably more illuminating to compare a review not to an experiment but to a complex argument. More precisely, a review will normally contain one or more conclusions and one or more supporting arguments. To use Campbell and Stanley criteria to criticize a review effectively, it has to be shown that the failure to meet some of the criteria destroys the cogency of at least one of the reviewer's arguments. This cannot always be done.

Consider, for example, the reviews by Eysenck (1952, 1966). One of his main arguments concerns psychoanalysis and can be reconstructed as follows:

1. If there is no adequate study of psychoanalytic therapy showing an improvement rate of more than two-thirds, or more than a suitable no-treatment control group, then there is no firm evidence that the therapy is therapeutically effective.
2. There is no adequate study showing either rate of improvement.
3. Therefore, there is no firm evidence that the therapy is therapeutically effective.

The objection by Smith et al., that Eysenck used a "design" with a non-equivalent comparison group, does nothing to show that the above argument is logically invalid or that either premise is false or unwarranted. The objection is simply irrelevant; it would also be irrelevant if the premises and conclusions concerned psychotherapy in general and not merely psychoanalysis. Smith et al. apparently believe otherwise because they take Eysenck's real conclusion to be that psychotherapy is ineffective rather than the weaker conclusion that, at the time of writing, there was no firm evidence of either effectiveness or ineffectiveness. They suggest (14) that Eysenck was being disingenuous in protesting later that he had argued only for the weaker conclusion. (For a detailed defense of his argument, see Erwin (1980).

If Rachman's argument (1971) is roughly the same as Eysenck's, then the first criticism by Smith et al. concerning selection bias does nothing to undermine it. To support his conclusion, it was not necessary for Rachman to discuss all studies of psychotherapy or a representative sample. It was sufficient to argue that none of the studies capable of providing evidence of effectiveness did so. (Rachman, in fact, did not argue for quite this strong a conclusion; he did agree that one study provided tentative evidence for the effectiveness of psychotherapy.) One could reply to Rachman by arguing either that he ignored high-quality studies with positive results or that he was mistaken in his criticisms of other studies. Smith et al. (1980) do neither; they simply say that the ex post facto impeachment of studies is unsupportable. They also add that Rachman used a double standard for evaluating evidence. In criticizing psychotherapy studies, he required an outcome better than the spontaneous remission rate; in examining behavior therapy studies he did not. The reason, presumably, for this difference is that there was no need to use a spontaneous remission rate in evaluating behavior therapy; there were controlled experiments available. Suppose, however, that the true reason is that Rachman was simply biased in favor of behavior therapy. Demonstrating that this was so would still do nothing to undermine any of his premises or his reasoning concerning psychotherapy.

Both the Eysenck and Rachman reviews are out of date. A more recent, somewhat skeptical review of the psychotherapy outcome literature can be found in Rachman and Wilson (1980). Smith et al. (1980) did not have the opportunity to criticize this review, but if they had, a change in strategy would have been required. It is not enough to argue that a review fails to meet criteria appropriate for judging experiments. Again, it would have to be demonstrated that such a failure adversely affects either the reasoning or one of the premises of at least one of Rachman and Wilson's arguments.

I conclude that Smith et al. have not shown that there is any difficulty in principle in employing standard methods to review the psychotherapy outcome literature. They have not even demonstrated the much weaker conclusion: that the arguments of two previous reviews (Eysenck 1952; Rachman 1971) were faulty. Nevertheless, Smith et al. have raised an important question about research integration, one that is not disposed of simply by criticizing their arguments against standard reviews. I turn now to this issue: Does the integration problem render standard review methods inadequate?

One difficulty in assessing solutions to the integration problem is that it is not precisely clear what the problem is. As several writers have described it, the problem appears to be one of interpreting a fairly large body of evidence that is seemingly inconsistent. But, again, what is the problem? Suppose that we examine 50 controlled studies of the use of implosion therapy to treat a certain sort of phobia, and 25 show positive results and 25 negative results. If the studies are equally good, it just might be that there is no known way to explain away the discrepancy. The proper conclusion would then be that *this* body of evidence provides no grounds for believing the therapy to be effective, or ineffective, for this sort of clinical problem. There need not be anything problematic about the argument for this conclusion. It should be noted, however, that translating the results into average effect sizes, as recommended by proponents of meta-analysis, might lead to the wrong conclusion. Suppose that only the studies with positive results included multiple outcome measures, but that the inclusion of extra outcome measures added no increment of evidence of a beneficial therapeutic effect. Because meta-analysis, at least as used by Smith et al., counts the number of outcomes (as opposed to the number of studies), the results would show a positive average effect size—even though there was zero evidence of effectiveness.

Consider a second case. We review 50 controlled studies of psychological therapies: some have positive and some have negative results. Again, there need not be any difficulty in interpreting the results. By distinguishing different types of therapy or clinical problems, or both, we might be able to explain why the data appear inconsistent when, in fact, they are not. Of course, we *might* face serious conceptual problems depending on the kinds of distinctions we draw. Is rational emotive therapy a form of behavior therapy? Do cognitive therapies form a natural kind? How useful are the distinctions commonly drawn between different forms of schizophrenia? As long as clinical psychology and psychiatry lack an adequate taxonomy, such questions will be difficult to answer, but two points should be stressed. First, the solution to such conceptual difficulties is not to replace traditional review methods with meta-analysis; use of the latter method raises the same sorts of conceptual problems. The solution is to find better theories and more and better empirical data. Second, conceptual unclarities need not defeat all attempts to explain away apparent inconsistencies. If 50 studies of systematic desensitization show inconsistent results, but the only negative studies concern agoraphobia, then, given what is known about this disorder, the plausible conclusion is that the data provide evidence of effectiveness for some phobias but not for agoraphobia.

Consider a third case. We review 50 studies of psychotherapy and the data are again apparently inconsistent. This time, however, we try to explain away the inconsistency by throwing out all of the positive results on methodological grounds. This is the sort of case that troubles Smith et al. and other proponents of meta-analysis. They complain about bias and the lack of objective rules for "impeaching" studies. This concern is not entirely unwarranted, but the epistemological difficulties are not as serious as they suggest. There are objective, empirically defensible rules for criticizing psychotherapy outcome studies. (If there were not, then the rationale of meta-analysis for treating good and bad studies alike would collapse from the outset. There would be no way of distinguishing good from bad studies, and, therefore, no way of comparing the results of both types, as required by meta-analysis.) These methodological rules are rarely stated explicitly (probably because of their obviousness), but they are clearly defensible, whether or not there is a consensus about them. For example, one rule is this: disqualify a study from providing evidence of psychotherapeutic effects if evidence is lacking for the occurrence of the putative cause. If we are reviewing psychotherapy outcomes, the rule would obviously disqualify studies of psychotropic drugs and, less obviously, studies of behavior therapy *if* behavior therapy can be shown to be not a form of psychotherapy. A second rule is this: disqualify a study lacking evidence of a beneficial therapeutic effect (or whatever sort of effect is being studied). This rule would disqualify any study using an outcome measure lacking empirical support. Smith et al. (1980, 19) apparently do not accept this rule. They suggest, on the contrary, that a study should not be disqualified on those grounds unless there is evidence that the measure is defective. For example, a study using a projective test to measure anxiety should not be disqualified merely for lack of evidence that the test measures what it purports to measure. If this is the suggestion of Smith et al., it is unacceptable. A reviewer who is trying to argue for the efficacy of psychotherapy cannot reasonably count a study as part of the supporting evidence unless it can be shown that a beneficial therapeutic effect occurred; that cannot be done if there is no warrant for thinking that the test used to measure the effect in fact does so.

A third rule for impeaching studies is this: disqualify a study if its controls are clearly inadequate to rule out competing plausible alternative explanations of the results. If beneficial therapeutic effects occur, but there is no more reason to believe that they were caused by the therapy than by spontaneous remission or other factors that are not part of the therapy, then the study provides no firm evidence of therapeutic efficacy. There is uncertainty, of course, about the the adequacy of certain sorts of controls. For example, as noted earlier, Eysenck has raised doubts, partly on theoretical grounds, about using a wait list control to rule out a spontaneous remission hypothesis. To take another example, various sorts of pseudotherapy controls can be faulted if the pseudotherapy is less credible than the treatment being tested, but it is often difficult to tell whether the treatment and pseudotherapy were equal in credibility. In all such cases, what is needed is not a new method for analyzing and integrating studies, but rather better clinical theories and more empirical evidence concerning the effects of being placed in a wait list group, the causal role of placebo factors, the credibility ratings of various therapies and pseudotherapies, etc.

Even if none of the types of cases discussed so far poses a perplexing integration problem, at least one remaining type apparently does. Sometimes a study contains important defects but nonetheless provides weak evidence of a causal connection. For example, the study may render a placebo explanation less plausible than its rival, but not rule it out altogether; or, it may contain double-blind safeguards, but doubts remain about their adequacy; or the evidence that its outcome measure has construct validity may be weak but not nonexistent. In such cases, how are we to weigh the results of the weak studies against the stronger studies if they conflict? There are several possibilities. One is to grade each study on the basis of the number of defects. Studies with 0-3 defects receive a grade of "A," those with 4-6 defects a grade of "B," and those with more than 6 defects a grade of "C." "A" studies can then be assigned three points, "B" studies, two points, and "C" studies, one point. Another method would be to grade the studies on the basis of the importance rather than the number of the effects. A third possibility is to weight the weak studies equally with the best studies. There are other possibilities as well. What they all have in common, as far as I can see, is their arbitrariness. There is no argument, or at least none that I am aware of, that demonstrates that any one of these methods is correct and that the others are all incorrect. If there is no justification for any particular weighting scheme, and if the argument of a review requires such a justification, then the argument will not support the conclusion. In such a situation, a reviewer may be unable to demonstrate either that there is or is not adequate evidence for a certain causal conclusion.

So, there is at least one apparently intractable integration problem: the problem of exactly how to weight evidence from weaker and stronger studies. This problem, however, does not inevitably arise in attempts to establish causal conclusions. It need not arise if: (1) the evidence clearly and consistently supports or disconfirms a hypothesis; or (2) the evidence is flatly inconsistent and is clearly neither confirmatory nor disconfirmatory; or (3) apparent inconsistencies in the evidence can be explained away by disqualifying a certain portion of the data or by distinguishing different types of therapy or clinical disorder. Where the problem does arise and prevents any reliable causal inferences, the use of meta-analysis may be of some help but it is not likely to solve the problem. What is needed are better theories, better taxonomies, and better empirical data.

References

Campbell, D., and J. Stanley. 1966. *Experimental and Quasi-Experimental Designs for Research*. Chicago.

Erwin, E. 1980. "Psychoanalytic Therapy: The Eysenck Argument." *Amer. Psychol.* 35:435-43.

Erwin, E. 1983. "Psychotherapy, Placebos, and Wait-List Controls." The *Behavioral and Brain Sciences* 6:289-90.

Eysenck, H. J. 1952. "The Effects of Psychotherapy: An Evaluation." *Jour. of Consult. Psychol.* 16:319-24.

Eysenck, H. J. 1966. *The Effects of Psychotherapy*. New York.

Eysenck, H. J. 1978. "An Exercise in Mega-Silliness." *Amer. Psychol.* 33:517.

Eysenck, H. J. 1983. "Meta-Analysis: An Abuse of Research Integration." Unpublished manuscript.

Fiske, D. 1983. "The Meta-Analytic Revolution in Outcome Research." *Jour. of Consult. and Clin. Psychol.* 51:65-70.

Garfield, S. 1983. "Does Psychotherapy Work? Yes, No, Maybe." The *Behavioral and Brain Sciences* 6:292-93.

Glass, G., and R. Kliegl. 1983. "An Apology for Research Integration in the Study of Psychotherapy." *Jour. of Consult. and Clin. Psychol.* 51:28-41.

Kazdin, A., and L. Wilcoxin. 1976. "Systematic Desensitization and Nonspecific Treatment Effects: A Methodological Evaluation." *Psychol. Bull.* 83:729-58.

Landman, J., and R. Dawes. 1982. "Psychotherapy Outcome. Smith and Glass' Conclusions Stand Up Under Scrutiny." *Amer. Psychol.* 37:504-16.

Luborsky, L., B. Singer, and L. Luborsky. 1975. "Comparative Studies of Psychotherapies: Is It True That Everyone Has Won and All Must Have Prizes?" *Arch. Gen. Psychiat.* 32:995-1008.

Prioleau, L. M. Murdock and N. Brody. 1983. "An Analysis of Psychotherapy versus Placebo Studies." The *Behavioral and Brain Sciences* 6:275-85.

Rachman, S. 1971. *The Effects of Psychotherapy.* New York.

Rachman, S., and G. T. Wilson. 1980. *The Effects of Psychotherapy.* New York.

Scriven, M. 1959. "The Experimental Investigation of Psychoanalysis." In *Psychoanalysis, Scientific Method and Philosophy*, edited by S. Hook. New York.

Smith, M., and G. Glass. 1977. "Meta-Analysis of Psychotherapy Outcome Studies." *Amer. Psychol.* 32:752-60.

Smith, M., G. Glass and T. Miller. 1980. *The Benefits of Psychotherapy.* Baltimore.

Vanden Bos, G., and C. Pino. 1980. "Research on the Outcome of Psychotherapy." In *Psychotherapy: Practice, Research, Policy*, edited by G. Vanden Bos. Beverly Hills, Calif.

Wilson, G. T., and S. Rachman. 1983. "Meta-Analysis and the Evaluation of Psychotherapy Outcome: Limitations and Liabilities." *Jour. of Consult. and Clin. Psychol.* 51:54-64.

A Syntactically Motivated Theory
of Conditionals

WILLIAM G. LYCAN

In this paper I shall propose and discuss a new theory of indicative conditionals in English, concentrating on the connectives *if, only if, even if,* and *unless.* By "a theory of" these connectives I mean a systematic assignment of logical forms to sentences containing them, which (a) accounts for such sentences' felt implications and other intuitive semantical properties, (b) explains the ways in which their truth-values depend upon context, and (c) accords with and accounts for noteworthy aspects of their surface-syntactic behavior. I shall also comment on the difference between indicative and subjunctive conditionals and shall suggest that indicatives and subjunctives are semantically identical though pragmatically distinct.

I

Logicians, without exception, give us to understand that *if . . . then* is a syntactically unstructured binary sentence operator; at least, they represent it as such in their respective formal languages: recall ⊃, ⤙, >, □→, and so on. A logician assigns any such operator its own distinctive clause in the recursive truth-definition for its containing language. In this way, *if . . . then* is assumed to resemble *and* and *or,* however more complex its truth rule may be. Presumed equivalents of *If A, then B* (*B if A, A only if B,* etc.) are treated equivalently. But there are several reasons for rejecting this treatment insofar as it purports to give a correct and complete account of *if . . . then* in English.

    1. *If* bears unmistakable surface-syntactic similarities to spatial and temporal adverb-forming expressions such as *where* and *when.* Indeed, it seems clear that the construction *If A, B* itself is produced by adverb fronting from the more basic *B if A,* just as *Where A, B* is produced from *B where A* and *When A, B* is produced from *B when A.* Straightforward binary setence operators such as *and* and *or* resist fronting: **And A, B;* **Or A, B.* *If* even occurs in coordinate constructions with *when*: *if*

and when, when and if (cf. *unless and until*; cp. **and and when, *when and or*).
The linguist Michael Geis has argued plausibly that *when-* and *where*-adverbials are
actually relative-clause constructions,[1] and that the genesis of *if* is parallel[2]; I shall
carry his insights over into the semantics for conditionals that will be offered below.

2. The antecedent of a conditional seems to tolerate (though does not require) some surface elements normally considered negative polarity items, thus:

(1) a. If you see any large mice, then the cat has run off again.
    b. *You (will) see any large mice and the cat has run off again.

(2) a. If you eat even a single clam-and-mint-jelly pizza, you'll be sick.
    b. *You (will) eat even a single clam-and-mint-jelly pizza or you'll be sick.

(3) a. If you are a whit conceited, Dick will massacre you.
    b. *You are a whit conceited or Dick will massacre you.

3. The sentence-pairs to which *if . . . then* can be applied are subject to
agreement and co-occurrence constraints of a sort that do not hold for *and*. For
example, (4a) is syntactically ill-formed, whereas (4b) is merely awkward:

(4) a. *If I could have sung, I have sung.
    b. I could have sung and I have sung.

Conversely, *and* and *or* forbid certain mixtures of moods that are allowed by *if*:

(5) a. If you're going out, are you going to get some beer?
    b. *You're going out and are you going to get some beer?

(6) a. If they have Port Salut, buy some.
    b. *They have Port Salut or buy some.

4. Many theorists agree that English sentences of the form *If A, then B* admit understandings of differing strengths, e.g., material, indicative, subjunctive, and
possibly even strict interpretations. If *if* were a simple unstructured binary sentence
connective in each case (if *if . . . then* expressed sometimes $\supset$, sometimes $\square\!\!\rightarrow$,
sometimes $\prec$, and so on), it would follow that *if . . . then* is simply ambiguous as
between all those different readings. We would have to suppose that one and the
same word homonymously expressed all those semantically distinct notions, which
is unpleasant to believe.[3]

5. Suppose *if . . . then* does reflect a syntactically unstructured binary sentence connective. Then its presumed equivalents, particularly *only if*, would reflect
the same operator. But in general, instances of *A only if B* are not understood as
being synonymous with the corresponding instances *if A, then B*; e.g.,

(7) a. If I leave, then Joe will leave.
    b. I (will) leave only if Joe leaves.

(8) a. If I have a headache, I will leave.
    b. I (will) have a headache only if I leave.

Thus, either *if . . . then* is not a simple binary sentence connective or *A only if B*
is not equivalent to *If A, then B*, contrary to every standard elementary logic text.

Note that it would be very surprising if *only if* were the surface realization of a syntactically primitive sentence operator, for the occurrence of *only* within *only if* would then be inexplicable. *Only* is ordinarily a *quantifier*, and I shall argue below that it has its normal quantificational function here.

6. *Then* in *if . . . then* seems to play a pronominal role, referring back into the *if* clause in much the way *then* and *there* refer back into time and space adverbials respectively:

(9) a. When Katherine wants to leave, then I will leave.
   b. Where Katherine lives, there I will live.
   c. If Katherine is four years old, then I am thirty-eight. [Cf. archaic *If Katherine be four years old, then am I thirty-eight.*]
   d. *Katherine is four years old or then I am thirty-eight.

It seems that *if* provides some pronominal antecedent (no pun intended) that *or* does not.

I hope I have dropped enough hints to cast some doubt on the idea that conditional connectives are syntactically unstructured. I shall now proceed to put forward a variant of Geis's own syntactic proposal and then take my semantical cue from this variant. The rest of this paper will be devoted to exploring the resulting semantical advantages.

II

Geis found impressive syntactic evidence of the presence both of universal quantifiers and of distinctness (negated identity) clauses in the underlying syntactic structure of the sentence-form P *unless* Q (and argued on these grounds that P *unless* Q is not equivalent to the logicians' $-Q \supset P$). In more recent work, Geis has gone on to posit similar quantificational constructions underlying P *if* Q, P *only if* Q, and P *even if* Q. He notes in this connection that there exist English paraphrases of such conditionals that overtly allude to and/or quantify over entities or pseudoentities usually called "events":

P if $Q = P$ in the event that Q
P only if $Q = P$ in no event other than that Q
P even if $Q = P$ in any event including that Q
P unless $Q = P$ in any event other than that Q

My theory modifies these paraphrases slightly, takes them seriously, and accounts for their equivalence to the conditionals in question.[4] It will be shown that the theory is able to explain a number of striking and otherwise puzzling facts about these conditionals.

I have an initial problem in working with Geis's paraphrases, viz., that in my speech they are dubious as they stand. For example, Geis would render *I will go even if you go* as ???*I will go in any event including that you go*, which sounds fractured to me. The following modified paraphrases, though ornate, seem grammatically much better:

P if Q = P in any event in which Q
P only if Q = P in no event other than one in which Q
P even if Q = P in any event including any in which Q
P unless Q = P in any event other than one in which Q

Thus, I replace Geis's apparent references to a *unique* "Q"-event by universal quantification across a domain of "events in which" Q.[5] 'Event' here is used in a slightly uncommon way, as being roughly equivalent to "case" or "circumstance." Events are not things that *happen* or *occur*; rather, they *obtain* or *materialize*. (Intuitively they are not unlike Perry and Barwise's "situations.")[6] Ordinary English represents events or situations as local goings-on that are much smaller than entire world-futures or world-slices; we speak as if there are a number of "events" that will materialize, not just one. (Worlds and world-futures may be conceived as being large aggregates or heaps of events.)

My hypothesis is that formalizations of our modified paraphrases exhibit the logical forms of the conditionals under analysis. This supposition would immediately explain why the conditionals and their respective paraphrases are felt to be equivalent or to have the same truth-conditions, especially if a conditional and its paraphrase can be syntactically derived from the same semantic representation. This hypothesis has a number of other explanatory advantages, as I shall go on to demonstrate.

Here are preliminary formalizations of the modified paraphrases:

P if Q = $(e)(\text{In}(e,Q) \supset \text{In}(e,P))$
P only if Q = $(e)((f)(\text{In}(f,Q) \supset f \neq e) \supset -\text{In}(e,P))$
P even if Q = $(e)(\text{In}(e,P) \,\&\, (f)(\text{In}(f,Q) \supset \text{In}(f,P)))$
P unless Q = $(e)((f)(\text{In}(f,Q) \supset f \neq e) \supset \text{In}(e,P))$

In these formalizations, 'e' and 'f' range over "events"; 'In' is a sentential operator with an added argument place, '$\text{In}(e,Q)$' being read "In e, Q." The last three formulas listed are trivially equivalent to simpler ones; I believe these equivalences help to explain why authors of logic texts may have uncritically thought that Geis's funny conditionals were simple truth-functional connectives, though I will not go into that here.

P only if Q = $(e)(\text{In}(e,P) \supset (\exists f) - (\text{In}(f,Q) \supset f \neq e)) = (e)\,(\text{In}(e,P) \supset \text{In}(e,Q))$
P even if Q = $(e)(\text{In}(e,P) \,\&\, (\text{In}(e,Q) \supset \text{In}(e,P))) = (e)(\text{In}(e,P))$
P unless Q = $(e)(-\text{In}(e,P) \supset (\exists f)(\text{In}(f,Q) \,\&\, f = e)) = (e)(-\text{In}(e,P) \supset \text{In}(e,Q))$

III

Notice that the quantifiers occurring in my proposed logical forms must actually be restricted quantifiers, at least if we are to countenance "events" that will not in fact materialize. If our quantifiers were to be left unrestricted, our analysans for *P even if Q* would entail its being true in all possible events or circumstances that P and hence that it is logically necessary that P, an unacceptable result; similarly, our analysans for *P only if Q* would be equivalent to the thesis that its being true that *P* logically necessitates its being true that *Q*. But this is just what we should expect. Speakers who put forward conditionals of the sort I am examining are clearly not speaking of *all logically possible* events or situations, including landings of men from Mars, suspension of the Law of Gravity, and the like; most such speakers would take themselves to be talking more "realistically." But this cannot mean restricting our "event" quantifiers to the class of *actual* events (call this class '@').[7] For one thing, conditional antecedents often express possibilities that their utterers know and/or explicitly assume are not actual. For another, utterers typically envision alternative possibilities, "alternative" in the sense of being *incompatible*; thus, among the "events" in the appropriate reference-class on an occasion of that sort will be two events that cannot both be actual.[8] It remains to specify, then, how an "appropriate reference-class" is to be determined that contains some nonactual events but not all of them.

Intuitively, the reference-class appropriate to a given utterance-occasion will contain only those events that the utterer regards as "*real*" or nonnegligible possibilities, or perhaps the union of this group with that of possibilities that are in fact "real" possibilities.

We have yet to specify this reference-class (call it '*R*') with sufficient precision. It might be suggested that we let *R* be the class of all "events" that the utterer believes to be "real" possibilities in his or her situation but does not believe to have materialized. But this will not do. For one thing, it lets into *R* all sorts of *irrelevant* possible events that, though it happens that the utterer does regard them as "real" possibilities and does not believe them to have materialized, have nothing to do with the speaker's subject matter or deliberations—e.g., the reference-class underlying my utterance of *I will finish this paper today unless I run out of anchovies* would include events in which Norway has an unusually early autumn in 2001. Were this to be allowed, that sentence would automatically be falsified by the fact that none of those events or situations contains either my finishing this paper today or my not finishing it today. Similarly, *I will finish this paper today even if they turn off the air conditioning* would entail *I will finish this paper today if Norway has an early autumn in 2001*. (The proof is straightforward: the former sentence would entail that I finish the paper today *in the event that* Norway has an early autumn in 2001, which event would be a member of *R*.) And *I will finish this paper today even if they turn off the air conditioning* would therefore be even more patently falsified by the fact that an event in which Norway has an early autumn in 2001 need not and very probably will not contain either my finishing this paper today or my not finishing it today.[9]

A second objection to the suggested value of *R* is that the utterer may be *wrong* about which logical possibilities are "real" relative to the occasion, or be *unjustified* in holding his or her modal beliefs, or both. One consequence of this is that the utterer may fail to include the real outcome (the relevant event that does in fact go on to materialize) among the envisioned possibilities, thus excluding it from *R*. For example, suppose Professor Arid says, "I will promote Sieg to full professor unless his productivity drops significantly during this next year," but then decides not to promote Sieg when he finds out that Sieg has lent Ilse a copy of *Counterfactuals*, despite there being no drop at all in Sieg's productivity. (Suppose also that there is nothing the least bit unusual about Sieg's lending Ilse a copy of *Counterfactuals*, nor any other reason why Arid should not have regarded this event as a real or nonnegligible possibility; he has simply and perhaps irrationally failed to envision it.) On the present suggestion for delineating our reference-class, Arid's sentence *I will promote Sieg to full professor unless his productivity drops significantly during this next year* will still count as true on the occasion imagined; but it seems clear that the sentence ought to be counted as false, both intuitively (Arid did not keep his word) and because its felt antecedent is true but its felt consequent false.[10]

Our tasks, then, are two: We must do something to ensure the *relevance* of each of the members of R, and we must modify the original "envisioning" condition in such a way as to abstract away from the possible irrational oversights of particular speakers.

Perhaps we might achieve the first task by restricting the quantifiers underlying P *if* Q etc. to events e such that either it is true in e that P or it is true in e that $-P$ or it is true in e that Q or it is true in e that $-Q$. The rationale for this particular characterization of "relevance" (call it the Moderate Relevance Condition) would be that express articulation of the antecedent and consequent states of affairs defines a conditional's subject matter by (vaguely) specifying two overlapping neighborhoods of hypothetical fact, the antecedent state of affairs with its closely related facts and the consequent state of affairs with its closely related facts; no hypothetical facts extraneous to these two neighborhoods would be considered relevant. Alternatively, we might restrict the class of relevant "events" still further, to just events e such that either it is true in e that P or it is true in e that $-P$. (Call this the Strict Relevance Condition.) This would leave open the possibility that some conditionals could be considered "wild," in that their consequents expressed states of affairs that were not "relevant" to their respective antecedent states of affairs. But it would also have the effect of making it easier for a conditional to be true, because it would shrink the domain of the governing universal quantifier. I think that probably both types of conditional (those interpreted according to the Moderate Condition and those interpreted according to the Strict Condition) occur in English, but I shall say a bit more about this below. One reason the exact formulation of a relevance condition is important is that it is that condition that plays a selection-functional role in my theory[11] and that generates some of the semantically important truth-value distributions, as we shall see.

Our second task is more difficult. Several questions arise. First, do we want to stipulate that all *actual* relevant outcomes are members of R, whether or not those outcomes are envisioned by the speaker? It does seem that the speaker is making a serious claim about reality. And yet it is not absolutely clear how responsible the speaker is for unforeseeable contingencies. Suppose he or she says, "I will call you next week come hell or high water, even if I have over 104° temperature," but (unforeseeably) the Venusians land over the weekend and destroy all telephones. Was the speaker's utterance true or false on that occasion? There is a disinclination to call it false, because we don't want to conclude that the speaker broke his or her word, and it would be perfectly reasonable for the speaker to say afterward, "Well, obviously I didn't *mean* 'even in the event that all phones are destroyed'". On the other hand, it seems more repugnant to call the sentence true because the speaker certainly asserted that he or she would call, and the fact that we don't (morally) *blame* the speaker for having failed to anticipate the Venusian invasion should not blind us to the fact that he or she did *not* in fact call. We might want to say that the sentence tokened was false, despite the speaker's good intentions and despite the speaker's perhaps having meant something by it that was true.

One way of seeing what is at stake here is to note that with the inclusion or noninclusion of all actual relevant events in R stands or falls the validity of Modus Ponens. If some actual but unenvisioned "event" escapes R, then even though it is true that P (even though there is some event $e@$ in which P) and any P-event $e@$ is also a Q-event, it may not be actually true that Q (there may be no actual Q-event eR). This reinforces our inclination to hold a speaker semantically (though not morally) responsible for the falsification of his or her consequent due to justifiably unenvisioned developments. Also, it is natural to be squeamish about a theory of conditionals that allows a conditional to be true even though its antecedent is true and its consequent is false. The preservation of Modus Ponens is probably worth the slight ad hoc quality of stipulating that R shall contain all the actual relevant events whether they are "envisioned" or not.[12]

It remains to comment, very briefly, on the final related task that would complete our delineation of R: that of abstracting away from the irrationalities of individual speakers.

We have a number of options. Should we require that any event that the speaker's beliefs *justify* him or her in foreseeing be included in R? Or should we follow legal custom and require the inclusion of any event that "a reasonable person" would have envisioned? Or what? I shall forgo pursuing these options for now. But the delineation of our reference-class is a matter that must be settled fairly crisply before any truly serious adjudication of my theory can be achieved (just as, I would claim, an antecedent delineation of Lewis's relativized notion of "similarity of worlds" is a prerequisite to truly serious adjudication of his)[13] until that matter is settled, we will not know exactly what cases would count as satisfying my analysantia, which will make it difficult to test the analysis for counterexamples.

IV

We have already noted one or two benefits of the "event" theory. I shall catalogue some more—some fairly routine, others quite striking.

Benefit 1. The theory frees our indicative conditionals from the paradoxes of material implication, and in an illuminating way, without (implausibly) treating them as being *strict* conditionals of any sort and without importing exotic semantical machinery. It is easy to see that the theory avoids validating the three most objectionable inferences involving the truth-functional *if . . . then*, viz., $-P$ / If P, then Q; Q / If P, then Q; and $-$ (If P, then Q) / P & $-Q$. These argument-schemata would be analyzed respectively as:

$$(A) \quad \frac{-P}{(e_{\epsilon R})(\text{In } (e, P) \supset \text{In}(e,Q))} \qquad (B) \quad \frac{Q}{(e_{\epsilon R})(\text{In}(e,P) \supset \text{IN}(e,Q))}$$

$$(C) \quad \frac{-(e_{\epsilon R})(\text{In}(e,P) \supset \text{IN}(e,Q))}{P \ \& \ -Q}$$

(A) is invalid because some nonactual event ϵR may contain P but not Q even though no actual event does. (B) is invalid because some nonactual event ϵR may contain P but not Q even though an actual event contains Q. (C) is invalid because the event in which both P and $-Q$, whose existence is guaranteed by (C)'s premise, may not be an actual event.

I have said that the "event" theory blocks the paradoxical inferences in an illuminating way. To illustrate: Consider (C)'s premise. Read crudely, what it says is that there is some event that is a real and relevant possibility (but which is not necessarily going to materialize in fact) and in which P but $-Q$. This is a natural reading of *It's false that Q if P*, and it seems intuitively to capture what is intended by a speaker who denies *Q if P*. Finally, this reading makes it clear why (C)'s premise fails to imply anything about its being true or false that P or that Q in the real world.

Benefit 2. The "event" theory does not treat *if . . . then* as a syntactic primitive but rather as a complex adverbial structure of the sort hinted at in section I above. One must not be misled either by the fact that a conditional's superficial antecedent and consequent are still represented by the "event" theory as sentential argument places, or by the similarity of my resulting semantics to other purely semantical treatments such as Stalnaker's and Lewis's in that it incorporates a device that plays a selection-functional role in order to block the standard set of intuitively invalid inferences (the paradoxes of material implication, Antecedent Strengthening, and, as we shall see, contraposition and others as well). The "event" theory is not vulnerable to the sorts of objections I put in section I to the prevailing unstructured sentential-operator picture, though I shall not have the space to show this in detail here. Nor, on the "event" theory, does *if . . . then* require its own special clause in the truth-definition for English, in addition to the clause controlling $\supset$. (I think this is a significant advantage.) The truth-value of an ordinary indicative conditional can be computed from the semantic values of its components using just our standard recursive clauses for quantifiers and for $\supset$ (provided one is willing to countenance the domain of "nonactual events" for which my theory's quantifiers are defined). *If . . . then* need no longer be regarded as one or more isolated semantical primitives having little connection to other locutions.

Benefit 3. The theory explains the appearance of pronominalization noted as point 6 of section I above, as well as the similarity of *if*-clauses to *when-* and *where*-adverbials construed as relative clauses, and some related paraphrase relationships. Crudely, *event* is grammatically the analogue of *time* or *place*.

(10) a. When Sheila leaves, I will leave, and Judy will leave $\left\{ \begin{array}{c} \text{then} \\ \text{at that time} \end{array} \right\}$ too.

　　　b. Where Sheila lives, I will live, and Judy will live $\left\{ \begin{array}{c} \text{there} \\ \text{at that place} \end{array} \right\}$ too.

　　　c. If Sheila leaves, I will leave, and Judy will leave $\left\{ \begin{array}{c} \text{then} \\ \text{in that case} \\ \text{in that event} \end{array} \right\}$ too.

Benefit 4. On the "event" analysis, *even* in *even if* means "even," and *only* in *only if* means "only." This feature is almost nonexistent among philosophers' going theories of conditionals. I suppose this is because as elementary logic students we are taught that *if . . . then* is a sentential connective and that *only if*, being its converse, is a sentential connective too; this gets us into the habit of translating *only if* automatically by the horseshoe, and subsequently by some more arcane conditional connective when we become sufficiently troubled by the paradoxes of material implication. But, as I have mentioned in section I, no one stops to ask why that word *only* occurs there. Why not *blup if* or *bagel if* or some single morpheme such as *schmif*? *Only* in *only if* feels like the ordinary word *only*, as in *Only Susan left early*, and that *only* reflects a quantificational construction; the point is reinforced by the fact that *only if* is paraphrasable by *only in the event that* and by *in only one event: that*, which sound more explicitly quantificational because of their equivalence with *in no event other than one in which*. The "event" analysis explains these facts; any analysis of indicative or of subjunctive conditionals that (seriously) renders conditional connectives as syntactically primitive officially declares them inexplicable.[14]

For that matter, the "event" analysis explains the presence of *if* in *only if*. V. H. Dudman has pointed out to me that if one paraphrases one's target conditionals, appropriately enough, in terms of *conditions, If P, then Q* and *P only if Q* differ sharply in direction of conditionhood:

(11) a. If you start throwing lamps, I'll leave.

　　　b. I'll leave, $\left\{ \begin{array}{c} \text{given} \\ \text{on the condition} \end{array} \right\}$ that you start throwing lamps.

(12) a. You (will) start throwing lamps only if I leave.

　　　b. You (will) start throwing lamps only $\left\{ \begin{array}{c} \text{given} \\ \text{on the condition that} \end{array} \right\}$ I leave.

As the received doctrine(s) of conditionals would have it, (11a) and (12a) are not only logically equivalent but effectively synonymous, in that they are translated by one and the same logical primitive. Yet the *condition* in (11a) is the condition that you start throwing lamps, whereas the condition in (12a) is the condition that I leave. The "event" theory accommodates and explains this fact; *you start throwing lamps* appears as the antecedent of a conditional in the "event" analysans of (11a), but *I leave* appears as the antecedent of a conditional in the analysans of (12a).

Benefit 5. The "event" theory explains an oddity about *even if.* The oddity is that, although *P even if Q* has the superficial aspect of a conditional, it does not seem intuitively to be conditional in meaning. A speaker who asserts *P even if Q* is felt to have asserted that *P*—unconditionally. So what is the role of *even if Q?* (This I take to be a pretheoretical puzzle for any theory of conditionals of any mood.)

The "event" theory explains (a) why *P even if Q* is felt to assert that *P*, (b) wherein *P even if Q* is conditional in form, (c) the uneasy feeling of redundancy or superfluity brought on by the foregoing pretheoretical argument, and (d) the actual positive role of *even if Q*—all at one stroke. (a): *P even if Q* is felt to assert that *P* because (on the "event" analysis) its first conjunct says in effect that in any ("envisioned") event, *P*. (b): *P even if Q* is conditional in form in that its other conjunct is a conditional (to which *even* is applied). (c): The feeling of superfluity is brought on by the fact that the conditional conjunct posited by the "event" theory is redundant, being entailed by the previous conjunct.

The "event" theory's explanation of (d) turns on the function of the parameter 'R.' Suppose the speaker were merely to assert some reflection of

$$(e_{eR})(\text{In}(e,P)).$$

Now, what the speaker had asserted (what proposition he or she had expressed, so to speak) would depend on the exact value of 'R,' since the formula as displayed is an open sentence until the parameter has been assigned a denotatum in the context. And a hearer who is concerned to grasp the speaker's meaning exactly must know the correct value of 'R.' But that value is something that that hearer would have to work out from the context, employing the almost inarticulable pragmatic rules (whatever they may be) that we use in computing the valuation function for demonstratives and other indexicals. These rules are irreparably vague. Now suppose the speaker is anxious that the hearer fully understand what proposition is being expressed: It would be a good idea to save the hearer the trouble and risk of this pragmatic guessing, by making *explicit*, if he or she can, what had been left merely implicit in the context. And to do this, I submit on behalf of the "event" analysis, is the function of *even if Q*.

Our analysans for *P even if Q*,

$$(e_{eR})(\text{In}(e,P) \& (f_{eR})(\text{In}(f,Q) \supset \text{In}(f,P))),$$

is equivalent to

$$(e_{eR})(\text{In}(e,P)) \& (e_{eR})(\text{In}(e,Q) \supset \text{In}(f,P)),$$

whose second conjunct ensures that among the "events" eR are at least one in which Q and at least one in which $-Q$. Thus, the redundant conjunct serves to assure the hearer more explicitly that "events" in which (= "the event that") Q *are envisioned by* the speaker in the context in question. Thus, rather than letting his or her utterance go at (heuristically) *In any relevant event that is a "real" possibility relative to this occasion, P,* the speaker is saying the more explicit *In any relevant event that is a "real" possibility relative to this occasion, and I specifically count the event that Q as such an event, P.* The redundancy of *P even if Q* is just the price that the speaker and hearer pay in extra time and computation for the advantage of greater clarity and ease of communication.[15]

Allan Gibbard has made the following objection to this account (in conversation): There are cases in which *P even if Q* is not felt to assert that P unconditionally.

> (13) I'll be polite even if you insult me, but I won't be polite if you insult my wife.

My analysans for (13) is

> (e) $(In_{eR}(e, \text{I am polite}) \& (f_{eR}) (In(f, \text{you insult me}) \supset In (f, \text{I am polite})) \& (g_{eR}) (In (g, \text{you insult my wife}) \supset In (g, - (\text{I am polite})))$.

This formula is not itself a contradiction, but it entails that there is no event ϵR in which you insult my wife, which contradicts both the Moderate and the Strict Relevance Conditions because they ensure via the second conjunct that there is such an event. Some response is required.

An obvious move would be to claim that even though '*R*' had not changed its value from its first occurrence to its second, it did change its value from the first conjunct to the second conjunct. The idea would be that an utterer of (13), while uttering the first conjunct, did not envision his hearer's insulting his wife, but suddenly came to envision it and therefore uttered the second conjunct. Though perhaps a bit forced, this is not implausible. Its plausibility increases if we choose not to require the inclusion of all actual relevant events in *R*, since on our analysis under that requirement, (13) would *entail* that the hearer will not in fact insult the speaker's wife, which seems wrong. If we drop the reality requirement (cf. section III above), this consequence is avoided. The intuitive content of (13) could then be expressed as *I do not as things are envision any real and relevant possibility that I will not be polite, not even one in which you insult me, but if I now make myself envision one in which you insult my wife, I do not see myself being polite in any such event.* This is not too bad as a gloss of (13). So we have a bit more motivation for choosing not to impose the reality requirement. If Modus Ponens seems a high price to pay, notice that (13) creates a *pretheoretic* difficulty regarding Modus Ponens, quite apart from the "event" theory. Suppose I token (13) and you do proceed to insult both me and my wife, whereupon I am very impolite. Then although (13) was presumably true, its first surface conjunct *I'll be polite (even) if you insult me* has a true antecedent and a false consequent. Somehow, (13)'s second conjunct cancels or suspends the reality requirement we would ordinarily impose on the first. (The case here is cognate with that considered in section III above, in which a speaker's conditional consequent is falsified in some bizarre and unforeseeable way. Notice too that the problem is not generated by the presence of *even*; it persists even when *even* is deleted from (13).)

However we settle the reality requirement issue, I think it will not be too hard to integrate the resulting account with standard treatments of *even* in other sorts of sentences, particularly with those that focus on the interaction of *even* with quantifiers. It is certainly safe to predict that the *even* of *even if* is not a different *even* from the normal ones.[16]

Benefit 6. Any logician would take

(14) If I leave, then Joe will leave,

(15) Joe will leave if I leave,

and

(16) I will leave only if Joe leaves

to be equivalent. Are they? Even the "event" analysis might seem to entail that they are, and yet they differ at least in connotation. Statement (14) hypothesizes my leaving and remarks on or suggests something that will be triggered by that event. Statement (15) focuses on the question of Joe's leaving and can be heard either as being part of a list of conditions under which Joe will leave, or as emphasizing a consequence of the already stipulated hypothesis that I leave. Statement (16) lists a necessary condition for my leaving.

Perhaps these differences in purport are *simply* differences in focus and/or in emphasis and/or in conventional implicature and/or in resolution of vagueness. But there is some temptation to insist that there is a difference in the proposition expressed as well. The "event" theory can account for this, despite its assigning (14), (15), and (16) each the formula

$$(e_{eR}) (\text{In}(e, \text{I leave}) \supset \text{In} (e, \text{Joe leaves}))$$

as a semantic representation. To see this, note that 'R' is a parameter or free variable and may be assigned a different value on each occasion of its use. Therefore, it is at least possible that different ranges of possible "events" are being envisioned by the utterers of (14), (15), and (16), and thus that distinct propositions *are* expressed even though the logical forms (in the narrow sense) of (14), (15), and (16) are the same. For example, (14) suggests that my leaving would be a reason for or cause of Joe's leaving, whereas (16) suggests the reverse; thus, the value of 'R' on an occasion of the utterance of (14) would very likely not include any event(s) in which Joe had already left some *time before* I left, whereas the value of 'R' associated with an utterance of (16) would include these but would exclude events in which Joe is still in the room when I leave but leaves some time thereafter.

It should be noted that the difference between *If P, then Q* and *P only if Q* holds for subjunctives as well. Compare (17) and (18):

(17) If Joe were to leave, then he would have a headache.

(18) Joe would leave only if he were to have a headache.

An analysis of subjunctive conditionals such as Lewis's offers no way of distinguishing these, but it seems plain that they can differ in truth-value.[17] This leads me to suspect the presence of quantification over possible outcomes in the semantic structures underlying counterfactuals and other subjunctives as well. A bit more on this shortly.

Benefit 7. Is *P if Q* transitive? On the "event" analysis, *P if Q* is relative, in that it is elliptical for *P if Q in all the relevant events envisioned.* If our parameter is held fixed, our conditionals will of course be transitive. But this does not mean that any instance of *P if Q; Q if R / P if R* found in nature will be a valid argument, since there is no guarantee that the parameter does stay fixed in the course of arguing. In fact, as I have tentatively explained "relevance," the parameter *cannot* very well stay fixed. The value of 'R' associated with *P if Q* will include all events in which *P, –P, Q,* or *–Q,* and which are "real" possibilities in the situation of utterance, or at least (on the Strict Relevance Condition) all the "real" possibilities in which *P* and those in which *–P,* whereas the value associated with *Q if R* may exclude some events in which *P* or in which *–P.* This is why our parameter 'R' plays a selection-functional role.

It is hard to form clear (unpolluted) intuitions about the transitivity of *if,* and certainly hard in particular to find clear counterexamples to transitivity for indicative conditionals. Something like the following may do:

> If Reagan resigns the presidency, he will take it easier.
> If Reagan takes it easier, his friends will be glad.
>
> ---
>
> If Reagan resigns the presidency, his friends will be glad.

Better:

> If Reagan is renominated for president, I will skip the front page of my newspaper.
> If all the other Republican candidates are squashed by a falling meteorite, Reagan will be renominated for President.
>
> ---
>
> If all the other Republican candidates are squashed by a falling meteorite, I will skip the front page of my newspaper.

This last is plainly invalid, and the "event" analysis provides an obvious explanation: The antecedent of the second premise forces the hearer to envision an event in which all the other Republican candidates are squashed by a meteorite. But the value of 'R' associated with the first premise did not contain any such event because it is not one that a speaker would normally envision, and it is with this assumption that the speaker has asserted the first premise. Since the conclusion continues to force the hearer (and speaker) to envision the event(s) in question, the argument is invalidated by straightforward parameter shift.[18]

It is interesting to ask whether any change in transitivity phenomena is occasioned by the replacement of one of our *if . . . then's* with an *only if.* The "event" analysis suggests that no such change should occur, since on it *P if Q* and *Q only if P* are assigned equivalent logical forms. But to conclude this would be again to overlook the parameter shift required by my account of relevance. Consider (14) and

(19) Joe will leave only if the booze runs out.

Transitivity would entitle us to infer

(20) I will leave only if the booze runs out,

which is counterintuitive. Actually we tend to hear (14) and (19) themselves as *contradicting* each other. This points importantly toward the nature of *only if only if*, as Geis originally saw. And yet any competent logician would infer (20) from (14) and (19) without seeing any irregularity at all.

Benefit 8. The "event" theory neatly explains our somewhat paradoxical feelings about this: The reason that (14) and (19), uttered in the same context, seem to contradict each other is that we presume that roughly the same set of events is envisioned by the speaker in making each utterance. The speaker must be envisioning at least one "event" in which I leave, and presumably at least one in which I leave but in which the booze does not run out. Statement (14) entails that Joe leaves in the latter event, but (according to the "event" analysis) (19) entails that he does not; hence the air of incompatibility. And even if we were to juggle parameters in such a way as to repair this, we would still leave open the possibility of parameter shift that would account for the failure of surface transitivity. Similar points may be made about *P unless Q*.

We may also ask whether indicative conditionals support antecedent-strengthening. As before, we can generate counterexamples by selecting our antecedents in such a way as to force parameter shift:

If Ted Kennedy runs against Reagan in the next election, Reagan will win the election.

If Ted Kennedy runs against Reagan in the next election and Reagan is crushed by an avalanche of jellybeans, Reagan will win the election.

This example works because, as before, the conclusion forces speaker and hearer to envision an "event" that is not counted by the utterer of the premise as a "real" possibility.

V

Earlier I have hinted at some affinities between indicative and subjunctive conditionals, and it is obvious that the semantical analysis to which our syntactic considerations have led us is strikingly close to the similarity-of-worlds approach to conditionals due to Stalnaker. (As I have said, most of its main advantages over the latter approach stem from its not treating surface conditional connectives as being syntactically primitive.) Yet there are well-known cases in which an indicative conditional and its corresponding subjunctive seem to differ in truth-value. What, then, is the relation?

This is a large issue on which a number of excellent works have been written.[19] Let me here just sketch the account of the indicative-subjunctive relation that falls out of the "event" theory. What seems clear is that an indicative conditional and its corresponding subjunctive are or would be tokened with different sets of relevant and/or envisioned possibilities in mind. The difference is characteristic and systematic enough that it splits the individually various values of 'R' into two general types. A conditional token whose associated value of 'R' is of the first type is lexicalized indicatively; a conditional token whose associated value of 'R' is of the second type is lexicalized subjunctively.[20] Thus, an indicative conditional and its corresponding subjunctive have the same logical form but differ in the types of value that their respective parameters can take, and this is why they can differ in truthvalue.

Let me hazard a quick guess regarding the two types of reference-class, based on the following examples.[21]

(21) a. If Oswald didn't shoot Kennedy, someone else did.
  b. If Oswald had not shot Kennedy, someone else would have.

(22) a. If it's nighttime now, I'm having a very strange visual delusion. [Said while looking out the window during the day.]
  b. If it were nighttime now, I'd be having a very strange visual delusion.

In uttering (21a), a speaker in effect holds the fact of Kennedy's assassination fixed, and eo ipso envisions no event in which Kennedy escaped being shot. By contrast, (21b) seems false (to anyone who is not a conspiracy theorist) because in evaluating (21b) we do not hold the assassination fixed; given the totality of events in our ken prior to the shooting, we had no particular reason to suppose that an assassination would occur, and so in considering events in which Oswald did not shoot Kennedy we easily—more easily than not—envision some in which Kennedy remained unhurt. Statements (22a) and (22b) differ similarly. In uttering (22a), I hold fixed the daylight-suffused experiences I am having and envision no event in which I am having them during the nighttime but am not having a delusion, while in uttering (22b) I envision only nighttime events that are in all other ways epistemically normal; since I am not given to having strange visual delusions, most of these events are not ones in which I am thus deluded.

The following generalization is tempting, though crude and vague (or perhaps *because* crude and vague): A conditional is lexicalized indicatively when its utterer holds fixed some *striking fact* that is looming very large in his or her epistemic field, a fact that is presumably though not necessarily "common ground" between utterer and audience. A conditional is lexicalized subjunctively when its utterer means to prescind from contextually striking facts and consider a wider range of alternative possiblities constrained only by a similarity relation of some Lewisian sort or other.

For (21a), the striking fact is that of Kennedy's having been assassinated; for (22a), the striking fact is that of my having the vivid daylight experiences. Both get held fixed, making (21a) and (22a) true. What is distinctive about the subjunctives (21b) and (22b), I think, is that their respective consequents would be quite remote —not easily envisioned against the background of the antecedent suppositions combined with the known facts leading up to those suppositions' "reference-times"[22] — *but for the striking facts* that underwrite their corresponding indicatives. Supposing just that Oswald did not shoot Kennedy, and *not* being given the historical fact of the assassination, we would have no particular reason to envision someone else's shooting Kennedy. Supposing just that it is nighttime, and not being given the fact of my having daylight experiences, I would have no reason to suppose that I would shortly be having delusions. It seems, then, that a subjunctive conditional with antecedent A and consequent C differs most obviously fron indicative *If A, then C* when the possibility of C, given A and the background information leading up to A's reference-time would be remote but for the "striking fact" that makes *If A, then C* true.

Let us apply our protohypothesis to a further example. J. L. Mackie suggests that instances of accidental generalizations yield indicative-subjunctive mismatches:[23]

(23) a. If x is in my pocket, x is silver.
      b. If x were in my pocket, x would be silver.

Mackie contends that (23a) is true of a typical coin, say, but (23b) might well be false. However, against Mackie, Wayne Davis[24] maintains that nonsilver coins do not satisfy (23a); (24) is not true, for example:

(24) If this penny is in my pocket, it is silver.

I believe Mackie's suggestion is true for some instances of (23a-b) and false for others, in a way that is predicted by our protohypothesis. I agree with Davis regarding (24), and I think the reason (24) is false is that an utterer of (24) would normally be ostending a penny, making it a "striking fact" that the penny is copper rather than silver. Thus, what is true is not (24) but

(25) (Even) if this penny is in my pocket, it is copper.

But now change our mode of reference to the penny, or rather its mode of presentation to us. Suppose a puckish friend enters the room and says she is thinking of a particular coin in here that she calls 'Arthur'; I am to guess things about it. In this case I would be perfectly right to say

(26) If Arthur is in my pocket, he is silver.

For in this utterance context, the striking fact is not the (unknown) composition of the coin but that all the coins I know of in this room, viz., the ones in my pocket, are silver. This adjudication of the intuitive disagreement between Mackie and Davis is a pleasing protoconfirmation.

No doubt the woods are thick with counterexamples, insofar as the protohypothesis is clear enough to admit of testing at all. Regarding clarity, I hope that the notions of "strikingness," "looming large in one's epistemic field," etc., might usefully be explicated in epistemological and psychological terms, perhaps with the aid of the probability calculus.

It is time to stop. The "event" theory can claim a number of further achievements and advantages that it has over other current theories of conditionals.[25] There are also some drawbacks and nasty difficulties, more than one of which will have occurred to the reader, and which only more clarification and tinkering will alleviate. In this paper I have tried only to make the case that such clarification and tinkering will repay the effort.[26]

Notes

1. "Adverbial Subordinate Clauses in English" (Ph.D. diss., MIT, 1970) and three subsequent articles published in *Ohio State University Working Papers in Linguistics*, No. 18 (1975); cf. "Time Prepositions as Underlying Verbs," in *Papers from the Sixth Regional Meeting of the Chicago Linguistic Society* (Chicago, 1970).

2. "*If* and *Unless*," in *Issues in Linguistics: Papers in Honor of Henry and Renee Kahane* (Urbana, 1973); "The Syntax of Conditional Sentences," (unpublished typescript); and elsewhere. I am indebted to Geis for some of the data in this paper, for my basic syntactic approach to the study of conditionals, and for many lengthy and helpful discussions.

3. At least one etymologist has suggested to me that *if* does have two genuinely different meanings, one deriving from Old English *gif* ("given") and the other deriving from German *ob* ("whether"). I have no way of knowing whether this is true.

4. From now on I shall be talking primarily about semantics, since Geis has already worked out syntactic derivations for this kind of relative-clause construction. He employs a Generalized Phrase Structure Grammar of the sort recently developed by Gerald Gazdar and others. (See G. Gazdar and G. K. Pullum, *Generalized Phrase Structure Grammer: A Theoretical Synopsis* [Indiana University Linguistics Club Publications, 1982].)

5. My paraphrases may be understood as being equivalent to Geis's, *if* Geis's *the* and *that* are interpreted nonuniquely, as in *The man who can get through* Sein and Zeit *has a stronger head than I*.

6. There are formal similarities also. See J. Barwise, "Scenes and other Situations," *Journal of Philosophy* 78 (1981), and Barwise and J. Perry, *Situation Semantics* (in press).

7. David Lewis coined '@' as a name of the actual world, in *Counterfactuals* (Cambridge, Mass., 1973). For our purposes here, we may simply identify "the actual world" with the class of actual "events."

8. There are more technical reasons as well. With the aid of two or three plausible reduction formulas or meaning postulates, it is easy to show that restricting our "event" quantifiers to the actual has the effect of collapsing our conditionals back into their truth-functional shadows and reinstating the paradoxes of material implication. I take this to be a bad thing, *pace* Frank Jackson in "On Assertion and Indicative Conditionals," *Philosophical Review* 88 (1979).

I have as many qualms about "nonactual situations" as anyone; but for now, we are having trouble enough trying to find a logical structure of any sort that will predict all that we want to predict concerning the behavior of indicative conditionals. Anyone who objects to "nonactual possibles" being posited even for this limited purpose may think of my "events" as small sets of propositions and the truth of a proposition "in" an "event" simply as set membership. (On ontological issues of this kind, see my "The Trouble with Possible Worlds," in *The Possible and the Actual* edited by M. Loux [Ithaca, 1979].)

9. This is not to deny that *Either I will finish this paper today or I will not finish it today* holds in these "irrelevant" events. Although events or circumstances are *incomplete*, they are presumably closed under deduction and so contain all tautologies. (However, we may want to relax this closure and admit a variety of impossible events in order to handle conditionals with impossible antecedents. On the probity of impossible states of affairs, see "The Trouble with Possible Worlds, " 313-4.)

10. It may be objected that Arid's utterance *was* true and that its defect was rather that it was *misleading* to any normal hearer (such as Sieg in the imagined situation), in that the hearer would have a right to expect that Arid's reference-class did include the unexotic possibility that Sieg would lend Ilse his copy of *Counterfactuals*. I will not discuss this objection here, since I take it to be just a special case of the general philosophical problem of whether it is intention, convention, or some unsuspected factor that predominates in fixing the denotatum of a demonstrative token.

11. See Stalnaker, "A Theory of Conditionals," *American Philosophical Quarterly Monograph Series,* No. 2 (Oxford, 1968), and David Lewis, *Counterfactuals* (Cambridge, Mass., 1973), sec. 2.7, for discussion of selection functions and their duties.

12. I believe the connection was noted by Brian Chellas during the discussion of an earlier version of this paper at the 1978 University of Western Ontario Workshop on Conditionals and Pragmatics. The suggestion that a special adjustment was needed in a theory of conditionals in order to make Modus Ponens come out valid caused considerable merriment at the time.

13. See *Counterfactuals*, sec. 4.2; also, "Counterfactual Dependence and Time's Arrow," *Nous* 13 (1979).

14. Richmond Thomason and others have pointed out to me that in its normal uses, *only* generates an entailment (or "presupposition") of existence as well as uniqueness. Thus, *Only Susan left early* implies not only that no one other than Susan left early, but that Susan did leave early. I believe (contrary to the letter of the semantic representation I have assigned to *P only if Q*) that in colloquial English *P only if Q* carries a similar implication; *I will pass you only if you get an A on the final* implies that I will pass you *if* you get an A on the final. (*I will pass you only in the event that you get an A on the final* clearly implies that I will pass you in that event but in no other.) What about the logician's contrasting monoconditional use of *only if*? I surmise that at some point *only if* acquired a technical use in mathematics, a syntactically fused sense that permits the otherwise redundant *if and only if* (cp. *Susan and only Susan*) and that this technical use has filtered into ordinary academic English from mathematics and logic, perhaps via various sciences. In this technical idiom, of course, *only* occurs merely orthographically or at least does not have its entire normal meaning.

15. This explanation substantively assumes that the values of '*R*' as it modifies both of the quantifiers in our anlaysans for *P even if Q* are one and the same, i.e., that '*R*' does not take one value for the first quantifier and then a second, distinct value for the second quantifier. But I see nothing objectionable about this; we should expect that the speaker would be envisioning one and the same set of relevant "events" throughout his or her utterance. It ought also to be acknowledged that the explanation depends crucially on my tentative explication of "relevant" possibilities in section III above: If that explication had not given us the assumption that the reference-class *R* mentioned in the analysans of *P if Q* contains events in which *P*, events in which −*P*, events in which *Q*, and events in which −*Q*, that analysans might be *vacuously* satisfied due to the absence from *R* of any events in which *Q*.

16. This is also noted by A. Hazen and M. Slote in "'even if'," *Analysis* 39 (1979). (Cf. also James McCawley, "*If* and *Only if*," *Linguistic Inquiry* 5 [1974].) Indeed, one might think that *even* simply applies to a conditional as a whole, being read as "It is even true that." But this is not quite right. Consider *If kangaroos have no feet, they topple over, and for that matter if they have no front paws they topple over; it is even true that if they have no tails they topple over*. The last clause of this recitation is not equivalent to *Kangaroos topple over even if they have no tails*.

17. Actually it is open to Lewis to distinguish the truth-values by stipulating that different similarity relations are mobilized by the two surface constructions *if . . . then* and *only if*. But (a) this would be ad hoc unless the distinction between the similarity relations could be independently motivated, and (b) no light would be shed in any case on the presence of *only*, the direction-of-conditionhood datum, etc.

18. This phenomenon is quite similar to that which invalidates the corresponding counterfactual argument on a "similarity" analysis of counterfactuals such as Stalnaker's or Lewis's. In each case it is the improbability of the second premise's antecedent that makes the counterexample work.

19. Particularly: Jonathan Bennett, "Counterfactuals and Possible Worlds," *Canadian Journal of Philosophy* 4 (1974); Allan Gibbard, "Two Recent Theories of Conditionals," in *Ifs*, ed. W. L. Harper, R. Stalnaker, and G. Pearce (Dordrecht, 1981); R. Stalnaker, "Indicative Conditionals," ibid.; and Wayne Davis, "Indicative and Subjunctive Conditionals," *Philosophical Review* 88 (1979). Also, my "Indicative *vs* Subjunctive," unpublished ditto, in which inter alia I apply the "event" theory to Gibbard's riverboat paradox ("Two Recent Theories," sec. 5).

20. The mechanism here, on my view, is what Boër and I have called "lexical presumption"; see *The Myth of Semantic Presupposition* (Indiana University Linguistics Club Publications,

1976), chap. 5, and particularly sec. 5.3, in which it is argued that the "subjunctive mood" is not a *mood* at all. Mood is in all other cases a matter of standard illocutionary force (declarative, imperative, interrogative, etc.); no standard type of speech act corresponds to subjunctivity. There is other evidence as well.

21. Statement (21) is due to E. W. Adams, "Subjunctive and Indicative Conditionals," *Foundations of Language* 6 (1970), 90; cf. Lewis, *Counterfactuals*, 3. Statement (22) was called to my attention by Allan Gibbard.

22. A conditional's "reference-time" is roughly the time (if any) of the state of affairs that would make the conditional's antecedent true. See M. Slote, "Time in Counterfactuals," *Philosophical Review* 87 (1978); V. H. Dudman, "Conditional Interpretations of 'If'-Sentences," photocopy; and especially Davis, "Indicative and Subjunctive Conditionals," 552ff.

The idea that some fact or facts are held fixed in evaluating an indicative conditional but let rip in evaluating a subjunctive conditional is hardly revolutionary. Indeed, it is an obvious special case of the view that the indicative-subjunctive distinction is at bottom a difference between two designated similarity relations. Thus, my proposal may be just a rather vague specification of Davis's. All that I claim as distinctive about it is its picking out "the facts held fixed," or the relevant respect of similarity, in epistemic rather than metaphysical terms. In this respect my view goes back to Stalnaker's original suggestion ("A Theory of Conditionals," 102), abandoned by Stalnaker himself almost without remark, on the same page.

23. "Conditionals," in *Truth, Probability, and Paradox* (Oxford, 1973), 115ff.

24. "Indicative and Subjunctive Conditionals," 547-48.

25. There are more subtle grammatical points to be made. Also, the "event" theory affords a precise and illuminating statement of the account of "conditional perfection" sketched in Boër and Lycan, "Invited Inferences and Other Unwelcome Guests," *Papers in Linguistics* 6 (1973), as well as a particularly useful way of formulating different "reliability" theories in epistemology (see my "Armstrong's Theory of Knowing," in *Profiles: D. M. Armstrong*, edited by R. J. Bogdan [in press], nn. 12, 21).

26. Various fragments of various versions of this material have been presented at the 1977 Ohio State University Mini-Conference on Conditionals, the 1978 University of Western Ontario Workshop on Conditionals and Pragmatics, the Second New Zealand Linguistics Conference (August, 1978), and the philosophy colloquia of the University of Iowa, Monash University, the University of Western Australia, and the Australian National University's Research School of Social Sciences. I am indebted to many people for useful comments and suggestions. I shall try to take account of all of them in more detailed work, in progress. In the meantime I should like to thank D. M. Armstrong, Max Cresswell, Philip Cummins, Wayne Davis, V. H. Dudman, Allan Gibbard, William Harper, Lloyd Humberstone, Frank Jackson, Ronald Laymon, David Lewis, Donald Nute, Richard Routley, Robert Stalnaker, David Stove, Richmond Thomason, Michael Tooley, and (again) Michael Geis.

How the Causal Theorist
Follows a Rule[1]

PENELOPE MADDY

Wittgenstein's rule-following problem presents a powerful and quite general argument against most forms of traditional semantics. At stake is the relationship between what we learn when we learn an expression and our subsequent use of that expression. There have been various accounts of this relation. For example, a Fregean might say that when we learn a word, we grasp its sense, that the sense determines the reference, and that we then use the word to refer to its referent. In contrast, a modern day antirealist might say that we learn the word's assertability conditions and that we then use the word when those conditions obtain. Around the period of the *Blue Book*, Wittgenstein himself seemed inclined toward the view that language learning involved the acquisition of semantic rules that guide future usage. If correct, the rule-following argument would undermine all three of these accounts.

As is to be expected of an argument with such wide-reaching implications, the rule-following argument can be formulated in a number of different ways. My interest here is in its application to any semantic theory that involves a causal theory of reference, so I will present it as an argument against the notion of determinate reference.[2] Though its conclusions are supposed to apply to reference of all kinds, detailed presentations of the argument usually rely on mathematical examples. I think this preference is simply due to the precision of mathematical cases; the central issue of rule-following can be clearly separated from extraneous issues concerning vagueness. Under the circumstances, I will begin with a mathematical example, then append two others to combat the impression that the difficulty is somehow peculiar to mathematics.

Suppose that I've learned to use the phrase 'plus 2' to refer to the infinite sequence of even natural numbers. I know that plus 2 begins 0, 2, 4, 6, 8, . . . , and I've calculated various later steps in the sequence, though (let us suppose), no step beyond 1000. I now claim that the next step after 1000 is 1002.

At this point, one of Wittgenstein's henchmen[3] sets out to show that this claim is false, that in fact the next step is 1004. This henchman is not Wittgenstein himself, because Wittgenstein's own conclusion will be quite different. The henchman begins:

H: The next step is 1004, not 1002. Your expression 'plus 2' refers to the sequence 0, 2, 4, 6, 8, . . . , 1000, 1004, 1008, . . . , 2000, 2006, 2012, ... (*PI* 185)

ME: Nonsense. Your sequence is a nonstandard one *plus 2. (Read this "star plus two.") I refer to the ordinary plus 2: 0, 2, 4, 6, 8, . . . , 1000, 1002, 1004, . . . , 2000, 2002, 2004, ...

H: But what fixed your past reference to plus 2 rather than *plus 2? You had never worked out or even thought of the steps after 1000. Nothing in your mind, practice, or training distinguishes between the two.

ME: That's not true. Granted I'd never taken or thought of the particular step 1000, 1002, but I did associate the phrase 'plus 2' with an explicit rule: $f(n) = 2 \times n$. That rule guarantees that the 501st step, the step after 1000, is 1002. (*PI* 189)

H: You've misapplied your own formula!

$$f(500) = 2 \times 500 = 1000$$
$$f(501) = 2 \times 501 = 1004$$

So the next step is 1004, just as I said.

ME: There you go again with your nonstandard interpretations. The symbol '$\times$' refers to multiplication, but you're using it to refer to a nonstandard function *multiplication where

$$n \,{}^*\!\times m = n \times m \qquad\qquad \text{for } m \leqslant 500$$
$$n \,{}^*\!\times m = n \times (m + 1) \qquad \text{for } m > 500.$$

H: But that's what your use of '$\times$' refers to also.

As before, assume for the sake of argument that I've never performed or thought of any multiplications with factors larger than 500, so that the henchman's claim is consistent with my past usage of '$\times$'. I will argue below that these assumptions are inessential.

ME: You're making the same mistake as before. I may not have worked out the particular example of 2×501, but I accepted rules for multiplication that rule out your nonstandard interpretation:

$$n \times 1 = n$$
$$n \times (m + 1) = (n \times m) + n$$

H: Once again you've misapplied your own rules.

$$2 \times 500 = 1000$$
$$2 \times (500 + 1) = (2 \times 500) + 2 = 1000 + 2 = 1004$$

ME: Now you've misinterpreted the symbol '+'. You've got a nonstandard $^*+$ for which

$$n\,{}^*\!\!+ m = n + m \qquad \text{for } n \leqslant 1000$$
$$n\,{}^*\!\!+ m = n + (m + 2) \qquad \text{for } n > 1000$$

H: But that's what your use of '+' refers to also.

Once again we make the inessential assumption that I've computed no sums with arguments of 1000 or more.

At this point I begin to wise up. The tactic of appealing to explicit algebraic rules is ineffective because, in the henchman's words,

However many rules you give me – I give a rule which justifies my employment of your rules. (*RFM* I 113)

I realize that

we can think of more than *one* application of an algebraic formula; and every type of application can in turn be formulated algebraically; but naturally this does not get us any further. (*PI* 146)

I decide to leave these esoteric algebraic maneuvers and get back to basics.

ME: All right, now I understand. My association of some explicit algebraic rule with the expression 'plus 2' is not what determined my reference to plus 2 rather than to your *plus 2, and your demonstration of this point was most ingenious. Still, you must admit that your claim that I have actually been referring to *plus 2 all along is preposterous. What determined my reference to plus 2 is really something simpler and more basic, a primitive method of calculating. I knew all along that if you want to calculate the next step in the sequence I call 'plus 2', you should proceed as follows: count out a pile containing as many marbles as the last number of your sequence. Add two more marbles to this pile and count the result. That number is next in the sequence. There! Nothing could be less ambiguous.

H: OK, I'll try it.

Under my supervision, he counts out a thousand marbles, adds two more, then re-counts.

H: . . . 997, 998, 999, 1000, 1002, 1004. See? This correct answer is 1004, just as I said.

ME: I don't believe it! You've done it again! You're *counting, not counting!

H: But your use of the expression 'counting' refers to *counting also.

One more time, assume I've never counted beyond 1000.

ME: This is going too far. I learned to count as a child, not to *count, and so did you. We didn't learn by being given any explicit formula that you can now misinterpret, but by lots of examples and practice, with help, encouragement, and punishment from our teachers. If I'd made the sort of mistakes you do, I'd have flunked kindergarten. In fact, I'm surprised you didn't! (*PI* 208)

H: Wait a minute! How can you say that counting 1000, 1002 is a mistake like the ones you were punished for? Did you or your teacher ever consider this case?

ME: No, but that's not important. Learning to count isn't just a matter of the particular examples chosen. My understanding reached beyond those examples; I guessed what the teacher had in mind.

H: By that I suppose you mean that various interpretations of your teacher's examples occurred to you – among them maybe count and *count – and that you opted for count. If that's what happened, you could simply have asked which was correct and received an answer. But as you know, no finite number of these explicit answers would be enough to rule out all the interpretations you call nonstandard. In fact, your teacher's references is not more determinate than the examples and explanations he or she gives, and neither is yours. (*PI* 209-210)

The problem is worse than I'd suspected. My attempt to return to basics has brought me back to the beginning where I admitted that a finite number of previously worked examples couldn't determine the correctness or incorrectness of a new case. But there must be more to my understanding of counting (and my teacher's) than a finite list of cases! Perhaps it is something that can't be fully expressed in words, a particular feeling like the look of lavender or the smell of the ocean. I make one last effort.

ME: I associate something beyond algebraic formulas and a finite batch of examples with the word 'count'. The formulas and examples may not determine that my uses of the word refer to count or to *count, but this something more does. Unfortunately, I can't tell you much about what it is. It's just a special inner feeling I have.

H: Have you had this sensation continuously since you learned the word 'count'? (*PI*, p. 59 [a], [b])

ME: . . . Well, no. But I had it a moment ago when I counted your pile of marbles . . . 1000, 1001, 1002. When I have that feeling, that's what I call 'counting'.

At this point I close my eyes and concentrate on my sensations.

H: What if you were given a drug that induced just that sensation while you were *counting , that is, while you were saying "1000, 1002, 1004"? (*PI* 160)

ME: Well . . .

H: And what if someone gave all the same answers you do when asked to 'count', but claimed to have no special inner sensation? Would you say that person wasn't really counting? (*PI* 160)

ME: Well . . .

H: Come on now! When you counted out that deck of cards yesterday, did you really have a particular feeling? . . . . Or try this: say "1000, 1001, 1002," and then say "1000, 1002, 1004." Was there really some special sensation that went with the first and didn't go with the second?

ME: In all honesty, I must admit that there wasn't. (*PI* 156-178)[4]

Let's step back from the debate for a moment and assess the damage. There is no denying that the defender of the standard reference to plus 2 is at least temporarily routed. It may seem, though, that the difficulty arises from the attempt to use finite means (examples, training, rules, etc.) to pin down an infinite referent (the sequence plus 2). Since mathematics is the sole custodian of the infinite, it might seem that the problem is peculiar to that discipline. This is not the case. To see this, let's consider two cases involving ordinary physical objects: first a general term, then a proper name.

The examples of general terms most often cited by Wittgenstein are color terms, but I will avoid these as they raise irrelevant issues about vagueness and the nature of sensation talk. Shape terms like 'cube' are also mentioned in the *PI*, and though vagueness can intrude in such cases, the problem is much less acute. To eliminate distracting issues involved in two-dimensional representation of three-dimensional shapes, let's replace Wittgenstein's 'cube' with 'triangle'. These terms are to be taken as ordinary language shape terms applicable to ordinary physical objects. In the case of 'triangle', these are usually physical inscriptions, or objects thin by comparison with their length, like guitar picks or crackers. I use the word 'triangle', then, to refer to members of the class of triangles. Presented with the inscription □ I naturally deny that it is a triangle. Once again, Wittgenstein's henchman sets out to prove me wrong.

ME: (To myself: I'm tempted to start by insisting that a triangle is a three-sided figure while this example has four sides, but I know from cruel experience how he can misconstrue a simple explicit rule. I'll try a different strategy this time.) I associate the word 'triangle' with a mental image like this: Δ. Your figure doesn't match it.

H: Why sure it does! Look:

ME: But that's not matching! This is matching:

You must be doing some sort of *matching.

H: But your previous use of the word 'matching' referred to *matching too . . .

I've never seen this particular inscription before, so the henchman's claim can be consistent with my past matching behavior and usage.

> . . . so you should admit that this new figure is a triangle. (*PI* 139)

This time I despair much more quickly. I could insist on a standard interpretation of 'matching', but any explicit rule I propose, he can systematically misinterpret. What I hadn't noticed until now is that a sample doesn't wear its application on its sleeve any more than a formula does.

From our position above the fray, we should note another new feature of this case. If there are only finitely many physical objects, then there are only finitely many things in the standard extension of 'triangle'. (I'm excluding triangular inscriptions hidden in homogeneous surfaces, and the like.) Here the accusation of nonstandard reference concerns a finite rather than an infinite referent. This suggests that the problem is not simply that finite means never fully specify something infinite.

Still, it might be thought that the indefinitely large extension of 'triangle' makes it impractical for my training to embrace all triangles, or for my definition to include an exhaustive list. To see that even this would do no good, we must consider one last example: my tortoiseshell cat Fauve. I see her sleeping on the couch and claim, "There is Fauve." My constant companion denies this, pointing to my grey cat sunning on the patio. "That," he claims, "is Fauve."

> ME: This time you're surely in over your head. Here we have no new case of counting I've never thought of before, no new triangle I've never seen before. This is the same tortoiseshell cat I adopted as a kitten and named 'Fauve'. My training, and my previous usage on many occasions, both explicitly determine that my use of 'Fauve' refers to the tortoiseshell and not the grey.

> H: Now wait a minute. Your introduction of the name, your previous uses of it, never referred to this . . .

He points at the sleeping cat.

> . . . but to previous temporal stages. When I say your current use of the name 'Fauve' refers to the grey cat, I'm claiming that once again, you've misunderstood your own usage. You introduced the name, and you have previously used it, to refer to a space-time worm consisting of stages of the tortoiseshell until five minutes ago and stages of the grey thereafter. Thus that (the sunning cat) is Fauve and that (the sleeping cat) is not.

> ME: (To myself: Oh no! My past interactions with Fauve have been just as much interactions with the composite worm. If I insist on some explicit rule connected with the name [e.g., that it refers to the tortoiseshell, or that it always refers to the same cat], he'll give a composite interpretation of that image. rally indexed interpretation of 'tortoiseshell' or 'same cat']. If I appeal to my mental image of Fauve, he'll give a composite interpretation of that image. If I allude to some special inner feeling that determines my reference to the

tortoiseshell rather than the grey, he'll point out that there is no such thing.)
. . . ? ? ? ? . . .

Let us leave the debate here. This final example shows that the standard referent need not be infinite, or even large, to generate the spector of nonstandard reference. Size of the referent doesn't matter because questions can be raised about my current reference even if the case is not a new one. The problem is not that fairly small finite means cannot determine infinite or relatively large referents, but rather that past facts cannot determine the correctness or incorrectness of future usage. Not only do we seem unable to tell the henchman what makes stepping from 1000 to 1002 the same as stepping from 2 to 4, or what makes ◣ the same as △, we can't even seem to say what makes the past tortoiseshell stage a stage of the same thing as the current tortoiseshell stage. (See *PI* 214-217) He will insist, with seeming impunity, on 1004, □, or a stage of the grey cat.

At this point, the henchman's job is done. He has argued that nothing in my past determines my reference to the standard referents rather than to his *referents. Of course, this doesn't mean that we have all in fact been referring to *plus 2 all along. If his arguments are correct, I can just as easily turn the tables on him and insist that nothing in his past determines his reference to *plus 2 rather than to plus 2. This is the conclusion that Wittgenstein draws; he notes that analogous arguments will undermine the claim of determinate reference to any particular referent. We thought that our training or past usage or associations gave us rules for the future usage of our words, so that 1000, 1002 is the correct step in continuing what we call 'plus 2', and □ is not what we call a 'triangle', and this cat rather than that one is called 'Fauve'. According to Wittgenstein, his henchman's success, and the applicability of analogous considerations to any claim of determinate reference, shows that

> no course of action could be determined by a rule, because every course of action can be made out to accord with the rule . . . if everything can be made out to accord with the rule, then it can also be made out to conflict with it. And so there would be neither accord nor conflict here. (*PI* 201)

The usages we thought correct are no more nor less so than those we thought incorrect; our words refer no more to one thing than to any other.[5]

This conclusion is a disaster for the defender of determinate reference. As mentioned earlier, the Fregean semanticist expects the referential connection to be accomplished via senses, the entities grasped during language learning. But if the grasping of a sense is to be the mental act of adopting some sort of rule or paradigm that determines the correctness or incorrectness of future usage, the henchman has cast serious doubt on this notion.[6]

Still, the Fregean account of reference is not the only one available; it is not even the most popular. The Fregean idea has been developed over the years, its most familiar descendants being the various versions of the cluster theory. On such theories, reference is determined by a group of descriptions associated with a word. Unfortunately, the language learner must still use these as rules governing future uses of the term, so the henchman's difficulties are not avoided. All these theories involve the idea that the referent of a term is that which satisfies various requirements, whether they be specified by a sense or by a group of descriptions. In recent years, all such description theories have come under considerable fire, for reasons unrelated to the rule-following problem, and the causal theories have arisen as alternatives. This brings me to my stated aim of assessing the rule-following problem, somewhat proleptically, as a debate between Wittgenstein and the causal theorists.

My goal will be to suggest that the causal theorist has the beginning of a reply to Wittgenstein's sceptical conclusion. This is not to say that the causal theorist's reply need be understood as a further contribution to the debate with the henchman. While the inconclusiveness of that debate seems to show that there are no facts available to me — no facts about my behavior or introspectible mental states — that I can cite to the henchman as fixing my reference to plus 2 rather than to *plus 2, this does not by itself imply the stronger conclusion that there are no facts at all that fix determinate reference. Wittgenstein's sceptical conclusion depends on their being no such facts. I will turn to the causal theory in search of some.

To see how matters stand between Wittgenstein and the causal theorist, I will sketch a typical example of the causal theorist's account, then ask where Wittgenstein would object. What, then, determines the referent of my uses of the word 'gold'? The causal theorist tells an idealized story that begins with the observation that, in most cases, I use the word to refer to that to which the person from whom I learned it used it to refer. This historical chain of borrowed usage stretches back to the introduction of the word in a initial event sometimes called a "baptism." This is when the word's reference is fixed, so it is on this event that we should concentrate.[7]

The baptism of gold is supposed to go something like this. The baptist picks out samples of the metal in question. He points at these, pronounces "gold!", and from that moment, the word refers to whatever is like this,[8] that is, to all members of the natural kind containing the samples. Someone may, in the future, think that samples of iron pyrites are gold, but they are not, because they do not belong to the natural kind in question. Of course, this is just the crudest beginning to an account of reference.[9] The theory is naturally much more subtle than this, but instead of spinning out its details helter-skelter, we can allow Wittgenstein's objections to guide us.

The first of these concerns the ostensive nature of the initial baptism. If the extension of the term 'gold' is to contain everything "like this," the referent of "this" must be determinate. Wittgenstein argues that it is not. The baptist points toward his sample, but who is to say whether he is pointing at the metal, or at its shape, or at its color? And if this question cannot be answered, then the term cannot be said to refer to any particular one among these several natural kinds.

The causal theorist would agree that the gesture of pointing is not enough to pick out the metal as opposed to its shape or color. The unambiguous specification of which of these the baptist meant is actually accomplished by a more structured perceptual connection. Is there any fact of the matter, then, about which of the various possibilities the baptist was actually looking at?

The answer to this question appeals to neurological theory and speculation.[10] The evidence suggests that our ability to perceive develops over time by the growth of neural structures called "cell assemblies." Repeated viewing of a triangular figure first produces an assembly that responds selectively to apexes, then assemblies for base angles, and finally an integrated assembly that responds to triangles. This large assembly incorporates the others, though they can still function independently. Without these assemblies, the pattern of stimulation from causal contact with a triangle is a short-lived and chaotic buzz; with them, that same pattern of stimulation produces a much longer, more organized reverberation. The development of the triangle assembly is what allows us to see the triangle as a unit, as similar to other triangles, to remember it, and so on. In other words, given only the original pattern of stimulation from the triangle, we could only be said to "see" it in the sense in which one "sees" a hidden figure in a complex drawing before one notices it. With the cell assembly, we can be said to perceive the triangle as such.

Suppose now that we have access to the baptist's neural state. We observe the pattern of activity brought about by his perceptual experience of the samples. Presumably some cell assembly has been stimulated.[11] What reason could we have to say that this assembly responds to the metal rather than the shape or color? This now seems quite simple. Imagine that we present the baptist with a number of objects of the same shape as his sample without producing a stimulation of the original assembly. We then present him with a number of yellow objects with the same result. On the other hand, exposure to other gold objects of different shapes does stimulate the orignal assembly. The neural theory just discussed also provides for the development of higher-order assemblies for more general concepts like color, shape, and metal.[12] Suppose we also discover that the assembly first stimulated by our subject's experience of the sample is connected via one of these higher-order assemblies to other assemblies we have reason to believe respond to silver and brass.

I can see no reason to deny that this sort of evidence would strongly support the claim that the baptist saw a metal sample in the first place, that he "meant" the sample for his baptismal act to be the metal, not its color or shape. This is not to say that in order to understand the baptismal act, we must investigate the baptist's brain.[13] The point at issue is whether or not there is a fact about which sample he picked out. The discussion so far is supposed to support the claim that there is such a fact. If there is, then I have properly understood if and only if my understanding matches what he meant. I might do this naturally, in Wittgenstein's words "blindly," or I might get it wrong the first time and have to be corrected, or I might never get the hang of the expression, but there is a fact about which I can be right or wrong.

Alas, the fairly natural potential misunderstandings, like shape and color, that Wittgenstein discusses explicitly in the context of ostensive definition (*PI* 28) do not exhaust his store. Recall, for example, the weird space-time worm the henchman claimed to be the referent of the name 'Fauve'. How can we rule out the possibility that the baptist actually perceived a space-time worm consisting of stages of the gold sample up until tomorrow afternoon and stages of Tom Watson thereafter?

Neural facts might help a bit here because the baptist's neural mechanism would not respond to Tom Watson stages on any day. Unfortunately, this sort of appeal will not go all the way to a solution to this difficulty, but I will postpone for a moment my explanation of why it does not, and what might.

For now I want to discuss several Wittgensteinian objections to the very idea of introducing neural considerations. He writes quite bluntly:

> "Just now I looked at the shape rather than at the colour." Do not let such phrases confuse you. Above all, don't wonder "What can be going on in the eyes or brain?" (*PI*, p. 211)

Unfortunately, it is easier to establish what Wittgenstein thinks here than why he thinks it. Still, I have tried to isolate a number of Wittgensteinian views that might explain this disdain for brain science.

To start with, Wittgenstein sometimes seems to think that everything mental is open to us, or conscious, that nothing mental is ever hidden:

> "How does thought manage to represent?" – the answer might be "Don't you really know? You certainly see it when you think." For nothing is hidden. How does a sentence do it? Nothing is hidden. (*PG* I 63(5-6))

> Now if it is not the causal connections which we are concerned with, then the activities of the mind lie open before us . . . All the facts that concern us lie open before us. (*BlBk*, p. 6)

Of course, we are unaware of the operation of our neural mechanisms, so if all that concerns us is open to view, then neural mechanisms are irrelevant. But this isn't much of an argument. Psychologists have shown that a considerable amount of activity that ought to be considered mental is not open to view. For example, under certain conditions, experimental subjects report no conscious difference between what happens when they add and what happens when they subtract. But in the performance of mental calculations, there must be such a difference, so it must be hidden.[14]

It might be that Wittgenstein holds, along with a number of contemporary physicalists, that there are no type-type correlations (or identities) between psychological and physical states. This is suggested by the following passage:

> No supposition seems to me more natural than that there is no process in the brain correlated . . . with thinking; so that it would be impossible to read off thought-processes from brain-processes . . . Why should there not be a psychological regularity to which *no* physiological regularity corresponds? (*Zettel* 608, 610)

If this were so, then we could not discover correlations (or identities) between physically specified types of neural assemblies and psychologically specified experiences, for example, between activation of a certain type of cell assembly and perceiving a triangle. Fortunately, universal type-type identities of this sort are not required by the above application of neural lore. It isn't necessary that your cell assembly for triangles be physically similar to mine; all that is needed is for the patterns of neural stimulation triangles produce in me to belong to a single physical type. This much is assumed by the fairly well supported scientific theory of cell assemblies. So, even if there are no general type-type correlations, certain very simple psychological states of an individual might be read off that individual's brain state.

Be that as it may, other remarks in the same vicinity as the ones quoted above suggest that Wittgenstein does more than deny the existence of general type-type correlations. Even granting that a given type of psychological state is not correlated with any physically characterizable type of physical state, one might still hold (as suggested above) that such type-type correlations are possible for each individual, or even weaker, simply that every particular psychological event is correlated with (or even identical with) some particular physical event. But Wittgenstein writes:

> It is thus perfectly possible that certain psychological phenomena *cannot* be investigated physiologically because physiologically nothing corresponds to them. (*Zettel* 609)

This could be just to deny the existence of the sort of physiological regularities I claimed above to have scientific support, but perhaps there is more to it than that.

Wittgenstein may be claiming that we could have the psychological properties we do, that we could perceive and refer, with very different bodies, and perhaps even with no bodies at all.[15] If so, even if cell assemblies and such do give a causal account of the mechanisms by which we actually happen to perceive and refer, this sort of account cannot tell us what perceiving and referring actually are:

> But that is only to give a causal connexion: to tell how it has come about that we now go by the sign-post; not what this going-by-the-sign really consists in. (*PI* 198)

In other words, perceiving can't be a matter of cell assemblies because Martians perceive without any neurons at all. Referring can't be the sort of process I've described because in some possible world, my noncorporeal self refers without the help of any causal processes.

If this, or something like it, is Wittgenstein's point, then I think he is making a demand that the causal theorist has every right to reject. The point at issue is the rule-following argument; it challenges the causal theorist to explain how our reference is determinate. The causal theorist pursues this goal by attempting to describe those mechanisms that make it so. Provided with scientific evidence that this is indeed how we perceive or refer, he can cheerfully admit that the Martian and the disembodied ego must accomplish this same task differently. Even those causal theorists who hold that their theory allows reference to be fixed to a given individual or kind across possible worlds explicitly hold that the paticular mechanism of reference-fixing in this world is purely contingent.

The demand that our account of reference be applicable to worlds quite unlike our own may be a preconception acquired from early association with theories like Frege's. Both Frege and the early Wittgenstein held that senses must be given independently of all truth values so that propositions can be understood before investigation into truth values begins. On this model, the sense would determine a referent in any possible world, and it would do so via the same mechanism in each. The causal theorists have rejected this idea; the referent of a name or natural kind term depends on the truth values of a number of statements describing various facts of the term's causal history and the features of the initial baptism. Though his rule-following argument undermines the Fregean theory, Wittgenstein seems inclined to retain one of its features as a requirement on future theories.[16]

A second inappropriate demand Wittgenstein places on the causal theorists is that their analyses of psychological notions be conceptual:

> "But this isn't *seeing*!" — "But this is seeing!" — It must be possible to give both these remarks a conceptual justification . . . "This phenomenon is at first surprising, but a physiological explanation of it will certainly be found" — Our problem is not a causal but a conceptual one. (*PI*, p. 203)

But if the point at issue is whether or not our reference is determinate, all that is needed is an account of how this is possible, and there is no reason such an account need be conceptual rather than scientific. Wittgenstein holds that philosophy in general is conceptual rather than empirical (*PI* 90), but it is jumping the gun to decide ahead of time that what makes reference determinate must be philosophical in this sense.

Wittgenstein might think he has outflanked the causal theorist by starting with conceptual analysis because his own conceptual analysis rules out the causal theorist's method of response to the rule-following problem. His analysis purportedly reveals that there could be no reference without a community of referrers, but even if this is true, it does not establish his stronger conclusion that the practice of this community is the mechanism that determines reference. Though conceptual analysis may reveal that referring is a practice employed by a linguistic community, the referents of particular expressions in that community's language might still depend on mechanisms peculiar to that community and the world it inhabits: no reference without community, but community reference determined by community-specific mechanisms and circumstances.

Assuming that these considerations open the way for an account of the sort the causal theorist has embarked upon, let us retrace our steps and see where the debate now stands. Wittgenstein has argued that reference is indeterminate. The defender of determinate reference has responded by discarding theories of the Fregean variety that seem particularly susceptible to the rule-following argument and setting out to elaborate a version of the causal theory instead. In the particular case of 'gold', the defender claims that reference is determined by means of an initial baptism in which the baptist picks out samples of gold and fixes the reference of the term to whatever is "like this."

Wittgenstein has responded that the baptist's pointing to a sample does not tell us how the sample is "meant," that is, whether the baptist wishes us to attend to the metal, the shape, the color, or whatever. The causal theorist replied that the baptist's "meaning" depends on what the baptist perceives when he attends to the sample, and that neural facts could give substance to the claim that he perceived the metal rather than its shape or color. At this point, I admitted that these considerations could not rule out the more unusual alternative percepts. This problem was temporarily shelved, however, and I went on to argue that various possibly Wittgensteinian arguments against the relevance of neural evidence were not conclusive.

Keeping the problem of wildly nonstandard alternative percepts on the shelf for a while longer, let us suppose that the problem of isolating the baptist's samples has been overcome, that is, that the "this" in "like this" is determinate. The next problem naturally concerns the "like." The extension of the term is to consist of whatever is like those samples. What determines this?

Let's consider a tempting but incorrect answer first. Recall that what the baptist perceives when presented with his samples is determined (except for our shelved question) by the particular cell assembly stimulated on that occasion. Obviously whatever else stimulates that same assembly is in some way similar to the sample. The temptation is to say that this similarity is the "like" in "like this," that the extension of the term 'gold' consists of whatever stimulates that assembly.

This tempting account seems to solve all our problems. To see this, recall that cell assemblies are formed for perceiving triangles; an elaboration of this process allows for a higher-order assembly responsive to my tortoiseshell cat. Suppose, then, that my past experience has produced such cell assemblies in me, and that my linguistic training has produced further neural connections between these and my auditory and visual assemblies for recognition of the words 'triangle' and 'Fauve'.[17] If Wittgenstein's henchman now shows me the figure □, I will deny that it is a triangle; presented with the tortoiseshell, I will insist that it is Fauve. When the henchman objects, I may not know what to say to defend myself, but the fact remains that his figure does not stimulate the assembly associated with my use of the word 'triangle', and the tortoiseshell cat does stimulate my 'Fauve' assembly. I appeal to no explicit rule that might be misinterpreted; I point to no ambiguous class of examples; rather, my learning experiences with examples have "wired in" a rule I simply obey.[18] Given my neural setup, I would be wrong to call □ a triangle, and I am right to call the tortoiseshell cat 'Fauve'.

Unfortunately, there are three quite serious objections to this proposal. First, there are too many physical limitations on the performance of the baptist's cell assembly.[19] Pieces of gold that are too small, too large, too far away, too tarnished, will not stimulate it, and pieces of iron pyrites will. Similarly, ◣ is a triangle and □ is not because one stimulates my triangle assembly and the other doesn't, but this method will not determine my usage for geometric figures of astronomical size. Finally, behavior of my cell assembly won't distinguish between Fauve and a space-time worm with stages of the grey cat beginning after I'm dead. (Suppose both cats outlive me.)

The second objection depends on the simple observation that machines, even neural ones, do malfunction:

We talk as if these parts could only move in this way, as if they could not do anything else. How is this—do we forget the possibility of their bending, breaking off, melting, and so on. (*PI* 193 [2])

Occasionally, the 'gold' assembly will misfire and either admit a piece of nongold to the extension of the term 'gold' or exclude a piece of real gold. But in this case we want to say that I've gone wrong, not that I'm actually referring to some nonstandard extension. The problem is that if the referent of my uses of the word 'gold' is determined solely by the behavior of the associated assembly, no sense can be made of the claim that it has misfired.[20]

The final objection to the tempting proposal that the extension of the term 'gold' is determined solely by the behavior of the baptist's cell assembly is perhaps the most serious: the explanation this account offers is of the wrong type. In Wittgenstein's words:

"How am I able to obey a rule?"—if this is not a question about causes, then it is about the justification for my following the rule in the way that I do. (*PI* 217)

The best the suggested causal account can do is to account for the fact that the baptist will use the term 'gold' to refer to gold objects in terms of a neural connection that has been formed between the cell assembly involved in the baptism and the cell assembly responsive to the word type 'gold'. But what we are out to explain isn't the fact: if he means gold by 'gold', he will say . . . . What we want to understand is: if he means gold by 'gold', he should say . . . . In other words, a purely causal account can only tell us how the baptist goes on to use the word, not why his baptismal act justifies him in so using it. In Kripke's words: "The relation of meaning and intention to future action is *normative, not descriptive.*"[21]

Thus this natural first attempt at determining what counts as "like" fails. It fails because it loses sight of the structure of the causal theorist's first sketch of his account. The interpretation of the word "like" in "like this" was by no means left up for grabs; the whole idea is that by isolating a sample, the baptist fixes the reference of the term to members of its natural kind. It isn't up to the baptist to determine what belongs in the same kind as his sample; the world determines that. His cell assembly only functions to pick out that determinate sample, so it need not be universally applicable or infallible. This is why, presented with another member of his sample's natural kind, the baptist should call it 'gold' even if the various causal mechanisms fail and he does not.[22]

This reply also applies to triangles. Our cell assemblies allow us to perceive the similarities between various triangles, but they are not the final arbiters of membership in the kind—that final arbiter is the world. It is a brute fact that triangular figures are more similar to one another than to squares and that a natural grouping corresponds to this similarity. Our neural structures allow us to perceive the similarity between triangular figures of medium size against suitable backgrounds because perceptually similar entities stimulate the same cell assembly. But our reference is to the underlying kind responsible for that perceptual similarity, so the extension of our term includes triangles too large to stimulate our similarity detect-ing mechanisms. Just as iron pyrites might stimulate the cell assembly for 'gold' without being gold, a quadrilateral with one angle so close to $180°$ as to be indis-tinguishable from a straight line might stimulate our triangle assembly without being a triangle because it is not a member of the kind to which our reference is fixed. And, of course, cell assemblies might occasionally misfire on their own. The assem-bly is a fallible detector of the phenomenal similarity, and the phenomenal similari-ty is a fallible detector of membership in the kind; none of this alters the fact that our reference is to the kind of the initial samples.

Wittgenstein's objection at this point might be that the world is not pre-packaged into natural kinds independently of our linguistic activity. This ia a per-fectly legitimate premise, but it is just that. The causal theorist, on the other hand, begins from the realist's idea that the world consists of individuals that behave as they do on account of enjoying various real and objective properties. Though an individual has all sorts of properties, the natural ones are those that correspond to objective similarities or traits, those that figure in correct scientific explanations of its behavior. Our causal theorist considers it a brute fact that pieces of gold are more like one another than they are like pieces of silver or bodies of water, and that these similarities account for the behavior of gold. These are no more nor less un-defended premises than Wittgenstein's, and the debate is once more at a standoff.[23]

To return to the beginning, the causal theorist's story starts with the baptist's perception of his sample. He perceives the gold on this occasion, rather than the sample's shape or color, because the cell assembly involved responds selectively to the constellation of goldlike qualities (luster, weight, color, etc.) rather than to the shape or color. This brings us back to the problem I set aside some time ago; what has not yet been answered is why we should take this perception to be of the gold sample rather than some weird space-time worm involving stages of it and later stages of Tom Watson. The assembly is responding selectively to this "object" as well. Once again, we may be tempted to appeal to further properties of the baptist's cell assembly—such as its reactions at different times, and so on—but this approach will not work against space-time worms that diverge, say, after the baptist's death.

These difficulties are analogous to those presented by the first proposal for the determination of "like"-ness. What counts as "like" cannot be left to the capac-ity of the assembly, nor can the determination of the object of perception. Instead, we must view the world from the causal theorist's scientific perspective. The bap-tist's cell assembly is stimulated by (and incidentally, developed by contact with) some aspect of the world. In our case, the experimental evidence suggests that that aspect is whatever aspect of the sample is responsible for what I called before its goldlike qualities. And what aspect of reality is that?

For the answer, we must turn to our current scientific theories. The best ex-planation they offer for the goldlike properties of gold, and for the formation and stimulation of the associated cell assembly, involves the membership of the samples in the natural kind "gold." Having atomic number 79 is what accounts for pieces of gold having the phenomenal properties that they do, and having the phenomenal properties it does is what accounts for the sample's stimulation of the baptist's assembly.[24] This is why the realist would say that the baptist perceived a piece of gold, rather than a shape, or one of the more bizarre alternatives. The point is that neither the shape nor the gold-Watson worm plays the appropriate explanatory role.

This line of thought suggests a treatment of the case of reference to individuals. Just as it is a brute fact that one triangle is more like another than like a square, a cat is a more natural individual than a composite worm.[25] The question of what fixes my reference to one rather than the other reduces to that of what I perceive on the occasion of baptism, and the scientific account of my perceptual experience involves the natural individual rather than the unnatural one. Thus the referent of the name 'Fauve' is the tortoiseshell cat, not the henchman's worm, because the former, not the latter, plays the appropriate causal role in the scientific explanation of my perceptual experience on the occasion of baptism.

Unfortunately, these appeals to the scientific account of perceptual experience are not conclusive. We must ask: What justifies our causal theorist in denying that it is the sample's membership in the kind of things with atomic number 79 up to a point and with features of Tom Watson thereafter that accounts for its stimulation of the baptist's assembly? Or that the odd space-time worm is causally responsible for my perceptual experience when I name my cat? Any current causal powers produced by membership in the kind "gold" will also be produced by membership in the weird kind; any current causal role enjoyed by Fauve is shared by the odd worm. What justifies the choice of one rather than the other?

It's easy to guess what the causal theorist would answer: his preferences are justified because "gold" is a natural kind, and the tortoiseshell cat is a natural individual, while the others are not. Natural individuals and kinds correspond to objective traits, figure in true scientific explanations, while the weird kind and odd worm do no such thing. But what justification is there for this claim?

Let us take stock for a moment. Suppose we grant the causal theorist's scientific assumptions rather than Wittgenstein's premises, grant that the world has an objective structure of natural individuals and kinds. Then our causal theorist can insist that on the occasion of baptism, the baptist has perceived an individual chunk of the stuff that our best scientific theory says is responsible for the stimulation of his cell assembly and that he has fixed the reference of the term 'gold' to the natural kind of which that sample is a member. Thus his reference *is* determinate. But the only way the causal theorist can go on to claim that his perception is of a chunk of gold rather than a weird composite worm, and that the determinate reference is to the kind "gold" rather than a weird kind, is by showing that chunks of gold and the kind "gold" are objective, while the weird objects and kinds are not.

How, then, can the causal theorist be sure that his kinds and individuals are the natural ones, and the henchman's are not? I think the answer here is that he cannot. In any particular case, say when the henchman claims that a chunk of aluminum is more like the sample of gold than another chunk of gold is, the causal theorist cannot be conclusively certain that the henchman is wrong. He can cite various reasons for thinking that the henchman has gotten the objective similarities wrong, for example, that our well-confirmed scientific theories would be much disturbed by the henchman's claim, that he doubts a similarly useful and elegant theory could be developed around the henchman's proposed similarities, that the success of the scientific theory based on his own similarities counts as evidence for their correctness.[26] But evidence of this sort can never produduce certainty. Science is always fallible, so long as truth is nonepistemic. Still, the scepticism involved here is ordinary epistemological scepticism about our ability to know what the objective similarities are, not metaphysical scepticism about whether there is a fact of the matter about which piece of metal is really gold.

As was suggested at the outset, none of this appeal to neural facts, natural kinds, the success of science, and so on, would do me any good in a renewed debate with the henchman. If the causal account were presented with an eye to winning that debate after all, the henchman might agree with all my neural theories, with my account of baptism, with my view that the world comes with objective divisions into natural kinds and individuals as this account requires, and so on, and still disagree with me on the next usage of "plus 2" or "triangle." ("Yes," he says, "triangles are the things that stimulate the cell assembly we agreed on, but you're confused again. *This*, not *that*, is the cell assembly we agreed on.") I seem no better off than when the first phase of debate ended. I am unable to convince the henchman; Wittgenstein seems free to step in and draw his sceptical conclusion about the complete indeterminacy of reference.

Obviously, then, this talk about neurons and natural kinds must be seen as part of my meta-debate with Wittgenstein, and not as part of the object level debate with his henchman. Wittgenstein draws his radical conclusion from his perspective above the fray, and I step up to meet him, denying that my inability to refute the henchman has the consequence he claims it does. At this level, I argue that reference is not radically indeterminate, that it is determined by various neural and causal facts. Thus there is a fact of the matter about which of us in the object level debate—me or the henchman—is right. I may not be able to convince the henchman that I am the one who's right, I may not even be absolutely certain at the meta-level about which of us is right, but there is a fact about which one of us is right and one of us is wrong. This is what Wittgenstein denied.

In fact, I think the reason I can't answer the henchman, even after I've given my answer to Wittgenstein, actually has to do with the rhetorical features of verbal debate. When I propose that it is such-and-such that determines reference, I must do so in words. The henchman can then interpret those words according to his own lights. It's as if I'd presented him with another explicit rule for determining reference: "the referent of my use of 'triangle' is whatever bears such-and-such causal relations to such-and-such neural structures." But we know that no such explicit rule will do. My proposal isn't that this rule is what determines reference, but the facts that I describe in this way. I'd refer perfectly well, I claim, in complete ignorance of those facts. It is the causal and neural facts themselves, not my scientific theory of them, that determine reference. But within a verbal debate, one can't point to those facts without describing them in words. Thus the henchman has a natural advantage simply because the debate is a linguistic exercise.

Finally, it should also be acknowledged that even with the added detail forced by Wittgensteinian objections, the causal theory of reference is still just the idealized beginning of an account. I would like to discuss just one point at which further elaboration is needed because it illuminates the central role of the perceptual mechanisms discussed here. The difficulty I have in mind comes out clearly even in the chosen example of the term 'gold'. The proposal is that reference is fixed to the natural kind membership in which is responsible for the sample's ability to stimulate the baptist's cell assembly. Since the sample is gold, and having atomic number 79 is what gives gold the phenomenal properties it has, and having the phenomenal properties it has is what makes the sample stimulate the appropriate assembly, reference is fixed to the kind whose members have that atomic number. The trouble is that the baptist might have had several samples, one of which was actually iron pyrites, or even one sample that was a combination of the two. In these cases, the iron pyrites would also have stimulated the baptist's assembly because it has the same phenomenal properties as gold. To which kind would the baptist's reference be fixed?

At the outset, I suppose the causal theorist may be forced to allow modification of the standard Tarskian framework to provide for some device like partial reference. But as science progresses, chemists will come to realize that gold and iron pyrites belong to different kinds, and they will do so on the basis of evidence from various mechanical detectors and measuring devices. At that point, the behavior of these devices can be called upon to sharpen the reference-fixing for a scientific term like 'gold'. The kind referred to will not only have to figure in the correct acaccount of the sample's ability to stimulate the baptist's perceptual cell assembly, it must play a similar role in the account of the behavior of those mechanical detectors and measurers. Reference can be narrowed down in this way.

But this use of machines to narrow reference could not universally replace the perceptual account. Neural connections between perceptual assemblies for samples and perceptual assemblies for word types are "wired in," as it were; they are not conscious rules subject to henchmanlike reinterpretation. The role of scientific instruments is not so primitive. When we narrow our reference by saying that real gold must affect this instrument in such and such a way, we are employing an explicit rule that could be reinterpreted in a henchmanlike way. ("By 'the blue needle' you really mean a composite space-time worm consisting of . . . .") The sting is removed from this reprise of the henchman's maneuvers only by the fact that the reference of the various simpler terms in the explicit rule has already been fixed by the more primitive method.

I have tried to sketch the beginning of an account of how the causal theory of determinate reference might be defended against Wittgenstein's rule-following argument. At several points, I have described the debate as coming to an impasse, a difference in the constitutive premises of the positions of which the causal theory and the rule-rollowing argument are parts. If Wittgenstein's argument is to force the defender of determinate reference into retreat, it must be supplemented with attacks on these constitutive premises. These can undoubtedly be found or constructed, but I hope something is accomplished by pushing the debate back a bit. As far as the preliminary considerations sketched here are concerned, I see no conclusive reason why the causal theorist cannot still maintain that □ is not a triangle because it is not a member of the natural kind by virtue of membership in which the original baptist's sample stimulated his cell assembly, and that the grey cat is not Fauve because she is not the individual who plays the appropriate explanatory role in the scientific account of my perceptual experience when I introduced the same. This leaves only the mathematical case, but that is a problem for another occasion.[27]

Notes

1. This research was supported by an AAUW fellowship and a sabbatical leave from the University of Notre Dame, both of which are gratefully acknowledged. The rule-following problem discussed here may be more Kripke's than Wittgenstein's, but I have avoided that issue for now, as well as comparisons with related contemporary problems such as Quine's indeterminacy of reference, Putnam's model theoretic argument, and Goodman's new riddle of induction. This version has benefited from my conversations and correspondence with John Burgess, Hartry Field, Michael Friedman, Anil Gupta, Pat Manfredi, Carolyn McMullen, Donna Summerfield, Steven Wagner, and Mark Wilson, though not as much as they might have hoped, and certainly not enough to produce much agreement from any of them.

References to Wittgenstein's writings are incorporated in the text. *PI* is *Philosophical Investigations* (New York, 1953), *PG* is *Philosophical Grammar* (Berkeley, 1974), *BlBk* is the first of the *Blue and Brown Books* (New York, 1965), *RFM* is *Remarks on the Foundations of Mathematics*, revised edition (Cambridge, 1978), and *Zettel* is *Zettel* (Berkeley, 1970).

2. Two remarks are in order. First, the causal theorist needn't demand that reference be completely determinate; some cases of partial or failed reference are surely allowable. Still, Wittgenstein's full indeterminacy is surely unallowable. Second, by confining our consideration of the rule-following problem to extensional rather than intensional matters, we are spared irrelevant worries over what constitutes sense or meaning. Kripke seems to agree that nothing of the core of the problem is lost in making such a move. See S. Kripke, *Wittgenstein on Rules and Private Language* (Cambridge, 1982), 9-10 and n. 8. My account here of the rule-following problem derives from Kripke's extremely helpful book. Thus the reservations expressed there — ". . . to attempt to present Wittgenstein's argument precisely is to some extent to falsify it" (p. 5) — are in order here as well.

3. I hope my choice of words here will not be felt to be offensive. A henchman is a "trusted helper or follower" according to my dictionary. I only mean to suggest that this helper of Wittgenstein's has taken on the task of engaging in the ensuing debate so that Wittgenstein is free to draw his own conclusions from a perspective outside the arena.

4. In this phase of the debate, the henchman's strongest argument is the simple empirical fact that I can find no such inner state when I introspect. If there were such a state, I could defuse the two thought experiments he suggests by denying that the cases he imagines are in fact possible. For a somewhat related conclusion, though from a different perspective, see Kripke, *Wittgenstein on Rules*, 41-51.

5. Of course this is only an interim conclusion for Wittgenstein, what he calls his "paradox." He will later introduce his new approach to language, based on the notion of criteria, in order to overcome the paradox. The criteriological approach is the source of his startling positions on private language and mathematics. See Kripke, ibid., chap. 3.

6. Compare Kripke, ibid., 54.

7. It may be that attention to the historical chain of borrowed reference would reintroduce

referential indeterminacy even if the baptist's reference is determinate. I will confine myself to the baptismal problem here.

8. Often accounts of the initial baptism involve the baptist reciting some formula like "these and everything like them are gold" or "gold is whatever is like this." As Kripke points out (ibid., 59, n. 45), no utterance of this sort can do the job here because each word is subject to the henchman's reinterpretations. I have suppressed these incantations because they are not essential to the account given in the text; the perceptual connections described below constitute the speaker's contribution to the determination of the extension of the term. This should be borne in mind when I use the expression "like this."

9. For one detailed version of the causal theory, see Devitt's *Designation* (New York, 1981). He replaces the overly simple notion of an initial baptism with a more subtle account involving multiple "groundings." Of course, no causal theorist would suggest that all reference is accomplished via causal chains. (See Devitt, 202-3; Putnam, *Reason, Truth and History* [Cambridge, 1981], 52-53.) I will limit my attention here to simple terms learned by ostension.

10. This neural theory is presented in D. O. Hebb, *The Organization of Behavior* (New York, 1949), especially chaps. 4 and 5. See also his more popular *Essay on Mind*, (Hillsdale, N.J., 1980).

11. Actually, many cell assemblies may be stimulated on a given occasion because the baptist will often see the metal, the color, and the shape. However, if his attention is predisposed to one of these, as it presumably is on the occasion of baptism, this should show up in a higher, perhaps more prolonged, level of activity in the associated assembly. (For a discussion of the mechanism of selection, see Hebb, *Essay on Mind*, 86-87.) This accentuated assembly is the one we are concerned with here. When I speak below of the object the baptist perceived, I mean the one that stimulated the accentuated assembly. (See *PI* 666)

12. These involve parts of many lower-level assemblies. For discussion, see Hebb, *Essay on Mind*, 107-10.

13. Kripke agrees that the henchman's challenge is not epistemological. See *Wittgenstein on Rules*, 21, 38-39.

14. See Hebb's *Essay on Mind* (18-19) for a discussion of this particular experiment. Unfortunately, the experiment cited doesn't really decide the case against Wittgenstein. He would agree that there is no introspectible difference between adding and subtracting here, but conclude that nothing mental determines the reference of these terms and that they must be understood criteriologically. I want to insist that the mental need not be introspectible, and thus that something mental might still help here with the job of fixing reference.

Kripke (ibid., 49-51) also suggests that some mental states are not introspectible.

15. The quoted passages from *Zettel* are hard to interpret conclusively, so it may be that Wittgenstein would not have endorsed the idea of disembodied reference. (Though see *PG* 64[2].) But even if he wouldn't have, it seems Kripke would. (See his defense of Cartesianism in "Naming and Necessity," in *Semantics for Natural Language*, 2nd ed., edited by D. Davidson and G. Harman (Dordrecht, 1972), 253-355). I will consider this line even if it is not Wittgenstein's because it is open to the Wittgensteinian.

16. Of course, Wittgenstein's own criteriological view of reference doesn't satisfy the requirement in question, but he might still expect it of a semantic theory of the traditional sort, that is, one according to which language is learned in such a way as to predetermine the correctness or incorrectness of future uses.

17. For a discussion of this sort of connection, see Hebb, *Essay on Mind*, 108-11.

18. In his review (*New York Review of Books*, October 23, 1980, 47-50) of *Rules and Representations* (New York, 1980), Hacking suggests a move of this sort for Chomsky, though Chomsky himself makes no explicit mention of the rule-following problem.

19. Though this objection is quite natural and obvious, I have not found it in Wittgenstein. Kripke apparently hasn't either (*Wittgenstein on Rules*, 6, n. 7), but he states it himself quite forcefully (26-27, 34).

20. See Kripke's discussion of this problem, ibid., 28-30, 34-35. It might be thought that

these first two objections could be handled by the addition of a ceteris paribus clause, but Kripke shows that such efforts are ineffective because they presuppose an understanding of which uses are correct.

21. Kripke, ibid., 37.

22. I have argued here that the causal theorist's account is normative rather than descriptive. One must follow the rule in this way because it alone agrees with the actual structure of the world. This meets Wittgenstein's requirement that an account of reference provide a justification if 'justification' is taken in the sense that a move is justified if it is correct, or a belief is justified if it is true. Wittgenstein may have more in mind, that is, 'justification' in the sense that a speaker has some support for having moved as he did, or for believing what he does. I don't have space to address this notion here, but I think that the causal genesis can be justificatory. See Goldman, "Innate Knowledge," in *Innate Ideas*, edited by S. Stich (Berkeley, 1975), 111-20, and "What is Justified Belief?" in *Justification and Knowledge*, edited by G. Pappas (Dordrecht, 1979), 1-23.

23. Natural kinds here are meant as objective similarities or traits of the world. They need not be essences of any sort, and their naturalness need not be all or nothing; it is somewhat more plausible as a matter of degree. For discussion of this notion, see Quine, "Natural Kinds," *Ontological Relativity and Other Essays* (New York, 1969), 114-38.

The assumption of objective natural kinds has come under considerable fire recently from Putnam in "Why There Isn't a Ready-made World," *Synthese* 51(1982):141-67, where he argues that our classificatory schemes depend on our interests and not upon objective features of the world. There are hints of this line of thought in Wittgenstein: "Concepts lead us to make investigations; are the expression of our interests, and direct our interests." (*PI* 570) Still, I think the odd classificatory behavior of some of Wittgenstein's tribes is designed to show that our schemes are contingent, not that they are interest relative. (See again *PI* 230.) In these cases, there is every reason to suppose that the physical circumstances and/or the tribe member's experiences are different from ours. When the facts to be explained are different, it is to be expected that different natural kinds will figure in the explanation. In any case, there is no room for doubt that Putnam argues for the interest relativity of our "natural" kinds. I hope to discuss interest-relativity in connection with his position elsewhere.

Finally, Donna Summerfield has suggested that Wittgenstein's objection to the natural kind picture would be that it is part and parcel of a non-Humean account of causation. If this is correct, the debate with the causal theorist will reduce (at least in part) to a debate over the nature of causation, and Kripke's analogy between Humean and Wittgensteinian scepticism is more than that.

24. It might be that a cell assembly, understood as a detecting device, can be seen as measuring several equally natural kinds. (See Mark Wilson, "Predicate Meets Property," *Philosophical Review* 91 [1982]; 549-89.) If so, I would propose to treat these cases of partial reference. (See Field, "Quine and the Correspondence Theory," *Philosophical Review* 83 [1974]:200-28, and Devitt, *Designation*.)

25. See Kripke's lectures on the primitiveness of object identity over time. It should be noted that the unnatural individuals considered by the henchman are not of the same type as Quine's undetached rabbit parts. (For a discussion of the connections between Wittgenstein's argument and Quine's, see Kripke, *Wittgenstein on Rules*, 14-15, 55-58.) One important difference between Quine's argument for indeterminacy of reference and the rule-following argument as presented here is that examples like that of undetached rabbit parts involve issues of individuation and numeration rather than simpler matters of qualitative similarity. For this reason, Quine's examples cannot be discussed independently of mathematics.

26. Some general methodological principles of the sort cited by Wilson in "Maxwell's Condition—Goodman's Problem," *British Journal for the Philosophy of Science* 30 (1979): 107-23, might also help.

27. Readers of "Perception and Mathematical Intuition," *Philosophical Review* 89 (1980), 163-96, will realize that I intend a very similar account for mathematics.

Semantical Anthropology[1]

JOSEPH ALMOG

The association between the smell and the bacon is "natural", that is to say it is not the result of any human behavhior. But the association between the word "breakfast" and breakfast is a social matter, which exists only for English speaking people.

—B. Russell, "An Inquiry into Meaning and Truth"

1. E. T. AND HIS TRANSPLANETARY INVESTIGATIONS

Imagine that Twin Earth is inhabited by beings who use a language that is phonetically, morphologically, and syntactically identical to English.[2] In fact, it is even a semantical duplicate of Earthly English, except for two words: 'I' and 'you'. For whereas on Earth 'I' means, roughly, "The agent of the context" and 'you' means "the addressee of the context," on Twin Earth their *linguistic meanings* have been permuted. That is, the community on TE uses 'I' to refer to the addressee and 'you' to the agent.[3]

Imagine the Earthling Hilary Putnam on a visit to TE face-to-face with his TE doppelganger, Hilary Mantup. Suppose Putnam says to Mantup with true generosity, "You are charming," to which Mantup responds with "You are charming." Interestingly enough, despite the fact that their phonetically identical sentences *mean* different things, the content (proposition) they express *is* the same, i.e., that Hilary Mantup is charming. In fact, it is precisely because their two sentences mean different things that the content so determined can be one and the same. They would have used two sentences with the *same* meaning if one and only one of them had used 'I' instead of 'You'.

We should not confuse the above situation with the recent Twin Earth cases due to Putnam. In those Putnamian cases, when we move from Earth to TE, we *vary* the objectual reference of the expression under consideration but we keep a crucial semantic factor (maybe the very linguistic meaning) *invariant*. When Putnam's doppelgangers Castor and Pollux both say 'I am hungry', they both use 'I' to refer to themselves. That is, both operate under the *same* linguistic conventions. In our case, we *vary* those very linguistic conventions.

The question is: *Why do the two (phonetically identical) sentences used by Putnam and Mantup mean what they mean?* I want to put forward a picture. Let us engage ourselves in the following piece of fictional (Martian) anthropology. A Martian, whom we shall call "E. T.," is sent down to investigate the ways in which Earthlings and Twin Earthlings use words. This Martian anthropologist is not handicapped by time constraints. He lives as long as he wishes and can really be thought of as an "omniscient observer of the history of Earth and TE."[4] After observing the users on Earth and the users on TE over a period of a thousand years, he goes back to Mars. He then reports his findings in the Martian Journal of Sociolinguistics.

E. T.'s first field assignment on Earth is to investigate the history of the Earthlings' use of 'I'. He reports that at some point in the history of the English language on Earth, 'I' became a well-formed expression endowed with a specific linguistic meaning. E. T. poses now the following question: How is this relevant to the *present* use of the word 'I' on Earth?

Well, says our learned Martian, let us ask ourselves: what was preserved across the Earthly history of uses of the word 'I' from its "conception" until this very day? It is surely not the *extension* (reference) of the first use of 'I' that was preserved. Each one of the Earthlings refers to himself when he uses 'I', not to that pioneer. Nor is what is preserved the *in*tension. The intension determined on that first occasion of use *is* the extension, if we accept what seems to E. T. the uncontroversial fact that 'I' is directly referential. The hallmark of directly referential expressions is that their *ex*tensions determine their *in*tensions (and not vice versa) and so if the extension was not preserved, the intension wasn't preserved either.[5]

Maybe, suggests E. T., we can make some progress by asking ourselves: What did each of the Earthlings *learn* when he became a competent user of 'I'? It seems that when R. Reagan learned the word 'I', he learned a linguistic rule, a rule that, for any context, tells us that 'I' refers to the agent of that context. It is this rule, says E. T., that has been preserved.[6] It is because the first English users of the word 'I' on Earth used it to refer to the agent of the context, rather than to the addressee of the context, that the rule:

[R(I)] For any context c, 'I' refers to the agent of c

describes the current actual meaning of 'I' in Earthly English and, in particular, H. Putnam's use. If 'I' *were* originally associated with the rule:

[R(I)*] For any context c, 'I' refers to the addressee of c,

'I' would have meant in the mouths of the present users of English on Earth what 'you' actually means in their mouths. This, our Martian friend reports, is exactly what happened on TE. Their actual history originated with an association of the word 'I' with the rule [R(I)*] and their current use, and in particular Mantup's use, is regulated by *that* history. For them, the association of 'I' with the Earthly [*R*(I)] is just a *counter*factual historical possibility.

Driving his point home, E. T. offers now his general picture:

A word is introduced into the language of the given community. The originators have a privileged role: They don't *learn* the meaning of the word, they *stipulate* it.[7] Having made this decision and generated this ongoing activity, they seem to have initiated a practice. As the originators grow old, new candidates are trained to join the community and its practices. Newcomers must come to use the word in the way the competent users in the community use it. If it is observed that a newcomer fails to conform, he is corrected by those with linguistic authority. Years go by. The originators are long gone but their original practices are preserved because the learning process is literally transitive. Any deviations can be ruthlessly uprooted in the name of authority. The authority stands for what was intended by the fathers and what came to be the standard in the community. There is nothing in the given meaning assignment *itself*, sociohistorical facts aside, that makes it privileged in any way over the others. Its "standardness" is due to the fact that the community has adopted it as a standard.

In short, testifies E. T., an almost *"recursive"* principle for the specification of the actual linguistic meaning reigning in a given community has been discovered:

[*M*] For any competent speaker *S* of community *C* at time *t* and any expression '*E*', the actual linguistic meaning of '*E*' at *S*'s mouth at *t* is that meaning that '*E*' was endowed with by the originators of the practice of *C* at t_0.[8]

E. T. sums up his discussion by making the following observation: The role that historical chains and principle [*M*] perform on this picture is a *presemantic* role. This contrasts with the rules we have encountered earlier. For these early rules, [*R*(I)], [*R*(you)], perform a *semantic* role. Principles like

[*R*(I)] In any context *c*, 'I' refers to the agent of *c*

[*R*(you)] In any context *c*, 'you' refers to the addressee of *c*

are rules that govern the *reference* of the words 'I' and 'you' on *Earth*. On the other hand, the historical chains, and in particular principle [*M*], operate at a *presemantic* level. They regulate the *very correlation of syntactic shapes with such rules of reference*. There is here a strict conceptual and formal order. Formally, the evaluation of sentences must start with a specification of the relevant value of the historical chain parameter. We must specify the meaning assignment that is assumed for the rest of the evaluation. Only when this meaning assignment has been specified can we go on to determine which proposition has been expressed in the given context by the given sentence and whether that proposition is true or false in the given possible world with respect to which we evaluate. Corresponding to this formal observation, a very neat (four-level) conceptual hierarchy emerges: Suppose we want to evaluate the sentence 'I am hungry'. First let us look at 'I'. The *presemantic* principles have as input the well-formed English expression 'I'. They yield as output, on Earth, the linguistic meaning encoded by [R(I)]. This output is taken in turn and applied in a given context c (say, where I am the user). Relative to the specific history and the context, we now have the propositional constituent: J. Almog. We can now take that propositional constituent and the propositional constituent obtained in the same way for the predicate "hungry" and move to our final stage. We now investigate whether J. Almog is in fact hungry in the state of affairs ("possible world") with respect to which we want to evaluate this proposition.

2. WHAT THE PRESENT PICTURE IS NOT I: RULES OF REFERENCE

E. T. argues that the picture presented so far is not a causal theory of reference. Why is E. T.'s picture not a causal theory of reference? It is not a theory of *reference* at all. Well aware of the impact of the earlier work on proper names by his colleague S. A. Kripke, he offers the following reconstruction of Kripke's picture. On E. T.'s reading, what Kripke has offered us is a basis for a general sociohistorical theory of *linguistic meaning*. Just as a sociohistorical (so called, "causal") theory of reference is supposed to preserve *reference* across the historical chain, a sociohistorical theory of linguistic meaning is supposed to preserve *linguistic meaning* across the historical chain.[9] E. T.'s picture of linguistic meaning transmission applies to *any* basic expression of the language. This raises the following question: How does this picture apply to proper names?

A direct reference semantics of proper names in English (like the semantics of Kripke) should maintain that names are just tags. As Mill and Russell taught us, this means that all that there is to the linguistic function of names is to refer.[10] It follows that Kripke and Donnellan were correct in their claim that historical chains preserve reference. It is *no* surprise that they were right: The historical chain preserves the *linguistic meaning* of any expression. In the case of names, all there is to this meaning is to stand for the given referent. Ergo, the chain preserves the fact that the name stands for that referent.[11]

When we investigate the role of the chain, it is crucial to distinguish the *assignment* process from the *value* of that assignment. The chain *assigns* a meaning to a name. It is not part of the rule of reference that formulates the meaning of the name.[12] Take the name 'Hilary Putnam'. The actual history of uses assigns to that syntactic shape, the meaning that I shall roughly describe as: to-refer-to-H. Putnam.[13] Counterfactual chains assign different meanings to this syntactic shape. For instance: To-refer-to-the-individual-S. A. Kripke. It could well have been the case that Kripke was named by his parents 'H. Putnam' (and, for that matter, Putnam might have been dubbed 'S. A. Kripke').

Now, the picture presented so far includes a *unique* actual historical chain and countless counterfactual historical chains. This picture may be adequate for the treatment of the intuition that 'H. Putnam' might have had the meaning:

to-refer-to-Kripke, and 'table' might have meant what 'chair' actually means. But the picture seems to be in trouble with the undeniable fact that many individuals on *a given planet in the actual world* bear the same name (type). That is, our picture may seem to run into problems with the fact that many people here on Earth are actually called 'John Smith', or the fact that several cities are called 'London'. What should we do to accommodate those facts into E. T.'s picture?

I see two options. The first is the "indexical gambit." On this picture, names are almost fully assimilated to indexical expressions. This approach rejects, in effect, our earlier insight *not* to regard the chain as part of the linguistic meaning of the expression. That is, we now try to incorporate a mentioning of the chain in the reference rules of names. In other words, the chain is now seen to play a *semantic* role. We now have a twin of $[R(I)]$ and $[R(you)]$ for proper names (and possibly some kinds of predicates):

> $[R(N)]$ At any context c, 'N' refers at c to the individual (kind, property) standing at the end of the historical chain leading to the use of 'N' by the agent of c.

E. T. could have suggested this approach to the above problem, but he did not. The reason, roughly, is this: We had a most intuitive sociohistorical picture concerning the presemantic role of chains. Just as with *indexicals*, the chain *preserves* the linguistic meaning, rather than being mentioned in the formulation of that meaning. The chain assigns a rule of reference to the syntactic shape; it is not mentioned in the rule of reference itself. To totally disregard these arguments because of a temporary obstacle seems to be a hasty way out. Moreover, and this is an independent point, it is not obvious at all that homonymous names can really be thought of intuitively as a *single-word-with-one-meaning* that happens to refer to different individuals in different contexts. E. T. proposes a solution that (i) preserves all the independently plausible aspects of his picture above and (ii) covers the case of homonymous words without forcing them into the mold of indexical expressions. This second option can be called "The lexical ambiguity gambit."

Referring here again to the earlier work of his colleague D. Kaplan, "Demonstratives" (sec. XXII), our Martian theorist suggests that our model for the homonymous word 'Aristotle' (on Earth) should be lexical ambiguity (e.g., 'bank'), rather than indexicality. We do not have a single word-with-a-fixed meaning (e.g., 'I'). When we look at two such homonyms we see that as far as their *linguistic* function is concerned they have nothing in common (as if they were two different words having no semantic relation to each other). Consider the word 'bank'. We look at the particular history leading to a particular utterance of 'bank' as a disambiguation procedure. We are involved in a presemantic decision as to which meaning is relevant here. A more dramatic example would involve the word 'no' which means in Knoh what 'yes' means in English. Looking at the particular history of an utterance of 'no' would help us to decide which language (and meaning) is relevant on the given occasion. The same, I believe, goes for 'Aristotle'. The historical information involves here the same type of choice between radically independent meanings. One use refers to the teacher of Alexander the Great, the other to the modern shipping magnate. The chain is therefore literally presemantic. It assigns meanings to expressions. It is only *then* that the semantical process begins.[14]

3. WHAT THE PRESENT PICTURE IS NOT II: FREGEAN SENSES

E. T. has told us above that the historical chains perform a *presemantic* task. He has stressed that the chains are not *part* of the rules of reference (or Kaplan's "character-rules") but rather that they operate *before* the rules of reference get into the picture. As stressed above, this distinction is quite important when one tries to (i) locate the *stage* at which the chains operate and (ii) sort out what *general theoretical proposal* may be peeled off from Kripke's rather informal picture.

However, the dispute between the indexical theorist and E. T. may seem like an interfamily dispute among direct reference proponents. The difference between the semantic and the presemantic may be significant from *within* the direct reference perspective. But what should we make of one who believes that those insights on chains of communication are fine *in themselves* but that they ought to be grounded in a Fregean theory of meaning? What should we say about someone who thinks that for every expression 'X', we can, relying on E. T., form the definite description "The object (kind, property) that stands at the end of the chain leading to the use of 'X' by the relevant agent" and look at it as formulating the *sense* of 'X'? In other words, what should E. T. say to a Fregean colleague who suggests:

> The description theory of meaning (not just of names, but of any single denoting word) holds that each expression 'X' is an abbreviation of a definite description 'The F'. This theory suffered some blows lately. But the problem wasn't really with the *general* structure of the theory. Rather it was with the *particular* candidates offered for 'The F'. Kripke's insights on chains and E. T.'s generalization of this analysis offer the description theory new, much fitter for survival, candidates for 'The F'.

E. T. is well aware of such sophisticated moves that his neo-Fregean adversaries may take in response to his report. In particular, he is well aware that the above mentioned move was anticipated by R. Nozick, as mentioned by Kripke:

> As R. Nozick pointed out to me, there is a sense in which a description theory must be trivially true if any theory of the reference of names, spelled out in terms independent of the notion of reference, is available. For if such a theory gives conditions under which an object is to be the referent of a name, then it of course uniquely satisfies these conditions.[15]

Now, the question is: *What should we make of this move?*

There are, E. T. believes, *positive* general theoretical reasons to shy away from a (neo) Fregean theory of meaning and reference and if, as E. T. believes, they are sound reasons, they will carry the major weight in a refutation of the above mentioned neo-Fregean picture. But to defend those positive proposals is beyond the scope of this work. Rather, E. T. will make some general *negative* comments on the above proposal. The comments will not try to do justice to the almost endless variety of (post-Kripkean) neo-Fregean epicycles, but they will still cover most of the well-known contenders. The neo-Fregean proposal is: *For each expression 'X', the description "The individual (kind, property) standing at the end of the historical chain leading to the use of 'X' by the agent" (henceforth "The h-description") formulates the sense of 'X'.* E. T. will try to refute the claim.[16]

Fregeans, traditional and modern, have held the view that the *sense* of an expression is a four-dimensional crystal ball that is:

(i)   That which *determines* the reference of the expression,
(ii) That which gives the *modal* value of the expression,
(iii) That which a speaker *learns* when he becomes a *competent* user of the expression,
(iv) That which gives the *cognitive significance* of the expression.

Now, it seems that E. T. would have made his point even if he would have only been able to show that the h-description failed to satisfy one or two of the desiderata (i)-(iv). But, in fact, E. T. is going to show that the h-description satisfies *none* of the desiderata!

Consider the word 'table' and its h-description. (The arguments below are meant to apply across the board to words like: 'I', 'Jones', 'elm', 'bachelor', etc.) E. T. starts with (i). Obviously, the Twin Earth cases above show that the h-description does not determine uniquely the reference of 'table'. The descriptional content is not enough by itself to single out a unique reference for the expression. In one and the same possible world, the description determines different referents on different planets. Senses (in a given world) are supposed to determine reference uniquely. The h-description does not.[17]

Turning to (ii), the question is: are 'table' and its h-description *cointensional*? Answer: certainly not. The property that might have stood at the end of the historical chain leading to my use of 'table' could have been that of being-a-horse (see the above remarks on counterfactual chains). *Some* neo-Fregeans have sought here an easy way out by *rigidifying* the h-description. But the rigidifiers leave a bad taste: they involve devices like 'actual' or 'in w' which smack of uneliminable direct reference. Besides, to put it a bit rhetorically, the thoughtful among the neo-Fregeans have admitted that this is a rather "cheap" way out.[18]

Thirdly, the h-description seems to fail the test of (iii). Is it part of the ordinary requirements of competence to know about each word 'X', the (correct) *theory of reference* governing that word? Surely not. After all, this is exactly where the ordinary Earthlings (and Twin Earthlings) differ from E. T., the Martian anthropologist who investigates them. Any other response would have left us with no competent English speakers before 1970 and with an extremely narrow class of competent users since that time. Again, here too *some* neo-Fregeans have tried to bite the bullet and put the whole theory of reference "in the head" of the ordinary user. But other neo-Fregeans have criticized such desperate moves and have admitted that even though Fregeanism always posited a high threshold for competence, this one is, frankly, quite absurd.[19]

Finally, consider (iv). "Sense" is characterized here through "cognitive significance judgments." That is, 'A' and 'B' have the same sense (for a competent user J) iff whenever J believes . . . A . . . , J believes . . . B . . . and vice versa.[20] It seems to E. T. that it can hardly be denied that most competent speakers can believe that Jones is happy without believing that the individual standing at the end of the chain leading to the use of 'Jones' is happy. Similarly for beliefs about oneself ('I believe I am happy'), elms, tables, and what not. But this was to be expected once we have seen the failure of the h-description to satisfy (iii). For indeed, if the h-description is not "in the heads" of most competent users, why should it be available to them when they form their beliefs? Again, it seems that certain neo-Fregeans admit the fact that J can believe that X is G without believing that the F is G, where 'The F' is the h-description of 'X'.[21]

4. WHAT THE PRESENT PICTURE IS: WHERE THE CHAIN COMES IN

Thus, concludes E. T., the dispute on the *role* of the chains is not an internal affair among direct reference proponents. Of course, says E. T., it was important to get straight on the fact that the chain is neither part of the rule of reference nor is it playing a semantic role. But equally important is the need to block sophisticated neo-Fregean epicycles in the theory of meaning. Neo-Fregeans have sought to incorporate unsuitable material into "senses" in order to make a last-ditch attempt against direct reference theory. Indeed, in this respect, the present picture offers a very interesting *twist* to those Fregeans who are *not* trying to save the description theory at all costs. This twist is all the more interesting since it reinforces E. T.'s point that historical chains play a *presemantic* role. The twist is this: E. T.'s view of the chains as presemantic is *compatible* with a Fregean semantics. Thus, a careful Fregean who does *not* try to incorporate the historical chain into the sense can argue as follows:

E. T.'s picture is fine. I do not dispute it. My differences start at the *semantic* level. I do not dispute the role of the chain. I dispute the nature of its *output*. For whereas a direct reference theorist thinks its output is a rule of reference, I think its output is a sense.

This seems to be an interesting move. For the differences between the Fregean and the direct reference proponent can now be seen to concern the nature of the *linguistic meaning* assigned by the chain. Their differences are semantic, not presemantic.

E. T. makes this point *not* because he supports a Fregean semantics. Rather, the twist is just as much important from the point of view of direct reference proponents. The fact that there are chains of communication across the ages is *not* going to settle dispute between Fregeans and anti-Fregeans. This is hardly surprising: the chains, being presemantic, are relatively uncontroversial and can be accepted by both sides. The dispute is over what *is* preserved by the chain. Direct reference theory can have the edge over Fregeanism if it will show that the meaning assigned by the chain is not a sense, but rather something like the above reference rules (Kaplan's characters). This point is often obscured because certain Fregeans and certain direct reference proponents turn the "causal theory" into the ultimate battleground: Fregeans put into their senses, and anti-Fregeans put into their character rules, the h-description. But once we see that the historical chain belongs neither here nor there, we realize that E. T.'s presemantic theory will not decide the semantic issues.

E. T.'s move may seem to take all the air out of the big balloon of "essential role of causal (historical) chains in semantics." Those who put the chain into senses or reference rules have looked at it as a semantic oracle, a universal key to the understanding of reference. They have endowed the chain with unlimited powers. E. T. turns the almighty into the rather trivial. But, he says, to *realize* that the almighty is rather trivial is not trivial at all.

Notes

1. My debt to D. Kaplan is well over and above what is indicated in the text. The major part is ineffable. I owe a heavy debt of thanks to H. Wettstein for long-suffering (and enlightening) hours of discussion. Thanks are also due to comments of H. Kamp and C. Peacocke. None of them is responsible for the following "extraterrestrial" speculations.

2. I would even say this language *is* English, but nothing below depends upon this controversial assertion.

3. Henceforth I will use 'TE' for 'Twin Earth'.

4. The term "omniscient observer of history" is due to K. Donnellan. Our Martian anthropologist had been invented by D. Kaplan. I use him here for a different kind of job, even though we shall see that this job connects with Kaplan's original story.

5. E. T. refers his readers to the work of D. Kaplan on directly referential expressions. See Kaplan's "Demonstratives," UCLA Draft 2 (1977). See the discussion of "Principle 2." He adds here a scholarly footnote reminding his reader that for indexicals, the intension is defined relative to a given *context*. Hence if Tom Smith was the first to use 'I' in English in some context c, his use determined an intension: that function that for any world-time pair gives Tom at that world-time pair. This function isn't preserved across the chain. When the Earthling Ronald Reagan first learned to use 'I', he didn't learn to associate with it that function, otherwise R. Reagan would have referred to Tom every time he said 'I'.

6. Of course, "learn" doesn't mean that Reagan is able to articulate this rule. Reagan is *not* in the position of our Martian theoretician. What is crucial is that Reagan came to conform in his use of 'I' to an ongoing practice that the rule articulates. See immediately below.

7. Some may believe that words are not *introduced* into the language and meanings aren't stipulated for them. Rather, words "enter" the language and just happen to "catch" a certain meaning. There might be some artificiality behind the stipulative picture. For most names and common nouns, the hypothesis about the stipulative mode seems to me *empirically* correct. That is, we do rely on an (informal) dubbing, though the dubbing may not be the *first* time, in the history of the universe, at which the relevant noise was emitted. For a recent case, consider the way in which various words relating to computer technology have found their way into English in the last 30 years. There are other cases for which the stipulative mode is a rough idealization. However, even in those cases this idealization should, I believe, be preferred over the intrinsic vagueness and obscurity of the "enter" and "catch" vocabulary. Nothing, however,

in the present picture hangs on this issue. Therefore I wish to be open-minded about the form of introduction of words. It may well be the case that the whole issue does not belong to the philosophy of language but to empirical investigations.

8. Without getting into the heart of the matter, E. T. notes that the use of 'actual' is important here. This shows up when we make modal assertions about linguistic meanings. In such contexts, "The actual linguistic meaning of . . ." embeds differently than "The linguistic meaning of . . . ." E. T. does not explore such assertions in the present paper. Another brief remark on modality: The above picture of E. T. fits nicely with a "perspectival" analysis of 'actual': when uttered on a given planet, it refers to the situation on *that* planet.

9. The emphasis in the text is on denying that the theory is a causal theory of *reference*. As an aside (at least in the present paper), E. T. wishes to note that neither his picture nor Kripke's seems to be a *causal* theory. But, questions from the floor display scepticism: Wasn't the earlier breakthrough, due to his colleague Kripke, based on a *causal* picture? Aren't there insoluble problems in extending the picture to *abstract* objects (of which his meanings are a case par excellence)? The picture that Kripke has offered is really a concatenation of two separate pictures (1) The historical chain from a recent utterance to the dubbing occasion (The chain of *transmission*). (2) The chain from the dubbing agent to the object so dubbed (The *initiating* chain). Nothing in Kripke's analyses suggests an adherence to a physicalistic reduction of either sort of chain. Even though I will not defend this view here, I believe that there is nothing in Kripke's remarks that imposes such constraints on the chain. Moreover, there are, implicit in Kripke's work, *positive* arguments why the chain *does* preserve reference to abstract objects. Kripke relies on the following methodological twist: instead of giving an a priori argument for or against the possibility of reference to abstract objects, we should look at our actual linguistic intuitions as to what we refer to when we use certain kinds of terms. Two cases, natural kind terms and numerals, suggest themselves in our context. We, the present users of English, seem to refer to the kind Tiger and the number 3.14 . . . (using 'Tiger' and 'π'). We do not refer to the original individual tigers that were spotted by the first users of 'Tiger' in English. But it seems that we and those pioneers refer to the same thing when using the word 'Tiger'. Hence, the chain connecting us and them may after all preserve reference to abstract objects. Of course, this instant note doesn't do justice to this very subtle topic. But by and large, there seems to be a widespread philosophical agreement that says that *if* meanings are introduced in this stipulative way and are some sort of abstract objects, then a causal picture is blocked. This may or may not be true. Kripke's picture and E. T.'s refinements are not *causal*. They are socio-historical pictures.

10. This is not argued for by our friend at this stage. He presupposes it and assumes that he doesn't have any dispute on this with Kripke, Donnellan, or Kaplan.

11. If certain atomic predicates (names of natural kinds or maybe even other types of properties) just refer directly, their meaning *is* just to stand for those kinds or properties. Then the chain that preserves their meaning will, inter alia, preserve the fact that they *refer* to those kinds or properties. Another extension of the present remarks concerns the following issue. E. T. does not discuss here apparent counterexamples to Kripke's picture, such as G. Evans' 'Madagascar'. Let us just note that if they are to be accepted as significant, then the present socially oriented framework is very flexible in this respect. There are many cases of *meaning* shifts in the history of English and other languages. Thus if Evans is right, his case would turn out to be a special case of a meaning shift that came to be socially pervasive.

12. I really mean that a description of the workings of the chain, i.e., "the individual standing at the end of the causal chain leading to the use of the name 'N'" is not part of the meaning of 'N'. See immediately below my discussion of what it is for the chain to be part of the meaning.

13. A most important warning: This should *not* be confused with the proposal that for a given name 'N', "The referent of 'N'" formulates the *sense* or *meaning* of 'N'. What the historical chain assigns to the syntactic shape is *not* a sense. To think otherwise would be like thinking that other outputs of the chain, the rules [R(I)] or [R(you)], are senses. Of course, they are

not. Rules of reference are *not* senses. See more on this below. One should note the following here. Originally the sentence in the text read: "the actual history of uses assigns the meaning: H. Putnam." More generally it was asserted that the meaning assigned to a name *is* the referent. A thoughtful commentator pointed out the following: This Russellian "language" is often regarded as very troublesome. Nothing in what was intended depnded on the extreme Russellian "style." The commentator is correct as far as the present content goes. However, it is not obvious at all that this "Strawsonian" displeasure with Russell is really justified. Its reasons may lie deep in descriptional conceptions that affected Strawson. In other words, the common platitude that Strawson was right and Russell was wrong is not obvious at all once it is realized that names are directly referential. But to avoid the controversy the terminology has been put into line.

14. E. T. draws some satisfaction here from the fact that note 9 in Kripke's 1980 introduction to his *Naming and Necessity* (Cambridge, Mass.) and the surrounding text are sympathetic to the above picture.

15. See Kripke, ibid., n. 38. See also further relevant remarks in Kripke's addenda to the main text.

16. In the following, E. T. disregards a further problem for the neo-Fregean: the non-uniqueness of the definite description "the agent" in the h-description. See the next footnote.

17. The Fregean may retreat and suggest that the h-description expresses an "incomplete" sense that *together with a context* determines a referent. Such a concession was bad enough for Frege himself in the very limited case of *true* indexical expressions. Even if this move made sense here, it would have made *every* expression modeled on the indexicals. Needless to say, this is a radical departure from Fregeanism, which sought the exact opposite: model the indexicals on the *nonindexical* expressions.

18. See D. Ackerman, "Proper Names, Essences, and Intuitive Beliefs," *Theory and Decision* 11 (1979):5-26. Similar remarks apply to temporal contexts and the use of "present" or "at t."

19. See D. Ackerman's comments on Schiffer in her "Natural Kind Terms, Concepts and Propositional Attitudes." *Midwest Studies in Philosophy* 5 (1981):469-85.

20. I am being sloppy here. One should distinguish *assent* from *belief*. But I have assumed that J is competent, so disquoting him is a matter of routine. We need not go here into subtle doubts about this since our case will be straightforward.

21. See the works mentioned above. In particular, D. Ackerman has stressed that h-descriptions do *not* characterize the cognitive significance of expressions. I should stress that failing to satisfy (iii) is not a *condition* for failing to satisfy (iv). One can envisage a variety of cases of two expressions '*A*', '*B*' with which competent users associate the *same* information (that information they ought to associate in order to count as competent) but such that one can still wonder whether *A* is *B* (all *A*'s are *B*'s.) But, of course, a candidate that fails to satisfy (iii) is making the whole case much more obvious.

Note added in proof: After completing the present manuscript, I had the opportunity of reading D. Kaplan's unpublished 1971 Princeton lectures. Without committing him to my reading of his work, it turns out that he anticipated the major ideas of the present paper, in particular *where* the chain comes in. More embarrassing even is the fact that his examples are, as can be expected, much more penetrating and amusing.

Causality and the Paradox of Names

MICHAEL McKINSEY

In the literature concerning the semantics of proper names, almost no attention has been paid to methodological questions, such as: What should be the formal structure of theories of reference for the various types of singular terms including names? What should be the subject matter of such theories, and what kinds of facts are relevant to determining their truth-values? In this paper, I wish to suggest some answers to these questions, answers that I believe provide an accurate conception of the form that a theory of names should take. Such a conception is valuable because it constitutes a constraint that any correct theory of names must satisfy, and so it provides a tool for evaluating particular theoretical proposals concerning names. Using this tool, I will argue that no *causal* theory of names can be correct and that the true theory must be a kind of description theory. The fact that the true theory of names takes the form it does has some surprising consequences regarding the semantic structure of natural languages and the concept of meaningfulness.[1]

1. THE REFERENTIAL PARADIGM

I will begin by considering *indexical* singular terms, since such terms provide fairly simple and clear models of what a semantic theory for a type of singular term should be about and what such a theory should look like. The semantic referent of an indexical term typically varies from context to context, even if the term has a single linguistic meaning. Consider the first person pronoun 'I', for instance. According to English convention, 'I' refers on a given occasion to whoever is its speaker on that occasion. So it is plausible to suppose that the word 'I' is governed in English by the rule:

(1) For any α, if α is a token of 'I', then for any object x, α is to refer to x if and only if x is the speaker of α.

Now the fact that a given utterance of 'I' in English refers to a given object would seem to be determined by the facts (a) that the speaker is in some sense following or invoking the correct rule for 'I' in English and (b) that the object in question satisfies the reference-condition contained in that rule.[2] In this way, the rule (1) determines the referent of 'I' relative to any given context. Moreover, it is plausible to suppose that the linguistic meaning of 'I' in English is completely specified by the fact that English contains the rule (1). In this manner, then, *the linguistic meaning of a term determines its referent.*

This doctrine contrasts with Frege's principle that the referent of a term is determined by its *sense* (Sinn).[3] On Frege's concept of sense, the proposition expressed by a sentence is functionally determined by the senses of its parts. As Frege knew, it follows from this fact that the sense of an indexical like 'I' varies from context to context because the propositional expressed by a single sentence containing the indexical varies from context to context.[4] But the linguistic meaning of an indexical does not vary in this way. So the linguistic meaning of such a term is not its sense. Rather, as David Kaplan has suggested, a term's linguistic meaning must be something that, together with a context, *determines* the term's sense in that context.[5] Since the sense of an indexical is determined by its linguistic meaning, and since the linguistic meaning of an indexical would seem to be given by a rule like (1) that determines reference, the most plausible view, contrary to Frege, is that the sense of an indexical in a context *is identical with* its referent in that context.

To say that a given term's sense in a context is identical with its referent in that context is to say that the proposition expressed in the context by a sentence containing the term is a function of the term's referent in the context. Terms of this sort I call "genuine terms" and propositions expressed in contexts by use of such terms I call "singular propositions." The example of indexicals like 'I' provides a useful paradigm of a semantic theory for a genuine term. To give a semantic theory for such a term amounts to stating the rule of reference analogous to (1) that speakers follow in using the term. I call this "the referential paradigm."

Now among genuine terms I count proper names. My reason for doing so is the same as the reason Kripke has given for thinking that names are "rigid designators," or terms that refer to the same object at every possible world.[6] Consider a particular use of any sentence containing an ordinary name, such as:

(2) Ben Franklin was bald.

Suppose that in our use of (2), the referent of 'Ben Franklin' is a certain man, say, the American patriot of that name. Then this use of (2) is true in the actual world just in case this man was bald. Kripke's point is that such a use of (2) is also true in any *other* possible situation if and only if *that very man* was bald in that situation. We might say that in any possible world in which our use of (2) is true, the state of affairs that makes it true is just that of *x's having been bald*, where x is the actual referent of the token of 'Ben Franklin' in question.[7]

Perhaps this consideration does not *prove* that the proposition expressed in a given context by (2) is a function of the referent of 'Ben Franklin' in that context.

Still, if one is casting about for likely candidates to play the role of the sense of 'Ben Franklin' in a particular use of (2), there seems to be no *other* choice that is consistent with that use's having the possible-world truth conditions that Kripke describes. For instance, as Kripke points out, a particular use of 'Ben Franklin' would not have the sense of any contingent *definite description* that Ben Franklin actually satisfies.[8] So I will take it that the proposition expressed in a context by (2) is functionally determined by the referent of 'Ben Franklin' in that context. And since similar considerations apply to all proper names, I will take all names to be genuine terms in the sense introduced above.[9]

Since names are genuine terms, they fall under the referential paradigm. However, in giving a theory of names, we are not interested in giving a theory of any *particular* name. So we are not interested in stating any particular semantic rules that speakers follow in using names. Instead, what is wanted in a theory of names is an adequate generalization concerning the *sort* of reference rule that speakers follow in using words as names.

Suppose that a certain language L contains the following reference rule concerning the word N:

(3) For any α, if α is a token of N, then for any object x, α is to refer to x if and only if x is the inventor of bifocals.

Would the fact that L contains this rule imply that tokens of N have the same *sense* in L as the English definite description 'the inventor of bifocals'? No, it would not. The presence of the rule (3) in L guarantees at most that tokens of N *have the same referent* as 'the inventor of bifocals' in fact has, since this is all that the rule (3) requires for its satisfaction. But the senses of such definite descriptions are notoriously *not* the same as their referents, and so the fact that L contains (3) does not imply that tokens of N have the same sense as 'the inventor of bifocals',

Kripke has suggested that a name's referent could in principle be "fixed" by use of a definite description, without thereby giving the name the *sense* of that description.[10] The hypothesis that languages might contain reference rules of the form (3) provides a clear and simple way of understanding the sort of possibility that Kripke has described. Whether or not any natural languages actually *do* contain such rules as (3) is an issue we shall discuss at length below.

In semantic treatments of modal languages containing singular terms, it is common to relativize the relation of reference to a possible world.[11] This is done primarily to handle definite descriptions, since to correctly state the possible-world truth conditions for sentences containing descriptions, we must allow the descriptions' referents to vary from world to world. Reference rules for genuine terms can be stated by use of a relativized reference relation, provided that in our statements we guarantee that the terms rigidly designate the same object at every possible world. For instance, letting 'w^*' represent the actual world, (3) would become:

(3^*) For any α, if α is a token of N, then for any object x and possible world w, α is to refer to x at w if and only if x exists in w and x is the inventor of bifocals in w^*.

However, I prefer to stick to the use of an unrelativized reference relation for genuine terms and to evaluate sentences containing such terms at different possible worlds simply on the basis of what, if anything, the terms in fact refer to. Since a genuine term's referent will only be an object that in fact exists, and since a term will have at most one referent, we get the same effect that we would get by requiring the term to refer to the same thing at every possible world.

We may if we wish keep a relativized reference relation for use in our treatment of nongenuine terms like definite descriptions. But in any case, it is clear that we will have to provide a semantic treatment for such terms that is quite different from the one just suggested for genuine terms. So I will assume that only genuine terms fall under reference rules that are formulated by use of the unrelativized reference relation.[12]

One advantage of using an unrelativized reference relation to formulate reference rules for genuine terms is that our formulations are simpler and more likely to express accurately the kind of rules that speakers of natural languages actually follow. For if we stated reference rules by use of a relativized reference relation, our statement would presuppose that the reference rules that people actually follow involve quantification over possible worlds, and this is a controversial assumption at best.

2. THE PROBLEM OF SEMANTIC AMBIGUITY

As I have characterized them so far, reference rules have the following general form:

(4) For any α, if α is a token of W, then for any object x, α is to refer to x if and only if φ,

where W refers to a word-type and φ is a formula containing x and perhaps α as free variables.[13] But the phenomenon of semantic ambiguity raises a serious problem for the idea that reference rules have this form.

On one widely held view, *demonstrative* indexicals all have in common the feature that their tokens' semantic referents are determined either wholly or in part by what their *speakers* refer to, or demonstrate, by use of the tokens.[14] Given this view of demonstratives plus the idea that reference rules have the form (4), it is plausible to suppose that the feminine demonstrative 'she' is governed in English by the following rule:

(5) For any α, if α is a token of 'she', then for any x, α is to refer to x if and only if x is the unique female to whom the speaker of α refers with α.

Now 'she' is also the name of a novel by H. Rider Haggard. So suppose on a given occasion I say out loud, "*She* is Haggard's most exciting book." Then my token refers to Haggard's novel, a genderless object. So my utterance of 'she' *violates* the rule (5), even though my utterance is in *English*. But if this is true, can (5) really be a rule of English? In my view, it can.

A term might have two meanings in a language, and in both meanings be a genuine term. There would then be two reference rules of the form (4) in the language, both of which govern the same term. These rules will contain nonequivalent reference-conditions, and so in a sense the rules will be "inconsistent," for they can yield contradictory results when applied to the same token. But how is this possible? I call this "the problem of semantic ambiguity."

In my view, we should just accept as fact the ideas that natural languages contain conflicting rules and that we can follow a semantic rule in full awareness that the rule we are following is inconsistent with another rule of our language. After all, we often do this sort of thing in other spheres of activity. Thus, a piece of wood having a certain shape might be used in two different games. Each game might require the piece to be moved in ways that conflict with what the other game requires. In the context of each game, we find it easy to think of our moves with the piece as subject to a certain rule that we know is violated in the other game.

Similarly, when I use 'she' as a feminine demonstrative, I am thinking of my utterance as subject to the rule (5), even though I know that I could use 'she' as a name and violate this rule. In fact, I suggest, thinking of my utterance as subject to the rule (5)—or, in other words, following this rule—is precisely what using 'she' as a feminine demonstrative amounts to.

These facts strongly suggest that in many spheres of activity, including both playing games and speaking a language, we "follow the rules" of an activity in a given context by letting certain of these rules guide our behavior in that context, rather than by actualizing a permanent disposition to obey the rules in every context.

But the following objection might be raised. On my view, a game such as chess contains rules like:

(6) A bishop is to be moved only on the diagonal.

And also on my view, we could easily invent another game perhaps much like chess but containing rules that conflict with (6). However, it might be objected that the rules of chess don't really look like (6), because these rules are really of the form:

(7) *When playing chess*, a bishop is to be moved only on the diagonal.

Similarly, it might be said, the rule for 'she' is not (5), but instead is a rule whose antecedent is 'if α is a token of "she" *that is used as a feminine demonstrative*'. On this suggestion, the rules of chess could not conflict with the rules of any other game, and the rule for using 'she' as a feminine demonstrative could not conflict with any other rule of English.

Now if the sentences that express the rules of chess all contain the phrase 'when playing chess' as a prefix, then every rule of chess mentions the game of chess itself. But this implies that chess cannot be defined in terms of its rules. For obviously any definition of chess as a game consisting of such-and-such rules, each of which mentions chess, would be viciously circular. But I think it is clear that chess, like any other game, *can* be defined in terms of its rules. Therefore, the rules of chess cannot be expressed by sentences like (7) that contain the phrase 'When playing chess' as a prefix.

Statement (7) does not express a rule of chess. On the one hand, it can be understood as stating an analytic truth *about* the rules of chess, namely:

(8)   It is a rule of playing chess that a bishop is to be moved only on the diagonal.

Understood as meaning (8), (7) correctly states *that* a certain rule — namely (6) — is a rule of chess. But it would be a fallacy to infer from this that (7) *itself* states a separate rule of chess. On the other hand (7) could be understood to mean:

(9)   When one is playing chess, one should move a bishop only on the diagonal.

But (9) is not a rule of chess either. It is instead most plausibly construed as a "hypothetical imperative" to the effect that if one wants to play chess correctly (that is, obey its rules), one should obey rule (6). On both ways of understanding (7), it is (6) and not (7) that expresses a rule of chess.

So there seems to be no plausible way of avoiding the fact that the rules of the different games we play can conflict, and hence there seems to be no inherent difficulty in my suggestion that the semantic rules of a language may also conflict. Moreover, there is a good reason for thinking that the semantic rules of English do in fact conflict. For to use 'she' as a feminine demonstrative is surely the same as using 'she' *with a certain linguistic meaning*, and this in turn is the same as the speaker's following a certain semantic rule in using 'she'. But then the sort of rule in question cannot itself involve the concept of a feminine demonstrative, and so the rule's antecedent cannot be expressed by 'if α is a token of "she" that is used as a feminine demonstrative'. The only alternative would seem to be that the relevant rule must like (5) be simply a rule for using 'she', and if this is so, then the rule conflcts with other rules of English. Again, we should just accept as fact the idea that natural languages may contain conflicting semantic rules.

However, there is still a serious problem connected with this idea that we have not yet faced. Let us say that a rule R is an *inviolable* rule of a language L if and only if any utterance that violates R cannot be an utterance that is in L. Thus (5) as well as other reference rules of the form (4) and rules for ambiguous words in general cannot be inviolable rules of their languages. But then the question arises: What makes a rule of this kind a rule of a language at all?

A language, I suggest, may be identified with a finite set of syntactic and semantic rules. Intuitively, the rules in such a set are the rules that define the language in question. Let us call a rule R a *basic* rule of L if and only if R is a member of the finite set of rules that defines or comprises L. I would speculate that the inviolable rules of any language L are just those rules that are either basic rules of L or logical consequences of basic rules of L.

The rules of English permit 'she' to be used as a feminine demonstrative and prohibit other words from being so used. But again, to use 'she' as a feminine demonstrative is just to follow rule (5). This suggests that at least some of the rules of English must be *second-order* rules that permit the following of certain rules and prohibit the following of others. The rules granting permission to follow a rule like (5) would be "second-order" in the sense that they would be rules about rules. So let us say that a rule R is a *nonbasic* rule of a language L if and only if: R is not a basic rule of L, but there is a rule Q such that Q is a second-order basic rule of L, and Q explicitly permits speakers to follow R.

I propose that (5) is a rule of English in the sense that it is a nonbasic rule of English. Similarly, any rule of a language that can be violated by an utterance in that language is, I suggest, either a nonbasic rule of the language or a logical consequence of such a rule. Below, when I speak simply of a "rule of" a language L, I shall mean a basic or nonbasic rule of L, or a logical consequence of a basic or nonbasic rule of L.

Reference rules like (5) provide examples of first-order, nonbasic semantic rules. But what do second-order semantic rules look like, and in what sense do they "explicitly permit" the following of some first-order rules and forbid the following of others? These are difficult questions that I cannot really do justice to here, but I will make a brief suggestion. The second-order rule of English permitting 'she' to be used as a feminine demonstrative would, I suggest, grant this permission in the sense that it would explicitly allow tokens of 'she' that are used in this way to have semantic referents. Roughly, the relevant second-order rule would be:

(10) For any α, if α is a token of 'she' that is used as a feminine demonstrative, then the referent of α is to be determined in accordance with the first-order rule being followed.

Since a token of 'she' is used as a feminine demonstrative if and only if its speaker is following rule (5), (10) says that tokens of 'she' that are produced by speakers following rule (5) may have their referents determined accordingly.

The general picture I would suggest goes roughly as follows. For each genuine term of English, there is at least one second-order rule like (10) permitting tokens of the term to have referents in accordance with a certain first-order reference rule of the form (4). To each such first-order rule for a term that is mentioned in the second-order rule of English, there corresponds *one* of the term's linguistic meanings in English. The fact that more than one first-order rule for a given term may be mentioned in the second-order rules of English allows the picture to account for semantic ambiguity. The list of second-order rules for genuine terms will of course be finite, and there will in addition be a rule to the effect that a token that is not used in any of the ways mentioned in the list has no referent.[15]

If I am right, the existence of semantic ambiguity in natural languages is best taken account of by a view according to which these languages contain nonbasic semantic rules. By definition, any such language also contains basic second-order rules like (10). So the existence of semantic ambiguity in natural languages provides good evidence that these languages contain second-order semantic rules. As we shall see below, the fact that there are second-order rules in natural languages provides a significant key to understanding names.

I said earlier that a theory of names should describe the kind of reference rule we follow when using words as names. Our discussion of 'she' strongly suggests that whether or not a word is used as a name depends upon the sort of rule the speaker is following. This gives us another way of describing the goal of a theory of names.

By providing an adequate generalization concerning the sort of reference rule that speakers follow when using words as names, an adequate theory of names would tell us *what it is for a word to be used as a name.*

Having described what the goal of a theory of names should be, I now wish to consider whether any form of causal theory of names is capable of reaching this goal.

3. CAUSAL THEORIES OF HAVING AN OBJECT IN MIND

One of the main motivations behind a certain kind of causal theory of names results from combining two ideas. The first idea is that the semantic referent of a particular name-token or utterance is in part determined by which object its speaker *has in mind* or *means* by the token. The second idea is that whether or not a speaker has a given object in mind in using a name is determined by whether or not the speaker's mental states are connected to that object by the right sort of causal relation. A view that results from combining these two ideas is best looked upon as a causal theory of having an object in mind that has been applied to the semantics of proper names.[16]

A causal theory of having an object in mind is a causal theory of what makes our mental states *about* or *of* certain objects and not others. I have criticized such theories elsewhere in some detail.[17] But here I wish to point out that even if a causal theory of having an object in mind were true, this fact would not suffice to show that any causal theory of *names* is true. For a causal theory of having an object in mind will not support a causal theory of names unless the concept of having an object in mind somehow generally figures in the semantic rules or conventions that people follow in using words as names. But as we shall see, it is far from clear that this concept does generally figure in these rules.

In his recent book *Designation*, Michael Devitt proposes a causal theory of having an object in mind and purports to use this theory as the basis of a causal theory of names.[18] The main concept of the book is that of designation, which Devitt explains in terms of a type of causal chain that he calls a "d-chain." The idea is that an utterance, or token, of a term designates an object if and only if the object "grounds," or is the ultimate source of, a d-chain that eventuates in the utterance. According to Devitt, his concept of a token's designating an object is a theoretical counterpart of the ordinary concept of a speaker's having an object in mind (or meaning an object) by a token (p. 33).

My question is: How is the concept of designation supposed to be relevant to the semantics of proper names? It is instructive to consider the way Devitt himself takes designation to be relevant to the semantics of *demonstratives*. His view is that the conventions for the various types of demonstrative terms all require that the terms' semantic referents be determined at least in part by what the terms designate. Since what is designated by a token corresponds intuitively to what the speaker refers to with (has in mind by) the token, Devitt's view is in essence the same as the view of demonstratives mentioned earlier, a view that I subscribe to. Devitt suggests, for instance, that the term 'this', 'that', and 'it' all mean (approximately) 'a designated object', whereas 'he' and 'she' mean 'a designated male' and 'a designated female', respectively (p. 46). It is easy to put these suggestions in the form of reference rules. For instance, the relevant rules for 'this' and 'she' would be:

(11) For any α, if α is a token of 'this', then for any x, α is to refer to x if and only if α designates x; and

(12) For any α, if α is a token of 'she', then for any x, α is to refer to x if and only if α designates x and x is female.

Notice that (12) is in effect equivalent to the rule (5) for 'she' that I introduced earlier.

Devitt proposes a causal theory of having an object in mind, and he describes how the latter concept figures in the various conventions or rules people follow in using demonstratives. By my criteria, Devitt has stated a causal theory of demonstratives, a theory that fits the referential paradigm. However, he nowhere states a comparable sort of theory for proper names. In sharp contrast to his treatment of demonstratives, Devitt never attempts to explain how the concept of designation figures in the conventions people follow in using words as names. In fact, nowhere in his book does he explicitly attempt to describe these conventions at all.

Thus, by my criteria, Devitt has not succeeded in stating a causal theory of names. Instead, he has given a causal theory of what he calls designation (having an object in mind) and then applied this theory to names to show the various ways that names can designate objects. But applying a theory of designation to names in this way is not at all the same as giving a theory of *names*. For, on Devitt's own view, ever so many different kinds of terms designate objects. Thus to merely describe how names designate objects in various ways is not to say anything that distinguishes names semantically from other kinds of terms, and so it is also not the same as giving a theory of names.[19]

There are of course various ways in which the concept of designation might conceivably figure in the rules people follow in using words as names. One obvious possibility is that these rules all have the following form:

(13) For any α, if α is a token of N, then for any x, α is to refer to x if and only if α designates x,

where N refers to some name-type. But this proposal fails to distinguish names from other semantically different sorts of term. In particular, if this proposal were true, then whenever anyone uses a word as a name, he is following just the same sort of rule as the rule (11). But then the proposal has the false consequence that every name is semantically indistinguishable from the demonstrative 'this'. Moreover, since the proposal is that to use a word as a name is to follow a rule of the form (13), and since the rule (11) for 'this' is of that form, the proposal also has the absurd consequence that the demonstrative 'this' is itself a proper name.

Another sort of difficulty for the idea that reference rules for names have the form (13) is raised by examples of the following kind that Kripke has described.[20] Suppose that Smith always uses the word 'Reagan' as a name of the American president, Ronald Reagan. But Smith mistakenly believes that his neighbor Jones—who perhaps looks just like Reagan—is the President, and because of this mistake Smith often refers to Jones with 'Reagan'. On one such occasion, Smith says, "Look, Reagan is mowing his lawn for the third time this week." Intuitively, as Kripke points out, Smith is using 'Reagan' *as a name of* Reagan but is *referring* with 'Reagan' to his neighbor Jones.[21] So if we assume that designation is a counterpart of speaker's reference, this is a case in which a name-token semantically refers to one object (Reagan) and designates another (Jones).[22] But then the speaker cannot be following a rule of the form (13). Yet he is using 'Reagan' as a name. So again, the idea that the rules for names have the form (13) is false.[23]

At one point in his book (p. 151), Devitt mentions in passing a convention of *designating a certain object* with a name. So perhaps he would say that conventions for using names have the form:

(14) For any α, if α is a token of N, then for any x, α is to designate x if and only if $x = b$,

where b is a term referring to a certain object.[24] Now (14) is a rule governing designation, or speaker's reference, as opposed to semantic reference. So it is difficult to understand how such a rule could determine a name-token's *semantic* referent, especially since, as we've just seen, a name-token's semantic referent can be an object that it *fails* to designate.[25] This problem suggests that perhaps Devitt did not have rules of the form (14) in mind, but rather rules of the form:

(15) For any α, if α is a token of N, then for any x, α is to refer to x if and only if $x = b$,

where again, b is a term referring to a certain object. But of course, the proposal that conventions for names are of this form does not help explain how the concept of designation is supposed to figure in these conventions.

Moreover there is a further overwhelming difficulty that confronts both the proposal of (14) and that of (15). Rules of this form are supposed to be rules that concern *certain objects*. So I take it that in the instances of (14) and (15) expressing such rules, the instances of 'b' are supposed to be *genuine terms*.[26] Consider any instance I of (14) or (15) containing a genuine term b. Since b is genuine, the rule expressed by I is a function of the referent of b. But then unless b has a referent, I expresses no rule at all. Hence no rule has the form (14) or (15), unless that rule concerns an existing individual.

Now it is clear that we do not *always* follow such rules in using words as names. For sometimes we use a word as a name without using it as a name of any existing object. (A child asserts "Santa Claus is going to bring me a laser gun for Christmas.") In such a case the rule being followed is not a rule concerning any real individual, and so the rule is neither of the form (14) nor of the form (15). So neither of these forms of rule can provide the basis of a generally adequate account of what it is to use words as names.[27]

Furthermore, it is highly implausible to suppose that speakers *ever* follow rules of this kind in using words as names. For any such rule essentially involves a certain individual. Hence the mere fact that one is following such a rule in using a word guarantees that one is using the word as a name of an existing individual. So if we ever followed such rules, then we could sometimes know whether we are using a word as a name of an existing individual, merely by finding out which rule we are following. But since it is implausible to suppose that we could ever gain such knowledge in this way, it is also implausible to suppose that we ever follow rules of this form.

There are no doubt other ways in which Devitt's concept of designation might conceivably figure in the reference rules for names. But rather than discuss more of these possibilities, let us instead turn to a more general consideration of how causal concepts of any kind might figure in these rules.

4. A GENERAL ARGUMENT AGAINST CAUSAL THEORIES

On every sort of causal theory of names, the semantic referent of a particular use or token of a name is determined by a causal or historical chain of communication reaching back in time from the use to an initial point at which an object, the use's referent, acquires the name in some way. But when confronted with this picture, we should ask ourselves, How *could* the referent of a name-use be determined by a causal chain of this sort? The only possible answer would seem to be that a name-use's referent can be determined by such a causal chain only if the rule or convention being followed by the speaker *makes* it the case that the use's referent is so determined. Thus causal theories seem to all be committed at a minimum to the view that every (or at any rate *almost* every) reference rule for using a name has the form:

(16) For any α, if α is a token of N, then for any x, α is to refer to x if and only if $x = (\imath y)Cy\alpha$,

where each instance of $\ulcorner Cy\alpha \urcorner$ expresses a relation involving causality, and $\ulcorner x = (\imath y)Cy\alpha \urcorner$ is equivalent to $\ulcorner (\exists y) ((z)(Cz\alpha \equiv y = z) \,\&\, x = y) \urcorner$.

Within the range given by this minimal assumption, there is room for considerable variety. But even so, the theories that make this assumption share one striking feature in common. For on all of these theories, every proper name turns out to be a species of *indexical.*[28] On all of these theories, an object is the referent of a token of a name only if the object uniquely bears a certain causal relation to that token. But if this is true, then the referent of a name in a given context is always determined in part by features of the particular token that is uttered in the context, and this is the defining mark of an indexical.[29] The relevant instances of $\ulcorner x = (\imath y)Cy\alpha \urcorner$ in the various conventions for names would each be something like 'x is the unique object that grounds such-and-such a kind of causal chain that eventuates in α'. Typically, one imagines, chains of the various relevant sorts could link distinct objects to distinct tokens of the same name. If so, then the conventions for names, like those for most indexicals, allow a name's referent to vary from context to context.

However, it seems to me that proper names are intuitively *not* indexicals, and that instead their referents are determined independently of context. Most philosophers writing on names, I believe, have shared this intuition, either explicitly or implicitly. For instance, in philosophical discussions of names, it is common to assume for the sake of simplicity that name-types have unique referents. Such an assumption is quite harmless, provided that each convention or rule for a name determines a unique referent for that name, for then the assumption amounts to just ignoring for simplicity's sake the possibility of a single name's falling under more than one convention. But if names were indexicals, the assumption would be far from harmless; it would be like assuming that the word "I" has a unique referent.

And when philosophers do remark the fact that a single name-type may have several distinct referents, they almost always classify this as a kind of *ambiguity*.[30] This classification assumes, correctly I think, that distinctness of a name's referents in different contexts is a sign that the name is being used with distinct linguistic meanings in those contexts, an assumption that is reasonable if each rule or convention for a name determines a unique referent for that name, but an assumption that commonly fails for indexicals.

It is worth noting that intuitions of the above kind have frequently been expressed by *causal theorists*, indicating a significant tension in their views between these intuitions and the picture they've proposed of how names' referents are determined.[31]

In addition to these intuitive grounds, there are strong theoretical reasons for thinking that names cannot be indexicals. We have seen that to use a word as a name is to follow a certain sort of semantic rule. Similarly, it would seem, a word *is* a name in a certain language just in case the language contains a semantic rule of the relevant sort governing that word. Now if a word is a name in a language by virtue of the language's containing a certain rule, and if one is following that rule in uttering the word, then surely one would be using the word as a name, and hence would be using the word *as a name of* whichever object is the referent of one's utterance.

But now consider the imaginary indexical term 'toof' that is governed in a certain language L by the following rule:

(17)   For any α, if α is a token of 'toof', then α is to refer to an object x if and only if x is the unique object that is precisely two feet in front of the speaker of α's nose at the time he utters α.

Suppose that a speaker s follows (17) on a given occasion in uttering a token α of 'toof', and that x is the unique object two feet in front of s's nose at the time of utterance. Thus x would be the referent of α. But would s be using 'toof' *as a name* of x on this occasion? Obviously not. But why not? The reason, I suggest, is that the existence of the rule (17) in L would not be sufficient to make 'toof' a name in L *of* any particular one of the indefinitely huge number of objects that it might refer to in different contexts. And in order to be *used as* a name of an object, a word must *be* a name of that object.

We said that if a word is a name in a language by virtue of the language's

containing a certain rule, then the existence of that rule in that language would allow the word to be used as a name of whichever object is referred to by any particular use of the word. But as we've just seen, this in turn implies that the existence
of such a rule in a language would be sufficient to make a word *the name of* whichever object is referred to by any particular use of the word.

Now as the example of 'toof' shows, the existence of a rule in a language can
make a word a name of an object in that language only if the rule contains a condition that determines a unique referent for that name. But then, the sort of rule in
question cannot be the sort of rule we follow in using indexicals. Hence, the existence
in a language of a rule cannot make a word a name of any object, if that rule is the
kind we follow in using indexicals. But again, the existence in a language of the
kind of rule we follow in using words as names *can* make a word the name of an object. Therefore, the kind of rule we follow in using names is *not* the kind of rule we
follow in using indexicals. Therefore, names are not indexicals.[32]

It will help to nail the point down if we consider an example of a kind of rule
that would be sufficient to make a word the name of an object in a language. In section 1 we saw that a name's referent could in principle be fixed in a language by a
context-independent definite description. For instance, Kripke has described the
possibility that 'Neptune' might have been first introduced as a name of whatever
planet uniquely causes such-and-such perturbations in the orbit of Uranus.[33] Thus
the following *could* be a rule of a given language L:[34]

    (18)   For any α, if α is a token of 'Neptune', then α is to refer to an object x
           if and only if x is the unique planet that causes the perturbations in the
           orbit of Uranus.

Now suppose we've just discovered that (18) is a rule of L. Would we say that
'Neptune' is a *name* in L? Yes, obviously. And assuming that a certain planet
uniquely satisfies the relevant description, would 'Neptune' be a name *of* that planet
in L? Again, the answer is obviously Yes.

Thus merely by knowing that a word's referent is fixed in a language by a
context-independent description, we know automatically that the word is a name in
that language. This fact supports my suggestion that for a word to be a name in a
language is for the language to contain a reference rule of a certain sort. It also confirms my contention that the sort of rule in question is not the sort of rule that
governs indexicals.

The evidence we've cited seems to lead inevitably to the conclusion that *to be
a name just is to be a context-independent genuine term.*

This view is theoretically satisfying because it not only allows us to distinguish
names from both descriptions and indexicals, but it also allows us to see the respects
in which names are significantly similar to both of these other types of term. Like
indexicals but unlike descriptions, names are genuine terms. Like many descriptions
but unlike indexicals, names are context-independent. The fact that names are significantly like both descriptions and indexicals explains why philosophers have
been prone to assimilate names to one or the other of these two types of term. The

fact that names are significantly different from both descriptions and indexicals shows that such assimilations are mistaken.

If names are not indexicals, then it is false to suppose that any reference rule for using a name is ever of the form (16). Thus, no causal theory of names according to which the conventions or rules for names are of this form is true. Yet as we've seen, the picture provided by causal theorists of how names' referents are determined is most naturally interpreted as suggesting that the conventions for names are of the form (16).

In fact, if the conventions for using names are not of this form, then there are very few alternatives left to a causal theorist. We saw in section 3 that the rules people follow in using names cannot involve actual individuals, and thus we eliminated the possibility that these rules are of the form (15), where b is a genuine term referring to a certain object. But if the reference rules for names must make names context-independent, and yet these rules are not of the form (15), then there is only one sort of form left that these rules could take. *They must be rules of the form (4) that are expressible by means of context-independent definite descriptions.*

So the only sort of view left for a causal theorist to take is a view according to which the various reference rules that people follow in using words as names are each of the form:

(19) For any α, if α is a token of N, then for any x, α is to refer to x if and only if $x = (\imath y)Cy$,

where in each such rule the instance of 'Cy' expresses a property involving causality. However, I should think that most causal theorists would be unable to accept this idea with equanimity. For causal theorists recommend their sort of view as a preferable alternative to description theories of names. In opposition to description theories, the proponents of causal theories assert that the referents of most uses of names are not determined by any properties or descriptions that are associated with the names by their speakers and that typically a name-use would have the referent it in fact has, even if the descriptions associated with the use were satisfied by objects other than the referent or by nothing at all.[35]

But surely, if whenever a speaker is using a word as a name he or she is following a reference rule of the form (19), then the speaker associates with that use the property mentioned in the rule's reference condition, and an object must uniquely satisfy this property to be the referent of the name-use in question. Of course this "association of a property with his or her use" amounts to no more than is implied by the fact that the speaker is "following the rule" in question, and it is difficult to say precisely what is implied by this sort of fact. I do not think that a speaker need know, or be explicitly aware of, the rule being followed, in order to be following it. Nor need the speaker be able to formulate the rule being followed.

But the fact that a speaker is following a rule of the form (19) would at least have to be reflected in the truth of various counterfactuals concerning the speaker's mental dispositions. Thus if in uttering a token of 'Reagan' Smith is following the rule that tokens of 'Reagan' are to refer to the president, then Smith must be disposed, among other things, to think that his utterance is not about a real man, if he comes to believe that the president never existed and is, say, a figment of his imagination. It is in this manner that a speaker who follows a rule of the form (19) would be "associating" the relevant property with his use of a name.

So I think it is clear that if to use a word as a name one must follow a rule of the form (19), then the correct theory of names must be a description theory, and causal theories that deny the truth of every description theory must be false. Of course, if some description theory based on rules of this form were correct, then an element of causality would be involved in the various rules that determine reference for names. But I should think it would be of small comfort to a causal theorist to know that the correct theory of names is a description theory of this form.

5. THE PARADOX OF NAMES

Our discussion so far shows that whatever semantic rules we follow in using words as names must be expressible by use of context-independent definite descriptions, and this is a serious difficulty for causal theories. Yet the idea that names' referents are determined by associated descriptions is itself not without difficulties. For Donnellan and Kripke have described examples that make a convincing case for the conclusion that an object can be the referent of a name, even though the object uniquely satisfies none of the properties that are commonly associated with the name.[36]

One of these examples is Kripke's Gödel-Schmidt case. Practically the only thing most people have heard about Gödel is that he discovered the incompleteness of arithmetic. So it is quite plausible to suppose that this is the only property commonly associated with the name 'Gödel' that Gödel in fact uniquely satisfies. But as Kripke points out, people's uses of the name 'Gödel' would still succeed in referring to Gödel even if it had not been Gödel but an unknown Viennese named 'Schmidt' who actually discovered incompleteness.[37] Moreover, no matter how many further properties might be commonly attributed to Gödel and associated with his name—properties, for example, involving additional achievements for which Gödel is famous—it is quite clear that people's uses of 'Gödel' would refer to Gödel even if he had possessed none of these properties, even if someone else had done all those things for which Gödel is famous.

So an object can be the referent of a name, or a particular use of a name, even though the object uniquely satisfies none of the properties that are commonly, or publicly, associated with the name. This in fact seems generally true of the names we use. But then it surely must be false to suppose that names are governed in public languages by reference rules that are expressible by use of definite descriptions. For if a name were governed by such a rule in a public language, English say, then speakers of English would commonly follow this rule in using the name, and so there *would* be a property that is commonly associated with the name by speakers of English, a property that the name's referent would have to uniquely satisfy. But again, there in general seem to be *no* such properties.

We saw earlier that the reference rules we follow in using names are not the kind of rules that govern indexicals and that they are also not rules that are expressible by use of genuine terms. The only alternative left is that these rules are expressible by use of context-independent definite descriptions. Yet we've just seen that names are in fact not governed in public languages by rules that are expressible with descriptions. It seems to follow that names are governed by no semantic rules or conventions at all! But if this is so, then it seems impossible that names should even *have* referents. This is the paradox of names.

It is important to be clear about what examples like the Gödel-Schmidt case do and do not show. I have said that these examples show that an object can be the referent of a name or use of a name, even though the object uniquely satisfies none of the properties that are *commonly associated* with the name. Causal theorists usually make the additional claim that these examples show that an object can be the referent of a use of a name, even though the object satisfies none of the properties that *the speaker associates* with the name. However, as I have argued elsewhere, this additional claim is not supported by the features of the examples.[38]

A typical use of the name 'Gödel' by a speaker who associates the property of having discovered incompleteness with this name would no doubt refer to Gödel even if Schmidt and not Gödel had discovered incompleteness. But this would not be a case in which Gödel, though the referent of the use, fails to uniquely satisfy *every* property that the speaker associates with the name 'Gödel'. For among the many other properties that a typical user of 'Gödel' would associate with the name are such properties as being one to whom the speaker has heard others refer with 'Gödel'; being a man of whom the speaker has heard that he discovered incompleteness; and so on. Now these are not properties that are commonly associated with the name 'Gödel', for they are properties that involve the particular speaker in question. But nevertheless, they are properties that Gödel would uniquely satisfy in the example. So it is open to a description theorist to maintain that the speaker's use of 'Gödel' would intuitively refer to Gödel in the example simply because the use's referent would be typically determined by one or more of these other properties that *the speaker* associates with the name.

Causal theorists sometimes object that description theorists cannot appeal to such "buck-passing" descriptions as 'the one to whom I have heard others refer with "Gödel"' without involving their view in some kind of circularity.[39] But in my opinion, no clear account of this alleged circularity has yet been given. Of course, if the description theorist's view were that a name's referent is *always* determined by buck-passing descriptions, then his view would in a sense be circular. But this just shows that a description theorist should agree that the success of any name-use based on borrowed reference depends ultimately on the existence of speakers who are in a position to make *independent* references to the object in question.

Perhaps a causal theorist would claim that description theories must inevitably give a false account of *unborrowed* name-reference, because if we trace any chain of reference-borrowing involving a name back to its initial point, the description theorist's account of how the name's referent is initially determined by descriptions that are *not* buck-passing will always be open to counterexamples of the Gödel-Schmidt sort. But this claim would be unjustified. A typical buck-passing use of 'Gödel' would surely be traceable eventually to one or more of Gödel's close relatives, colleagues, or other acquaintances. But can we *really* describe an example that shows that, say, the uses of 'Gödel' by one of Gödel's closest colleagues would have referred to him, even had he uniquely satisfied *none* of the no doubt enormous number of properties that are not buck-passing that the colleague associated with his name? It surely seems unlikely that any such example is forthcoming.

I have yet to see a decisive objection to the point that in the Gödel-Schmidt case and others like it, the referents of the names involved would intuitively be determined by buck-passing properties. So it is consistent with these cases to suppose that the referents of names are in general determined by properties that are associated with the names by their speakers. This fact provides the basis of my solution to the paradox of names.

6. THE PRIVATE-RULE THEORY

We have seen that to use a word as a name is to follow a certain sort of reference rule of the general form (4). We have also seen that the rules in question cannot be expressed by genuine terms and cannot be the kind of rule that governs indexicals. Thus the rules we follow in using names *must* be rules of the form (4) that are expressible by context-independent descriptions. In fact, I suggest, one uses a word as a name if and only if one follows such a rule, a rule of the form:

(2)   For any α, if α is a token of N, then for any x, α is to refer to x if and only if $x = (\imath y)Fy$,

where each instance of 'Fy' expresses a property.[40] This suggestion does justice to the conclusion reached earlier that to be a name is just to be a context-independent genuine term.

But again, examples like the Gödel-Schmidt case show that names are not governed in public languages by rules of the form (20). This may sound inconsistent with the principle that to use a word as a name is to follow a rule of the form (20). But in fact there is no inconsistency. What follows instead of a contradiction is the conclusion that *the semantic rules we follow in using words as names are not rules of the public languages we are speaking in using the words.*

Now I admit that this consequence seems inplausible at first glance. It is certainly not a possibility that strikes one as immediately obvious. But nevertheless, I maintain that our unlikely-seeming consequence *must* be true. For if it is not, then we have to deny one of the above set of compelling assumptions that together imply it, and the paradox of names is unresolved.

To make this solution to the paradox acceptable, we need to make it plausible that people could be meaningfully speaking a language in using a word, even though the semantic rule they are following is not a rule of the language they are speaking. This can be done by use of the concept of a second-order rule that was introduced earlier. In section 2, I argued that the basic rules regarding singular terms in natural languages are second-order rules that permit the following of certain first-order reference rules and prohibit the following of others. The only kind of second-order rules considered before were rules that explicitly mention the first-order rules that they permit speakers to follow. But it is conceivable that a language could contain a second-order rule that permits speakers to follow any of a certain general *sort* of first-order rule, without mentioning any *particular* rule of that sort. This, I suggest, is the kind of second-order rule regarding names that occurs in natural languages.

Simply put, the second-order rule for names that occurs in natural languages is just the following: it is permitted to use any word as a proper name. More precisely, the rule is:

(21) For any token α of any word N, if α is used as a proper name by a speaker, then the referent of α is to be determined in accordance with the first-order rule being followed.

Here it is of course understood that to use a word as a proper name the speaker must be following a first-order rule of the form (20).

On the view I am proposing, (21) is the *only* semantic rule concerning names that occurs in natural languages like English. But (21) mentions no particular first-order reference rule involving any particular name. So the existence of (21) in English is not sufficient to turn any particular first-order rule of the form (20) into a non-basic rule of English. Thus when a speaker of English uses a word as a name, he or she is following a reference rule of the form (20), but the rule being followed is not a rule of English. Yet such a speaker would nevertheless be meaningfully speaking English, for in following a rule of the form (20), he or she would be doing something permitted by the rules of English, and the name-use in question would have its referent determined accordingly.

The basic idea is that proper names are like "wild cards" that the rules of English allow to be used in accordance with unspecified rules of a certain sort at the speaker's discretion.

The following is my official explication of what it is for a speaker to use a word as a proper name:

(22) α is used as a proper name by $s = df.$ There are a property F and a word N such that: (i) α is a token of N; (ii) s utters α; (iii) in uttering α, s is actualizing a stable disposition to utter tokens of N in certain circumstances with the understanding that these tokens are subject to the rule that:

(R) For any β, if β is a token of N, then for any x, β is to refer to x if and only if $x = (\imath y)Fy$;

and (iv) is logically possible that, for some object x, both s utters α and $x = (\imath y)Fy$ even though α does not refer to x.

This definition has two new features that require further explanation. Statement (22) conforms to the idea already proposed, that to use a word as a name is to follow a reference rule of the form (20). But in addition, (22) requires that a speaker who uses a word as a name must be exercising a stable disposition to follow the rule in question in certain circumstances. This requirement is necessary to avoid violation of the principle enunciated earlier that a word cannot be *used as* a name of an object unless it *is* a name of that object. For a word to be a name of an object, I suggest, it is sufficient that there be at least one person for whom the name is a name of that object. And further, I would say that a word is a name of an object for a person just in case the person has a stable disposition to in certain circumstances follow a rule of the form (20) concerning that word, where the object uniquely satisfies the property *F* mentioned in this rule. Given these assumptions, it follows from definition (22) that a person cannot use a token of a word as a name of an object unless the word is a name of that object.

The second feature of (22) requiring explanation is the presence of clause (iv). This clause is intended to rule out the occurrence of what we might call "blatantly question-begging" properties in rules of the form (20) that determine reference for uses of names. For instance, consider the property of being referred to by all tokens of 'Socrates' that are uttered by *s*. We surely would not want to allow such a property to occur in any rule of the form (20) that determines reference for use of *s* of 'Socrates'. Clause (iv) prevents such properties from occurring in rules of the relevant kind.

On the other hand, (22) does allow what we might call "factually question-begging" properties to occur in rules of the form (20) that determine name-reference. For instance, (22) allows buck-passing descriptions like 'the one Jones's tokens of "Socrates" always refer to' to occur in rules of the relevant sort. If Smith always follows such a rule in uttering 'Socrates', and it should happen that Jones passes the buck right back to Smith by always following a similar rule concerning 'the one Smith's tokens of "Socrates" always refer to', then of course neither Smiths's nor Jones's tokens of 'Socrates' would ever have referents. But the fact that this unfortunate sort of thing *can* happen is not a good reason to insist that buck-passing properties could *never* determine a name's referent. For surely not all, and perhaps very few, buck-passing properties actually turn out to be factually question-begging in this way.

The theory of names that I am proposing has two main parts, each of which is independent of the other. The first part is the explication (22) of what it is to use a word as a name. The second part is the thesis that the only rule about names to be found in natural languages like English is the second-order rule (21). As we've seen, it is a consequence of this second thesis that the rules of the form (20) that we follow in using words as names are, as a matter of fact, not rules of the languages we are speaking. But I should stress that my theory allows there to be *possible* languages that contain rules of this form governing words that are names in those languages.

7. SOME FEATURES AND CONSEQUENCES OF THE PRIVATE-RULE THEORY

The private-rule theory is a description theory of names on which names' referents are determined by privately associated descriptions. Theories of this kind are of course not new to the literature. I take the chief novelty of the present paper to lie not in the type of theory proposed but in the new *argument* I've given in favor of this type of theory, an argument that if sound refutes other types of theories of names, such as causal theories. But the private-rule theory does have some novel features that both distinguish it from other forms of private-description theories and make it preferable to these other theories.

The main intuitive difficulty that faces any private-description theory is this: how can a description that is idiosyncratically associated with a name by a given speaker determine the semantic referent of that speaker's uses of the name in a public language? The private-rule theory gives a novel solution to this problem via the hypothesis that natural languages contain a second-order rule permitting speakers to invent and follow their own rules for proper names. I should stress that this second-order rule is *not* the same as a permissive rule that allows a speaker's use of a name to semantically refer to whatever the speaker intends it to refer to on a given occasion. A rule of this latter sort is the kind of rule that governs demonstratives like 'this', and as we've seen, the hypothesis that names are governed by such rules would not allow us to properly distinguish names from demonstratives. Instead of permitting speakers' uses of names to refer to whatever they like, the second-order rule in English for names in effect directs speakers to supplement English with new rules of the form (20). When a person does this and then follows such a rule, the person's name-use does not just refer to whatever he likes. Instead, it is *as if* the person were speaking a language containing the new rule in question, and his linguistic behavior is accordingly constrained by this rule.

A related difficulty that often plagues private-description theories is that of adequately distinguishing speaker's reference from semantic reference in the case of names. Consider again the example of Smith, who always uses 'Reagan' as a name of the president, but who by mistake often uses 'Reagan' to refer to his neighbor Jones. Of the descriptions associated by Smith with 'Reagan', some are true of the semantic referent, Reagan, and some are true of Smith's neighbor Jones. The problem for a description theory is to provide a method of distinguishing those descriptions that determine a name's semantic referent from those that determine what the speaker is referring to. The private-rule theory helps to provide such a method. When Smith says such things as "Look, Reagan is mowing his lawn again," Smith's primary intention is to say something about his neighbor. This is why it is intuitively correct to say that Smith is referring to Jones with his use of 'Reagan'.[41] But it is consistent with Smith's having this primary intention that when he utters 'Reagan', he is *following a semantic rule* of the form (20) that requires his utterances of 'Reagan' to refer to the president, and not Jones. This explains how it is possible for Smith to use 'Reagan' as a name of the president while at the same time he is referring with 'Reagan' to his neighbor.

One of the most important consequences of the private-rule theory is the distinction it implies between a word's being meaningfully used in a language and the word's having a particular meaning in that language. As we explained earlier, the private-rule theory allows a word to be meaningfully used as a name, even though the rule being followed is not a rule of the speaker's language. The theory also says that natural languages like English do not contain rules of the form (20) for proper names. And since a name has a particular linguistic meaning in a language only if the language contains a rule of the form (20) governing that name, the theory implies that as a matter of fact, proper names have no linguistic meanings in English or other natural languages. Another way of putting this is to say that *proper names are not words of natural languages.*

The idea that names do not have particular meanings in their speakers' languages has not been discussed very much, but a few philosophers have expressed intuitions that support the idea. These intuitions confirm the private-rule theory. For instance, Strawson has pointed out that "ignorance of a man's name is not ignorance of the language."[42] Vendler has noted that names do not require translation into another language and that, accordingly, dictionaries do not list proper names.[43] And Ziff has given the following argument to support the idea that names are not words of their speakers' languages:

If I say 'Are you familiar with Hsieh Ho's view on art?' I am speaking English: I am not speaking a combination of Enlish and Chinese. Yet if 'Hsieh' and 'Ho' are words then they can only be words of Chinese . . . and I must speak a combination of English and Chinese, which is absurd.[44]

Ziff is clearly right that having adopted a name used by speakers of another language, we may use it in sentences of pure English. But is he right when he claims that 'Hsieh Ho' could only be a word of Chinese? Why isn't it true that when we adopt the use of this name, it then *becomes* a word of English as well as Chinese?

If 'Hsieh Ho' becomes a word of English when we adopt its use as a name, then when we adopt this use, we are changing English. For we will have added a word to English, and to do this we will have had to add a new semantic rule to the rules of English, namely, a rule for 'Hsieh Ho'. But it seems clearly false that we have changed English in any way when we begin using 'Hsieh Ho' as a proper name. This seems true in general: when we introduce a new name for an object, we are not changing English. We are instead doing something that is already permitted and anticipated by the rules of English. Since the private-rule theory predicts that we do not change our language when we adopt new uses of names, the intuition that this is so is evidence in favor of the theory.

In order to explain how proper names work, I have had to argue for hypotheses about the semantic structure of natural languages that make such languages look far different than they are usually described. I have had to explain how words that are literally without meanings can yet have referents and be used to express propositions. And I have had to explain how it is possible to follow a semantic rule and thereby be speaking a language, even though the rule is not a rule of that language. Kaplan has aptly remarked that proper names "are like bicycles. Everyone easily learns to ride, but no one can explain how he does it."[45] One further small piece of evidence in favor of my theory is that if it is true, then it is easy to see why proper names have proven so difficult to understand.

Notes

1. The research on this paper, at various stages of its development, was supported by a Summer Stipend Award from the National Endowment for the Humanities and by a grant from the American Council of Learned Societies under a program funded by the National Endowment for the Humanities. Material in this paper forms part of a larger work currently in preparation on the semantics of singular terms and the intentionality of mental states. Many of the ideas and views expressed here, especially those in section 1, will receive much more extensive elaboration and defense in the larger work.

I am especially indebted to Lawrence Powers, whose valuable criticism of my earlier views led me to write this paper and who made useful comments on an earlier draft. I am also grateful to Lawrence Lombard and John Tienson for helpful comments and discussions.

2. I use the expression "to follow a rule" in such a sense that it means more than just acting in accordance with a rule. To follow a rule in the sense I mean is something like thinking of one's behavior as subject to the rule, or letting one's behavior be guided by the rule. I do not have an analysis of the concept, but I think its intuitive content is clear enough to justify my use of it here.

3. See Gottlob Frege, "On Sense and Reference," in *Translations from the Writings of Gottlob Frege*, edited by P. Geach and M. Black (Oxford, 1966).

4. See Frege's "The Thought: A Logical Inquiry," translated by A. M. Quinton and M. Quinton, *Mind* 65(1956):289-311.

5. David Kaplan, "On the Logic of Demonstratives," in *Contemporary Perspectives in the Philosophy of Language*, edited by P. A. French, T. E. Uehling, and H. K. Wettstein (Minneapolis, 1979), 403. What I am calling "linguistic meaning" and "sense," Kaplan calls "character" and "content," respectively.

6. Saul Kripke, "Naming and Necessity," in *Semantics of Natural Language*, edited by D. Davidson and G. Harman (Dordrecht, 1972), 270.

7. Gareth Evans puts the point this way in "Reference and Contingency," *Monist* 62 (1979), 173.

8. A description is contingent if and only if: it is possible for an object to satisfy the description, and necessary that any object that does satisfy it could exist without doing so.

9. It is worth noting that Kripke's modal intuitions about names apply equally well to indexicals, thus providing more evidence that indexicals are genuine terms.

10. "Naming and Necessity," 276-77.

11. See, for example, R. Thomason and R. Stalnaker, "Modality and Reference," *Nous* 2(1968):359-72.

12. For a fuller statement and defense of this approach, see Evans, "Reference and Contingency," 167-70.

13. Here I am assuming that any reference-condition φ that occurs in a rule of the form (4) for an indexical term can always be expressed in terms of a two-place relation that the referent of any token of the term uniquely bears to *that token itself*. I eliminate the need for variables ranging over other contextual features such as the speaker, time, and place by using the token to fix these features. Thus, a token α of 'I' refers to x just in case *x is the unique speaker of α*; a

token α of 'now' refers to x just in case x *is the unique time at which* α *is uttered*; and so on.

14. For an example of this view of demonstratives, see Tyler Burge, "Demonstrative Constructions, Reference, and Truth," *Journal of Philosophy* 71(1974):205-23. On the distinction between speaker's reference and semantic reference, see Saul Kripke, "Speaker's Reference and Semantic Reference," *Midwest Studies in Philosophy* 2(1977):255-76.

15. On this picture, notice, English contains *no* basic first-order reference rules for genuine terms. This is because in English, *any* term that is not a name *could* be used as a name, so that any first-order rule for a term that is not a name may be violated. We shall see below in section 6 why English contains no basic first-order rules for names themselves. Of course, my view allows there to be *possible* languages containing basic first-order rules for terms, provided that these terms are *unambiguous* in the languages in question.

16. Views of this kind have been suggested by David Kaplan, "Quantifying In," *Synthese* 19(1968):178-214; Keith Donnellan, "Speaking of Nothing," *Philosophical Review* 83(1974): 3-31; Gareth Evans, "The Causal Theory of Names," in *Naming, Necessity, and Natural Kinds*, edited by S. Schwartz (Ithaca, 1977), 192-215; and Michael Devitt, "Singular Terms," *Journal of Philosophy* 71(1974):183-205.

17. See my paper, "Names and Intentionality," *Philosophical Review* 87(1978):171-200.

18. New York, 1981.

19. For further discussion, see my "Review of *Designation*, by Michael Devitt," *Canadian Philosophical Reviews* 3(1983):112-16.

20. See "Speaker's Reference and Semantic Reference," 263.

21. Here I am disagreeing with the theory of names that I proposed in "Names and Intentionality," 190-97. That theory implies that a name-token semantically refers to an object only if its speaker refers to that object with the token. But I now believe that this implication is false. Lawrence Powers changed my mind by pointing out to me that on each occasion when Smith refers to Jones with 'Reagan', he is doing so *just because 'Reagan' is his name for the president*. So it is intuitively correct to say that on each such occasion, Smith is still using 'Reagan' as a name of the president, and thus his use semantically refers to the president, even though *he* refers to Jones.

22. Here it matters whether we take designation to be a counterpart of speaker's reference or of having an object in mind. These latter two concepts are not precisely the same, since one can refer to only one object with a name-token, but one can have more than one object in mind in using the token. (I ignore this distinction in the text for the sake of simplicity.) In the present case, Smith has *both* Reagan and Jones in mind in using 'Reagan'. So if we take designation to be a counterpart of "having in mind," the proposal of (13) is still false, for then Smith's token of 'Reagan' would designate Jones even though the token does not semantically refer to him.

23. Devitt disagrees with Kripke's view (and mine) that in cases like this, the speaker is referring to an object that is not the name's semantic referent. He would prefer to say that the speaker *partially* refers to both Jones and Reagan. (See Devitt's paper, "Donnellan's Distinction," *Midwest Studies in Philosophy* 6(1981):511-24.) But this view still yields the result that the proposal of (13) is false, for on this view, Smith's token of 'Reagan' would semantically refer to Reagan without (fully) designating him.

24. Evans also suggests that the conventions for names are of this sort in "The Causal Theory of Names," 209.

25. I have argued at length that reference rules do not govern speaker's reference, or any other kind of psychological state, in my paper "Psychologism in Semantics," *Canadian Journal of Philosophy* 13(1983):1-25.

26. One could of course give interpretations of the proposals of (14) and (15) on which b is not assumed to be genuine but is instead, say, allowed to be a definite description. I doubt that Devitt had a proposal of this kind in mind, but in any case we'll take theories based on such rules into consideration below.

27. My earlier theory of names in "Names and Intentionality" also suffered from this kind of defect.

28. I ignore rules of the form (16) in which the occurrence of α in $\ulcorner (\imath y)Cy\alpha \urcorner$ is *vacuous*, as when for example the instance of $\ulcorner (\imath y)Cy\alpha \urcorner$ is of the form $\ulcorner (\imath y)(Fy \ \& \ \alpha = \alpha) \urcorner$.

29. See note 13 above.

30. See, for example, John Searle, "Proper Names and Descriptions," in *The Encyclopedia of Philosophy*, vol. 6, edited by P. Edwards (New York, 1967), 490.

31. For instance, I mentioned above Devitt's intuition that the convention for a name is a convention that the name is to designate *a certain object*, and this of course is a convention that would make the name in question context-independent rather than indexical. And at one point in his book, Devitt remarks: ". . . for two tokens of an ambiguous physical name type are intuitively of different semantic types if they designate different objects. This is not the case with demonstratives and definite descriptions . . . ." (*Designation*, 136.) Another causal theorist, Kripke, has also suggested that a name-type with several distinct referents should be thought of as homonymous. See the preface to *Naming and Necessity* (Oxford, 1980), 7-10.

32. The above argument is not conclusive as it stands because it is possible for there to be indexicals that could not refer to more than one object. One might claim that names are indexicals of this sort and thereby avoid my argument. Still, a similar point can be made about this (very unusual) sort of indexical. Suppose we have an indexical W that is governed by a rule of the following form in a language L:

(R) For any α, if α is a token of W, then α is to refer to an object x if and only if $x = (\imath y)(y = (\imath z)Fz \ \& \ Cy\alpha)$.

Though W could not refer to more than one object (since any object it ever refers to is $(\imath z)Fz$), it could refer to an object x in one context and yet refer to *no* object in another context (since x and the token uttered might fail to satisfy $\ulcorner Cy\alpha \urcorner$). But no *name* could have this sort of property. For if W is a name of x in L by virtue of L's containing a certain rule, and one is following this very rule and thereby using W as a name, then surely one would have to be using W as a name *of x*, and so one's token would *have* to refer to x. So indexicals of this special sort cannot be names either.

33. "Naming and Necessity," 347-48, 33.

34. Causal theorists usually qualify this suggestion by saying that after a name has been introduced in this way, *future* uses of the name do not *in fact* have their referents determined by the introducing description, but rather by their causal relation to the introduction ceremony. But no causal theorist would, I think, wish to deny that a name *could*, at least in principle, have its referent permanently fixed in a language by a rule like (18). See the discussions by Donnellan in "The Contingent *A Priori* and Rigid Designators," *Midwest Studies in Philosophy* 2(1977): 12-27; and by Evans, "Reference and Contingency."

35. See Kripke, "Naming and Necessity," 293-303; and Devitt, *Designation*, 13-23.

36. Kripke, ibid.; and Donnellan, "Proper Names and Identifying Descriptions," *Synthese* 21(1970):335-58.

37. "Naming and Necessity," 294.

38. See my paper, "Kripke's Objections to Description Theories of Names," *Canadian Journal of Philosophy* 8(1978):485-97.

39. See Kripke, "Naming and Necessity," 297-300; and Devitt, "Brian Loar on Singular Terms," *Philosophical Studies* 37(1980):271-80. I replied to Kripke's objections about circularity in my "Kripke's Objections," ibid.; Loar replies to Devitt's similar objections in his "Names and Descriptions: A Reply to Michael Devitt," *Philosophical Studies* 38(1980):85-89.

40. I will add some qualifications to this proposal below in definition (22). Notice that the proposal is consistent with the possibility that the properties in the rules that determine names' referents often, or even typically, involve an element of causality. I myself am inclined to believe that this is true because it seems that names' referents are typically determined by buck-passing properties, and these properties usually seem to involve an element of causality. ('The one I have *heard* others refer to with "Gödel"', for example.) If speakers do typically rely on buck-passing properties in their uses of names, this is no doubt because they generally desire to

use names in conformity with other speakers' uses to facilitate communication. I take this to be the grain of truth that lies behind causal theories. Of course, as I point out in the text, no description theory can imply that names' referents are *always* determined by buck-passing properties, on pain of circularity.

41. On the connection between referring to an object and primarily intending to say something about the object, see my "Names and Intentionality," 191-93. See also my "Causes and Intentions: A Reply," *Philosophical Review* 90(1981):408-23.

42. P. F. Strawson, "On Referring," in *Readings in the Philosophy of Language*, edited by J. Rosenberg and C. Travis (Englewood Cliffs, N. J., 1971), 190.

43. Zeno Vendler, "Singular Terms," in *Semantics*, edited by D. Steinberg and L. Jacobovits (Cambridge, 1971), 117.

44. Paul Ziff, *Semantic Analysis* (Ithaca, N. Y., 1960), 86.

45. David Kaplan, "Dthat," in French, Uehling, and Wettstein, *Contemporary Perspectives*, 385.

MIDWEST STUDIES IN PHILOSOPHY, IX (1984)

Causal Theories of Knowledge[1]

FRED DRETSKE AND
BERENT ENÇ

C ausal theories of knowledge require some causal connection between belief and the conditions whose existence make that belief true. Lacking this connection, the belief may be true, it may be altogether reasonable, but it is not knowledge.

Philosophers have a variety of reasons for imposing this requirement. Aside from its intrinsic plausibility in cases of perceptual knowledge, the condition has a solid, naturalistic ring to it. It does a fair job in avoiding Gettier-type examples; it helps fix the object of belief; it shows promise as a device for avoiding skepticism and foundational regresses; and it bids fair to capture the intuition that a belief, to qualify as knowledge, must have no admixture of accidentality in its correspondence with the facts. Whatever the reason, many philosophers have endorsed some version of the causal theory.

Our purpose in this essay is to examine the basic elements of a causal theory. We shall argue that it isn't clear whether a causal theory *can* do the job it is supposed to do, but, if it can, some fundamental revisions must be made in the role the causal condition plays in the production of belief.

The following is a first formulation of a causal condition on knowledge. It isn't intended to be complete. It is, at best, a *base* clause in most formulations of the causal condition. Nevertheless, it represents the causal theory in its purest form, and it is the pure form of this theory that (allegedly) applies to our clearest cases of knowledge (e.g., perception).

C(0): S knows that P only if the fact that P is the cause of S's belief that P.

I can see (hence, know) that I have five fingers on my right hand only if the fact that I have five fingers on my right hand causes me to believe this.

Though we commonly talk of events—and sometimes facts—as the cause of things, these modes of description tend to obscure important distinctions that are, we believe, vital to an appropriately formulated causal analysis of knowledge.

517

Consider the cause of Tom's intoxication. On Tuesday afternoon, Tom drinks a quart of clear liquid. The liquid in question happens to be gin, a 94 proof liquid. We have one event (fact?) referred to (expressed?) in different ways: Tom's drinking a quart of clear liquid and Tom's drinking a quart of gin. Since it is the event itself (however we may happen to refer to it) that enters into causal relations, it seems to follow that it was Tom's drinking a quart of clear liquid on that afternnon that caused him to become intoxicated. This, though, isn't right. What causes Tom's intoxication is not his ingestion of a quart of clear liquid, but his ingestion of a quart of gin. *In* drinking a quart of gin he drinks a quart of clear liquid, but the former, not the latter, is (what we will call) the *effective cause*. If Tom's ingestion of a quart of clear liquid is (because the liquid in question is gin) *the same event* (fact?) as his ingestion of a quart of gin, then we need some way of specifying the *causally effective* or *causally relevant* elements of this single event (or fact). The notion of an effective cause is our way of doing this.

To see why this distinction is important for a causal theory of knowledge, consider Sally's allergy to lecithin—a substance found in milk and egg yolks and often added to chocolate bars. Sally has noticed that whenever she eats chocolate, she breaks out in a rash. After a dinner party, noting the distinctive rash beginning to appear, she comes to believe that there was chocolate in the food. In fact, there was chocolate (with lecithin) in the mole sauce served with the chicken. The chocolate in mole sauce doesn't really taste like chocolate and it is hard to detect. Nothing else Sally ate contained lecithin. Under the circumstances, it seems clear that Sally does not know that the food contained chocolate.

Is the fact that there was chocolate (with lecithin) in the food Sally ate the *same* fact as that there was lecithin (in the chocolate) in the food she ate? Is her ingestion of the chocolate with lecithin in it the *same* event as her ingestion of the lecithin in the chocolate? These questions do not seem to have clear answers. What is clear is that if these facts (or events) *are* the same, then we need a more discriminating way of referring to the cause of belief. We can, of course, refer to the event that caused Sally's rash (and resulting belief) with any of the following expressions: Sally's eating the mole sauce, Sally's eating the chocolate (in the mole sauce), Sally's ingesting the lecithin (in the chocolate). And since her belief that the food she ate contained chocolate was caused by the event these expressions pick out, it was, it seems, caused by her eating the chocolate. But though these expressions pick out the same event (token), her belief that the food she ate contained chocolate is distinct from her belief that the food she ate contained mole sauce or lecithin. A causal theory of knowledge should, therefore, prescribe different causes for these different beliefs. To do this one needs a finer grained analysis of the causal condition, an analysis that looks to those properties of the event that make it a causally effective agent. *The food's containing chocolate* (with lecithin) is not what caused Sally's rash (and subsequent belief). It isn't (what we are calling) the *effective* cause. The effective cause was *the food's containing lecithin* (whether or not in chocolate). The food's having chocolate in it is causally irrelevant—its only relevance being that, as a matter of fact, this particular chocolate had lecithin in it.

Describing the cause as an event or fact (without focusing on the effective properties) obscures these essential distinctions.

Speaking of effective causes is merely a way of shifting from an extensional to an intensional mode of discourse about events and causes, a way of referring to event tokens that exhibits their relevant type affiliation and thereby reflects the lawful regularities that underly their causal power. The event token, c, has its effects (the rash, Sally's belief) by virtue of being a realization (instance, token) of a certain property (event *type*)—the ingestion of lecithin—and there is, under the circumstances, some causal regularity between events *of that type* and such effects.[2]

It may be thought that we are putting a burden on the causal condition that it was not designed to bear. It isn't that C(0) is wrong or too weak. Rather, what disqualifies Sally's belief (that there was chocolate in the food) as knowledge is not the failure of the causal condition, but the failure of some *other* condition on knowledge. Perhaps, that is, Sally fails to know there was chocolate in the food because she has a false background belief, the belief that *only* chocolate produces the rash, and a correct analysis of knowledge requires, besides a causal condition, some condition excluding the presence of false background beliefs.

The exclusion of false background beliefs may be required at some point in the proceedings, but we don't think it is relevant here. The causal theory has the resources for handling this case without invoking other conditions. What disqualifies Sally's belief (as a form of knowledge) is *not* that she has a false background belief, but that this false belief affects her *causal* relationship to the world—thereby disqualifying her on causal grounds. Compare: what makes the instrument inaccurate is a faulty spring, but the spring is responsible for the instrument's inaccuracy only because it changes the way the world *affects* the instrument—changes the way the instrument responds to external conditions. If *that* didn't change, the faulty spring would be irrelevant. And so it is with false background beliefs. They are relevant to the acquisition of knowledge, but only because they influence the way we causally interact with the world. A false background belief merely makes it more difficult to satisfy the causal condition on knowledge.

C(0) should therefore be reformulated to reflect this more discriminating specification of the cause. The causally effective properties must be made explicit. We do so by abandoning the factive and adopting the gerundive mode of specifying the cause: something's *being* F, *turning* G, *ingesting* H, or whatever. We also, in order to avoid unnecessary complications, restrict ourselves to *de re* beliefs.

C(1): S knows of a that it is F only if a's being F is the cause of S's believing of a that it is F.

Sally doesn't know that the food contained chocolate because it was not the food's containing chocolate that (via the rash) caused her to believe this. It was the food's containing lecithin. Hence, Sally fails to satisfy C(1).

C(1) forces one to distinguish between a house's being painted blue and a house's being painted Toby's favorite color even when blue *is* Toby's favorite color. Even though we have one event (or fact?) described in different ways, we have two (potentially) effective causes (or event *types*): its being painted blue and its being painted Toby's favorite color. This is a distinction a causal theory of knowledge needs. For we surely want to make distinctions, *cognitive* distinctions, between two beliefs, one of which is caused by *a*'s being painted blue, the other of which is caused by *a*'s being painted Toby's favorite color. The causal conditions on knowing that *a* is blue are *not* the same as knowing that *a* is Toby's favorite color.

Though an improvement, C(1) is still inadequate. Not only does it fail to cover what Alvin Goldman calls Type II cases,[3] it also fails to accommodate obvious counterexamples involving overdetermination.

If I am caused to believe that a patient will soon die by observing massive, and inevitably fatal, brain damage, I know he will die (other possible conditions being satisifed) even though I am not caused to believe he will die by his impending death. Rather, his death is caused by a condition that causes me to believe he will die. I am causally connected to the condition I believe will obtain (patient's death), but not in the way described by C(1). Instead, I am caused to believe of *a* that it will be F by a condition, massive brain damage, that causes *a* to be F.

We could, following Goldman, supplement C(1) to include this more indirect type of causal relationship. This would be premature. For one can know the patient will soon die even if he is hit by a truck as he leaves the hospital and dies from the injuries sustained in this accident—even if the massive brain damage that causes one to believe he will die does *not* cause his death. This, of course, is merely a version of Brian Skyrms's example.[4] If a man dies of poisoning and is later beheaded, his death is not causally related to his decapitation. He died of poisoning. Yet, one can know he is dead by observing his decapitated state. One knows a condition obtains to which one's belief bears no causal relationship.

Such examples have convinced some that a causal condition is much too demanding. It isn't that there must actually be some causal connection (however indirect) between the belief and the condition believed to obtain. Instead, the belief may be caused by some condition (event, state) that, though it doesn't actually cause the condition believed to exist, is causally *sufficient* for it. So, for example, if one is caused to believe that the patient will die by the presence of massive brain damage, then one knows he will die even if the brain damage doesn't actually cause death. It is enough that it *would* cause death if nothing else did.

It seems to us that some modification of the causal theory along these lines is necessary. A *pure* causal theory, one requiring an *actual* causal connection between *a*'s being F and the belief that *a* is F, cannot be sustained. It is enough, and perhaps within the spirit of a causal theory, if the cause of belief is a causal guarantor of the truth of that belief.

In cases where the belief that *a* is F is caused, not by *a*'s being F, but by a condition (*b*'s being G) that is causally sufficient for *a*'s being F, we will speak of the cause (of belief) as being a *causal surrogate* for *a*'s being F. Modifying C(1) accordingly gives:

C(2): S knows of *a* that it is F only if S's belief of *a* that it is F is caused by
    (a) *a*'s being F or (b) some causal surrogate of *a*'s being F.

It is important to emphasize, though, that whether we are speaking of the condition itself, or some causal surrogate for it, it is the *effective cause* that figures essentially in the satisfaction of C(2). As we saw in the case of Sally, she failed to know that the food contained chocolate because it wasn't the food's containing chocolate that was the effective cause of belief. And in cases where a causal surrogate is operating, it must be the surrogate's effective property (that property whose realization makes the event an effective cause) that figures in *both* the event's causation of belief *and* in its sufficiency for *a*'s being F.

To illustrate this with a Type II case, suppose Clarence sees Tom drink a quart of gin and is caused to believe by this observation that Tom will soon be drunk. A pure causal theory, a theory that looks to the actual causal relations existing between events in a given situation, would reach the judgment that the causal condition was satisfied by Clarence's belief. Yet, if Clarence does not see that (or otherwise know that) it is gin that Tom is drinking, if it isn't Tom's *drinking one quart of gin* that causes Clarence to believe this, then C(2) renders the verdict that Clarence does *not* know that Tom will get drunk. The condition that causes him to believe that Tom will soon be drunk must be the condition that is sufficient for Tom's getting drunk.[5]

By giving Clarence what turns out to be true background beliefs (e.g., the belief that the bottle contains gin), we make him susceptible, so to speak, to only the *right* causes. Seeing Tom drink one quart of gin is not enough to know that Tom will get drunk, not if the effective cause of this belief is Tom's drinking one quart of liquid. To satisfy C(2), one needs a discriminating network of background beliefs, a network of background beliefs that "tune" one to those properties of the event that are causally responsible for Tom's getting drunk. Justificationalists may insist, as a further condition, that Clarence's belief about what it is that Tom is drinking be somehow justified. Reliability theorists may be willing to dispense with this additional requirement. But the point remains that C(2) makes the kind of discriminations one expects of a causal condition on knowledge. It is a way of capturing, within the spirit of a causal theory, what Nozick was after in requiring an ability to "track" the world.[6]

This same point can be made with a Type I case. If Clyde's fuel gauge functions properly on weekdays but not on weekends, does Clyde know he needs gas when he consults the gauge (reading "empty") on Tuesday? Once again, a causal condition [e.g., C(0)] that ignores effective causes gives the wrong answer. Since (it may be supposed) it is the fact that the tank is empty that causes the gauge to register "empty" and this, in turn, causes Clyde to believe his tank is empty, the causal condition is satisfied. But C(2) requires us to judge this case otherwise. If Clyde is unaware of the gauge's erratic behavior, if he trusts it *every* day of the week, if, in other words, it is the gauge's reading "empty", *not* its reading "empty" *on a weekday* that is the effective cause of belief, then Clyde does not satisfy C(2). To satisfy C(2), it is not enough that the gauge read "empty" on what is, in fact, a weekday and that its reading "empty" cause Clyde to believe he is out of gas. The property of the gauge that is causally sufficient for an empty tank (reading "empty" on a weekday) must actually be the property of the gauge in virtue of which it causes Clyde to believe. Clyde is being caused to believe by a condition which, under *some* description, is causally sufficient for an empty tank, but it isn't under *that* description that it functions as a cause of Clyde's belief.

C(2), then, appears to be an improvement on less analytical (and, hence, less discriminating) statements of the causal condition on knowledge. By abandoning the requirement of an *actual* causal connection (no matter how indirect) while retaining (in the notion of a causal surrogate) the idea of causal sufficiency, and by insisting on the importance of an event's effective properties in the articulation of the causal relationships, C(2) yields a better fit with the data without altogether losing touch with the original spirit of the causal theory.

We must now confront a problem that plagues all causal theories. For we sometimes come to know that *a* is F by a condition or state of affairs (*b*'s being G) that bears *no* causal relation to *a*'s being F, fails even to qualify as a causal surrogate of *a*'s being F. We are not thinking of familiar difficulties causal theorists have with mathematical, general, and abstract truths (does 2 + 2 being 4 *cause* you to believe that 2 + 2 is 4?). There are problems enough with empirical knowledge of particular facts. We are thinking, instead, of situations in which *b*'s being G is a reliable (perhaps only a *locally* reliable) sign of *a*'s being F when this reliability is not a manifestation of any *causal* regularity. That is, *within* certain environments there seem to be de facto, noncausal correlations that are sufficiently extensive and unexceptional (in *those* environments) to confer on *b*'s being G the power to produce a knowledge that *a* is F.

Think of our ability to recognize automobiles by their silhouette and styling. Does the car's *being an Oldsmobile* cause it to have that silhouette and styling? Apparently not, since some Oldsmobiles don't look like that. Is its having that appearance *a causal surrogate* of its being an Oldsmobile? No, since we can easily construct a forgery. Nevertheless, if, as a matter of fact, no other car looks just like that particular model Oldsmobile, why isn't this fact alone (quite aside from the question of whether this fact is a manifestation of a *causal* regularity) enough to enable one to recognize it *as* an Oldsmobile? Face recognition exhibits the same pattern. I recognize my uncle by his face although his having that face and his being my uncle are causally unrelated. His having that face, the one by means of which I recognize him, could be the result of a disfiguring accident.

A frog's cognitive capacities exhibit a similar structure. Lettvin et al. have identified the effective properties of the stimulus in the production of the frog's response to flying insects.[7] What causes the frog to flick at the flying bug with its tongue is the bug's projecting (to the visual receptors of the frog) a small, dark, moving profile. *Anything* exhibiting these visual properties will do. Carefully produced shadows that are used in the laboratory turn out to be as effective in triggering the response as bugs are in the frog's natural habitat. The frog's (so-called) bug detectors, those systems of neurons that have their optimal firing rate to this kind of visual stimulus, are *bug* detectors only by grace of the fact that in the creature's natural surroundings only edible bugs exhibit that constellation of properties. But something's being a small, moving, dark spot is not causally sufficient for its being an edible bug. The shadows show that. And the creature's being an edible (to the frog) bug does not cause it to be a small, moving, dark spot. *Dead* bugs are perfectly edible and they don't move. The frog doesn't recognize them. Something's being a small, moving, dark spot plays the same role (in the frog's recognition of bugs) that one's uncle's face plays in recognizing him as one's uncle.[8]

Or consider Tinbergen's well-known studies of the stickleback fish. During the mating season, the males turn a bright red on their underside.[9] Males use this feature to recognize male intruders, and females use it to identify interested males. The fish react this way to a variety of objects of similar coloration: artificial wooden models eliciting aggressive behavior in the males and sexual interest from the females (a red mail van passing the window of the laboratory provoked similar behavior). Tinbergen notes that "the stickleback responds simply to 'sign stimuli,' i.e., to a few characteristics of an object rather than the object as a whole. A red fish or a red mail truck, it is the signal, not the object, that counts."[10]

This is a fairly primitive form of recognition, of course, but is it much different (aside from number and complexity of characteristics involved) from the way *we* identify the sex of people we meet? It illustrates nature's way of solving an epistemological problem. There are no red "models" (much less mail trucks) in the stickleback's natural habitat. As long, therefore, as there are no other objects with this peculiar coloration, nature can economize on the cognitive resources it devotes to satisfying the organism's needs. The "sign stimuli" are enough. It is a matter of indifference whether there is a causal connection between having a red underside and being a male stickleback. What is important is that the fish's sensitivity to this characteristic developed *because* it was, at least in the fish's natural surroundings, a reliable index to the presence of a male conspecific.

It may be objected that frogs and fish don't have beliefs. Hence, their so-called cognitive exploits are irrelevant to a theory of knowledge. Perhaps. But the causal theory is an attempt to naturalize knowledge, and if, for whatever reason, we do not yet have knowledge at this biological level (because, for example, we don't yet have beliefs) we surely expect to find the kind of natural relations between organism and environment that will confer upon beliefs, once they arrive on the evolutionary scene, the status of knowledge. Even if one insists on a justificational account of knowledge, the frog surely has (without being able to exploit it *as* a justification) as good a justification for thinking there is an edible bug in the vicinity as we have for most of the things we purport to know.

Nature adopts the most economical strategy in designing systems to satisfy their needs. So do engineers. If a system needs F's, and hence requires the cognitive wherewithal to recognize F's, it is enough to design a system to recognize G's if, in point of fact, *only* F's are G in the system's sphere of operation. Furthermore, it is clear that for the purpose of this design problem, it is irrelevant whether in that sphere of operation this correlation between F and G is a symptom of some underlying causal regularity. Why build a fuel gauge whose responses are limited, specifically, to *gasoline* in the tank when one that will respond the same to *any liquid* in the tank will, given the normal operation of the gauge, serve as well? The fact that our automobile gauge cannot distinguish between gasoline and water in the tank does *not* prevent us from learning what we need to know (that there is still some gas left) from the gauge. (Once again, it is irrelevant to point out that it is gasoline in the tank that is causing the gauge to register "full"; the point is that it is not *its being gasoline* that causes this.) If it requires a greater expenditure of cognitive effort to distinguish F's from non-F's than it does to distinguish G's from non-G's, it would be profligate of nature (or an engineer) to design a system for which *a*'s being F was the effective cause when *a*'s being G will do the job. And it *will* do the job as long as the system in question remains in an environment in which there exists this correlation between F's and G's. Why complicate the frog's nervous system to enable it to distinguish real bugs from deceptive shadows when such hardware is irrelevant to the frog's efficiency in its natural surroundings? *If* mock (unedible) bugs start to appear in swamps and ponds (exhibiting the same effective properties as bugs now do), nature will see to it that either the requisite means of discrimination develops or that frogs will vanish from swamps and ponds. To retain their fitness, frogs will need a new mechanism, one that is sensitive to more subtle, discriminating properties of the stimulus. The same can be said about the stickleback.

These considerations suggest that the causal factors associated with knowledge, if they are to be found at all, must *sometimes* be found in the etiology of those mechanisms that *now* enable an organism to know something from which it is causally insulated. If a belief that *a* is F is produced by *b*'s being G, and the causal unrelatedness of *b*'s being G and *a*'s being F does not *itself* prevent this belief from being knowledge, then perhaps this is because the cognitive structures responsible for this disposition *themselves* have the right causal antecedents. Natural selection, through processes that are fairly well understood, has "tuned" organisms to be sensitive to properties in their environment that are (locally) reliable signs of other properties that the organism needs to detect, recognize, and respond to. This tuning process sometimes exploits noncausal correlations to achieve its ends. Exposure to these correlations leads to the development of mechanisms in members of the species that enable them to satisfy their needs by responding to properties that are not necessarily causally related to the satisfaction of these needs. The long time span, the magnitude of the numbers involved, and the high price paid by false starts require that the correlation responsible for the development of these mechanisms be a widespread and prolonged one. Spurious correlations, those not persisting throughout the geographical range and temporal duration of the species' evolution, will not be causally effective in shaping such cognitive dispositions.

The learning process occurring in the lifetime of an individual is in some ways similar to the adaptive development of a population. Certain relationships, the persistent co-occurrence of F with G, produce a change in the organism's cognitive dispositions: i.e., in its tendency to believe (anticipate) that *a* is (will be) F upon perceiving *b* to be G. Our earlier examples of recognizing a person by his face and a car by its styling was meant to illustrate this phenomenon. As learning theorists like to put it, the contingencies between stimuli (the degree of co-occurrence of F and

G) produce a change in the organism's pattern of responses—a change, if you will, in the function mapping stimuli onto beliefs (or responses).

One learns to recognize coffee cups, trucks, and umbrellas. One does so by acquiring a sensitivity to certain properties that are (often) only locally correlated with the condition whose presence one learns to recognize. Philosophers are fond of pointing out that many of our ordinary concepts are *functional* concepts. To be a coffee cup, a truck, or an umbrella is not to have a certain shape, color, and size. It is to function, or be used (or be designed to be used) in a certain sort of way. Yet, though such objects are not classified in accordance with their sensible properties, we *use* these sensible properties in identifying them. One can see that *a* is a coffee cup, not because one sees it being used in a way a thing must be used (or usable) to qualify as a coffee cup, nor because one apprehends the intentions of its designer, but because it has the kind of sensible properties that, as a matter of fact, only things of that (functional) kind have. Knowing that *a* is a coffee cup in this way is no different than a stickleback's recognition of another stickleback. We each exploit properties of the object whose correlation with the object's being as we believe it to be has produced in us (by evolutionary adaptation in the case of the fish, by learning in our case) the requisite sensitivity. If things go right, our cognitive *dispositions* have the right cause.

Where does this leave us? Our discussion suggests yet another modification of the causal condition on knowledge, something along the following lines:

C(3) S knows of *a* that it is F only if S's belief of *a* that it is F is caused by (a) *a*'s being F or (b) a causal surrogate of *a*'s being F or (c) some condition (*b*'s being G) whose effective property's (i.e., G's) correlation with F has produced in S the disposition S manifests in acquiring this belief.

This is *still* a causal condition of sorts. The final clause (c) is merely a causal condition on the background beliefs that "map" (current) stimuli onto (current) beliefs.

We are, however, very reluctant to propose this as even a partial analysis of knowledge. The whole structure is getting too creaky and unwieldy. It threatens to collapse under its own weight. Can such a monstrous condition possibly be *a* condition on knowledge? We doubt it.

Furthermore, the suggested change departs significantly from the kind of intuitions that originally motivated a causal theory of knowledge. If this is *a* causal theory of knowledge, it certainly isn't what most philosophers will recognize as *the* causal theory of knowledge.

Finally, we are uncertain about whether causal theorists shouldn't be content with a causal condition on background beliefs *alone*. That is, the drift of our argument has been, implicitly, an argument *against* the necessity of C(2). If it is, as we argued, the fact of correlation (within an organism's environment), not the causal or lawful grounding of this correlation, that is responsible for the development of those cognitive mechanisms on which an organism depends to satisfy its needs, then it is, or *should* be, this *same* fact that figures in a naturalized picture of knowledge.

If it is the correlation, *whether causal or not*, that is responsible for the development of cognitive systems exhibiting a "displaced" sensitivity (a sensitivity to something's being G when what the organism needs, or needs to know about, is F), then it should be these correlations, not their causal foundation, that is relevant to evaluating the organism's cognitive condition. But if this is so, the causal connection [expressed in clauses (a) and (b) above] between individual beliefs and their satisfaction conditions turns out to be irrelevant. The relevant question is whether the correlations that make a belief reliable were themselves instrumental in shaping the cognitive mechanisms that determine what and when an organism believes. That is, the relevant question is whether (c) is satisfied.

Nevertheless, despite our uncertainty on this matter, we think that something resembling C(3) is the best chance, perhaps the *only* chance, a causal theory has for giving a realistic picture of knowledge. So let us close by mentioning one counterintuitive, but (we think) perfectly acceptable, consequence of clause (c) in C(3). Consider the following situation: Toby lives on the Island of Elysium, geographically and ecologically isolated from the rest of the world. In Elysium all yellow fruit contains citric acid. There are, for example, no bananas on the island. Addition of citric acid causes milk to curdle. Curdled milk is the basic ingredient of the most popular cheese in Elysium, and Toby's family has been in the business of producing curdled milk for cheese manufacturers for many years. They have handed down the secret of making curdled milk from generation to generation. The "secret," though, happens to be that the juice of *any* yellow fruit will curdle milk, something that is (considered literally) false though, when applied to the yellow fruit on *that* island, true enough. What promoted this belief, of course, is the repeated (and varied) success in curdling milk with the juice of yellow fruit. Toby, preparing to curdle the batch of new milk, believes, as he has always believed, that the milk will curdle. What causes him to believe this is his careful extraction of the juice he is using from some yellow fruit—lemons in this case. What causes the milk to curdle is *not* the additive's being the juice of yellow fruit. It is the additive's containing citric acid that causes this. So Toby's (false) background belief makes him sensitive to something (being the juice of a yellow fruit) that is neither the cause, nor is it a causal surrogate for, the condition (curdling of the milk) he expects to occur.

Yet, given the unexceptional correlation between the juice of a yellow fruit and its milk-curdling powers *on that island*, and given the fact that it was the existence of this persistent correlation over generations that caused Toby to have this background belief, it seems to us altogether reasonable to say that Toby *knows* the milk will curdle.

The similarity between this case and the lecithin example is instructive. In each case, the agent's belief that *a* is (will be) F is caused by a property that is causally unrelated to *a*'s being F. In Sally's case, however, the correlation between something having chocolate in it and the appearance of her rash was largely coincidental. Many things not having chocolate in them would produce the rash. Sally just hasn't eaten them. Nevertheless, two properties F and G that are not persistently correlated in a person's *natural environment* may, for whatever reason, be perfectly correlated in that person's *experience*. As a result, the person (like Sally) may become disposed to believe that something is F upon encountering an instance of G. The causal antecedents of Sally's disposition are no different than the antecedents of Toby's disposition. Both have *experienced* a uniform correlation. Why, then, say that Toby knows but Sally doesn't?

Since, in natural selection, the stakes are so much higher (survival? extinction?), it is difficult to find organisms whose genetically coded dispositions are analogous to those of Sally. But we find a variety of creatures in Toby's condition. The difference is partly a matter of degree, something having to do with the extent and reliability of the correlations that produced in one the disposition to believe. Such issues are familiar ground in epistemology. The attention given to "relevant alternatives" and "defeasibility conditions" is a symptom of the importance of this issue. But there are deeper intuitions operating in distinguishing Toby's from Sally's condition. It is, we think, the biological paradigms that function in our classifications of epistemological reality. Toby knows, whereas Sally doesn't, because Toby is more like the frog and the stickleback than Sally. If *nature* had designed a cognitive system for Toby, one to be used in the satisfaction of (let us imagine) a biological need to curdle milk, nature would have yielded precisely what we find in Toby —a sensitivity to the color of fruit. That is all nature did for the frog and the stickleback. Why should it do more for Toby? And if nature wouldn't have done it any different, who are we to demand higher design standards? But Sally is a different matter. If she had a biological need for chocolate, her reliance on the rash would be short-lived indeed.

If we are correct in thinking that the biological examples form a paradigm for our ascriptions of knowledge, then the problem of relevant alternatives ought to be approached by a causal theorist by looking to see how closely each case approximates that paradigm. One has to ask what the natural environment is and, secondly, whether, if there were genuine biological needs at stake, a continued disposition of *that* kind in *that* environment would long survive.

Notes

1. Our thanks to David Sanford for helpful comments on an earlier draft.

2. The distinction we have in mind here was made by J. L. Mackie in terms of the difference between "explanatory causes" and "producing causes" (see his *The Cement of the Universe* [Oxford, 1974], 262-68). Mackie writes, "We can . . . say that the concrete event, this hammer blow, was the producing cause of the chestnuts' change of shape, it was what actually led on to this change; but the explanatory cause was the fact that there was a blow of at least such-and-such a momentum . . . . The concrete event was not necessary in the sense in which the fact was; the event could have been different without altering the result, whereas the fact as stated could not" (265). Mackie goes on to note that explanatory causes generate opaque contexts, whereas producing ones are purely extensional.

Our reference to effective causes is a way of talking about Mackie's explanatory causes. But we don't like the word "explanatory." It suggests that the cause is an artifact of our explanatory or epistemic stance—hence, something unavailable for the analysis of such epistemic concepts as knowledge. Reference to effective causes *is* relevant to explanation, but not because reference to such causes is covertly a reflection of our epistemic attitudes. Rather, a causal explanation is (among other things) an attempt to identify the relevant connection between cause and effect – to identify, in other words, the *effective* cause – those *properties* of the events whose lawful relation underlies their causal relationship.

Elliott Sober has a helpful discussion of a closely related distinction in "Why Logically Equivalent Predicates May Pick Out Different Properties," *American Philosophical Quarterly* 19(April 1982). Sober argues, rightly we think, that expressions like "Sally's eating the chocolate" (not his example) are ambiguous between a rigid and a nonrigid designation of the property in question.

3. Alvin Goldman, "A Causal Theory of Knowing," *Journal of Philosophy* 64(1967):357-72.

4. Brian Skyrms, "The Explication of 'X knows that P'," *Journal of Philosophy* 64(1967): 373-89.

5. A causal theroy of *perception*, a theory about what Clarence *sees*, need not advert to effective causes. For if Clarence sees Tom drinking a clear liquid, and the liquid in question is gin, then (whether or not Clarence knows it) he sees Tom drinking gin. But knowledge, seeing *that* Tom is drinking gin, is different. We return to this point again.

6. Robert Nozick, *Philosophical Explanations* (Cambridge, Mass., 1981), 178.

7. J. Y. Lettvin, R. R. Maturana, W. S. McCulloch, and W. H. Pitts, "What The Frog's Eye Tells the Frog's Brain," *Proceedings of the Institute of Radio Engineers* 47(1940-1951).

8. In the frog's natural surroundings, of course, it *is* (usually) a nearby bug that causes the frog to believe (or, if this is too strong, to respond as if) there is a bug nearby. But this, as we have argued, is irrelevant. It is also gin that Clarence sees Tom drinking. This doesn't mean that Clarence is in a position to *know* that Tom is drinking gin. What is of relevance to a causal theory of *knowledge* (though not to a causal theory of *perception* – i.e., what objects and events we perceive) is whether *its being a bug* (its being gin) is the effective cause of belief.

9. N. Tinbergen, "The Curious Behavior of the Stickleback," *Scientific American*, December 1952; reprinted in *Frontiers of Psychological Research* (San Francisco).

10. *Frontiers of Psychological Research*, 9.

The Concept of Knowledge

COLIN McGINN

1. TYPES OF KNOWLEDGE

Analysts of knowledge have typically confined their attentions to propositional knowledge (knowledge that such-and-such is the case). Answering the question "What is knowledge?" has thus been assumed to be possible by treating only of a single type of knowledge; the other types of knowledge have accordingly been deemed secondary, and their correct elucidation has been supposed strictly irrelevant to the proper analysis of propositional knowledge.

It seems to me that this is a dubious procedure. The concept of knowledge occurs in a variety of different locutions—knowing how, knowing who (which, where, etc.), knowing one thing from another—and it is a condition of adequacy upon an account of knowledge that it display the unity in this family of locutions. For the word 'know' is surely not ambiguous; and it is reasonable to expect that there is some discernible common theme upon which the different types of knowledge can be exhibited as variations. And once we take on the responsibility of confronting the whole family of knowledge locutions, it is by no means guaranteed that propositional knowledge will emerge as fundamental: perhaps the core notion will attach most directly to some other locution, so that knowledge-that comes out as a species of some more basic type of knowledge. The methodological situation here is comparable with that in the theory of causation: the word 'cause' likewise occurs in a variety of locutions, and it is a desideratum of any analysis of the concept of causation that it somehow unify these different uses.[1] To refuse the obligation of seeking this unity, by concentrating exclusively upon one type of causal or knowledge locution, is to run the risk of parochialism in one's analysis of the concepts and hence of drawing a distorted picture of what causation or knowledge essentially involves. In particular, the analysis of a given locution of the families concerned should be sensitive to the conceptual links of that locution with others.

I think that this methodological constraint already throws suspicion upon certain of the standard and received analyses of knowledge. It is hard to see, for instance, how the justified true belief account of propositional knowledge can be extended or modified to encompass the other types of knowledge (notably knowing how); and the causal theory, to take a more topical proposal, does not appear any better placed in this respect.[2] What is wanted, from the present point of view, is some component of our account of knowing-that which can be seen to play a role in our account of the other knowledge locutions. The most obvious and direct way to achieve this unification would be to select one type of knowledge locution as basic and to explain the others in terms of the selected type.

This is the approach I shall favor in this paper. Taking my lead from J. L. Austin[3] and (more explicitly) A. Goldman,[4] I shall suggest that the underlying notion is that of what might be called *distinguishing* knowledge, i.e., knowing one thing (or sort of thing) *from* another. The result is a unified theory of knowledge in which the notion of *discrimination* is central and basic. This kind of theory is by no means novel—it is, indeed, a variant of what have come to be called *reliability* theories of knowledge—but I think the virtues of the theory have not been sufficiently appreciated and its motivation has not, to my mind, been properly articulated.[5] Furthermore, reliability theories in which the notion of discrimination is invoked have also relied upon the use of counterfactual conditionals of certain sorts in providing conditions for knowledge, and I would like to separate the discrimination analysis from its association with counterfactual analyses of knowledge.[6] My reason for wishing this separation is that I find the discrimination theory attractive while finding the associated counterfactual analysis in various respects unsatisfactory.

I shall proceed by critically examining Robert Nozick's[7] recent presentation of a counterfactually formulated reliability theory, arguing that it fails on a number of counts to provide an adequate analysis of (propositional) knowledge. The lessons thereby learned will then help us to arrive at a more satisfactory theory, as judged from a variety of standpoints. A good deal of my discussion will retrace themes familiar from the (swollen) literature on this subject, but I hope I can succeed in putting certain issues and problems in a (somewhat) new light.

2. TRACKING THE TRUTH

According to Nozick, knowledge is (true) belief that 'tracks the truth', where the relation of tracking between a believer S and a proposition p is defined subjunctively, as follows:

(i)   If p weren't true, S wouldn't believe that p and
(ii)   If p were true, S would believe that p

When we add to these two conditions the usual requirements that p be true and that S believe that p, we are claimed to have (subject to some minor refinements) necessary and sufficient conditions for S to know that p. The basic idea is that knowledge is not merely *actually* believing what is true but being *disposed* to believe what is true and being *indisposed* to believe what is false: knowledge is belief that is counterfactually sensitive to the truth value of the proposition believed.[8] This sensitivity thus has two aspects, corresponding to the counterfactuals (i) and (ii), which Nozick refers to as the *variation* and *adherence* conditions, respectively. Putting these two conditions in terms of the usual possible worlds semantics for counterfactuals, we can say that S has knowledge that p iff (i) in all the worlds closest to the actual world in which p does not hold S does not believe that p, and (ii) in all those close worlds in which p does hold S believes that p: belief that p is not preserved in the close not-p worlds and it is preserved in the close p worlds.[9] Thus tracking is supposed to provide a sense in which S's true belief is not merely *accidentally* true, since it varies subjunctively with the truth value of the proposition believed.

It is natural to see Nozick's tracking theory as a direct descendant of the causal theory; for the causal theory also conceives knowledge as a certain kind of linkage between a belief and the fact that makes the belief true, the linkage consisting in a 'causal connexion' between belief and fact.[10] Indeed, adjoining a counterfactual account of causation, in the style of David Lewis,[11] to the causal theory of knowledge yields a theory looking very like Nozick's; and once this step has been taken the resulting theory becomes, as the original causal theory was not, hospitable to nonempirical knowledge.[12] I emphasize this affinity with the causal theory because I think that Nozick's tracking theory encounters difficulties very like (some of) those that have been acknowledged to beset the causal theory; so (as I shall argue) we need to make a more radical break with the causal theory if we are to capture the true character of the concept of knowledge. We need, in particular, to give up the idea that knowledge consists in a relation between the person's belief and that which makes his belief true.

My criticism of the tracking theory falls into three parts: first, I shall contest the necessity and sufficiency of Nozick's conditions; second, I shall press some difficulties regarding knowledge of necessary truths; third, I shall voice some misgivings concerning the primitive use of subjunctive conditionals in Nozick's analysis.

There seems to me room for doubt as to whether the variation condition is *necessary* for knowledge, though I recognize that intuitions may differ here. The following (rather extravagant) case convinces me at any rate that the condition is too strong. Suppose we are living in a universe in which there also exists a benevolent deity who watches over our sensory input: he has the intention to preserve this input by artificial means in the event of a cataclysm in which the material objects that actually produce it should suddenly go out of existence. Let us suppose that this cataclysm is, in fact, physically possible and that the deity has the power to carry out his intention. Then it seems that we have the truth of this counterfactual: 'If the objects around me were to go out of existence, I would still believe that I was surrounded by those objects'—since the deity would see to it that my experience sustained this belief were the cataclysm to occur. (We also, of course, have the adherence condition satisfied in this case.) Yet I am reluctant to say that, because of these facts, we do not *know* that we are surrounded by material objects:

for the truth of the counterfactual does not, intuitively, make our true belief that we are surrounded by material objects merely *accidentally* true.[13] Suppose that in the whole history of the universe the cataclysm never in fact occurs, though *if* it had the deity would have intervened to preserve our beliefs: can we really say that we do not then know, e.g., that the earth exists?

Or consider a parallel example concerning our knowledge of other minds: the deity intends to keep other people behaving normally in the event, which we can suppose physically possible, that they suddenly cease to have mental states, and in so doing to preserve my beliefs about their mental states. It turns out that this mind-destroying cataclysm never occurs, but if it had I would have persisted in my beliefs about the mental state of others, thanks to the deity's intervention. Again, it does not seem to me wrong to say that in these circumstances I nevertheless *know* that other people have various mental states: for it is, intuitively, not merely an *accident* that these beliefs of mine are true. If it be thought that the introduction of a deity somehow makes these cases illicit, then the following case might be found more compelling. Suppose S believes on the usual sorts of grounds that trees exist, but it is also true that if trees were not to exist he would still believe they did because the absence of trees would alter the chemical composition of the atmosphere in such a way as to interact with the chemicals in his brain so as to preserve this belief in him (he gets hallucinations of trees, etc.). In this case Nozick's variation condition fails, but my intuition is that S still knows that there are trees. These counterfactuals just seem not to be relevant to assessing S's claim to knowledge.

Explaining why there is knowledge in these cases requires a positive theory of what makes knowledge possible, which I will try to set forth later; for now I am merely testing Nozick's theory against what I take to be our spontaneous verdicts on such cases. The suspicion is already raised, however, that Nozick's conditions succeed in predicting our intuitions, in the cases where they do, because of a more or less fortuitous coincidence between the truth of the tracking counterfactuals and some conceptually distinct property that is covertly doing the real work of distinguishing knowledge from nonknowledge.[14]

Turning now to sufficiency, I think the inadequacy of Nozick's analysis stands out yet more starkly. Remember that knowledge is claimed to be belief that tracks the truth of *the proposition believed*, and consider the following case. You visit a hitherto unexplored country in which the inhabitants have the custom of simulating being in pain. You do not know that their pain behavior is mere pretence, and so you form the belief of each person you meet that he or she is in pain; imagine you have acquired a great many false beliefs in this way. There is, however, one person in this country who is an exception to the custom of pain pretence: this hapless individual *is* in constant pain and shows it (we can suppose that he falsely believes others to be in his unfortunate condition—he has not been told of the pretence by the others). You also believe of this person, call him N, that he is in pain. Now I take it that we would not say that your true belief that N is in pain counts as knowledge, for it is, intuitively, a mere accident that your belief is true in this instance. But now consider the relevant counterfactuals, in particular 'if N were not in pain, you would not believe that N was in pain': this counterfactual is *true* in the envisaged circumstances, since if N were not in pain then (unlike the pretenders around him) he would not behave as if he was, and so you would not believe that he was.[15] So your belief that N is in pain *does* track the truth of that proposition even though it does not rank as knowledge.

It may be thought that this is a somewhat special case in that it involves (at least on most views about our knowledge of other minds) an inference from evidence: so can we produce a counterexample to the sufficiency of tracking that is not thus inferential? Well, if ordinary perceptual knowledge is agreed not to be inferential, then I think we can, as follows. Suppose you are surrounded by straight sticks immersed in water that therefore look bent to you; you, however, take them to be in air, and so you falsely believe of each of them that it is (really) bent. There is, though, one stick that is *not* immersed in water and it really *is* bent; on the basis of how that exceptional stick looks you believe it to be bent. Again, I take it that you do not *know* that that stick is bent, since, in view of the circumstances, your belief is only accidentally true. But Nozick's variation condition is satisfied in this case, since if *that* stick were not bent you would not believe it to be, because *it* would not, being in air not water, look bent. So here we have a perceptual belief that tracks the truth of the believed proposition but does not rank as knowledge.

Here is another case of a somewhat different kind. Suppose there is a chemical C in your brain that has the property that only if it is present in your brain can you have beliefs involving the concept of C (surely there are such chemicals in our brains). Now imagine that the neuroscientists are causing you to hallucinate seeing C in your brain but that you erroneously take your experience to be genuinely perceptual; you therefore believe (truly) that C is in your brain. We can suppose that the scientists have been causing a lot of hallucinations in you recently, most of which lead you to form false beliefs; so there is a clear sense in which your true belief that C is in your brain is only accidentally true. I think it is patent that this is not a case of knowledge, despite the truth of the tracking counterfactual 'if C were not in your brain, you would not believe that C was in your brain'.[16] (We can easily describe the case as one in which the adherence condition is also satisfied: suppose the scientists decide to cause you, by means of brain stimulation, to believe that C has reached a certain concentration whenever it does in fact reach that concentration, so that if C were at that concentration you would believe it was. This adherence to the truth would not give you knowledge, especially in the presence of the other false beliefs similarly caused in you by the scientists.)

The lesson of the foregoing examples is that if we to have a reliability theory of knowledge it cannot be a tracking theory: when assessing claims to knowledge we have to reckon with both more and less than the counterfactual dependence of belief upon the truth value of the proposition believed.

The second line of objection I want to mention concerns the applicability of the tracking theory to knowledge of necessary truths, such as the truths of mathematics. The causal theory, notoriously, has its troubles with this sort of knowledge, and so too does Nozick's theory, though for a different reason. The problem is simply that the variation condition, which carries the main burden of the theory, cannot be applied to such knowledge on pain of producing unconstruable counter-factuals—e.g., 'if it were not the case that $7 + 5 = 12$, it would not be the case that S believes that $7 + 5 = 12$'. It is not merely the general problem that we have no adequate theoretical account of counterfactuals with impossible antecedents, since it might well be thought a deficiency of current accounts that they provide no truth conditions for apparently *true* counterfactuals with impossible antecedents;[17] the problem is the specific one that the counterfactuals demanded by the tracking theory appear not to state clear truths.

Nozick himself immediately concedes that his variation condition is inapplicable to necessarily true propositions, but he quickly brushes the problem aside, claiming that the adherence condition will suffice on its own. His rationale for simply deleting the variation condition is just that if the believed proposition is a necessity we are not going to be called upon to consider what the person would believe in the circumstance that it is false.[18] This raises two doubts: first, the tracking analysis now possesses an undesirable asymmetry as between knowledge of necessary and contingent truths—so the univocity of the concept seems not to be properly represented in the analysis; second, the radical weakening of the theory raises the expectation that there will now be problems of sufficiency. The first doubt might, I suppose, be partially allayed by noting that the adherence condition is common to the analysis of knowledge of necessary and of contingent truths; but the second doubt cannot, I think, be brushed off so unconcernedly. For it was precisely the variation condition that, in respect of contingent truths, made the analysis (allegedly) invulnerable to Gettier-type cases; so we should expect that deleting that condition would leave the analysis wide open to such difficulties.

Suppose I perform a computation upon some number n and decide upon this basis that n is prime; I then deduce the existential proposition that some number is prime. But suppose the computation was wrongly executed and n is not prime. Then I have a (justified)[19] true belief that fails to qualify as knowledge; but Nozick cannot exclude this case by adding the condition that if it were not the case that some number is prime I would still believe this. Or suppose I fortuitously acquire a true mathematical belief on the basis of generally unreliable testimony—my informant was trying to deceive me but happened to convey the truth: again we have a Gettier case, but it cannot be excluded in the way Nozick excludes exactly parallel cases involving contingent truths. Moreover, it is hard to see how the adherence condition alone could handle these cases, since it is easy to see how I might also be *disposed* to have these true beliefs—I might have a tendency to make the kind of computational mistake in question, and I might have implicit faith in my mendacious informant who himself has a tendency to have mistaken mathematical beliefs.[20]

Nozick considers only a priori necessities in connection with his tracking analysis, but it is clear that the same problems arise for a posteriori necessities too.[21] Suppose someone forms the belief that a lectern is made of wood on the basis of a hallucination that happens to be veridical; here we have a classic Gettier case in which the proposition believed is a necessity. Nozick cannot exclude this case in the way he would for a parallel case in which the believed proposition is contingently true, namely by observing that if that lectern were not made of wood the person would still believe it was; so it seems that Nozick is powerless to exclude such cases. And if the adherence condition is insufficient by itself in the contingent case, it is difficult to see how it can suffice for the exactly analogous cases in which the believed proposition is necessary—and indeed it is readily seen that this condition is insufficient. Nozick has thus introduced an asymmetry into his account of knowledge that prohibits him from treating intuitively analogous cases in the same way: whether a proposition is necessary or contingent should not be relevant to the conditions required for someone to know it—the metaphysical should not intrude in this way upon the epistemological.[22]

I can summarize the problem necessary truths pose for the tracking analysis in this way: Gettier cases of the familiar sort show that justified true beliefs can be true by accident, and that if they are they fail to count as knowledge; but whether a true belief is thus accidentally true is surely independent of its modal status—it depends, intuitively, upon how the belief was acquired; so we should not try to capture the idea of accidental true belief, and hence the concept of knowledge, in terms of apparatus whose application *is* dependent upon modal status. That is, the same kind of thing is going wrong in cases in which (e.g.) a true existential belief is inferred from a false singular belief (in a justified way), whether the former belief is in a necessary or a contingent truth; so we do not want our *account* of what is going wrong to treat these cases differently. If this uniformity constraint is accepted, it shows that the failure of the tracking analysis to deal with knowledge of necessary truths reflects, and is symptomatic of, a deeper and more general inadequacy: that counterfactual dependence is not the right way to handle Gettier cases and so does not give the correct analysis of knowledge. In short, accidentally true belief cannot be defined as belief that fails to track the truth.[23]

The third and last point I want to make against Nozick's analysis is a very general one and I do not expect that it will be found compelling by everybody; nevertheless, the point does seem to me of some methodological importance across a wide range of issues, including the analysis of knowledge. The point is that it is unsatisfactory to employ counterfactuals in a primitive way in one's analysis of a concept. It is a generally accepted thesis that counterfactuals are true in virtue of categorical propositions; they have *dependent* truth value.[24] We can always legitimately ask what *makes* a given counterfactual true and expect to be presented with a suitable categorical fact. Now it seems to me that this general thesis imposes a constraint upon philosophical analyses, to the effect that we should be able to say what categorical propositions ground the counterfactuals we employ in the analysis. Thus counterfactual phenomenalism, for example, invites the question what grounds the reductive counterfactuals about sense experiences, and a phenomenalist owes it to us to provide some answer to this question. Indeed, it is frequently the case for such counterfactual analyses that the only categorical statements capable of supplying the requisite grounding are precisely those that are allegedly being analysed (or reduced)—in which case a charge of circularity appears in order. On the other hand, if noncircular categorical grounds *can* be produced it seems that the counterfactuals are in principle dispensable in the analysis; they serve merely as an eliminable intermediate or interim step to the real analysis, which is categorical in form.[25]

In the light of this general constraint (of which I have not, of course, offered a full defense), I think we are entitled to press Nozick on the question what makes his tracking counterfactuals true: what *categorical* facts about the believer S and S's relation to the world *make* it true that if it weren't the case that p S would not believe that p and if it were S would? Not to be able to answer this question is not to have completed the analysis of knowledge, according to our constraint; whereas answering it would render the counterfactuals strictly redundant. Since Nozick does not consider this kind of opposition to his style of analysis, we cannot say what sorts of categorical facts he might offer; but it seems to me essential to fill this need if we are to claim a fully satisfying analysis of the concept of knowledge. In the next section I shall try to supply an analysis that does meet this constraint.

3. DISCRIMINATING THE TRUTH

Nozick's theory defines knowing that p as belief that varies with the truth of p; only a single proposition is mentioned in the analysis, along with the person's disposition to believe *that* proposition. Tracking is thus reliable belief with respect only to the proposition believed; the person's reliability with respect to other propositions does not enter the picture. Let us say, in view of this feature of the analysis, that Nozick's tracking theory is a *local* analysis of knowledge—it localizes the conditions for knowledge into a relation between the knower and a unique proposition. Then I think it is easy to see that the counterexamples I gave to Nozick's analysis arise (at least in part) because of the local character of that analysis; for what disqualifies the belief that N is in pain or that that stick is bent from counting as knowledge is that the person is (in a sense to be made more precise) placed in a context in which that person is apt to form (and indeed has formed) many false beliefs in a range of *distinct* propositions.[26] Thus, while in these cases the person's belief that p allows us to infer (nondemonstratively) that p is true, there are other beliefs, which are relevant to whether the person knows that p, which do not provide sound reason for inferring to the truth of what is believed—for the person is *un*reliable with respect to q, r, s, etc. Let us accordingly say that a theory that attempts to incorporate this sort of reliability with respect to other propositions into the analysis is a *global* theory: a global theory takes knowledge that p to require, essentially, some condition that speaks of the person's propensity to believe the truth with respect to a range of distinct 'relevant' propositions. Then the theory I want to put forward is a global reliability theory based upon the notion of discrimination.[27]

The guiding idea of the theory is simple: to say that a person S is globally reliable with respect to a range of propositions is to say that S can *discriminate* truth from falsehood within that range of propositions; global reliability is a capacity to *tell the difference* between true propositions and false ones within some given class of propositions. We then say that S knows that p just if his (true) belief that p is acquired by the exercise of a capacity to discriminate truth from falsehood within some relevant class R of propositions. It is precisely such a discriminative capacity that is lacking in my cases of the pain pretenders and the bent sticks: in the circumstances specified, the person is unreliable with respect to the relevant class of propositions. S cannot in these circumstances tell a real pain feeler from a simulator or a really bent stick from one that merely looks bent; so S's true beliefs that N is in pain and that that stick is bent do not qualify as knowledge, despite the counterfactual dependence of S's belief upon the truth value of those *particular* propositions. The lesson of these cases is then that someone's belief may track the truth of p and yet not result from a general capacity to discriminate the true from the false; and when this capacity is lacking, it is merely accidental that the particular belief is true—hence we do not have a case of knowledge. In other words, we need to consider the truth-discriminating power of the *method* employed by S in arriving at the belief that p, and this will have us looking at the truth value of *other* beliefs acquired by use of this method. Placed in unfavorable circumstances, S might employ a method, e.g. observing how things look, that is apt in those circumstances to produce false beliefs—and getting it right in a particular case will not then constitute knowledge.[28]

The difference between the tracking and discrimination theories comes out, not just in the local/global distinction, but also in that the latter theory makes no essential use of counterfactuals. To introduce a counterfactual element into the discrimination analysis, or to try to *reduce* that analysis to a set of counterfactual conditions, would be to go beyond what has so far been endorsed—and to go, in my view, in the wrong direction.[29] I have spoken only of a global capacity to tell true from false—and nothing in this compels us to go counterfactual. We might, however, choose to take this further step; and if we do there are two places at which counterfactuals might be supposed to come in. We might, first, propose a sort of global tracking theory: we speak of what S would believe were the associated propositions false, and what S would believe were they true—we require, that is, that S's beliefs track the truth of the propositions in the relevant class and not just the truth of p. And second, we might introduce counterfactual conditions that, while keeping the truth values of the associated propositions fixed, specify what S would believe were *he* differently situated: we might say, for example, that S does not know that N is in pain because if he were to meet a pain pretender he would believe that pretender to be in pain. It seems to me that neither of these supplementations is obligatory and that both raise problems we can avoid by sticking to our noncounterfactual formulation.

The first suggestion may be able to handle the sorts of counterexamples to sufficiency that I raised against the local tracking theory, but then Nozick's theory has effectively merged with a global reliability theory and is not an alternative to it.[30] However, the global tracking theory, unlike the global discrimination theory, still runs up against my other objections to Nozick—namely, the problem of knowledge of necessary truths, and those general methodological scruples regarding primitive counterfactuals. It is fortunate, then, that the discrimination theory can be detached from the tracking conception simply by declining to formulate the theory in counterfactual terms: we can instead speak categorically of the person's propensity to form true beliefs across a range of propositions whose truth values are taken as fixed in the actual world. Once we introduce these other propositions, and S's belief propensities with respect to them, we do not need to consider what S would believe were the truth values of these propositions other than what they actually are. Nozick needs the extra strength given by tracking because his is a local theory, but a global theory gets the necessary strength by bringing in *other* beliefs and propositions.

The second suggestion for introducing counterfactuals does not face these objections because it does not employ counterfactuals whose antecedents suppose the relevant propositions to have truth values other than their actual truth values: all that is suggested is, in effect, that we explicate the notion of discriminative capacity by speaking of what S would believe were he situated differently. Thus, the suggestion goes, having a truth-discriminating capacity with respect to a class R of propositions is being such that, were one presented with propositions from R as candidate objects of belief, one would believe the truths and refrain from believing the falsehoods. This is a pleasingly simple view of what such a capacity consists in, but I am sceptical about its adequacy.

In the first place, it seems to me that this explication gets the logical priority the wrong way around; for I would hold, quite generally, that an ascription of capacity is what grounds the associated counterfactuals—it is not that the capacity ascription is true in virtue of the truth of the counterfactuals. This claim is, I think, just a corollary of the general position about counterfactuals and categoricals that I allied myself with earlier: the counterfactuals about what someone would do in such-and-such circumstances are true *because* (inter alia) the person has a certain capacity—the person does not have the capacity because he satisfies the associated counterfactuals.[31] (I do not, of course, claim to have established this view of capacity concepts here; I am merely gesturing at the sort of position that motivates my reluctance to accept the proposed counterfactual explication.)

The second thing I would say is that, even waiving the question of logical priority, it is not in fact correct to propose a counterfactual analysis of what it is to possess a discriminative capacity, since the sorts of simple counterfactual exemplified above do not supply either necessary or sufficient conditions for possessing such a capacity. The point here is familiar: someone can have the capacity to ϕ and yet not ϕ when appropriately placed, and it is possible for someone to ϕ in appropriate conditions and yet not have the capacity to ϕ.[32] This logical gap opens up because the capacity to ϕ is at best only one component of what makes it true that someone will (or would) ϕ: so someone could, for example, have the capacity to hit the bulls'-eye and yet fail to hit it, and someone could hit it and not have that capacity. Possessing a capacity is a more complex condition that the simple counterfactual explication suggests.

Returning to truth-discriminating capacities, it seems to me that possessing such a capacity can likewise be pulled apart, logically, from satisfying counter-factuals about what would be believed under certain circumstances: for a person might satisfy such counterfactuals without genuinely having the *capacity* to tell true from false, since the person might, so to speak, receive outside help; and some-one could have the capacity yet not satisfy the counterfactuals, perhaps because of some sort of extraneous interference in its normal operation. And the third point I would make is that it is simply unnecessary to explicate the notion of discriminative capacity counterfactually: there is no objection that I can see to taking the notion of capacity as primitive in the analysis. In view of the difficulties attendant upon re-ducing the notion of capacity to a set of counterfactual conditions, it seems to me advisable to keep counterfactuals out of the analysis altogether.[33]

It will clarify the conception of knowledge I wish to advocate to contrast it with an attractive and widely held view of perception; the points of contrast con-cern the global character of knowledge and the role of causation in explicating the two concepts. The concept of perception is plausibly understood as both causal and local: to perceive the fact that p requires that that fact should play an appropriate causal role in the production of an experience, and whether a particular experience counts as genuinely perceptual depends solely upon how that experience is related to the fact that causes it. That is, what perception requires is a certain kind of causal relation between an experience and a particular state of affairs—we do not need to establish that *other* 'relevant' experiences are veridical in order to know that a given experience is genuinely perceptual. Knowledge depends upon the status of other relevant beliefs, but perception is possible without such global reliability. I there-fore think that it is a mistake to make perception one's model or paradigm of knowledge; the two concepts operate quite differently.[34] A tracking theory may, indeed, be more workable for perception than we have seen it to be for knowledge.[35]

I just said that knowledge requires more than perception; what I want to say now is that in another respect it requires less. Causation is pretty indisputably a necessary condition for perception, but it seems not to be a necessary condition for knowledge. We give every appearance of having mathematical and other a priori knowledge, but a causal theory is inapplicable to such knowledge; so causation can-not be a necessary condition for the applicability of the notion of knowledge per se.[36] But we surely cannot make sense of the idea that mathematical facts or enti-ties might be (literally) *perceived*. The discrimination theory, by contrast, carries smoothly over to a priori knowledge, so that theory cannot plausibly be said to be somehow tacitly causal.[37] Also, we cannot require even for empirical knowledge that the known fact be the cause of the belief that it obtains, because of the exist-ence of inferential knowledge; for such knowledge the causal requirement must be weakened to mere 'causal connexion'.[38] No such weakening would be possible for perception; what is necessary for perception is that the fact or object straightfor-wardly cause the experience—it is not enough, for example, that fact and experience have a *common* cause.

But I think that in the case of knowledge the weakening of the causal link can in principle go further, even to the point of obliterating it altogether. The discrimination theory explicitly requires only global reliability, so that nothing in that theory, as so far stated, excludes knowledge of empirical facts in a universe in which there is a preestablished harmony: that is, the theory seems to permit knowledge of facts that are totally causally isolated from one's beliefs. And I think that reflection upon such a setup does not contradict the deliverances of the discrimination theory: if one's beliefs correlate with the facts in a sufficiently reliable way, then it seems intuitively that they may rate as knowledge. It is not just that knowledge does not *generally* require perception of the fact known; we can even say that it *never* (logically) requires perception of the fact known—God could give us the capacity to know without giving us the capacity to perceive. Knowledge is thus not an *inherently* causal concept, whereas perception is; and this difference is of a piece with the global character of the former concept and the local character of the latter.[39]

Why should our concept of knowledge be global and not local after the manner of Nozick's analysis? What is the *point* of having a concept of this global kind instead of a local concept 'knowledge*' defined as Nozick tries to define 'knowledge'? The answer (or *an* answer) can, I think, be found by looking at the use we make of the information that someone knows that *p*—what this information equips us to do. If knowledge is global reliability within a range of propositions, then to be told that someone knows that *p* is to be told that this person's beliefs with respect to that range are reliable indicators of the truth; so if we know that *S* knows that *p* we can infer (with good probability) a *number* of truths about the world given information about *S*'s other (relevant) beliefs, since the particular knowledge ascription encapsulates, so to speak, a whole range of true beliefs (or at least propensities to form true beliefs).

Thus the concept of knowledge has a pragmatic role in our acquisition of a range of true beliefs on the basis of what another believes: if someone is certified as a knower, then you can rely upon that person's beliefs in forming your own beliefs about the world. But the tracking theory does not, because of its locality, confer upon 'knowledge*' a pragmatic role of this kind: since only *S*'s disposition to adjust beliefs to the truth value of a *single* proposition *p* is constitutive of *S*'s knowing* that *p*, we can infer from *S*'s belief that *p only* the truth of *p*, when given the information that *S* knows* that *p*. So to be told that someone tracks the truth in respect of *p* is, in itself, no help to us if we are interested in relying upon that person's *other* beliefs in forming ours—and this no matter how 'relevant' those beliefs may be to the belief that *p*. If a community had in use only the concept expressed by 'knowledge*', they would not be in possession of a concept that was designed to enable them to place reliance upon each other's beliefs across of *range* of propositions; and given the utility of a concept that is global in the way I have outlined, we might expect them to introduce the concept expressed by 'knowledge'. Someone who knows can be depended upon on other occasions; someone who merely knows* can be depended upon only in respect of a single belief. Of course, if someone does track a single truth *p* we have *some* sort of reason to believe that his belief-forming methods are *generally* reliable, since this is likely to be the best explanation of why he tracks

the truth that p; but this assumption is strictly *external* to the notion of knowledge[*]
—it is not something that can be read into its very analysis. The concept of knowledge as we have it, on the other hand, is ideally suited to serving our interest in learning from other people.

I have so far steadfastly refrained from *defining* the notion of a truth-discriminating capacity, preferring to leave the notion in a relatively intuitive and unexplicated state. It may be complained that this is objectionable, not because (or just because) it is impermissible to take such notions as primitive, but rather because there is a danger that the analysis as stated is tacitly circular. The objection may take the form of a dilemma: either a truth-discriminating capacity is understood simply as a disposition to have true beliefs within a given range of propositions, or it is something more than this. If it is such a disposition then, arguably, it is insufficient for knowledge; but if we intend to employ a stronger notion, the suspicion is raised that a truth-discriminating capacity is to be defined precisely as a capacity whose exercise produces *knowledge*. Is this line of criticism just? I think there is something to the point that the intended notion of a capacity to discriminate the truth is a stronger notion than that of a disposition to form true beliefs, and that the latter notion is not *strictly* sufficient for knowledge.

Consider this case: a certain child cannot do addition problems—lacking the ability to add, if the child were to get an addition problem right it would be by sheer accident. However, a benevolent and numerate deity intervenes in the child's efforts to add up numbers and directly produces true arithmetical beliefs involving addition in the child's mind; moreover, the deity does this in a regular and dependable way—you could reliably infer the answer to addition problems from the child's beliefs. This is a case where we would say the right answer just pops into the child's head, as a result of the deity's interventions, but the child lacks the *capacity* to employ the method that in us leads to such true beliefs: in such circumstances I think there is some temptation to deny that the child really *knows* what he or she thereby comes to believe. And what is lacked might well be described as a capacity to discriminate true from false arithmetical equations: the child does not have the ability to *tell* which is the right answer to the problems that are set. Indeed, we can even say that there is a sense in which the child's beliefs are only accidentally true, since the child has no *capacity* that explains why the beliefs are true. Now if this is correct, as I have some inclination to think it is, the notions of discriminating and telling are not (at any rate simply) definable in terms of the notion of a disposition to form true beliefs, so that the notion of reliability I am using is stronger than anything that can be delivered by those notions. And it is certainly a question whether the extra strength is got by hearing the words 'discriminate' and 'tell' in such a way as to presuppose the concept of knowledge: to have the capacity to discriminate truths from falsehoods, or to be able to tell whether arbitrary propositions from a certain range are true or false—these capacities might well be thought to be nothing other than capacities *to acquire knowledge*. So there is at least a challenge to me to explain the concepts of discrimination and telling in a way which shows the non-circularity of the account I have proposed.[40]

My response to this accusation of circularity will, perhaps, be shocking to some – an abnegation of the responsibilities of the analyst of knowledge. For I do not think that the kind of circularity alleged is necessarily a bad thing; indeed, I am inclined to think that it is quite a *good* thing. The reason I say this is that I am generally sceptical of attempts to provide analytical *reductions* of philosophically central concepts – attempts to define fundamental concepts entirely in terms of concepts that are in no way contaminated with the concept to be defined. I am sceptical for two reasons: (a) such attempts have seldom, if ever, met with success; and (b) it would be surprising if they had, since it is implausible to explain the existence of the defined concept (or better, its lexicalization) merely as a convenient shorthand for the conditions that exhaustively define it – a much more plausible explanation, it seems to me, is that the concept is in some way primitive.[41]

But I do not think it follows that the whole enterprise of conceptual analysis is therefore misguided and should be abandoned; we should rather adopt a less ambitious and more relaxed attitude to the enterprise of analyzing concepts. We should be content with whatever illumination we can obtain by relating the given concept to others with which it has conceptual liaisons; and we can construct an illuminating conceptual map of a domain of concepts without claiming that the illuminating concepts contain no tincture of the concepts to be illuminated. In other words, conceptual analysis need not be construed as *foundationalist*; it can be, as one says, 'holistic'.[42] Moreover, a theory of the concept of knowledge might derive its rationale less from a project of conceptual breakdown as from a desire to achieve some sort of conceptual unification of the various types of knowledge; and from this perspective, there is no objection even to employing the word 'know' itself in one's theory.

Be this last point as it may, the real test of a piece of philosophical analysis is its capacity to throw light upon our employment of the concept to be analyzed and to provide some sort of explanation of our intuitions: judged by this test I think that the discrimination theory has much to recommend it, notwithstanding a lingering suspicion of 'circularity'. The notion of discrimination does tell us what kind of thing is 'going on' in an attribution of knowledge, and I think that it is unreasonable to insist that conceptual illumination can be got *only* from conceptual reduction.[43] In the next section, we shall see that the discrimination account can also help us to understand and assess sceptical arguments.

4. SCEPTICISM AND CLOSURE

Dretske,[44] Nozick,[45] and others have argued that knowledge is not closed under known logical implication: it is possible for someone to know that p, to know that p implies q, and not to know that q. This nonclosure has been supposed to offer a rebuttal of one form of scepticism, namely the argument that since I do not know I am not a brain in a vat I ipso facto do not know that (e.g.) there is a table in front of me. I find these arguments against closure convincing and the application to scepticism attractive, but I want to dissociate the nonclosure thesis from a tracking analysis of knowledge: I prefer, for the reasons set out earlier, to rest nonclosure upon the discrimination analysis of knowledge. So I shall in this section indicate how to do this; then I shall make some remarks about the relevance of the discrimination analysis to the question whether I know that I know that there is a table in front of me.

The tracking analysis leads to nonclosure by way of the following train of reasoning: for S to know that there is a table in front of him he must be such that he would not believe this proposition if it were not true; and in normal conditions S satisfies this condition, since the antecedent of the counterfactual takes us only to worlds in which, e.g., there is a chair or a dog or some such there instead of a table, but otherwise things are much as they actually are. Similarly, for S to know that he is not a brain in a vat he must be such that if he were he would not believe he was not; but it seems that S *fails* to satisfy this condition, since if he were a brain in a vat he *would* still believe that he was leading a normal life, since (by hypothesis) his evidence would remain unchanged under this counterfactual supposition. But now 'there is a table in front of me' *entails* 'I am not a brain in a vat floating in empty space with no tables within a million miles of me'; so knowledge is not closed under known logical implication, given the assumption that S knows this entailment to hold.

Now those wedded to closure might want to object that this consequence of the tracking analysis is sufficient to show its untenability; so if we want to insist upon nonclosure we need a more intuitive argument for it, one which does not rely upon already accepting the tracking analysis. I want to suggest that the natural intuitive argument introduces considerations of discrimination in a way that conforms with my earlier contentions about knowledge. The following seems an intuitively correct principle: one can *know* that p only if one can *tell whether p* – I can know that (e.g.) it is raining outside only if I can tell whether it is raining outside.

Let us apply this principle to my putative knowledge that there is a table in front of me and that I am not a brain in a vat. Can I tell whether there is a table there? I think that in the ordinary use of the phrase 'tell whether', what this requires is that I can distinguish there being a table from there being a chair or a dog or some such.[46] So, granted that conditions are normal – there is a table there, my eyes are functioning normally, etc. – I *can* tell whether there is a table there. But can I tell whether I am a brain in a vat? Again, assume conditions are normal: I am not a brain in a vat, there is a table there, my eyes are functioning normally, etc. Then what is required for telling whether I am a brain in a vat is that I be able to *distinguish* my being a brain in a vat from my not being a brain in a vat. But it seems clear that I lack this ability – I cannot tell whether I am a brain in a vat because I have no means of distinguishing being in that condition from not being in that condition.

I claim that this reasoning does no violence to our ordinary intuitive understanding of the key locutions it employs; accordingly, we have a pretheoretical argument for nonclosure. It seems to me, furthermore, that the discrimination account of knowledge is hovering in the background of this intuitive reasoning; for what is critical to the argument is the idea of a capacity to *distinguish* one state of affairs from others. To know that there is a table there requires discriminating tables from chairs and dogs and empty corners; to know you are not a brain in a vat requires discriminating this state of affairs from envatment—and a person could have the former discriminative capacity without having the latter.

What is crucial to this defense of nonclosure is the assumption, or thesis, that possessing the capacity to tell whether there is a table there does not require that one be able to tell whether one is a brain in a vat: that is, the discriminative capacity required for the former piece of knowledge does not need to be powerful enough to rule out the possibility that one is a brain in a vat. And this assumption is tantamount to the idea that different propositions carry with them different requirements as to the discriminative capacities necessary for knowledge of them and that knowledge of logically weaker propositions can require greater discriminative power than knowledge of logically stronger propositions. Put less ponderously, it can be easier to know p than q though p implies q (and not vice versa) because q requires more in the way of discrimination than p. The possibility that I am a brain in a vat is, as one says, not *relevant* to telling whether there is a table there.[47]

Now it seems to me that this point about relevance is a virtual datum about discrimination and knowledge: it is simply what the concept intuitively involves, and I cannot see how one could hope to prove it from independent epistemological principles. When we ask whether someone knows a particular proposition p, we just do tacitly presuppose a range of propositions R somehow determined by p whose truth values must be discriminable by the would-be knower. These relevant propositions are in some intuitive sense 'at the same level' as the given proposition—they are propositions 'of the same kind' as the given one: this is why 'there is a dog there' is relevant to knowing 'there is a table there' but 'I am a brain in a vat' is not.[48] I have no precise criterion for this kind of relevance, but I think we do have an intuitive grasp upon how the requirement operates, and hence some understanding of the rationale for nonclosure: nonclosure holds because of the different discriminative requirements imposed by propositions and (some of) their logical consequences.[49]

What nonclosure shows is that it is invalid for the sceptic to infer from our not knowing that his sceptical hypothesis, e.g., that we are brains in vats, does not hold the conclusion that we do not know those ordinary things that we commonly take ourselves to know, e.g., that there is a table there. Nonclosure allows us to accept that the sceptic's initial contention has force without being committed to the alarming conclusion that our ordinary knowledge claims are false. This seems to me some advance against the sceptic, but it leaves an important question open: do we *know* that our ordinary knowledge claims are true? We commonly think, not only that we may have knowledge that there is a table there, but also that we know that we do—so that we are in a position to *assert* that we know that there is a table there. It therefore seems that if we are to be at all consoled by the antisceptical consequences of nonclosure, we need to sustain our conviction that we know that we know. The question, however, is not straightforwardly answered.

The discrimination theory tells us the form of what is required for such

second-order knowledge: to know that you know you have to be able to discriminate the cases in which you have a (first-order) discriminative capacity from the
cases in which you do not. Second-order knowledge thus consists in a capacity to
tell whether you have a capacity. Now I think it is clear that first-order knowledge
does not *entail* second-order knowledge; for one could have a capacity to tell without being able to tell that one has such a capacity—having a capacity does not guarantee knowing one has it. So if we are to secure second-order knowledge it cannot
be by claiming that it simply *follows* from first-order knowledge. Indeed, it might
begin to seem that there is a yawning gap between knowing and knowing one knows
when we recall the concession already made to scepticism; for (it might be thought)
if I cannot tell whether I am a brain in a vat how can I hope to be able to tell
whether I have the first-order discriminative capacity in which my knowing that
there is a table in front of me consists? If I *am* a brain in a vat—a possibility I am in
no position to exclude—then I do not have the truth-discriminating capacity I think
I have; so how *can* I tell whether I have this capacity? I think there is force in this
reasoning—it explains why we feel that agreeing with the sceptic about being a
brain in a vat inhibits us from *asserting* that we know that there is a table there—
but I want to suggest that there is a possible intermediate position that has thus far
been glossed over.

Under what circumstances would we in fact allow that someone has learned
that he (earlier) lacked a truth-discriminating capacity? Well, if he became apprised
of the fact that he had been given a hallucinogenic drug or that he had been the victim of a brain stimulation experiment: he would, in coming to know such things,
come to know that he (earlier) lacked his usual capacity to discriminate the truth,
so that any accidentally true beliefs he acquired in this condition did not count as
knowledge. But, equally, I can (sometimes) tell that I have *not* been subject to such
disruptions of my usual discriminations of the truth: that is, in normal circumstances I am reliable in my beliefs about whether my (first-order) beliefs are the result of normal sensory functioning or of drugs, etc. So being under the influence of
a drug is *not* like the sceptic's vat hypothesis, since I can be credited with the general capacity to distinguish drug-induced beliefs from regular beliefs, whereas I
could not distinguish vat-induced beliefs from regular beliefs in the circumstances
envisaged by the sceptic.[50]

If this is so, then there is a foothold, however narrow, for knowing that one
knows: I can know that I know that there is a table there because I have the general
capacity to distinguish (e.g.) drug experiences from regular experiences. This is an
intermediate discriminative capacity because it is not entailed by the capacity to
tell whether there is a table there, and it does not entail the capacity to tell whether
I am a brain in a vat. And so far as I can see, this intermediate capacity is *stably*
intermediate: there is no cogent reason to suppose that it must collapse into either
of the two extremes—it really does require *less* than the capacity needed to tell that
the sceptic's radical hypotheses are false and *more* than the capacity to tell that
ordinary propositions about the external world are true. This seems to me a moderately happy result, since it allows us to persist in asserting that we know such

ordinary truths while (regretfully, but honestly) conceding that we do not know we are not brains in vats. My only residual worry is that a clever sceptic might show how my incapacity to tell whether I am a brain in a vat *somehow* undermines my claim to be able to tell whether I am now exercising a (first-order) truth-discriminating capacity; but as of this moment, I have not met such a clever sceptic. What I am confident of – and this has been the prime point of the foregoing remarks – is that the discrimination theory provides the right setting for answering the question.

5. FURTHER REMARKS

I began this paper by stating a condition of adequacy upon any analysis of propositional knowledge – the condition, namely, that the analysis should in some way unify the various types of knowledge. This adequacy condition was prompted by the thought that the word 'know' cannot be regarded as ambiguous in its occurrence in the various knowledge-ascribing locutions – there must be some common thread running through the various members of the family of knowledge concepts. I am now in a position to say how I think this unification may be effected: the sought-for common thread is precisely the notion of discrimination. The unification is obvious enough for knowledge-that and knowing one thing from another (what I earlier called distinguishing knowledge); for the burden of my thesis has been precisely that the former is a special case of the latter – it is knowing the true propositions from the false ones within a certain range. Knowledge-which (who, where, what, etc.) also falls smoothly into place; for it is very plausible to say that (e.g.) knowing who the burglar is (in the context, say, of an identity parade) is a matter of being able to *distinguish* that person from other individuals relevant in the context; it is knowing the burglar *from* the guiltless bank manager next to the burglar. Or again, for me to know whom you are speaking of in a conversational context is for me to be able to pick out, identify, or discriminate, from among the range of possible referents, the person spoken of. In much the same way a dog's knowing where its bone is buried consists in its being able to distinguish that place from other places where the bone is not buried. Thus, knowing-which essentially involves a discriminative capacity, where the objects of discrimination are (not propositions but) *things* that are in some way the target of some kind of cognitive state: it is, as we say, knowing the *identity* of some specified item.

Knowing-how admittedly falls into place somewhat less smoothly, but I do not think this should be found so very disturbing, since it seems to me intuitively correct to see this type of knowledge as somewhat removed from the types so far considered. That is to say, knowing-how belongs less to the realm of the strictly cognitive than do the other types of knowledge, as is shown by its connections with the motor faculties. However, I think that something can and should be said to explain why the word 'know' gets used in the ascription of (paradigmatically at any rate) motor skills. First, the notion of *capacity* is common to the application conditions of both knowledge-that and knowledge-how – a capacity (roughly) to believe the truth in the former case and a capacity successfully to do something in the latter case.[51] Second, it seems not unduly strained to characterize knowing-how capacities as discriminative: if someone knows how to ride a bicycle, for example, that person (or the sensori-cognitive-motor system) has the capacity to *select* which movements will lead to bicycle-riding success when sat in the saddle; the person (or the system) can *distinguish* which movements will, and which will not, maintain balance and mobility on a bicycle. Or again, if I know how to reach my office I have the capacity to discriminate selectively from among the courses of action available to me which will get me to my office. As we might say, to know how to ϕ is (at least in part) to know ϕ-ing movements *from* non-ϕ-movements: knowing how to ϕ is knowing *what you have to do* to ϕ. It therefore seems to me that the main varieties of knowledge can be adequately accommodated by the discrimination theory; and this conceptual unification should, I think, increase our confidence in the analysis of specifically propositional knowledge as a truth-discriminating capacity.

Finally, some remarks about knowledge and belief. If the root notion of knowledge is the notion of a discriminative capacity, then it will not be surprising if knowledge is logically independent of belief. That knowledge does not imply belief seems plain for *non*-propositional knowledge, since belief is a propositional attitude, and these other types of knowledge are not ascribed by completing 'know' with a that-clause; if they were to involve belief at all, it would have to be indirectly. It seems to me, though, that we are prepared to make literal ascriptions of knowing-how, knowing-which, and knowing one thing from another to creatures whose status as believers we are (rightly) reluctant to acknowledge: we say without strain of various species of animal that they have such nonpropositional knowledge, though an element of the metaphoric attaches to any ascriptions of belief to them.[52] The reason for this difference is, I suggest, this: possessing authentic beliefs presupposes the capacity to reason, to weigh evidence, draw inferences, and so on; but the concept of knowledge per se requires only a capacity to discriminate, to respond differentially—and this sort of capacity is possible in the absence of a capacity to reason.

Knowledge is thus a *subrational* achievement, whereas beliefs are essentially cognitive states that are formed and interact according to the dictates of rationality. In *this* respect, knowledge belongs with perception (and also memory), for perception is also possible in the absence of belief and reasoning: many animals that can be said to see, hear, smell, etc., what is going on around them could not literally be credited with beliefs. Such animals can, it is true, be credited with informational states that are, if you like, *analogous* to genuine belief; but processing information about the environment is not the same thing as reasoning about it. So both perception and knowledge are, in a clear sense, more primitive than belief; they require less cognitive sophistication than belief. (Knowledge and perception predate belief in evolutionary history.)

But what of *propositional* knowledge: does not it imply belief? The foregoing considerations encourage me to doubt that it does: what is required by knowledge-that is *some* sort propositional attitude, but we need an argument to persuade us that this attitude must be belief. Why not require only something like registering and retaining the information that p, where these 'attitudes' are conceived as sub-rational cognitive states?[53] When we say that the mouse knows that the cat is behind the door, we do not imply that it *believes* that the cat is there; we imply only that the mouse's senses have functioned to register the information that the cat is there. This seems to me an intuitively plausible account of our practice with such ascriptions, and it comports with the analysis of knowledge as a discriminative capacity. If this is correct, then propositional knowledge is also more primitive than belief: it is not, as the tradition has supposed, an especially rarefied form of belief, calling for some higher cognitive faculty than mere belief; rather, it is a condition that even dumb, nonrational animals can aspire to.

These reflections lead one also to doubt the rationalistic conception of (propositional) knowledge as inextricably associated with the having of reasons or justification for belief. For if knowledge does not require belief, then it does not require *justified* belief. It may be replied that we can separate out the requirement of justification from the belief requirement; we can hold that justification is itself more primitive than belief. My response to this is that if we are really speaking of justification—of the *having of reasons*—then we cannot licitly make this separation: to have genuine *reasons* is precisely to have reasons for *belief*. I think this inseparability is again borne out in our descriptions of the cognitive life of (subrational) animals: as we do not readily ascribe beliefs to (certain) animals, so we do not (a fortiori) speak of them as having justifications. Such animals may of course be in receipt of information that provides good grounds for supposing a state of affairs to obtain; but it does not follow that they *have reasons* corresponding to this information. It has been usual for analysts of (propositional) knowledge to inquire what needs to be *added* to truth, belief, and justification to arrive at knowledge; but it seems to me that there are plausible considerations that recommend *subtracting* the second two conditions from the analysis.

The independence of the concept of knowledge from that of justified belief also bears upon the way in which scepticism has traditionally been supposed to arise for our claims to knowledge. Sceptics have characteristically argued that we do not know what we think we do because our justification for the beliefs we hold is in some way inadequate: thus, e.g., none of our ordinary beliefs concerning the external world is really justified because our evidence is (logically) compatible with some other hypothesis. But we are now in a position to protest that this kind of argument presupposes a mistaken conception of knowledge: for if knowledge requires not justified belief but a discriminative capacity, then it is strictly irrelevant to object to a claim to knowledge on the ground that the underlying beliefs are unjustified; what the sceptic has rather to show is that such a discriminative capacity is actually lacking. This means that it is consistent for us to agree with a sceptic that no belief is ever justified and at the same time maintain that we nevertheless have knowledge.

I think this point is best appreciated by considering again cases of subrational animal knowledge. Suppose we say of a mouse that it knows that there is a cat behind the door: is it appropriate to question this knowledge ascription on the ground that the mouse's beliefs are not adequately justified because the reasons it has for its belief are logically compatible with some other hypothesis, as that it is being deceived by an evil demon? Certainly the mouse cannot itself raise such epistemological doubts since (as we are supposing) it is not a reasoning creature capable of weighing evidence and so forth. Where there *is* no (possibility of) justification, it makes no sense to ask whether the justification is adequate; so scepticism of *this* kind simply gets no purchase upon the knowledge of subrational creatures. It seems odd to ask whether the mouse knows that it is not a brain in a vat precisely because this question presupposes a structure of justification whose credentials are being called into question.

But what of those creatures, such as ourselves, who do have justified beliefs: is *their* knowledge imperiled by scepticism about justification? Here two positions offer themselves. The first is that such scepticism is misplaced even for this type of knower since our claims to knowledge rest only upon the existence of appropriate truth-discriminating capacities and not upon whether we can justify what we believe. The second position is that where knowledge gets associated with justified belief, the question of the adequacy of the justification *becomes* relevant to the possession of knowledge—the fate of knowledge becomes intertwined with the fate of justified belief. This latter position is that justification becomes, in effect, one's method of discriminating the truth: rationally weighing evidence is the *means* by which one attempts to make one's beliefs sensitive to the truth. It seems to me that this second position has much to be said for it, so that *our* knowledge claims do (or can) come to rest upon the adequacy of our reasons for belief, and hence come under threat from justification scepticism, whereas the mouse's knowledge is free of such doubts.

This position produces a somewhat ironic result: that when knowledge is made to rest upon full-blooded justifying reasons it comes to be *more* vulnerable to sceptical attack than when it is independent of reasons and justification. Thus, if we suppose a child to move from the subrational to the rational while possessing knowledge during both phases, we have to say that justification scepticism gets a purchase only in the rational phase; and so we have the prospect that what was once knowledge ceases to be, because it comes to rest upon an inadequate foundation The irony is that the enterprise of foundationalism, construed as an answer to scepticism, so far from securing knowledge, renders it more assailable by the sceptic, since where there exists an evidential foundation the question of its shakiness becomes a live issue. One of the penalties of acquiring rationality may be that it becomes harder to know things.[54]

Notes

1. We speak causally of events, objects, facts, and properties in a variety of grammatical forms; we apply the word 'cause' in both mental and physical contexts; we use the word to indicate an explanatory relation as well as simply to cite the *entity* that was the cause (see Donald Davidson, "Causal Relations," in *Essays on Actions and Events* [Oxford, 1980]).

2. See A. Goldman, "A Causal Theory of Knowing," *Journal of Philosophy* 64 (1967).

Indeed, as Goldman acknowledges, the causal theory does not even extend to nonempirical knowledge.

3. See his "Other Minds," in *Philosophical Papers* (Oxford, 1961). The notions of telling, discriminating, classifying and recognizing are prominent in Austin's account of knowledge; he even has the idea of a 'relevant alternative'.

4. See his "Discrimination and Perceptual Knowledge," *Journal of Philosophy* 73 (1976).

5. For discussion of reliability theories see John Watling, "Inference from the Known to the Unknown," *Proc. Aristotelian Soc.*, 1954-55; D. M. Armstrong, *Belief, Truth and Knowledge* (Cambridge, 1973), Part III; R. Grandy, "Ramsey, Reliability and Knowledge," in *Prospects for Pragmatism*, edited by D. H. Mellor (Cambridge, 1980).

6. I thus diverge from Goldman's official development of the discrimination theory in "Discrimination and Perceptual Knowledge," in which counterfactuals are given a central role.

7. See his *Philosophical Explanations* (Oxford, 1981), chap. 3. As Nozick remarks (n. 53), Fred Dretske anticipates Nozick's principal theses in "Epistemic Operators," *Journal of Philosophy* 67 (1970) and "Conclusive Reasons," *Australasian Journal of Philosophy* 49 (1971). I focus in this paper upon Nozick's presentation because it is fuller and sharper than Dretske's.

8. Nozick does not, in fact, employ the notion of a disposition to believe the truth in his official analysis; but it is a natural and convenient way to state the kernel of his theory.

9. Tracking is thus a cross-world relation as Nozick defines it; but we might also consider a cross-time tracking relation, defined as follows. A person's belief that *p* held at *t* temporally tracks the truth of *p* just if the person *persists* in believing that *p* at times later than *t* at which *p* is true, and the person *ceases* to believe that *p* at later times at which *p* is not true: that is, the belief tracks the truth of *p* across time just if the person believes that *p* just so long as *p* is true. This notion of temporal tracking thus contains temporal analogues of Nozick's subjunctively defined variation and adherence conditions. It is not perhaps too far-fetched to see this notion of temporally tracking the truth as the analogue for whole propositions of the notion of tracking an *object* through time, as invoked by Gareth Evans in *The Varieties of Reference* (Oxford, 1982), esp. 1974f.

10. Nozick himself appears to take this view of the tracking theory: see *Philosophical Explanations*, pp. 172-3.

11. See his "Causation," *Journal of Philosophy* 70 (1973).

12. As we shall see, however, problems do arise for the tracking theory over the *modal* status of nonempirical propositions; so it may be that in the end the tracking theory is no better off than the causal theory when it comes to, e.g., mathematical knowledge.

13. I appeal to the idea of accidentally true belief frequently in this paper, so I should say something about how I construe this idea. My view is that the idea functions as a sort of adequacy condition on whether a theory of knowledge is correct—a theory of knowledge should have the consequence that when its conditions are met the belief is not accidentally true. I do not think the nonaccidentality idea *itself* constitutes an adequate theory of knowlege, because all it really does is give expression to our intuition that a given case fails to qualify as knowledge. The condition of nonaccidentality is to a proper theory of knowledge as (roughly) Tarski's Convention T is to a proper theory of truth.

14. I mean that the critical defining property *generally* brings with it the truth of the tracking counterfactuals but that it does not *necessarily* do so—hence the possibility of knowledge without tracking. What this underlying property is we shall presently see.

15. This example is expressly designed to parallel Goldman's case of the real barn surrounded by facsimiles of barns and other objects: see his "Discrimination and Perceptual Knowledge," 772. The difference is that in my example it is clear that the tracking counterfactuals hold: this separates out the failure of discrimination from the failure of the counterfactuals in such a way that the former is seen to be what is crucial.

16. After thinking up this example I came across a very similar example reported by Armstrong, *Belief, Truth and Knowledge*, 178, and attributed to Ken Waller: there is a moral to be drawn here about reading the literature *first*.

17. It does seem that such counterfactuals exist and that we cannot give their truth conditions in terms of what holds good in close *possible* worlds. Suppose a scientist is devising an experiment to test a theory of the nature of a certain substance and reasons 'if this substance were not of that nature, it would not behave thus-and-so when subjected to such-and-such conditions': it may be that the scientist's theory is correct and that the substance *necessarily* has that nature. It even seems that we could have such contrapossible counterfactuals in respect of mathematical necessary truths, as in 'if 16 were not divisible by 2, it would not be divisible by 4'.

18. Nozick, *Philosophical Explanations*, 186.

19. The belief could be justified because I generally get such computations right and have merely made a slip on this occasion. Note that this example is of exactly the form of the classic Gettier case of truly believing *someone* owns a Ford on the basis of the false but justified belief that *Jones* owns a Ford.

20. Here it is instructive to ask whether the adherence condition would suffice on its own for parallel cases involving contingent propositions.

21. Of the kind discussed by Saul Kripke in *Naming and Necessity* (Oxford, 1980).

22. That is to say, it should not be a consequence of the analysis that we *mean something different* when we say of S that S knows that p, according as p is necessary or contingent. For one thing, we may not in ascribing knowledge that p to S ourselves know the modal status of p. An analogous requirement holds for the word 'true': we do not want our account of the *content* of that word to vary with the modal status of the proposition to which it is ascribed.

23. The argument I am using here could be paralleled in the case of the causal theory: granted that there are Gettier cases for nonempirical knowledge, we cannot use the notion of a causal connection to diagnose the Gettier cases that arise for empirical knowledge – on pain of having no univocal account of accidentality for the two sorts of case.

24. See Michael Dummett, "What is a Theory of Meaning" (II), 89f in *Truth and Meaning*, edited by G. Evans and J. McDowell (Oxford, 1976).

25. David Lewis has proposed counterfactual analyses of causation and of perception that infringe the constraint I am endorsing: see his "Causation" and "Veridical Hallucination and Prosthetic Vision," *Australasian Journal of Philosophy* 58 (1980). Part of the motivation for the constraint is the conviction that the modal is somehow supervenient upon the actual: whatever is possible should be *made* possible by what is actual. I cannot, however, get into a defence of this supervenience thesis here.

26. Although it is somewhat less obvious, the other examples I have are also explicable in this way. The case of the brain chemicals fails to count as knowledge because the hallucinations produced in the subject render him incapable of discriminating the truth in respect of propositions not involving the concept C. And the counterexamples to the necessity of the tracking conditions work because the requisite powers of discrimination are preserved in these examples.

27. I have not found the distinction between local and global reliability theories made in the literature, though what is in effect global reliability is sometimes invoked. This distinction, plus the rejection of a counterfactual account or reliability, constitute what is (I believe) new in the analysis I am proposing.

28. My position, then, is that possessing and exercising a discriminative capacity is what *explains* tracking when tracking serves as an indicator of knowledge: the capacity grounds the counterfactuals about what would be believed. There are possible circumstances, however, in which the capacity is absent though the counterfactuals are true (hence Nozick's conditions are not sufficient) and the capacity is present though the counterfactuals are false (hence his conditions are not necessary).

29. Goldman's formulation of the discrimination theory in terms of counterfactuals renders him unable to make the sharp distinction I make between tracking and discrimination theories. No wonder Nozick cites Goldman's theory as a variant of his own: *Philosophical Explanations*, 689.

30. More exactly, for the tracking theory to go global is (a) for it to lose its original essential

form and (b) for it to employ machinery that it does not then need, since the global counter-factuals become redundant once a local analysis is abandoned.

31. I would say the same about traits of character and their associated counterfactuals: what makes it true that if Jones were put in a situation calling for bravery he would act bravely is precisely the fact that Jones has the trait of bravery – it is not the other way about. To hold these views about capacities and traits is part and parcel of being a *realist* about them.

32. Saul Kripke's discussion of meaning and dispositions to use in *Wittgenstein on Rules and Private Language* (Oxford, 1982) is relevant here. We need to allow for dispositions to make systematic *mistakes* in the exercise of a capacity, and all *sorts* of things could give some-one a disposition to φ – not just the capacity to φ. Put differently, the notion of *competence* is not definable dispositionally.

33. I am not saying that counterfactuals are quite *irrelevant* in the ascription of capacities; I am just resisting the idea of a *reduction* of the former to the latter.

34. It is thus wrong to conceive knowing as a kind of *seeing*. This has the consequence that one does not secure knowledge, in some epistemologically problematic domain, by claiming that the facts in question are perceptible; for it is possible to see a state of affairs and yet not know that it obtains (this is indeed the situation in my bent sticks example). I therefore think, contrary to much traditional epistemology, that debates about the 'directness' or 'indirectness' of our perceptions do not have the relevance to the question whether we know that they have commonly been taken to have. Perceiving that p is one thing; knowing that p is quite another.

35. Lewis's analysis of perception, in "Veridical Hallucination and Prosthetic Vision," is in effect a tracking theory.

36. If Platonism in mathematics is epistemologically problematic, as argued by Paul Bena-cerraf in "Mathematical Truth," *Journal of Philosophy* 70 (1973), it cannot be because the very *concept* of knowledge requires a causal connection with the fact known. It must rather be that our *means of access* to numbers is inexplicable – that is, we have nothing relating us to numbers as perception relates us to material objects.

37. We thus avoid what was an embarrassment for the causal theory. This still leaves a theo-retical role for the notion of causation, though, namely that of distinguishing between a priori and a posteriori knowledge: see my "*A Priori* and *A Posteriori* Knowledge," *Proc. Aristotelian Soc.* (1976), for this sort of causal definition of the distinction.

38. As Goldman did in "A Causal Theory of Knowing," thereby compromising the origi-nal conception.

39. The asymmetry between perception and knowledge can be brought out as follows. The problem of analyzing knowledge is the problem of supplementing the two conditions: S believes that p, and it is a fact that p; the problem of analyzing perception is the problem of supple-menting the two conditions: S has an experience as of its being the case that p, and it is the case that p. In the perception case, we need some kind of local connection between experience and fact, and it seems that a causal relation is what is required to make this connection. In the knowledge case, we need to introduce further facts and S's beliefs with respect to those facts, so that a local condition will not suffice; in addition no requirement of causal connection be-tween belief and fact seems built into the concept of knowledge. Perception is, but knowledge is not, a kind of *linkage* between representational state and fact represented.

40. It may help to put this circularity objection in some perspective if I point out that a parallel kind of objection might be made against the condition of justification. For it may be claimed that when we come to explaining what it is for one belief to justify another, we will be forced back to the concept of knowledge: one belief justifies another just if the former belief is of a kind to confer the status of *knowledge* upon the latter. And if we were compelled so to define justification, then it may seem that we are not entitled to employ the concept of justifi-cation in our analysis of knowledge. Now just suppose for the sake of argument that this point is correct – the concept of justification is tainted with the concept of knowledge – should we then conclude that it is 'uniformative' to be told that knowledge requires a justification condition? As I go on to argue in the text, such 'circularity' is *not* a good reason for rejecting an analysis as trivial and unilluminating.

41. Surely if we were dealing with merely ellipsis, the philosophical analysis of concepts would be a lot easier than it is (think of 'bachelor' and 'unmarried male'). I also think that the 'paradox of analysis' – that any analysis of a concept must be either trivial or incorrect – is much less of a worry when analysis is construed in the more relaxed way I am recommending: instead of seeing ourselves as excavating the substructure of a concept, we can conceive our enterprise as that of linking the concept with others – finding its conceptual *location*. (These remarks are, of course, highly impressionistic: the whole question of how conceptual analysis is to be understood is a deeply perplexing one, and I do not claim to have said anything very helpful on the question here.)

42. The foundationalist picture of conceptual analysis, according to which we decompose complexes into simples until we reach conceptual bedrock, is I think prompted by the old Russellian doctrine of logical atomism: if you find that doctrine unpalatable, you should be suspicious of the foundationalist picture that goes with it.

43. We can compare this view of what an analysis of knowledge should aim at, or resign itself to, with Kripke's recommendations a propos the theory of reference: see *Naming and Necessity*, 93-94. For both reference and knowledge, it can be enough to present the right *picture* of the concepts.

44. Dretske, "Epistemic Operators"; see also, G. C. Stine, "Skepticism, Relevant Alternatives and Deductive Closure," *Philosophical Studies* 29 (1976).

45. Nozick, *Philosophical Explanations*, 204f.

46. This claim is made more intuitively compelling by stressing 'table' within the contexts 'tell whether' and 'know': it is an interesting fact that these contexts accept such stress, whereas belief contexts do not (felicitously).

47. The discriminative capacities of animals bear out this nonclosure thesis: a bee can tell flowers from leaves and birds and concrete, but it would be extremely odd to say that the bee can tell whether it is a brain in a vat – even though there being a flower in front of it implies that it is not a brain in a vat. So the bee knows there is a flower there, but does not know it is not a brain in a vat. (Choose another example if you jib at attributing knowledge to bees.)

48. It seems that propositions partition according to subject matter with respect to what determines the discrimination class. Suppose that someone is reliable about propositions concerning material objects but hopelessly unreliable when it comes to getting other people's mental states right. It does not seem that this unreliability about the latter class of propositions infects the person's knowledge claims regarding the former class. The difference of subject matter insulates the knowledge about material objects from the vagaries of the beliefs concerning other minds. So it is not *only* sceptical possibilities that are irrelevant to one's ordinary knowledge claims about the material world.

49. Perhaps the nonclosure of knowledge under known logical implication will seem less surprising if we observe that neither perception nor memory is closed under known logical implication. The reason is simply that known logical implication does not preserve what perception and memory require (chiefly the right kind of causal connection): so why should it be *so* surprising that another epistemic concept imposes requirements that are similarly not preserved by known logical implication? Note also how perverse it would be to argue that we do not perceive what we think we do because we do not perceive the known logical consequences of what we (claim to) perceive!

50. Of course I cannot *while* under the influence of the drug distinguish which of my beliefs are true and which false – if I could I would not form the false beliefs; rather, I *subsequently* distinguish the drug-influenced condition as one in which my truth-discriminating capacities have gone awry. But it does not follow that I do not, at the time of being under the influence of the drug, have the general capacity in question – on the contrary, I *do* have the capacity to distinguish drug-induced beliefs from regular ones, though I cannot then *exercise* this capacity. It is otherwise the the possibility of envatment: as the situation is set up I can *never* exercise a capacity to tell real life from envatment.

51. A caveat is needed here. I do not in fact believe that knowing how to φ *entails* the ability to φ: a person may know how to swim or to get to the office but be unable to do these things because of motor failures (e.g., paralysis). Knowing how to φ is indeed an activity-involving concept — it concerns what one has to *do* to φ — but it is a further accomplishment to be able to carry out what one knows how to do. If one has appropriate general motor capacities, then knowing how to φ will *typically* confer the ability to φ upon one — but these general capacities may be lacking. This is not to say that knowing-how is a species of propositional knowledge, concerning actions and goals; and I do not think that knowing what to do to φ is to be conceived as a kind of knowing-that either — as I do not think that knowing-which is a species of knowing-that.

52. Thus birds (for example) know how to build nests, know predators from prey, and know which other bird is their mate; but I would be uncomfortable ascribing beliefs to birds.

53. See Jonathan Bennett, *Linguistic Behaviour* (Cambridge, 1976), 46f, for the notion of registration. Bernard Williams, in "Deciding to Believe," in *Problems of the Self* (Cambridge, 1973), 144f, has some remarks about knowledge and belief that are very much in the spirit of the position I am advocating. Note that my reasons for disputing the necessity of a belief condition are not the same as those sometimes given, e.g., by C. Radford in "Knowledge — By Examples," *Analysis* 27 (1966-67), in which the knower is reluctant to claim that he knows or even is (allegedly) prepared to dissent from the known proposition. My position is more radical: it is that you do not need to be a believer at all to be a knower (though you need some cognitive state that is the *analogue* of belief). (Perhaps this notion of subdoxastic propositional knowledge is what is wanted to explain the Chomskyan claim that we have unconscious knowledge of the grammatical rules of our language?)

54. These remarks about knowledge, justification, and scepticism are, I realise, sketchy and allusive; I am just hinting at a line of thought that seems to me worth pursuing.

Reliability, Justification, and the Problem of Induction

JAMES VAN CLEVE

According to the main tradition in epistemology, knowledge is a variety of justified true belief, justification is an undefinable normative concept, and epistemic principles (principles about what justifies what) are necessary truths. According to the leading contemporary rival of the tradition, justification may be defined or explained in terms of reliability, thus permitting one to say that knowledge is reliable true belief and that epistemic principles are contingent. My aim here is to show that either of these approaches will yield a solution to the problem of induction. In particular, either of them makes it possible to ascertain the reliability of induction through induction itself. Such a procedure is usually dismissed as circular, but I shall argue that it cannot be so dismissed if either approach is correct.[1]

As one would expect, the solution based on the traditional approach differs from the one based on the reliabilist alternative, but they have important features in common. The common elements are presented in sections I, II, and III, the elements specific to the reliabilist approach in sections IV, V, and VI, and those specific to the traditional approach in section VII.

I

The problem of induction is the problem of showing that inductive inferences are justified. More precisely, it is the problem of showing that *some* inductive inferences are justified, for no one, I presume, holds that *all* inductive inferences are justified, at least not if 'inductive' is used broadly to cover everything that is not deductive. I shall be concerned here only with inductive inferences conforming at least roughly to the "straight rule" pattern,

$x\%$ of the A's I have examined were B's.
Hence,
$x\%$ of *all A*'s are B's.

and especially with inferences of the form

> Most of the A's I have examined were B's.
> Hence,
> The majority of *all A*'s are B's.

I shall assume that we know how to restrict the predicates involved in these inferences so as to avoid Goodman's paradox about the grue emeralds.[2] That is, I shall
assume that we have at least a partial answer to the "new riddle" of induction—
which are the good inductive inferences, the ones that are justified if any are?—in
order to tackle the traditional problem—are even *these* inferences justified?[3]

Before we can go further we need to answer the question, What is it for an
inference to be justified? Taking the notion of justified *belief* for granted, I suggest
the following as a preliminary account of justified *inference*: an inference is justified if and only if any person who drew the inference and who was justified in believing its premises would also be justified in believing its conclusion. We cannot rest
content with this, however. To acquire justification by drawing an inference, it is
not enough simply to be justified in believing the premises; in addition, (a) one
must believe the conclusion *because* one believes the premises, and (b) one must
not be in possession of further evidence that defeats the justification the inference
would normally provide. These points are accommodated in the following account:
an inference is justified if and only if any person justified in believing its premises
who drew the inference and believed its conclusion as a result would be prima facie
justified in this belief. The additional qualifications will seldom be important in the
discussion that follows, however, so I shall generally omit them.

II

The case for inductive skepticism has not been improved upon since Hume. Para-
phrasing the fifth and sixth paragraphs of Section IV, Part II, of the *Inquiry Concerning Human Understanding*, we may state it as follows:

> All justified inferences are either demonstrative or probable. But no inductive
> inference is demonstrative, for it is always conceivable that the conclusion of
> such an inference be false even though its premises be true.[4] Nor can any in-
> ductive inference be said to be probable. A probable inference, in order to
> establish its conclusion, presupposes the principle that the future will resemble
> the past (or, more accurately, that "instances, of which we have had no ex-
> perience, resemble those, of which we have had experience").[5] This principle
> is not a necessary truth, for a change in the course of nature is easily conceiv-
> able. How, then, is it to be established? Not by demonstration, for it is not
> entailed by any premises that are accessible to us; and not by probable infer-
> ence, since such inferences presuppose that very principle.[6] It must therefore
> be concluded that no inductive inference whatsoever is justified.

Part of this argument—that inductive inferences are not demonstrative—should be as undisturbing as it is incontestable. The real bite comes with the contention that inductive inferences are not even *probable*, since as such they would presuppose a principle that could itself be established only by induction, thus involving us in a circle. When we reflect on this part of the argument, however, a striking irrelevancy comes to light. In what sense can it be maintained that inductive inferences *presuppose* that the future will resemble the past, or any such general principle? Evidently, it is in this sense only: an inductive inference would not be *valid*—would not be *demonstrative*—unless its premises were augmented by some such principle. But so what? This is irrelevant to the position supposedly under attack. When it is claimed that some inductive inferences are probable, what is meant is this: there are inferences that, *despite being nondemonstrative*, confer justification on their conclusions for anyone who is justified in believing their premises.[7] That such inferences would require further premises to be valid is beside the point, since validity is not claimed for them. All that is claimed is that justified belief in the premises would make belief in the conclusion also justified, at least to some extent. Against the possibility that inductive arguments are in this sense probable it appears that Hume has made no case whatsoever.[8]

I think inductive skeptics would have to concede that this answer to Hume (sometimes known as "inductive probabilism") is correct in its negative points, but they might nonetheless try to save their case by making two claims. First, the existence of probable inductive arguments, though not disproved by Hume, has not been proved by his opponents either, and must remain an article of faith. Second, even if we knew that a given inductive argument was probable, this knowledge would scarcely be worth having. For to say that a conclusion is warranted (though not entailed) by a certain set of premises is one thing; to say that it is *likely to be true*—in the sense that in believing such a conclusion on the strength of such premises one would usually be right—is another. What we *want* from an inductive inference is what Carnap called probability 2 (probability in the statistical sense), but all we *get* (or at least all we *know* we get) is probability 1 (probability in the "reasonable to believe" sense).[9]

We shall be in a better position to deal with these objections after considering another approach to the problem of induction.

III

Ask a layman why he believes in induction and you are likely to be told, "Because it works." Implicit in this response is the following argument:

Argument A
Most of the inductive inferences I have drawn in the past from true premises have had true conclusions.
  Hence,
The majority of *all* inductive inferences with true premises have true conclusions.

Since Argument A is itself an inductive inference, most philosophers would be quick to condemn it as circular. But I shall argue that the form of circularity present is not vicious, thus joining ranks with a small minority that has come to the defense of the inductive validation of induction.[10]

Under what circumstances is an argument viciously circular? I submit that it is so under one circumstance only: a necessary condition of using it to gain knowledge of (or justified belief in) its conclusion is that one *already have* knowledge of (or justified belief in) its conclusion.[11] Let us say that an argument with this trait is *epistemically circular*. The most obvious examples of epistemically circular arguments are those in which the conclusion or a mere stylistic variant of it occurs among the premises. More subtle examples are those in which the conclusion, though not occurring in any guise among the premises, is nonetheless epistemically prior to one of the premises, in the sense that one could arrive at knowledge of the premise only via an epistemic route that passed through the conclusion first. In either of these cases we may speak of *premise circularity*. Now Argument A does not appear to suffer from premise circularity, though I shall consider later the possibility that it does. The more likely charge against Argument A is that it is circular in a different way: it is sanctioned by a rule of inference that one could know to be correct only if one already knew that its conclusion was true.[12] Let us call this feature *rule circularity*. If to be correct a rule of inference must be such that most arguments sanctioned by it and having true premises also have true conclusions, then rule circularity is undeniably present in Argument A.[13] The question is whether rule circularity is a vice.

In answering this question, it is important to keep two points in mind: (i) rule circularity is not a vice unless it makes for epistemic circularity, and (ii) an argument that is rule circular is not on that account epistemically circular *unless knowing that its rule is correct is a precondition of using the argument to gain knowledge*. So what we must determine is whether knowing its rule to be correct is a precondition of using Argument A to gain knowledge. I shall argue that the answer is no.

In section II we saw that Hume's arguments do not exclude the possibility that some inductive arguments are probable. Let us suppose for the moment that this possibility is realized and that Argument A is a probable argument. In that case, persons who reason in accordance with Argument A and who are justified in believing its premise will acquire justified belief in its conclusion. Moreover, they will do so *without need of having a justified belief in the correctness of the rule of inference sanctioning Argument A*. This follows from our supposition: if Argument A is probable, justified belief in its premise is *all* that is required to produce justified belief in its conclusion. Or more accurately, since there are also the two requirements mentioned at the end of section I, justified belief in the premise is all that is required *by way of justified belief*. One need *not* have a justified belief about the rule. Thus Argument A, though rule circular, is not epistemically circular.

This is all very well, critics may say, but it only works given your supposition that inductive arguments like A are probable. How is one to know that this condition obtains? There are two things to be said in response to this question. First, our condition is an *external* condition, that is, one of which an inference-drawing sub-ject need not be cognizant. In a world in which inductive arguments were probable, persons who used them would be able to acquire justified beliefs thereby, regardless of whether they *knew* inductive arguments to be probable. Second, from the stock of justified beliefs thus acquired there is a way to advance to the knowledge that in-ductive arguments are indeed probable. (This will be shown in the next section.) So the critics are doubly mistaken: the knowledge they think we need but cannot get is *not* needed and *can* be got.

IV

We have seen how someone might come to know, by way of an inductive argument, that most inductive arguments with true premises have true conclusions, or in other words, that induction is *reliable*. The task we took on at the end of the last section was to show that induction is *probable*, and the task that has been with us since the beginning has been to show that induction is *justified*. To accomplish one of these tasks is automatically to accomplish the other, since a probable argument is simply a justified argument that is not demonstrative. So to complete our work we must cross (or close) the gap between 'Induction is reliable' and 'Induction is justified', and for this purpose there is obviously nothing better suited than the reliability theory of justification.

The tenets of the reliability theory can be set down in the following way, which is due to Goldman.[14] First, we distinguish two kinds of belief-forming process: those that do not "operate on" other beliefs (e.g., perception) and those that do (e.g., inference). Then we say that a process of the first sort is reliable iff it tends to produce only true beliefs and that a process of the second sort is reliable iff it tends to produce only true beliefs when applied to true beliefs. Finally, we say that a belief is justified iff it either (i) results from a reliable process of the first sort or (ii) results from justified beliefs via a reliable process of the second sort.

Now let us put 2 and 2 together. The conclusion of Argument A tells us that inductive inference is a reliable process. The reliability theory tells us that beliefs re-sulting from justified beliefs by a reliable process are themselves justified. It follows that beliefs arrived at by inductive inference from justified beliefs are themselves justified. But that is to say that inductive inferences are both *probable* (in the sense defined in section II) and *justified* (in the sense defined in section I).

Here, then, is one solution to the problem of induction: by means of Argu-ment A one can come to know that induction is reliable, and by supplementing this result with the reliability theory one can advance to the further conclusion that in-duction is justified.[15]

It is instructive to note that by combining the two approaches to the problem of induction we have considered so far, the "inductive probabilism" of section II and the "inductive validation of induction" of section III, we manage to avoid ob-jections that are damaging to either taken separately. The objection generally thought fatal to the second approach is that any attempt to argue for the reliability of induction by using induction itself is viciously circular. But if inductive arguments are probable in the sense maintained by the first approach, they may be used to gain knowledge about induction itself without epistemic circularity, which is the only vicious kind. The objections left unanswered above to the first approach were that to regard inductive arguments as probable can only be an act of faith, and that in any case, they cannot be known to be probable in any sense implying that their conclusions are usually true. But what is shown in the second approach is *precisely* that the conclusions of inductive arguments (with true premises) are usually true, which answers the second objection; and when this result is coupled with the reliability theory, it follows that inductive arguments are justified, hence probable, which answers the first objection.

But there are other objections that must be addressed as well. The next section shows how they may be answered, at least within the reliabilist's framework.

V

Objection 1: You have made things too easy on yourself by characterizing justified inference as you did in section I. Being justified in believing a premise is never by itself sufficient for being justified in believing a conclusion drawn from it; in addition, one must be justified in believing that there is some appropriate relation of support (be it deductive or inductive) between the two.

Reply: One can go at least part way toward meeting this objection by making a point reminiscent of Lewis Carroll. Suppose that premise P is justified for subject S, that P entails Q, and that S infers Q from P. Shall we say that Q is not justified for S unless he is also justified in believing that P does entail Q? But if so, shall we not also have to add the requirement that S be justified in believing that if P is true and P entails Q, Q is true, too? A regress impends, and to avoid it we must say that in some cases the mere *existence* of an appropriate relation between premise and conclusion, whether the subject has a justified belief about it or not, enables justification to be transmitted from one to the other. And if this must be true in some cases, why not inductive cases, too?

However that may be, there is something else to be noted about the objection. What it calls into question is the proposition that being justified in believing a premise can be a sufficient condition (or at any rate, the sole *epistemic* condition that is required) for being justified in believing a conclusion. But this proposition is an immediate consequence of the reliability theory, in particular of its second clause. (See section IV.) So if the theory stands, the objection falls.

Objection 2: How do you know that the *premise* of Argument A is true? There would be no problem here if your past inductions had all been inferences of the form 'Most A's I have observed were B's; hence, the *next* A will be a B', since to verify the conclusion of such an inference one need only wait and see. But your stated concern is with inferences to conclusions of the form '*Most A's are B's*', and such conclusions can only be confirmed by further use of induction. Thus, there is a kind of epistemic circularity present in Argument A after all—the kind you called premise circularity.

Reply: It is true that the success of past inductions with general conclusions can only have been confirmed through induction. This is not to say, however, that *justified belief in the reliability of induction* was required for this purpose. I have already argued that to produce justified belief in the conclusion of an inductive inference, all that is required by way of justified belief is justified belief in the premise. This point applies not only to Argument A itself, but also to the various arguments that contribute to justified belief in its premise. Thus the present objection really raises the same point as the previous one, and may be answered in the same way.

Objection 3: Your proposed justification of induction could be used with equal right by a *counterinductivist*. Counterinductivists believe that if most of the *A*'s one has observed were *B*'s, one should infer that the majority of all *A*'s are *not* *B*'s. If his habits of inference permitted him to live long enough, a counterinductivist would no doubt come to realize that counterinduction had led him mostly to false conclusions. But he would not be discouraged by these failures; he would regard them as evidence of future success. He would argue as follows:

Agument B
Most of the counterinductive inferences I have drawn in the past from true premises have had false conclusions.
Hence,
The majority of all counterinductive inferences with true premises have *true* conclusions.

Now Argument B is as good by his standards as Argument A is by yours, but it is absurd to think it amounts to a justification of counterinduction.

Reply: Argument B may be as good in the eyes of the counterinductivist as Argument A is in mine, but it does not follow that the arguments are epistemically on a par. To think that they are is to embrace a subjectivism that rejects all external constraints on justification, admitting nothing as relevant but the subject's own beliefs. If we admit reliability as an external condition, however, and if our world is one in which induction is in fact reliable, then Argument A will be justified and Argument B will not be—regardless of what the counterinductivist thinks about the matter.

Objection 3 continued: Yes, but by the same token if our world were one in which *counterinduction* were reliable, Argument *B* would be justified and Argument *A* would not be. So there is a standoff between the arguments after all, though at a higher level: although at most one of the arguments is justified, and although it may be the case that one of them is justified and the other not (if one is reliable and the other not), no one is in a position to say that it is A and not B or vice versa.

Reply continued: I am not sure that counterinduction *could* be reliable (in the long run, as the objection requires), but for the sake of argument I will grant that it could be.[16] To meet the objection it suffices to point out that in a world in which induction were reliable, not only would Argument A *in fact* be justified, but users of it could *know* that it was (and that Argument B was not). How this is so has already been explained in sections III and IV. If the reader asks, "But how could anyone ascertain the truth of the antecedent on which all this depends—that induction is reliable?" I remind him or her that (for the reliability theory, at any rate) this antecedent is an *external* antecedent. It makes knowledge possible not by being known, but simply by being true.[17]

VI

In one way or another, each of the objections just considered presupposes that the reliability theory is false; if the theory stands, the objections fall. But perhaps it is the theory that deserves to fall. In this section I wish to consider some possible misgivings about it.

The most likely point of dissatisfaction with the reliability theory can be brought out by the following example.[18] Suppose there is a man who predicts rain whenever his bunions throb and nearly always predicts correctly—not by luck, but because his bunions are sensitive to falling pressure—but whose poor memory makes him oblivious to his own record of success. His beliefs about the next day's weather are the result of a reliable process, but are they justified? There is a strong inclination to say no—they would not be justified unless he knew that predictions so based were generally correct. The general point would be that no matter how reliable a belief-forming process may be, its products are not justified unless the subject *knows* (or is justified in believing) that the process is reliable. But if this is so, justification cannot be grounded in reliability alone. Reliability is important only in so far as the subject has knowledge of it.

More broadly, it might be said that what is wrong with the reliability theory is that it makes one of the conditions of knowledge purely external. That is, it makes S's knowing p dependent on a fact q that obtains outside S's knowledge. If q obtains, S knows p; if it doesn't, he doesn't; and for all S knows, q might either obtain or not. But if one's knowing p depends on a certain fact, shouldn't one have to know that fact?

To this question we must answer no. Some external conditions of knowing are admitted by nearly everyone. The extra conditions of knowledge that some have proposed to circumvent the Gettier problem (e.g., the condition that the subject's justification be undefeated) have generally been proposed as external conditions; it has not been required that the subject know them to obtain. The causal conditions on knowledge that others have proposed (e.g., that a belief, to count as knowledge, must be caused by the fact that makes it true, or by the other beliefs that serve as reasons for it) have likewise been meant as external. In a way truth itself is an external condition, at least according to any but the most rigorous conception of knowledge: if truth is not entailed by justified belief, then whether someone who has justified belief also has knowledge depends on whether what he believes happens to be true. Of course, one cannot have knowledge of something without knowing the truth condition for this knowledge to obtain, but the latter piece of knowledge is one with the former and not a precondition of it.

To the last point it may be replied that although *knowledge* of the truth condition is not a precondition of knowledge, *justified belief* in it is. So why not require of the subject justified belief in the other conditions of knowledge as well? The answer is that if it were held that *every* condition of someone's knowing something must be a condition the knower is justified in believing to obtain, it would follow that no one could know *anything* unless one were justified in believing each of the propositions in the series

Kp, JKp, JJKp, JJJKp, etc.,

which is absurd. Thus, it is inevitable that some conditions of knowing be external, not only to knowledge, but also to justification.

Of course, to show that knowledge must have *some* external conditions is not yet to show that reliability can be plausibly regarded as one of them, so what I have offered here in defense of the reliability theory hardly goes far enough. Rather than defending it further, however, I wish to go on and consider what becomes of our solution if we drop the reliability theory in favor of its less fashionable rival.

VII

The solution to the problem of induction outlined so far involves the following three steps: Hume's skeptical arguments do nothing to rule out the possibility that there are probable inductive inferences, i.e., inductive inferences that are justified despite being nondemonstrative (section II); if this possibility were realized, it would be possible to come to know by means of induction but without any vicious circularity that induction is reliable (section III); and from this in turn one could infer, with the help of the reliability theory, that induction is justified (section IV). The solution now to be advanced can retain the first two steps, but it will have to put something else in place of the third. It will also have to handle the objections of section V in a way that does not depend on the reliability theory.

How can we satisfy ourselves that induction is justified if not on the basis of its reliability? To this question some philosophers would reply that there is no need to ground the reasonableness of induction in its reliability or anything else, since its reasonableness is intuitively evident. Here is a representative quotation:

> I think that in some sense our justification of inductive rules must rest on an ineradicable element of inductive intuition—just as I would say our justification of deductive rules must ultimately rest, in part, on an element of deductive intuition: we *see* that *modus ponens* is truth-preserving—that is simply the same as to reflect on it and fail to see how it can lead us astray. In the same way, we *see* that if all we know about in all the world is that all the A's we've seen have been B's, it is *rational* to *expect* that the next A will be a B.[19]

Since things known by intuition are presumably known a priori, I shall refer to this view as apriorism.

Apriorism often calls forth the following objection: "Induction is justified only to the extent that the regularities we have noted in the past will continue to hold in the future. But that these or any other regularities should continue is at best a contingent feature of our world; it is conceivable that chaos should break out any minute. So how can induction be known to be justified a priori?"

It is clear, however, what the apriorist should say in reply: "You must distinguish the *reasonableness* of induction from its *reliability*. The latter depends on the contingencies you have mentioned, but the former does not. Induction would be reasonable (rational, justified) in any possible world, even if reliable only in some."[20]

The apriorist's approach to the problem of induction is of a piece with the larger epistemological tradition I mentioned at the beginning. According to this tradition, justification cannot be defined or even partly explained in terms of reliability; instead it must be either taken as primitive or defined in terms of other irreducibly epistemic concepts.[21] This makes it possible to hold that the ultimate principles of epistemic justification, of what confers evidence on what, are necessary truths known a priori.

Of course, if justification and reliability are thus driven apart, some will wonder why justification is worth having. What good is it to know that inductive inferences are justified if one does not thereby know that they usually lead to true conclusions?[22] But to this question section III of this paper has already given an answer. If induction is conceded to be justified in a sense *not* entailing that it is reliable, this will enable one to come to know that it is *also* reliable. For by means of Argument A one may arrive at justified belief in its reliability, and if it really *is* reliable this belief will be knowledge.

It was this part of the paper, however, that was the target of the objections in section V. I answered them before by invoking reliabilism; how shall we answer them if we embrace apriorism instead?

Objection 3 may be dealt with quickly: if it is evident a priori that induction is reasonable, it is also evident a priori that counterinduction is *unreasonable*.

Objections 1 and 2 require more attention. They both challenged, one explicitly and the other implicitly, the following vital point: to obtain justified belief in the conclusion of an inductive inference, we do not need justified belief in any rule or principle about the premise-conclusion nexus, but only in the premise itself. I pointed out earlier that this proposition is an immediate consequence of reliabilism; I want to point out now that it is also a consequence, though in a way less likely to be noticed, of apriorism.

The way to see this is to focus on just what it is that the apriorist finds intuitively evident. It is not that inductive inferences are *frequently truth-preserving*, for that could hardly be evident a priori. It is rather this: inductive inferences are *necessarily justification-extending*.[23] That is, if someone draws an inductive inference and is justified in believing its premise, he will also be justified in believing its conclusion. But this is to say that justified belief in the premise is *sufficient* to produce justified belief in the conclusion. And if justified belief in the premise is sufficient, justified belief about the premise-conclusion nexus is not necessary. Q.E.D.

Of course, if the intuited feature of inductive inference were what Peirce called its "truth-producing virtue," there would be room to insist that induction gives knowledge only to those who know that it has this virtue. But there is no room for such insistence if the intuited feature of inductive inference is its justification-extending virtue. This is what it is generally claimed to be; and if it were not this, what else could it be?

VIII

For the apriorist, we know a priori that induction is justified, and can learn from Argument A that it has the *further* virtue of being reliable. For the reliabilist, we learn from Argument A that induction is reliable, and can infer from this that it has the *equivalent* virtue of being justified. What the two parties should agree on is this: there is no vicious circle in using Argument A to ascertain the reliability of induction.

I do not expect everyone to be convinced that Argument A is noncircular, but anyone who is *not* convinced is obliged to reject reliabilism and apriorism alike. It is worth noting what this double rejection would commit one to. What makes the reliabilist solution work is its tenet that reliability is *sufficient* for justification; what makes the apriorist solution work is its tenet that reliability is *not necessary* for justification. Hence, in order to reject both solutions, one would have to maintain that reliability is *necessary but not sufficient* for justification. And in that case the following question would become pressing: what is the x that must be added to reliability to obtain justification?[24]

Notes

1. This paper is something of a sequel to "Foundationalism, Epistemic Principles, and the Cartesian Circle," *Philosophical Review* 88(1979):55-91. There I argue that the reliability of intuition ("clear and distinct perception") can be known through intuition itself without vicious circularity; here I use some of the same strategy to make a similar point about induction. For a related result, see Francis W. Dauer, "Hume's Skeptical Solution and the Causal Theory of Knowledge," *Philosophical Review* 89(1980):357-78.

2. Nelson Goodman, *Fact, Fiction, and Forecast*, 2nd ed. (Indianapolis, 1965), 59-83. It is not clear to me that the paradox arises if the inferred frequency is anything less than 100%, but even so we do not want to project 'grue'.

3. Thus, as I see it, Goodman's "new riddle" is an *additional* problem; it may be prior to the old problem, but does not replace it.

4. I have tried to allay misgivings about the use of conceivability as a mark of possibility in "Conceivability and the Cartesian Argument for Dualism," *Pacific Philosophical Quarterly* 64(1983):35-45.

5. *A Treatise of Human Nature*, edited by L. A. Selby-Bigge (Oxford, 1888), 89.

6. "To endeavor, therefore, the proof of this last supposition by probable arguments . . . must be evidently going in a circle and taking that for granted which is the very point in question." *An Inquiry Concerning Human Understanding*, edited by Charles W. Hendel (Indianapolis, 1955), 49-50.

7. "There exist arguments which, although not valid (that is, their premises do not entail their conclusions), necessitate, for any rational being of limited knowledge who knows their premises, belief, rather than disbelief or the suspension of belief, in their conclusions—belief to which, nevertheless, a degree of assurance attaches, less than that (maximal) degree which a

valid argument necessitates. In short, there are probable arguments." So writes D. Stove in "Hume, Probability, and Induction," *Philosophical Review* 74(1965):160-77. The late J. L. Mackie took a similar stand; see his "In Defense of Induction," in *Perception and Identity*, edited by Graham Macdonald (Cambridge, 1979), 113-30.

8. Stove, "Hume, Probability, and Induction," maintains that Hume did not even *intend* to argue that inductive arguments could not, in the sense explained, be probable. I do not wish to debate this point. What matters for my purposes is that try or no, he did not succeed.

9. This charge is made by John Cassidy in "The Nature of Hume's Inductive Scepticism: A Critical Notice," *Ratio* 19(1977):47-54.

10. The chief representatives of the minority are Richard Braithwaite, *Scientific Explanation* (Cambridge, 1953), 264-92, and Max Black, "Self-Supporting Inductive Arguments," *Journal of Philosophy* 55 (1958):718-25." These pieces are reprinted in *The Justification of Induction*, edited by Richard Swinburne (Oxford, 1974). More recently Nicholas Rescher has advocated an inductive validation of induction; see *Induction* (Pittsburgh, 1980), especially chap. VII. My strategy here differs from that of all three authors, but it is closest to that of Braithwaite.

11. Thus, an argument is not viciously circular just because the *truth* of its conclusion, or *belief* in it, or both, are necessary conditions of using the argument to gain knowledge. For more on this see Braithwaite, especially pp. 114-20, in Swinburne.

12. The rule in this case is 'From *Most observed* A*'s have been* B*'s* you may infer *The majority of all* A*'s are* B*'s*'.

13. The same could not be said of Black's "self-supporting" inductive argument, since its conclusion pertains only to the *next* use of induction.

14. Alvin Goldman, "What is Justified Belief?" in *Justification and Knowledge*, edited by George S. Pappas (Dordrecht, 1979), 1-23.

15. There is a complication I have so far ignored. For induction to be justified in the sense defined in section I, it is not sufficient that it lead from justified belief to justified belief in every *actual* instance of its use; it must also be such that it *would* lead from justified belief to justified belief in nonactual instances. To obtain this result we need the lemma that induction is reliable not just in the sense that it usually *does* lead from truth to truth, but also in the sense that it usually *would*. But this stronger lemma is presumably reachable by Argument *A* if the weaker one was; grounds that justify 'Most *A*'s are *B*'s must also justify 'Most *A*'s *would* be *B*'s'.

16. If he has noticed that most of the cars he has seen have not been red, the counterinductivist will infer that the majority of all cars are red; if he has also noticed that most of the cars he has seen have not been green, he will infer that the majority of all cars are green. He will thus often be led into inconsistent conclusions, but I do not see how to prove that he will be wrong more often than right.

Black (pp. 133-34 in Swinburne) points out that if counterinduction (of a somewhat different variety from what I have considered) had a run of successful predictions it would predict its own future failure, and thus suffers from a kind of incoherence. But "incoherence" in this sense is compatible with reliability.

17. Cf. what Mackie says on p. 129 of the article cited in note 7: the principle of the uniformity of nature need only be *true* in order for induction to give us knowledge in the sense of "non-accidentally true belief."

18. For elaboration and discussion of similar examples, see Laurence Bonjour, "Externalist Theories of Empirical Knowledge," *Midwest Studies in Philosophy* 5(1980):53-73.

19. Henry E. Kyburg, Jr., "Comments on Salmon's 'Inductive Evidence'," *American Philosophical Quarterly* 2(1965):274-76; reprinted in Swinburne, 62-66. A similar position is advocated by P. K. Sen, "An Approach to the Problem of Induction," in *Logic, Induction, and Ontology* (Calcutta, 1980), 82-90.

20. Compare P. F. Strawson, *Introduction to Logical Theory* (London, 1952), 261-62. It should be noted that the apriorist need not share Strawson's view that the rationality of induction is explicative of the concept of rationality.

21. The best exemplar of this approach is R. M. Chisholm, *Theory of Knowledge*, 2nd edition (Englewood Cliffs, N. J., 1977), chap. 1.

22. This is Cassidy's complaint again. See also Wesley C. Salmon, "The Concept of Inductive Evidence" and "Rejoinder to Barker and Kyburg," *American Philosophical Quarterly* 2 (1965):265-80; reprinted in Swinburne, 48-57 and 66-73. For Salmon, it seems, the more pressing question to ask those who would divorce justification from reliability is not "What *good* is justification?" but "What *is* justification?"

23. I omit the needed qualifications about prima facie justification.

24. For criticisms of an earlier draft, I am grateful to Diana Ackerman, Philip Quinn, and Ernest Sosa. My research was supported by a grant from the American Council of Learned Societies.

Perception, Causation, and Supervenience

BRIAN P. McLAUGHLIN

What relation between an experience and a physical object makes the experience a perception of the object?[1] One common answer is that it is a certain kind of causal relation. The idea is that to perceive an object is just to undergo an experience *appropriately caused by* the object. This answer is incorrect. The reason is that perceiving an object does not *supervene* on the causal connection the object bears to the perceiver's experience. Whether or not a person perceives an object depends, in part, on conditions that could obtain or fail to obtain without variation in the causal processes (if any) by which the object causes the person's experience. In what follows, I explain and defend these claims.

I

One of the central questions facing any philosophical investigation of human sense perception is:

(Q1) What is it for a person to perceive a physical object?

One common answer is:

(A) A person perceives a physical object iff that object *perceptually causes* a sense experience the person undergoes.[2]

Answer (A) purports to state *a causal analysis of perceiving a physical object* [henceforth, a (CAP)]. But (A) does not succeed in stating a (CAP). One reason is that it is circular. The goal of those concerned to provide a (CAP), causal theorists, is to recast (A) by specifying what counts as *perceptual causation*, so as to yield a correct, finitely statable, nonquestion-begging answer to (Q1). My main task is to show this cannot be done.

Given this task, it is essential that we share a common understanding of what (A) means, and, thereby, of what counts as a (CAP).

Answer (A) implies that a necessary condition for perceiving an object is that the perceiver's experience be causally dependent upon the object. Moreover, (A) implies that a necessary and sufficient condition for perceiving an object is that the perceiver's experience be causally dependent upon the object in *a certain kind of way*, that is, that there be *an appropriate mode of causal connection* between the object and the experience, where the appropriate mode varies somewhat from one sense modality to another. The idea is that a perceived object causes a perceptual experience by means of a certain kind of causal process (or chain, or mechanism). Perceptual causation is understood to be causation by means of a kind of causal process (or chain, or mechanism), the occurrence of which is necessary and sufficient for perceiving an object. (This raises the issue of what is to count as *a kind* of causal process (or chain, or mechanism), but more about this in section III.)[3]

Answer (A) purports to state what makes it the case that a person perceives an object. It is inteded to assert that perceiving an object just consists in undergoing a sense experience perceptually caused by that object; that undergoing a sense experience perceptually caused by an object amounts to perceiving it. According to (A), then, if I am seeing various objects in the scene before my eyes, it is because those objects are perceptual causes of my visual experience. If I am not seeing my optic nerve, the inside of my brain, the source of illumination, objects behind my back, or objects blocked from view, it is because those objects are not perceptual causes of my visual experience. And if I am seeing an object, rather than hallucinating and not seeing any object at all, it is because some object is a perceptual cause of my visual experience.

Causal theorists hope to provide a noncircular specification of what counts as perceptual causation. They face at least two kinds of problem cases. First, when a person undergoes an hallucination, the person undergoes a sense experience. But while (completely) hallucinatory experiences are caused, they have no perceptual causes. Second, whenever a person perceives an object, the person's experience is caused by many objects that the person does not perceive. Not every cause of a perceptual experience is a perceptual cause.

We can distinguish two questions:

(Q2) How must a person's experience be caused to make it the case that the person perceives, rather than hallucinates, by undergoing the experience?

(Q3) How must an object cause a person's experience to make it the case that the person perceives that object by undergoing that experience?

An adequate specification of what counts as perceptual causation must provide an answer to (Q3). And, if whenever one perceives, one perceives an object, an answer to (Q3) would yield an answer to (Q2). But an answer to (Q2) need not yield an answer to (Q3). An answer to (Q3) must explain how an object must cause an experience to make it the case that the subject of the experience perceives that object by undergoing that experience. But since an answer to (Q2) need only explain how an experience must be caused to make it the case that the subject of the experience perceives, rather than hallucinates, by undergoing the experience, it need not explain how the subject perceives all and only the objects she perceives by under-going the experience. The task of providing a (CAP) is distinct from that of provid-ing a causal criterion for distinguishing perception from hallucination. (I say more about this at the close of section V.) While progress has been made on (Q2), (Q3) remains intractable.[4]

To make my position concerning perception and causation clear from the start: I think that a necessary condition for perceiving a physical object is that the perceiver's experience be causally dependent upon the object. Moreover, I think it may be possible to distinguish perceptual experiences from hallucinatory experi-ences by appeal to their distinct kinds of causal ancestries. But I do not think that a (CAP) is possible.

Attempts to provide a (CAP) have been many and varied. I shall not canvass them here. To do each justice would take a distracting amount of space. Besides, even if each were shown to fail, that would not show no (CAP) is possible. And I hope to show that no (CAP) is possible.

My strategy for showing this involves two stages. The first stage consists of showing that any would-be (CAP) will imply a certain supervenience thesis. The second stage consists of showing that supervenience thesis is false, and, hence, that no (CAP) is possible. The reason that no (CAP) is possible is that (A) is false: it is not the case that there is a kind of causal process by means of which all and only the physical objects a person perceives cause the person's experience. In a nutshell, there is no such thing as perceptual causation.

I carry out the first stage of the strategy in sections II and III, the second stage in section IV. Finally, in section V, I draw a distinction and use it to make some positive proposals.

II

To begin, any would-be (CAP) will imply a supervenience thesis of the following form:

(ST) If an object and a person's experience bear the same causal connection to each other (in relevant respects) as do a second object and a second person's experience, then the first person perceives the first object iff the second person perceives the second object.

Every would-be (CAP) will purport to state necessary and sufficient conditions for perceptual causation, so each will fill in 'in relevant respects' with a specification of the alleged defining conditions.

Any statement of form (ST) will be equivalent to one that says (roughly): *necessarily there is no perceptual difference without a relevant causal difference.* The force of the modal term 'necessarily' will be logical (or metaphysical) necessity, since causal theorists aim to provide logically (or metaphysically) necessary and suf-ficient conditions for perceiving an object.

To show that any supervenience thesis of form (ST) is false, one need only describe a possible situation in which there is a perceptual difference without a relevant causal difference. Any test of the implied supervenience thesis will presuppose an understanding of what is to count as a *relevant* causal difference. And to show no (CAP) is possible, one must refute a supervenience thesis that will be implied by any would-be (CAP), a supervenience thesis that employs a common interpretation of 'in relevant respects'. I shall attempt to do just that, but first some remarks concerning strategy and the notion of supervenience may be helpful.

The general strategy I employ is implicit in critical discussions of a wide range of would-be analyses. Since the general strategy is interesting in its own right, I shall digress by citing some examples.

John Searle's well-known Chinese Room thought experiment can be viewed as an attempt to show that the following supervenience thesis, (allegedly) implied by any artificial-intelligence analysis of language understanding, is false: there can be no difference in language understanding between two systems without a relevant AI-difference between them.[5] Searle claims that we must investigate the underlying causal processes and mechanisms in the brain if we are to understand what it is for someone to understand a language.[6]

Hilary Putnam's familiar Twin-Earth thought experiment can be viewed as an attempt to show that the following supervenience thesis, (allegedly) implied by any Fregean analysis of reference, is false: there can be no referential difference between two speakers' words without a relevant difference in the narrow psychological states of the speakers.[7] One conclusion Putnam draws is that any account of reference must appeal to the causal ancestries of the speaker's psychological states, including causal interactions with the environment.[8]

Tyler Burge's thought experiment concerning a speaker with partial understanding of a term can be viewed as an attempt to show that the following supervenience thesis, (allegedly) implied by any physicalistic, individualistic analysis of the content of psychological states, is false: there can be no difference in the content of two persons' psychological states without a relevant difference in their dispositions to behave or in the causal ancestries of those dispositions.[9] If successful, the example shows that what content a person's psychological states have depends, in part, on linguistic conventions that can change without change in the dispositions or causal ancestries of those dispositions of the person.

It is of specific interest for present purposes to note that the strategy in question has been employed against causal analyses of empirical knowledge and causal analyses of de re perceptual knowledge. Subtleties aside, according to causal analyses of empirical knowledge, someone knows that p (where p is an empirical proposition) iff the fact that p is appropriately causally connected with that person's belief that p. Thus any would-be causal analysis of empirical knowledge will imply that if a person's belief that p and the fact that p bear the same causal connection to each other (in relevant respects) as do a second person's belief that q and the fact that q, then the first person knows that p iff the second person knows that q. Both Gilbert Harman's use of his Assassinated Social Worker example and Peter Klein's employment of Lehrer and Paxon's Tom Grabbit example can be understood as attempts to show that this supervenience thesis is false, and, hence, that no causal analysis of empirical knowledge is possible.[10] Both examples purport to show that whether or not S knows that p depends, in part, on factors that can change without change in the causal process by which the fact that p causes S's belief that p, for example, upon such factors as what evidence is available to other members of S's epistemic community.

According to causal analyses of de re perceptual knowledge (roughly), a person perceptually knows of an object that it is an F iff the object is an F and is appropriately causally connected with the person's belief it is an F. Alvin Goldman's Phoney Barn Country example can be viewed as a would-be counterexample to a supervenience thesis that would be implied by any causal analysis of de re perceptual knowledge.[11] The example purports to show that whether or not S perceptually knows of an F (e.g., a barn) that it is an F (a barn) depends on factors that are independent of the causal process by which the F causes S to believe of it that it is an F; for example, it can depend on such factors as whether or not there are any phoney Fs in S's vicinity.

Examples are readily multiplied. The strategy deserves a name. Let us call it 'refutation by appeal to a false implied supervenience thesis', or, for short, 'refutation by appeal to a (FIST)'. The success of any would-be refutation by appeal to a (FIST) requires: (i) that the supervenience thesis be indeed implied by any analysis of the sort in question, and, (ii) that the supervenience thesis be false. I do not here claim that any of the above examples of would-be refutation by appeal to a (FIST) succeed. I cited them only to illustrate a general strategy. My aim here is to provide a refutation by appeal to a (FIST) against any would-be (CAP).

But first, it will prove useful to have a partial general characterization of the supervenience relation and some related notions. Supervenience is best understood as a kind of *dependency relation* between two sets of conditions (or properties, or relations, or event types). By 'a condition' I mean what is expressed by an open sentence, a predicative expression, or that which can be explicitly stated by means of a nominalized predicative expression. Consider, then, the following partial definition of 'supervenience', which is quite similar to a definition offered by Jaegwon Kim:

> A set of conditions P is *supervenient upon* a set of conditions Q only if necessarily, for any condition A in P, if any x satisfies A, then there is a condition B in Q such that x satisfies B, and necessarily any y that satisfies B satisfies A.[12]

The sets of conditions P and Q are to be understood as closed under complementation, conjunction, disjunction, and any other permissible condition-forming operations. (Definitions of supervenience can be provided, mutatis mutandis, for properties, relations, and event types. And I shall sometimes speak of properties, or relations, or event types as supervening on other properties, or relations, or event types.) Following Kim, we may leave the force of the modal term 'necessarily' as an unspecified parameter.

When a set of conditions P is supervenient upon a set of conditions Q, and A and B are related in the way specified above, A is *supervenient upon B*, and B is a *supervenience base* of A. Each condition in the supervenient set P will have a sufficient condition in the supervenient base set Q. But it is left open whether or not two items satisfying the same supervenient condition will satisfy the same supervenient base condition. A given condition in the supervenient set can have *multiple supervenience bases* in the supervenient base set.[13] For example, according to certain functionalist theories of mind, mental conditions (e.g., believing that the cat is on the mat) supervene on physical conditions; but a given mental condition can have numerous, perhaps infinitely many, distinct physical supervenience base conditions.

A claim that condition A analyzes condition B will imply that there is a supervenience relation between A and B, though not conversely if we require for analyzability that the analysans be finitely specifiable. Refuations by appeal to a (FIST) show that the intended analysandum does not supervene on the intended analysans.

III

I want now to attempt to identify a common assumption among causal theorists concerning the interpretation of 'the same causal connection in relevant respects' in (ST).

Perceived objects cause perceptual experiences by means of causal processes. The causal processes are enormously complex; much about them is not well understood. But their broad outlines are well known. For example, in the case of sight, a perceived object causes a perceiver's experience by directing (reflecting, or emitting) light rays to the perceiver's eye. The light rays are absorbed by the eye and focused onto the retina by the lens of the eye; various retinal cells are stimulated and send electrical chemical impulses along the optic nerve to the cortex where a pattern of brain cell stimulation occurs that either is, causes, or constitutes a visual experience. The causal process just sketched is a micro-causal process relative to the macro-level causal transaction between the perceived macro-object and the perceiver's experience, though it is a macro-causal process relative to causal processes involving, say, atoms and more elementary particles. In general, causal processes described in the vocabulary of the physical sciences will be at a micro-level relative to causal transactions described in everyday, nontechnical vocabulary.[14]

What bearing do investigations of the micro-causal processes by which perceived objects cause experiences have on saying what counts as perceptual causation? While causal theorists differ in their answers to this question, a brief discussion of some remarks by a few representative causal theorists will help illustrate that causal theorists are in agreement on one point: *Perceptual causation supervenes on at least one of the kinds of micro-causal processes by which a perceived object can cause a perceptual experience.* This supervenience requirement gives a somewhat precise sense to the notion that perceptual causation is causation by means of *a certain kind of causal process*; and it yields a common interpretation of 'the same causal connection in relevant respects' in (ST).

In *Perceiving*, R. M. Chisholm characterized perceptual causation in terms of such features of micro-causal processes as the transmission of light waves, the propagation of sound waves, and so on.[15]

H. P. Grice objected that such details have no place in the causal theorists' answer to (Q1) because someone able to use perceptual verbs may be ignorant of them.[16] We need not pause to consider whether or not this is a good reason for excluding such details. For our purposes, it suffices to note that Grice went on to say that:

> for an object to be perceived by X it is sufficient that it should be causally involved in the generation of some sense-impression had by X in the kind of way in which, for example, when I look at my hand in good light, my hand is causally responsible for its looking to me as if there were a hand before me, or in which . . . (and so on), *whatever that kind of way may be*; and to be enlightened on that question we must have recourse to the specialist.[17]

Grice thus suggests that causal theorists should indicate what counts as perceptual causation by citing examples, leaving the task of specifying the nature of perceptual causation to the relevant specialists. He claimed that we do not ordinarily need recourse to the specialist in making perceptual ascriptions "for we may be in a position to say that the same kind of mechanism is at work in a plurality of cases without being in a position to say what that mechanism is."[18] Specifying the mechanism is, according to Grice, the job of the specialist. Grice's remarks suggest that the relevant specialists will tell us what counts as perceptual causation by specifying the details of the appropriate micro-causal processes by which perceived objects cause perceptual experiences. Essentially the same proposal is made by George Pitcher and many other causal theorists.[19]

Not all causal theorists see so intimate a connection between perceptual causation and micro-causal processes. Christopher Peacocke has noted that Grice's proposal bears a resemblance to the Kripke-Putnam semantic model for natural kind substance-terms.[20] On the Kripke-Putnam model, the extension of a natural kind substance-term (e.g., 'water', or 'gold') can be fixed by citing examples, leaving the task of revealing the properties in virtue of which the examples are instances of the kind in question to be carried out by the relevant experts through empirical investigation of the examples.[21] But Peacocke points out that the Kripke-Putnam model is inappropriate for determining the extension of 'perceive' and the more specific perceptual verbs 'see', 'hear', etc.[22] He says that an account of what scientifically identified relations underlie and explain actual examples of the perceptual relation would not properly fix the extension of 'perceive':

> To mention a few reasons: we wish to apply the concept of perception to creatures with different physico-chemical realizations from our own; we wish to allow prosthetic devices and reroutings in, at the very least, internal stages of the chain; and so forth. The concept of perception, unlike that of a substance,

is not one that determines a notion of kind such that what is quite generally necessary and sufficient for perception can be discovered by empirical investigations of the examples of that kind. Thus, we cannot wholly avoid the traditional hard work of the method of imagined examples and the testing of the appropriate intuitions of the masters of the concept perception against them.[23]

Peacocke alludes to what David Lewis has called 'prosthetic perception'.[24] It is possible for a person to perceive via the operation of a prosthetic sense organ, for example, to see via the operation of a prosthetic eye. A prosthetic eye must function sufficiently like a natural eye if it is to serve for seeing. But at the level of physico-chemical structure, many different structures may be able to realize the requisite function. The possibility of prosthetic visual perception indicates that there may be no uniform micro-physical structure had by all and only eyes. (Of course it does not *show* that there is no uniform micro-physical structure.) Moreover, there is controversy among causal theorists concerning whether or not the external stage of perceptual causation in the case of sight, for example, must proceed by means of the transmission of light rays. It has been argued that the external stage can proceed by other means.[25] (Similar considerations arise, of course, in the case of perception within the other sense modalities.) And as Peacocke remarks, a (CAP) must "state the conditions in virtue of which hypothetical routes are in the hypothetical circumstances sufficient for perception."[26]

The point to be noted is this: There may be no uniform micro-causal process that underlies all and only cases in which someone perceives something. Three remarks are in order concerning this point.

First, it is not required for there to be a kind of causal process that there be a uniform micro-causal process underlying all and only instances of the kind in question. There may be no uniform micro-causal process underlying all and only cases of soil erosion; nevertheless, soil erosion is a kind of causal process.

Second, that there need be no uniform micro-causal process underlying all and only cases of perceiving an object shows, at most, that perceptual causation has multiple supervenience bases.

Third, this is compatible with what I claim to be a common assumption of causal theorists: Perceptual causation supervenes on at least one of the kinds of micro-causal processes by which a perceived object can cause a perceptual experience.

What, then, is to count as the same causal connection in relevant respects? The notion of 'perceptual causation' is understood by causal theorists in such a way that a micro-causal process by which an object causes a person's experience can be an instance of perceptual causation solely in virtue of its *intrinsic* properties. When, or where, or in what social environment a micro-causal process occurs is allegedly irrelevant as to whether or not it counts as an instance of perceptual causation. Moreover, no instance of perceptual causation can be relevantly different from any other. The reason is simply that if something is an instance of perceptual causation, there is no necessary condition for being such that it fails to satisfy. So an object and a person's experience can bear the same causal connection to each other in relevant respects as do a second object and a second person's experience, solely in virtue of the first object's causing the first person's experience by means of a micro-causal process, the second object's causing the second person's experience by means of a micro-causal process, and the two micro-causal processes being the same in appropriate respects. The appropriate respects will be those intrinsic properties of each in virtue of which each is an instance of perceptual causation. The idea is that, for example, if two objects direct light to a person's eye (on different occasions) in essentially the same way and the light triggers internal causal processes that are without intrinsic difference, the person saw the first object iff she saw the second.

This, then, completes the first stage of my strategy. We know enough about the micro-causal processes underlying actual cases of perception to be able to test (ST). Before doing so, however, it will help in clarifying what is at issue in assessing (ST) to note that neither perceiving an F (for countless values of F) nor perceiving the whole or entire object supervene on the micro-causal processes whereby the F or the object in question cause the perceiver's experience. These failures of supervenience do not show (ST) to be false. I conclude this section by illustrating this.

A coin may bear the same micro-causal connection to Dick's experience as a second coin bears to Jane's experience and yet Dick see a genuine coin and Jane not see a genuine coin. This can happen if the coin that Jane sees is a counterfeit coin with the same micro-structure as the coin Dick sees. But this does not show that (ST) is false. The perceptual difference at issue in (ST) is *not* that between perceiving an F (for every value of F) and not perceiving an F, but rather between perceiving an object and not perceiving an object. One perceives an F just in case one perceives something and that something is an F. The reason that perceiving an F (for countless values of F) does not supervene on the micro-causal processes by which the F causes the perceiver's experiences is just that the condition of being an F may fail to supervene on any conditions of the F in virtue of which it participates in the micro-causal process. Causal theorists will claim that if an F bears the same micro-causal connection to one person's experience as a *non-F* bears to a second person's experience, then the first person perceives the F iff the second person perceives the *non-F*. (Whether or not this is so is what remains to be seen in section IV.)

What about perceiving the whole (or entire) object? Whenever one sees something, for example, there will be parts of it that one does not see. These unseen parts may be internal parts, parts not facing one, occluded parts, subvisible parts, and so on. Even when what is seen is transparent and in full view, there will be parts of it that are not seen, if only subvisible and molecular parts. (If objects are four-dimensional, then when one sees an object there will be many stages of the object that one does not see; and one will not see every part of the stage one sees. But this noted, I shall continue to speak of objects as three-dimensional and persisting through time.) Nonetheless, it is often pointed out that sometimes one sees the whole (or the entire) object. For example, one may see the entire surface of the wall or the whole house. But if one sees the whole (or entire) object, one sees every part of it. (How could one have seen the whole [or entire] object if there were some part of it that one failed to see?) The claim that we sometimes see the whole (or entire) object seems at variance with the claim that whenever one sees something, there will be parts of it that one does not see.

The apparent discrepancy is resolved by appeal to ambiguity. One natural place to locate the ambiguity is in 'every'. 'Every', like all quantifier words, is pragmatically ambiguous.[27] It has determinate content only in a context of use. (Consider: 'Everyone voted for the amendment to the bill'.) The universe of discourse for quantifier words can vary from one conversational-context to another. When we count someone as seeing the whole house, for example, many parts of the house are not counted as within the universe of discourse. There is *a pragmatic parameter* that determines the universe of discourse for the implied quantifier in ascriptions of the form 'S perceived the whole (or entire) x', and its value is determined by the pragmatic presuppositions of the speaker.[28] Thus, Tom might say 'Dick saw the whole house' and Harry might say 'Dick did not see the whole house' without contradicting one another.

Perceiving the whole (or entire) thing does *not* supervene on intrinsic conditions of the micro-causal processes linking the thing in question to the perceiver's experience. The pragmatic parameter that determines the universe of discourse for the implied quantifier can vary in value without variation in those micro-causal processes.

But this tells us more about the notions of 'the whole thing' and 'the entire thing' than it does about perception. (Compare: 'Tom painted the whole house'.) The distinction between perceiving the whole (or entire) thing and not perceiving the whole (or entire) thing is not a perceptual difference in the sense at issue in (ST). As we noted before, the perceptual difference at issue in (ST) is that between perceiving an object and not perceiving an object. And one can perceive an object without perceiving the whole (or entire) object. For example, one can see the front of a house, and thereby see the house, without thereby seeing the whole (or entire) house.

The question at issue, then, is whether or not perceiving an object supervenes on any of the micro-causal processes whereby the object causes the perceiver's experience.

IV

I want now to show that (ST) is false. To lay all of my cards on the table, the conditions under which perceiving one thing counts as perceiving another do not supervene on the micro-causal processes by which objects cause perceptual experiences. Once we see this, it should then be clear how to generate counterexamples to (ST).

Let us begin by noting that perceiving part of an object or an effect of an object can count as actually perceiving the object itself. On occasion, Paul can see the dog by seeing its head, or hear the alarm clock by hearing the ringing sound of the alarm clock. On an occasion of the first sort, it is not as if Paul sees the dog's head while also seeing the dog, at least not in the way that Paul sees the dog's head while also seeing, say, the door that occludes the rest of the dog's body. Rather, *in* seeing the dog's head, Paul sees the dog. For Paul to see the dog's head in the circumstances in question is ipso facto for him to see the dog. Likewise, in hearing the ringing sound of the alarm clock, Paul thereby hears the alarm clock. For Paul to hear the sound of the alarm clock is ipso facto for him to hear the alarm clock. Cases in which perceiving part of an object or an effect of it counts as perceiving the object itself are readily multiplied.

However, to perceive part of something (even when the part is suitably attached) is not ipso facto actually to perceive the thing itself.[29] New Jerseyites draw a distinction between seeing the New Jersey Turnpike and seeing New Jersey. And outsiders draw one between seeing New Jersey and seeing the United States. Examples involving physical objects abound. Seeing one inside wall of a house may not count as actually seeing the house itself. Perhaps the unfortunate kidnap victim did not get an opportunity to see the house, but saw only the one wall of the house. To see the doorknob of a door leading into a building is not thereby to see the building. If Jack's hand is before Jill's eyes, in seeing the palm of his hand she sees his hand; but while his hand is a part of his body, she may not thereby see his body. Perhaps Jack prevented her from seeing his body by placing his hand before her eyes.

Likewise, to perceive an effect of something is not ipso facto to perceive it. As one gazes at the scene before one's eyes, one does not thereby see the Big Bang. There are less cosmic examples. When one hears the sound of a passing car, one thereby hears the car. But one may not thereby hear the pistons in the engine or the wall that reflects the sound, even though each causally affects the sound. Seeing the glows of a car's headlights may count as seeing the car but not as seeing the battery inside, even though the battery is a causal source of the glows.

The preceding discussion raises at least two questions:

(Q4) Under what conditions does perceiving part of an object count as (and so suffice for) perceiving the object itself?

(Q5) Under what conditions does perceiving an effect of an object count as perceiving the object?

Causal theorists are committed to a certain initial answer to each.

According to any would-be (CAP), there is, fundamentally, or basically, one and only one way to perceive an object: by undergoing a sense experience of which it is a perceptual cause. However, it is clear that one way to perceive an object is to perceive part of it, another is to perceive an effect of it. Causal theorists are committed to the view that these ways of perceiving an object just consist in ways of undergoing a sense experience of which the object is a perceptual cause. They are so committed because they purport to be providing a necessary condition for perceiving an object.

Causal theorists are committed to the following initial answer to (Q4) and (Q5): S's perceiving A counts as S's perceiving B (where A is a part of or an effect of B) on a certain occasion just in case on that occasion for A to be a perceptual cause of S's experience is ipso facto for B to be a perceptual cause of S's experience.

Thus, they must hold that if, on occasion, Paul sees the dog by seeing its head, on that occasion, for the dog's head to perceptually cause Paul's experience is ipso facto for the dog to perceptually cause Paul's experience; and if, on occasion, for the dog's head to perceptually cause Paul's experience is ipso facto for the dog to perceptually cause Paul's experience, then, on that occasion, Paul sees the dog by seeing its head. I call this an 'initial answer' because causal theorists owe us an account of the relevant features of the occasions in question.

But, in any case, if the causal theorist's initial answer to (Q4) and (Q5) is correct, the set of conditions queried in (Q4) and (Q5) *must* supervene on intrinsic conditions of micro-causal processes by which perceived objects cause perceptual experiences. If these sets of conditions fail to so supervene, perceptual causation would not so supervene; and by hypothesis it must. Label the set of conditions queries in (Q4), C^*, and that queried in (Q5), C^{**}. Neither C^* nor C^{**} so supervenes. I shall attempt to illustrate this with a wide variety of examples.

Consider C^*, the set of conditions under which perceiving part of an object counts as perceiving the object itself.

We sometimes count situations in which part of an object participates in a causal transaction as situations in which the object itself participates in the causal transaction. For example, the table may cause a scratch in the wall by virtue of the fact that the corner of the table caused a scratch in the wall. Or, to put it in terms of events, the corner of the table hitting the wall causing it to become scratched may count as the table hitting the wall causing it to become scratched. And the surface of an object causing light to be directed to one's eyes may count as the object itself causing light to be directed to one's eyes. It is clear that causal theorists must acknowledge this sort of indirect participation in a causal transaction if they are to maintain that perceived objects cause perceptual experiences. So a partial answer to (Q4), one I accept, is that the parts being a cause of the person's experience must count as the object itself being a cause of the person's experience.

Presumably, one reason perceiving a detached part of an object (e.g., a tire detached from a car) does not count as perceiving the object itself is that the object does not cause the perceiver's experience in virtue of the detached part causing the experience. But it should be noted that the conditions of proper attachment of a part to an object may not themselves supervene on the micro-causal processes by which the part and thereby the object cause the perceiver's experience. Often the relation in virtue of which one thing counts as part of another is, in part, conventional. But if one can perceive B in virtue of perceiving A, in part, because A is a properly attached part of B, and the conditions of proper attachment are partly conventional, then the condition in virtue of which perceiving A counts as perceiving B will not supervene on the micro-causal processes by which B causes the perceiver's experience. The reason is simply that the relevant conventions governing proper attachment can change without change in the micro-causal process. And were they to change, seeing A would not count as seeing B, since A would not count as part of B. This would involve a perceptual difference without a relevant causal difference. But even if the conditions of proper attachment are held fixed, there are still counterexamples to (ST).

Suppose that on one occasion Judy sees the facing surface of one mural and on a second occasion she sees the facing surface of a second mural. Let A_1 = the facing surface of the first mural and B_1 = the first mural itself. And let A_2 = the facing surface of the second mural and B_2 = the second mural itself. Suppose further that the micro-causal processes whereby A_1 and A_2 are causally linked to the visual experiences Judy undergoes, on the respective occasions, are without intrinsic difference. Each directs light to her eyes in the same way, and so on. Finally, suppose that B_1 reflects light rays to Judy's eyes by means of A_1 reflecting light to her eyes, and that B_2 reflects light rays to her eyes by means of A_2 reflecting light rays to her eyes, so that B_1 and B_2 causally influence Judy's experiences, on the respective occasions, by micro-causal processes without intrinsic difference. (Of course, B_1 and B_2 may exert different gravitational pulls on Judy on the respective occasions, but this difference is irrelevant.) Still it is possible that Judy saw B_1 by seeing A_1 and that she did not see B_2 by seeing A_2. Suppose, for instance, that A_1 is the entire painted surface of B_1, while A_2 is a very small portion of the painted surface of B_2. A_2 is, say, two square feet and B_2 is one mile long, filled with various and diverse pictorial scenes, each one of which is well known. If so, we would count Judy as seeing B_1 in seeing A_1, and we would not count Judy as seeing B_2 in seeing A_2. Seeing A_2 does not suffice for seeing B_2. But, by hypothesis, both B_1 and B_2 are linked to Judy's experience by means of essentially the same micro-causal process (via, respectively, A_1 and A_2 being so linked to her experience). This, then seems to be an example of a perceptual difference without a relevant causal difference.

Consider *any* situation in which a person perceives part of an object, and the object itself is causally linked to the person's experience via the part being so linked. If the person does not actually perceive the object in virtue of perceiving the part, the situation is one in which there is a perceptual difference without a relevant causal difference. So the situation described above in which Judy sees A_2 and does not see B_2 is itself a case in which there is a perceptual difference without a relevant causal difference. Such cases are legion.

It should not be thought that a (CAP) can be easily supplemented by an additional condition concerning part-whole relations. Let us consider some candidate partial answers to (Q4) for the visual modality. It won't do to say that if S sees A, and A is a sufficiently large part of B, S sees B. What is to count as a sufficiently large part of smething? One cannot appeal to the ratio of the size of the part to the size of the whole. (There is a problem with vagueness, of course; but that is not a serious problem in this context. It is a vague matter whether or not someone perceives an object, and undecidable cases abound. The problem lies elsewhere.) Seeing one brick of a brick building may not count as actually seeing the building. But we count someone as seeing the Atlantic Ocean who sees only a very small part. It seems to me that seeing part of the landscape of the Moon, say, a certain valley, may count as seeing the Moon, while seeing part of the landscape of the Earth, say, a valley, that is larger relative to the size of the Earth than is the Moon landscape to the Moon, would not count as seeing the Earth. Moreover, we sometimes count seeing A as seeing B but not seeing C as seeing B, when A is a smaller part of B than C is of B. We might count seeing the face of a building as seeing the building and not count seeing the basement floor of the building as seeing the building, even when the floor is larger than the face. Typically, seeing a person's face counts as seeing the person; but seeing one thigh of a person may not count as seeing the person, even though the thigh is larger than the face. What is significant about the parts seen in the last two examples is that they are faces of the items in question, not their relative size. We often count seeing the face of an object as seeing the object.

It won't do to say that if S perceives A, and A is part of B by which S can recognize B, S perceives B. First, one can recognize, for example, that one is seeing part of a car, say, a tire, without thereby actually seeing the car itself. The tire may not be attached to the car. But the principle does not hold even in cases in which the part is properly attached. One may be able to recognize a human body by seeing a nose. But if all of Tom is occluded except for his nose, and one sees his nose, one does not thereby see a human body. Moreover, a condition concerning the recognition of an object has no place in any analysis of what it is to perceive something. You can see me without recognizing me. Moreover, if a person perceives an actual physical object that is an F, then the person perceives an F, regardless of whether or not the person recognizes it is an F, seems to perceive an F, perceives the F as an F, or has the concept of an F (for countless values of F). For example, a person may see the Queen of Hearts in a deck of cards (picture side not facing the person), without recognizing it as the Queen of Hearts, without seeming to see the Queen of Hearts, without perceiving it as the Queen of Hearts, and even while lacking the concept of the Queen of Hearts. (This is not to deny that all perceiving is perceiving-as or that what one perceives must appear some way to one.) After all, we can learn about the objects we perceive.

Intuitions can vary concerning when perceiving part of something counts as perceiving the thing itself. One reason, I think, is this. Whether or not a person perceives an object by perceiving a certain part of the object depends on *pragmatic, contextual factors*. Let us stipulate that if a part of something is a *relevant* part, perceiving the part counts as actually perceiving the thing itself. What parts of something count as relevant depends on the capricious factor of interest, on what parts are *deemed* relevant. Who deems which parts are relevant? To some extent the individual who is making the perceptual-ascription, to some extent the linguistic community of which the speaker is a part. What factors are relevant is determined by the pragmatic presuppositions of the individual who is making the perceptual ascription. These pragmatic presuppositions will include the speaker's knowledge of conventions, social norms, and practices; and they may also include the conversational-point of the perceptual ascription. What makes a part count as relevant can depend on social norms, practices, and conventions; and it can depend on speaker interest. Whether or not a part of an object is a relevant part does not supervene on conditions in virtue of which the object or the part participates in micro-causal processes yielding perceptual experiences. So C^* does not so supervene.

A related thesis warrants note. In defense of (A), causal theorists sometimes attempt to draw analogies between the relation in virtue of which a photograph is a photograph of an object and the relation in virtue of which an experience is a perceptual experience of an object. It is claimed that as a photograph's being a photograph of an object just consists in the object's being an appropriate cause of the photographic image, so an experience's being a perceptual experience of an object just consists in the object's being an appropriate cause of the experience.

But consider the following. A photograph can count as a photograph of an object by virtue of being a photograph of part of the object. Suppose Paul photographs the Berlin Wall. The resulting photograph may be a photograph of the facing surface of the wall (that part of the surface that reflected light to the camera lens), a certain section of the wall, the western side of the wall, and the wall itself. While the facing surface of the wall, the section in question, the western side of the wall, and the wall itself are intimately related, they are distinct entities. But for the photograph to be a photograph of the facing surface in question is ipso facto for it to be a photograph of the other items as well. Nevertheless, for a photograph to be a photograph of part of something is not ipso facto for it to be a photograph of the thing itself. For example, were Judy to photograph A_2 in our mural example, the resulting photograph would not actually be a photograph of B_2, but only of part of B_2. But were she to photograph A_1, the resulting photograph would be a photograph of B_1. The relationship a photograph bears to an object in virtue of which it is a photograph of the object does not supervene on intrinsic conditions of any of the micro-causal connections the object bears to the photographic image. The argument for this claim parallels the one for perception, so, for fear of tedium, I won't state it.

Consider C^*, the set of conditions under which perceiving an effect of something counts as perceiving the thing itself.

One can see people when they are wearing clothing and so when one sees no part of their flesh.[30] One can see a woman wearing a burnoose. In seeing the burnoose she is wearing, one sees her. One sees her despite the fact that one does not see her eyes or any part of the surface of her body. Yet we do not count seeing a pillow with a piece of foam rubber inside as seeing the piece of foam rubber. But the piece of foam rubber may causally affect the spatial position and configuration of the pillow covering in essentially the same way that the person causally affects the spatial position and configuration of the clothing she is wearing; and both the surface of the burnoose and the surface of the pillow covering may be linked to one's visual experience by micro-causal processes without intrinsic difference. This, then, seems to be a case of a perceptual difference without a relevant causal difference.

We often count seeing the book cover covering a book as seeing the book. But high school students often cover their books with brown paper taken from brown paper bags. When one sees such a book cover covering a book in the standard way, one sees the book. But if one were to lay a piece of brown paper on top of a book so that no part of the book could be seen beneath the piece of paper, one would not be able to see the book. The relevant difference is that in the first case, one sees part of the book's cover, in the second one does not. What one sees is a piece of brown paper that completely occludes the book. There is a perceptual difference in the two cases without any relevant causal difference.

Consider cases of perceiving causal sources by perceiving their effects. Seeing the search beam of a lighthouse may count as seeing the lighthouse and not as seeing the bulb inside the searchlight. Hearing sounds produced by someone's beating a drum typically counts as hearing the drum. But hearing sounds produced by someone's beating a rug hanging on a wash line does not typically count as hearing the rug, though it will count as hearing someone beating the rug. Tom knocks on a wooden door. Paul hears him knocking by hearing the sounds thereby produced. If the wooden door were functioning as a door, we may count Paul as hearing the door as well. But if, for instance, the wooden door were functioning as a desk top, propped at each end by short bookshelves, and Tom were rapping his fist on it, we would not normally count Paul as hearing the desk top in hearing the sounds thereby produced. The factors that make for the perceptual differences in question do not supervene on intrinsic properties of micro-causal processes by which objects causally influence perceptual experiences. More generally, C^{**} does not so supervene.

However, this does not preclude providing interesting partial answers to (Q5). Consider the following:

(1)   If S hears a sound, and the sound is the sound of a physical object O, S hears O.

(2)   If S smells an odor, and the odor is the odor of a physical object O, S smells O.

We sometimes ask questions such as 'What is that odor?' and 'What is that sound?' And in a particular conversational-context, appropriate answers might be, respectively, 'It is the cat' and 'It is a plane passing overhead'. Ellipses are involved here. The questions are, perhaps, 'Of what is that the odor?' and 'Of what is that the sound?' The answers are, respectively, 'That odor is the odor of the cat' and 'That sound is the sound of a plane passing overhead'. If the answers are correct, then anyone who smells the odor in question or hears the sound in question, thereby smells the cat or hears the plane passing overhead.

A sound is the sound of O only if O makes, produces, emits, gives off, or causes the sound. Likewise, an odor is the odor of O only if O makes, produces, emits, gives off, or causes the odor.[31] But, a sound is not the sound of each of its causal sources; nor is an odor the odor of each of its causal sources. Moreover, the 'ofness' relation here does not supervene on intrinsic conditions of micro-causal processes by which odors and sounds are produced. Consider again Tom knocking on the wooden door. If the wooden door were functioning as a door, the sound would count as the sound of the door; but if it were functioning as a desk top, the sound would not count as the sound of the desk top. The sounds produced by Tom beating the drum count as the sounds of the drum; but the sounds produced by Tom beating the rug (on the wash line) do not count as the sounds of the rug. Consider how natural it is to speak of the sound of the harp, the piano, the typewriter, or the engine, and how unnatural to speak of the sound of the book, the pencil, the rug, or the file cabinet. But each of the latter group can be used to produce sounds. What a sound is the sound of, or an odor is the odor of, depends, in part, I suggest, on pragmatic, contextual factors that can change without change in the means whereby objects cause sounds and odors.

To sum up, the covey of cases presented above suffices to show that C^* and C^{**} do not supervene on the intrinsic conditions of micro-causal processes whereby objects cause perceptual experiences. (ST) is false: there can be a perceptual difference without a relevant causal difference. Hence, no (CAP) is possible. Whether or not a person perceives an object often depends, in part, on conditions that are independent of the causal processes (if any) by which the object causes the person's experience. At least some of the conditions in C^* and C^{**} are just such conditions. Causal theorists hold that there is a kind of causal process K, by means of which an object can cause a person's experience, and K is such that (i) K's occurrence is necessary and sufficient for the person to perceive the object, and, (ii) K supervenes on at least one of the kinds of micro-causal processes by which a perceived object can cause a perceptual experience. Perceptual causation is understood to be causation by means of an instance of K. I hope to have shown that there is no such thing as perceptual causation. This, then, completes my central argument.

V

In this final section, I want to make some positive suggestions, drawing from notions that I elaborate elsewhere.[32]

Given that no (CAP) is possible, one may attempt something altogether different.[33] But less radical alternatives may be available.

Even if my central argument is sound, it may nevertheless be possible to provide a causal analysis for an interesting subclass of cases of perceiving public entities (i.e., entities that can, in principle, be perceived by more than one person). Of course, causal theorists themselves restrict their would-be analyses to a subclass of cases of perceiving public entities, namely, (roughly) cases of perceiving ordinary middle-sized physical objects, in particular, to use Austin's apt phrase, various varieties of dry goods. They take these to be the primary cases of perception. But it is remarkable how many and various are the sorts of things we say we perceive: the holes in a piece of Swiss cheese, marching bands, the sky, shadows, rainbows, rain, fog, lawns, universities, cities, the skylines of cities, the borders between countries, etc. Causal theorists hope to handle such cases in a derivative fashion, not necessarily the same in each case.

My central argument, if sound, may show that causal theorists have not drawn the primary/secondary distinction in the right place if they are concerned to understand the role of causation in our perception of public entities. What is wanted is a principled and well-motivated distinction between primary and secondary cases.

A strategy I think is promising, but can do no more than quickly sketch here, is to distinguish different kinds of primary cases of perceiving public entities for each of the five sense modalities. One might attempt to provide a causal analysis of unaided perception of public entities of the following sorts: seeing surfaces, hearing sounds, smelling odors, tasting tastes, and feeling surfaces. It may be the case that such cases of perceiving public entities supervene on the micro-causal processes by which such entities cause perceptual experiences. In any case, nothing I have said in this paper is incompatible with the claim that a causal analysis for such cases of perception is possible. The reason is this. In cases of unaided perception of the entities in question, it is not the case that one perceives such entities in virtue of perceiving any other public entities. For example, in cases of unaided aural perception of a sound, the perceiver hears the sound but not in virtue of hearing any other public entity. So one cannot construct examples of the sorts I used to show that (ST) is false.

Let us stipulate that:

(D1) S basically perceives x by undergoing experience E at t iff
    (a) S perceives x by undergoing E at t;
    (b) x is a public, concrete particular;
    (c) $\sim (Ey)$ $[(y$ satisfies (b)) and $(S$ perceives x by undergoing E at t by perceiving y by undergoing E at $t)]$.

(D2) S nonbasically perceives x by undergoing E at t iff
    (d) S perceives x by undergoing E at t;
    (e) x is a public, concrete particular;
    (f) S does not basically perceive x by undergoing E at t.

(It should be understood that the above definitions are to be relativized to a given sense modality.) (D1) and (D2) are stipulative definitions. The distinction between basic and nonbasic perception is not one I claim to find in our common conception of perception. Rather, I draw the distinction for theoretical purposes. Since the definitions are stipulative, they should be judged in terms of their theoretical fruits; in particular, in terms of the theoretical fruits of the distinction drawn along the lines specified by these definitions.[34]

Given (D1) and (D2), it follows that: S perceives a public, concrete particular x iff S basically perceives x or nonbasically perceives x. The basic/nonbasic perception distinction is jointly exhaustive over the class of events of someone's perceiving a public, concrete particular. Whether it is mutually exclusive over this class of events will be left an open question. The answer to this question turns on the controversial issue of event individuation. Those who prefer a fine-grained approach to event individuation will hold that no event can be both a basic perception and a nonbasic perception. Those who prefer a coarse-grained approach will allow that a given event can be both a basic perception and a nonbasic perception, depending upon how it is described. Tagged one way, an event may be a basic perception, tagged another way, a nonbasic perception.

Some brief remarks are in order so as to avert misunderstanding. First, (D1) and (D2) are neutral with respect to competing would-be theories of sense experience. Condition (b) rules out sense data, if there are such, as what are basically perceived. But acceptance of (D1) is compatible with acceptance or rejection of sense data theory.

Second, the distinction between basic and nonbasic perception does not imply that 'perceives' or the more specific perception verbs (e.g., 'see', 'hear', etc.) are ambiguous. There is a distinction between poisonous and nonpoisonous plants, but 'plant' is not thereby ambiguous.

Finally, the distinction offers no special support for any would-be theory of knowledge or epistemic justification. Let it be clear that I do not claim, nor do I believe, any of the following: (i) that we always attend to what we basically perceive, (ii) that we can be more certain about the properties of what we basically perceive than about the properties of what we nonbasically perceive, (iii) that we are less likely to be mistaken about the properties of what we basically perceive than about the properties of what we nonbasically percieve, (iv) that beliefs about what we nonbasically perceive are inferred from beliefs about what we basically perceive, or (v) that beliefs about what we nonbasically perceive are always justified by beliefs about what we basically perceive. Acceptance of (D1) and (D2) does not require acceptance of any of (i)-(v).

I think (D1) is satisfied by cases of unaided perception consisting of seeing surfaces, hearing sounds, smelling odors, tasting tastes, and feeling surfaces. I say "cases of unaided perception" because, for example, if one hears the sounds of Caruso singing by hearing the distinct sounds emitted by the recording, one nonbasically hears the sounds Caruso produced, though one may basically hear the sounds emitted by the recording. Likewise, if one sees the surface on Connor's forearm on the television, one nonbasically sees the surface in question.

There is room for rational disagreement concerning what sorts of things can be basically perceived within a modality. I shall not defend here my claims about what can be basically perceived. For present purposes, it suffices to note that the distinction between basic and nonbasic perception is intentionally drawn in such a way as to isolate in one of the two kinds of cases the factors that blocked a (CAP). Basically perceiving something does not require the obtainment of conditions in either C^* or C^{**}. Thus nothing I have said in this paper is incompatible with the claim that a causal analysis restricted to basic perception can succeed.

We can use the basic/nonbasic perception distinction to draw another distinction, one between two questions:

(Q6) What is it for a person to basically perceive something?

(Q7) What is it for a person to nonbasically perceive something?

Anyone concerned to answer (Q1) should distinguish (Q6) and (Q7). Answering one of these questions will have little to do with answering the other.

An answer to (Q7) will require the specification of *perceptual principles*. There are at least two ways to nonbasically perceive something: (i) by perceiving it by perceiving a part, and, (ii) by perceiving it by perceiving an effect of it. Questions (Q4) and (Q5) are requests for perceptual principles, and (1) and (2) are examples of such. Perceptual principles are principles that state under what conditions perceiving something of one sort counts as perceiving something of another sort. Perceptual principles may relate basic perceptions to nonbasic perceptions, and nonbasic perceptions to other nonbasic perceptions. As we saw in section IV, it is by no means easy to state general nonquestion-begging answers to (Q4) and (Q5). But less than perfectly general principles can be of interest in their own right.

The notion of 'a perceptual principle' is, I believe, useful for understanding certain disputes in the epistemology of science and of mathematics. For example, one can view Achinstein's arguments against the distinction between what is observable and what is unobservable as involving appeals to perceptual principles.[35] Achinstein raises considerations such as this: Since seeing the cloud trail of the jet passing overhead typically counts as seeing the jet, why should not seeing the path of an electron in a cloud chamber count as seeing the electron? If we could formulate perceptual principles concerning the perception of ordinary kinds of physical entities, we could then see what reasons there are for or for not employing them by extension to perceptual situations involving cloud chambers, electron microscopes, oscillographs, and other devices.

To turn to the epistemology of mathematics, Penelope Maddy has asked whether or not we ever see sets by seeing their members.[36] It will not do simply to say that we do not ever say we see sets. The issue is whether, given that there are sets, we in fact ever see them. Nor will it do simply to say that sets do not cause visual experiences. Maddy points out that it is only a stage of an object that causes one's experience when one sees it; the object itself causes one's experience only in virtue of the stage causing one's experience; and we may add that the stage causes one's experience in virtue of part of the surface of the stage or an event involving part of the surface of the stage causing one's experience. Why cannot a set sometimes cause an experience in virtue of its members or stages of its members causing the experience? Sometimes seeing members of a group, swarm, collection, system, or assembly counts as seeing the group, swarm, collection, system, or assembly itself. Why cannot seeing the members of a set sometimes count as seeing the set itself? Any attempt to answer Maddy's question would have to consider analogies and disanalogies between the relationship between mereological sums and their elements and that between sets and their members. But it would also have to investigate perceptual principles. I shall not take sides in these disputes here. I mention them only to indicate the potential interest of formulating specific perceptual principles.

A causal analysis of basic perception, if possible, would accomplish some but not all of what was expected of a (CAP). Of course, it would not yield an answer to (Q1), though it would yield an answer to the more restricted question (Q6). And a causal analysis of basic perception would yield an answer to (Q2), though not to

(Q3). Whenever one perceives anything at all, one basically perceives something. So a causal analysis of basic perception would yield a causal criterion for distinguishing perceptual from hallucinatory experiences. But whether or not a causal analysis of basic perception is possible must be left an open question.

The foregoing sketch raises more questions than it answers. But I must leave these questions for another occasion. My objective in this paper has been the limited one of showing that no causal analysis of perceiving physical objects is possible.[37]

Notes

1. I follow the philosophical convention of using 'perceive' as an all-purpose perceptual verb to stand in for the more specific perceptual verbs 'see', 'hear', 'smell', 'taste', and 'feel'. And I use the term 'sense experience' as a label for the kind of psychological event one undergoes when something appears some way to one, or when one is appeared to in some way. Subspecies of sense experience include visual, aural, olfactory, gustatory, and tactual experience. Each mode of sense perception has a corresponding kind of psychological event. In what follows, I shall remain neutral concerning competing would-be theories of sense experience. My principal concern is not with the psychological component of perception, but with the relationship the psychological component bears to what is perceived.

2. Proposals similar to (A), for one or more sense modalities, can be found in H. H. Price, *Perception* (London, 1932; New York, 1973), chap. 4; Roderick Chisholm, *Perceiving: A Philosophical Study* (Ithaca, 1957), chap. 10; H. P. Grice, "The Causal Theory of Perception," *Aristotelian Society Supplementary Volume* 35 (1961):121-68; George Pitcher, *A Theory of Perception* (Princeton, N. J., 1971), chap. II; Charles Chastain, "Reference and Context," in *Minnesota Studies in the Philosophy of Science*, edited by Keith Gunderson, vol. 7 (Minneapolis, 1975), 194-269; David Pears, "The Causal Conditions of Perception," *Synthese* 33 (1976): 25-40; Alvin I. Goldman, "Discrimination and Perceptual Knowledge," *Journal of Philosophy* 18 (1976):771-91; and in Michael Tye, "A Causal Analysis of Seeing," *Philosophy and Phenomenological Research* (1982):311-26.

The term 'perceptual causation' is taken from Goldman's "Discrimination and Perceptual Knowledge," where he says "One problem for the theory of perception is to explicate the notion of perceptual causation, that is, to explain which of the causes of a percept a person is said to perceive" (pp. 783-84). Goldman has an excellent discussion of issues in the causal theory of perception, but does not venture necessary and sufficient conditions for perceiving an object, in his "Perceptual Objects," *Synthese* 35 (1977):257-84.

3. By 'a causal process', I mean, roughly, a sequence of causally related events. It may be left open whether or not causal processes are deterministic and whether or not they can have spatio-temporal gaps. What I say below concerning causal processes is compatible with all the major would-be analyses of causation and all the major would-be theories of events. Should it prove to be the case that events are not the primary *relata* of the causal relation, the discussion in this paper could, I believe, be recast in terms of whatever prove to be the primary *relata*.

4. For an attempt to answer a question similar to (Q2), for the visual modality, see David K. Lewis, "Veridical Hallucination and Prosthetic Vision," *Australasian Journal of Philosophy* 58 (1980):239-49.

Christopher Peacocke's notion of *a sensitive causal chain* may be useful for providing an answer to (Q2). He introduces the notion in "Deviant Causal Chains," *Midwest Studies in Philosophy* 4 (1979):123-56. Peacocke acknowledges that his notion of a differential explanation won't itself provide an answer to question (Q1) or (Q3). One of the conditions he appeals to in answering (Q1) is this:

(iii) phi(x) is a condition at the right stage of the causal chain as determined by the examples of "perceives" used in fixing the concept. (p. 149)

I shall provide examples below in which two objects are at the same stage of a nondeviant causal chain, but one is perceived and the other is not. If successful, my examples will show that Peacocke fails to provide a sufficient condition for perceiving an object.

5. "Minds, Brains, and Programs," reprinted in *The Mind's I*, edited by Douglas R. Hofstadter and Daniel C. Dennett (New York, 1981), 353-73.

6. Ibid., 366-68.

7. "The Meaning of 'Meaning'," in *Mind, Language and Reality, Philosophical Papers*, vol. II (New York, 1975), 215-71.

8. Ibid., 223-35.

9. "Individualism and the Mental," *Midwest Studies in Philosophy* IV (1979):73-123.

10. Gilbert Harman, "Knowledge, Inference, and Explanation," *American Philosophical Quarterly* 5 (1968):164-73; Peter D. Klein, "Knowledge, Causality, and Defeasibility," *Journal of Philosophy* 20 (1976):792-811; Keith Lehrer and Thomas Paxson, "Knowledge: Undefeated Justified True Belief," *Journal of Philosophy* 8 (1969):225-37.

11. Alvin I. Goldman, "Discrimination and Perceptual Knowledge," *Journal of Philosophy* 20 (1976):771-91.

12. "Causality, Identity, and Supervenience in the Mind-Body Problem," *Midwest Studies in Philosophy* IV (1979), 42-43. See Kim's "Supervenience and Supervenient Causation," Spindel Vol. *Southern Journal of Philosophy* (1983):45-56; see also "Epiphenomenal and Supervenient Causation" in the present volume.

13. Cf., "Supervenience and Supervenient Causation." I discuss Kim's views on supervenient causation in "Event Supervenience and Supervenient Causation," Spindel Vol. *Southern Journal of Philosophy* (1984):71-92.

14. See ibid. for a discussion of macro-causation and micro-causation.

15. *Perceiving: A Philosophical Study* (Ithaca, 1957), chap. 10.

16. "The Causal Theory of Perception," 143-44.

17. Ibid., 144.

18. Ibid., 144.

19. See the references to Pitcher and Chastain in n. 2.

20. "Deviant Causal Chains," 144.

21. See "The Meaning of 'Meaning'."

22. "Deviant Causal Chains," 144.

23. Ibid., 145.

24. "Veridical Hallucination and Prosthetic Vision."

25. See Michael Tye, "A Causal Analysis of Seeing," 320-21.

26. "Deviant Causal Chains," 145.

27. See Robert Stalnaker, "Pragmatics," in *Semantics of Natural Language*, edited by Donald Davidson and Gilbert Harman (Boston, 1972), 380-97.

28. Ibid.

29. See, e.g., G. E. Moore, *Commonplace Book 1919-1953* (London, 1962), 320-25; G. J. Warnock, "Seeing," *Proceedings of the Aristotelian Society* 55 (1954-55):208; Thomson Clarke, "Seeing Surfaces and Physical Objects," in *Philosophy in America*, edited by Max Black (Cornell, 1965), 98-114; Roderick Firth, "The Men Themselves: or the Role of Causation in Our Concept of Seeing," in *Intentionality, Minds, and Perception*, edited by Hector-Neri Castañeda (Detroit, 1967), 257-82; Paul Ziff, "There is More to Seeing than Meets the Eye," in his *Understanding Understanding* (Cornell, 1972), 120-42; and David Sanford, "The Primary Objects of Perception, *Mind* 75 (1976):189-208.

30. See Firth's discussion in "The Men Themselves."

31. These points are made in J. O. Urmson, "The Objects of the Five Senses," *Proceedings of the British Academy* 54 (1968):117-31; and they are made in Sanford's "The Primary Objects of Perception."

32. "What Distinguishes Perception from Hallucination" (forthcoming).

33. For an alternative to the causal approach see Dretske's theory in *Knowledge and the*

Flow of Information (Cambridge, 1981), chap. 6. I discuss Dretske's approach in "Information Content and Perceptual Objects" (forthcoming).

34. I am deeply indebted to Sanford for his suggestion to draw a distinction of the sort in question. In "The Primary Objects of Perception," Sanford draws a distinction between immediate and mediate perception. I do not use his definitions since they do not succeed in distinguishing only the intended cases. His definitions depend, in part, on the definition of a class of perceived primary objects of a sense. He says:

> C is a class of perceived primary objects of a sense if and only if
> (i)   The perception of any physical existent with this sense requires the perception of a member of C.
> (ii) The members of C are physical existents.
> (iii) Normally when one perceives with this sense, there is some member of C which one can pick out or identify as something one perceives.
> (iv) No proper subset of C satisfies the above three conditions. (p. 194)

But consider the set of smelled skunks and odors the smelling of which is not the smelling of a skunk. This set satisfies (i)-(iv). In fact, there is no end of sets that satisfy it. This difficulty infects Sanford's distinction between immediate and mediate perception.

Somewhat similar definitions to (D1) and (D2) can be found, for the visual modality, in Frank Jackson's *Perception* (Cambridge, 1977), 19-20.

35. *Concepts of Science* (Baltimore & London, 1968).

36. "Perception and Mathematical Intuition," *Philosophical Review* 469 (1980):163-96.

37. I wish to thank the following people for helpful discussions of the issues discussed in this paper: David Benfield, Peter Klein, Douglass Long, Judy McLaughlin, Fadlou Shehadi, and Robert Van Gulick. Thanks are also due to David Lewis for some lectures I attended in which he attempted to formulate various supervenience theses that both proponents and opponents of physicalism might take as definitive of the position. Finally, special thanks are due to Richard E. Grandy and David H. Sanford.

Causation and Identity

CHRIS SWOYER

C ausal accounts of the transtemporal identity of physical objects and of persons are not completely new. Passages in Hume can be read as suggesting causal accounts of the identity of physical objects and of the self, as can Kant's arguments that the successive states of an objective substance must be causally connected; and in this century, a variety of causal accounts of the identity conditions for persons and for physical objects have been proposed. Such accounts, especially for physical objects, have not been very fully developed, however, and here I want to provide a more detailed motivation for, and development of, a causal account of identity through time and to examine some of its implications. I think that my general line of argument applies both to persons and to physical objects, though to keep the discussion manageable I shall concentrate on the latter.[1]

I

If we are to find anything like conditions of adequacy for an account of the identity conditions of physical objects or of persons, we need to be clear about our reasons for wanting to know such conditions in the first place. It would be an overstatement to say that such accounts are designed solely to shed light upon the notions of a physical object or of a person, rather than on identity. After all, an investigation into the identity conditions of persons or objects might convince us that a universe consisting of two qualitatively indiscernible iron spheres or neutrons or minds is metaphysically possible and thus lead to an interesting conclusion about identity itself, viz., that possession of the same purely qualitative properties is not always sufficient for it. Nevertheless, we do begin with a pretty definite conception of identity—it is, I shall assume, an equivalence relation and identical things are indiscernible—and the goal is to use the logical features of identity to provide formal constraints on a story that says something of philosophical interest about what it is to *be* a physical object or a person.

The motivation for telling such a story is not that we must provide a "criterion of identity" for a given sort of entity if we are to understand talk about such things or know what they are. There is a perfectly good sense in which most everyone knows what persons and physical objects are even though they cannot provide necessary and sufficient conditions for the identity of either. As I see it, our situation with respect to persons and physical objects is something like the situation of miners and artisans who knew what lead was before scientists discovered any of its essential features, like its atomic number. On this view, the goal of an investigation of the identity conditions for a given sort of thing like physical objects or persons is to learn something about what members of such basic categories as physical objects or persons *are* by learning what features are essential to a person or an object (of a given sort) and which are necessarily or metaphysically sufficient for being a given person or object. It may, of course, turn out that the transtemporal identity of persons or of objects is primitive and that there are no interesting necessary or sufficient conditions for it, but it would be important if there are, and we are not likely to find any unless we look. Thus we are concerned with metaphysical questions about the nature of the identity of persons or physical objects rather than with epistemological questions about the bag of tricks we use to identify and reidentify them. Moreover, we are after conditions that give us philosophical insight into what physical objects or persons are in a way that claims—whether correct or not—that physical objects are identical just in case they have all of their properties in common or just in case both have the property of being identical with a (for some object a) or just in case both occupy the same regions of space-time do not.

Trying to discover the fundamental features of objects or persons is a venerable philosophical task, but why approach it by way of identity through time? If there are such things as numbers or sets or properties, we might well learn much of philosophical interest about them by learning about their identity conditions, but neither their identity conditions nor their fundamental features seem to have anything much to do with time. So why suppose that the identity or essential features of other sorts of things have anything to do with time? One reason why many philosophers think of temporal considerations as irrelevant to philosophically interesting identity conditions for numbers is that those who believe that numbers exist at all are convinced that numbers cannot fail to survive changes in the world. Those who believe in the existence of sets and properties disagree about whether they exist eternally. For example, some hold that a set ceases to exist if any of its members do; however, only one sort of change in the world is relevant here, viz. the beginning or ceasing to be of the members of the set; more important, such questions are questions about the identity conditions of the set's members rather than about those of the set itself. Hence we may learn much about sets by learning of identity conditions that do not involve time or change, e.g., that sets are identical just in case they have exactly the same members.

Matters are different with persons and physical objects. There can be—and sometimes are—serious questions about whether a person can survive certain changes like the destruction of the body or whether a person after a left hemispherectomy or amnesia or waking up from a "brain transplant" is identical with a person who existed before. Such questions about identity and change bear on what it is to be a person, on whether either psychological continuity or bodily continuity are necessary or sufficient for the continued existence of a person (and, with appropriate changes, for physical objects) in a way that considerations about change do not bear on what it is to be a number or set. A feature is metaphysically sufficient for being a given object only if anything having that feature is that object despite any changes it has undergone; a feature is essential to an object only if it retains that feature throughout any changes it survives. And because change requires time, it makes good sense to approach questions about the fundamental nature of persons and of physical objects by way of questions about their identity through time.

A common and useful approach to problems about the transtemporal identity of physical objects or of persons is to look for relations that hold among temporal stages just in case they are stages of the same object or person. This approach has often suffered from guilt by association with bad motivations. Certain empiricists have favored it because they thought that momentary things—ideas or representations or sense data, which were typically viewed as subjective—were better known and perhaps more real than enduring objects like rocks or cows; others, especially champions of a causal theory of time, often thought of momentary events in space-time as more real or more fundamental than enduring things. My goal, however, is not to reduce ordinary enduring objects to something more real—whatever that might mean—and certainly not to reduce them to something better known and understood, since physical objects are clearly better known and understood than atomistic stages. The notion of a temporal stage or phase, or a momentary cross section or temporal part of an enduring thing, is an abstract philosophical concept that is useful, not because stages enjoy some elusive sort of ontological or conceptual priority, but because it is a piece of theoretical apparatus that helps us to mobilize the notions that do the real work in our treatments of identity; it furnishes pegs on which to hang the properties a thing has at an instant and on which to string key relations like spatiotemporal or compositional or psychological continuity.

It is true that we understand what an object stage is only because we understand what an enduring object is, but there is nothing amiss here, since the idea is not to *define* the notion of a stage in terms of the notion of an enduring object. Indeed, we needn't define it at all, any more than we need to define 'belief' or 'truth' before asking whether knowledge requires true belief or need a theory of memory before evaluating Locke's account of personal identity. The situation is more like this: We begin with an everyday understanding of physical objects—lots of knowledge and opinions and intuitions about them—but without precise and philosophically interesting identity conditions for them. Our intuitive understanding is good enough, however, to enable us to say quite a bit about the features a stage has—where it exists and when, its shape, color, mass. And with luck this notion of a stage is sufficiently precise to enable us, with one last tug of our bootstraps, to give the sort of identity conditions for physical objects that we were after. Philosophical progress here does not lie in constructing—logically or otherwise—physical objects out of stages or in explaining their identity conditions to someone who has no idea what objects are; it lies in using stages to learn something important about objects that *we* didn't know before.

Much of our best science is formulated in differential equations that treat changes as continuous, and since a *complete* account of identity through time ought not leave unanswered questions about the identity of stages through change, it will require stages that are infinitesimally slender. Stages sliced so thin would lack many of the familiar properties of enduring things and would be hard to handle without some complicated apparatus involving limits and related notions. We are very far from a complete account of identity for physical objects or persons, however, and the familiar puzzle cases used in comparing and evaluating the prospects of current accounts usually only require us to consider less evanescent changes before and after some watershed like a complete replacement of a ship's planks or a person's brain transplant. When dealing with such cases it is convenient to treat stages as having considerable duration and possessing a number of ordinary properties, and in much of what follows I shall do so. The task is then to explain the identity conditions for physical objects in terms of some relation — often called *gen-identity* — that stages bear to each other just in case they are stages of the same enduring object.[2]

II

According to the most popular view about the transtemporal identity of physical objects, a necessary condition for the gen-identity of objects stages is that they be spatiotemporally continuous: contiguous or connected by an intervening series of stages that are contiguous (some philosophers speak instead of spatiotemporal continuity of physical objects, and while for convenience I shall sometimes follow suit, I mean this to be a loose way of speaking about the continuity of their stages). Clearly, though, mere spatiotemporal continuity of stages is not sufficient for their gen-identity. When the steamroller ran over Aunt Gussie's candelabrum, (the stages of) her candlestick and this shard of metal left behind enjoyed spatiotemporal continuity. But the shard and the candelabrum are not identical.

We need to isolate the sort of spatiotemporal continuity that is *appropriate* for the gen-identity of object stages and thereby for the identity of physical objects through time. Cases like Aunt Gussie's suggest that we want to rule out abrupt and sudden change, and so we might add requirements of qualitative or structural or compositional continuity (e.g., Broad 1949, 393; Quine 1981, 125). Qualitative and structural continuity are not easy to explain precisely, but in any case such requirements are not sufficiently discriminating. A deflated balloon retains identity through rapid change whereas the candelabrum would not have been identical with the shard even if it was transformed into it by a long, slow series of tiny changes. A more subtle approach is to require spatiotemporal continuity "under a (substance) sortal" (roughly, while remaining the same "sort" of thing; (cf. Hirsh 1982, chap. 2). Despite unclarities as to what a sortal is and doubts about whether an object of a given sort must always be an object of that sort, this suggestion seems an improvement on the preceding ones. It promises to capture what seemed right about them, since it is often thought to be analytically true that a given sort of thing like a cow cannot undergo sudden changes in composition, structure, or the like, but it is more flexible since it allows the amount of change compatible with identity to vary in the case of different sorts of things.[3]

We need not linger over the differences among continuity theories as to precisely which additions are needed to characterize the sort of spatiotemporal continuity that is sufficient or appropriate for identity, however, for our goal is to compare accounts of this sort with a causal theory. Hence, it won't matter what items are added, so long as none of them involves causality in a way that would turn a continuity theory into a causal account.

There is no denying the intuitive appeal of continuity theories; if we cannot see how an object could have gotten from one region of space-time to another by a continuous path, then no matter how similar the object at one region with that at the other, we have a powerful reason not to count them as one. Furthermore, some philosophers have thought that the requirement of spatiotemporal continuity is needed to guarantee a fact of the matter about the transtemporal identity of physical objects. For suppose that it is not necessary for their identity and that the truck in my driveway could suddenly jump two feet to the left without traversing the distance in between. Now, such philosophers urge, imagine a second situation, just like the first, but in which the original truck disappears and *two* trucks qualitatively indiscernible from it immediately appear, one two feet to the left of the original truck's location (precisely as before), the other two feet to the right. Each truck has an equally good claim to be counted identical with the original truck, and since both can't be (by the transitivity of identity), we seem forced to conclude that neither is. If popping into existence nearby isn't sufficient for identity in the second case, however, why suppose it to be so in the first (cf. Williams 1973)?

Despite its appeal, there are strong reasons for believing that the continuity theory is mistaken, not just in matters of detail, but in fundamental respects. A graphic illustration of one of its shortcomings is provided by thought experiments concerning immaculate deceptions, the basic idea of which was proposed independently by Armstrong (1980) and Shoemaker (1979). Imagine that a group of fanatical environmentalists invent an extraordinary machine that can instantaneously destroy pickup trucks and that Detroit counters with a machine that can instantaneously create pickups out of nothing. Using methods like Mill's, we find that the first machine has unfailingly wiped out trucks, leaving nothing in their wake, while in independent tests the second machine has created trucks where none had been before, and the properties of the created trucks depended entirely on the settings of the machine. In short, we have just the sort of evidence that normally supports causal attributions and generalizations (we might also imagine that we have a well-confirmed physical theory that predicts and explains all of this).

One day the truck annihilator destroys the pickup out there in the driveway, and quite coincidentally the operator of the truck creator sets its controls and creates a qualitatively indiscernible pickup that picks up exactly where the first truck had been. We have an immaculate replacement, or so it seems. If we do, we have a case of spatiotemporal continuity under a sortal, plus qualitative, structural, and chemical continuity. Yet we have distinct trucks. Hence all of these conditions put together are not enough to ensure the transtemporal identity of physical objects. True, we don't have compositional continuity here, for if the trucks are two, they are presumably composed of different matter, but any attempt to save the continuity theory by pleading the lack of compositional continuity faces problems of its own. The question is bound to arise about the identity of matter, and the continuity theorists will surely wish to explain it in terms of spatiotemporal continuity plus something else — but what? The matter of the two trucks exhibits spatiotemporal continuity plus complete qualitative and structural and chemical similarity, and so the continuity theorist can offer no principled reason for saying that the matter or atoms or whatever of the two trucks are different. Moreover, we could imagine that the first machine dissipates the matter of the trucks it destroys whereas the second machine creates trucks by transmuting and rearranging atoms in the region where the truck is created and that in this case, by some remarkable coincidence, the same matter constitutes the two trucks. Thus it seems that spatiotemporal continuity under a sortal plus all the other sorts of continuity is *not sufficient* for the identity of physical objects through time.

A more complex story suggests that spatiotemporal continuity is *not necessary* either. Suppose that our two machines can also instantaneously relocate trucks a few feet from their original position (as judged from the inertial frame of the truck). One day the first machine relocates my neighbor's pickup in my driveway, the second machine creates a new truck in his driveway exactly where his old one had been, and then the first machine relocates *it* in my driveway just as the second machine transfers the first truck back to its original position. We have an immaculate interpolation in which a single truck exhibits spatiotemporal discontinuities, and so spatiotemporal continuity is not necessary for identity. Nor are philosophers the only ones to imagine such strange goings-on. Some physicists have speculated that the matter — though not the same object — absorbed by a black hole passes through a "worm hole" into a distant region of space-time, and science fiction is full of seemingly coherent stories about spatiotemporal gaps in the histories of objects.

To be sure, the replacements in our first examples seem to violate conservation laws, and the interpolations of our second, with their instantaneous relocations, are not always easily reconciled with the relativity of simultaneity; moreover, the continuity theorist may reasonably ask why we take interpolations to involve relocations rather than a simple case of creation and destruction. Some of these difficulties can be avoided by more complicated examples where the trucks are created from matter in a given location rather than from nothing or where we imagine a more detailed theoretical background that supports a given interpretation of an example. Such details aren't critical here, however, for the point of the example is not really that such machines are metaphysically possible but that it is not an a priori truth that they are not; hence, it is not a conceptual truth that spatiotemporal continuity (of the appropriate sort) is either necessary or sufficient for the transtemporal identity of physical objects.

We need not rely upon anything so exotic as interpolations to cast doubt on the claim that spatiotemporal continuity is necessary for the identity of objects. Everybody said that Sam's prefabricated house was flimsy, and even his insurance agent declared it destroyed—utterly demolished—when the twister hit it. But after years of searching, Sam found all of the boards, nails, and other components of his original house. By comparing the code numbers on each with the original instruction manual, he was able to build a house where the first one had been with each part in its original place. Most people agree that the same house existed before the cyclone hit and after Sam put the parts back together, and many also feel that it did not exist during the time the parts lay scattered all over seven counties. Others feel that the house did exist during this interval, though in a wildly scattered state, but the more the parts are broken down and strewn about, the less plausible this seems. Jonah's body has broken down at least to ashes and dust and this has even been incorporated into other organisms, so that it is hard to make sense of talk of its current parts or the view that his body is just temporarily disassembled and lying about. Yet believers in the literal resurrection of the body are confident that his very body could be recreated come judgment day (some think this possible even if every particle that was ever a part of it has been completely annihilated). Thus the ordinary conception of identity does not seem to require spatiotemporal continuity. This ordinary conception may be inconsistent, contain tensions, or need to be revised for some other reason, but since this is not obviously so, some argument is needed to show that it is. Meanwhile, such examples rob the continuity theory of much of its commonsense support.

Reasonably normal examples also suggest that the continuity theory does not provide a sufficient condition for the identity of objects. Suppose one begins with a small submarine and gradually replaces its parts in such a way that one ends up with a submarine of a *very* different shape and size. Many find it plausible to suppose that the original submarine is not identical with the latter one even though their stages exhibit spatiotemporal continuity under a sortal (I assume 'submarine' is a sortal noun; if not, similar examples will do) and all of their changes were gradual enough to preserve all the other sorts of continuity as well.

The intuitions on which these and other putative counterexamples to continuity theorists rest are not widely enough shared to make any one of them conclusive, but together they cast considerable doubt upon such theories. Moreover, there are difficulties in principle with continuity accounts. For example, there may be physical objects that don't always have definite spatiotemporal locations. On the dominant interpretation of our best theories of microphysics, for instance, elementary particles do not have a definite position at all times but rather a superposition of many until we collapse the wave packet by performing a measurement. If so, talk about the spatiotemporal continuity of the fundamental building blocks of the universe is scarcely straightforward. For various reasons, talk about the identity of elementary particles is often thought not to be straightforward either, and although some of these reasons depend upon dubious doctrines like verificationism or the principle of the identity of indiscernibles, our current interpretations of microphysics are too controversial for us to put great weight on them. Let us turn, then, to ordinary, medium-sized objects. These contain lots of empty space, have indefinite borders and can undergo quite abrupt changes in volume—as when a muffler is suddenly attached to a truck or a portion of a mirror is broken off and shattered. Such facts make it difficult to explain a sense in which the stages of material objects enjoy spatiotemporal continuity in a way that does not include too little or too much to capture intuitions about identity (cf., e.g., Nelson 1972).

In addition, at least many attempts to explain continuity presuppose some account of the identity and individuation of places or volumes or regions of space-time and thus seem committed to an absolute theory of space and time (or of space-time) or else to explaining the identity of places in terms of the identity of objects and vice versa. Furthermore, what counts as spatiotemporally continuous judged from one frame of reference won't seem so judged from a second frame that is discontinuous with respect to the first, and I have yet to see a terribly good philosophical (as opposed to practical) reason for favoring some possible frames over others. Finally, it has recently been argued that the continuity theorist does not have the resources to account for a variety of facts about motion. For example, he cannot distinguish a situation in which a sphere of a completely solid, homogeneous material is rotating from one in which it is at rest. The problem is that he must view both situations as involving a series of instantaneous, spatiotemporally continuous sphere stages (cf. n. 2). Because the stages are instantaneous, they are incapable of motion, and since the simple relation of spatiotemporal continuity is present in the same way—stage for stage—in each case, no difference between the two situations can be described using just the resources available to the continuity theorist (Armstrong 1980).

III

Taken together, these problems are serious enough to motivate a search for an alternative to continuity accounts of the transtemporal identity of physical objects. I shall argue that a better account can be found, one based on causation.

Pick a phenomenon of philosophical interest and chances are that someone has proposed a causal account for it. And often with good reason. Causal theories of reference, knowledge, preception, memory, inference, action, emotion, and so forth not only seem plausible in their own right; many of them also promise to solve problems that infect more traditional accounts of the notions. Thus we have well-known theories that tell us that the referent of a proper name is the thing that satisfies some proportion of the cluster of description that constitutes the name's meaning, that knowledge is justified true belief, that actions are to be explained by citing beliefs and desires in light of which the action (under some description) can be seen to be rational, and so forth. However, some goatherd in Albania might, quite by chance, satisfy the descriptions associated with the name 'Empedocles' even though he is not causally related to the name in any interesting way; Jones' justified belief that the man who will get the job has ten coins in his pocket may accidentally turn out to be true; and some of Sebastian's beliefs and desires may, quite fortuitously, be good reasons for him to butter the toast without being *the* reasons that led *him* to butter it. In such cases we have what Kim has aptly called the problem of *fortuitous satisfaction*; something can have all the features traditionally felt to be sufficient for reference or knowledge or action or whatnot *by accident*, rather than because it is the genuine article. In such cases, the traditional picture does not really provide sufficient conditions for what it was supposed to, and, it is argued, some sort of causal connection between the referent and the use of a name or between the world and Sam's belief or between Sam's mental states and his action is needed to rule out such fortuities.

Many traditional, noncausal accounts also fail to provide necessary conditions for the phenomena they are supposed to explain. An entire society can use the name 'Empedocles' without any of its members knowing any description that he alone satisfies, and perhaps not all knowledge requires justification (so-called perceptual knowledge may be an example). But if we can have reference or knowledge without meeting the traditional requirements, it is natural to suppose that there must be something else, something these left out, that makes a name refer to its bearer or in virtue of which a person has knowledge. And some sort of causal connections seem a plausible candidate.

Causal theories of the transtemporal identity of physical objects have similar motivations. Immaculate replacements show that their traditional competitor, the continuity theory, succumbs to the problem of fortuitous satisfaction, for in such examples (the stages of) diverse objects are spatiotemporally contiguous quite by accident. Immaculate interpolations, along with a variety of less exotic phenomena, suggest that spatiotemporal continuity is not necessary for identity through time; if such identity is not a brute and mysterious fact, something else is needed to explain it, and causal connections seem a plausible candidate (we appear to have distinct trucks in an immaculate replacement because of the lack of any interesting *causal* connection between the two).

We would not ordinarily speak of the earlier stages of an object as causing its later stages anymore than we would talk of Aristotle as causing any recent use of his name. In each case, however, there are causal or, more generally, lawful connections between the relevant things. The features that an object has at one time are partly determined by the features that it has at earlier times; they also depend, of course, upon its interactions with other things, but how it interacts with other things also depends upon its earlier properties. Talk of causal relations between the temporal stages of a given object may seem more fitting now that we know that the parts of even the most stolid object are in constant flux, its particles rapidly vibrating, its atoms exchanging electrons, and the like, but our account doesn't rely solely on this. The key is the existence of lawful relationships between the properties of the different stages of a single object, and sometimes these may simply involve the persistence of properties. We commonly think of the velocity of an object as partly determined by its velocity at earlier times and, in the absence of interactions, as wholly determined by it and remaining the same. And the stages in the development and degeneration of organisms or stars, the decay of elementary particles or the carbon 14 in a piece of wood at a fairly definite rate, the gradual spreading of heat throughout a piece of metal are all causal processes in which earlier states lead to later ones in lawful ways.[4]

This is not to deny that spatiotemporal continuity plays an important part in our thought about physical objects, but the view that objects are things that undergo regular and lawful changes has an equally vital role. Indeed, many philosophers have suggested that it is the coherent, lawful behavior of genuine objects that distinguishes them from illusions and the like. More important, when an object does enjoy a great deal of qualitative, compositional, and spatiotemporal continuity, this is (presumed to be) explicable by the laws of nature. The development of an organism exhibits many continuities because of the lawful ways in which its properties at later times depend on those at earlier times. It is no accident that the chair I am now sitting in doesn't fly off into a million pieces or suddenly jump ahead into the twenty-first century; such things can be explained, at least in part, by natural laws governing motion, the electromagnetic forces that hold the chair's molecules and atoms together, the conservation of various properties, the structure of space-time, and the like. Indeed, the very idea of spatiotemporal continuity requires the continuity of space-time and so depends upon natural laws (and very general facts). Hence, even if it should turn out that the transtemporal identity of objects is *in fact* always accompanied by spatiotemporal continuity, it would still be reasonable to regard a causal account of identity as basic and use it to explain the presence of the continuity. In fact, a causal account of the identity of objects might seem to guarantee their spatiotemporal continuity, since it might seem that any causal chain that links stages into a single object must itself be spatiotemporally continuous. One has only to recall the prevalence of beliefs about action at a distance to see that it is not an a priori truth that all causal chains are spatiotemporally connected, however, and it is a virtue of a causal account of identity that it leaves it an empirical question whether the causal chains linking stages of a single object must be spatiotemporally continuous or not.

A causal account of the transtemporal identity of physical objects avoids many of the dubious assumptions of continuity theories. For example, a causal account does not favor an absolute theory of space-time (although it is compatible with one); indeed, a causal account might first be given for the identity of objects and these might then be invoked in developing a relational (perhaps even causal) account of space-time. Moreover, a causal account does not require that objects have definite spatiotemporal locations; so long as there is some appropriate causal or nomological story—deterministic or indeterministic, known or unknown—about their history, it allows for identity. Finally, causal accounts can allow such relations between stages as forces and so hold out a good promise of enabling us to distinguish a rotating sphere from a sphere at rest (cf. Armstrong 1980 and Shoemaker 1979).

What about the claim that reduplications—where two pickups pop up on either side of an original truck's location—require a continuity account of identity? Since the two trucks have the same purely qualitative properties, this tells against any purely qualitative account of the transtemporal identity of physical objects, but a causal account is not purely qualitative. Depending upon the details of the case, a causal account might count the truck on the left or the truck on the right or neither as identical with the original. If a truck creator had its controls set to create a truck to the right and a truck relocater was set to move the original truck to the left, the truck to the left would be the original. Less fancifully, we may recall views about the atom according to which an electron could leap from one orbit to another without traversing the distance in between but in which only certain leaps were permitted and their size depended in a lawful (though perhaps not deterministic) way on initial conditions like the amount of energy absorbed or emitted by the electron. In short, knowledge of laws of nature might allow us to trace the history of an object despite spatiotemporal discontinuities, and the laws themselves might determine facts about identity even if we didn't know them.

Reduplications raise a more serious problem if our original pickup stage could bear the sort of causal relationship to each of two later, coeval pickup stages that would be sufficient for gen-identity if it bore it to only one of the two. It is not clear that such situations couldn't arise, and I think that the causal theorist will simply have to rule them out by requiring that the causal chains for gen-identity, and thereby identity, be nonbranching (Swoyer unpublished). However this may be, the continuity theorist cannot take much comfort in the possibility of branching or coalescing causal chains, since fission and fusion present him with an analogous difficulty.

A causal account of the transtemporal identity of physical objects is also recommended by the light it casts on the familiar maxims that one object cannot be in different places at the same time and that diverse objects (of the same sort) cannot be in one place at the same time. The maxim that a thing cannot be in more than one place at the same time could fail if certain sorts of time travel were possible. For example, in 1949 Gödel discovered solutions to the field equations of general relativity that would permit the existence of approximately closed timelike curves (individual histories or worldlines that loop back almost onto themselves). In a universe in which these solutions describe the structure of space-time, Gödel could in principle travel in a very fast spaceship with his worldline temporally oriented to the future and yet arrive back in his past (Gödel 1959).

Here Gödel's earlier self and his later self could exist in different places (in a single inertial frame) at what would *ordinarily* be taken to be the same time (as measured in that frame). Of course if we are to preserve the indiscernibility of identicals, we will want to qualify this, perhaps by saying that although Gödel has incompatible properties (e.g., looking young and looking old) at the same time as told by the grandfather clock in that frame, the two versions of Gödel have their different properties at different *proper* times (roughly, the proper time of Gödel is that measured by a clock in the frame in which he is always at rest). The important point here, however, is that this story seems coherent and that it can be explained in terms of the causal connections between the Gödel stages along with facts about his motion through a universe with a particular space-time structure. Perhaps such situations never occur, but if they do not, that would seem to be a consequence of laws of nature, e.g., that the world is a general relativistic one, along with such very general features of the universe as the distribution of matter in it (which may be determined in part by other laws).

The second maxim is that numerically diverse objects of the same sort cannot occupy the same place at the same time. The continuity theory makes this true, but there are reasons to think that it is true, if it is, because of natural laws about matter and motion rather than because of analytic truths about 'material object' or related concepts. In *New Essays*, Leibniz notes that when two light rays cross at an angle so that they penetrate each other, we can often trace each before and after their intersection because of the direction of their paths. Moreover, he adds, we can imagine a world where normal physical objects also overlap in this way (I, xxvii, 1). Perhaps we make a movie of two spheres moving toward each other and when we run the film in slow motion it looks for all the world like the spheres passed right through each other, momentarily occupying the same position.

One might alternatively describe this as a case of fusion quickly followed by fission, but there seem to be no principled reasons for describing the situation in this way, and there might be good reasons not to. For example, we might have well entrenched theories according to which two objects of a certain sort have additive properties like mass, density, or charge, and this could suggest the presence of two objects (this might be more plausible with particles, where there might be theoretical reasons to suppose there could not be particles with, say, a mass of 2 m—perhaps they would be unstable—but no reason to suppose that two particles each with mass m couldn't momentarily coincide). The basic defect of the view that it would be contradictory to say that two material objects were in the same place at the same time is captured by Kant's riposte that the principle of contradiction does not repel any material object. Kant's own explanation of the impenetrability of physical objects in terms of repulsive forces that tend to keep bodies apart now appears too simple, and we would point instead to things like the Pauli exclusion principle that forbids two electrons (or any fermions of the same sort) from occupying the same location. But Kant was right that it does not seem to be an a priori truth that two objects cannot occupy the same space at the same time; when (if ever) this is possible depends upon the laws of nature.[5]

It is not difficult to see how a causal account might explain some of the examples that raised problems for the continuity theorist. Identities are present or absent in the case of immaculate deceptions, for example, just in case causal connections between the relevant object stages are, and presumably bodily resurrection is possible only if there are appropriate causal links (like divine intentions) between a body before judgment day and a body afterwards. Other cases, alas, are not so easily handled.

IV

The main problem facing our account is one shared by most causal theories; such a theory may well provide interesting necessary conditions for a given phenomenon, but the near ubiquity of the causal relation makes it unlikely that it will furnish a *sufficient* condition for anything of much philosophical interest. Using random electrical stimulation of my cortex, you might cause me to utter some name or to have an experience qualitatively indistinguishable from one I would have if I were to see you just at that moment. But the causal connection between you and my use of the name doesn't mean I am referring to you nor does the causal connection between you and my experience mean that I see you. Similarly, the current properties of this zygote are causally dependent (in part) upon properties of the gametes that produced it, those of the metal shard upon those of Aunt Gussie's candelabrum, and those of my truck upon the bus that smashed into it, the cat on its floor mat, and the gravitational influence of the moon. The problem of fortuitous satisfaction has been eliminated in one place only to pop up in another, now in the form of accidental or inappropriate causal connections. Hence causal theorists need to explain what *sort* of causal connection is *appropriate* to—sufficient for—the presence of whatever the phenomenon is that they are trying to account for.

Some philosophers have thought that since perception, personal identity, and the like are ordinary concepts, we ought to be able to explain the sorts of causal chains appropriate for them in terms of ordinary things that we all know. Thus conceptual analysis might reveal that visual perception requires a causal chain between the object perceived and the perceiver in which his open ideas are focused in the direction of the object. So long as we remain at this intuitive level, however, we are likely to find ourselves with a growing, but never ending, list of principles that do not add up to anything like a unified theory, since we will have to allow for all sorts of exceptions. The object is behind a person and he sees it in a mirror; the light is powerful and his eyelids thin so that he can see with his eyes closed, and so on and on. One value of scientific theories is that they unify what intuitively seem to be unrelated phenomena, allowing us to redescribe them in common theoretical terms (e.g., bodies being acted on by forces; conditioned stimuli). This suggests that questions about the sorts of causal connections appropriate for a given phenomenon might receive a tidier and more complete answer from science—a view that is especially appealing if one already has doubts about the possibility of pure conceptual analysis.[6] A detailed specification of the sorts of causal chain appropriate to visual perception is a task for optics, perceptual psychology, and neurophysiology. Similarly, a detailed specification of causal connections appropriate for the transtemporal identity of objects would be a task for such fields as chemistry and solid state physics—perhaps it would appeal to laws governing the temporal evolution of particles and of the forces binding these together, laws of motion, laws about the structure of space-time—though less abstruse answers about identity conditions for certain sorts of things could also be given by geology, astronomy, embryology, and the like.[7]

If one wants an account of appropriate causal chains that includes a detailed specification of specific causal mechanisms like optic nerves or intermolecular forces, then there really is no alternative to leaving the task to science and hoping that it can one day tell us some reasonably unified story about what sort of causes are appropriate for perception or for the identity of physical objects. This runs counter to the fairly common view that the meaning of a sortal noun furnishes specific identity conditions for things of that sort (or, since the word may not have been invested with enough meaning to determine its application in every conceivable situation, that such meaning at least provides identity conditions for objects in normal circumstances). On this view, questions about identity conditions of objects can be answered by philosophers doing conceptual analysis. One argument for the claim that the meanings of sortals establish identity conditions begins from the premise that we could not first point in the direction of a cow, say *'that* is a cow', and *then* go on to discover identity conditions for cows. Given their identity conditions, our subject matter is pinned down enough so that we can compare cows and learn much about them, but if we began without such conditions, we would not so much as know what counts as one cow and what counts as two—and if we didn't know that it may be doubted that we even know what cows are. Indeed, unless we knew what cows were and that our friend meant to be pointing to one, we would not even know what his utterance of 'that' referred to—it could be a cowbell or a temporal stage of a cow or the entire pasture.

One problem with all this is that we have reason to doubt that sortals always have a rich enough meaning to determine identity conditions. Kripke, Putnam, and others have given us excellent reasons to suppose that sortals associated with natural kinds—'cantaloupe', 'human being', 'electron'—designate what they do because of an appropriate causal connection between the term and the relevant kind (or its members) rather than because of the term's meaning; indeed, such terms have little or no meaning (as traditionally conceived). I think that this is correct and that it shows that, at least in the case of natural kinds terms, the traditional picture of the relationship between meaning and identity conditions is wrong.

This also suggests an answer to the contention that we couldn't come to learn anything about cows if we didn't begin with detailed analytic truths about their identity conditions. Such claims are similar to the contention that unless at least some people had first known necessary or at least sufficient conditions for something's being lead, scientists could never have proceeded to make any interesting discoveries about this element, inasmuch as they would not have been sure whether any given sample of metal was a sample of lead and so relevant to their investigation. We now have good reason to believe that this picture is mistaken. Several hundred years ago no one knew any interesting metaphysically necessary or sufficient features like the atomic composition or spectral properties of lead, but some people had accurate enough beliefs about lead's obvious qualitative features, the sorts of places it is typically found, and so forth, to mine it and make bullets from it and for scientists to eventually discover some of its essential properties.

Something similar occurs with identity conditions for members of natural kinds. To know what my friend's 'that' refers to, I have to realize that he is not pointing to a cow stage or to a pasture, but I do not need to understand the sortal 'cow' to disambiguate his reference; much broader terms like 'animal' or perhaps 'medium-sized object' will often do. Of course, once a term like 'cow' is introduced, people probably have various beliefs about what counts as the same cow and what kinds of changes a cow can survive.[8] Further investigation can lead us to sharpen some of these beliefs and to discard others, as perhaps occurred when people discovered that caterpillars could turn into butterflies, that atoms of one element could be transmuted into atoms of another, or that sex change operations were possible. So, at least for sortals associated with natural kinds, it seems reasonable to conclude that the details about their identity conditions must await empirical discovery.

Artificial kinds differ from natural kinds in that pencils and spinning jennies do not share any underlying structure or follow developmental laws that could be invoked to explain their identity through time. This suggests that there are important differences between the identity conditions for artifacts and members of natural kinds—those for the former, for example, might be thought to involve a much greater element of convention. I suspect that there may be something to this, but it does not follow that causal connections are not necessary for the gen-identity of artifact stages or that a causal account of artifact identity isn't called for. It might mean that the sorts of causes appropriate for an artifact's identity involve our linguistic conventions and it would probably mean that it would be much more difficult to find general appropriate causal conditions for the identity of artifacts than for objects belonging to natural kinds. For example, the sorts of causes appropriate for the identity of everyday artifacts might differ considerably from those appropriate for historical landmarks or famous works of art. It may also be that one sort of causal chain is sufficient for the gen-identity of object stages, though in its absence some other sort of chain would be enough (though perhaps this can happen with natural kind substances as well; cf. Swoyer unpublished).

Even if all of this is true, it is not clear that linguistic conventions would be of paramount importance in determining identity conditions. I understand 'spinning jenny', I think, though I couldn't tell you if this room in the museum contains one spinning jenny or two, and it is not even clear that my mastery requires that there be experts who could do so. But even if such nouns go some way toward pinning down the identity conditions for various sorts of artifacts, they also leave room for empirical discoveries to change traditional views about such conditions; for example, the discovery of immaculate replacements would show that trucks needn't exhibit spatiotemporal continuity (without, surely, changing our original concept of a truck).

Detailed specification of at least many of the causal mechanisms appropriate to a given phenomenon must be left to science, but one might hope to say something less detailed but of more philosophical interest about appropriate causal chains. For example, it has been suggested that a causal chain is appropriate for a given phenomenon just in case it explains certain features of that phenomenon. Explanation is an epistemological (and perhaps partly pragmatic) enterprise, however, and rather than making it the key ingredient in a metaphysical account of the identity of objects, it would be better to look for features that appropriate causal chains have that give them their explanatory power.

Taking our cue from causal accounts of other phenomena, we might hope to make use of such notions as counterfactual dependence or sensitivity (this may be partially redundant if causes are somehow necessary for their effects). Counterfactual dependence is illustrated by a working thermometer that would have been different, though correct, readings had the temperature been different. Counterfactual dependence might be hoped to rule out cases of fortuitous satisfaction because it involves what would occur in a wide variety of situations rather than what just happens to be the case. When you put an electrode in my brain and accidentally cause me to have an experience that seems like a visual experience of you, it is unlikely that there are any interesting ways in which aspects of my experience depend upon how you look. If I genuinely see you, however, many features of my visual experience will depend upon how you look; had you differed in certain ways (while everything else stayed as much the same as possible), my visual experience would have been correspondingly different.

A similar treatment seems promising in the case of identity, because the states of an object at a given time frequently depend on its earlier states in such a way that had the earlier states been different (while everything else was as nearly the same as possible) then the later states would have differed in fairly definite ways. If the momentum or color of this football had been different from what it in fact was a moment ago, then its momentum or color half a second later would have been different (since, in circumstances where it differed in such respects but everything else was as much like the actual ones as possible, the football would have been acted on by very nearly the same forces; no one would have spray-painted it, and so on).

In general, the existence of a given stage of an object is not a metaphysically necessary condition for the existence of its subsequent stages. A given stage of a ship composed of certain planks in a certain arrangement might come to exist as a later stage of one ship (after we replaced the ship's original planks) or as the original stage of a different ship that we built from scratch. However, counterfactual dependence does not require metaphysical necessity, and at least often the existence of an earlier stage of an object is necessary (in the circumstances) for the existence of subsequent stages. Thus, *in those circumstances* where I've replaced many of the planks of my original ship, the existence of the stage right before the last replacement is necessary for the existence of the last stage. Moreover, setting aside indeterminism, the existence of the earlier stage is often sufficient for that of later ones in the rather vague sense that in slightly different circumstances the existence of the earlier stage would still be sufficient for that of later stages (cf. Mackie, 1974, 75).

We might even hope to invoke counterfactual dependencies to explain more complicated cases like the identity of Sam's house or his body before and after resurrection, since in addition to the causal links between the relevant stages, the features of the later stages would depend upon the features of those before. Of course, things will get messy. Sam's pencil may be green right now because it was green thirty seconds ago but if it hadn't been green then it still would be now since he has just decided to paint everything on his desk green unless it's already that color. Then too, counterfactual dependence, unlike gen-identity, is not transitive. I believe that enough details can be worked out to extend counterfactual dependence to a transitive relation in a way that excludes many sorts of causal chains that are inappropriate to identity, but I shall not rehearse a series of refinements, counterexamples, and responses, since quite simple examples suggest that it will be impossible to use the notion of counterfactual dependence to exclude *all* inappropriate causal chains.

Imagine that our truck creator and annihilator have fallen into the hands of some creature like Laplace's demon, who can ascertain the complete state of the universe at any given time. Bent upon deceiving us, he decides to set the controls on the second machine to produce a truck qualitatively indiscernible from the pickup he plans to wipe out with the first machine. In such an immaculate replacement, the two trucks are causally related and we will have virtually every sort of counterfactual dependence between the (first stage of the) second truck and the (last stage of the) first one. In these circumstances, the location, shape, color, rest mass, and even existence of the second truck depend upon those of the first; had the former differed with respect to any of these, the second would have as well. Moreover, the properties of the later stage yield the same information about those of the first as they would were they gen-identical. Perhaps some interesting counterfactuals do fail here; it can be false that if the first truck had existed in slightly different circumstances, the second would have existed as well. The notion of slightly different circumstances is too fragile to support an account of identity, however, and besides requiring the truth of such counterfactuals would exclude genuine cases of gen-identity. If the time bomb that very nearly exploded had gone off, its earlier stages would have existed (in very similar circumstances) but its later stages would not; yet the earlier and later stages are in fact gen-identical. This example also shows that we cannot solve our problems by appealing to such backtracking counterfactuals as: if the second stage hadn't existed, the first one would not have; for presumably this also fails in the case of the bomb.

The causal chain in this immaculate replacement seems to be demonic rather than appropriate because it has the wrong sort of *causal route* rather than because counterfactuals fail to hold. To exclude causal chains that run through demons or the like, we might require that every link in a causal chain appropriate for gen-identity consists of stages of the same sort, e.g., truck stages. This is too strong, since it would mean that Sam did not have the same house after the storm and that his body couldn't return at judgment day, so perhaps we should allow there to be a number of causal chains beginning with the parts of the original object and require each of *these* to run through the same sorts of stages. Whether a given stage is a stage of a given sort, however, may depend upon its relationships (*including gen-identity*) to other stages. For example, Dummett and others have urged that a species' evolutionary history is essential to it, and if this is correct, then whether a given stage is a horse stage will depend upon its relationships to many other stages.[9] One could avoid *this* difficulty by taking stages to be gen-identical just in case any object composed of them would be a single sort of thing throughout its career, but his proposal won't rule out our demonic causal chain because the stages of the two trucks would, if gen-identical, yield an object that was a truck. Besides, the notion of a sortal is not all that clear, and it isn't even obvious that an object of a given sort is essentially of that sort. Nor is it the case that a causal chain involving qualitative, structural, and compositional continuity is in general sufficient for the identity of an object (though perhaps something of the sort is necessary for it) since all of these conditions are satisfied by (the stages of) Aunt Gussie's candelabrum and the metal shard if the first is very gradually transformed into the later. In short, appropriate causes are hard to come by.

Any progress in the search for the sorts of causal connections appropriate for the transtemporal identity of physical objects will probably require a detailed examination of many examples, perhaps especially ones from biology, since living organisms provide one of the clearest examples of things whose existence and development and replacement of parts is governed by fairly general causal laws. Progress here is also likely to require advances in other areas of philosophy. Many causal theories can plausibly be thought to furnish necessary conditions for this or that without relying on any very detailed picture of causation, but explaining the notion of appropriate causal chains is a far more delicate task that probably must await a better understanding of the relationship between natural laws and causation, between causation and counterfactual dependence, and so on.

Causal accounts of identity are no exception, and discovering the precise sorts of causal connections appropriate for identity will be extremely difficult; indeed, were current usage not so well established, it would be better to speak of a causal research program rather than a causal theory. There is no guarantee that such a program will succeed, but even if it only delivers necessary conditions for the transtemporal identity of physical objects—as it has—that should not be thought a trivial result. For it would show that their identity is not utterly primitive and inexplicable and it would also mean that a very well-entrenched account, viz., the continuity theory, is incorrect.

Even without sufficient conditions we can say a bit more than this. One reason that philosophers have wanted accounts of values or semantic phenomena or mental events is that it is hard to see how claims about them can be "*barely* true"; their truth values seem to depend upon other facts—facts, for example, about the actual physical world. In the wake of failures of reductionist programs, it is common to hear arguments that facts about mental events and so forth are supervenient upon— completely fixed by—certain facts about the physical world. It is an important insight of Shoemaker's (1979) that we could also construe causal theories of identity as supervenience claims (I believe this might usefully be done for various other causal theories as well). Facts about causation exhaust those about identity in this sense; if the members of two series of stages have the same nonrelational properties, stage for stage, and their respective stages bear the same causal connections to each other, then one series consists of gen-identical stages just in case the other does. This is not to say that we should abandon the search for appropriate causes, but in the meantime the supervenience claim nicely captures the idea that facts about identity are determined by facts about causation. I hope that our earlier discussion helps to motivate this claim, but perhaps its chief motivations are simply that it seems very plausible, no one has found any reasons to think it false, and it would be a very great mystery if two series of stages could be exactly the same in these respects yet differ about matters of identity.

V

Our account of the trans*temporal* identity of physical objects aimed to tell us something about metaphysically necessary and sufficient conditions for things of that category and so we might expect it—and, indeed, any account of the identity of objects that is sensitive to the myriad possibilities involved in puzzle cases—to tell us something of interest about the trans*world* identity of physical objects as well. I believe that our causal account does so, and I shall conclude with a few suggestions about its bearing on questions about transworld identity (taking our modal reasoning at face value, I shall assume that many claims about the transworld identity of objects make sense). I do not mean to suggest that we must discover conditions for identity across possible worlds before we can legitimately engage in counterfactual deliberations, anymore than we need to specify conditions for identity through time before we can talk about one thing existing now and in the future. As Kripke has argued, we typically stipulate that we are considering some counterfactual situation that contains that bomb without knowing of any properties that are necessary or necessarily unique to it. It does not follow that identity of physical objects through time or across worlds is primitive, however, and if it is not, an account of it will be of philosophical interest.

Claims—whether correct or not—that objects enjoy a transworld identity just in case they have exactly the same properties in every world or possess the same nonqualitative property of being identical with a (for some individual a) or share some world-indexed property like being the greatest buffoon in the actual world will not shed much light upon the nature of physical objects or our model reasoning. A more enlightening account of transworld identity for physical objects would involve a specification of the individual essences of objects—necessary and sufficient conditions for being the same object—in terms of purely qualitative properties. Intuitively, a purely qualitative property is one that does involve any individuals. The notion of such a property is hard to define, but fairly easy to grasp: greenness and being an elementary unit of positive charge are purely qualitative monadic properties; being two miles from an iron sphere is a purely qualitative relational property, whereas being two miles from the Cotton Bowl is not because it involves the Cotton Bowl.

The claim that there are purely qualitative essences is that it entails a version of principle of the identity of indiscernibles according to which objects with exactly the same purely qualitative properties are identical. The problem is that there are many counterexamples to claim. Some involve cyclical times, others symmetrical worlds in which an individual on one side of an axis of symmetry has a qualitative counterpart on the other side—an individual with exactly the same (purely qualitative) monadic and relational properties that it has. To keep things simple, let's consider Max Black's well-known example of a universe whose sole inhabitants have always been two iron spheres two miles apart. Each sphere has the same (purely qualitative) monadic properties and relational properties (like being two miles from an iron sphere) as the other. We may also imagine that the spheres have exactly the same (purely qualitative) properties at all times—if one turns green, the other does so too—and exactly the same (purely qualitative) modal properties (if any)—if one could have been green, the other could have too.[10] Since the two spheres have exactly the same purely qualitative properties, neither has a purely qualitative essence. The moral is quite general. It is epistemically possible, for example, that the actual world is a symmetrical universe, and it seems metaphysically possible that there could be a world very much like ours but with qualitative counterparts to all our actual objects on the other side of an axis of symmetry or in some later cycle of time. In short, physical objects do not have purely qualitative essences.

Since there seem to be no causal relations between the actual world and other worlds and no spatiotemporal relations that will allow us to zero in on a definite object in a unique (non-actual) world (as opposed to a distinct but similar object in a very similar world), it is tempting to conclude that our only access to objects in other possible worlds is in terms of their purely qualitative properties or else by stipulation. Stipulation won't explain transworld identity, and since there are no purely qualitative essences, it is natural to conclude that the transworld identity of physical objects is primitive even if their transtemporal identity is not. To drive the point home, let us consider an example given by Robert Adams (1979). Label our two-sphere world w and imagine two further worlds, w_1 and w_2, that are exactly like w up until a given moment t. At t, however, one of the spheres in w_1 ceases to exist, while in w_2 the *other* sphere disappears. After t, w_1 and w_2 contain different spheres; yet w_1 and w_2 and their respective occupants are qualitatively indiscernible. Hence the identity of the sphere in w_1 with one rather than the other sphere of w must be primitive (or at least depend solely upon primitive relations like being identical with a, where a is one of the two spheres).

A causal theorist might reply that this scenario merely shows that no purely qualitative account of the transworld identity of objects can be given, and that the surviving sphere of w_1 is identical with one sphere of w rather than the other because the survivor's stages after t bear the appropriate sorts of causal relation to the earlier stages of one sphere but not to those of the other. There is something to this reply, but the present example conflates two sorts of cases, and we need to separate them before examining it.

Consider first a case in which neither sphere of w is actual or is causally related to anything that is. Imagine further that w_3 has always contained one of the spheres of w as its sole inhabitant and that w_4 has always contained just the *other* one. In this case, we can't explain transworld identity in terms of causal relationships between stages since, stage for stage, the spheres are indiscernible, and so surely this example shows that the identity of the sphere of w_3 with a particular sphere of w is simply primitive. But at this point we must ask whether it is really so clear that there *is* any fact of the matter about which sphere of w is identical to the sphere of w_3. I believe that some people feel that there must be a fact of the matter here because in actual cases we can point to one of two things, name it, and then stipulate that we are talking about it in various counterfactual situations. We can't fix the reference of a name for either sphere of w, however, for there is no analogue to ostension here—I can't, for example, let 'Alfred' name the sphere I am now thinking of, for how does my thought link up with one sphere rather than the other? Nor are there any definite descriptions that could be used for reference fixing, since prior to naming a sphere, every open sentence true of one is true of the other.

There are three familiar views about such cases. Some hold that it just is a brute, primitive fact that the sphere of w_3 is identical with one of the spheres of w rather than with any of the other—infinitely many—possible spheres indiscernible from it. Others claim that the relevant spheres are (or, had they existed, would have been) identical because they share some nonqualitative essence. Still others deny that there are any facts about transworld identity in this situation.

The second alternative, with its nonqualitative essences, faces well-known difficulties. While there may be such properties as being identical with Alvin Plantinga in a world in which Alvin Plantinga exists, it is most unclear what unexemplified, nonqualitative properties would be like or why we should believe that there are any. Furthermore, unexemplified nonqualitative essences seem to be surrogates for merely possible objects, and so it is not obvious that the second suggestion is really all that different from the first, which holds that the spheres of w and its kin are irreducible, merely possible individuals. The view that there are merely possible individuals, often labeled *possibilism*, plainly makes the transworld identity of such individuals a great mystery. Moreover, it is quite unclear how the existence of merely possible individuals could account for the truth of our sentences involving *de re* modalities or how it could explain our modal reasoning or justify our modal claims. What we know about merely possible worlds is based on evidence garnered in the actual world, and so it seems that any facts about such worlds—at least any that we could ever know—must be rooted in facts about the actual world (cf. Swoyer, 1982a).

Such considerations provide excellent reasons for adopting the view, often labeled *actualism*, that the only things that exist (in any sense) are those that exist in the actual world. Thus there *are* no merely possible spheres of the sort claimed to be in w or w_3 or w_4. This is not to deny that there *could* have been a pair of indiscernible spheres, but as Peirce and Prior and others have urged, this is a purely general or qualitative or *de dicto* possibility—a possibility that *could* have been realized but not one that is in fact realized by some merely possible spheres (Peirce 1935, sec. 172; Prior 1968, 71).[11] If this is correct, as I think it is, then our descriptions of w_3 and w_4 are not descriptions of distinct worlds but merely descriptions of the same purely qualitative possibility (as are those of w_1 and w_2, unless they involve actual individuals). Thus the present example does not show that transworld identity is primitive because it does not involve objects that could enjoy transworld identity at all.

A *second* sort of case involves spheres that are actual or that are in some way related to actual objects. Here we cannot appeal to actualistic considerations to try to show that there are no such spheres and, consequently, no facts about their transworld identity. By the same token, however, the champion of primitive identity cannot simply repeat his earlier argument to show that such identity is primitive, since in this case we might be able to explain it in terms of actual things. For example, various philosophers have proposed that a sufficient condition for the identity of objects in distinct worlds is that their histories converge back via a spatiotemporally continuous path of stages (of a given sort) to some stage in the history of the same object in the actual world, and since this might explain the transworld identity of all actual objects, the actualist might take this to be a necessary condition as well.

The possibility of immaculate replacements shows that such proposals will not furnish a sufficient condition for transworld identity, however, while interpolations and less exotic sorts of discontinuities show that it does not furnish a necessary condition. Indeed, as we should expect, this proposal faces all the problems that beset continuity theories of transtemporal identity. Furthermore, unlike causation, spatiotemporal continuity is a symmetrical notion. Hence this proposal offers no principled reason for counting continuous branches that diverge into the future as sufficient for identity while excluding continuous branches that converge from the past to a point in the actual history of some object. This will seem a drawback to those who believe that certain features of an object's origin are essential to it.

This proposal is based on a picture of possible worlds as ways that things could have developed or branched off from the actual world at some time; their history is the same as the actual world's history up until a given moment and diverges in some possible way thereafter (e.g., Prior 1968, 69). This picture fits nicely with actualism, for it grounds transworld identity in objects in the actual world whose identity is not a problem. No doubt it is too restrictive in various ways. For instance, there are surely possible worlds whose histories are completely unrelated to that of the actual world. As we have seen, however, such worlds do not contain any actual individuals and so they contain no occupants that enjoy transworld identity. Hence it might be the case that all possible worlds containing individuals that enjoy transworld identity—those that can be subjects of *de re* modal attributions—are possible offshoots of the actual world.

The branching picture need not be combined with the view that spatiotemporal continuity provides the key to transworld identity; at first blush, at least, it seems to fit just as well with the view that causality is what really matters. There are possible worlds in which that bomb goes off because there could have been a causal chain of the sort appropriate to transtemporal identity that ran from some point in the bomb's actual history to an exploding bomb. Below we will have to modify the proposal a bit, but the basic idea is this. Call any causal chain that runs from a stage through further stages a *causal development* of the original stage. Then an object in a merely possible world w_p is (identical with) an object in the actual world if some segment of gen-identical stages of the former (in w_p) is a possible causal development or outcome (of the sort appropriate to trans*temporal* identity) of a segment of stages of the object in the actual world. And objects in different merely possible worlds are identical if they are appropriate causal developments of the same object in the actual world.

If there is a sort of causation appropriate to trans*temporal* identity, this *sort* of proposal surely provides a satisfactory sufficient condition for the transworld identity of objects. In view of earlier arguments that transtemporal identity requires causal connection, hard-core actualists who believe that only actual objects can enjoy transworld identity may view the proposal as furnishing a necessary condition for transworld identity as well, but perhaps this is too stringent. Suppose that I have a kit to build a table that contains a top and four legs and that just as I am about to insert the legs into the coded slots, I am struck down by lightning. The parts were never before assembled, and I assume that the table did not already exist when it came in the kit (if it did, more complicated examples will make the same point). Yet it does not seem that a definite table would have come into existence had I placed the legs in the slots in accordance with the instructions. Put another way, it seems impossible for there to be distinct tables originally made of just these parts (which never before made up any piece of furniture) assembled by me at that time and place according to these instructions; taken together, these features seem to be *metaphysically sufficient* for being that table. Our intuition about metaphysical sufficiency are no doubt rooted in views about supervenience, e.g., that the matter and form (and their history) of a physical object determine all of its other properties, but whatever their source, they make it tempting to suppose that our nonactual table could enjoy an identity across various worlds since its properties could have been exemplified in more than one world, but not by distinct tables.[12]

Such cases need not violate the spirit of a causal account of transworld identity, for causal connections will still account for the identity of the actual objects like the legs and top that figure in the metaphysically sufficient conditions for being the table. More important, various causal mechanisms are involved in our metaphysically sufficient conditions. For example, it is sometimes said that being the offspring of a (specific) actual sperm and egg is metaphysically sufficient for being a given human being. If this is true, it's because of causal laws governing the behavior of gametes, the development of zygotes, and the like (I think the claim is false because of the way in which the relevant causal mechanisms allow for the development of identical twins, but this too shows the importance of causal processes). With radio parts on an assembly line we can speak of the radio that would have been *produced* from these parts had the machines and people continued to *operate* in the normal way. With the table kit, causes seem a bit less central, but even here the legs have to be inserted—somehow—into the slots. Allowing the relation of being a causal development to be a multigrade one, our possible objects are *causal developments* of one or more actual objects, and the sort of causal development they are is metaphysically sufficient for being a given object. So when all possible causal developments of a given sort from certain actual objects would yield a unique object, we can also have transworld identity.

A number of considerations recommend a causal account of the transworld identity of physical objects. First, it would provide a *unified* account of the identity conditions of physical objects through time *and* across worlds. Second, it does justice to the fact that even when we do rely upon spatiotemporal continuity to "trace" the possible careers of actual individuals, causal considerations are still basic, since they help determine which continuous paths are possible. Third, such an account seems to accommodate many cases of counterfactual reasoning in which we imagine that the world was pretty much like it was up until a given time but differed thereafter in some particular way, for this often involves imagining that events took a slightly different turn that set off a chain of causes and effects leading the world and some of the individuals in it to be different from the way that they actually are. Fourth, a causal account allows for immaculate deceptions, resurrections, and other cases that raise problems for continuity theories of transworld identity. Finally, such an account does not require any favored frame of reference, presuppose anything about the transworld identity of places or times, assume that objects must always have a definite location, or the like. What the account does not do — or aspire to do — is to explain the transworld identity of objects in nonmodal terms. It unabashedly appeals to the notion of a metaphysically possible causal development, and no attempt has been made to give a nonmodal account of this, since it seems clear that modal notions cannot be explained in nonmodal ways.

Despite its attractions, there is room for reservations about a causal account of the transworld identity of physical objects. For example, your last cigarette would still exist if Sebastian had not just smoked it down to the filter. An explanation of this fact may seem to require merely possible cigarette stages that could have borne the appropriate sorts of causal connections to earlier stages of your cigarette here in the actual world, and this would be a most unfortunate lapse from actualism. The natural way of stating our account may well suggest this conclusion, but it does not follow from the account. Nixon could have had a son, and if he had, that son would have stood in an intimate causal relationship to him. It does not follow, however, that there *is* some merely possible person who might have been causally connected to Nixon in this way. Similarly, to say that there could have been cigarette stages of a certain sort that were causally related to your cigarette's actual stages is not to say that there are merely possible stages that in some world are causally connected to its earlier stages. Most actual objects *could* have had stages that don't in fact exist, but (aside from specific worries about stages) this is no more a mystery than the fact that your house could have had rooms that don't in fact exist — though they *would* have if you had ever gotten around to building that addition out back.

It is often convenient to talk as though we begin with an object x in a unique (merely) possible world w_p and proceed to inquire whether x is identical with some actual individual. We never — on anyone's account — begin with a *single* merely possible world, however, but with many that are alike in certain respects. Moreover, on our account we don't really begin with some object x in a bunch of worlds and ask whether its stages are causal developments of some actual object. We begin with an object in the actual world, and if there could have been stages with certain features that bore the appropriate causal relations to that object's stages in this world, the actual object could have had (many of) those features. The feeling that we invoke merely possible stages may be reinforced by the fact that we sometimes seem to be able to specify such stages in terms of their metaphysically sufficient conditions, but even if this is so, we have seen that it need involve no serious lapse from actualism (cf. n. 12).

Causal accounts of the transtemporal and transworld identity of physical objects are realistic in the sense that they invoke objective relations in the world whose presence we might, even in principle, be unable to detect. Now realism with respect to a given subject matter (like identity) is sometimes equated with the view that all grammatical sentences about that subject matter are either true or false (e.g., Dummett 1978, 358). This, though, is a mistake. The heart of the realist's view is that the truth conditions of a sentence can outstrip our recognitional capacities, but this is compatible with the existence of truth value gaps for all sorts of reasons (vague predicates, nondenoting singular terms, failed presuppositions, and so on). Indeed, our causal account is not committed to the claim that there must be a fact of the matter about the transtemporal or transworld identity of physical objects in every conceivable case. To begin with, the notion of a physical object is itself rather fuzzy at the edges, but even when we clearly have physical objects there may, for all I know, be no fact of the matter about whether their stages are causally related in a way that is appropriate for transtemporal identity. If something like a causal account is correct, we should expect many unclear or borderline cases in (imagined) situations where our causal laws have broken down, for here the notion of appropriate causes would run into trouble. One way to test the account is to ask whether or not this is so.

A far more serious difficulty concerns the picture of possible worlds as possible offshoots from the actual world. The good news is that this picture nicely pins things down to objects in the actual world whose identity and diversity is an objective fact. The bad news is that it pins things down *too* well. This is more easily seen if we imagine that the laws of our world are deterministic, for then *any* possible branching off from the actual world at a given time will require that at least some of the laws of nature *change* at that time. Indeed, since many things in the actual world are lawfully related in many ways, if the world is to continue on with different things in it interacting in an ordered way, it may require large changes in a variety of laws. To be sure, the laws of our world may not be deterministic. If they aren't, we could think of different possible branches from points in the actual world as representing different outcomes that are nomologically allowed, but not necessitated, by prior states (this would be a little like the Everett-Wheeler many-worlds interpretation quantum mechanics, except that all but one of the various offshoots from any given "choice point" would be merely possible).

One might adopt an antirealism about natural laws, but this option is not available to those who would invoke causal laws to explain identity, and so we are left with two ways to accommodate the branching picture with the possibility of alternative causal developments. Unfortunately, neither is entirely satisfactory. One problem with trying to explain branches solely in terms of the possibilities allowed by indeterministic laws is that it is far from clear that our laws will allow for all of the divergences that we take to be possible. There are various problems with explaining branches in terms of changing laws; indeed, I am not convinced that this is even possible (Swoyer 1982a; cf. Kripke 1980, 164). But the important point here is that doing so doesn't seem to capture the intuitions that led to our picture of branching worlds in the first place. Whatever I mean by the claim that if I had flipped the switch, the light would have gone on, I don't *always* mean to be talking about a possible — perhaps enormous — change in some law of nature.

It seems to me that the intuitive picture of different possible histories of an object is one in which its "intrinsic" properties and actual laws determine how it would behave in a variety of situations in which it might find itself. If the world is deterministic, however, then any difference in a current situation — indeed, any difference from the actual history at any moment — would require that the entire past be different. But if two histories differed *all* the way back, there *is* no point at which they branched from a common spot in the actual history of the world. This leads to various problems not directly related to identity, and rather than pursue them I shall conclude by noting the options available here to someone who wants to give a causal account of transworld identity.

One could cling to the branching picture and explain branches solely in terms of indeterministic laws, one could explain them in terms of changes in actual laws, or one could do both. Someone who wishes to avoid changes in laws is left with just those branches from the actual world that are permitted by indeterministic laws. If this seems too restrictive, such a philosopher might hope to secure a wider range of possible causal developments for objects by abandoning the branching picture and allowing for histories that have differed all the way back in time. The difficulty here is finding a way to do this that allows for enough different histories to explain as many different possible circumstances as we can while ensuring that all of the various histories or worlds contain at least some of the *same* objects. At best, this is likely to leave open fewer possibilities for an object than the view that laws can change. This is not likely to worry a philosopher who rejects the picture of changing laws, however, for he is also likely to suppose that it is not possible for objects to undergo as many changes as other philosophers fondly suppose that they can. Indeed, he will probably think that many of the things we seem to be able to imagine are not really metaphysically possible at all (cf. Kripke 1980, 104; Swoyer 1982a). But wherever one comes down on such issues, the causal theorist must find some way to live with the fact that accepting the branching picture of possible worlds leaves less room for possible causal developments than might be supposed, while abandoning it leaves little room for speaking of the same object that can develop in different ways.

VI

The remarks about transworld identity are programmatic, but, as we have seen, all that anyone can reasonably be said to have at present are causal research programs (rather than causal theories) of identity. Misery loves company, and it is some comfort—though not much—that the same could be said for (so-called) causal theories of most phenomena of philosophical interest. What is more comforting, if earlier discussion is on the right track, is that we can see how parts of a causal account of identity would go and that we have very good reasons to believe that such an account is much closer to the truth than any of the noncausal accounts of identity of physical objects that have been proposed.[13]

Notes

1. A remote ancestor of causal theories of identity might be found in the view that each stage of an enduring thing requires a sustaining cause, though Descartes and others reserved this task for God rather than for the thing's earlier stages. There is room for considerable dispute over Hume's considered views about identity (cf. Swoyer 1982b); here I shall simply note that what he calls the "fictitious identity" of the self in many ways resembles what most people nowadays would think of as its actual identity and that he locates this identity partly in the causal connections between stages ("fleeting impressions and ideas") of the self. Hume's explanation of our belief in the transtemporal identity of physical objects in terms of the causal or at least lawful relations (the "coherence") between their stages foreshadows recent causal accounts, although he thought this belief mistaken, whereas most of us do not. Kant discusses the role of causality in the sequence of states of an object (in a broad sense that includes the empirical self) in various places in the first *Critique*, particularly in the Second Analogy. Earlier in this century causal accounts of the identity of physical objects were developed by Russell (in many places, e.g., 1948, 453ff.), W. E. Johnson (1964, 96 ff.), and various proponents of causal theories of time (e.g., Reichenbach 1956); more recently they have been defended by Mackie (1974, 155ff), Armstrong (1980), and Shoemaker (1979). Meanwhile, Russell (1948, 458), Wiggins (1971, 55), Shoemaker (1970) and others have championed causal accounts of personal identity. One might also try to develop causal accounts for the identity of such things as matter, stuff, (noninstantaneous) events, and processes, but I shall not pursue this here. I shall assume that identity is not relative (in Geach's sense that x and y can be ⌐the same F but different G's⌐ (where F and G are sortal or count nouns).

2. When dealing with longer stages I shall sometimes speak as though features of one stage could be caused by those of the immediately preceding stage. Of course some problems, for example those involving various sorts of motion, will require instantaneous stages and technical notions like limits, and since a gen-identical series of instantaneous stages would not be discrete, we will have to complicate our discussion of causality when we come to them. (Matters here are delicate, but by way of illustration, someone who believed that causes were necessary conditions for their effects and that causal chains were always spatiotemporally continuous might claim that a cause of the relevant sort requires that the properties of the members of any arbitrarily short sequence of stages before a given stage be necessary in the circumstances for that stage's having the properties that it does.) Stages are useful because they allow us to give a reasonably definite sense to the vague notion of "criteria of identity" for persons and objects and because they let us link our discussion to a number of traditional treatments and so provide a common and simple idiom for comparing a variety of accounts. It should also be noted that many of the standard objections to stages do not apply to our nonconstructivistic program, in which they function mainly as pegs on which to pin properties and relations. My use of 'stage' is typically noncommittal enough that if better pegs can be found, my talk can (I think) be viewed as an infelicitous way of talking about them. I shall assume here that gen-identity is an equivalence relation; this can be avoided if distinct objects can overlap by sharing a stage, but there are many problems with the claim that this is possible.

3. None of these additions is quite enough, for when a parent amoeba splits into two or two drops of water merge into one, we certainly seem to have spatiotemporal continuity under

a sortal, together with qualitative and compositional continuity. The continuity theorist might hope to find a characterization of spatiotemporal continuity that does not count cases of fission or fusion as preserving continuity, though I have yet to see any way of doing this that rules out fission and fusion without ruling out some things that seem to be clear cases of (gen-)identity as well. Thus the continuity theorist may need to add that spatiotemporal continuity is sufficient for gen-identity only when it is a one-one relation, i.e., a stage existing at one time is gen-identical with a stage existing at another time only if each is spatiotemporally continuous with *only* one stage existing at the other time. This requirement may seem ad hoc, but since something rather like it may be needed by any satisfactory account of the identity of physical objects (Swoyer unpublished), it would be unfair to deny it to the continuity theorist.

4. This sort of account does not require determinism and is compatible with various views about laws of nature and of causation, though it fits especially nicely with the following sort of picture (which can be given quite independent motivation; Swoyer 1982a). Laws involve a special relation among properties and physical magnitudes so that (to take a *very* simple example) a generalization of the form ⌜All P's are Q's⌝ expresses a law just in case a thing's having the property P is nomologically sufficient for its having the property Q. In everyday life and in science we often think of an object's or event's having some property P as causing (or being causally relevant for) it or some other object or event coming to have some property Q: the liquid turned the litmus paper blue because it is an alkaline, impressed force causes acceleration, smoking tends to cause lung cancer. On this view, the properties of later stages of an object causally arise or evolve out of its earlier properties in a lawful way.

5. Much of the above can be modified to furnish an argument for a causal account of the transtemporal identity of persons. Some philosophers have wanted to locate personal identity in the transtemporal identity of a living body, but we have seen reasons to suppose that identity conditions for bodies involve causation. Others have hoped to explain personal identity in terms of the psychological continuity of person stages. If psychological continuity does not require causal connections between stages, though, it will not be sufficient for personal identity because of the possibility of immaculate replacements. Just as one person dies, some fantastic machine or god or simply a random coming together of atoms might accidentally produce a different person whose mental life is as similar to or continuous with that of the original person as you please. Nor is such continuity necessary, for a person can—most people agree—retain his identity despite psychological discontinuities, as when someone goes to sleep or becomes quite psychotic or suffers amnesia. Causal connections overcome at least many of these difficulties.

6. It is far from clear that we have univocal or static concepts of perception, knowledge, personal identity, and so forth, and even if we do, it seems doubtful that philosophers ever do much pure conceptual analysis. Much of our knowledge about language and concepts is thoroughly entwined with our beliefs and memories and expectations and bits of lore about the world around us, and we bring all this, as well as any pure linguistic knowledge, to our philosophical thought experiments. If this is so, philosophical accounts of perception or knowledge or the transtemporal identity of physical objects are not merely analyses of the relevant concepts, and this raises the question what their status is. In at least some cases, I suspect that they involve using many things—linguistic understanding, commonsense knowledge, any relevant bits of science we can muster—in an effort to discover the metaphysically necessary and sufficient conditions for something. But fortunately we don't have to settle such matters before embarking on the current project, for as the history and philosophy of science make clear, people can have fairly definite and widely shared views about how to engage in a discipline even if they are unable to codify these views or to explain the exact nature of the discipline.

7. The point of our earlier example of literal resurrection of the body was not that resurrection *is* metaphysically possible but that it is *not* an a priori truth that it is impossible. If it can occur, there will be some causal chains appropriate to identity that won't likely be explained by any current branches of science. Similar problems would arise for other causal theories if we could directly *perceive* or *know* certain things about God (e.g., what he wants us to do), can have postresurrection *memories* of preresurrection experiences, and so on.

8. One may well have to have some such beliefs about the identity conditions of cows if one is to have mastery of a word like 'cow', but that does not mean that *all* of the beliefs must be true (such beliefs are in this and other respects rather like Putnam's [1975] stereotypes). Elsewhere I have argued that natural kinds are properties and that properties are objective things in the world (Swoyer 1982a, 1983). On this view, a natural kind term is causally connected to a property, and this can leave open questions about the identity conditions for members of that kind (as can Putnam's account of natural kind terms). In stressing that many sortal terms associated with natural kinds do not have enough meaning to determine identity conditions, I do not mean to suggest that a given individual's natural kind is essential to it. Indeed, if a horse could be turned into a member of some other kind, say a mule or a zebra, it would no longer be the same sort of thing (according to many views about sortals), though I believe it would survive this change. If so, we have yet another reason for thinking that sortals do not always determine the identity conditions of things that happen to be members of that sort.

9. For definiteness, I have often spoken of truck stages and the like, but if Dummett's claim is correct, such talk should be recast in terms simply of (object) stages.

10. In describing Black's universe as containing *two* spheres, the partisan of the identity of indiscernibles will charge that I have begged the question against him. I see little reason to view the dispute here as a standoff, however, for the description of the universe seems entirely coherent to most people while the reasons for taking the principle of the identity of indiscernibles seriously are quite weak (the classical defenses depend on dubious theological and verificationist principles). Hence the burden of proof is on the proponent of this principle to show us that such a universe is not metaphysically possible. In a recent paper, Hacking (1975) has argued that the champion of this principle need not – indeed, cannot – do this, but that his opponents can take small comfort from this since, with sufficient ingenuity, redescriptions of their examples can always be given that preserve the principle. For example, I said that we had *two* iron spheres two miles apart, but we cannot simply help ourselves to notions like distance and direction. We must, for example, explain the notion of a straight line (geodesic) in terms of light rays, and so someone could redescribe Black's universe as one with enough positive curvature that a light ray leaving one sphere would arrive back at *it*, rather than at another sphere, thus suggesting that it is not an objective fact that the universe contains two spheres. The question is whether such redescriptions are always legitimate. For pretty much the reasons various philosophers have given for preferring a realistic to a conventionalistic account of various aspects of space-time, I would argue that we can sometimes stipulate that our imagined universe has a certain topology, a given "intrinsic" metric, or that it is governed by certain laws.

11. Strictly speaking, on the version of actualism that I favor, purely qualitative possibilities (and their apparent modal properties) are grounded in the *de re* modal features of properties. There is no general possibility of a sphere that is both red and green all over because redness and greenness cannot be coexemplified. The guiding picture here is that possible worlds are complex, highly structured properties made up from simpler (purely qualitative) monadic and relational properties as well as such properties as being identical with *a*, where *a* is an *actual* individual. On this view, we learn about possibilities by learning about properties here in the actual world, and we learn about these by learning about the behavior and potentialities of the objects that exemplify them (cf. Swoyer 1982a, though the existence conditions suggested there for properties are too restrictive and the identity conditions work only for purely qualitative properties). These remarks are intended only to indicate very roughly what an actualist position that takes properties as basic might look like; to do more they will need to be backed by a detailed semantics.

12. Phrases like 'the possible table' are so natural and convenient that they are difficult to avoid. As figures of speech they are innocent enough, so long as they are not taken as a commitment to the existence of any merely possible object. One way to avoid this problem is to hold that, strictly speaking, what does exist is an unexemplified essence of the table, viz., the property of being identical with the table made from these parts according to this plan by, etc. Since this involves actual individuals, it would not be mysterious in the way that unexemplified

nonqualitative essences usually are. What seem to be metaphysically sufficient features of stages may also allow us to zero in on merely possible stages—or at least give us the illusion that we do—as when we specify a ship stage in terms of certain planks in a certain arrangement at a certain time.

13. I am indebted to J. I. Biro for helpful comments on an earlier version of this paper.

References

Adams, Robert M. 1979. "Primitive Thisness and Primitive Identity." *Journal of Philosophy* 76:5-26.

Armstrong, David. 1980. "Identity Through Time." In *Time and Change*, edited by Peter van Inwagen.

Broad, D. C. 1949. *Scientific Thought*. London.

Dummett, Michael, 1978. *Truth and Other Enigmas*. Cambridge, Mass.

Gödel, Kurt. 1959. "A Remark About the Relationships Between Relativity Theory and Idealistic Philosophy." In *Albert Einstein: Philosopher Scientist*, edited by P. A. Schilpp. New York.

Hacking, Ian. 1975. "The Identity of Indiscernibles. *Journal of Philosophy* 72:249-56.

Hirsh, Eli. 1982. *The Concept of Identity*. Oxford.

Johnson, W. E. 1964. *Logic, Part III*. New York.

Kripke, Saul, 1980. *Naming and Necessity*. Cambridge, Mass.

Mackie, J. L. 1974. *The Cement of the Universe*. Oxford.

Nelson, Jack. 1972. "Logically Necessary and Sufficient Conditions for Identity Through Time." *American Philosophical Quarterly* 9:177-85.

Peirce, Charles S. 1935. *Collected Papers: Vol. IV*. Cambridge, Mass.

Prior, Arthur, 1968. "Identifiable Individuals." In *Papers on Time and Tense*. Oxford.

Putnam, Hilary. 1975. "The Meaning of Meaning." In *Philosophical Papers II: Mind, Language and Reality*. Cambridge.

Quine, W. V. 1981. *Theories and Things*. Cambridge, Mass.

Reichenbach, Hans. 1956. *The Direction of Time*. Berkeley.

Russell, Bertrand, 1948. *Human Knowledge: Its Scope and Limits*. New York.

Shoemaker, Sydney, 1970. "Persons and Their Pasts." *American Philosophical Quarterly* 7:269-85.

Shoemaker, Sydney. 1979. "Identity, Properties, and Causality." *Midwest Studies of Philosophy* 4:321-42.

Swoyer, Chris. 1982a. "The Nature of Natural Laws." *Australasian Journal of Philosophy* 60: 203-23.

Swoyer, Chris. 1982b. "Hume and the Three Views of the Self." *Hume Studies* 8:43-61.

Swoyer, Chris. 1983. "Belief and Predication." *Nous* 15 (1983):197-220.

Swoyer, Chris. n.d. "Rival Claimants." Unpublished photocopy.

Wiggins, David. 1971. *Identity and Spatio-Temporal Continuity*. Oxford.

Williams, Bernard, 1973. "Bodily Continuity and Personal Identity." In *Problems of the Self*. Cambridge.

Contributors

Peter Achinstein, Department of Philosophy, The Johns Hopkins University

Laird Addis, Department of Philosophy, University of Iowa

Joseph Almog, Department of Philosophy, University of California, Los Angeles

George Bealer, Department of Philosophy, Reed College

Hector-Neri Castañeda, Department of Philosophy, Indiana University

Arthur Collins, Department of Philosophy, City University of New York, Graduate Center

Michael Devitt, Department of Traditional and Modern Philosophy, University of Sidney

Fred Dretske, Department of Philosophy, University of Wisconsin

John Dupré, Department of Philosophy, Stanford University

Berent Enç, Department of Philosophy, University of Wisconsin

Edward Erwin, Department of Philosophy, University of Miami

Evan Fales, Department of Philosophy, University of Iowa

Jaegwon Kim, Department of Philosophy, University of Michigan

William G. Lycan, Department of Philosophy, University of North Carolina

Penelope Maddy, University of Illinois at Chicago Circle

Colin McGinn, Department of Philosophy, University College, University of London

Michael McKinsey, Department of Philosophy, Wayne State University

Brian McLaughlin, Department of Philosophy, Rutgers University

Ernan McMullin, Department of Philosophy, University of Notre Dame

John Pollock, Department of Philosophy, University of Arizona

Hilary Putnam, Department of Philosophy, Harvard University

Alexander Rosenberg, Department of Philosophy, Syracuse University

David H. Sanford, Department of Philosophy, Duke University

D. S. Shwayder, Department of Philosophy, University of Illinois at Urbana-Champaign

Brian Skyrms, Department of Philosophy, University of California, Irvine

Ernest Sosa, Department of Philosophy, Brown University

Patrick Suppes, Department of Philosophy, Stanford University

Chris Swoyer, Department of Philosophy, University of Oklahoma

Michael Tooley, Department of Philosophy, University of Western Australia

Peter Unger, Department of Philosophy, New York University

James Van Cleve, Department of Philosophy, Brown University

Zeno Vendler, Department of Philosophy, University of California, San Diego

Peter A. French is Lennox Distinguished Professor of Philosophy and chairman of the philosophy department at Trinity University in San Antonio, Texas. He has taught at the University of Minnesota, Morris, and has served as research professor in the Center for the Study of Values at the University of Delaware. His books include *The Scope of Morality* (Minnesota, 1980). **Theodore E. Uehling, Jr.**, is professor of philosophy at the University of Minnesota, Morris. He is the author of *The Notion of Form in Kant's Critique of Aesthetic Judgment* and articles on the philosophy of Kant. **Howard K. Wettstein** is associate professor of philosophy at the University of Notre Dame. He has taught at the University of Minnesota, Morris, and has served as a visiting associate professor of philosophy at the University of Iowa and Stanford University. Wettstein has published papers in the philosophy of language.